BUSINESS STATISTICS

Using EXCEL & SPSS

SAGE was founded in 1965 by Sara Miller McCune to support the dissemination of usable knowledge by publishing innovative and high-quality research and teaching content. Today, we publish more than 850 journals, including those of more than 300 learned societies, more than 800 new books per year, and a growing range of library products including archives, data, case studies, reports, and video. SAGE remains majority-owned by our founder, and after Sara's lifetime will become owned by a charitable trust that secures our continued independence.

Los Angeles | London | New Delhi | Singapore | Washington DC

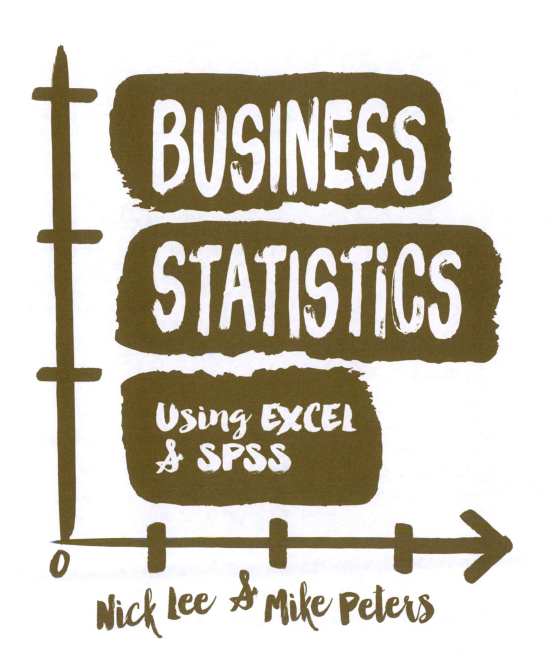

BUSINESS STATISTICS

Using EXCEL & SPSS

Nick Lee & Mike Peters

SAGE

Los Angeles | London | New Delhi
Singapore | Washington DC

SAGE

Los Angeles | London | New Delhi
Singapore | Washington DC

SAGE Publications Ltd
1 Oliver's Yard
55 City Road
London EC1Y 1SP

SAGE Publications Inc.
2455 Teller Road
Thousand Oaks, California 91320

SAGE Publications India Pvt Ltd
B 1/I 1 Mohan Cooperative Industrial Area
Mathura Road
New Delhi 110 044

SAGE Publications Asia-Pacific Pte Ltd
3 Church Street
#10-04 Samsung Hub
Singapore 049483

Editor: Kirsty Smy
Editorial assistant: Molly Farrell
Production editor: Nicola Marshall
Copyeditor: Neville Hankins
Proofreader: Andy Baxter
Indexer: Gary Kirby
Marketing manager: Alison Borg
Cover design: Francis Kenney
Typeset by: C&M Digitals (P) Ltd, Chennai, India
Printed and bound in Great Britain by Ashford
Colour Press Ltd

Library of Congress Control Number: 2015939926

British Library Cataloguing in Publication data

A catalogue record for this book is available from the British Library

ISBN 978-1-84860-219-9
ISBN 978-1-84860-220-5 (pbk)

At SAGE we take sustainability seriously. Most of our products are printed in the UK using FSC papers and boards. When we print overseas we ensure sustainable papers are used as measured by the PREPS grading system. We undertake an annual audit to monitor our sustainability.

DEDICATION

NICK

This book is dedicated to Professor Charles 'Danger' Darwin.

Who is my dog.

I don't mean that in a 'hip hop' sense, I mean he is actually my Cocker Spaniel. He's been my constant companion for the entire time I have written this book, from start to finish. He was a puppy when I started and has sat on this very beanbag next to me for virtually the entire process, snoring, huffing and grumbling about needing a walk. Perhaps he will now get one…

MIKE

This book is dedicated to my partner Joyce who has put up with my mad ramblings about mathematics and statistics being wonderful subjects. I would also like to dedicate this book to our families, especially our children Glenn, Adam, Wayne and Kayleigh.

CONTENTS

ABOUT THE AUTHORS

PROFESSOR NICK LEE

Nick is the Professor of Sales and Management Science at Loughborough University's School of Business and Economics, and Honorary Chair of Marketing and Organizational Research at Aston Business School. Nick's research aims to bring theories from psychology, neuroscience, economics and sociology to bear on important problems in management, motivation and human behaviour in sales forces and other organizations. As a result of wanting to do this, he figured he'd have to learn a bit about actually doing research, like collecting and analysing data. In doing so, he realized that not everyone felt the same way. So he let out a big sigh and wrote a book about it called *Doing Business Research*, which – like the first Velvet Underground album – wasn't bought by too many people, but everyone who did buy it ended up starting their own band, so to speak. In a fit of hubris, Nick then decided to write a complementary book on business statistics. Many sighs later, he finished it. In the meantime, he became the Editor in Chief of the *European Journal of Marketing*, won a bunch of awards for his research, and was featured in *The Times* as 'one of the 15 scientists whose work will shape the future' (possibly as some kind of journalism in-joke). You might also have seen him pop up in the *Financial Times* and *Forbes*, and he has appeared on BBC Radio 4, BBC Radio 5 Live and BBC Breakfast television – which is probably why it took so long to finish this book.

Nick tweets at @nj_lee

DR MIKE PETERS

First and foremost, Mike is a Cornishman and very proud of it! He is currently the Director of Engineering and Applied Science Foundation Programmes and the Academic Director for Aston International at Aston University. He is a Chartered Mathematician, Fellow of the Institute for Mathematics and its Applications, and a Senior Fellow of the Higher Education Academy. He sincerely believes that anyone can 'do mathematics and statistics' and his greatest ambition in life is to get everyone to love maths and stats. To achieve this ambition his research is focused on how we learn mathematics and how such fascinating subjects should be taught. Some of the results from his research have been used in the writing of this book and hopefully you will benefit from them and become a member of the 'I love mathematics and statistics movement'.

Finally, Mike lives on a canal boat and if you see a red one with the flag of St Piran on the stern, give a wave or, if he's moored, ask for a cup of tea!

FOREWORD

WHAT IS THIS BOOK? HOW SHOULD YOU USE IT?

This is a book about introductory quantitative analysis for business studies (let's call this 'business statistics' or 'business stats' for now). As such, it is designed to be read by first- and (perhaps) second-year students on a business studies degree course. In particular, it has been written with an intention to assume as little background knowledge as possible. In this way, it is somewhat different to almost every other business stats book we know of. Both of us have been teaching introductory quantitative skills for many years, and the key problem we've faced (and one which is growing worse, not better) is the lack of foundational knowledge. Whatever the reason for that, it's not really important to us. The simple fact is that we are commonly trying to teach reasonably basic quantitative techniques to students who for example are not confident in absolutely foundational skills like mathematical notation, basic algebra, or even the concepts of equations and formulae. Without this, students quickly get left behind, and, without those skills, they find it incredibly difficult to catch up. We know; that was us. So, this book was written without any major assumptions about exactly what the reader would know before picking it up. We assume of course that you actually know that numbers exist, and you can do basic numerical operations, but we don't assume you know what for example $\sum$ means.

There are plenty of formulae and equations in the book, but these are all explained in detail, and what they actually *do* is explained. In this way, we want to teach you not just to remember equations, but to *understand* them. Our approach is based heavily on the latest knowledge about how people learn, and in particular how people learn mathematics. In fact, one of us has a PhD in exactly this. This approach is totally unique, and hopefully you will see the benefits in how we have created the exercises and questions. For example, while there are traditional end-of-chapter questions, these are not just about memorizing equations, but about applying what you learnt to typical problems. Further, throughout each chapter there are regular 'Think it Over' boxes, which help you immediately to translate into real knowledge the concepts you are reading about, instead of having to wait until the end of the chapter to think about things.

We've also created a set of different boxouts which are aimed at different audiences. If you are struggling to understand something, there's often going to be a 'Back to Basics' box for it. These boxes are intended to explain key concepts in the most basic way possible, often relating to interesting or humorous examples – or at least what we think of as humorous. Alternatively, if you're racing ahead, you might be interested in an 'Above and Beyond' box, which is where we'll introduce more interesting or advanced concepts that are a little bit outside of what you might 'need' to know, but will be of interest if you 'want' to know more. We've also interweaved our journey through business stats with the (somewhat fictional) journeys of two students, who you'll see typifying many classical situations of introductory business stats students. Partly, of course, this is a little bit of fun on our part, but there are important messages in those stories if you care to find them…

As you probably already expect, computer software is integral to our approach. In fact, we've spent many hours creating examples of the analysis techniques on both Microsoft Excel and IBM ® SPSS ® software. These are arguably the two most commonly used packages in business schools around the world, and this book also serves as a useful introduction and primer for using them. We've also created a set of useful data files and templates for the examples, which should help you really to accelerate your learning process by going through them step by step along with us. They're available as online resources for the book, as are other files and useful tips – including the spreadsheets and files we used to create most of the tables and diagrams in many of the chapters, and which you can download and use/modify yourself. We hope these online resources will grow and change as time moves on, which is the great beauty of the Internet in terms of textbooks – we can continuously improve the resource.

Essentially, both of us are at heart great lovers of numbers and believers in the power of numbers to help us. The creation of mathematics is in our view one of the greatest and most important achievements in history. As such, it's a great source of concern to us that so few people are really confident in using the power of numbers to make decisions and improve the world around us. In fact, an understanding of maths and stats will *definitely*, *without possible failure*, improve your life in whatever context you care to mention. Of course, it will be probably the major influence on your success as a student in most subjects (directly and indirectly), but also in your ability to make good decisions as a person, or as a professional. Our intention with this book is ultimately to make a difference to your life, and by extension the world around us, by improving understanding of these vital concepts.

However, while that sounds like a serious business, and it is, we are also people who like to enjoy ourselves. Most importantly, writing a book (even with a co-author) is a fundamentally solitary business. When we write, we like to have fun, and we also think numbers are fun (seriously). We've hopefully gone at least some way towards translating our fundamental enthusiasm and enjoyment for numbers into this book, by way of fun examples, exercises and asides. We are human, like you. With this in mind, we've tried our hardest to write in a friendly, personal style. What this means is that we have tended to write in the first person, using 'I' quite a lot. This might seem a bit weird to some people, especially if you note that there are two authors! But, in essence, we shared responsibility, with one of us focusing on the text of the chapters (Nick) and the other focusing on the exercises and other material (Mike). So at any one point in time, it really is only one of us writing! We think using 'I' helps keep it friendly and less formal, and certainly avoids some of the clumsy wordings we were forced to use when we tried to write it in other ways. We think being informal and human is vital with material like this, because you have to understand that – honestly – we are no different from you! If we can learn this stuff, so can you – neither of us is some numerical prodigy who was doing calculus at 9 years old. We had to work hard to learn this stuff, and if we can do it, so can you. We are not special. As you'll see, we learnt things even when writing this book. No one is born gifted at this, even those who pretend they were. So, don't be intimidated. The way to become good at this is quite simple – work, practise and practise some more. Understand each stage before moving on to the next. And ask for help if you need it.

Finally, while it's hard to look back this far, this book has been in progress for around six years. It's difficult to class it as a 'labour of love', but in many ways the fundamental importance of what we're doing has spurred us on. We both remember the challenges of quantitative analysis when we were starting out, and every day we see evidence that these challenges are not easier now, they are harder. We've learnt a lot while writing this, and discovered things we wish we'd learnt many years ago. We hope that this book can help you through what is a challenging time, and save you the heartache that so many students go through when studying quantitative subjects.

We truly hope you enjoy this, but more importantly that it helps.

Best wishes and good luck!
Nick and Mike

ACKNOWLEDGEMENTS

NICK

After I wrote my first book *Doing Business Research*, I enjoyed tremendously the process of writing acknowledgements, as you can tell if you read them. However, at this point of the process for this book, it is definitely more of a catharsis than anything else. The process of writing this book was far more difficult than the last, and it almost feels like I need to thank people for just keeping me going! To be totally honest, the people that most deserve thanks are the huge numbers of people in this world who struggle with mathematics, statistics and general quantitative 'stuff'. For many years, whenever I felt like throwing in the towel on this project, I would be reminded somehow that I was intending to make a real difference in people's lives with this book. I know that seems horribly grandiose for what amounts to 'just' a stats textbook, but I've seen the problems that can be caused by poor knowledge of quantitative analysis, for students, researchers, managers, businesspeople, the general public, even politicians who are making decisions about our very society. Each time I was close to giving up, something would happen that reminded me that we *need* better knowledge and education about numbers. That kept me going.

Of course, there are so many people individually who have made major contributions to this book. Without Delia Martinez at Sage, I wouldn't have even thought about this project. While Delia was never formally involved with this book, it was she who floated the idea of my writing it after completing *Doing Business Research*. It was Natalie Aguilera at Sage, however, who took this project on, convinced me to do it, and supported me for the first couple of years. It's not too much to say that without Natalie, this book would not exist. That said, this project has seen quite a few editors come and go. I'm not sure whether it was me, the project or natural turnover, but through the process Robin Lupton tried to keep my mind on the job – with more or less success – until she moved on like Natalie to a role where she wasn't forced to deal with me. Finally, the project arrived at the door of Kirsty Smy (who may very well be some kind of 'troubleshooter' at Sage, I have no idea), and she managed to cajole this book over the line in her inimitable 'iron fist in a velvet glove' style, along with Molly Farrell. I know that I must have been something of a nightmare to work with, and they all deserve immense credit for keeping this to themselves.

Mike Peters also deserves major thanks for his incredible input into the exercises, tutorials and material in general. I know he's a co-author of this book, so it's kind of weird to acknowledge him, right? However, I also know that this book would never have happened without his arriving on the team. His massive input is most clearly shown from his inexorable move from a contributor to a full co-author. This book just would not have happened without him. It helps a lot that Mike is completely unique in his approach to mathematics education, and unlike most people who work on books like this, he is a genuine maths educator, with a PhD in maths education, not a dabbler like myself. He makes this book unique, and is a true kindred spirit – as well as living on a boat, which in my mind places him in a stratum of coolness occupied only by the TV character MacGyver (Google it) and him.

I'd like to acknowledge IBM and Microsoft for allowing us to use screenshots of their software in the book. I'd also like to thank them profusely for continually updating their software so we needed to take new screenshots. Thanks. That helped. A lot. Thanks also to Steffen Fixson and John Cadogan for letting me use their diagrams in Chapters 2 and 11 respectively.

A lot of this book was written while I was employed at Aston University, and it seems appropriate to thank my colleagues there for their support over the years that I was working on this. In particular, John Rudd, who was department chair (as such, my boss) for many of those years, and is a great friend of mine, deserves lots of thanks for letting me indulge myself in writing this book, even though he probably thought it was madness. He's also been a constant source of encouragement, and inspiration, in my life in general. I also worked on a fair amount of the book while on sabbaticals at the University of Houston and Michigan University, and Mike Ahearne, Niladri Syam, Zach Hall, Jeff Boichuk, Yashar Atefi (University of Houston) and Rick Bagozzi (Michigan University) deserve thanks for being both excellent hosts and great inspirations during my time there. I also spent quite a lot of time visiting at Ruhr University in Bochum (Germany) over the years I was working on this, and Jan Wieseke, Sascha Alavi, Johannes Habel, Sven Mikolon, Laura Marie Schons and Julia Sprenger were all outstanding hosts for me during those times. Finally, I spent quite some time in Finland, both at Lappeenranta University of Technology and in Helsinki for KATAJA, the Finnish doctoral programme in business studies, teaching statistics. Anssi Tarkiainen, Sanna-Katriina Asikainen and Olli Kuivalainen were wonderful hosts during that time. These visits all made significant contributions to the material in the book in various ways. In 2014 I moved to Loughborough University, and I'd particularly like to thank the Dean there (Angus Laing) for letting me indulge myself with this project without asking any questions. Anne Souchon, my head of department and great friend, also deserves thanks for the same reasons, as well as for being an amazing friend and supporter over the years.

In fact, those already mentioned, and my other friends in academia, have been a constant source of encouragement and enthusiasm over the years. It feels like every single one has at one point or another been really enthusiastic about this project, which has kept me going during various stages of despair. There are too many to mention, but a few in particular stand out. Laura Chamberlain has been a constant source of support, enthusiasm and advice over the years, and has been a major contributor to so many of the ideas in this book. John Cadogan, as always, has been a great inspiration to me, and as I said in my last book, without him there is no way I would be doing this. There are so many others, but in particular (of those not already mentioned) I'd like to thank Carl Senior, Mirella Kleijnen, Rob Morgan, Diamantis Diamantopoulos, Astrid Dickinger, Milena Micevski, Dagmar Fraser, Nigel Driffield, Geoff Durden, Amanda Beatson, Ian Lings, Adam Rapp, Ryan Mullins, Julien Schmitt, Andrew Farrell, Greg Marshall, Tom Steenburgh, Florian Kraus, Manfred Krafft, Erik Mooi, Dave Gilliland, Koen Pauwels, Seshadri Tirunillai, Aarti Sood, Anouche Newman, Allan Lee, Rachel Ashman, Nadia Zainuddin, Emi Moriuchi, Bernadette Frech, Stuart Greenhill, James Brown, Dan Merriman and Alex Connor for contributing in some direct or indirect way to the ideas in this book. You probably have no idea how, but you did – maybe even some random conversation you don't even remember.

Finally, without my friends outside the strange environment of academic research, I probably would have gone crazy. There are just too many here to mention by name, because so many of you have made my life better over the last few years while writing this book, through various random acts of support, kindness, entertainment, sports, intoxication or otherwise taking my mind off things. But, thanks to you all for making my life what it is. Thanks also to Mark Zuckerberg for inventing Facebook so people can see I am still alive, and Alan Turing for pretty much inventing computers because they are kind of important. Special thanks to Dave Davies from the Kinks for inventing guitar distortion, and Jimi

Hendrix, Pete Townshend, Jimmy Page, Eddie Van Halen, Steve Vai and Billy Corgan for working out how to use it properly. I'd also like to thank the people who invented whisky, wine and beer, but my publishers keep telling me to stop talking about booze, so...

MIKE

Without wishing to give the impression of a 'mutual appreciation society', I would like to thank Nick for giving me the opportunity to contribute towards this book. We have had numerous discussions on how to present the material, what are important concepts and most importantly, the pedagogical drivers behind the book. We have both suffered from lecturers who seem to assume that every topic is 'obvious' and cannot understand why some of us struggled with statistics.

The main reason I stay in academia is the opportunities to work with students. Over the years I have learnt so much from this often misrepresented group of people and although there have been times when I could have quite easily given up (especially when the prospect of marking 300 exam papers looms!), overall my experience has been that teaching is the best job in the world.

The staff members of Sage (already mentioned by Nick) deserve a medal for the patience they have exhibited over the years this book has been in production. Without their continual belief and encouragement that a book such as this one was needed, the whole project would have ground to an ignominious end.

Finally, I would also like to thank some of my colleagues who have acted as critical friends for some of my ideas on approaches to learning and teaching and have offered encouragement when changes haven't happened as quick as I thought they should.

ABOUT THE COMPANION WEBSITE

Business Statistics Using EXCEL and SPSS is supported by a wealth of online resources for both students and lecturers to aid study and support teaching, which are available at: https://study.sagepub.com/leepeters

For Students
- **Datasets** ready to upload into Microsoft Excel and IBM SPSS to generate meaningful information that will help you master your statistics skills. Most of the spreadsheets and data that were used to create the tables and diagrams within the book are available online for you to download, use and adapt yourself.
- **Q&A** answers to in-text exercises and questions within the book.

For Lecturers
- **Workbooks** with extra questions and examples accompanying each chapter for tutors to download, print off and use in tutorials, or give to students as homework.

GUIDED TOUR OF THE BOOK

This is the first chapter, and our learning
and they do cover some pretty foundation
mind when studying this chapter:

☑ Understand why people might be scared
turned off by studying quantitative metho

☑ Understand how quantitative analysis
business is primarily to help you r
decisions in your future career, e
what you think might be the most
and creative professions.

Learning Objectives
Each chapter begins with a handy
checklist which sets out all the
key information you will soon
understand so that you can easily
track your progress.

**'The Ballad of Eddie the Easily
Distracted' and 'Esha's Story'**
Following you on your journey
through the book will be the two
(somewhat) fictional business
statistics students, Eddie and
Esha. In these engaging storylines,
you will recognise many typical
situations and uncover some
important lessons about learning
statistics along the way.

The Ballad of Eddie the Easily

for the first lecture of QUAN101 Quantitative Analy
his. Perhaps he had died and gone to hell. Or even, he thou
wrong lecture. Yes that was it – he was in the wrong lecture
n his future career with all these formulae and numbers?
– a young lady who herself looked only a few years older tha
an individual assignment and an exam. He wouldn't even be a

med so much to cover in the subject. Dr Jones, the lectu
chers in the past, and he had never done too well the
e nauseous.

cture anyway so he might as well try to pay a
who was taking copious notes, but look
Union bar last night; she'd left
What was her na

...re. Life is full of dec...
realize. Every time you measur...
you actually perform quite a comp...
mize your financial potential as well. ...

think it over 1.1

Can everything that varies (i.e. what are cal...
Think about feelings. When you say you ...
can you measure it accurately?
What about when you get exam result...
asked to complete a questionnaire abou...
What if you got 35%, a fail – would thi...

Think it over
These boxes are here to make you stop, engage and reflect upon the different connections you are making between topics. They will include important questions and points of discussion to encourage you to think actively about your study of statistics.

Above and Beyond
Above and Beyond boxes are included for readers who are racing ahead in learning the basic issues and want to find more out about advanced or abstract concepts in business statistics.

...d Box 1.1) whe...
...matics, statistics, economics an...
...g. However, log can also mean base 10 ...
often in mathematics.
Finally, Above and Beyond Box 1.1 goes into so...
might come in handy somewhere along the line...

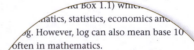

above and beyond

Box 1.1   Strange Numbers

In this box, and others throughout the book, there ...
sary to understand the material here, but which mi...
statistics by illustrating interesting terms and c...
...ey also may put more familiar terms into ...

back to basics

Box 1.1   Equations

In contrast with the Above and Beyond boxes ...
absolutely key foundational concepts in an alte...
stand. Given that the 'omigod, letters are actual...
student, why not start here?[6] This first one will ...
Consider that you have £37 in your studen...
the town for the last Friday night of term, and...
fess your love to the girl/boy/whatever you h...
experiences that it will take the consumpti...
the courage to do this. Yet you also know...
for the holidays, which will cost £9. Th...
your pints, and where the beer is ...
...nable you to purchase e...

Back to Basics
These boxes are intended to explain key concepts in the simplest way possible, often relating to examples that we hope you will find either interesting or entertaining!

The Ballad of Eddie the Easily Distracted: Part 1

As Eddie sat in the back row for the first lecture of QUAN101 Quantitative Analysis, he wondered exactly how his life had come to this. Perhaps he had died and gone to hell. Or even, he thought with a flash of hope, he might be in the wrong lecture. Yes that was it – he was in the wrong lecture, surely? I mean, what possible interest would he have in his future career with all these formulae and numbers?

His heart sank as the lecturer – a young lady who herself looked only a few years older than him – explained how the course would be assessed by an individual assignment and an exam. He wouldn't even be able to freeload off other students!

But where to start? There seemed so much to cover in the subject. Dr Jones, the lecturer, seemed pleasant enough certainly, but so had his teachers in the past, and he had never done too well there either. In fact, just the sight of numbers made him feel a little nauseous.

Still, Eddie thought, he was in the lecture anyway so he might as well try to pay attention. Nevertheless, his gaze kept going to the girl in the front row who was taking copious notes, but looking just as bored as he felt. He thought he recognized her from the Student Union bar last night; she'd left early while he had spent many hours with his new friends – which he rather regretted now. What was her name again? Esha he seemed to remember. Seemed nice enough, if a little serious.

Anyway, he tried to get his attention back to the task in hand, but he just couldn't seem to concentrate. The trouble was that each new concept seemed to build on an earlier idea, and if he hadn't understood that one, he was totally lost! Given that Eddie was easily distracted, this was a bit of a problem. Eddie resolved to try his best to keep up, but what he really needed was a place where all these basic concepts were addressed slowly, so he could take them in at his own pace.

Eddie left the lecture a little downcast, accidentally bumping into that girl Esha on the way out, who Eddie thought looked at him rather unnecessarily angrily. Later that evening, before meeting his friends in the bar again, he resolved to open the first chapter of his QUAN101 textbook and see if there was anything useful in it.

Esha's Story: Part 1

Esha had sat in the front row (as she always did) through the first of what she thought, with barely concealed disdain, would probably be a series of interminably boring lectures for QUAN101. Her mood had not been improved when the scruffy-looking daydreamer from the Student Union bar last night had walked straight into her on the way out as if she was invisible.

As Esha walked back to her room on campus, she reflected on the lecture. She had always hated this mathematical stuff. Not because she didn't understand it – she understood it very well, thank you very much – but because for the life of her she just could not see the point of all this in the real world. She came to university to study management, not maths!

She called her father that night. He had always been useful in situations like this; he owned his own successful firm and had been really pleased when Esha had gone to university to study management, although she had always thought it odd that he had a degree in engineering himself. 'Dad' she said with some exasperation, 'I don't understand the point of all this maths business, what's the point of it? I want to study management, not numbers!'

'Well,' Esha's Dad began, as Esha got the feeling she was in for a second lecture of the day, 'first of all, what do you think I do all day?' Esha thought about this, and realized she didn't really know any actual details about what Dad did at work; she just heard him tell interesting stories about the decisions he'd had to take, and what happened afterwards. 'I'm not sure, Dad. I guess you make decisions about people.' 'Quite right,' he said, 'but how do you think I make those decisions? Just by guessing?' Esha got the uncomfortable feeling that she knew where this was going. 'In order to make big decisions which affect the company, and even people's lives, you need to have information – and most of that information comes in numbers. Business people who just go on their instincts may do well for a short time, but hardly ever do they stay successful – and in my experience that is true for almost any business career. And if you always rely on others to look at the numbers for you, how do you make your own decisions?' Esha was beginning to understand the point of QUAN101.

'But there is a second answer,' continued her Dad, who was clearly warming to the subject, 'didn't you ever wonder why I have an engineering degree, yet I run my own snack food firm? The fact is, sometimes learning things is its own reward. My degree gave me the skills to critically analyse situations and information, even though it wasn't directly business related at the time. Similarly, understanding mathematics helps you in the interpretation of information, as well as in becoming comfortable with systematic and repeatable answers to general problems. It helps you to think in abstract terms, and to simplify complex specific problems into more general answers – as well as many other useful things.' Esha had already begun to feel a little better about things, and after she had spoken to her sister about some new shoes (which seemed to be all her sister was ever interested in), she thought she might have a quick look at the first chapter of the QUAN101 textbook.

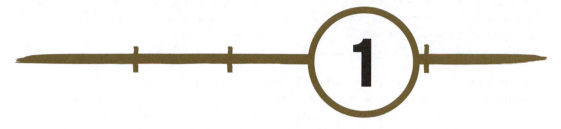

DEMYSTIFYING QUANTITATIVE DATA ANALYSIS

CONTENTS

 **learning objectives**

This is the first chapter, and our learning objectives are simple really; however, there are quite a few, and they do cover some pretty foundational issues, so please try to bear the following objectives in mind when studying this chapter:

- ☑ Understand why people might be scared or turned off by studying quantitative methods.
- ☑ Understand how quantitative analysis for business is primarily to help you make decisions in your future career, even in what you think might be the most exciting and creative professions.

- ☑ Understand exactly what data is, and what is an element (or data point), a variable and an observation, and how these together make a data set.
- ☑ Understand the difference between qualitative and quantitative variables, and discrete and continuous data.

(Continued)

(Continued)

- ☑ Begin to see how we often approximate the amount of qualities (like happiness) by numbers, but that these numbers are not the exact same thing.
- ☑ Learn the names and properties of the four different scales of measurement – nominal, ordinal, interval and ratio.
- ☑ Understand the difference between cross-sectional and longitudinal data.

- ☑ Understand what a sample is, what a population is, and the relation between the two.
- ☑ Learn why variation is important in quantitative analysis.
- ☑ Learn the concepts of BEDMAS, exponential notation, powers/exponents and logarithms.
- ☑ Understand what equations and functions are, and how they can often be expressed in sigma notation.

If you are reading this, then you are probably beginning a basic, introductory or otherwise foundational quantitative methods course. It will probably be concerned with business studies in some way, but may not be. Many of you will be quite apprehensive at this stage. Like so many people in this world, you may not feel confident with numbers, mathematics and statistics. If you are anything like me, you might have not done so well at these in the past, and may even have forgotten much of what you learnt previously. Or perhaps you might not really see the point of studying quantitative analysis anyway; after all, your course is probably in something else like human resources, work psychology, general management or (like my undergraduate degree) marketing. So the aim of this chapter is to get you off on the right foot in your quantitative analysis studies from now on – whether you are straight out of school, coming back after some work experience, or whatever. I will go through some really key concepts of number theory, mathematics and statistics, and hopefully give you the basic tools to approach quantitative analysis with some confidence. But at the same time, I will do my best to help you understand why quantitative analysis is important for business studies and many other areas of life.

But the first thing to remember is, if you are scared, you are not alone. At this stage, most students are apprehensive about beginning a quantitative course. In fact, this chapter begins with the stories of two students who are pretty typical in my experience – of course they are not real people, but more a combination of characters I have met (parts might even be based on me, but I am not telling which).

NUMEROPHOBIA[1]

Quantitative data analysis is frightening. Yes it is. Go ahead, admit it, you are *scared* of numbers. If you aren't, (a) you are lying to yourself, (b) you don't even know enough to be scared yet, or (c) you might be one of the lucky people who were always quite good at it. If you are among the latter, then you'd better get used to getting a lot of late-night visits or calls from your colleagues (actually, if you play your cards right, you can work that to your advantage). But even if you are pretty good at it, don't get lazy – because, unlike many subjects, quantitative analysis can get very tough very quickly, and if you don't lay the foundations effectively, you *will* come unstuck at some stage.

However, I'll let you in on a little secret. It's not just students who are scared of quantitative analysis – your lecturers may be too! I know it's hard to believe, but it's quite probably true. In fact, you could call the quantitative analysis course in many business school (or other university) departments 'the graveyard shift'. Certainly in my own experience it's where bright new lecturers start out teaching (unless they claim some kind of stress-related psychiatric condition or something like that). I started out my career teaching market research, and did it for nearly 10 years. Occasionally, at 9 a.m. on a Monday morning,

---

[1] Fear of numbers. Not to be confused with hexakosioihexekontahexaphobia, which is fear of the number 666.

I would walk into the lecture theatre and see tumbleweeds blowing across the floor, so desolate was the environment. Perhaps I am exaggerating, but when I wake up screaming 'Central Limit Theorem' in the middle of the night, I'm not so sure.

In fact, the only thing more scary than quantitative analysis is actually writing a book about it. Box 1.1 shows some of the most common sources of fear that individuals have about quantitative analysis, and some alternative ways of thinking about them.

 box 1.1

Fear of Numbers

'I'm scared of being wrong.' Well, this is totally acceptable. In fact, when we learn something new, we are all scared of being wrong. However, what is needed is for you to try to divorce your feelings of success from being 'right' immediately. Try to break a numerical task up into small steps, and go back to the last part which you did get right, then go forwards from there.

'How do I know if I have it wrong?' Try to look at a problem as a set of steps which need to be followed in order to get to the answer, or a decision which needs to be carefully worked through to get to the end. I sometimes like to think of a problem as a recipe, in the knowledge that if I follow the steps, then I can't fail. All that is needed is a calm head and a knowledge of what steps to follow. Of course, just like cooking, with practice it gets easier.

'I can only do simple sums.' Well, everything in maths is built upon these simple foundations. In fact, it is a lot harder to learn the simple things without any prior knowledge than it is to build in little steps on top of those foundations – so you have already done the hardest part and you don't even remember it. Try to think of each new step as a simple layer on top; don't panic as it gets more complex, just make sure you learn it before moving on.

'I can't remember my times tables.' Neither can I. The trick in maths is not to fixate on memorizing those kind of things, but to understand the rules of the game. Once you do that, you don't need to memorize hundreds of numbers. Of course, memorizing basic things can help, but you can't rely on that for everything, so make it your task to understand the rules. Focusing on memorization will actually usually lead to a point where you get stuck because you didn't bother learning the concepts.

'But I don't know the answer.' Try to think of maths and quantitative analysis as a set of rules of increasing complexity. Each rule depends on your knowledge of previous rules. So, if you take your learning slowly, and try to understand all the steps which lead up to the solution, you'll actually know the answer in the end.

Finally, always remember that maths is very simple when you break it down to its component parts – it is a set of consistent rules about what to do. Understanding maths and quantitative analysis is the process of taking your time, and being confident with each small new step before moving on to the next. Remember, there was a time when you didn't know how to add numbers, or even what a number was.

If you are anything like I was when I arrived at university to study my first[2] undergraduate mathematics course, you don't know a heck of a lot about quantitative analysis. You might have studied it at school – you might even have got pretty good grades as well – but after the summer break you probably forgot most of it, or never really *learnt* it properly in the first place. Now there's a whole bunch of stuff that you need to know before you can approach a data set with some confidence and analyse it in a meaningful way. The

---

[2] To be honest, despite my future career being heavily based around applied mathematics and statistics, it remains my *only* proper university mathematics course.

early chapters of the book lay down these foundational concepts in both a theoretical and a practical way. As a student of an applied discipline (like management, marketing and the like) you are also probably not very interested in quantitative analysis. However, I would not be exaggerating when I say that the difference between someone who is a success in business and someone who is not, is often the ability to take data and manipulate it to draw useful conclusions.

The simple reason for this is that the business world is awash with data and numbers, and I'm going to show you how different professions use quantitative analysis in the next section. If you're a person who can cut through all those intimidating numbers, you are automatically in demand. Trust me. That's of course not to say there won't be plenty of examples from here on in, but this book is about explaining key quantitative analysis concepts as clearly as possible, and teaching you to think correctly about them – it's not a book about 'your' specialist subject (e.g. market research, financial mathematics, etc.). So use this book as the foundation stone for your course, and supplement it with the unique subjects you'll need as you move through the course and specialize more and more tightly. Then, at any time you can come back to this book and refresh your memory. In fact, I still do that with my own first-year undergraduate statistics books.

HOW IS QUANTITATIVE ANALYSIS USED IN BUSINESS?

When I first went to university as a 19 year old, I wanted to be in advertising (obviously, that didn't work out too well). I figured it was all about drawing cool pictures and playing 'creative games' in the middle of the day, and I thought that going to university to study business and marketing would be a good start to this, for some reason. One thing I did *not* expect was how important quantitative analysis skills would be in my degree. In fact, I was *forced* to study two quantitative modules in my first year – *two*! Maths *and* Stats! You might be having the same issues. Then, as I specialized in marketing, I had to study yet more quantitative techniques. Not to put too fine a point on it, I struggled for quite a few years with numbers. I just never seemed to be able to get my head around all the concepts. While this was likely to be because I am just fundamentally lazy and had what I thought were better things to do, it may also have been partly because I didn't see quite how business was not the 'seat of the pants' career I expected, but one where the smart and successful decisions are most often made based on the analysis of data. After all, I was quite keen on studying strategic decisions, or designing creative marketing campaigns, but I didn't understand how *those* decisions depended on an earlier process of data analysis. In this section, I'm going to try to give a brief picture of how quantitative analysis is vital to almost all business careers, which may help you to understand the importance it has to your own success. In fact, now that I know multiple creative directors from advertising agencies, I realize that even what I thought was a completely non-numerical field is often heavily dependent on data analysis to make decisions.

As I've already alluded to, the key way in which quantitative analysis is used in business is to help *make decisions*. In almost all cases, if you want to maximize your chances of making an effective decision, you need to base that decision on *information*. Different professions or situations need different types of information, but in almost all cases a large part of that information is numerical, either in the form of data which is specifically collected for the purpose (e.g. consumer satisfaction scores), or as part of the inherent nature of the profession (e.g. stock prices and trends as data for investment decisions). Some examples of how quantitative analysis is used in business are given below, along with some references to the appropriate part of this book where they are introduced. While almost all of these specialized fields will have dedicated courses and books about them, they all rely on the base material covered in this book – without having that under control, it is very hard to move on to more specialized methods, as I know from hard experience. In fact, numeric skills are useful in making decisions in all the different aspects of your life, now and in the future. Box 1.2 gives some interesting examples.

box 1.2

Decisions, Decisions...

Life is about decisions, and many of those decisions are about numbers. I've split things into three categories (your university life, your future career and your actual life in general), and below are some very simple examples of how good quantitative skills can help you out.

University: One of the more useful skills in university life is time allocation. In order to allocate time, at minimum you must know basic mathematics. You will also find that your numeric skills will come in handy in allocating your finances, or dividing up who will pay what at dinner (the cleverest mathematician can sometimes make a profit here).

Career: Whatever career you have in mind, numeric skills will serve you well. Apart from the specific demands of the job, if you have to decide between jobs the decision often comes down to finance, and relying on headline salary figures is often misleading. Sometimes you will need to weigh up more complex packages against one another. People without numeric skills often 'can't be bothered' weighing up things like distance, travel costs, benefits and the like, along with salary.

Life: Life is full of decisions which require numbers, so much so that most of the time you do not even realize. Every time you measure something, or convert one unit (e.g. kilograms) to another (e.g. pounds), you actually perform quite a complex procedure. Of course, quantitative skills can also lead you to maximize your financial potential as well. In fact, this book may end up making you a lot of money!

think it over 1.1

Can everything that varies (i.e. what are called variables) be reduced to numbers?

Think about feelings. When you say you love something or at the opposite end hate something, how can you measure it accurately?

What about when you get exam results? For example, you score 98%, top of the class, and you are asked to complete a questionnaire about the quality of teaching in your class – what will your response be? What if you got 35%, a fail – would this make you feel different about the quality of teaching?

think it over 1.2

Some people just 'know' something is right. When you ask them how they 'know' it is right, they reply with statements such as 'it feels right', 'my gut instinct tells me it's right' or 'just intuition'. How, if possible, can you account for this?

Accounting

It is no surprise that accounting is highly quantitative. Balance sheets, cash flows, incomings and outgoings are inherently numerical. There is a vast difference between a profit and loss account that shows a profit of £24.6 million and one that uses the words 'quite a lot'. Many of the basic accounting tools and techniques are reliant on quite simple mathematics (the skill is in their correct application), but there are also lots of statistical methods employed in many large firms. For example, an auditing firm needs to validate whether or not a company's figures are accurate. However, for a large company it is impossible to examine every single transaction to see whether it tallies with the 'accounts receivable' amount shown on the balance sheet. Thus, auditors will extract a sample of the total accounts to analyse for accuracy. From this sample, the auditors can make a judgement with a certain level of confidence as to whether or not the full figure is accurate. As well as this, accountants often need to work out things such as depreciation and amortization of assets or finances. You'll be pretty confident with the basic mathematics by the end of this book, and sampling is covered in Chapters 6 and 7.

Economics

If you watch or listen to the news, you will likely hear the results of the quantitative analysis done by economists every day. They are often concerned with forecasting future values of numbers such as the gross domestic product (GDP) of a country, or the inflation of prices on important goods such as fuel or food. Despite what many may think sometimes, economists do not pull these forecasts out of, uh, 'thin air', but instead rely on complex mathematical models. These models are generally based around a regression framework, which is introduced in Chapters 10 and 11, and expanded upon in Chapter 15.

Finance and Banking

Finance is generally considered to be a highly mathematical field. Much of financial mathematics concerns techniques and models for more accurately forecasting future profits (or some other monetary value such as share price). The more accurately one is able to do that, the better the decisions about where to invest can be made. In fact, with the amounts of money being invested by the large investment banks today, even a tiny increase in the performance of these models can lead to a huge increase in profits. The foundational mathematics of this is similar to that of economics, but finance is also the most obvious business application of all that calculus you learnt at school and didn't understand why. Finance also uses a lot of statistical information – particularly in comparing the key figures of one potential investment target against market averages over a longer term. This helps analysts decide how much emphasis to place on things like short-term fluctuations of stock price. Critical forecasting concepts are introduced in Chapter 15, but those of you studying finance subjects will be using a lot of specialized texts beyond this one.

think it over 1.3

In the banking crisis of 2008–9, do you think investment decisions were made purely on the available numeric data? If they were, do you think the crisis would have happened? If they were not, what factors do you think caused the problems?

Human Resource Management

Human resource (HR) professionals are also reliant on numerical data. In particular, in order to design and conduct successfully any large-scale HR initiative, data must be collected about the organization first. In fact, in my own organization I seem to be responding to a questionnaire about staff satisfaction or opinions almost every week. Members of the HR department collect and analyse this information in order to determine in which direction to take the overall HR strategy – or at least I assume they do. In doing so, they must understand sampling, and especially sampling and non-sampling error (see Chapters 6 and 7), to understand how accurate their results are. They will probably also need to understand the correlation and regression methods in Chapters 10 and 11 to discover if some factors are linked to others, and also they will probably need to compare different groups of employees (e.g. males and females, or different departments) which may necessitate t-test or ANOVA analysis methods, which are covered in Chapters 12–14.

Production

There are many areas of production which require quantitative skills. Perhaps most interesting is the need for increasing standards of quality. As competition has intensified, quality has assumed an ever more prominent place in the mind of the consumer. Modern statistical methods have allowed the organization to monitor accurately the quality of a production process. For example, control charts, which are covered in Chapter 16, help managers to make decisions about whether or not a process is performing within an acceptable range of quality. Using control charts and other methods of quality control involves concepts from throughout this book, including sampling methods, and many of the basic statistical foundations covered in the early chapters, such as confidence intervals (Chapter 7) and statistical hypothesis testing (Chapter 8).

Marketing

I was shocked to discover quite how quantitative that marketing, my own field of choice as an undergraduate, was. Effective marketing decisions should almost always involve research which looks at customers – often done through administering questionnaires to a sample of consumers. You have probably participated in this yourself on your own main street. But even more sophisticated methods are now becoming the norm. For example, major market research agencies collect data from supermarket scanners and sell their analysis of this to other organizations. Such analysis is often based on the regression and forecasting methods introduced in Chapters 10, 11 and 15. In this way, consumer goods firms can get reasonably accurate information on key indicators such as market share, and track how effective their promotions are. This in turn helps in developing future strategies. Many firms now also have gigantic consumer databases (Google for instance has an almost unimaginable store of consumer information) and sophisticated data mining methods allow firms to use this data effectively.

Retailing

Of course, retailers themselves can also use the scanner data I referred to above, to help them to understand how consumers may behave in their stores. For example, does positioning a product in a different area of the store result in changed sales results? Or do various methods of promotional discounts result in increased profit? Such analysis relies on regression (Chapters 10 and 11) and also sometimes on the ANOVA methods in Chapter 14. Retailers may also be interested in understanding traffic flows over time and the profit potential of various locations. In order to understand these issues, knowledge of forecasting (Chapter 15) is very helpful.

Strategy

Tying it all together is strategy. In order to make strategic decisions with a high chance of success, managers need information. This information is most likely to be in numerical form, perhaps drawn from one of the areas already mentioned. For example, in order to make investment decisions, strategic managers should have some knowledge of financial analysis. In order to make decisions about what business the firm should be in, forecasting and economic analysis will be useful. Naturally, many other situations will require excellent quantitative skills. While of course the strategic manager will use many more specialized managers for advice, in order to make a decision the manager must *understand* the advice given to him or her by the – say – financial expert. Thus, even at the very highest levels of the organization, the foundational skills and tools presented in this book are vital to success.

THIS SECTION IS REALLY IMPORTANT!

Sorry, I didn't mean to shock you. I just wanted to make sure I caught your attention, because this section actually *is* really important. The common thread running through all the above examples is the idea of *data*. Quantitative analysis manipulates numbers, but those numbers are not just any numbers without meaning, they are data. Data is information in its raw form. It is the information that you have collected or obtained in some way to answer the question you have. In the context of this book, the data we will be working with is numerical, but it does not have to be, as we will see soon. The different subsections to follow all describe key ways in which you can describe the characteristics of data, and they are all important, so do make sure to read through them as they will come in handy later on.

The collection of data to be used for a given task or study is known as the data set, and Table 1.1 shows a typical data set. In this case it is a set of figures describing the characteristics of various companies. A data set like this is rarely of use by itself; it needs to be *analysed* or somehow presented. You can see this in Table 1.1. Even with only 20 companies it is hard to get a feel for the data, but imagine that there were 100, 1000 or even 100000 firms! That raw data set is essentially meaningless by itself, without analysis.

 think it over 1.4

Is there a difference between data and information? If you just read the number 10 would it have any meaning? But if you read £10 would that be different?

There are three components to every data set. The elements of a data set are the entities (i.e. 'things') about which the data is collected. In Table 1.1, the elements are companies, but they may be individuals, countries or anything that you have collected data about. Sometimes in more academic circles you can hear elements referred to as data points, but this is not common in business circles. The data set shown in Table 1.1 contains 20 elements, or data points. Possibly the most important term to understand right now though is *variable*. A variable is any specific characteristic of the elements you have collected data on. In the case of Table 1.1, the variables are *firm* (the name of the company), *turnover* (the value of the annual sales of the company) and *employees* (number of employees of the company). Finally, the set of measurements of each variable for one element is called an observation, or sometimes a case. In other words, looking at Table 1.1, observations run *along the rows*, whereas variables run *down the columns*. Or at least that is how a good data set should usually look.

Now we have the basics out of the way, let's start to think a little more deeply about data. Perhaps the most important thing to keep in mind when you are dealing with a numerical data set is that *the numbers in the data set are not always numbers in the real world*. What is that supposed to mean? Well think about it carefully. In Table 1.1 it is pretty self-explanatory: the number of employees is a number, and the turnover is also a number, so no worries there. But what about if we consider the data set in Table 1.2? Here I have added some average customer satisfaction scores. Imagine that each company asked randomly selected customers to say how satisfied they were on a scale of 1 to 5, 1 being 'not at all satisfied' and 5 being 'very satisfied', like that in Figure 1.1. Then we took that score and added it to the data set from Table 1.1 to get Table 1.2. We could use that data set to examine lots of interesting questions, as you will see later in the book.

Table 1.1 An example data set

Firm	Turnover	Employees
Jones Bros	14000000.00	74.00
Dataforce	14000000.00	1000.00
Smiths	13000000.00	130.00
AMBD Ltd	12000000.00	69.00
X-FS	12000000.00	40.00
Signum	12000000.00	30.00
Korg	10000000.00	48.00
Imatix	10000000.00	48.00
147.com	10000000.00	48.00
Stevensons	10000000.00	48.00
Analysis Ltd	10000000.00	48.00
Marketize	10000000.00	48.00
Jones Partners	10000000.00	48.00
Endoff	10000000.00	300.00
BDM Co	9000000.00	40.00
Kozelek Inc.	7000000.00	700.00
Chambers	7000000.00	3000.00
Controls	5000000.00	32.00
Star Products	4000000.00	20.00
Nick's Emporium	3303000.00	30.00

 think it over 1.5

In statistics we talk about data all the time. Quite often it is given in a numeric form. Would you say these numbers are purely data (no meaning) or do they need to be understood in the context of the situation which is being analysed?

Strongly Disagree		Neither Agree nor Disagree		Strongly Agree
1	2	3	4	5

Figure 1.1 Example Scale

However, you should not confuse the *number* in the 'satisfaction' column with the *real customer satisfaction* of a consumer. The number is simply an indicator of the satisfaction. The most basic illustration of this is that the 1–5 scale only contains whole numbers. What if my real satisfaction is not 1 or 2, but somewhere between? The scale cannot capture this. So the number is a crude approximation of what is probably quite a complex thing.

Table 1.2   Example data set 2

Firm	Turnover	Employees	Satisfaction
Jones Bros	14000000.00	74.00	1.00
Dataforce	14000000.00	1000.00	4.00
Smiths	13000000.00	130.00	5.00
AMBD Ltd	12000000.00	69.00	2.00
X-FS	12000000.00	40.00	3.00
Signum	12000000.00	30.00	4.00
Korg	10000000.00	48.00	5.00
Imatix	10000000.00	48.00	3.00
147.com	10000000.00	48.00	1.00
Stevensons	10000000.00	48.00	2.00
Analysis Ltd	10000000.00	48.00	2.00
Marketize	10000000.00	48.00	1.00
Jones Partners	10000000.00	48.00	1.00
Endoff	10000000.00	300.00	4.00
BDM Co	9000000.00	40.00	5.00
Kozelek Inc.	7000000.00	700.00	3.00
Chambers	7000000.00	3000.00	3.00
Controls	5000000.00	32.00	2.00
Star Products	4000000.00	20.00	5.00
Nick's Emporium	3303000.00	30.00	4.00

This is the essence of what we are doing when we use numbers to represent many concepts that we are interested in. We are no longer playing with 'real things', but instead with numerical *representations* of things. Using numbers allows us to use the amazingly useful tools of mathematics and statistics to answer our questions, but we should never forget that we need to link these tools and the answers they provide back eventually to the 'real world'. The numbers by themselves are not useful. Figure 1.2 illustrates this very simply.

How 'happy' do you feel?

1   2   3

Figure 1.2 Linking Numbers to the Real World

Here, the number '3' would represent 'less happy' than the number '1'. Yet the number '3' is higher than the number '1'. The number by itself is meaningless, it only has meaning when you keep it linked with the 'thing' you are trying to measure.

Qualitative and Quantitative Variables

The most obvious way to understand the difference between numerical data and the real-world qualities it often represents is to consider the difference between *qualitative* and *quantitative* variables. This is a book about quantitative analysis, but often the things we want to analyse do not come naturally in numerical form like, say, profit (a quantity of money) or age (a quantity of time) does. Qualitative variables are those like the 'firm' variable in Table 1.1. These types of variables are often labels or names of things. There is not much we can do with such variables in terms of mathematics or statistics, other than count them, work out their proportions or use them as labels. Nevertheless, they can be important in your analysis, for instance to summarize the data set – which will be discussed later when we come to Chapter 4 on descriptive statistics.

On the other hand, quantitative variables contain numerical data which indicates *how much*, or *how many*, of a variable there is. These variables are like the 'employees' (how many) or 'turnover' (how much) variables in Table 1.1. With such variables we can perform all kinds of useful mathematical and statistical analyses, which will make up the bulk of the tools explained in this book.

But what if I were to use numbers instead of words to represent qualitative variables in our data set? Take a qualitative variable like biological gender – male or female. Instead of writing 'Male' or 'Female' in the spreadsheet, I could make '1' represent 'Male' and '2' represent 'Female'. Then I have numbers in the spreadsheet, not words, so surely I can use my fancy mathematical tools on them? Unfortunately not. You see, the numerical value in that case is still just a label; it does not represent anything quantitative about the variable. There is not 'more' of anything to do with females than males, *even though the number for 'Female' is bigger than for 'Male'*. This is the crux of the distinction between quantitative and qualitative.

You might at this point be thinking back to that customer satisfaction example earlier, or the happiness example in Figure 1.2. Surely, these are qualitative concepts as well? Well, yes and no. Satisfaction is not *naturally* numerical, like profit, or share price, might be. But it is quantitative in that it is meaningful to consider 'how much' of it there is. In such a case we can *measure* it with a number, not just assign a label to it.

This concept is illustrated well by an explanation of the different scales of measurement.

think it over 1.6

In the satisfaction survey, if a person rated their satisfaction as 4, does that mean they are twice as satisfied as someone who responded with 2?

Scales of Measurement

So, we now know that we can represent 'quantities' of things in the real world with numbers in our data set. But we cannot take off our thinking caps yet. You already know many basic rules for working with numbers: you know how to count, add, subtract, multiply, divide (at a minimum, you can do these on a calculator) and the like. Now, these operations and rules all apply to numbers – give us a number and we can operate on it. But the same rules do *not* always apply to the real-world variables we are working with. For example, remember above that I labelled 'Males' with '1' and 'Females' with '2'? Well, I can certainly do all kinds of things with those *numbers*, but many of them will just not be logical if I was to do them with the real-world concept of biological gender. For example, if I had 3 males and 3 females, I could take the average of the gender variable and come up with 1.5 as my answer. But a value of 1.5 does not make sense in the context of my real-word concept, which can only take the value of male (1) or female (2). What is 1.5 meant to be? So, we need *rules* that can tell us what we can logically do with the different qualitative and quantitative variables we have in our data set, even though they may all be using numbers. Most of the time, we tend to reject rules, but in the case of quantitative analysis, rules are good because they make life easier. Try to think of them as instructions for a recipe. If you do not know the rules, the recipe will not work!

First of all, there is the *nominal* scale. This scale refers to the situation where we are using numbers to label a qualitative element. The simplest example is biological gender as above. Biological gender is a characteristic of an element in a data set – you can be either male or female. Similarly, the 'colour of your underpants' and many other things. In such cases we *could* use words as labels. But we often like to assign a numeric code to the different possible values of the variable (e.g. 1 = 'red', 2 = 'orange', 3 = 'blue', etc.); this can make life easier for us in the long term. However, in such cases the numbers are only *labels*, there is no logic behind their order or value. The only mathematical thing you can do with this sort of variable is *count* it. You can thus examine the comparative amounts or proportions of each different value. This is the simplest rule.

If there is some meaning to the *order* of numbers we use to represent the variable, we can term the scale *ordinal*. In this case we are now working with quantitative concepts. For example, we could ask for ratings of consumer satisfaction on a scale of 'excellent', 'so-so' or 'rubbish'. In this case, we know that 'excellent' is better than 'so-so' which is better than 'rubbish'. So there is a meaning to the order. But we do not know whether the difference in satisfaction between 'excellent' and 'so-so' is the same 'amount' (also called magnitude) as the difference between 'so-so' and 'rubbish'. We can label these as '3', '2' and '1' from excellent to rubbish respectively if we want. However, even though the differences *between the numbers* are the same (i.e. 3 is one bigger than 2, which is one bigger than 1), this still does not mean the differences *between the values* of excellent, so-so and rubbish are the same.

If we can see that our variable has some kind of fixed unit of measurement (i.e. the differences between values are consistent) we can use an *interval* scale. Consider the typical temperature scale in degrees Celsius. This is a great example of an interval scale. The difference between 20 and 30 degrees Celsius is 10 degrees. This is exactly the same amount of heat that there is between 60 and 70 degrees Celsius. So just like an ordinal scale, we can rank the scores from low to high (or vice versa), but the *differences between the scores* are also meaningful. This scale enables us to use more mathematical techniques again, and is yet more powerful. But it still lacks the full range of properties of the standard number sequence. For example, consider the statement 'it was twice as cold as it was yesterday, and yesterday it was 0 degrees Celsius'. So how cold does that make it? Another interesting example is the Western date in years. We know the difference between AD 1950 and 2000 is the same as that between AD 150 and 200, that is 50 years. But think about what the date 'AD 0' represents.

What I am getting at is that an interval scale lacks a meaningful zero point. Even though it may have 'zero' in the range, this zero point does not mean there is 'nothing'. Zero degrees Celsius simply means that water freezes; AD 0 does not represent the beginning of time, just the beginning of a certain number sequence representing time. To be *meaningful* the zero point must indicate no value of the variable at all. In such cases, we have a *ratio* scale. The term ratio refers to the fact that once we have a meaningful zero, ratios of the variable have meaning. For example, the ratio temperature scale is the Kelvin scale. Zero Kelvin refers to a total absence of temperature (which is in fact around −273 degrees Celsius). If we think about 80 degrees Celsius, this cannot mean there is 'twice as much temperature' as 40 degrees Celsius, the ratio is just nonsense without the meaningful zero. But, 200 degrees Kelvin *is* twice as much temperature as 100 degrees Kelvin. In a business context, *profit* is an excellent example of a ratio scale. Although things get a bit more complicated if you start thinking about negative profit (i.e. loss). Even so, there is such a thing as 'no' or 'zero' profit.

One key thing to realize here is that the most powerful scale we can use is defined by the real-world variable in question. For example, for a variable like gender, we can only ever use a nominal scale. However, for heat, we can use ratio if we wish, but also we could use interval (Celsius), or even ordinal (say 'hot', 'cold', 'brrrrrr!'). This means you should always think carefully about what you are trying to measure and why. Furthermore, the scale you use has impacts on what you can do with the data mathematically. For example, even though ordinal scales have some meaning to their magnitude, gaps between the values are *not* meaningful, so you cannot take the mean of the ordinal scale. The important point to keep in your mind is – again – that the numbers you see in front of you, that you will be working with throughout your courses, are only *representations* of real-world concepts, properties and objects.

The Temporal Dimension

Another key distinction between different types of data concerns time. In case you did not know, 'temporal' is just a fancy way of saying 'time' and something which has always impressed me – so I figured it might impress you too. Anyway, imagine these two different types of research project: (a) we collect data about the balance sheets of 100 companies at the end of the 2008–9 financial year; and (b) we collect data on the profit of one company over the course of a decade, collecting data each month.

The first situation results in what is called a cross-sectional data set. This data set is collected at a single point in time – or at least, an approximately single point in time. Perhaps the best way to think about it is that the *intention* is for the data to represent a 'snapshot' of the situation at one point in time. Of course, it is usually impossible to collect data at exactly the same point in time across many cases.

On the other hand longitudinal data is collected over a long time period, which is why this type of data set is sometimes called time series data. The intention here is for the data to represent how the data changes over time. For example, Figure 1.3 shows a time series for the amount of sales calls made by a salesperson in one month.

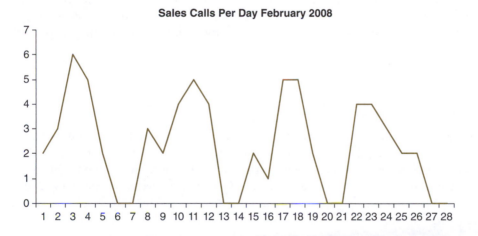

Sales Calls Per Day February 2008

Figure 1.3
Example
Time Series

While this is not a concrete rule, you often find that cross-sectional data is collected about many variables at one time, whereas time series data can be collected on a single variable over many time periods. Most of the analysis tools in this book will look at cross-sectional data, but time series data is specifically covered in the later chapters, for example on forecasting. Whether you need cross-sectional or time series data depends on your research goals, but that is outside the scope of this book, which is mainly aimed at telling you what to *do* with the data when you have it.

 think it over 1.7

Which is better, cross-sectional data or longitudinal data? Why do we have these two techniques?

Samples and Populations

The concept of sampling, and the linked concept of the population, will come up again and again in this book. However, it will be handy for you to have come across it before getting to later chapters. I already snuck in a reference to sampling earlier on, when we talked about what auditors sometimes do, so it should not be totally new to you (you probably learned about it before as well).

In essence, it is usually impossible for us to collect data on every element we are interested in. For example, perhaps we want to know the turnover of every company with less than 100 employees in the UK. Theoretically, this may be possible to collect if we have the resources (maybe we are the UK government), but most likely it is impossible. Even if it is possible, what about if we wanted to know about every company in the *world* with less than 100 employees? Or what if we wanted to collect satisfaction scores from every purchaser of Heinz Baked Beans? The population is a term which refers to the set of all of the elements we are interested in. In one of the earlier situations, the population was 'every company in the UK with less than 100 employees', and in another 'every company in the world with less than 100 employees'. It is important that analysts and researchers understand clearly exactly what population they are interested in, even when they cannot collect data on it in its entirety.

In fact, most of the time it is just not feasible to collect data on every element. If we can collect data on every element, we are doing what is called a census. Such exercises are done by many national governments, and their relative infrequency should give you an idea of how resource intensive they are. More commonly, we have to take what is called a sample. A sample is any subset of the entire population. There are many different ways of collecting samples, and I will go through sampling theory in Chapter 7. In fact, most of the specific research courses you take later on in your career (e.g. market research) will spend a long time talking about sampling. This is basically because we are more interested in applying the results of the analysis of our sample back to the population than we are in the sample results. As a consequence, there will be a lot of information in this book which is related to the issue.

Discrete and Continuous Data

The final distinction I will cover in this section is between discrete and continuous data. This is covered in some depth later on in this book (e.g. when I introduce ideas of sampling, probability, distributions and the like), but it will help you a lot if you get the idea bubbling away in your head right now. That said, it is quite a difficult thing to get your head around at first, so do not worry too much if you do not 'click' with it immediately, I will be going through this again at various points of the book. It is important that you meet it right now, though, because having this idea somewhere in your mind throughout the rest of your reading will help you ultimately to understand it when you *really* need it.

Consider this: I collect data on the age of 1000 people, asking them to give me their age to the closest full year. I can then count the frequency of occurrence of each year and I could plot it on a graph or something like that. So, basically, I would have something where maybe there were 45 people who were aged 30, 15 were aged 19, 20 were aged 50, and so forth. This kind of data is discrete. In other words, there is separation between the possible values which an element can take – you can be either 20 or 21, but not both, and not 21.5. Get it?

Now, work with me here and imagine the following situation. Try really hard because it is quite challenging to get your head around. Imagine we made the way we measured age finer and finer – first to months, then weeks, then days, minutes, seconds, and keep going. You can imagine that as the way to measure age got more fine-grained, the number of people of each age would get smaller and smaller. OK? So, at the same time imagine that we kept increasing the number of people we were measuring as we made the measure finer. Imagine if you will that in fact we kept *infinitely* making the measure finer and finer, while increasing the amount of people we were measuring at the same time. Eventually (remember, *infinity*) there would be no distinction between one age and the next.[3] This kind of data is continuous. In other words, there is no separation between the possible values of a variable each element can take. There are many real-life situations where data is essentially continuous if we do not artificially divide it into units (e.g. time), but the real benefit of this concept is evident when it comes to the statistical theories which we will come to eventually in Chapter 5.

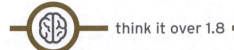

think it over 1.8

Does continuous data really exist or is it just a convenient way of thinking about data? How many numbers are there between 0 and 1? What about 0 and 0.00000001? If I wanted to measure the temperature of a room accurately, what are the decisions I would have to make?

A RECAP OF KEY MATHEMATICAL AND STATISTICAL CONCEPTS

One of the things which kind of scared (or should that be 'scares'?) me about quantitative analysis is that I always felt a little bit lost in the terminology of basic foundational concepts. In other words, I never felt that I had learned the 'language' of mathematics and statistics. So, just seeing an equation or function on a sheet of paper was enough to scare me away. As a consequence, I think it is really important for beginning students to have a grasp of these things before moving on to anything else. I will begin by discussing the concept of statistics itself. After this, there will be a set of critical mathematical tools, concepts and operations which you should understand intimately. Finally, I will conclude with a section about the basics of mathematical functions and symbols, which is something I always struggle with myself.

What Are Statistics?

Since I mentioned statistical theory above, now would seem to be a good time to introduce the idea of statistics. First let's think about why we might need statistics. If you go back to Table 1.1, you will see that I made the point that it was hard really to draw any conclusions about raw data without analysing it. A huge set of raw numbers in rows and columns is pretty meaningless to us. What we really need is some way of summarizing the characteristics of the set, or extracting a smaller set of information from it. For example, we might want to calculate the average turnover of the companies in Table 1.1. Actually, it is very imprecise to use the word average, since there are many different ways of calculating average – but I will deal with this in Chapter 4. Anyway, moving swiftly onwards, if we were to take the average of every company in the population, this would be called a parameter. However, when we are dealing with the analysis of a sample, it is called a statistic.

Most of the time, we are actually not very interested in the statistic by itself. We are in fact more interested in the population parameter. Recall the accounting example above. The auditors were not interested in the sample statistic itself, they were interested in whether it was *the same as the value the company they were auditing claimed for the parameter*. This task is what we call statistical inference. It is the task of understanding the *likelihood of our sample statistics being the same as the population parameters*. Or at least that is it in a nutshell. Most of Chapters 5–8 are concerned with this, and the rest of the book after Chapter 8 generally depends on that information as well. So it is kind of important.

---

[3] I know infinity is a tough concept, but just run with it for now.

Variation and Statistics

Building on the previous brief discussion of what statistics are, I want now to talk about the concept of variation in data. You can see from lots of examples already in this chapter that the variables take on different values for different elements. In fact, the clue is in the name – we call them variables, remember. The idea of variation is an absolutely vital one in statistical inference and other quantitative analysis fields. Again, variation will be covered in much more depth later on, but basically try to imagine the situation where you wanted to see whether one factor (maybe something simple like gender) was associated with a change in another (something more controversial like, say, intelligence test performance). Continue to imagine the situation where we have 50 males and 50 females, but that each of those elements scored exactly the same on our intelligence test. So how could we tell whether differences in test scores were associated with differences in gender? Simple answer: you cannot! So it is easy to see how the concept of variation is key in quantitative analysis methods. In fact, we can measure it in many ways, which will be introduced in Chapter 4.

In theory, variation can be partitioned into at least two types. The first is systematic variation, which is basically variation which we think is due to something important – usually what we are testing for. In the case above, systematic variation is that which is due to the gender effect (i.e. if females are smarter than males). The second is unsystematic variation, which is the variation due to everything else – sometimes called error or random variation.

When we are 'doing statistics' – or in other words when we are performing statistical inference – we are basically trying to work out the chances that the numbers we observed in our sample are the same in the population. We do this by first calculating what are called test statistics. There are many (hundreds at least) different test statistics, each used for different purposes. I will be covering many of them in the later sections of the book, but the basic concept is simple. A test statistic is simply a number with specific characteristics. Most importantly, we know how often the different values of it occur in any given situation.

As I said, there are many of these, but it is easy to understand when you think about something a bit more simple, like a characteristic of people. Take something like reaction time, for example. Studies have shown the average reaction time for all kinds of tasks; let's take 'pushing a button in response to a sound' as an example. We know that the average reaction time for a human to push the button after hearing the sound is some amount of time, which we can represent with the symbol x. We also know the distribution of reaction time, in that we know the probability of the various different reaction times. This makes basic logical sense if you think about it. If the *average* time is x, then, if we take any given person, it is *most likely* that they will have a reaction time of x or close to it. Therefore it is *less likely* that they will have a reaction time either a lot slower or quicker than x. Flip that logic around and, once you know x, then if you were to measure your own reaction time, you could work out the probability of observing that time, given that reaction time has a known distribution. In other words, are you around the average x, or are you much lower or higher? This will be covered in much more depth in Chapters 6–8.

Moving back to variation, these test statistics are basically calculated by working out how much of the variance in your data is systematic, versus that which is not. Of course, it is more complex than that, and each statistic works it out differently. Because we know the distribution of these test statistics, we can calculate how likely it was that we observed that particular value for the test statistic. This is the whole point of statistical inference, and I will begin to discuss it in depth in Chapters 7 and 8.

 **think it over 1.9**

If I used a reliable statistical technique to measure the reaction times of 1000 people, could I use the answer to predict the reaction time of one person?

Basic Mathematical Concepts and Tools

Now, let's get some critical mathematical revision out of the way. Of course, it is impossible to cover absolutely every basic mathematical and numerical concept here; perhaps one day I will write a book about that too (good lord, I am only at the very beginning of this one so far!). I do have to assume some basic knowledge. Nevertheless, there are some pretty handy things which might have slipped your mind, or been taught while you were, ahem, 'sick' at school, which will be quite useful here. These are basic mathematical tools which are very simple but the cause of great trouble if one does not know them.

First, when I was younger at school in New Zealand, I was taught the acronym BEDMAS, which stands for Brackets, Exponents, Division, Multiplication, Addition, Subtraction. It refers to the order in which you should calculate in an equation. In the UK system, I am told it is in fact referred to as BODMAS,[4] which is the same thing, but Exponent is termed 'Order'. I think that is confusing, because 'order' refers to a specific mathematical thing, but this is within an acronym about order in a different sense. It seems a bit silly to me, especially when there is a ready-made alternative. So let's work with BEDMAS. Basically, BEDMAS tells you how to calculate in any simple equation, and is quite important. First, however, let me define exponents (aka orders, aka indices). This is simple: for example, 5 squared is written mathematically as 5^2, where 5 is the coefficient and 2 is the exponent (also termed 5 to the order of 2, or 5 to the power of 2). So let's see an example, in Figure 1.4.

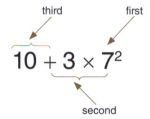

Figure 1.4
BEDMAS

think it over 1.10

Why are exponents useful? What about algebra in general, using letters to represent quantities?

Of course, the answer here is 157 if you follow the order shown in Figure 1.4. If you place brackets in that equation, you can actually change the answer. If you bracket it to make $(10 + 3) \times 7^2$ you will get 637, whereas if you bracket it to make $10 + (3 \times 7^2)$ you will get 157 again. The latter is because, in this case, the brackets do not change anything (you were already doing the exponent before the multiplication before the addition anyway).

think it over 1.11

Why are there rules like BEDMAS? What happens if we violate these rules?

---

[4] Actually, when I looked at my friends' daughter Lucy's maths homework last week, they used BIDMAS, where the I stood for 'indices' – which is again another term for exponents/order. BIDMAS works OK for me too (it's definitely an improvement on BODMAS), so you might have heard of that term.

Scientists and other quantitative gurus often represent numbers in exponential notation. This is because such people often work with huge or very small numbers which are rather unwieldy to write out. Think about the mass of the Earth, which is around 5973600000000000000000000 kilograms, or the mass of an electron, which is something around 0.00000000000000000000000000000091093822 kilograms. Imagine having to write out those kinds of numbers repeatedly, or even once. Mistakes will happen, I promise you. Instead, if you use exponential notation you can express the number as *something multiplied by 10 to the power of something else*. Or more scientifically, as a coefficient multiplied by $10^{exponential}$, where the coefficient is a number between 1 and 10, with the relevant exponent. So in this notation, the Earth's mass is 5.9736×10^{24} kilograms, and an electron's mass is $9.1093822 \times 10^{-31}$ kilograms.

What confuses some people (myself included) is that calculators often express this a bit differently. Usually, they use an 'e' or 'E' to represent the 'times 10 to the power of' bit. So the Earth's mass would be 5.9736e24. I always used to think the 'e' represented 'error' and that I had done something wrong. This caused much heartache at school and university (as if I didn't have enough already).

Exponents or powers (sometimes called 'orders' as well, as we found out above) are basically representative of growth, with x, x^2, x^3, being named the first, second, third (and so on in sequence) powers of x. Of course, you will probably remember that these lower powers (second and third) are called *squared* and *cubed*. To introduce for the first time some algebraic notation, using n to stand for 'any number', you could say that x^n is the nth power of x. Incidentally, if you read Above and Beyond Box 1.1 you might wonder about the power of 0. Well, any non-zero number raised to the power of 0 equals one, which can be proved mathematically if you want.[5] Do not even ask about 0^0, when things get even more complicated!

You can think of logarithms as the inverse of exponentials. Logarithms (called 'logs' by those who want to look cool) are important because they help to describe a lot of interesting properties in the real world, as you will see later on. A logarithm is the power (explained above) to which you must raise a given number in order to attain a specific other number. A logarithmic expression contains two main elements, the *base* and the *power* (or exponent). For example, the logarithm of 10000 to the base 10 is 4, because 10^4 equals 10000. This would be expressed as $\log_{10}10000 = 4$. The logarithm to the base 2 of 128 is 7, because 2^7 equals 128 ($\log_2 128 = 7$). The main bonus from the development of logarithms is the fact that they can reduce multiplication to addition, which makes complex calculations much easier if one has to do them by hand. They do this by virtue of the formula $\log(xy) = \log x + \log y$. Handy. Base 10 and 2 are the most common simple logarithmic bases, but you will also very commonly come across what is called the natural logarithm, which is a logarithm to the base e, where e is an irrational constant (see Above and Beyond Box 1.1) which is *approximately* equal to 2.718281828. This logarithm is super-useful in mathematics, statistics, economics and various other fields. It is sometimes noted as ln, Ln, $\log_e$ or even just log. However, log can also mean base 10 – which is confusing. It is called 'natural' because it appears so often in mathematics.

Finally, Above and Beyond Box 1.1 goes into some very interesting different types of numbers, which might come in handy somewhere along the line…

 above and beyond

Box 1.1 Strange Numbers

In this box, and others throughout the book, there are terms and concepts which are not strictly necessary to understand the material here, but which might help you build your confidence in mathematics and statistics by illustrating interesting terms and concepts you might have heard about but not understood. They also may put more familiar terms into a new and interesting context.

---

[5] Don't email asking me to do it, find it for yourself!

Consider the number 0. What actually *is* it? It is generally accepted to have been invented at the same time by the Chinese and Hindi cultures, around the sixth century AD. Being more concerned with practical uses of maths than rules, the Chinese came up with it simply as a 'placeholder' to represent the missing place in numbers such as 'one hundred and one' (i.e. 101). By contrast, the Hindi civilization considered it in a more philosophical manner, concerning their idea of 'The Void'. This latter idea is vital to the meaning of zero, because it is very weird (and is a good example of how seemingly simple mathematical concepts become very odd if we think them through to their extreme). On the one hand, zero is just like any number, in that it can be added and subtracted without any weird things happening. But what about multiplying? Multiply anything by zero and you get zero, and divide anything by zero and you get infinity! And also, you do not *count* using zero, you start at one. That for example is why I used to get so confused about centuries – I was born in the twentieth century, because we started counting in the first, not the 'zeroth'. The more you investigate zero, the weirder it gets. But there are plenty of other odd numbers which you could find out about.

Prime numbers are those which cannot be divided by any other number apart from themselves and one. What this means is that if you divide a prime number by any other number apart from itself or one, you get a fraction. You may think this has no real point, apart from being interesting, but there are applications for this, for example in creating encryption algorithms – such as those useful for Internet applications. There are an infinite number of primes, and there is an ongoing competition for finding the largest known prime.

Rational numbers are another name for fractions. They are numbers which can be represented by ratios of two integers (whole numbers), like 4/5. They are used for calculation, but not counting. They have their own arithmetic, which can be quite hard to follow. In this book, fractions will appear very infrequently, as we will work with decimals mainly.

Irrational numbers are those which *cannot* be represented by the ratio of two integers. This sounds weird to most people (hence the name I guess). But you almost certainly know one – pi or π, which is the ratio of the circumference of a circle to its diameter. As you also probably know, if you were to calculate it as a decimal, it would never end. The decimal expansion of an irrational number neither repeats nor terminates. Another example is the square root of two.

Complex numbers are produced when a real number is added to what is termed an imaginary unit, which is basically the square root of –1. Like most of the above, they do not really concern us here other than for interest's sake, but they are almost essential to most higher-level mathematics applications. For example, in solving some equations, even though the answer may be a real number, complex numbers are necessary or useful during the solving.

 think it over 1.12

Are complex numbers called complex numbers because they are complicated? Why are they called complex numbers? Can a rational number also be a complex number?

Equations

Equations cause much pain and suffering among the less quantitatively oriented students. Which is somewhat unfortunate since they are the fundamental core of mathematics (and thus business statistics and the like). You will see equations throughout this book on almost every page. Some basic concepts will help you overcome any fear of equations and have you playing with them like a pro. Well, almost.

Equations contain variables, which in this case mean something slightly different from the data set example given earlier. Variables in equations are 'quantities which are unknown' and usually represented by *letters*. Representing unknown numbers with letters is sometimes the point where your mind warps to the point of no return and mathematics becomes 'stupid'. But just think of the letters as numbers which we do not know (yet). If the purpose of the equation is to determine what number that letter represents, we call it an unknown, otherwise it is just a variable. A constant in an equation is simply a number we do know, represented by – you guessed it – an actual number. Sometimes constants are called parameters. Equations are basically essential for anything more than extremely basic maths, and are actually very useful in everyday life as well, which makes it a shame that so many students switch off as soon as a letter appears in an equation. They are essential, at least in part because they allow us to solve mathematical problems far easier than otherwise, and given that a lot of our lives is concerned with solving mathematical problems, understanding them is useful. This is of course quite apart from how integral they are to this book's material. Back to Basics Box 1.1 is a simple explanation of one of the most basic equations possible, in a way which might clarify things for some.

think it over 1.13

The term modelling is used quite a bit in statistics and mathematics. What do we mean when we say we have created a statistical model?

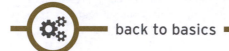

back to basics

Box 1.1   Equations

In contrast with the Above and Beyond boxes scattered throughout, Back to Basics boxes aim to present absolutely key foundational concepts in an alternative manner which might be easier for some to understand. Given that the 'omigod, letters are actually *numbers*!' stuff has been the downfall of many a maths student, why not start here?[6] This first one will concern pints of beer, which I am quite partial to.

Consider that you have £37 in your student account left after the first term. You want to go out on the town for the last Friday night of term, and during this night you want to pluck up the courage to confess your love to the girl/boy/whatever you have been infatuated with all term. You know from previous experiences that it will take the consumption of a minimum of 5 pints of beer in order for you to get up the courage to do this. Yet you also know that on Saturday morning you have to buy a train ticket home for the holidays, which will cost £9. There are a variety of bars around town where you could purchase your pints, and where the beer is of varying prices. *You need to know how expensive the pints can be* to enable you to purchase enough to give you the courage for your confession, as well as leave £9 in your pocket for the trip home to Mum.

This is an extremely simple equation, which you can set up as follows:

$$5x + 9 = 33$$

where x is the maximum average price of a pint which would enable you to buy five. Our objective is therefore to discover what x should be, so in the end we would like an equation to look something like:

$$x = ??$$

where ?? is the answer. Right?

There are various ways of solving this. Because it is so simple, we could do it by trial and error, but that is not the point here (and they are not always so simple!).

---

[6] That said, if you think expressing numbers with words is nonsensical, you are in good company. One of the greatest philosophers and mathematicians ever, René Descartes, originally thought the same. And he went on to make huge contributions to mathematics in the end.

So, let's solve it by using basic algebraic manipulation. Think of the equation like a scale with the equals sign as the pivot. The rule is: you *must keep it balanced*. In other words, everything you do to one side of the 'pivot' (i.e. the equals sign) must be done to the other. So let's work this out...

First, subtract 9 from both sides: $5x = 24$

Then, divide by 5 on both sides: $x = 4.8$

So, the maximum average pint price is £4.80 to still leave funds for the train trip. At the time of writing this book, that would certainly be fine, and in fact would probably leave you with funds left over to buy the object of your desire a drink. Bonus!

So, never let it be said that mathematics is not romantic.

An equation such as that in Back to Basics Box 1.1 is termed a linear equation. It contains only a variable to the power of 1, and as you will see later in the book, it can be plotted as a straight line on a graph. A quadratic equation contains a variable to the power of 2 (i.e. x^2). Because of the properties of multiplication, they always have two possible answers, or 'roots', although they can be the same. For example, $x^2 = 25$ could have the answer 5 or −5. A cubic equation unsurprisingly has a single variable to the power 3. Cubic equations always have three roots, and two or all of them may be equal. A quartic equation is one with a variable to the power of 4, and you can imagine by now no doubt that there are four roots here. You can also term these equations first-, second-, third- and fourth-degree equations respectively, and there is basically no limit to the degrees as we go on.

You will no doubt have noticed that so far we have been dealing with equations with one variable. However, equations can have more variables than this, and in fact there is no limit to how many variables there can be in an equation. Nevertheless, in most cases, if there is more than one variable in a single equation, this equation by itself is unsolvable, or *insoluble*. The only way to solve such equations is if we have additional equations which contain the same variables. If we have the same number of equations as we do variables, it is usually possible to solve the equations and discover the values of the variables. In such cases, we say we are dealing with a system of simultaneous equations, like the following:

$$5x + xy + 7 = 0$$

$$x + 2xy = 0$$

The first thing to remember is that these systems are internally consistent. In other words, x and y are the same in both equations. So, we can solve this one quite easily, even though it might look quite complicated to the uninitiated at first. But remember the rules from Back to Basics Box 1.1: everything you do on one side of a single equation has to be done to the other. However, you do not have to do the same thing to both equations at the same time.

To begin then, multiply the first equation by 2 to get:

$$10x + 2xy + 14 = 0$$

Do you see what has happened here? If we subtract the second equation from the new first equation, we get:

$$9x + 14 = 0$$

This leaves us with a very simple piece of manipulation to do, like we did in the box above:

$$9x = -14$$

$$x = -14/9 = -1.56$$

The next thing to do is *substitute* that value for x into the first equation, replacing x with -1.56, to give $y = -0.51$. Note, though, that these values have been rounded to two decimal places, so they are not absolutely exact.

That said, most simultaneous equations cannot be solved as easily as this, and require complex computer models to get approximate solutions (usually by trying over and over again with different values, to try to get as close as possible, termed an iterative method).

think it over 1.14

If you plotted a graph of the two equations given above, could you predict where they would cross? What is the significance of this value?

Sigma Notation

One thing that always confused me (for what you would think was a surprisingly long time) was what I later found out could be termed sigma notation, or summation notation. This appears all over statistics and involves a rather gratuitous use of the Greek letter Σ (sigma). Σ is used in many statistical contexts to indicate 'the sum of'. So Σx means the *sum of all x values*, and Σx^2 means the *sum of all the squared x values*. In the latter case, you would square each x first, and only then sum the squared values (remember, BEDMAS). You are normally in the situation where you have a set of x values (maybe some data), and the sigma notation shows you that you have to add them together in some specific way. Here is a simple example.

If x takes the values of 2, 5, 10, 256, then:

$$\Sigma x = 2 + 5 + 10 + 256 = 273$$

$$\Sigma x^2 = 2^2 + 5^2 + 10^2 + 256^2 = 65665$$

This is simple enough in this instance, but it is in fact a rather informal version of sigma notation. I always got more confused when things got more general. Consider the more formal notation in Figure 1.5.

Figure 1.5
Formal
Sigma
Notation

$$\sum_{i=m}^{n} x_i$$

The index variable appears at the bottom of the Σ (termed the *subscript*). The index variable i is called the index of summation, and m is the lower bound of summation. In this case $i = m$ means that the index i begins equal to m. The n represents the upper bound of summation. In this case, we find successive values of i by adding one to the previous value of i, starting out equal to m and finishing up when $i = n$. If it is an infinite series, the infinity symbol ∞ is used as n. The x_i part of the formula is changeable, and it depends on what you are summing. As you know, the i part of the formula is the index of summation and varies between m and n, but the x part can be replaced by pretty much any relevant expression.

Functions

Functions are kind of similar to equations in concept, and you should also be aware that the word 'function' means different things to different people. So do not get it confused with a subroutine in computer science, or, more importantly, a party. Turning up to mathematics classes dressed in your party clothes might be seen as inappropriate. Anyway, a function is a way of expressing some dependence between two variables or quantities. The concept of functions is vital to most of the more advanced mathematical and statistical operations in this book, so let's get it straight now.

As I just said, a function expresses some dependence between two variables. One of these is called the independent variable, sometimes called the argument or the input. You might also hear it called the predictor, or exogenous variable in some contexts. The independent variable is usually given. The other variable is called the dependent variable, or sometimes the value or output. It may also be called the criterion or endogenous variable in some situations. A function basically tells you what output you get for a specific input.

According to convention, we represent variables by letters at the end of the alphabet, such as x, y and z. Functions can also contain constants, which are of a constant value (hence the name), and where necessary these are represented by letters at the start of the alphabet, such as a, b and c.

As a very simple example of a function consider the following:

$$f(x) = x^2$$

This is the standard notation to describe a function; it can be read as 'the function of x is x squared'. So, in other words, for every input we put into the function, we get an output of the input number squared. Thus the input of 2 results in the output of 4, which can be written as $f(2) = 4$.

A different example you might recognize occurs in cooking. I like cooking – it is very relaxing after a long day writing about statistics. In New Zealand, I learnt to cook using grams and kilograms as units of weight, but in the UK (when the European Union is not looking) we often use ounces and pounds. So, of course, I need to convert these units. If I have x grams, I can use a formula to express easily the conversion from grams to ounces, for example as:

$$f(x) = 0.053x$$

This case shows that 1 gram equals 0.053 ounces. I think you can pretty easily work out other values, and this is of course an extremely simple formula.

We use the f notation above when we need to give the function a name for some purpose. This is quite common in mathematics. For example, we might need to use a long function repeatedly, and it would be handy just to use $f(x)$ for simplicity. So I could equally define $f(x) = x^3 + 5x + 3$. Then $f(2) = 21$. However, sometimes we do not need to name a function (which is much more common in more applied situations like those in this book). In such cases we sometimes drop the f business and use the form:

$$y = x^2$$

This defines the dependent variable as y and the independent variable as x. It might help you to work out what is going on here. The confusion may arise when you wonder whether you have an equation or a function. If you have an equation like $y = x^2$ to deal with, then you already know that this is insoluble without any other information. However, if it is a function it is not meant to be solvable by analysis, instead it simply *describes what happens when you input a value of x*. Or in other words, the value of y which results from a given value of x.

As you might have already guessed, functions can be shown in many different ways. So far I have given you functions in the form of formulae, but sometimes it is more useful to show them as a plot or graph. Figure 1.6 shows $f(x) = x^2$ as a plot, and you will probably recognize it. We plot the inputs on the x axis and the corresponding outputs on the y axis. Plots and formulae are the most useful representations for our purposes, but functions can instead have their properties described in words (as was done before), or be represented by algorithms, or even by their relationships to other functions (e.g. the inverse of some other function).

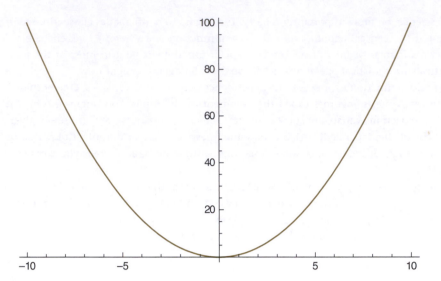

Figure 1.6
Plot of
$f(x) = x^2$

think it over 1.15

Look at Figure 1.6. If you drew a vertical line up from −5 and another one up from +5 until they hit the curve, and then joined the two end points to form a rectangle, where would the horizontal line cross the vertical axis? What is significant, mathematically speaking, about this value?

Extremely common or useful functions are often given their own permanent name. You have almost certainly come across these in your prior mathematical career. For example, the function $f(x) = x^2$ is generally written as Square(x). Although, to be honest, this is not the greatest example since the permanent name is actually longer! Nevertheless, you will probably have come across the trigonometric functions sine, cosine and tangent, which are represented as $\sin(x)$, $\cos(x)$ and $\tan(x)$. In other words, you input x into the relevant function and get an output y. These are good examples of how function notation can be very useful to us.

think it over 1.16

Why do we call one variable independent and the other dependent? Is there a mathematical relationship between them?

SUMMARY

At this point I suspect you either have all kinds of confusing things going around in your head, or otherwise think I just totally wasted an hour of your life because you knew it all already. Whichever of those you find yourself closer to – or if you are instead somewhere in the middle – you need to keep in mind the following things which will really help you progress through the sometimes treacherous forests of quantitative analysis:

- Remember, a surprisingly large number of other people are scared of numbers, so if you are too, you are not alone. If you are not, then perhaps you have a fruitful avenue to get to know others?
- Quantitative analysis is vital to almost all business careers, almost certainly including the one you hope to pursue, or the one you will eventually find yourself in.
- The key to beginning to understand the relevance of quantitative analysis to your career is to remember that you need *data* to make effective decisions. Data is information, and you use it to answer important questions.
- The numbers that make up quantitative data are representations of things that are in the 'real world'. Sometimes numbers can behave differently from these things, and we need to understand the relationship between 'raw numbers' and the things they are supposed to represent, if we are going to do good analysis.

Finally, it is absolutely vital that you take seriously my words that learning how to do quantitative analysis is fundamentally a *step-by-step* process. If you do not master the early steps, the later steps will be very difficult, and in fact will end up being impossible and frustrating for you. If you did not do well at school, please take seriously the idea of doing some recapping in more depth of the basic concepts which are covered here – it will really help you out in the future. However, on the other hand this also means that maths and stats are not an impossible mystery that only a few 'clever' people can do. They are things which anyone who is prepared to sit down and work at can end up being pretty decent at – and most definitely decent enough to be very successful in business. So good luck. I am looking forward to accompanying you on this journey.

 final checklist

You should have covered and understood the following basic content in this chapter. If not, go back and retry the relevant sections:

- ☑ Reasons why people might be scared or turned off by studying quantitative methods.
- ☑ How quantitative analysis for business is primarily to help you *make decisions* in your future career, even in what you think might be the most exciting and creative professions.
- ☑ What is data, and what is an element (or data point), a variable and an observation, and how these together make a data set.
- ☑ The difference between qualitative and quantitative variables, and discrete and continuous data.
- ☑ How we often approximate the amount of qualities (like happiness) by numbers, but that these numbers are not the exact same thing.
- ☑ The names and properties of the four different scales of measurement – nominal, ordinal, interval and ratio.
- ☑ The difference between cross-sectional and longitudinal data.
- ☑ What a sample is, what a population is, and the relation between the two.
- ☑ Why variation is important in quantitative analysis.
- ☑ What BEDMAS, exponential notation, powers/exponents and logarithms are.
- ☑ What equations and functions are, and how they can often be expressed in sigma notation.

EXERCISES

This section will contain useful exercises for you to do, to help you understand the content. However, they probably will not be like the ones you have seen in other similar books. Here, I am not trying to test your knowledge, but to help you further understand the content of the chapters. Your lecturers and teachers can test your knowledge, I am here to help you develop it.

With that in mind, I offer the following observation regarding the exercises in this chapter: from my own experience, it was not until I had to teach a subject that I started to understand it. In fact, I can remember fervently praying to the lecturing gods that students would not ask me about certain things (probability theory mainly!). Thus, when I want to learn something, I often put myself in the situation where I will have to teach it to someone else, and it helps a lot. The following questions are based on this theory. You can make them even *more* helpful by finding a friend who struggles with maths, and trying it for real.

Imagine the following scenario (this may be hard for some of you).

You have successfully obtained your qualification – top of the class. Some friends of yours have asked if you would help their school-age daughter with some maths. In particular, she is struggling with some of the notation.

1. First, your task is to explain to her what algebra is all about. She just does not get it – maths is about numbers, not letters. She is really stuck on the idea of variables. She wants to know if there is a difference between the variables she uses in maths, like *x*, *y*, *z*, and the ones she has seen in statistics, like firm, gender, etc. Can you explain to her the difference (if there is one)?
2. Next, she tells you she is confused about data – qualitative data, quantitative data. Does it mean some data is 'quality' and other data – well, that there is just lots of it? Give three examples of each type of data and explain why they are different.
3. Importantly, she tells you that she is doing a project based on the different attitudes of students and lecturers towards exams. What sort of scale do you think she should use to classify the variable, 'student or lecturer'?
4. For her project, to measure attitude she used a scale where 0 represented extreme hatred and 5 represented exquisite love of exams. In her sample five students circled 0 and three lecturers circled 5. Does this mean that hatred for exams scored 0 ($0 \times 5 = 0$) and exquisite love scored 15? You will need to explain your answer in simple terms here.
5. She has also been shown the symbol $\sum$, but it is all Greek to her. Can you give her an easy way to remember what the symbol means?
6. Her teacher has been banging on about functions (not bodily ones) as well. This is causing lots of problems, and she asks, with desperation in her voice, 'What does *f(x)* tell me and what does it mean?'
7. As you walk home, you think back to your own performance in your quantitative courses. You remember that one time during your degree, you did a class test for quantitative analysis. You scored 80 in the test and your friend scored 40. Does that mean you are twice as clever as your friend? How would you classify this scale?

To access additional online resources please visit: **https://study.sagepub.com/leepeters**

The Ballad of Eddie the Easily Distracted: Part 2

Eddie felt a little better about life as he wandered up to the back of the lecture theatre to take his seat in QUAN101 for the second lecture. He actually felt that he had made a little progress at this numbers thing over the week, and some of the bits that he'd struggled with made some more sense – like formulas! Or formulae as his smug roommate had told him it should be said, last night at the Union. That had been a bit embarrassing, especially in front of those girls.

Despite his good mood, Eddie was quickly getting a little bored. Dr Jones seemed to be going on about *collecting* data, rather than analysing it. Eddie felt that all his hard-earned knowledge was ebbing away from him a little. Worse, this collection business seemed to require quite a lot of attention to detail and planning. Not his particular strength he thought glumly. Eddie looked at his lecture notes. Dr Jones was trying to explain the principle of 'garbage in, garbage out', which kind of made sense to him. After all, if you didn't know what it was you were analysing, how were you supposed to trust the results?

Pleased with himself for that insight, Eddie leaned back in his seat a little with a little smile. At this point, he knocked over his bottle of water, which fell to the floor with a clatter as Dr Jones finished her sentence. The entire class turned around and looked at Eddie, who was scrabbling around trying to stop the bottle from emptying all over the floor. As he felt his cheeks warm, Eddie heard them start to laugh. He managed to pick the bottle up – at least there was some water left – and sit down. As the class all turned back to look at Dr Jones (who Eddie felt was enjoying this a little too much) he noticed what's-her-name – Esha? – speaking to her friends, who all laughed again.

'That went well,' thought Eddie. 'Pride comes before a fall.'

Esha's Story: Part 2

Esha had had a pretty boring first week of classes. All the basic stuff she already knew. She'd moaned to her Mum about the whole thing, and Mum had just told her to have some sympathy – not everyone was as clever as her. While Esha had secretly enjoyed that a little, it didn't make her classes any more interesting. And when that clown at the back of QUAN101 knocked over his water bottle, she'd enjoyed it immensely, telling her friends that he'd probably done it as he fell asleep.

Frankly, that had been the highlight of the lecture itself. She just didn't see why it was necessary to think about collecting data before analysing it. After all, she was hardly going to be working on the high street getting people to fill in questionnaires for a living, was she now?

Still, she did find some appeal in the details of the task. All that careful planning and preparation for the task was something she did enjoy, and she could certainly see herself perhaps managing the process in the future. Maybe there was something to this after all? After she'd gone home, still giggling about the water bottle incident, she sat in her room with her friends having a coffee and talking about it. They'd set up a little study group to go over the week's material, and Esha enjoyed helping some of her friends understand things better.

'I guess,' Esha said, 'it kind of helps if you know where the data comes from – even if you didn't collect it yourself. I mean, it's what Dr Jones said: garbage in, garbage out.' Esha's friends nodded sagely. 'But also, I suppose it's quite likely that we might have to be in charge of getting data to answer questions in our jobs, even if we don't collect it, and also I think that understanding the spreadsheets is going to help us a lot.' Esha had a final insight: 'Hey, I bet we can use all of that project management stuff at the end to help with our group assignments.' She was rather pleased with herself at that, and enjoyed her coffee all the more.

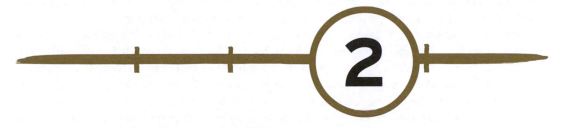

2

GATHERING AND PREPARING DATA

CONTENTS

 learning objectives

The key learning objectives for this chapter are as follows:

- ☑ Appreciate why it is important to understand data collection before data analysis.
- ☑ Learn the difference between primary and secondary data.
- ☑ Understand the advantages and disadvantages of interactive and non-interactive primary data collection methods.
- ☑ Learn the basics of designing good surveys or data collection forms, and how to write good questions.
- ☑ Appreciate why collecting data over time, and from experiments, requires special attention from you as a researcher.

- ☑ Learn how to evaluate the quality of secondary data.
- ☑ Learn what a spreadsheet is and how it is constructed.
- ☑ Learn how to prepare your data for analysis, using ID numbers and codes to help you identify problems.
- ☑ Understand the basic principles of project management.

It is actually quite unusual to see the collection of data given its own dedicated chapter in an introductory quantitative analysis and statistics textbook. There are probably at least two reasons for this.[1] First of all, almost all students who take an introductory 'quantitative analysis for business' course (which this book is basically aimed at) will go on to take later courses dedicated to their specialism – such as market research, economics or financial analysis. The data needs for these different business specialisms are quite different (as we will see in this chapter), meaning that it is impossible to cover everything in depth. So most authors and editors probably think that it is better to leave such issues to the specialists to cover. Secondly, it might be the case that quantitative analysis experts see the actual collection of data as outside the scope of their work. In other words, 'Hey, once you've got the data, come to us, we don't care how you got it.'

Personally, I can understand these reasons, but I do not agree with them on the whole. In fact, the collection of data is a vital part of the analysis process itself. If poor data is collected, then analysis can never succeed. Yet too often we concentrate on fancy analysis techniques to the detriment of getting good data in the first place. In many cases it is my view that a simple analysis with good data is much more useful than even the fanciest complex analysis of poor data. If this is the case, then you should surely be introduced to data collection very early on in the piece. Hence this chapter. Furthermore, it really helps you to understand how to analyse your data if you have an understanding of the data collection process (even if you never collect your own data). In particular, you can save much trouble later on if you prepare your data effectively – which is part of this chapter.

Of course, it is impossible to fully cover everything about data collection which you might need to know about in your entire career – that is still the place of your specialist subject research textbooks. Instead, the aim of this chapter is to introduce you to the key practicalities of gathering the major types of data that you will need to use in quantitative analysis for business. Importantly I will also cover some key aspects of preparing the data and entering it into a spreadsheet – which leads us into the next chapter rather nicely.

SOURCES OF DATA

It is often the case that data collection is described as falling into one of two camps: either you collect your own data for a specific purpose, or you use data which has been collected for a different purpose in the past (usually by someone else) and apply it for your own current purpose. The first case is usually called collecting primary data, whereas the second is termed using secondary data.

Primary data is defined as data that has been collected for the specific purpose you are using it for. For example, if you want to look at consumer opinions of your brand, you go and collect data about this. Note that it does not specifically have to be *you* that collects the data – for example, you could commission a research company to do it for you – but the key is that the data is specifically collected for your purpose. This type of data is very commonly used in marketing research, but also in professions such as human resource management (e.g. staff surveys), operations management and quality control (defect rate monitoring, etc.), and many other business areas.

 **think it over 2.1**

If you decide to collect primary data, is there anything you can do to ensure the data you collect is going to give you the information that you are looking for?

---

[1] There is actually a third reason – that writing a book like this is enough work as it is, so why add even more to the task?! Of course, I would *never* dream of such a thing – or perhaps it is more accurate to say that my editors would never allow me to dream of it!

On the other hand, secondary data is data that has been collected in the past for *another* specific purpose, which you are using for your own purposes. For example, the governments of many countries regularly collect huge amounts of data on individuals and households by way of what is called a national census. Such data is usually available to researchers and companies for them to use for their own purposes. I could use that data to do things such as target a mailout to geographic areas of specific average income levels. Companies also often hold a lot of data on their staff and customers, as well as about the companies they may also work with (e.g. suppliers and resellers). Externally, there are many sources of business-related data which you will almost certainly be able to find in your university library, like economic, financial and market data. Many specialist research companies even regularly collect general data which they then sell on to others. One example which has become almost ubiquitous in our lives is the data from retail stores collected from the scanning of barcodes when we purchase stuff. This can be employed for all kinds of useful purposes, and when you link it with a loyalty card as carried by most of us these days, the potential is somewhat frightening! Also, everything we do on the Internet is – if we are not careful – recorded, resulting in yet more data about us. Think about that before you click…

One of the major types of data which will be analysed in this book is *financial* data. In many cases, financial data is collected for some purpose other than what we will be analysing it in relation to – making it secondary data. For example, companies listed on the stock market have to provide financial figures to the public, and most private companies will also file balance sheets and various other financial statements. This data is clearly collected for the purposes of compliance with standards and the law, yet if you can gain access to it, you might use it for all kinds of other things, like making investment decisions. Sometimes, the same data is collected specifically to help you make a decision, in which case it is primary data. Thus, financial data kind of sits outside the usual secondary/primary distinction, and can be both, or either one, at various times.

There are various advantages and disadvantages of the different types of data. Secondary data is usually quicker and cheaper to acquire than primary data. In fact it can sometimes be free and instant if you can access it online, or through your library. Box 2.1 gives some examples of free sources of secondary data, and you will usually be surprised by just how much secondary data is available to you quickly and cheaply for most purposes. As a result, a general rule is to look for secondary data first, and only when you cannot use it should you go and collect primary data. Even so, you should be aware of the limitations of secondary data, the most pertinent of which is that secondary data is rarely exactly 'right' for your purposes. This is of course because it was collected for some other reason! Secondary data may give you too much or too little detail, it may look at something slightly differently (e.g. it may have household income figures when you need individual ones), or it may be too old to be of use. Secondary data may also be inaccurate. After all, you do not know how it was collected, and therefore it is hard to know how accurate it is. As we already know, poor data leads to poor conclusions from the analysis.

 **box 2.1**

Free Sources of Secondary Data

Governmental sources like the UK Office of National Statistics:

www.statistics.gov.uk

Intelligence sources, like the CIA:[2]

www.cia.gov/library/publications/the-world-factbook/

(Continued)

---

[2] Seriously! Of course, it is not what you might think, but it is a good source of information about different countries.

(Continued)

Commercial services who offer some free information, like ACORN:

http://acorn.caci.co.uk/

Of course, the Internet has thousands of other free sources of information. However, you need to be careful in collecting this information, because there are few quality checks for the Internet. Always remember this. Also, remember, the Internet is constantly changing, and links come and go out of date. These links were correct when the book was written, but they might be different by the time you read this book!

Probably the best source of free secondary data is your library. If you are at university or college, your librarian will have a great knowledge of the different sources of secondary market data available to you, for example. Even your public library will also have plenty of useful information.

If you cannot use secondary data, primary data has the advantage of being a 'custom fit' to your problem. However, it is usually more expensive, time consuming and difficult to collect. Yet you have more control over the process used to collect it – meaning you can be more confident in the quality and accuracy of the data (or at least know whether it is or is not of good quality). Knowledge of how primary data is collected is vital in designing your own collections, and also in assessing the quality of secondary data. While a full knowledge of these methods is best left to dedicated books, the foundations of this understanding are given in the next section.

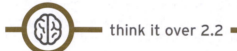 **think it over 2.2**

Two terms that are frequently used when dealing with data are 'reliability' and 'validity'. What is the technical definition of these terms within the context of data collection?

GATHERING DATA

This section is mainly about going out and collecting primary data. The reason for this is that if you are using secondary data, the main task is finding a good source and evaluating its quality, not collecting it – someone else already did that. The key point to make here is that *if you use secondary data, remember that it was once primary data for someone else*. In other words, if you are assessing its quality, it would be useful to know whether or not the original data collector had taken into account at least the basic issues covered below.

It is pretty much impossible to discuss every single issue of relevance in this introductory chapter, but the aim is to give you a basic picture of the key issues of importance, so that you can keep them in mind when you are actually analysing data. I will begin by making an important distinction in data collection – the one between using data collection methods which involve *interacting* with the subject(s) of the data and ones which do not. Sometimes you can find in research textbooks the classification between *communication* and *observation*, but I prefer the interactive/non-interactive distinction.[3]

Interactive data collection methods involve the data collector in some kind of interaction process with the subjects of the data. This is most often by questioning them, and somehow recording their answers.

---

[3] Partly because I came up with it in an earlier book, *Doing Business Research* (which would make a great gift for someone special…).

You might have been walking down the street one day and been waylaid by a data collector of this type, who asks you a bunch of questions about some brand or other. Or you could participate in a staff survey for your employer. On the other hand, non-interactive methods involve the data collector recording data about the subjects, without actually communicating with them. This is often done by observation. For example, sometimes a local government wants to count traffic flows at certain points (presumably so it can laugh at how busy things are rather than do anything about it), and it employs someone to sit there counting how many cars go past in a defined time period. Or instead it might use a mechanical or electronic device for the same job. Or you might access a large economic information database and record all the net profit figures for a set of companies over a 10-year period. None of these activities involved asking the subject of the research (e.g. car drivers, company managers) for any information.

 think it over 2.3

When conducting an interview, is it possible for the interviewer to influence the answers of the person being interviewed? Think of a possible scenario where the interviewer is deliberately attempting to 'put words in the mouth' of the person being interviewed. Think about the strategies the interviewer is using and avoid them if you intend to use interviews to collect data!

While specialist research books give far more detail here, it is pretty clear that interactive methods are more flexible. Usually, if you can think of some question to ask, you can collect that data even if you cannot observe it. In a staff survey for example you could ask people questions on their satisfaction or motivation, which is hard (if not impossible) actually to see. Also, you can sometimes find out information about the past or the future, by asking relevant questions of the right subjects. Most of the time, non-interactive methods are stuck with trying to collect data on what can be seen right now. For example, taking the satisfaction example above, we could certainly record whether our employees *look* satisfied, but is this the same thing as whether they really *are* satisfied? And what about whether they were satisfied last week? What about the traffic flow two months ago? Of course, this is not *always* the case: if you have access to a database of information over time, you can actually take account of things which happened in the past, such as last month's net profit, for example.

On the other hand, the non-interactive methods are often more accurate. Most obviously, if we ask questions to get our answers (interactive research) then how much do we trust the answers? This is a subject which has exercised the minds of many thinkers greater than I, and there is not really an answer to it – although you can take steps to reduce the problem. For example, you need to take account of all kinds of question design theories which are available in other books. Non-interactive methods tend to be more accurate because they are recording things which can be observed. However, this relies on the data collector being willing and able to collect accurate data in many cases. What if the 'car-counter' falls asleep? This is why electronic and mechanical methods are increasingly popular. Also, if you are collecting data from another source (e.g. a company performance database), the accuracy of *your* data depends on how accurate the original source is – and sometimes that may be questionable.

 think it over 2.4

Accuracy is an extremely important aspect of data collection. The flip side of accurate data is inaccurate data; how would you recognize inaccurate data?

So with all of those ideas safely in hand, let's move on to look at some actual practical ways of getting hold of primary data. The focus is on essential issues that will influence the quality of your data, rather than specific techniques.

Designing Survey Questionnaires and Data Collection Forms

I am going to begin by talking about surveying because I consider it to be the foundational method of collecting data. When you think of surveys, you probably think of filling in questionnaires for some boring reason or another, and certainly this is a major part of survey research. But what I really mean in this case by the word surveys is *any method of data collecting which involves collecting a consistent set of data from some research subject or subjects*. Surveys are most often considered an interactive method of data collection (i.e. you question subjects using questionnaires). But they can also be a non-interactive method too; for example, you can set up a consistent data collection form to use when you are observing activity or collecting data from a database.

Figure 2.1 shows a section of a typical example of a survey questionnaire that you might create for interactive research, and Figure 2.2 shows a typical example of a data collection form (which can also be considered a survey in this context). Even so, while in this case I have put these two methods under the same heading (because for our purposes the key issues are the same), in other more specialist areas you will most probably see 'surveys' referring to interactive research methods such as in Figure 2.1.

SECTION 4: YOU AND YOUR FIRM

9. **The final few questions ask you details about you and your firm. It is important that you answer them honestly, remember this data is confidential.**

How old are you? _____ years	Are you? _____ Male _____ Female Is your sales manager? _____ Male _____ Female

How long have you worked in sales?

_____ years

How long have you worked in this organization?

_____ years

How long have you worked in your current job?

_____ years

what is your highest educational qualification?
(*please tick*)
_____ Postgraduate degree
_____ University degree
_____ Some university courses
_____ Trade qualifications
_____ 'O' or 'A' levels
_____ GCSE or equivalent
_____ High school
_____ Other

Approximately, what is your company's annual **_TOTAL_** sales turnover?...   £ _____

Approximately, how many sales people would a first level sales manager supervise in your company?... _____ *people*

Approximately, how many people are employed by your company?... _____ *people*

THANK YOU FOR COMPLETING THIS QUESTIONNAIRE!

If you would like to receive a summary of the findings of this study, please enclose your business card along with this questionnaire in the reply envelope.

YOUR CONTRIBUTION IS GREATLY APPRECIATED, THANKS!!!

Figure 2.1
Example
Questionnaire

TRAFFIC COUNT FORM:

Name of Researcher: _____

Date: _____

Location: _____

Start time: _____

End time: _____

CAR

TALLY: _____

_____

_____

_____

VAN/TRUCK

TALLY: _____

_____

_____

_____

HGV

TALLY: _____

_____

_____

_____

NOTE: HGV for this count is defined as an articulated vehicle (not a car or trailer)

Figure 2.2
Data
Collection
Form

The first thing to remember is that a poor questionnaire or form will lead to poor data. This point is important on two levels. First of all, of course, you have to ask the right questions to get the right data. But the actual *design* of the form is important too. One of the key decisions in this regard is length, and – despite what you may have been told – size *does* matter. More specifically, the longer and more time consuming the form or questionnaire is, the harder it will be to fill in accurately, and the less likely you will be to get good data. If you have to get subjects to fill it in, then they will be more likely to get bored and stop or walk away. Or, if you are collecting non-interactive data, then the longer the form is, the more likely the collector is to make mistakes.

Unfortunately, as a rule, questionnaires and data collection forms are also often very badly designed in an aesthetic sense. For example, cramming questions together in very small type to shorten the length is very bad practice in all situations. Many forms and questionnaires are also full of typos and just, well, look *ugly*. This might seem unimportant, but a nicely designed piece of work (like Figures 2.1 and 2.2, if I may say) is much more likely to result in good data than an ugly one. That said, you also need to consider cost and practicality issues. Sometimes the optimal design decisions may be impossible. In such situations it is even more important to do the best you can within the parameters of your project.

think it over 2.5

When designing a questionnaire, would the order of the questions have an influence on the respondent's answers? For example, if you needed to collect personal data, where in the questionnaire would you put the questions you know are contentious? Could you use the ordering of questions to encourage the full participation of the respondent?

Structuring the questionnaire or form will also have a major impact on the quality of your data. For example, if you are using interactive research, then you should structure the questionnaire in order to give yourself the best chance of getting the data you need. Remember that your data quality depends on the subjects giving you the right information. One key issue is not to ask questions which might be too difficult, sensitive or personal early on – since this may put off respondents from continuing. That said, another line of reasoning suggests you should ask the most important questions earlier, so if respondents get bored and stop halfway through, you still have some data. Of course, these two points sometimes conflict, so you need to trade them off as best you can.

When considering the type of data you want to collect, you also need to think about some important issues. First and foremost, is it even *possible* to collect good and accurate data on the subject you are interested in? For example, if you wanted to know how many chocolate bars a person bought yesterday, this would probably be pretty easy to get by asking. The same could be said if you wanted to know how many chocolate bars a person bought last week. But what if you wanted to know how many they bought last *year*? Or how many they bought on 8 August 1996? A person is highly unlikely to know this. Worse, people who are asked such questions sometimes feel they *have* to give some answer, so they make one up! In this case your data is meaningless. In other words, you must always consider the people who will be providing the answers to your questions. Will they be able to answer? Box 2.2 gives some very brief tips on how to write questions to collect good data.

box 2.2

Designing Questions to Get Good Data

- Make the questions simple and clear.
- Never ask two questions at the same time (e.g. 'do you like the colour and shape?').
- Your questions should use terms the subjects will understand.
- Keep your wording objective to avoid leading the subject to a particular response.
- Always try to make answering as easy as possible.
- Never use slang or technical language unless it is essential.
- Always write for the least well-educated person who is likely to use the form.

think it over 2.6

Two other terms commonly used within the analysis of statistical data are 'subjective' and 'objective'. What do these terms mean and how do they impact on data collection? Is it possible to be truly objective in all circumstances? What if you had to interview someone you took an instant dislike to?

All of the points I just mentioned above for questionnaires also apply to data collection forms which you will use to collect non-interactive data. For example, you need to make the form simple and easy to fill out by the data collector, to avoid mistakes. You also need to make extremely clear exactly what data is needed, wherever there is possible confusion. For example, in the earlier traffic flow case it might be critical to note what type of traffic was of concern. Are heavy goods vehicles included? If not, what is the definition of a heavy goods vehicle, and is it possible for the data collector to assess this quickly? If on the form a heavy goods vehicle is defined as one which weighs over 10 tonnes, then how would the data collector assess that? It is much better to use a simpler definition such as 'more than two axles'.

The final point I will make about designing data collection forms and questionnaires is that you *must test them before use*. One of the things that is almost certain in life is that mistakes will be made – either obvious ones like typos or more subtle ones like poor wording and design. As the data collector you may not pick these up, but the testing process will. One good way of testing such things is to approach the sort of people you hope you will collect data from, and ask them to look at the questionnaire. Or, if you are using non-interactive research, go out and use the form in a practice run, or ask someone who will be collecting data to do so. Even taking such simple steps as this will improve your success rate significantly. If you ever do this in practice, it will save you time, money and stress.

 think it over 2.7

Books on data gathering often suggest doing a pilot study. A pilot study is a good way of checking not only your data collection tools, but also to see that you are actually getting the information you require. What criteria would you use to select an appropriate group for a pilot study?

Collecting Data Over Time

There are quite a few situations where you might want to collect data which occurs over a set time period, rather than at a single point in time. In the above section I used the word survey quite a lot, and this word is usually associated with collecting data at a single time point. However, all of the key points about designing questionnaires and forms are equally relevant to collecting data over multiple time points – also known as collecting longitudinal data. More importantly, there are several additional points you should be aware of before you start either collecting or analysing longitudinal data, or time series data. Commonly, this sort of data is collected by administering the same questionnaire to the same people at multiple time points (e.g. every month or every year). You can see examples of government-conducted studies like this online, and they are commonly called cohort studies. A cohort is some group which shares a characteristic (like having the same date of birth). You can also find panel studies, which are similar, but they use a more general group of people who do not necessarily share characteristics. However, the principle is the same.

 think it over 2.8

If you decided to do a longitudinal study of people's shopping habits in a particular town, could the location of where you collect your data have an influence?

When collecting data over time like this, there are some specific things you need to be careful of. The most critical of these is what is called sample attrition, which is when you are unable to collect data on an element or subject for the entire time period. For example, what if you get data from a person who then moves house without telling you? Or a company which goes into receivership partway through the study? In this case, you will lose data from these elements. The problem is if these are elements who are different in some important way from the ones who stay. Say you were studying the factors which influence company success; well of course if you lose data on the very unsuccessful companies (i.e. the ones which fail) your data will then be inaccurate and not trustworthy. As well as this, if you lose some subjects each time, you may be left with a much smaller data set at the end than what you started with. As you will see later, sample size is a key issue in analysis, so you really need to keep an eye on this.

It is also common to collect non-interactive data over time, for example financial or economic data, either for companies or individuals and households. In this case, we need to be aware of similar issues. First of all, it is vital that you are aware of data elements which are missing at certain time points (e.g. a company may not return profit figures for one month out of twelve). Dealing with this can be highly complex and is subject to a lot of debate and research under the general heading of 'missing data analysis', which is far beyond the scope of this book. But you might want to check it out when you get more advanced in your own development. The key to accurately collecting non-interactive data over time (if it is available in the first place) is thus a well-designed and clear data collection form. This minimizes the potential for problems of missing data by making it as easy as possible to collect the data that is available. Nevertheless, in some cases you may want data that is not available – for example, you may need weekly sales figures for a product, but they are only available monthly. In this case, your only option is to make do with what you have, or to change your strategy. For example, you could use an interactive approach to ask managers about their sales figures each week, in which case you would be subject to all the issues concerning such methods.

Collecting Experimental Data

Experiments are often seen as the most 'scientific' of research designs, although they are quite rare in business-oriented research. There are many books which discuss the important issues regarding experimental designs, but they are a little outside the scope of this book. Here, I am more interested in introducing issues concerning collecting data. Experimental data can be collected at either a single time, or at multiple times (e.g. before and after some kind of treatment). So the issues discussed above are all relevant here as well. The points I am going to make here are also potentially relevant to the other types of data collection, but they are most often discussed in relation to experiments, which is why they are here in their own section.

First of all, there is the measurement effect. This concept concerns the possibility that the measure you use might influence the results. What I mean here is that if for example you give a memory test to someone at one point in time, and then measure them again later using the same test, they will almost definitely score better the second time around, simply because they have had practice. So the measure has influenced the results. This is a possible problem which needs to be dealt with (e.g. by using different measures, or some kind of distraction task).

Experimental (and longitudinal) data collection can also be subject to history and maturation effects. These are pretty simple to explain. Say you measure one individual's sales at one point in time, and then at a second point in time a month later. During that month, many things might happen in the situation you are researching, which could influence sales. History effects are all of those things (e.g. an economic downturn, a major customer going bankrupt) that you are not interested in as part of your research – they are outside your scope, but still might have an influence on sales. Maturation effects are concerned with the actual individual's change over time. For example, people learn and grow over time, which can influence their performance. You need to take this into account in your data collection designs. For example, the longer the time between measures, the more chance you have of encountering these problems.

COLLECTING AND EVALUATING SECONDARY DATA

All of the different techniques and methods covered in the previous section may have been employed in the collection of a secondary data set that you want to use. But the problem for you is that you do not often have a large amount of information about the exact nature of the data collection. Certainly, many data providers – such as the government or large research agencies – do give a lot of information about their methods, because that is a key aspect of getting their data used and trusted. But many more data sets that you will use do not have such detailed information on their sources. In fact, even the ones that do usually provide much less information than you would know if you had collected the data yourself. So this section is about various methods and criteria you can use in assessing your secondary data – to work out if you can 'trust it' or not.

 think it over 2.9

You've decided to use secondary data from a well-known and respected source. Does this mean you do not have to worry about issues such as reliability and validity?

The first thing to think about is whether you are collecting the data from the original source or some second-hand source. For example, if you use census data, are you getting it from the census results, or from some source which used that data and reported its *own* results? The reason this is important is that going to the original source makes it more likely that you will be able to get more information about the methods used to collect this data, and it is usually more accurate and complete than a second-hand source. Every time a data set is used is one more place for mistakes to be made, so if you are using secondary data you should try to get as close to the original source as possible.

In evaluating the accuracy of secondary data, you should look for its original purpose, and who collected it. This is first and foremost to get an idea of how objective the data is. For example, when you see figures saying that '45% of people think the government's policy on climate change is poorly thought out', would it make any difference if you found out that the study was done by an opposition political party or an independent research agency? Often, it is hard to determine conclusively the objectivity of a particular set of data, but it helps if you use data collected by companies whose main function is to collect data – in this case the quality of their data is their competitive advantage.

 think it over 2.10

When working with data, especially in areas such as market trends, it is essential to have 'up to the minute' data. If you are using a secondary source for your data, is it possible to have 'up to the minute' data? Perhaps you need to use data from the most recent population census to investigate trends in employment; how up to date would you expect this data to be?

Apart from these judgements, you also need to gather as much information as possible on how the data was collected, to enable you to assess how trustworthy it is. The less information that is available, the less confident you can be in the data's quality. Ideally, you should have information on the sample used, how the data was collected, who collected the data and how well trained they were, how much data is missing, how many subjects did not respond, and such things. You would also like to know how the variables were measured if this is relevant – for example, if they measured 'customer satisfaction', what questions were asked?

PREPARING YOUR DATA FOR ANALYSIS

Along with actually going out and collecting data, the preliminary preparation of data can also have a vital impact on the analysis you conduct. For example, I have seen situations where students have collected data which might have been excellent, but unfortunately they prepared it incorrectly, which led to their data being far less useful than it might have been. In this section I will look at basic issues for the preparation of data from both cross-sectional and longitudinal collections, and show ways of preparing it which give you the most flexibility for analysing it later on. This section should also prepare you for the next chapter, which talks about the data analysis software environment I will be using throughout the book.

The Spreadsheet

The most important tool of the modern data analyst is the spreadsheet. A spreadsheet is a visual representation of your data, arranged in rows and columns. Virtually all data analysis software represents data by way of a spreadsheet, or a number of linked spreadsheets. Figure 2.3a shows a blank spreadsheet from the almost ubiquitous spreadsheet program Microsoft Excel. I will be using this program and another analysis program throughout the remainder of this book, and will begin to cover them in depth in the next chapter.

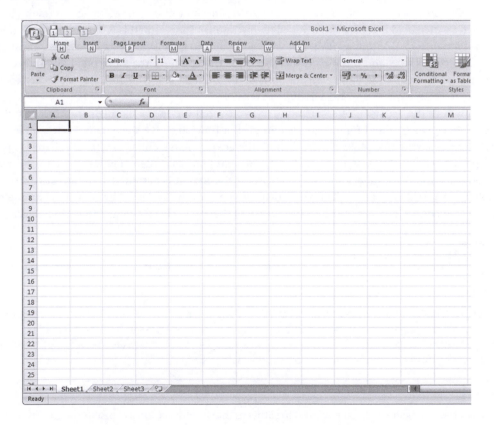

Figure 2.3a
Blank Spreadsheet

Copyright Microsoft Excel ®. Used with permission from Microsoft.

A spreadsheet consists of a matrix of cells. The cells are the small boxes, and they are of course arranged in rows and columns. The most important thing to remember is that each row represents data from one *element* (see Chapter 1), which may be an individual, a company or many other things. Each column represents a *variable*. In order to make this crystal clear, Back to Basics Box 2.1 covers it thoroughly

 back to basics

Box 2.1

Let's imagine you are interested in the number of pairs of shoes and pints of beer the average student purchases per month of university life. In order to do this, you have decided to do a survey of your classmates. Of course, this may or may not be the best way to do it, but for better or worse that is what you have chosen. You create a very short questionnaire with the following three questions:

1. Are you male or female? M___ F___
2. How many pairs of shoes did you buy last month? _____
3. How many pints of beer did you buy last month? _____

In order to gather all this data together you would use a spreadsheet such as the one in Figure 2.3a. You would probably set it up to look something like the one presented in Figure 2.3b, from Excel.

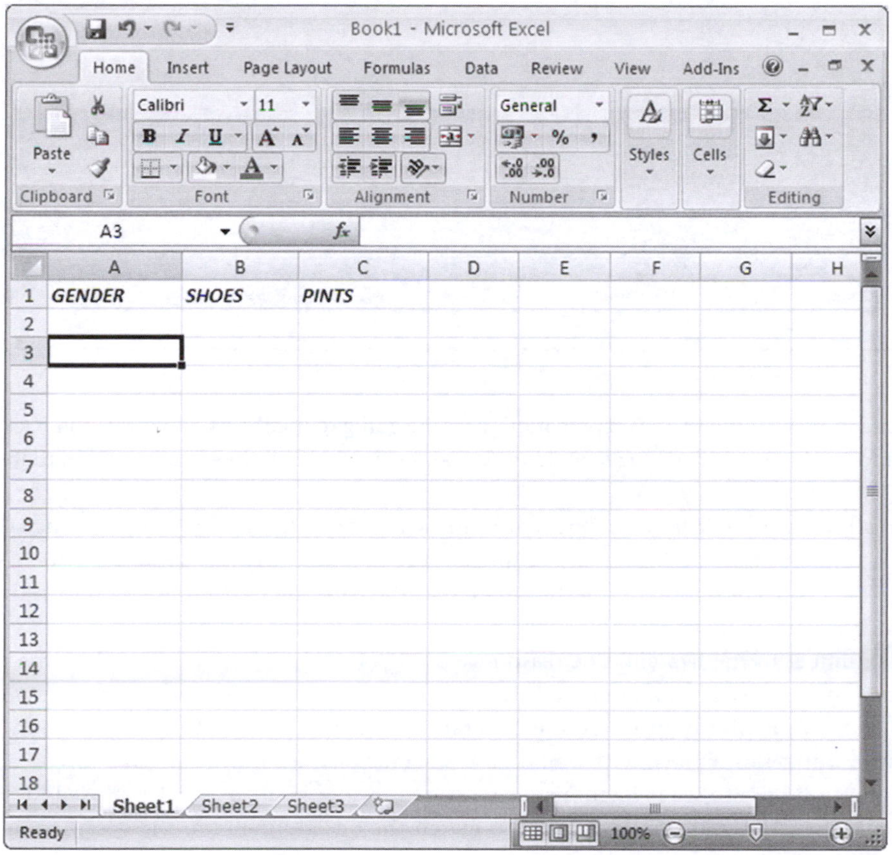

Figure 2.3b

As you can see, each questionnaire has three possible variables, and the spreadsheet represents those variables as headers for three columns. Figure 2.3c shows the same spreadsheet with data from five questionnaires entered into it. As you can see, data from each questionnaire runs *along the row*. So, if you have five questionnaires, you will have five rows of data (not including the column headings in Excel).

(Continued)

(Continued)

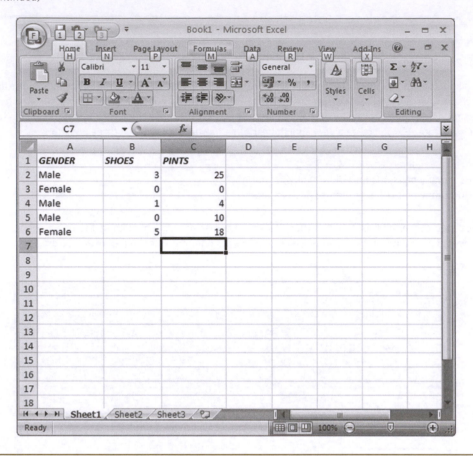

Figure 2.3c

To illustrate some key aspects of data preparation, we are going to use the example given in Back to Basics Box 2.1 and modify it as we go. Look at Figure 2.4, and you will see it differs a little from that shown in Figure 2.3c.

First of all, it has more data in it, but that is not what I am talking about really. Notice that there is an extra variable at the beginning of the spreadsheet called 'ID'. This is a number which identifies the actual data collection form or questionnaire that the data comes from. For example, if you used 100 questionnaires, you would number them all 1–100 and when you entered the data you would enter this number in the ID field. The reason we do this is to enable us to go back to the questionnaires and look for any possible mistakes. Have a look in Figure 2.4 for the answer for 'pints' from ID number 13. You will find it is 1000. Is this rather a lot for one month's consumption? Perhaps not for you, but certainly for me. I would be suspicious of this, and would like to go back to the original questionnaire to see if I had made an error entering the data (maybe pressed '0' too many times in a hurry). Without the ID number to match the questionnaire to the data, I would not be able to do this.

Just that simple tip will save you a lot of heartache later on, I bet.

Another thing you will notice is the 'gaps' in the data. These may mean many things. It could be that the respondent missed it out in this case, but it could also sometimes be that the respondent did not think the question applied to him or her. You can leave these blank, but many data analysis packages allow you to specify a specific number as representing 'missing data', and if so you should use this feature. I will cover this more when I discuss SPSS in the next chapter.

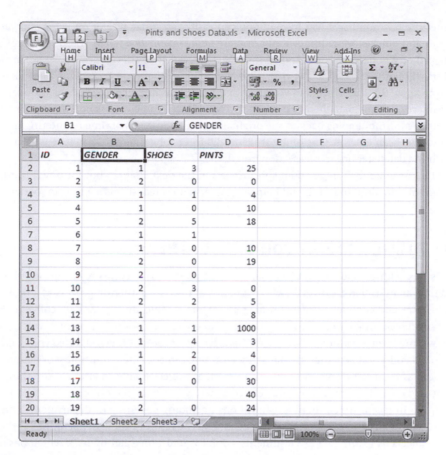

Figure 2.4
Pints and Shoes Data

 think it over 2.11

Do these gaps really matter? After all, the respondent has answered nearly all the questions. Can you think of reasons why someone may answer, say, 18 questions out of 20 and then not answer 2 of them?

You will also notice that there are no 'M' or 'F' values in there, only numbers. This is because I have coded male to be '1' and female to be '2'. This relates back to the discussion on numbers and scales of measurement in the previous chapter. The reason I have done this is because many analysis packages work only with numbers, not with letters or anything else. While for these labels it is not really an issue, I like to be consistent and always use numbers – so I give code numbers to all non-numeric variables. Of course, you need to keep records of this as well so you do not forget that 1 = Male and 2 = Female! Nevertheless, I will talk in more detail about setting up the spreadsheet in the next chapter.

One thing you might not have thought about is other ways in which the data might have been entered, but this is quite important. Think about it: question 2 asks how many pints you bought last month, which is a number. I have entered that exact number in the spreadsheet, as it appeared on the form (barring errors like '1000'). However, I could also have chosen to categorize the number and code the categories. I will say much more about this in Chapter 3, but in brief, for example, code 1 could = 0–5 pints, 2 = 6–10, 3 = 11–15 and so on. In this case, if the raw number was '14' I would enter a 3. Why do this? Well, sometimes people think that they are only interested in the category in the end, not the raw number. This may well be so but *you should never categorize raw data when entering it into a spreadsheet*.

Always enter the raw number if you have it. You can easily categorize it later on using software, which will be easier and quicker. More importantly, you are *losing information* when you do it, and you might find later on that you need it. For example, if you use the categories developed above, an answer of '7' and '6' pints will both be coded '2', leaving no way to tell the difference. You might think that you will never need to know this difference, but you might be wrong! It is fine to make that decision later on, and you can easily convert the data then, but if you do it at this stage, you are losing information which can never be retrieved without going back to the originals and spending lots of time re-entering the data – an irritating process, I can tell you. One of my students did this a long time ago, and it caused me no end of trouble with the data later on. So please, don't do it.

You will be learning much more about spreadsheets in the next chapter, but for now I think this will suffice for an introduction. In fact, it will help you understand spreadsheets a whole lot better I imagine.

PROJECT MANAGEMENT FOR DATA GATHERING

Finally, let's talk a little about the project management process. This seems to be an odd thing to talk about in a data analysis book. However, when you look at the data gathering process as a project, which can be quite large and complex, it makes more sense. More specifically, if your data collection activities are mainly small scale and personal (e.g. you collect your own data from 100 elements), you can often get away without any formal consideration of the 'management' process. However, once you begin to work with larger data collection activities, perhaps in your future careers, where multiple workers are involved in gathering masses of data, you will very likely see that project management is a key thing to think about. That said, even if you work by yourself, considering the data gathering process as a project can be very helpful. In recent times, many organizations (including government departments and the like) have recognized the need to manage projects effectively. The result of these deliberations is the PRINCE 2 method (PRojects IN Controlled Environments – don't you just love acronyms?), which has received a lot of support and use. Box 2.3 has some very brief details on this, as an introduction to project management itself. I will be using some of the PRINCE 2 ideas in the rest of this section. However, do remember that the exact details of what is required in your own specific area are likely to be different to the ones presented here in some way or another – the aim of this section is just to give you an introduction and get you thinking about the practicalities involved.

 **box 2.3**

PRINCE 2

PRINCE 2 is a system and method aimed at enabling the consistent and cost-effective management of projects. It has had a fair few name changes since its original incarnation as PROMPT, so I guess by the time you read this it may be known as TPMPFKAP, or 'The Project Management Process Formerly Known as Prince'.[4] It is basically a process-based system which specifies how a project should be most effectively run. A definition of PRINCE 2 would have these main points:

- A focus on the business justification for any project.
- A well-defined and structured project management team.
- A planning approach based on defined deliverable 'products'.
- An emphasis on dividing the project into discrete, controllable, stages.
- A flexibility to enable application at the appropriate level.

---

[4] I hope you laughed at that. I was quite pleased with it, and it maintains my main goal in life to get 1980s music referenced in as many research books as possible. So far, my hit rate is 100%.

While learning fully about PRINCE 2 would probably be considered overkill at this stage, some understanding of the process can help you get clear in your mind how to deliver a successful project (particularly where a group is concerned), and the basic principles are very helpful.

Fortunately, probably due to its governmental origins, the PRINCE 2 system is pretty much in the public domain, and you can get a good insight into it by looking at the various Internet sites available. Start (unsurprisingly) with www.prince2.com

The first thing to do when managing data collection is to plan it in more or less depth. What you need to know is how long it will take you to collect the data and, as an extension of this, how much it will cost. So you will need to know *how* you will get the data, whether you will collect it yourself or hire others, and how long it will take to collect each piece of data on average. This of course often requires some broad assumptions regarding how easy it is to collect the data, and the like, but even an educated guess at this is better than no planning at all. It is in fact surprisingly common to see lack of planning at this stage, particularly at the undergraduate or postgraduate level. Students appear to think that their data will magically 'appear' for them if they sit down at a computer for a few hours, or spend a couple of hours on the street asking people to fill in questionnaires. Unfortunately, it never happens like that, so seriously thinking about it is a key success factor.

 think it over 2.12

You have spent hours putting together a well-structured and detailed project plan. There are several dependencies: that is, where one process depends on the completion of a previous one. What happens if one process fails to be completed on time? Does this mean the project plan is useless and should be scrapped? Should you insist on sticking to the project plan rigidly or can 'contingencies' be built in to allow for 'slippage'?

From here, you also need to define a key set of tasks which need to be done to ensure the collection is a success, and at the same time you should set the dates that these things should be delivered by to make the project a success. Of course, the project itself consists of more than just data gathering, including analysis and report writing. So your structure for the project should also include these things too. A handy way of showing exactly what you have to do and the time frame you need to do it in is the Gantt chart (named after Henry Gantt who invented/popularized[5] it). A Gantt chart is a diagram which shows the tasks that need to be done, in relation to the time you have to do them. Figure 2.5 shows an example data gathering and analysis project, based on the tasks discussed below.

Number	Task	Start	End	Duration	Year 2: 2009/2010											
					Oct	Nov	Dec	Jan	Feb	Mar	Apr	May	Jun	Jul	Aug	sep
7	Survey modifications	Oct	Oct	1month												
8	Data collection	Nov	Jan	3 months												
9	Data analysis	Jan	Mar	3 months												
10	Evaluation of results	Mar	May	3 months												
11	Conclusions & Implications	Apr	Jun	3 months												
12	Write-up	Jun	Sep	4 months												

Figure 2.5 Example Data Gathering and Analysis Project

Figure courtesy of Dr. Steffen Fixson

[5] Depending on who you ask.

The sort of project I am discussing here is a simple one, typical of what you might conduct for an under-graduate or postgraduate project. Therefore, you will not be employing people to work for you, which simplifies things considerably. The early stages of a project involve defining the problem that the project is intended to solve, and from here you should write a clear brief or project plan (within which the various concepts discussed here will reside). From there, you need to get on with things, which encompasses designing the plan for the data collection (where and how you will get the data), designing a preliminary data analysis plan, designing the data collection instruments, testing them (*very important!*), and actually collecting the data. After you have got the data, you need to check it, finalize what analysis you need to conduct, enter it into the spreadsheet you are using, check for errors, and then begin analysing the data (within this stage there may be many sub-stages based on the chapters of this book as well). Finally, you need to prepare some kind of report on the analysis for whichever purpose you need.

 think it over 2.13

Defining a problem – that is easy; my life is one big problem! You have been asked to investigate and analyse a company's investment strategy; how would you define the problem? Could you do it in a sentence, a paragraph or perhaps a side of A4? What constitutes a 'good' problem definition?

At each point it helps to have defined 'milestones' which you can use to help you work out whether you are on schedule or not. The best way to use these is to have another person keep tabs on the project, as a 'project manager', to whom you can report regularly. As a student, this works well if you have a group assignment, but if you are doing something like an individual dissertation, it can help to use your academic supervisor as this project manager (I sometimes 'project manage' my PhD students in this way).

SUMMARY

By now, I hope you have some kind of understanding of where the data you will analyse during the course of working through this book might have come from. As I mentioned early on, without some idea of where data comes from and how it is collected, you run the risk of the classic 'garbage in, garbage out' approach. No matter how good you are at analysis, or whatever high-tech methods you use, your results are meaningless without good-quality data. With this in mind, remember the following points:

- Primary data is collected for your own specific purpose, whereas secondary data is data you use which was collected for some other purpose in the past.
- Primary data can be collected using interactive methods (which involve interacting with the subjects of your data) or non-interactive methods (which only record or observe data without interacting with the subject).
- Interactive methods are more flexible, but may be less objective and accurate.
- Primary data is usually collected with the use of a questionnaire or structured data collection form. The design of these forms is crucial to the success of your collection, and they should always be tested before final use.

- Collecting longitudinal or experimental primary data is subject to its own important issues. In particular, you should be aware of conditioning effects.
- When collecting secondary data, you should always be aware of checking its quality.
- The spreadsheet is the key tool for most quantitative analysis, and you need to prepare your data carefully for later analysis.
- A little attention to project management tools and techniques can help you more clearly understand your data collection process, and ensure its success.

 **final checklist**

You should have covered and understood the following basic content in this chapter; if not, please go back and read the relevant parts again:

☑ Why it is important to understand data collection before data analysis?

☑ The difference between primary and secondary data.

☑ The advantages and disadvantages of interactive and non-interactive primary data collection methods.

☑ The basics of designing good surveys or data collection forms, and how to write good questions.

☑ Why collecting data over time, and from experiments, requires special attention from you as a researcher.

☑ How to evaluate the quality of secondary data.

☑ What a spreadsheet is, and how it is constructed.

☑ How to prepare your data for analysis, using ID numbers and codes to help you identify problems.

☑ What PRINCE 2 stands for, and the basic principles of project management.

☑ Which 1980s pop star is formerly known as Prince?

EXERCISES

1. The company you work for is planning to launch a new product. In order to focus its marketing strategy the company wants to know the number of males aged between 30 and 40 years of age. You have accessed the Office for National Statistics and found its census data (follow this link: http://www.ons.gov.uk/).

If you use this data, what are its limitations? How would you classify this data?

2. Eddie is on his way into town one Saturday morning. He is approached by a girl carrying a clipboard. 'Here we go,' he thought, 'another survey.' The girl is standing outside one of the popular brand name clothing stores. She approaches Eddie who decides to stop and talk to her. She doesn't say explicitly what the survey was about but here is a snippet of the conversation:

She says: 'You look cool, if you don't mind me saying so. Can I ask you where you would shop for clothes if you had a hot date?'

'Well', says Eddie, 'as it happens I shop just over there.' [He points to another brand name clothes shop.]

'Oh, OK,' [her smile fades slightly]. 'That's interesting. Are there any particular reasons why you shop there rather than, oh I don't know, say the shop behind me?'

'No not really, I've always shopped over there,' says Eddie.

'Do you mind answering a few questions?' the girl asks.

'No not at all,' Eddie replies, still hoping.

'How much would you say you spend on clothes a month: is it £100, £150, £200 or more?'

'Would you consider paying £85 a lot of money for a pair of really good-quality jeans?'

'Most people believe that you get what you pay for; would you agree or disagree with this?'

'I can spot someone who knows how to dress. Would you say that the clothes a person wears reflects their personality?' [And many other things similar to that.]

Finally, she says: 'I don't know if you know, but in this shop they sell really good clothes. Even better is that you can get a 20% discount today if you take out one of these cards. How to look good without breaking the bank!'

a. What would you say was the purpose of the interview?
b. Is Eddie being 'guided' to a particular decision?
c. What was the purpose behind the questions concerning money?
d. Was the interview designed to produce unbiased data? Explain your answer.

3. Esha has been given the task of designing a questionnaire for a group assignment. The assignment is about finding out about effective profit-making strategies. Below is part of the questionnaire:

Question 1. If your company is losing money and you are on a bonus scheme and you've been told you won't be getting the gratuity you deserve because you're really good at your job, how does that make you feel?

Question 2. In the box provided [Figure 2.6] please give five examples of strategies your company uses to maximize profit, with the most effective being number 1.

Question 3. Why does strategy 1 work better than the others?

```
1.

2.

3.

4.

5.
```

Figure 2.6

a. If you were on the receiving end of such questions, what would your reaction be?
b. What do you think about the order of the questions?
c. What would you consider to be a major problem with question 2?
d. How would you answer question 3?

4. Eddie and Esha have decided to get together to discuss a project plan that they both have to submit (working together, not copying!). Eddie's is shown in Figure 2.7 and Esha's in Figure 2.8.

Figure 2.7 Simple Gantt Chart For A Data Collection Project

Eddie's Project Plan											
		Week Number									
		1	2	3	4	5	6	7	8	9	10
	Data collection	▓	▓								
	Analysis of data			▓							

Esha's Project Plan										
	Week Number									
	1	2	3	4	5	6	7	8	9	10
Group meeting	■									
Decide roles		■								
Literature review			■	■						
Discuss lit review					■					
Write lit review						■	■			
Discuss data collection		■								
Design questionnaire			■							
Decide who does data collection				■						
Print off questionnaires					■					
Collect data						■				
Meet to discuss data							■			
Discuss how to analyse data								■		
Analyse data									■	
Discuss on final report layout									■	
Write final report										■

Figure 2.8 Simple Gantt Chart For A Data Collection Project

5. Compare the two project plans. Which one is better or are they both bad in different ways? Remember to think about level of detail, time allocation (is it realistic?) and timing of actions (especially Esha's).

 To access additional online resources please visit: **https://study.sagepub.com/leepeters**

The Ballad of Eddie the Easily Distracted: Part 3

Eddie logged off from the online gaming server with a glow of satisfaction. His ranking in the top 10 for kills in 'Medal of Duty XIV' was safe for another day. He got up from his desk and walked over to his bed, to look at what was in store for him for the first computer tutorial of QUAN101. For once, Eddie was quite looking forward to this, because he knew plenty about computers – certainly more than he knew about people. Or quantitative analysis!

It seemed that this first tutorial would be simply an introduction to the software they would use in the course, namely Excel and SPSS. Eddie knew plenty about Excel, as one of his geekier friends had shown him a cool spreadsheet for tracking his online kills over time, and Eddie had progressively modified it to be quite an impressive model (as he would later discover it could be called). However, the SPSS one was new to him. Even so it shouldn't be too different should it? Eddie thought briefly about not even bothering to go (after all, how hard could it be?), and he couldn't think of anything worse than sitting in a PC Lab with some tutor trying to show him how to use a mouse! Even so, Eddie thought it might be nice to understand something for once, so he resolved to go along, to see what it was like.

When he got to the tutorial (a little late as usual), the tutor had already put everyone in pairs, since there were not enough PCs for everyone. Unfortunately, the only person left without a partner was that girl from the lecture who'd laughed at him when he dropped the water bottle (although, to be fair, she'd hardly been alone in that!). She looked equally irritated when the tutor paired them up, and brusquely introduced herself as 'Esha'. The mood didn't improve when the tutor informed them all that these pairings would persist throughout the course, for the rest of the year.

Anyway, when they sat down to work through the problems, Eddie was rather pleased to note that he seemed to be rather quicker to pick up things than Esha. Maybe all those games had paid off. He made a mental note to let his Mum know about that. It seemed that SPSS was pretty easy to pick up, although Eddie thought the company could have made it a bit easier to follow, and he felt sorry for those who weren't as experienced with computers as him. Even so, he rather enjoyed showing Esha some of the little tricks he had learned about Excel, before the tutor got to them. While Eddie wouldn't have said Esha looked exactly impressed, she did seem at least to listen to him. Perhaps this wouldn't be so bad after all?

Esha's Story: Part 3

Esha was struggling. She'd dreaded this PC tutorial for a week or so, and the reality was not turning out much better. She considered herself pretty smart; she'd often used the home computer to research her school projects and to present them really professionally. Her parents had even bought her a laptop before coming to university. But even though last week's lecture and reading had been about spreadsheets, she had never actually used one before, and that blank screen of rows and columns was pretty intimidating. There were so many options, and things just never seemed to work the way she was expecting – especially in SPSS!

It was bad enough that she was on her own at first, but things seemed to be getting even worse when that joker ('Eddie' he called himself; who is called 'Eddie' these days?) from the lectures turned up late and got allocated to her! And for the rest of the year!

But weirdly, Eddie seemed actually to be pretty useful in this regard. He certainly seemed to know plenty about how these computer programs worked (although Esha suspected it was mainly because of playing games), and he showed her quite a few tricks. He even seemed to know some things the tutor didn't know.

In fact, after some time of having the basics explained to her, and trying them out for herself, things seemed to get easier, and Esha felt she was getting the hang of things quite well. Actually, even though Eddie was quicker to pick up 'how' to do things, Esha seemed to find it easier to relate this to what was actually being done in terms of the data and analysis, and was able to explain this to Eddie. Oddly, Esha thought as she walked back to her room, they seemed to make quite a useful team.

THE SOFTWARE ENVIRONMENT

CONTENTS

 learning objectives

Try to keep these key learning objectives in mind when you read this chapter:

☑ Learn the foundations of how Excel and SPSS work.

☑ Understand the basic principles of data entry in Excel and SPSS.

☑ Learn how to create and manipulate data in Excel and SPSS.

☑ Get acquainted with the basics of formulae and functions in Excel.

☑ Learn how to create and define variables in SPSS.

☑ Learn how to transfer data between SPSS and Excel.

☑ Learn about the conventions used to instruct you for the rest of this book.

This chapter will introduce the two pieces of software that I am going to use to demonstrate the quantitative analysis techniques in this book, Microsoft Excel and IBM's Statistical Package for the Social Sciences (SPSS). Of course, each one of these software packages has essentially generated an industry by itself, focusing on its usage for basic and advanced analysis methods. Thus, there are what seems like hundreds of dedicated books available which cover each of the packages in great depth, and at various levels of complexity. Even so, I suspect that not too many of the readers of this book will be keen to invest in yet more books, so this chapter is an attempt to explain the basic concepts of both Excel and SPSS to you, to enable you to work with the analysis methods discussed in this book.

That said, before going on you should be aware of the possible dangers of relying on software to do your analysis for you. Now, I am not one of those boring people who says 'back in my day we never had calculators, it's so easy for students these days, blah blah blah blah' *ad nauseum*. Those people are irritating, and, besides, calculators only automate basic functions, you still need to know what you are doing. However, computer software is a slightly different issue. Packages like SPSS and Excel are almost unbelievably powerful, and with a few clicks you can be doing complex statistical analyses which only 30 years ago would have been almost impossible for a non-statistician to do. This significantly increases the chances of people using analysis methods that they do not understand, on data which is inappropriate, and coming up with results which they interpret incorrectly, or do not know how to interpret at all. In my job as an editor of a major research journal in marketing, I see this almost every day, and it is depressing.[1] Prior to the advent of such software, even to perform complex analysis required the sort of learning which took years, rather than simply understanding the phrase 'click here'. Knowing how to follow instructions is not the same thing as knowing what you are doing.

So the message I am sending here is to learn to understand what you are doing and why, before rushing off actually to do it. Just because you *can* do something does not always mean you *should* – simple analysis which is well thought out and interpreted is always better than complex analysis done badly. So with that cautionary note ringing in your ears, let's move on.

BASIC CONCEPTS

The most fundamental concept of interest here is the spreadsheet, which was introduced in the last chapter. Both Excel and SPSS feature what could be called spreadsheets, although Excel is a dedicated spreadsheet package, and SPSS would probably consider itself as something else. However, this is in my opinion splitting hairs, and SPSS basically displays its data as a spreadsheet, so that is good enough for me.

Beginning with Excel, I suspect many of you have some limited experience with either Excel or something similar to it. Excel is almost synonymous with the spreadsheet. I suspect most companies use it, and most professionals have access to a copy. In *Doing Business Research*,[2] I was a little disparaging about Excel, and I have occasionally taken quite a bit of heat for that from people from different backgrounds to me who disagree with my assertion that Excel is not that useful for statistical analysis. Even so, I stand by my argument that Excel is not really designed for academic research – even though it can perform some quite complex statistics. Excel is, however, very well suited to many key quantitative analysis tasks of use to us in a business context, and is certainly excellent at manipulating and displaying data.

On the other hand, SPSS is a package that is specifically designed to conduct the kind of statistical analyses used by social science (in which business studies and most of its various subfields are found). As standard, SPSS can do many things Excel cannot do, and is probably the most popular statistical package around. It is also increasingly commonly used in commercial applications. However, as is usual, this does not necessarily mean that it is the best. There are many others available, some of which can do different things, but SPSS is probably the 'standard' package at universities, and is thus the best one to use in this book. As well as this, experience in SPSS will be a great base to work from for you, if you have to use other packages later. If you move on to more specific fields (such as economics, finance, operations research and the like), you might find different packages more common – and you may even find your way back to Excel in some cases.

In this chapter, I will begin by discussing the basics of Excel, and then move on to SPSS, pointing out key differences as I go. Key topics of interest here are how data files are handled by each package, and

---

[1] My friends who work in other sciences say the same thing in fact.

[2] Nick Lee and Ian Lings (2008) *Doing Business Research*. Sage: London.

how data itself is entered and displayed. Throughout the book, techniques will usually be demonstrated using one or the other package, not both. I will use whichever of the packages I think is the most logical and suited for the task. Therefore, you should not assume that just because I show an example using, say, Excel, that the same thing is not possible on SPSS – simply that I think Excel is the most logical package to use for this task.

One other thing to note is the choice of computer. I will be working throughout this book with Intel computers running Microsoft Windows operating systems. This is not because I have anything against Apple Macintoshes. Anyone who knows me knows I am in love with them in a very real and legally binding fashion. In fact, most of this book was written on a Mac, listening to an iPod, talking on an iPhone (I'm listening to iTunes now!),[3] or whatever. But more importantly, in my experience, Windows machines are the more common within a business education environment and can be seen as the default 'standard'. Furthermore, while there are Mac OS versions of both Excel and SPSS, they work *generally* similarly to the PC equivalents, and therefore you should have no problems switching. Also, with recent versions of the Mac you can even run Windows, so covering Windows is pretty much the best option.

With regard to the version of Windows to use, this book was started using software running on Windows XP, but in the meantime we have gone through many different versions of Windows! Which is not very helpful. At the moment, most businesses and universities are running Windows 7, so all the screenshots are taken with that operating system. Many of you, however, will be using either Windows 8 or whatever Microsoft has come up with subsequent to that.[4] As such, your screens may look a little different. This is because software takes on some presentational features from the operating system. These should be merely cosmetic differences, and all the features and tools I am referring to should still be available.

Oh, the last thing to clear up – and apologies if I am being presumptuous here – is that I do assume you know how to start each program, use a mouse and use a computer in a basic sense. I assume you know how to select things, copy and paste, understand things like drop-down menus at the top of the screen, what windows are, and all of that foundational knowledge. I am really sorry if you do not, but I have to start somewhere, and if it is the case, then I think your time will be better spent for the next couple of hours learning how to do *that* than on learning statistics!

GETTING STARTED WITH EXCEL

So, once you start up Excel, you should find out what version you are using. Figure 3.1 shows a screenshot of the version of Excel I am using. Yours may look slightly different; you can find out what version you have by clicking the 'Help' menu at the top of the screen or the 'File' tab and selecting 'About Microsoft Excel'. Figure 3.1 also has a bunch of labels on it, showing various different parts of the Excel window. I have not included basic operating system features like scroll bars and the like, since I am assuming you have used a computer plenty of times before.

The main part of the Excel window in Figure 3.1 is taken up by a big grid, the spreadsheet. This is where the data is entered. The spreadsheet is made up of cells arranged into rows and columns. The active cell is outlined in a thicker line, and is the one into which you will enter data. Each cell has an 'address', which is the row and column in which the cell is located. The active cell in Figure 3.1 has an address B2, as it is in column B and row 2. This is shown in the name box. To make another cell active, you click on it, and you will see the name box change to that cell's address. You can select multiple cells by clicking on one and dragging (while holding the mouse button) to another. Of course, due to the characteristics of a spreadsheet, this will always be a rectangular selection. An example is shown in Figure 3.2.

---

[3] To the soundtrack of the movie *Frozen*, if you're interested. It cheers me up.

[4] In fact, just last week, Windows 10 came out to much fanfare. The whereabouts of Windows 9 are a mystery though – maybe Microsoft doesn't like the number 9?

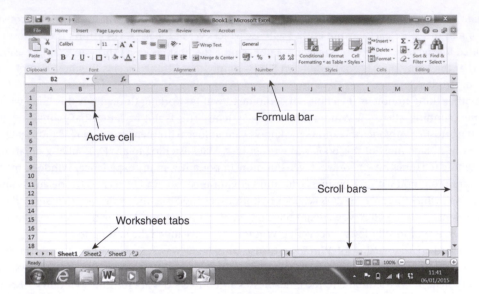

Figure 3.1
Basic Empty
Microsoft
Excel
Spreadsheet

— think it over 3.1 —

Why do you think the term active cell is used?

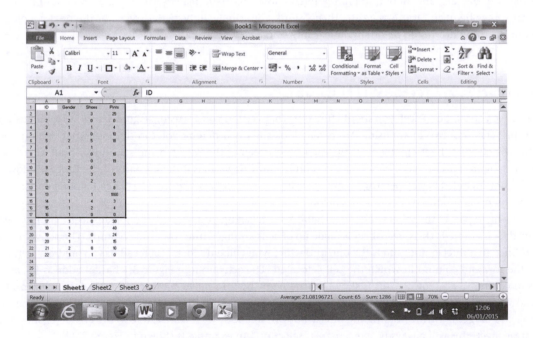

Figure 3.2
A Block
Selection

A selection is sometimes called a block. The useful thing about its being rectangular is that it can be labelled not by giving all of the cell addresses, but simply by using the top left and bottom right cell addresses. For example, the block in Figure 3.2 is denoted A1:D17. In such cases, the active cell is the one on which you clicked first, and it is white while the others are shaded.

Entering and Organizing Data in Excel

That said, you probably want to know about entering data, right? After all, that is what you will be playing with for most of the rest of this book. Most data you enter in Excel will be numbers, the raw material of quantitative analysis. To enter a number, click on the cell you want to enter it in and type the number. The number appears in the cell and the formula bar. When you press 'Enter', you tell the computer you are done. You can do exactly the same thing with text. You might ask me why you would want to enter text in a quantitative analysis. Well, as you will come to realize, text can be very useful to label your data. Where necessary, you should always use text in Excel to define the rows and columns, because Excel uses this information to create pretty graphs and charts.

 think it over 3.2

About a year ago you did an investment analysis for the company you work for. The analysis consisted of looking at the amount of profit made for different investment types. When you designed the spreadsheet you did not bother to give each investment type a descriptive name; you used headings like investment 1, investment 2 and so on. Unfortunately you have lost the bit of paper that mapped the headings to the investment type. What problems do you think this will cause? Can you resolve the problem? You have been asked to carry out a similar analysis based on your original work. What would you do differently?

One thing that always irritates me about Excel is editing the contents of a cell – either numbers or text – that you have already entered in the past. It is simple, but if you get it wrong you can inadvertently delete the contents of the cell, which I do often. Basically, to edit a cell with data in it already, click on it to make it active. But if you do not want to start from scratch and completely change the data (say you only want to add a number in the middle or the end), *do not start typing yet!* Instead, you have to tell Excel that you do not want to delete all the data in the cell and start again, and you do this either by clicking in the formula bar where the active cell data will have appeared, or by double-clicking on the active cell itself. Alternatively, if you are not a fool like me, you could just double-click on the cell in the first place. Either way, you should then see a flashing vertical line cursor appear in either the cell or the formula bar. Once you see this, you can type and move the cursor as normal.

Importantly, the basic file for Excel is termed a *workbook*. A workbook contains multiple *worksheets*. Think of it like, er, a workbook, containing lots of, um, worksheets, which you can keep various different data sets on – just like an old-fashioned exercise book. An Excel worksheet is basically a spreadsheet, and unlike an old-fashioned exercise book it contains far more cells than you can see at any one time. You can see the worksheet tabs in Figure 3.1. You can rename them to help you work out what they are. Worksheets are a great organizational tool, and you can insert them whenever you like using the 'Insert' menu. Worksheets do not have to be just spreadsheets, they can contain charts as well. Sometimes an operation (like the creation of a chart) creates new sheets automatically.

Entering Data in Excel

Table 3.1 shows some data about my favourite subjects, pints and shoes. This data set (different from that in the previous chapter) will be used in this chapter to demonstrate the differences between entering data in Excel and SPSS. But before you get started, you might want to go back to Chapter 2 and refresh your memory on the characteristics of spreadsheets.

Table 3.1 Pints and shoes data

Gender	Pints (p.m.)	Shoes (p.p.y.)
Male	25	6
Female	40	2
Male	10	10
Male	0	5
Female	15	8
Male	20	4
Female	4	10
Female	0	13
Female	1	20
Male	50	1

The first thing to do is to set up the spreadsheet. This means basically to give the columns and (sometimes) rows headings to allow us to see what the data means, and to allow Excel to use them as table and chart labels. So, in cell A1, enter the word 'Gender', in B1 enter 'Pints (p.m)', which means pints per month, and in C1 enter 'Shoes (ppy)', which means pairs of shoes per year. You can play with the format commands to make the labels look pretty, say by bolding them or the like. Then you should be able to enter the data pretty much as it is in Table 3.1, typing 'male' or 'female' as appropriate, and entering the numbers as they appear in the table. If so, the data should look like Figure 3.3.

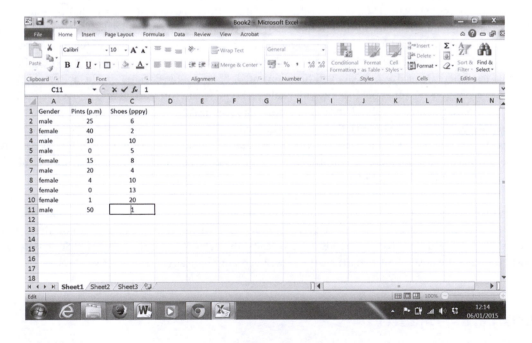

Figure 3.3
Pints and
Shoes
Spreadsheet

A couple of things to note here: first of all, you will have noticed that I told you to type in 'male' and 'female' rather than numbers. The reason for this is that Excel works fine with words as group labels (which are 'nominal variables' as shown in Chapter 1), and it makes the charts look nicer. However, if you are going to work with SPSS as well as Excel, it is best to use only numbers, as will be shown later in the chapter. SPSS gives you more features than Excel when entering data, and it will help you see the differences. Secondly, remember that the key characteristic of a spreadsheet of data is that data about a single person, company or case goes *along the row* and data on a particular characteristic or variable runs *down a column*. This is the same in both Excel and SPSS.

think it over 3.3

What is meant by the phrase 'data about a single person, company...'? Can you think of a more meaningful phrase?

Formulae and Functions in Excel

Functions are one of the key benefits of Excel and are one of the fundamental ways in which you can manipulate data in the package. However, one thing to note is that the term 'formula' is often used in Excel when what we really mean is 'equation'. So just bear that in mind, and do not get confused. Because Excel uses the term 'formula', I will tend to use that too when talking about Excel.

There are two basic types of formula in Excel, and we will look at both here. They are both entered by first making active the cell in which you want the result of the formula to appear, and then typing in the formula bar (or active cell, it is the same basic principle). You tell Excel that you are entering a formula, not a number or text, by making the first character the '=' sign (the equals sign). Looking at Figure 3.4, you can see that cell A1 is active, with '=6*6' in the formula bar, and '36' in the active cell A1. In other words, the formula is 'multiply 6 times 6', and A1 shows the answer. You should easily be able to do this yourself on Excel. One thing to note is that the keyboard does not have a standard multiply sign, so Excel (and most other software) represents this with the asterisk '*'; division is represented by the forward slash '/', and you could easily edit that formula by changing the * to / and getting the answer '1' in the cell.

think it over 3.4

When entering a formula into Excel it is always preceded by an equals sign. Why is this so? Why do you think Microsoft chose this sign? Could it mean something like 'the result of this calculation will equal...'?

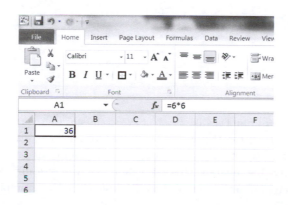

Figure 3.4
My First
Formula

If you remember Chapter 1, you will recall BEDMAS, the order of precedence for mathematical operations in an equation. Excel cleverly also uses this system, and you can organize your formulae by using brackets to make sure Excel operates on the numbers the way you want.

 think it over 3.5

If Excel adheres strictly to the rules of BEDMAS, can you think of reasons why it still might be a good idea to use brackets?

Within a formula, you can also insert *functions*, which we talked about in Chapter 1 too. Excel helpfully has a huge number of functions which will operate on your data. You can enter them either directly in the formula (if you know their names in Excel), or through a menu – which will be covered later in the book. Figure 3.5 is similar to Figure 3.4, but in this case the formula reads '6*6-SQRT(36)', and the answer is of course 30. SQRT is the Excel label for the *square root* function. Of course, the square root of 36 is 6. Most of the time, a function has a 'name' like SQRT and an *argument* in brackets – which is the number you want the function to operate on (think back to Chapter 1). Some functions have more than one argument, but they all appear between the same set of brackets, separated by commas, such as '=AVERAGE(4,2,4)' which will return the arithmetic mean (wait until Chapter 4 if you do not know what that is) of the three arguments. If a function has no arguments, the function name is followed by empty brackets like '()'.

 think it over 3.6

With some formulae you have to supply arguments. Why do you think the order you enter the arguments in is important? How would you know if you entered them in the wrong order?

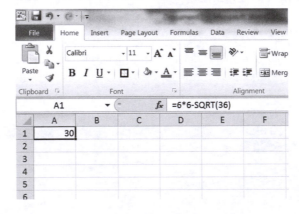

**Figure 3.5
A More
Complex
Formula**

Now, typing in formulae with numbers like those above is all very well, but not *that* useful; it is really just like a fancy scientific calculator. The real power of functions in Excel is when you understand that, instead of numbers, you can use cell names in formulae and functions – and the formula or function will use *the contents of that cell* as the input into the calculation. You will probably fail to see how incredibly useful that idea is until later, but if you look at Figure 3.6 you will see an example.

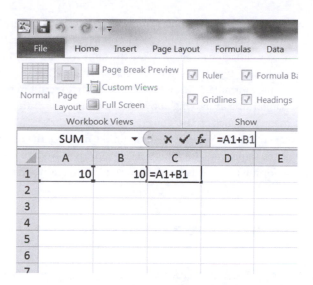

Figure 3.6
Cell Addresses in Formulae

In this example, I have set up a very simple addition between the contents of A1 and B1. Assuming you know what cells you are interested in, you do this by making a cell active and starting a formula with an equals sign as normal. However, instead of typing a number, *you click on the cell which contains the first piece of data for the formula*. In this case, I clicked on A1. You can then type whatever operator you are interested in and it will appear in the formula bar and the cell. However, make sure that the cursor is in the formula bar before typing the operator. In this case, I typed a plus sign. Then, click on the next cell of interest; in this case B1. Then when you are done, hit 'Enter'. The answer will appear in the active cell. I did not press 'Enter' in the example in Figure 3.6, because it helps to illustrate that when you are creating the formula, the cell names will be pretty colours, matching each cell border, which helps to keep things under control in your head. You can do this with every formula and function in Excel, instead of using real numbers, which is *brilliant*!

It is brilliant for loads of reasons which you will come to appreciate as the book moves on. Most obvious at this point is the ability to change the information in a cell, and the answer to the formula will change! For example, if you created Figure 3.6 as I suggested earlier, change B1 to 40 instead of 20, and the answer in C1 will also change, to 50. Clever! So you can set up automatic worksheets and workbooks to deal with specific types of problems, and then change the numbers in the cells to refer to whatever the actual situation is. This is an absolute stroke of genius, can save you masses of time, and make you look really clever. It is also the foundation of what many companies call 'scenario planning' – which is basically just setting up a neat model in Excel and changing the numbers to see what happens.

Tips on Moving and Copying Formulae

I am not going to teach you the basics of cutting, copying and pasting data. I hope you can already do that, and in Excel it is pretty much the same thing. But when it comes to formulae with cell names like I just described, a few tips will make your life a lot easier and allow you to do some cool stuff too.

First, let's cover moving. Moving data or cells is a handy technique and applies to many different situations as well as formulae. Consider Figure 3.6 again. Imagine I wanted to move C1 to somewhere else on the worksheet, yet still keep it working with the data in A1 and B1. This is easy: click on the cell to make it active, then depending on your version of Excel either select 'cut' from the edit menu and click on the 'cut' icon on the toolbar, or press the 'Ctrl' key at the same time as the 'X' key ('Ctrl-X'). Then either click the paste icon or press 'Ctrl+V' to paste into the chosen cell. If you do that correctly, you will see the same answer in the cell and exactly the same formula in the formula bar. Handy.

But, even more handy is when you *copy* a formula, not move it. Check out Figure 3.7. This figure is similar to Figure 3.6, in that it has the same information in A1 and B1, and the formula in C1. But in A2 and B2 there is also information. Now, imagine I wanted to use the same formula in C1 to add up the information in A2 and B2. Of course, I could type it in again in cell C2: '=A2+B2'. In this case, pretty simple, but imagine you had a really complex formula. What a hassle, and likely to result in mistakes. But there is an easier way. Do exactly the same thing as moving above, select the cell with the formula in, then either select 'copy' from the edit menu and click on the 'copy' icon, or press 'Ctrl+C'. Then either click the paste icon or press 'Ctrl+V' to paste in cell C2. You will see that, unlike moving, the original will not disappear and the new formula will be the same, but with different cell addresses. Note that this is exactly the same as 'copying and pasting' the formula. This is fantastically useful in so many circumstances.

think it over 3.7

What do you notice about the border of the cell you are copying? What if you chose the wrong cell? How can you deselect the cell?

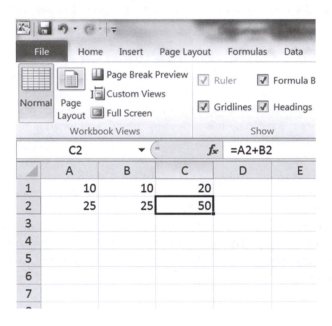

Figure 3.7
Copying
Formulae

The reason this works is that Excel uses something called a relative cell address. Most of the time Excel uses these relative cell addresses, and sometimes you will want to override this, for example if you were copying a formula and wanted to keep some of the same cell addresses but keep others relative. For instance, you might have a constant percentage or something which you wanted to multiply each row of data by. But if you copied the formula each time it would change all the cell addresses, even the one you wanted to keep constant. Have a look at Figure 3.8, where we have two columns of data which you might find familiar, and a label for a third column called 'Proportion'. What I want to do in that column is to work out the proportion of the total for the 'Pairs of Shoes' column that each year (the row labels) contributes. So in cell D2 I want the proportion of total shoes that Year 1 students purchase. This is easy: I just click on D2 and enter the formula '=B2/B5', press 'Enter', and there you go. As I have done.

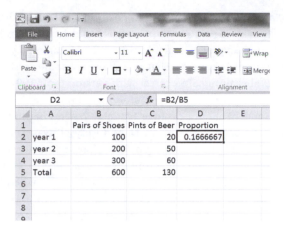

Figure 3.8
Relative
Cell
Addressing
Part 1

think it over 3.8

What does the word relative mean in the context of relative cell addressing? Is there any link with Eddie's Aunty Elsie?

Now, if I want to do the same for Year 2 and 3 in D3 and D4 respectively, why not just copy the D2 formula? Well, if you try it and see you would get a nasty error message in D3 and D4 of '#DIV/0!'. This is because Excel has treated all the cell addresses in the formula as relative. So the formula in D3 would read '=B3/B6'. This is good for B3, which is the Year 2 value, but bad for B6, which is nothing. We need it to keep B5 in the formula as an *absolute* cell address, but still change the other *relative* address. Naturally there is a way to do this. If you click on D2, you can see the formula and tell Excel which one of those to make absolute, and which to keep relative. You do this by changing B5 in the formula to $B$5 – note the added '$' signs. Now, when you copy the formula, B5 will stay the same, but B2 will change as required. Very, very clever.

think it over 3.9

What is meant by the phrase 'absolute cell address'? If we can use absolute cell addressing why do we need relative cell addressing?

So, this is a good introduction to the basics of Excel data input and manipulation, and certainly enough to get you started and make you confident enough to begin to analyse data as you move through the book. Many more features will be looked at throughout the book, and by the end you will know a lot of neat stuff.

GETTING STARTED WITH SPSS

Now you have a basic appreciation of Excel, I am going to cover the basics of SPSS. I will start off in a slightly more basic manner than Excel, since it is more than likely that you are coming to SPSS completely cold, with no experience at all. In terms of versions of SPSS, its makers have an irritating habit of releasing new versions of the software pretty frequently. Interestingly, this seems to have increased over the years, perhaps as SPSS has tried to position itself as a commercial business tool for customer research as much as a scientific analysis package. But let's not go into that. Most of these versions do not change the fundamentals, but add some new features, so you can almost always use books based on different versions in general. That said, there are some version updates which change major things. For example, I began my SPSS career with version 6, in 1997, and there was quickly a major change for version 7, which became much more 'windows-oriented'. Then there was a huge change between versions 9 and 10 about how to enter data. When I began writing this in 2009, SPSS was selling version 17, my university had version 16 and I myself was using version 12 as I had for the previous five years or so! I grudgingly moved up to version 16 to write the first draft of this book. However, in 2015 (for indeed it has taken some time) we are at version, er, well, SPSS seems to have now eschewed version numbers! Either way, it was at least version 22 when I last checked.

To avoid any confusion, let's make it clear from now on that this book will cover version 22. Either way, the upshot is you will be able to use this book to cover almost certainly the version of SPSS which you have.

The Basic Structure of SPSS

While SPSS might look exactly the same to you as Excel once you load it up, it is actually structured quite a bit differently. Importantly, while Excel allows you to work with multiple data sets on worksheets within the same workbook, with SPSS this is not really possible, unless it has been added in the ensuing time! Anyway, in my experience each instance of SPSS can only work with one data file at a time. If you try to open a new data file like you do in Excel, Word or lots of other programs, earlier versions will actually close the other file automatically, and later versions will open an entirely separate window with a new instance of SPSS, as far as I can tell. In the old versions, if you had made changes, SPSS would ask you to save them, but if not it will just load the new file and get rid of the old one. This can be a little irritating. One way around it with the old version is to open manually a new instance of SPSS, so you have it running twice, or more. Each instance can have a data file, but remember that it is completely separate. However, from version 14 onwards, you *could* open multiple files. So most of you should be OK. And since my recent move into the twenty-first century, me too!

 think it over 3.10

If you have done anything with databases you are probably familiar with the phrase 'instance of...'. What is meant by an instance of SPSS? How many instances can we have? If we have multiple instances running, could that cause problems?

SPSS is generally structured around *two* key windows, unlike Excel, which has one. The one which looks a little like a spreadsheet is the Data Editor, which is where you put your data in and do most of your statistical analysis. The results of that analysis (including charts and graphs) are then displayed in a new window which opens up, called the Viewer, or the Output window. I will deal with these separately, very soon. There is also another, more mysterious, window called the Syntax Editor. 'Syntax' is basically a name for the SPSS programming language. Most users of SPSS never use or see the Syntax window, because you can do almost everything by simple pointing and clicking. *But* there are some cool tricks and techniques which use the Syntax Editor to save you time and help you repeat analyses later on. I did one of my dissertations by programming SPSS in the Syntax window, many years ago, before lovely pointing and clicking was so well implemented, so I do have a soft spot for it. Then again, people do tell me I am weird. Also, it did help me a lot in learning to program other statistical software later on in life.

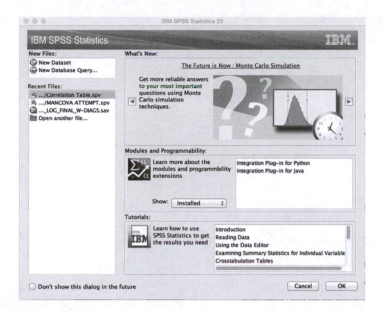

Anyway, moving on to practicalities, if you start SPSS (post version 10) you will immediately be presented with a 'helpful' window like Figure 3.9. If you are using pre-10 versions, you will get a blank Data Editor window. The specific details of the window change according to the whims of the software designers it seems. However, in the version I have, you will need to look at the left of the window. Here you'll get an option to start a 'New File', or lower down open a 'Recent File'. What I would do here if I wanted to start from scratch is click on 'New Dataset' which should appear somewhere in the top-left part of the window. That should open a blank data file. If you want to open an existing file, look a little lower to the list of 'Recent Files', and click the one you want. If it is not there, simply select 'Open another file' and click on 'OK', which should bring up the usual Windows file browser.

The Data Editor Window

The Data Editor window, confusingly, has two different views, which are called the Data View and Variable View. This was a major change with version 10 which completely confused me and lots of other smarter people. But let's not go into that as it was a bit embarrassing. Figure 3.10 shows the Data Editor window, and also the two small tabs down at the bottom left which you can use to switch between the Data View and Variable View (they look a little bit like the worksheet tabs in Excel). The white tab shows which view you are in. The Data View is the view you use actually to enter the data, and the Variable View is the view you use to define the variables. I will cover both of these shortly.

 think it over 3.11

We keep using this word variable. We are now talking about defining them. What do we mean when we say define your variables? Is it define them in the mathematical sense of integers, decimals, complex numbers, etc.?

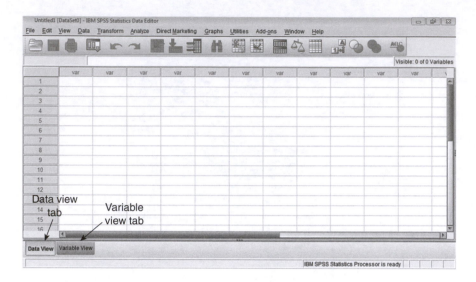

Figure 3.10
The Data
Editor

But first, let's look at some of the basic features of the Data Editor window, common to both views. As is usual, along the top of the screen is a menu bar, with all kinds of different menus. Some of these will be familiar to you from other software, like 'File' and 'Edit'. I am not going to look at those. However, there are lots of menus which are likely to be new to you, so those are presented in Box 3.1. I will not describe what all the options are, but rest assured that I will cover them as and when they are necessary.

 — box 3.1

New Menus

Data: This menu contains tools to manipulate your data set and create data, many of which are self-explanatory. Some of the important tools you have here include *split file*, which can split the file into different parts according to a specific variable, and *select cases*, which allows you to run an analysis only on a certain subset of your data.

Transform: This menu contains a lot of really useful tools to manipulate the data itself. *Recode* is very useful, allowing you to change values of variables according to rules you specify, and the *compute* function is fantastically useful (similar to the function editor in Excel in fact).

Analyze: This is where the action starts to happen. Located here are many of the statistical functions I will look at later, in detail.

Graphs: SPSS can produce some neat graphs, but we will often be using Excel for graphs and charts. That said, it is sometimes easier to use SPSS, so where it is, we will be poking around in here.

Entering Data in SPSS

Now, you are going to repeat the exercise you did earlier in Excel with SPSS, to demonstrate the differences. One thing you will immediately see is that SPSS gives you a lot more options when entering data, and it is important to set up the file correctly in the first place, to save heartache later. So, go back up to Table 3.1 for the data set to enter. You should have a nice clean Data Editor, with the Data View selected (see above if you are confused). Just like Excel, you should think of the spreadsheet as structured with each row representing data from one case, and each column representing a variable. I know I keep hammering this point home, but it is vital you get this clear before actually getting into your analysis.

However, there are plenty of differences between entering data in Excel and SPSS, most of which are driven by the slightly different intended purposes of the software. These will become apparent as you move through the book, but the major differences you will see at this point are in the treatment of the gender variable, and also in the way that variables are set up in general. Even so, with your experiences with Excel already, it should not take you too long to get the hang of things. It is slightly different to enter data in SPSS – there is no 'formula bar', for example. So to enter data, simply click on the cell you want to use, which will be outlined in black (like the active cell in Excel). Just type in the number. However, instead of hitting 'Return' you can use the arrow keys to move to the next cell in whichever direction you want. This is handy if you are entering questionnaire data because you can simply enter a value and hit the right arrow key to move on. Of course, this means you cannot navigate around within the cell, but SPSS is not designed for long entries, just for numbers, so it is not often an issue.

Just like in Excel, we need to set up the spreadsheet with row and column headings. But you are going to do something different with the 'gender' variable in this case. Gender is what you could call a grouping variable. In other words, each member of the data set can only be a member of one or another group, not more than one – the variable defines which group you are in. You will see many different grouping variables throughout this book. Taking things back to Chapter 1, grouping variables are nominal scales. Anyway, in Excel you typed in 'Male' and 'Female' as appropriate. However, in SPSS we are going to represent group membership with numbers instead of words. While you do not strictly have to do this, SPSS expects you to do it as default, and if you use words (which are called 'strings' in SPSS)[5] you cannot use the variable in many important types of analysis. So what we have to do is decide which group is represented by which number, and then tell SPSS which number represents which group. If you remember the features of a nominal scale from Chapter 1, you will remember that it does not really matter what these numbers are (as long as they are different of course). That said, it is usually simplest to make them logical, say '1' for males and '2' for females. So whenever there is a 'male' in the data, you enter a '1' into SPSS, and whenever there is a 'female' you enter '2'. You then tell SPSS that 'male' is represented by '1' and 'female' by '2'. So, let's do this step by step.

think it over 3.12

We have defined males as '1', females as '2'. Does this mean females are twice as good as males? Or does it mean males are always number 1? Why are we using numbers in any case – 'male' and 'female' are surely far more descriptive?

The first step is to create variables. We need to do this in SPSS to tell it what features our data has (since often numbers represent other features and attributes). You create variables using the Variable View and enter data using the Data View. So, again, let's use the data in Table 3.1.

think it over 3.13

Are there any differences between features and characteristics? If so, what are they?

---

[5] The programmers among you will recognize that term from old-fashioned computer programming terminology.

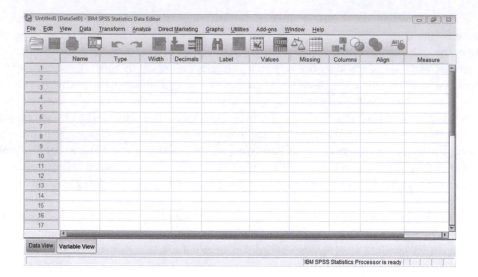

Figure 3.11
The
Variable
View

Click on the Variable View tab at the bottom of the Data Editor in SPSS and the contents of the window will change, to what is presented in Figure 3.11 (note the now gold-coloured tab at the bottom left). In the Variable View, each row represents a variable, and the columns represent features of that variable. In Figure 3.11 you can see these features running along the top of the window, things like 'Name', 'Type', 'Width', etc. Many of these are relatively unimportant visual characteristics (e.g. how many decimal places are displayed), but the others are vital aspects of your data, and it is important to get them right at the beginning of the process. The key ones are:

Name: In this column you name the variable, and that name will appear at the top of the relevant column in the Data View. SPSS has rules about variable names, which may or may not change. However, I think it best to stick to the following conventions, which are guaranteed to work in all versions: variable names must be eight characters or fewer, and not contain blank spaces.

Type: Here you tell SPSS what type of data you are using. The most common type is 'numeric' which is the default. This means you are using numbers. But you can also use 'string' for words and letters. There are other options which may be of use in specific circumstances, but so far in my 40 years (of life) I have never used them.

Label: Because in the old days you could only use eight characters in the variable names (a convention I still recommend today), SPSS allows you to give each variable a 'label', which can be longer and very descriptive. Because I am a lazy person, I never used to bother to do this, but I found out to my cost later that it is a very important habit to get into, especially if you work in teams. So, for the variable of 'pints of beer consumed per month' in our data set, we may be restricted to 'pints' in the variable name, but in the label we can be far more descriptive. SPSS can then use these labels in the analysis output, allowing you to see much more easily what you are doing, especially as time goes on.

Values: Here, we tell SPSS what the numbers in our variables represent (see below).

Missing: Here, you let SPSS know what number you have decided to use to represent missing data (see below).

Measure: This recalls Chapter 1, and it lets you tell SPSS what type of measure your variables are: nominal, ordinal or *scale* (which SPSS uses as a catch-all for interval and ratio). This is important because it restricts what you can do with the data, so make sure you get it right.

think it over 3.14

If I had two variables, both concerned with age, how could I give them a meaningful name rather than just 'age1' or 'age2'?

To enter the data from Table 3.1, you will need to create at least three variables. Let's begin by doing one of the simple ones, the 'pints per month' variable. You can use these steps:

- In the Variable View, click on the first cell in the 'Name' column.
- Type the word 'pints' – because we cannot use 'pints per month' since it is longer than eight characters and contains spaces.
- Move off the cell by using the right arrow key.

OK, that's it! Notice that SPSS has now filled in a bunch of default values in the other columns (e.g. it has assumed your variable is numeric). So let's label it. Move to the relevant cell in the 'Label' column (to the right of the 'Name' column), and type 'Pints per month'. Then move to the far right column labelled 'Measure', click on the drop-down menu and select 'Scale'. Everything else is pretty much OK as the default.

You can now click back to the Data View and see how things change. You should see that the first column now has the label 'pints'. Great work! After this, you should be able to add the 'pairs of shoes purchased per year' variable from Table 3.1 pretty easily. Just follow the same steps, and call it 'shoes'. You could now enter some data, but I do not think it is ever smart to do that before you set up the whole spreadsheet properly. So let's now move on to the more complex 'gender' variable. You should notice that in the data in Table 3.1, gender is the leftmost variable, but here we have already entered 'pints' there, so how do we get around this? It is not hard. First of all, go back to the Variable View and make sure you have selected the cell with the 'pints' name. Then select 'insert variable' from the Data menu at the top of the screen. A new variable will automatically appear above the 'pints' menu, labelled something like VAR0001. We now can modify this variable for our 'gender' one, as shown below.

Creating a Grouping Variable

Creating a grouping variable is more complex than anything you have experienced so far, because it needs values to be labelled. So it is a good exercise in doing this too. Group variables (sometimes called coding variables) can be very useful for dividing the data set, and later analysis. To do this we need to add an extra step to let SPSS know that the numbers in the cells represent something else in the real world. We do this to let ourselves know what is going on, and to prevent us from making erroneous conclusions.

So, first we create a variable and give it the name 'gender'. If you have been following above, you will have inserted the variable above 'pints' using the 'insert variable' command from the Data menu; it will be at the top of the list, with the automatic name 'VAR1' or the like. To rename it, just click on VAR1 and type 'gender'. You do not really need to give it a label, but to keep your habit going, move to the 'Label' column and type 'gender of respondent' in it. Next comes the more complex bit. Move to the column marked 'Values' – which you will notice says 'none' currently – either by clicking on it, or by using the arrow keys. When it is active a tiny button will appear on the right of the cell, with three dots on it. Click on this and you will be taken to the Value Labels dialog box. See Figure 3.12 for a visual of this.

Figure 3.12
Value
Labels
Dialog Box

It is an easy process to do this, but it can be a bit counterintuitive at first. What is more, this basic process works for many of the other dialog boxes in SPSS, so pay attention. First, you need to have decided what numerical values to give your groups, so let's use '1' for male and '2' for female. Now, click on the little white space to the right of 'Value' and type in '1'. Then click on the white space just below, and type 'male'. Now, we need to add that value label to the SPSS list, and we do this by clicking on 'Add'. You should see it appear in the large white box at the bottom of the dialog box. In Figure 3.12 I have already done this and am about to click on the 'Add' button to add the '2' value label for females. When you have finished, click on 'OK' and you will be back to the Variable View.

Finally, remember that grouping variables are always nominal, so make sure you set the measure correctly.

think it over 3.15

Why are grouping variables always nominal?

You can now enter all the data from Table 3.1 into SPSS, and if you do it correctly, it should look like the top panel of Figure 3.13. What is quite neat is that you can click on the little button shown in the top panel of Figure 3.13 and have SPSS show you the value labels, not the numeric codes, and in this case the data will look like the bottom panel of Figure 3.13. Personally I never use that feature, but it is quite clever.

Dealing with Missing Data

While of course we hope that we have complete data for every case we collected data from, this is hardly ever the case in real life. If you use questionnaires, people miss out questions either deliberately or accidentally. If you are creating a data set from a large database (say company profit figures) then there may be particular companies who do not provide figures for every time period. There can be many reasons. Missing data is a complex statistical issue, which can be dealt with in many ways. I will not deal with them in any depth in this book, and certainly not right now. However, to enable you to deal with them later on, it is important you let SPSS know when there is missing data.

In order to do this, simply choose a number to represent missing data, and then, when you get to a place where data should be but is not, input this value. SPSS will then ignore that piece of information as it knows it represents a missing data point. The trick is to set a value for missing data that will not occur in your real data. For example, it is common to use '9' as missing data. But if your data set actually has genuinely occurring scores of '9' – for example, in a nine-point scale – this would not be possible. You can set any number you want, as long as it is not possible that your actual data could include that number.

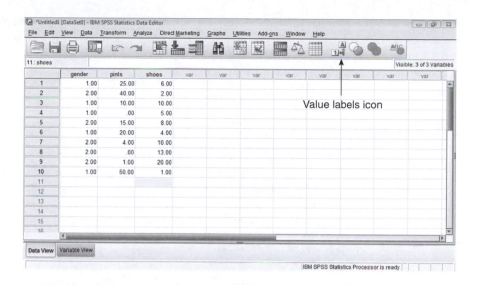

Value labels icon

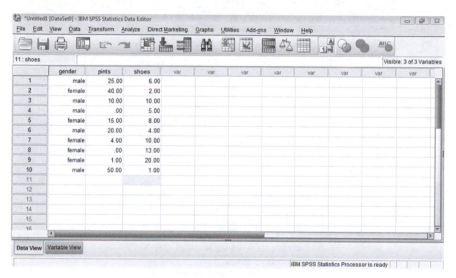

Figure 3.13a and b
SPSS Data

Figure 3.14
Missing
Values
Dialog Box

To set the missing data value, make sure you are in the Variable View and click on the column labelled 'Missing' for the variable you want to define missing values for. Then click on the small button on the right of the cell to activate the missing values dialog box which you can see in Figure 3.14. This box can appear quite complex, because there are three ways of setting missing vales. To set a number as a missing value label, click on the radio button next to 'Discrete missing values'. Then you can select up to three discrete single numbers to represent missing values. This is clever because you can then have different 'types' of missing data represented by different numbers, which can act as reminders to you in later analysis. In Figure 3.14, I have chosen to use 9, 99 and 999 to represent three types of missing values. Most people do not do this, though. You can also choose a range of values to represent missing values (say between 1 and 9), or you can have a combination of both. The latter two options can be useful in specific circumstances, but most people use a discrete number.

The Output Viewer

A separate window from the Data Editor window, the Output Viewer is basically where your results appear. It presents nicely laid-out tables, and pretty graphs, as well as highly complex analysis results. Figure 3.15 shows a basic example of the Output Viewer, with a nice graph on it (I will talk about this graph, a histogram, in the next chapter). You might find that in your version of SPSS it is just called the Viewer, but in the old days it was called the 'Output Window', and in my head the name 'Output Viewer' remains resolutely stuck.

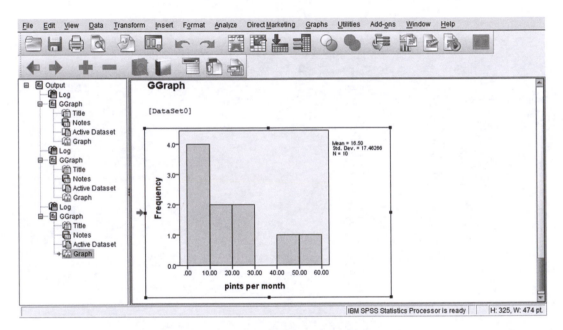

Figure 3.15
Output
Viewer

Anyway, you can see from Figure 3.15 that the left hand side of the Output Viewer contains a kind of tree diagram, which is uncannily like the Microsoft Windows Explorer folder structure. This is quite clever. On the right hand side, in the larger space, is where your actual results appear. There are two things you need to know about the Output Viewer. First of all, never forget that the output window is separate from the Data Editor. They can be saved separately, and they can have separate filenames. If you open a new data file to work on, and the old one closes, any analysis you do on the new file will have its results shown in the *same Output Viewer* as the last lot. So you can get very confused, very easily. What I always do is save my output from a given data file with the *same filename* as the data file, in the same folder. Then when I work on that data file, before analysing anything I can call up the old output window and continue to have the results appearing in it if I want. The other thing to remember is that you can click on any results or on a table or graph to expand it, or double-click on it to edit it. Sometimes, with very large sets of results, the Output Viewer only looks like it displays a part. To expand the results to their full extent you must click on them. A border will appear around the results, with handles you can grab with your mouse to expand the area displayed. This trick will come in handy later on.

There are many icons and presentational tools you can use within the Output Viewer to modify its presentation. However, my usual preference is to cut and paste the relevant output into a word processor or page layout program, and work within there.

While this may all sound very complicated, you will very quickly get the hang of working within this dual-window system. Once you do, it is actually quite handy.

 above and beyond

Box 3.1   SPSS Syntax

SPSS also has its own programming language, which you can use to perform analysis instead of using the point-and-click methods I will mainly be using. Sometimes, especially for very repetitive tasks, this can be actually easier.

SPSS language is called 'syntax' and it is written in the Syntax window. You can open a blank Syntax window from the File menu, by clicking on 'New' then 'Syntax'. A blank window will appear just like the top panel of Figure 3.16. If you know syntax, you can then type stuff in, and run it using the Run menu. To run everything, click on 'Run' and then 'All', or you can select 'Selection' to run only the highlighted bit. Or you can click on 'Current' to run the current command. If you want to run everything from where your cursor is to the end, click on 'Run' and then 'To End'.

But how do you start programming syntax? It is actually surprisingly easy. When you are in a dialog box you can often see a button with the word 'Paste' on it. If you click on that, SPSS will paste the syntax for the analysis you have specified into a Syntax window, such as in the bottom panel of Figure 3.16. This is a great way to learn what syntax is doing.

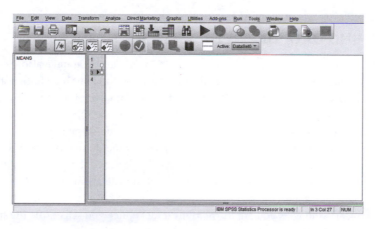

Figure 3.16
The Syntax Window

Differences and Compatibility Between Versions of SPSS

Currently, we seem to be up to version 22 of SPSS, although the version you are using will depend on your institution (in fact it will probably be later than 22 by the time this book comes out). Thus, bear in mind that all I am saying refers to SPSS up to version 22.

In terms of compatibility, since version 7.5 all *data* files are forward and backward compatible, so you can open them in any version between 7.5 and 22. However, one important caveat is that before version 12, variable names had to be 8 characters long, and from version 12 onwards they could be up to 64 characters. So if you try to open a data file which has long variable names in a version of SPSS from 11 or earlier, the variable names will be cut off – which could cause problems. As I said earlier, I think it is best to stick to eight characters anyway; then you are guaranteed that things will work OK.

However, *output* files are generally not backward compatible. So if you save an Output Viewer file in version 22, it may not be viewable in an earlier version. Furthermore, output files are only forward compatible among certain versions. For example, from 7.5 to 15 output files are forward compatible (i.e. you can open a version 8 output file in version 15), and the same is true between 16 and 17. However, if you save an output file in version 15 or earlier, you will *not* be able to open it in later versions. This might be a major pain for you if you upgrade. It could even prevent you from doing so, since you might have to redo all your analysis to get new output. That said, SPSS has created a legacy viewer application, which will allow you to view the data files from prior versions. You can download that from the SPSS website. Phew!

If you are interested in syntax files, great! They are usually forward and backward compatible, but in some cases specific commands have changed or disappeared in newer versions, which might make the program itself run weirdly. You will need to check specifics in the documentation of your new version of SPSS to know exactly, though. In fact, the SPSS website is a great resource for all kinds of compatibility issues.

TRANSFERRING DATA BETWEEN SPSS AND EXCEL

Now you have a good idea about how both Excel and SPSS work, and you have also created a couple of data files in the programs, it is important to spend a little time working out how to transfer data between them. Both software packages should be easily able to import data from the other, but the trick is how it is presented. Remember that in Excel, for example, the column headings were input directly onto the spreadsheet, whereas in SPSS they are specifically taken care of in the Variable View.

Beginning with importing Excel data into SPSS, this has become quite a bit easier over the years. In fact, SPSS now has a dedicated ability to import Excel data. Simply go to the File menu, then 'Open', then 'Data' and a dialog box will come up like Figure 3.17. Click on the arrow to the right of 'Files of type' and a drop-down menu will appear which you can use to select 'Excel' as shown. If you do this, the Excel spreadsheet will appear, as long as you are in the right folder. Once you select this file to open, another dialog box will appear as in Figure 3.18.

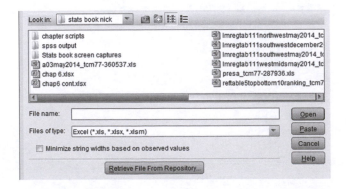

Figure 3.17
Importing
Excel Files

C:\stats book nick\chap 6.xlsx

☑ Read variable names from the first row of data

Worksheet: Sheet1 [A1:P28]

Range:

Maximum width for string columns: 32767

OK   Cancel   Help

Figure 3.18
Importing
Excel Files
Dialog Box

This can look complicated, but as long as you have kept your Excel file organized it is quite simple. The key is to load the right data with the right labels. To do this, make sure that the box 'Read variable names from the first row of data' is ticked. But, if you do tick this, you *must make sure the first row of your Excel data has the variable names, not actual data.* This will be the case if you are following my instructions.

Then, make sure the right worksheet is selected. Remember: an Excel workbook can have multiple worksheets. The little box below for the 'Range' is to specify where in the worksheet SPSS should grab data from. If you want to import the entire data set from the worksheet, and the data set is in one single rectangle of data from the top left corner, SPSS should automatically pick it up, like in Figure 3.18. However, if you wanted to import only a segment of the worksheet, you could do this by specifying the top left corner cell and the bottom right corner cell of the rectangle you wished to import.

Once you have done that, click on 'OK' and your data will appear in SPSS, hopefully with the labels and values correct. You will probably have to go through it to neaten it up, especially with the variable names and the like. But at least it is there!

Unfortunately, things are not as simple in transferring SPSS data to Excel. There is no import option in Excel of any use, and if you just load the SPSS file into it you will get garbage. One way of getting around this is to save your data from SPSS in a format which Excel will like. The most obvious way of doing this is to save it as an Excel file – which is actually quite simple and I wonder why I made such a fuss.

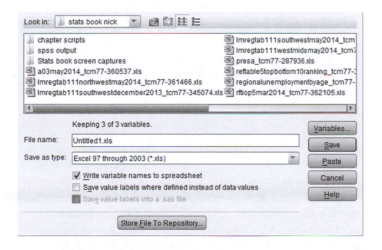

Figure 3.19
Exporting
SPSS Files
as Excel
Files

To do this, in SPSS go to the File menu, then 'Save As'; a window will appear, as shown in Figure 3.19. Make sure you select 'Excel 97 through 2003' or 'Excel 2007 through 2010' (depending on your own version) as the file type in the 'Save as type' box. Also, if you have variable names – which you should – make sure you check the 'Write variable names to spreadsheet' option. Then the variable names will appear as the first column of your worksheet. You *could* also check the other box next to 'Save value labels where defined instead of data values'. This is useful if you want Excel to display the words you used to label your numeric values, for example in the gender grouping variable you created above. If you checked that box, the spreadsheet would contain 'male' and 'female' instead of '1' and '2'.

Once you have done this, click on 'Save', and then you should be able to open the data set relatively painlessly in Excel. Although, of course, it will probably need tidying up.

CONVENTIONS FOR THIS BOOK

Up until now, I have tried to write the instructions on how to use the software in as close to 'plain English' as possible. The reason for this is to ease in those who might not be so comfortable with computers and this type of software. However, if I were to do this all the way through the book, things would rapidly start to get long-winded for you, and also me. Thus at this point it will be handy to set up a few conventions, so you know how I am going to describe software operations in the rest of the book. However, this approach will change slightly as the book moves on and you develop your knowledge. We will begin with the system described below, which is quite detailed. But, in line with learning theories, as you get more experienced with using the software, the instructions will be less detailed and more focused on the analysis methods themselves, rather than on clicking and moving the mouse. This is to help you cement the basic concepts in your mind, and then rely on them as you move forwards. If you ever find yourself having problems remembering the basics, just go back to the earlier chapters and run those exercises, or play with new data sets using the older techniques you have already covered. You will find that, in this way, you can speed up your learning a lot.

By now, you should have realized that in Windows software like Excel and SPSS there is almost always a bar at the top of the program window which contains menus – the menu bar. These menus include things like File, Edit and the like, and you can show them by moving your mouse to put the arrow (called the 'pointer') on the menu word, and clicking the left button to display the menu. When I want you to click the left mouse button, I will simply write 'click', and if I want you to click the *right* mouse button, I will specifically say 'right click'.

Once you click on a menu, the menu will appear, and you can then move the mouse to put the pointer on the right option and then click. Sometimes, another small menu will open (called a 'sub-menu'), but, more often, another window will pop up, called a 'dialog box'. Within a dialog box you will usually be able to click on 'buttons' which may have symbols or words on them, or you could click to put marks in 'check-boxes' or even to put a mark in a 'radio button'. A radio button is a small white circle which, when you click it, gains a tiny black dot. Radio buttons are used usually to allow you to select options.

To make things quicker to read and write, I will direct you to move your mouse pointer using a formal convention, involving words and arrows in the text. For example, if I wanted you to go to the Edit menu and click on 'Copy', I would use underlined type to designate the options to select, and an arrow to show where to move the mouse pointer. In other words, an arrow → means 'put your pointer on the next word and click'. So, moving back to the example, 'select <u>Edit</u> → <u>Copy</u>' means 'go to the Edit menu and click, then move the mouse to the Copy option and click'. That should clear things up a little.

SUMMARY

For many of you, I expect this chapter would have been a total breeze. However, I also suspect that a very large proportion of you would have learned at least one or two little things from it. I even learnt a few myself! More importantly, there will doubtless be many of you for whom this was a struggle. This might be because you have never really thought about how you use computers. Maybe you only ever use the Internet and a word processor? Although, actually, even using a word processor will give you a good knowledge of the Excel interface.

I guess it is unrealistic to think that even a small number of you will have never used a computer – although I did not use a computer for assignment work myself until I was a postgraduate (in 1997). Even then I never owned my own until that year. However, I have been lucky enough to have computers in my family home since before I can remember (in 1982 we owned a Sinclair ZX-81, with 1 kilobyte of memory, and no non-volatile storage at all!).[6] So, I have always been totally comfortable with computers and how they work. However, there are many of you who probably are not so comfortable, and I really tried to write this chapter to be approachable for you people.

---

[6] Hilariously, if you wanted the ZX-81 actually to 'do' anything, you had to program it, and leave the power on to retain the program in memory! I remember my Mum tripping over the electricity cord once, just as I finished writing a program. You can guess my feelings at the time!

The important thing to remember is that the software is only able to do what you tell it to do; it cannot 'do the analysis' for you. Analysis is about interpreting, not just the mathematics. You should not be intimidated by the huge power of these software packages, because they are merely your servants. If you take it slow and steady, you will be able to do some amazing things by the end of this book. And, what is more, you will be doing them right and understanding what you are doing too!

I promise. Remember, I have seen the end of the book...

 **final checklist**

You should have covered and understood the following basic content in this chapter:

☑ The foundations of how Excel and SPSS work.
☑ The basic principles of data entry in Excel and SPSS.
☑ How to create and manipulate data in Excel and SPSS.

☑ Formulae and functions in Excel.
☑ Creating and defining variables in SPSS.
☑ Transferring data between SPSS and Excel.
☑ The conventions used to instruct you for the rest of this book.

EXERCISES

1. You have been asked to produce a spreadsheet to analyse a marketing strategy. Using the data given below, sketch how your spreadsheet would look.

Variables: *flyers, posters, mail shots, telemarketing, potential sales, definite sales and no sales.*

Which are the 'variables' and which ones are the 'characteristics'?

2. You want cell G12 to display the result of the following calculation:

The net percentage profit from last month's sales is equal to the buy-in price of the product, plus the cost of packaging, plus a fixed cost of £5.35 per item to cover such things as staffing costs, utility costs, rent, etc., subtracted from the retail price, all divided by total cost to the company of the item.

Write this as a mathematical expression. How would you write the formula to be entered into Excel? Is there anything missing from the formula?

3. a. Figure 3.20 is a snapshot of a simple spreadsheet. From the diagram can you work out the formula to get the *y* value from the *x* value?

x value	y value
1	1
2	4
3	9
4	16
5	25
6	36
7	49
8	64
9	81
10	100

Figure 3.20

b. Construct a spreadsheet that produces the multiplication tables up to and including 15 × 15.

c.   The *Fibonacci* series is 0, 1, 1, 2, 3, 5, 8, 13, 21, 34.... Construct a formula to produce this sequence. Test your formula in a spreadsheet. What assumptions must you make? Feel free to research the Fibonacci series online.

d.   Figure 3.21 shows a spreadsheet for calculating the VAT and total cost of an item. From the spreadsheet construct the formula to get *total cost*.

VAT rate		Cost of item		Amt of VAT		Total cost
0.15		10		1.5		11.5
		20		3		23
		30		4.5		34.5
		40		6		46
		50		7.5		57.5
		60		9		69
		70		10.5		80.5

Figure 3.21

e.   (In the 'Cost of item' column, why do you think simple numbers are used, since in reality items are likely to have costs such as £12.78, £125.45, etc.?

4.   You have been given the job of setting up SPSS to analyse the profits of the following three companies. You do not have to perform the analysis itself, because that is done by a different department, you just have to set up SPSS for the analysts.

Richard Head Ltd   £1.50

Bodgit and Leggitt Ltd   £230.25

C.U. Cumming Ltd   £736.95

How would you construct the spreadsheet? What variables would you use? What type of variables would they be?

5.   Create an instance of SPSS to analyse the relationship between a Student Union's bar sales and the number of assignments due. You will need to use three variables: the week you are looking at; the number of assignments due in; and the amount of money generated from the Student Union bar. You are not expected to run the analysis.

6.   Consider a typical sales force management situation. Salespeople in the field have to visit a number of people each day, making calls on existing customers and potential new customers. Sales calls are very expensive, and a leading bicycle manufacturer is interested in reducing costs. The managers at BikeCo believe that fuel costs are a major area where they could make savings. It was immediately obvious to them that the distance a salesperson drives per week should have a major impact on fuel consumption. However, during a meeting, the sales director also suggested that the proportion of calls the salesperson makes inside large cities versus outside large cities also makes a difference. More specifically, driving in urban areas uses much more fuel than motorway mileage, so the higher the proportion of city driving the salesperson does, the more fuel is used.

Create an instance of SPSS to perform the required analysis. You will need to decide on the variables required, what type they are and what sort of measure to use. You are not expected to run the analysis.

To access additional online resources please visit: **https://study.sagepub.com/leepeters**

The Ballad of Eddie the Easily Distracted: Part 4

After his pleasant experiences with the first computer tutorial, Eddie was feeling pretty good about himself, and he was even looking forward to the next one. That said, the next lecture had been a bit of a shock to the system – so much information to take in! It was pretty boring too, Eddie thought, because 'descriptive statistics' seemed to be just looking at all those numbers, not doing anything with them. If you were going to have to play around with numbers, you might as well do something interesting.

Even so, the lecturer had tried to present it as 'getting to know your data' before doing anything complicated. But, as usual, Eddie wanted to get to the later stuff more quickly, even though he wasn't that confident with this early material. All that basic stuff was just tedious going-through-the-motions, he thought.

As he sat in the computer workshop actually putting it into practice, he turned to Esha next to him and said, 'So, um, how are you enjoying the first month of university?' 'It's been OK actually,' Esha replied, surprised Eddie had actually made some conversation. 'It's pretty weird not having to get up and go to class every day, though.'

Eddie thought that was interesting, since he loved not having a routine, so he followed it up: 'You know, I really like being able to make my own plans.' 'Yes, but having a routine makes it easier to plan what you are going to do,' replied Esha.

Well, thought Eddie, he'd learnt something about Esha there: she liked routines, whereas he liked taking things as they came. That could prove handy later on. All of a sudden, the value of taking time to get to know something before ploughing ahead began to make sense to him.

Esha's Story: Part 4

In the computer tutorial, Esha was completely shocked when Eddie blurted out something random like 'so how are you enjoying things so far?' The boy had hardly spoken in the last tutorial, other than to show her how to use the software, and she had put him down as pretty uninteresting. But while going through the exercises in the computer workshop, they'd had an interesting conversation about routines and whether they helped or hindered one's life. Eddie was clearly one of those people who just took things as they happened. Esha had always been a bit jealous of those people, since she had to have a routine and a plan to feel comfortable.

While they were talking, Esha had a bit of a brainwave. Getting to know someone was like getting to know your data – just like what they were doing now. If you didn't take the time to get to know someone first, you could find yourself in all kinds of trouble later on. Or, worse, you could miss something that could turn out to be really interesting and useful. For example, she'd originally thought Eddie was a bit of a waste of space, but it turned out he was actually quite good with computers, and he seemed to really enjoy talking about that kind of thing. He got very enthusiastic when he was showing her how to create these spreadsheets to do automatically some of the calculations they'd been shown in the lecture.

Esha was surprised to find that Eddie appeared to have more about him than was immediately apparent, although she made sure to remind him of the time he dropped that water bottle, just so he didn't get any funny ideas.

4

DESCRIBING YOUR DATA

CONTENTS

 learning objectives

There are a few learning objectives here – keep these in mind as you study this chapter:

- ☑ Learn why descriptive analysis is important.
- ☑ Learn what frequency distributions are and how to create them.
- ☑ Learn how to display frequencies graphically in various forms and how to create a stem-and-leaf display.
- ☑ Learn what cross-tabulations are and how to create them.
- ☑ Understand how to describe your data with numbers, including measures of locations (e.g. mean, median, mode) and spread (e.g. range, variance, percentiles, quartiles).

- ☑ Learn how to use these descriptive numbers to create a five-number summary, and from that a box plot.
- ☑ Learn what skewness and z-scores are.
- ☑ Understand how to generate descriptive statistics and charts in SPSS.
- ☑ Learn how to weight data to describe it more accurately with numbers.
- ☑ Learn how to deal with grouped data when describing it.

One of my earlier books, *Doing Business Research*, contains a chapter on the descriptive analysis of data. Apart from making a blatant begging appeal for more sales of *DBR*, I mention this for one important reason at this point. At the beginning of that chapter, two top-quality academics wrote about how describing your data was probably the single most important step in quantitative analysis. Those two individuals (Professor Felix Brodbeck and Dr Yves Guillaume, who was then a PhD student) had themselves introduced *me* to the importance of it in the course of a long overnight data analysis session. Before that, I'd been pretty lackadaisical about my approach to descriptive analysis, assuming 'it would all work out OK in the end'. But these guys really taught me how important it was to 'get to know' the characteristics of your data, and prevent any obvious mistakes. From them, I learned that my lazy attitude to data was a ticking time-bomb (so to speak), sure to lead to later problems.

 **think it over 4.1**

Before reading any further, have a think about the notion of 'getting to know your data'. Think back to when we discussed data. Write down five reasons why you think knowing about your data is important. Just one more thing: ask yourself what the purpose of this analysis is. This may help you to appreciate the importance of 'knowing your data'.

Descriptive analysis can easily be thought of using the metaphor of the relationship between two people. You are one and the data set is the other. Try to keep this in mind through the chapter, although I have done my best to keep reminding you with random stories, some of which are even true. The point I am making is that you cannot really get to grips with any serious relationship-type activities without first getting to know the characteristics of your potential partner, and it is the same with quantitative data analysis. You really cannot trust what your analysis results are without understanding your data first. For example, some characteristics in your data can actually mean the analysis results you see are not useful or trustworthy. So before rushing ahead of ourselves, let's learn how to take things slowly, and build up our relationship with our data on solid ground.

Will that not be far more fulfilling in the end?

WHY DO I NEED TO WASTE TIME ON *THIS?!*

This is what I used to think when I was a young(er) PhD student and lecturer. Of course, now I am a responsible professorial role-model, I cannot actively express such opinions. Apart from moral leadership, there is another reason for spending plenty of time exploring and describing your data before getting into the real analysis. But before we get started in earnest, let me explain how this chapter will work. This is the first of the real 'analysis' chapters, where we will be digging into IBM SPSS Statistics Software (SPSS) and Excel to actually get our hands dirty. Of course, it is impossible to show you how to do every single thing on each program. So what I am going to do is use one or the other program to illustrate each point, and, by the end, I think you will have picked up enough to use both programs to do all of the tasks within reason. Certainly by the end of this chapter you will be pretty comfortable with each program, and in a great position to attack the rest of the book.

So, returning to the issue at hand, why spend time digging into our data to describe it before we start analysing it? There are many key reasons for this, but they can be grouped into two main areas: (a) to *check for mistakes or weird data*; and (b) to *summarize the characteristics of the data*. You need to check for mistakes for obvious reasons – mistakes are not 'real data', therefore including them in your analysis will naturally lead to possibly problematic results. There are also plenty of instances where what you could call 'weird data' might occur; this type of data is real, but it seems to lie far outside the rest of it. For example, imagine you collected data on company profit from 100 companies: 99 of them had a profit of up to £2 million, but 1 company had a profit of £100 million. This might be a mistake, but assuming it is real, it is what we call an outlier, a value very far outside the others. Such values can influence our results, so we need to work out what to do with them. But before that, we need to find out if they are there.

think it over 4.2

Eddie had a look at a set of data. 'Hmm,' he thought, after seeing a graph of the data, 'that value is obviously a mistake. I'm not going to spend ages checking to see if it is valid – I haven't got the time. I'll just change it so that it's more realistic.' He altered the value and redrew the graph: 'That's better, much more sensible.'

What do you think? Was Eddie's action reasonable? After all, it was obvious to him that it was a mistake and besides he had a deadline to meet.

We need to summarize the characteristics of our data for many reasons. On the one hand, you might simply be interested in finding these out for your results, like if your project was to find out the average age of your classmates. Descriptive analysis would do this job for you in many cases. In fact, much of the quantitative analyst's job concerns summarizing data for others. As you saw earlier, looking at raw data is tough, and managers (and the general public) need useful summaries of data. Consider the reports often seen in newspapers – like share price trends, employment figures and so on. Also, though, many more complex analysis methods rely on data having certain characteristics, called assumptions, to allow you to use the analysis method. Descriptive analysis is needed here to show that your data set does have these characteristics. However, I have not yet covered a lot of these key concepts and will not do so until later on. So what I will do is give you the tools to check many of these assumptions, and then address them later, when they become specifically relevant and make sense.

Data can be described in three different ways for our purposes. First, it can be represented as a *picture* of some sort. Most of the time, we use graphs for this, which can also be called charts. Excel and SPSS do some very nice graphs, although Excel's are prettier to most people. We can also use tables of data, to show important characteristics of our data, sometimes more than one at a time. Excel has a very powerful function called pivot tables, and SPSS is also capable of tabulating data. Finally, we can use numbers to describe our data. There are many summary numbers which can be used depending on what feature of your data you are interested in; you will learn a number of them in this chapter and many more throughout the rest of the book.

GETTING TO KNOW YOUR DATA

I will begin with some very basic tools as a first look at the basic characteristics of your data, and in some situations this may even be enough. However, before we can effectively summarize data, we need to think about what *type of data* we are dealing with. Back in Chapter 1, I talked about qualitative and quantitative data and, straight after that, I mentioned the different scales of measurement – nominal, ordinal, interval, and ratio (NOIR). Just to recap, qualitative data uses labels (which are sometimes numbers) to represent categories, or whether an object possesses a certain quality or characteristic (e.g. male or female), whereas quantitative data uses numbers which represent how many or how much of something there is. Go back to Chapter 1 if you need a fuller recap.

The key is that both types of data need some slightly different preparation before you can get started on describing and summarizing them in the more basic ways which we are covering in this section. So what I am going to do is begin with qualitative data examples, which are simpler, and then move on to quantitative examples when you get the hang of things.

Frequency Distributions

Take a look at the data in Table 4.1, which is a very (*very*) simple data set of the favourite types of movies of 100 fictional undergraduate sociology students, selected from a list provided to them. This is basically qualitative data, since it places each student into one or another category (sometimes called a class). Here there are five categories. An important feature is that each subject (i.e. student) can be in only one class at a time – you only have one favourite. Thus, the classes are *non-overlapping*. This non-overlapping property is very important for our purposes, so keep it in mind. Table 4.1 is called a frequency distribution, and it is prepared simply by *counting* the occurrence of each movie type in the raw data set. Even this most basic type of description is far more insightful than just looking at the 100 pieces of raw data, and allows us to see that the most popular type of movie for undergraduate sociology students is 'musicals', closely followed by 'existentialist meditations'. The least popular are clearly 'action blockbusters' and 'science fictions', which is very unfair in my opinion.

think it over 4.3

Since 'musicals' were the most popular types of movie, does this mean they were the 'best' (however you decide to interpret 'best')? What do you think the reason is for collecting and describing this data? Could the data be used for another purpose (think back to secondary data)?

Table 4.1 Movie preference data

Movie preference	Frequency
Romantic comedy	19
Musical	23
Existentialist meditation	22
Action blockbuster	17
Science fiction	17

Learning to create the frequency distribution in Excel is a useful exercise in many ways, so that is what we will do. Interestingly, it is not particularly intuitive because the data is often entered into Excel in such a way that it makes it rather complex to create such a table, and one which will require our skills from the previous chapter. An Excel spreadsheet showing the first 20 elements in the data set from the movie preference study is presented in part in Figure 4.1. You can see that it is basically just a single column, in total 100 data points (although you can only see 20 here).

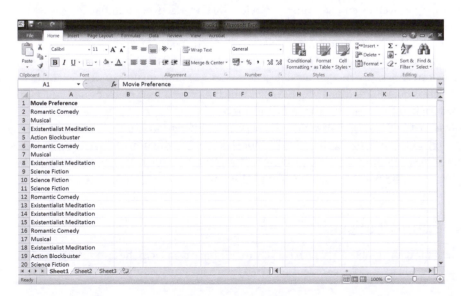

Figure 4.1
Movie
Preference
Data

To create a frequency distribution in Excel from this type of data we have to use a function which Excel has ready-made for our pleasure. This function is called COUNTIF, and it can be accessed in two ways, by either typing directly or using the *paste function* tool. I will teach the latter of these, because it will be handier in the long run. Figure 4.2 shows the paste function dialog box, which you access by clicking the Formulas tab as shown, and then Insert function. The dialog box will appear as shown. You can select different types of functions, called 'categories'; I have selected Statistical, and then highlighted the COUNTIF function. You can see that in bold below the functions there is a short description of how the formula should be used.

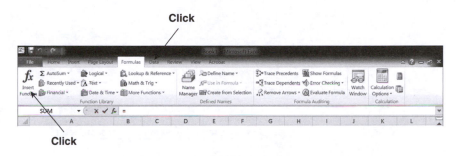

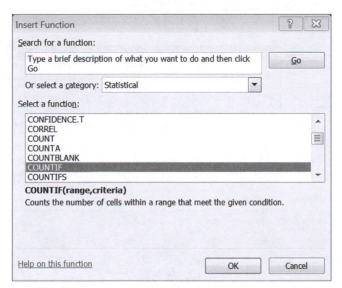

Figure 4.2
Excel's
Paste
Function
Dialog Box

To create the frequency distribution, you are going to use the COUNTIF function. Figure 4.3 shows the basic look of Excel as you do this. The top panel shows part of the working, and the full result is in the bottom panel. You can see that column 'A' has the data in it, but now I have added the basics of my frequency distribution to column 'C'. In column 'D' will appear the frequencies of each preference. First, select cell D2, and then bring up the paste function dialog as shown above. Make sure you choose COUNTIF from the Statistical category of functions, and then you will get another dialog box as shown in Figure 4.3, which has the title 'Function Arguments'. This is how you tell Excel what values to count. As you can see, I have entered $A$2:$A$100 in the Range box and C2 in the Criteria box. What I am saying is: look at the rows 1–100 in column 'A' and count the occurrence of whatever is in cell C2. Note the '$' signs, which mean that when I copy the formula, the range will not change, but the criteria will. Also note that Excel will *look to count whatever is in cell C2*, so it must be exactly the same label as in your data. In other words, Excel will look to count the occurrence of 'Romantic Comedy' in the range. If you put 'romantic comedies' in C2, it would turn up 0 results. Anyway, once you have done that, click on 'OK', and also then copy the formula from D2 to D3, D4, D5 and D6. As if by magic, Excel will do everything for you, resulting in the bottom panel of Figure 4.3.

think it over 4.4

How can you check that you have entered all of your data? [Hint: look at the bottom of the column headed 'Frequency' in Figure 4.3.]

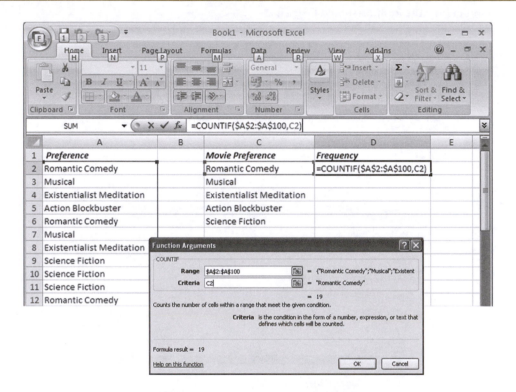

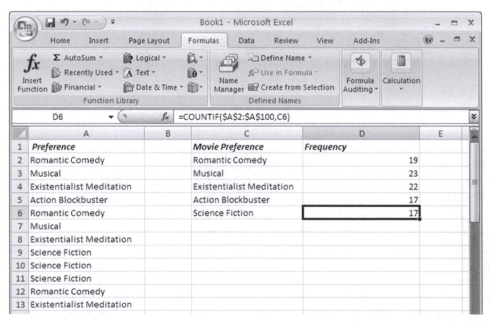

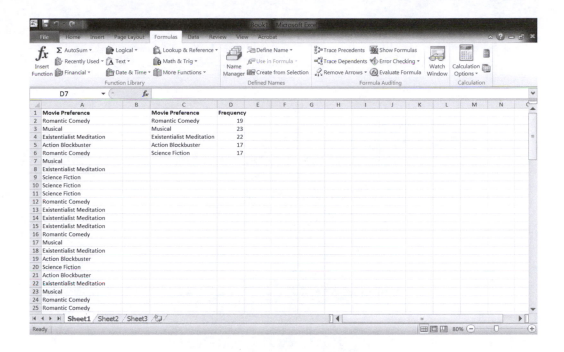

Figure 4.3
Creating a
Frequency
Distribution

When we have quantitative data, the situation can be a little more complex. Take a look at Table 4.2, which is a set of data resulting from a survey of 20 fictional PhD students about their drinking habits. To show that I have some class and sophistication, it is not about pints of beer this time, but glasses of fine wine. The data is about how many glasses of wine each of the students drink per week, and you can see there is quite some variation. In fact, virtually no two answers are the same. This is very different from the qualitative situation above, where there were only five classes. Here, there are nearly 20! So a frequency distribution using only these classes would probably not be that useful. What we often do in this situation is to define *new* classes, *each of which contains a range of values from the original data*. To do so, we need to make three important and linked decisions:

- Decide on the number of classes.
- Decide on the width of the classes.
- Decide on the class limits.

 think it over 4.5

When do you think a frequency distribution would not be very useful? Think about the term frequency. In terms of statistics, what do we mean by frequency?

The first thing to do is to decide how many classes you need. There are no official rules here, it is a judgement call. If you do not have enough, you will lose a lot of information which might be useful later on. If you have too many it becomes too complicated, there are hardly any data points in each class, and you might as well not have bothered. A general guide is to use between 5 and 20 classes, and the larger the variation and amount of data, the larger the number of classes. In this case, I am going to use five, since there are only 20 data points.

Table 4.2 Wine data

ID	Glasses p/wk
1	0
2	3
3	7
4	15
5	2
6	1
7	0
8	0
9	10
10	3
11	4
12	8
13	1
14	7
15	7
16	4
17	4
18	2
19	0
20	10

 think it over 4.6

The above data set was used in the pilot study of the experiment (think back to why we use pilot studies). The actual experiment involved 100 PhD students. How many classes would you use now? Should you stick to the same size as the ones used in the pilot study? What would you consider to be the key question(s) from the following:

1. What is the purpose of this study?
2. How is my data distributed?
3. How much detail do I need?

The next decision – width – might seem a bit of a no-brainer. Normally, you would use the same width for all the classes. In other words, it depends on the number of classes you decide on: more classes means narrower classes. So if you are following this principle, you can use the basic formula below to decide how wide your classes should be:

Largest data point – Smallest data point/Number of classes

If you do that with the data in Table 4.2 you should get three. If you do not have a whole number, you would usually round the answer up or down, depending on preference. In essence, therefore, class number and class width are intuitive decisions, and you use trial and error to see which balance between information (more classes) and convenience (fewer classes) is best for the frequency distribution. Of course, you can do some very cunning things by using non-equal class widths, like change the look of your frequency distribution, but I should not really talk about that, because often it is cheating and done to mislead people. So, when interpreting such charts, you should always make sure to see what the analyst has done with the class widths.

Having done the first two tasks, you have also unwittingly done the third. The class limits are basically the highest and lowest value data points which go into each class. It is important to set these so each data point can go in one and only one class. Take a look at the frequency distribution in Table 4.3, which I have created from the wine data using the classes I defined above. You can see that each of the data points can go in one and only one class. Remember: the classes must be non-overlapping. The class limits should be easy for you to see – for example, the lowest class is 0–3 glasses, so the lower class limit is 0 and the upper class limit is 3 for this class.

Table 4.3   Frequency distribution of the wine data

Glasses p/wk	Frequency
0–3	10
4–6	3
7–9	4
10–12	2
13–15	1

Class limits can, however, be a thorny issue. What if some of our data included something like '3.5 glasses'? Where should this value go? It is here that you need to be careful about defining class limits, since the decision clearly depends on how accurate your data is. You might in the latter case want to use classes such as 0–3.9, and 4–6.9, instead of 0–3 and 4–6. You can be as exact as necessary to incorporate the accuracy of your data – for example, 0–3.99, 4–6.99 and so on.

 think it over 4.7

Can you think of another issue that may affect your class sizes? For example, I record the length of time a group of companies have been in business. How accurate should I be? Should it be to the nearest year, month, week, day, hour, minute, second?

You might also need to incorporate what are called *open-ended classes* at the top and bottom. What if one of my PhD student sample drank 26 glasses of wine a week? Apart from the fact that I might refer the student to some professional help (although doing a PhD can be pretty stressful!), it would also cause me problems for defining my classes. If I keep to classes with a width of 5, I would have to add a bunch of classes between my original upper limit of 15, like 16–18, 19–21, 22–24, 25–27. Most of those would be empty. So instead I might use a class of '16 and over'. At the other end of the distribution (i.e. the class 0–3), there is no need for an open class in this instance, because it already starts at 0, but you get the idea.

So, now I have dealt with qualitative and quantitative types of data, and showed you how to prepare these for further analysis. From here on in, the analysis is relevant to both types, except where I specifically mention it.

Relative and Percentage Frequency

It is all very well looking at the frequency as we have above, but sometimes we will be interested in the proportion of data points which are in each class, compared with the others, which is called the relative frequency. This is the fraction of the total data which belongs to each class. It is simple to calculate. For a data set with n observations (in other words, n stands for the number of observations, so in the wine example, $n = 20$) you calculate the relative frequency of each class with the following equation:

$$\text{Frequency of the class}/n$$

See, simple! And what is more, you can find the percentage frequency by multiplying the relative frequency by 100. You can easily create relative and percentage frequency distributions from those I have already shown you. Perhaps you should go and do that now.

 **think it over 4.8**

That word 'relative' again! How would you explain relative frequency to someone who did not know the meanings of any statistical or mathematical terms?

Bar Graphs and Pie Charts

I love both bars and pies, as my friends will tell you. But when it comes to analysis, bar graphs and pie charts are really useful tools to summarize *qualitative* data. Although, they can also be employed to summarize quantitative data too if you want. Basically, they are both used to present a frequency distribution (or relative/percentage frequency) in a graphical format, which can sometimes be easier to understand than a table.

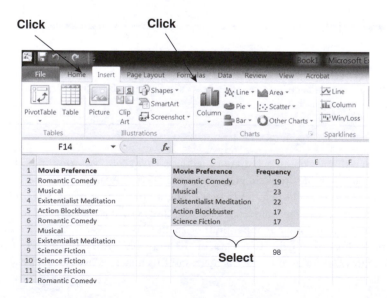

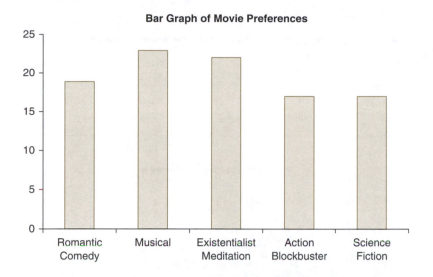

Figure 4.4
Creating a
Bar Graph
in Excel

The bottom part of Figure 4.4 shows a bar graph of the movie preference results shown above. You can see that on one axis (usually the horizontal axis, often called the *x* axis) are specified the labels for the classes, and the other axis (usually the vertical, or *y* axis) is the frequency (or relative/percentage frequency) scale. To draw the bar graph, we draw a bar of *fixed width* above each class label, to the length of the frequency. You should also note that in Figure 4.4 the bars are clearly separated, and this is always done with qualitative data.

 think it over 4.9

Why is having a fixed width important?

Once you have got a frequency distribution in Excel, it is simple to get a bar graph, so let's have a go. In fact, this will be the first time you use the chart function in Excel, so pay attention. In older versions this was the chart wizard, but in the newer versions it is integrated in the menus and icons. I am working with the movie preference data as described above. So I need to select the range which contains the column labels, the categories and the actual frequencies, which in this case is C1:D6. The top part of Figure 4.4 shows the parts you need to click to get to the bar charting function: select Insert → Column as shown. Then a little menu will come up with many different types of format to choose from. This is quite confusing to the uninitiated. For the most part, you will need the simplest, so select Clustered column and a chart will appear on your worksheet. It will not look exactly like the one in Figure 4.4 because you are first going to change a few things to make it look nice. If you double-click on the title (currently 'Frequency'), you can type a new title like 'Bar Graph of Movie Preferences'. You will also need to resize the graph possibly. To do so, click anywhere on the graph and you will see small 'handles' appear on the corners and the sides of the chart. Click on one of the corner handles, keep holding the left mouse button as you drag away from the chart, and you will see it get bigger. The final thing to do is to remove the 'legend'. On your chart, you will probably see to the right a small box of the same colour as the bars in the graph, with 'Frequency' next to it. This is telling you what those bars represent, and is useful if you have multiple variables. However, in this case you have only one, so it is redundant. Click on it and Delete. You will see the graph expand to fill all of the available space.

think it over 4.10

Putting a title on your graph, labelling axes – what a pain! Why do we do it? After all, I know what the data is and I know what the graph is supposed to show. OK, I'll put a title on – any old thing will do, it does not really have to indicate what the graph is showing; or does it?

Pie Chart of Movie Preference

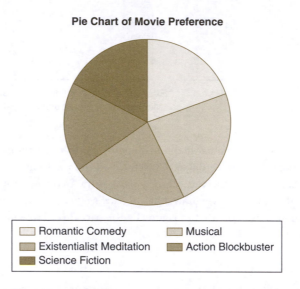

☐ Romantic Comedy ☐ Musical
☐ Existentialist Meditation ☐ Action Blockbuster
☐ Science Fiction

Figure 4.5
A Pie Chart

Figure 4.5 shows a pie chart of the same data. It is broadly analogous to a bar graph, only that you use a circle to represent all of the data (i.e. 100%) and then you use relative or percentage frequencies to cut that circle into slices (called sectors) which correspond to that relative frequency.

Getting a pie chart in Excel is also simple, and just requires a few different options when using the chart menu as above. Instead of selecting Column, click Pie then select the one you like; here I have just picked the simplest. You will see that I changed the title again, but this time I left the legend in, because I need it to tell the different categories apart.

Histograms

Beginners often get histograms confused with bar graphs – after all they look pretty similar, the only difference being that there is no gap between the bars. But in reality, that small difference is actually really important. Histograms are only used with *quantitative* data, to display the frequency distribution. You draw a histogram in the same way as a bar graph, but the *x* axis is labelled with the class limits for the quantitative data – as in Figure 4.6, which is a histogram of the wine data. You will see that it looks different from the others, because it was created in SPSS, not Excel.

The fact that there are no gaps between the bars is meant to represent the data as quantitative, and therefore the classes are not naturally separate. It is meant to show that, even though in the case of the wine data it is rounded to the nearest full glass (e.g. 14 or 15, not 14.5), it is theoretically possible that there may be values between the class limits of adjacent classes. This means that the distribution of the raw data is continuous, in that all numbers are possible, even though you have rounded them. This compares with the qualitative data (like the movie preferences) above, where no values between the classes were possible, called a discrete distribution. You will learn a lot more about continuous and discrete distributions in the next chapter.

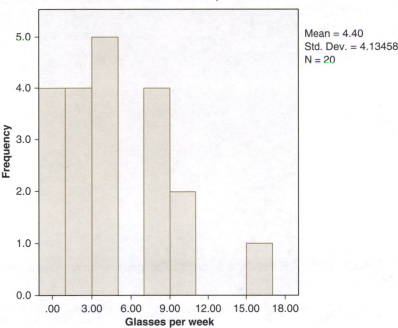

Number of Glasses of Wine per Week

Mean = 4.40
Std. Dev. = 4.13458
N = 20

Figure 4.6
A Histogram

think it over 4.11

I prefer to use bar graphs; they look prettier. So I decide to use a bar graph to show a set of continuous data. Is this a good idea? Does the bar graph convey the full meaning of the data? What does it not show?

I am going to teach you how to do a histogram in SPSS, because in Excel you just have to modify a basic bar graph to produce a histogram while SPSS has a dedicated option for histograms, betraying its main use as a quantitative analysis tool. Building charts in SPSS can be quite complex, and there are many different ways of doing them. I will describe one method here, and you will come across others as you move through the book. You do graphs in SPSS by using the Graphs menu. Select Graphs → Legacy Dialogs → Histogram as in the top part of Figure 4.7. You could click on the Chart Builder option as well, but that is a new feature in later versions which is to me very complex. For a simple histogram the old menus are better. When you click the item, you will get the histogram dialog box as shown. The format here is common to SPSS, with the variables displayed in a box on the left, and you need to move the relevant variables into certain boxes on the right to tell SPSS what to do. Here, you just need to click on the 'Glasses of Wine Per Week' variable, and click the little arrow button to move it to the Variable box, as shown. Select Titles if you want to add a title. Then click OK which will not be greyed now. A histogram will appear in the output window. You can click or double-click on different parts of it to change them (e.g. double-clicking on the title will allow you to type a new one in).

In the case of quantitative data, a key reason for producing a histogram is to look at the *shape* of the distribution of the data, which is also called the form. If you check out the four different panels of Figure 4.8 you can see one key thing we are looking for, namely skewness, which basically means how far to the left or the right the tail of your distribution extends. Panels A and B show distributions whose tails extend to the right (B more than A), which is called positively skewed. Panel C shows a moderately

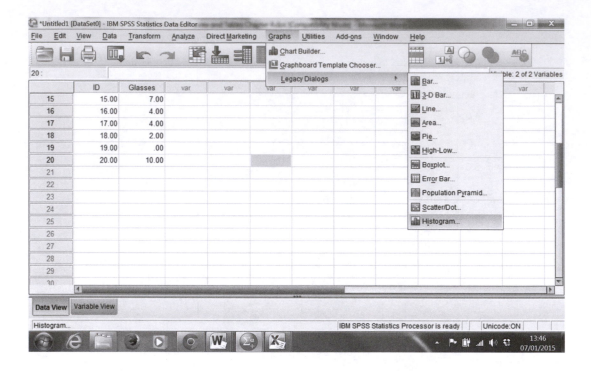

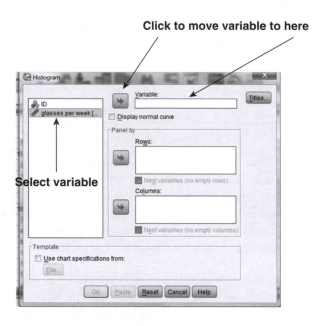

Figure 4.7
Building a
Histogram
in SPSS

negatively skewed distribution (i.e. the tail extends to the left). Panel D shows a symmetrical distribution. Understanding distribution shapes is very important to some of the more advanced things you will be covering later on, but for now think about the sorts of things which might be positively, negatively or symmetrically distributed. For example, you might be surprised to find that exam scores on a range of 0–100% tend to be quite negatively skewed. It makes sense, though: the range stops at 100, and there are not too many really low scores. On the other hand, salaries tend to be positively skewed – the range extends very far to the right, and there are not many really high salaries at that end. Finally, many natural characteristics (e.g. height, weight, etc.) are symmetrically distributed.

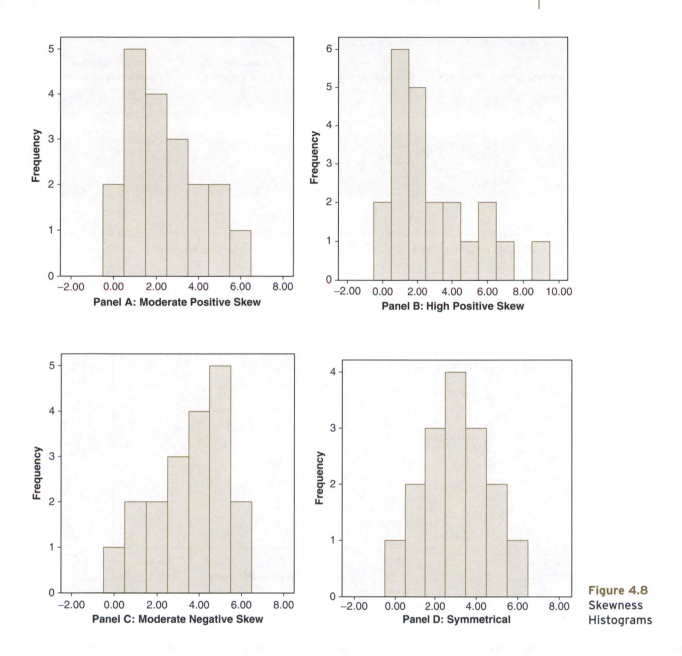

Figure 4.8
Skewness
Histograms

Cumulative Frequency

Cumulative frequency is a variation of the frequency distributions we have already covered, and it uses the same information, like classes, class limits and so on. In this case, though, the cumulative frequency distribution shows the number of data points which are *less than or equal to the upper class limit of each class*. You can also create cumulative relative and percentage frequencies, which are based on the same principles. Table 4.4 shows the three types of cumulative frequency for the wine data you have been dealing with so far. You should note that the last entry in a cumulative frequency distribution always sums to the total number of observations *n*, the last in a cumulative relative frequency distribution equals 1, and the last in a cumulative percentage frequency equals 100. You can easily create these by hand from the normal frequency distributions you have created earlier, and of course Excel and SPSS can easily create them for you.

Table 4.4 Cumulative frequency distributions of the wine data

Glasses p/wk	Frequency	Cumulative frequency	Cumulative relative frequency	Cumulative percentage frequency
0-3	10	10	0.5	50
4-6	3	13	0.65	65
7-9	4	17	0.85	85
10-12	2	19	0.95	95
13-15	1	20	1	100

You can graph the cumulative frequency as well, to create what is called an ogive, which I always thought was pretty cool for some reason. An ogive is shown in Figure 4.9 for the wine data.

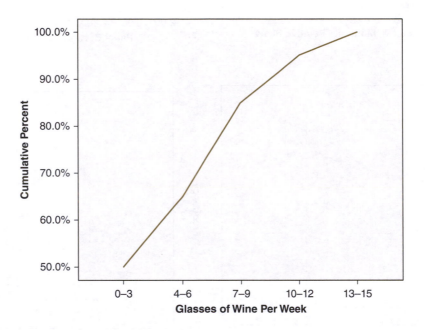

Figure 4.9
Ogive for the Wine Data

GETTING SERIOUS WITH YOUR DATA

OK, after all that descriptive analysis, you are doubtless getting to know the characteristics of the data a little better. However, before you want to make any kind of commitment to your data, surely the basic characteristics of the distribution are the *least* you should know? Take the histogram, for example: it is all very well, and very nice to see, but really it is only the surface of your data, isn't it? Hopefully, you will want to know *more* about your data before making any big decisions?

Table 4.5 Raw test data

53	67	39	52	100	54	65	45	50	76
80	26	58	55	54	63	70	52	61	66
43	50	55	62	68	65	58	55	57	64
57	52	54	63	79	63	41	17	54	68
57	62	80	74	54	65	58	53	54	69

You can get more of a picture of your quantitative data by using a stem-and-leaf display. This is actually quite easy to do by hand, as well as being another option you can select in SPSS. Take a look at Table 4.5, which is the raw data from a test I might have administered to 50 of my quantitative analysis students. It is easy to create a stem-and-leaf display from this smallish amount of data, as shown in Figure 4.10.

```
 1  |  7
 2  |  6
 3  |  9
 4  |  5 3 1
 5  |  3 2 4 0 8 5 4 2 0 5 8 5 7 7 2 4 4 7 4 8 3 4
 6  |  7 5 3 1 6 2 8 5 4 3 3 8 2 5 9
 7  |  6 0 9 4
 8  |  0
10  |  0
```

Figure 4.10 Stem-and-Leaf Display Working

You begin by drawing a vertical line towards the left of the paper. To the left of this line you write the *leading digit(s)* of each data point, without repeating. 'Leading digits' in this case means all the digits apart from the rightmost one for each number (i.e. for 114 and 115 the leading digits are 11). So, look at the first digits of the data in Table 4.5; the first digits (reading left to right along the top line) are 5, 6, 3, 5, 10. It is easiest if you put these in order as you work, so as you can see in Figure 4.10 they are in ascending order from top to bottom. Important things to note here are that you do not repeat numbers even though they appear many times, and also you do not just reuse '1' for the 10, but instead use '10'. To the right of the vertical line you note the last digit of each data point as you go through the data. This last digit is placed on the line which corresponds to the first digit(s) of each data point. So look again at the first five values, and you can see that the last values are 3, 7, 9, 2, 0. You place the '3' to the right of the leading digit '5' which you wrote earlier, the '7' to the right of the leading digit '6', and so forth. Note that you *do* record duplicate values in this case. From here, you should arrange the digits to the right of the line in ascending order, as done in Figure 4.11, which is the final stem-and-leaf display.

```
 1  |  7
 2  |  6
 3  |  9
 4  |  1 3 5
 5  |  0 0 2 2 2 3 3 4 4 4 4 4 4 5 5 5 7 7 7 8 8 8
 6  |  1 2 2 3 3 3 4 5 5 5 6 7 8 8 9
 7  |  0 4 6 9
 8  |  0
10  |  0
```

Figure 4.11 Final Stem-and-Leaf Display

It gets its name because the numbers to the left of the line are called the 'stem' and those to the right are called the 'leaf'. It directly shows the data values, so if you look at the first line, it shows that one data value has a first digit of 1, and that the actual value is 17. You can also see that it is kind of similar to a histogram, but in this case we get to see the entire data set in an easy-to-interpret form. This allows us to get under the skin of anything which might be obscured by a histogram.

As a final note on this, you can construct a stem-and-leaf display in any way you want, depending on how many stems you use. For example, you could use two stems for each digit. This would stretch the distribution, and would allow you to distinguish between, say, values ranging from 50 to 54 and from 55 to 59. On the other hand, you can provide *less* detail for complex data if you want. It really does depend on what you want to show. It is quite simple to get one on SPSS, but the results are a little more complex than the simple one I created by hand. Figure 4.12 shows the basic steps. Select Analyze → Descriptive Statistics → Explore and the Explore dialog box will appear as shown. I have moved the 'Test Result' variable already into the 'Dependent List' box, which tells SPSS I want to work with it. Make sure

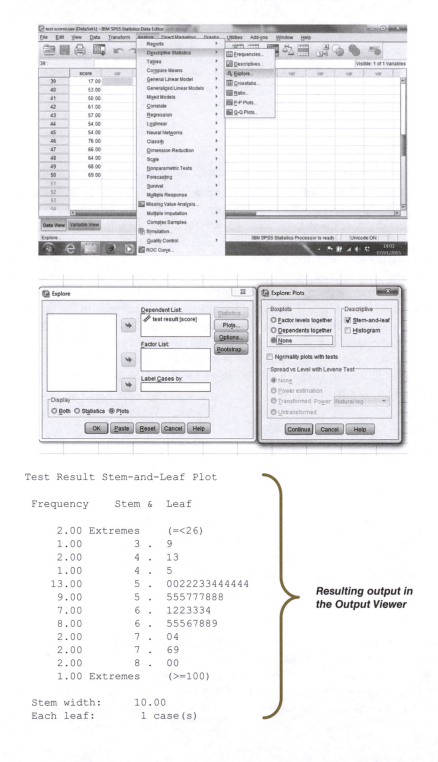

Figure 4.12 Stem-and-Leaf Displays Using SPSS

that the 'Plots' radio button is selected towards the bottom as shown, or you will get a bunch of other output which might confuse you until later. Then click <u>Plots</u> and the next dialog will pop up as shown. Make sure 'Stem-and-leaf' is checked, and 'None' is selected for 'Boxplots' on the left, as shown. Select <u>Continue</u>, then <u>OK</u>. You will get the output as shown appearing in the output window. This is more complex, because SPSS has automatically removed the values at the extreme ends and also split each of the others into two rows instead of one as I did. But it is the same thing, just presented differently. If you have a lot of data, this is a heck of a lot easier than doing it by hand.

From One Variable to More: Cross-tabulations

Cross-tabulations (also called cross-tabs) help us to look at more than one variable at a time, which can be extremely useful in making business decisions. In fact, when you combine well-designed and carefully interpreted cross-tabs with some of the graphs and summary numbers covered in the rest of this chapter, you may have enough skills to present some pretty powerful conclusions in your future work. Certainly I have done more than one piece of management consulting (for pretty high-powered clients) with nothing more advanced than that.

Table 4.6 Partial movie preference and wine data

ID	Preference	Glasses p/wk
1	Romantic Comedy	10
2	Musical	0
3	Existentialist Meditation	15
4	Action Blockbuster	3
5	Romantic Comedy	7
6	Musical	2
7	Existentialist Meditation	15
8	Science Fiction	0
9	Science Fiction	0

A cross-tab is normally a table which presents a summary of two different variables, although you can also combine cross-tabs to summarize more than two, as you will see later on. To illustrate this, look at Table 4.6, which presents part of a set of data similar to the previous examples. In this case, we have a set of 100 students' movie preferences *and* their average consumption of wine in glasses per week, and Table 4.6 shows the first nine. Note the ID number column, as discussed in Chapter 2. As you should know, movie preference is qualitative and glasses of wine is quantitative. Table 4.7 is a cross-tab of this data. You can see that the margins at the left and top define the classes of each variable (I have defined the wine glass classes as I did before), and each student has provided a movie preference and a wine consumption figure. Thus, each student belongs in one of the cells in the cross-tab. For example, student 6 from Table 4.6 likes Musicals and drinks 2 glasses of wine per week, so would go in the circled cell in Table 4.7. In other words, to construct a cross-tab by hand, you simply count the number of data points in each cell.

Also, note how the margins at the right and the bottom show the frequency distributions for wine consumption and movie preference respectively, and of course the bottom right corner shows the total *n* for the sample. Of course, you can therefore find the relative and percentage frequency distributions for the sample variables as you have already learned to do. If you cannot remember, go back up and check.

Table 4.7 Example cross-tabulation

Count of ID			Glasses p/wk			
Preference	0-2	3-5	6-8	9-11	12-15	Grand total
Action Blockbuster	6	7				13
Existentialist Meditation				9	22	31
Musical	9	3				12
Romantic Comedy			9	12	4	25
Science Fiction	16	3				19
Grand total	31	13	9	21	26	100

While all that stuff about frequencies for each variable separately is interesting, the main use of cross-tabs is to compare variables to help us to draw interesting conclusions. This is far easier than looking at the raw data. For example, Table 4.7 shows that those who prefer existentialist meditations also tend to have higher wine consumption. Those who like romantic comedies also have high wine consumption, especially compared with those who like musicals (perhaps they stick to vodka?).

 **think it over 4.12**

Some of the columns do not have any data, for example none of the participants who liked Action Blockbusters drank between 12 and 15 glasses of wine. The cell has been left empty. Could the fact that the cell is empty be misinterpreted? Is there a way in which you could show that the cell, for example, was not forgotten and in fact there was no data for that particular cell?

Converting the numbers in the cells to percentages can provide more insight, because sometimes we can be misled by the large or small amount in each cell, when as a percentage it may actually be quite small, or large, respectively. It is quite a simple task, but you need to remember that the number in each cell is actually *two separate percentages*. It is a percentage of both the row and the column it appears in. To convert a cross-tab like Table 4.7 to row percentages, you simply divide the number in the cell by the total for that row (right hand margin) and of course multiply by 100. To convert to column percentages, you do the same thing, but divide the number in the cell by the column total (bottom margin). Table 4.8 shows the row percentages for the cross-tab in Table 4.7 in the upper panel and the column percentages in the lower panel.

Table 4.8 Percentages in cross-tabulation

Row percentages

Count of ID			Glasses p/wk			
Preference	0-2	3-5	6-8	9-11	12-15	Grand total
Action Blockbuster	46.15%	53.85%	0.00%	0.00%	0.00%	100.00%
Existentialist Meditation	0.00%	0.00%	0.00%	29.03%	70.97%	100.00%
Musical	75.00%	25.00%	0.00%	0.00%	0.00%	100.00%
Romantic Comedy	0.00%	0.00%	36.00%	48.00%	16.00%	100.00%
Science Fiction	84.21%	15.79%	0.00%	0.00%	0.00%	100.00%
Grand total	31.00%	13.00%	9.00%	21.00%	26.00%	100.00%

Column percentages

Count of ID	Glasses p/wk					
Preference	0-2	3-5	6-8	9-11	12-15	Grand total
Action Blockbuster	19.35%	53.85%	0.00%	0.00%	0.00%	13.00%
Existentialist Meditation	0.00%	0.00%	0.00%	42.86%	84.62%	31.00%
Musical	29.03%	23.08%	0.00%	0.00%	0.00%	12.00%
Romantic Comedy	0.00%	0.00%	100.00%	57.14%	15.38%	25.00%
Science Fiction	51.61%	23.08%	0.00%	0.00%	0.00%	19.00%
Grand total	100.00%	100.00%	100.00%	100.00%	100.00%	100.00%

Cross-tabs are very powerful and useful, and they can be created for both qualitative and quantitative variables. But remember: to use quantitative variables you still need to create classes as you did earlier.

Simpson's Paradox

You also need to be aware of the dangers in drawing conclusions from cross-tabs. One example of this is called Simpson's Paradox. This has nothing to do with Homer, Bart, or even Lisa. On the contrary, it is a well-known statistical paradox, first described by Edward H. Simpson in a 1951 paper. Interestingly, Karl Pearson in 1899, and Udny Yule in 1903 had also alluded to similar concepts much earlier, and Simpson's Paradox is also sometimes called the Yule–Simpson effect. Pearson doesn't get a mention here, but then again, he's quite famous enough in my opinion. Simpson's Paradox has proven quite interesting to many people, and has even appeared in the television series *Numb3rs*.[1] Above and Beyond Box 4.1 shows how Simpson's paradox works.

 above and beyond

Box 4.1   Simpson's Paradox

Simpson's Paradox is basically the situation where the conclusions which can be drawn from separate analyses of two groups of data are reversed when we combine the groups. It is pretty basic stuff to statisticians, but most laypeople are unaware of it. It is relevant to many statistical situations. To give a basic example, the TV series *Num3ers* used a set of baseball statistics from Ken Ross's 2004 book, involving the batting averages of Derek Jeter and David Justice in 1995 and 1996. Check them out below:

	1995		1996		Combined	
Derek Jeter	12/48	0.250	183/582	0.314	195/630	**0.310**
David Justice	104/411	**0.253**	45/140	**0.321**	149/551	0.270

(Continued)

---

[1] If you've not seen this show, it's basically about a university professor who helps out his detective brother using his mathematical and scientific knowledge. Some have rumoured that it's loosely based on my life, but they are wrong (mine's more like *Game of Thrones*). In fact, by the time you have finished this book, you'll be able to outsmart the main character in *Numb3rs* with your own statistical knowledge, which is bound to impress people.

(Continued)

You can see that Justice has the higher average in both years, but that when you combine the years, *Jeter* has the higher! How is this possible? Well, notice that, in 1995, Justice batted many more times than Jeter, and the reverse is true in 1996. Clearly, the batting averages in 1995 are far lower than 1996, and poor old Justice batted a heck of a lot more than Jeter in 1995. So when you combine both years, most of Justice's data is taken from the year when it was harder to score, and most of Jeter's is from the year it was easier to score, but he still could not beat Justice's average that year. So, if you combine the data, Jeter looks the better player, but that is an artefact of the aggregation. When you take into account the season, by separating the data, it seems that Justice is the better player. That is basically how Simpson's paradox works, although of course you can look into it in far more depth if you want.

Simpson's Paradox as it is applied to cross-tabs often occurs when we combine two tables together. Because we are aggregating data across separate situations in this case, it can hide the importance of key variables. For example, looking at the baseball example in Above and Beyond Box 4.1, the *season* is a hidden variable of importance, on top of the two comparisons we were looking at (the individual batter and the average). So you must be extremely careful when aggregating data, because it is not always appropriate.

Using Excel to create cross-tabs gives you access to one of the most powerful features of Excel, so I will go into some detail here. Working with the movie and wine data, it is pretty easy to recreate the cross-tab in Table 4.7. Figure 4.13 shows the first steps: select <u>Insert</u> → <u>Pivot Table</u> → <u>Pivot Table</u> as shown (Excel calls cross-tabs 'pivot tables') and the 'Create Pivot Table' dialog box will appear as shown. Make sure the right worksheet is selected (I called mine 'Movies and Wine') and the right range is selected: $A$1:$C$101 as shown. This tells Excel what to use to create the table. To recap, it means that on the worksheet entitled 'Movies and Wine', the data runs from cell A1 to C101 – in other words, there are three variables and 100 cases (one row is the variable labels). I have also selected the 'New Worksheet' radio button, to insert the table as a new worksheet. This can help you keep things neat, but is not essential.

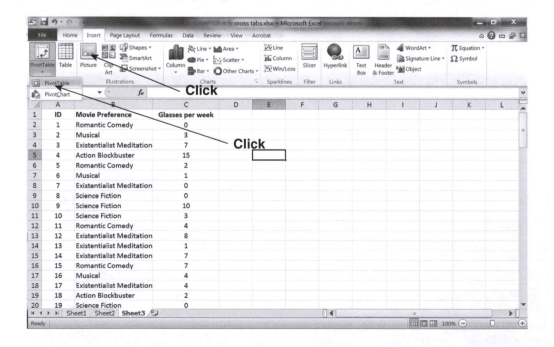

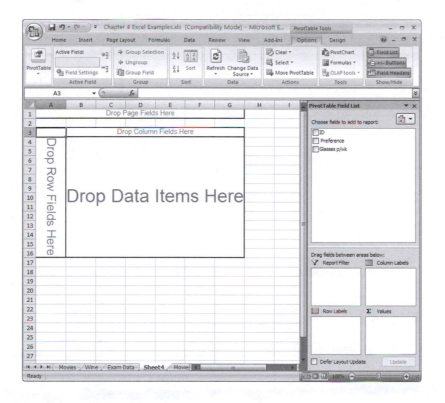

Figure 4.13
Pivot
Tables
Using Excel

When you click <u>OK</u> you will see a screen like the lower part of Figure 4.13. This works in a reasonably self-explanatory manner. You drag things from the right hand side (you will see you variables there) over to parts of the pivot table on the left. First, we want to make the rows represent the movie preferences, so click on 'Preference' on the left and drag it to the table, letting go of the left mouse button when you get to the part which says 'Drop Row Fields Here'. Drag 'Glasses p/wk' to the 'Drop Column Fields Here' part. Then drag 'ID' to the 'Drop Data Items Here' section. You will see something similar to the top part of Figure 4.14. But we are not done yet! Select <u>Field Settings</u> to bring up the dialog box as shown. Make sure you select <u>Count</u> as shown. Click <u>OK</u> and the numbers in the pivot table will change to represent how many data points are in each cell, rather than the sum of the ID numbers that was there in the first place. This is all very well, but you will notice that there are many, many columns, not nice classes as we wanted. Of course, Excel does not know the classes we want to divide our 'glasses per week' variable into, so it has used all the values we gave it. This makes the table a bit meaningless.

We need to group the columns according to the classes we want. You do this by right clicking on the 'Glasses p/wk' cell which is located in B3 in the example shown in Figure 4.14. Then select <u>Group</u> in the menu which appears, to bring up the Grouping dialog box as shown. You fill this in as shown, giving the lowest data value (0), the highest (15) and the intended class width (in this case 3). Click <u>OK</u> and magically the table will look much nicer, exactly like Table 4.7, and shown in the bottom part of Figure 4.14

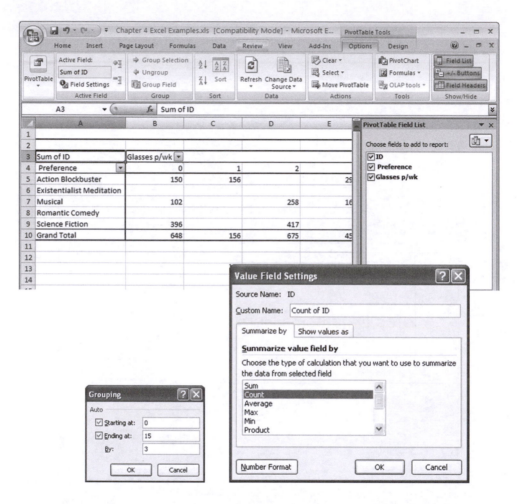

Figure 4.14
Pivot
Tables
Using Excel

FALLING IN LOVE WITH YOUR DATA

Up until this point, I have shown you a lot of ways of examining your data using tables and to some extent pictures. These things are great. But to *really* get to know your data, you need to start understanding some of the key numbers that can be used to describe it. Each of these measures concerns a single variable at a time. If your data set has more than one variable, you need to explore them using these numbers one variable at a time. I will look at things you can do with more than one variable simultaneously later in the book, though.

However, before we get going on this together, I need to clarify a couple of key terms relating to the difference between samples and populations. Remember, back in Chapter 1, that we usually draw a sample to analyse from a larger population, because it is not feasible to examine the whole population – even if we can define it accurately. The numerical measures I will discuss below are called sample statistics when they are calculated on a sample, but are called population parameters when they are calculated on the whole population. Later, I will deal with those two concepts in a lot more depth when I talk about *statistical inference*, in which case the sample statistic is also known as a point estimator. But do not forget: the measure is the same, it is just given a different name.

 think it over 4.13

How to remember which is which: all the s's – sample goes with statistics; and all the p's – population goes with parameters.

Measures of 'Location'

Measures of location are basically numbers which describe something which you could think of in simple terms as 'the typical value' of a variable. However, we can define this in different ways, which depend on what we want, and also the characteristics of the variable. Sometimes, you hear these called the 'average', but this is misleading since it can refer to different things, so let's focus on using the correct terms from now on, OK?

The Mean

The most commonly known of these is called the mean. This measure is basically an indication of the central location of the data. In a formula or equation, the sample mean appears as $\bar{x}$ whereas for the population mean it is denoted as μ. The formula to find the sample mean for a sample with n observations is:

$$\bar{x} = \frac{\sum x_i}{n}$$

If you go back to Chapter 1 and look at the explanations of formulae and equations you might be able to make sense of this yourself. But just to recap again, the $\sum$ means 'the sum of' what follows, and remember that in a formula we denote the value of a given variable x for the ith observation as x_i. So the value of x for the first observation is x_1, the second x_2 and so on.

Let's work through this formula together to clarify things for later on. The numerator (i.e. the top line of the fraction) is simply *the sum of all the values of the n observations*. In other words:

$$\sum x_i = x_1 + x_2 + x_3 + \ldots + x_n$$

Take the example set of data for a single variable – my favourite, the number of pints of beer consumed in one week. I collected data from a sample of five of my friends (so $n = 5$), and these data are:

$$5\ 10\ 18\ 2\ 9$$

So, using the x_i notation explained above:

$$x_1 = 5,\ x_2 = 10,\ x_3 = 18,\ x_4 = 2,\ x_5 = 9$$

To get the sample mean, we can use the formula in the following way:

$$\bar{x} = \frac{\sum x_i}{n} = (5 + 10 + 18 + 2 + 9)/5$$

Thus, the sample mean is 8.8 pints of beer per week.

To compute the mean for a population, the formula is exactly the same, but we use different notation. You already know the population mean is denoted as μ. The number of observations in the population is denoted as N. So the population mean is:

$$\mu = \frac{\sum x_i}{N}$$

The Median

The median is another measure of central location. It can be thought of as 'the middle value'. In other words, you find the median by first arranging the data in ascending order (i.e. from the lowest to the highest value). Then, for an odd number of values, the median is the middle value in this list. For an even number of values, the median is the mean of the two middle values. If this sounds simple, it is because it is simple. For example, go back to the above pints data and arrange it in numerical order to get this:

$$2\ 5\ 9\ 10\ 18$$

Here $n = 5$, an odd number. The median is therefore 9.

How about this data set of number of measures of whisky drunk per night by a good friend of mine over the course of a week? Namely:

$$0\ 1\ 2\ 4\ 4\ 5\ 7$$

Here $n = 7$, which is again odd, but what about the two '4' values? We treat them as separate for the purposes of calculating the median, so the median is 4.

For an even n, like in the data set below where $n = 4$:

$$2\ 5\ 9\ 10$$

we calculate the mean by calculating the mean of the two middle values, in this case it is the mean of 5 and 9. Which of course is (5 + 9)/2 which is 7.

The median is much less commonly used than the mean. However, it can be useful because the mean is influenced by extreme values in the data set (outliers – either very large or small values). To illustrate this, calculate the mean and then the median of the data set below:

$$2\ 5\ 9\ 10\ 150$$

Of course, the median is 9, but the mean is much larger, 35.2. Thus in such cases the median provides a better measure of central location than the mean.

The Mode

The mode is slightly different in nature. It can be defined as the value which occurs with the highest frequency, and it is particularly useful when we are dealing with data about characteristics and qualities. To illustrate this, I will return to the movie data already mentioned, represented in Table 4.9.

Table 4.9 Movie preference data redux

Movie preference	Frequency
Romantic Comedy	19
Musical	23
Existentialist Meditation	22
Action Blockbuster	17
Science Fiction	17

You can see the mode is 'musicals', since that type of movie was preferred by the most people. It should also help you to understand why the mode is useful to qualitative data. It makes no sense in this type of case to take the mean or the median, since there is no real order to the numbers in the table. What does it matter that the median is 'romantic comedy', or the mean is somewhere between 'romantic comedy' and 'existentialist meditations'? What do those values represent? There is no particular order to the different categories, they are just labels – remember, they are *nominal* measures, from Chapter 1.

 think it over 4.14

Thinking back to when we looked at skewness, sketch three graphs: one positively skewed, one negatively skewed and the last one symmetrical about the centre. Now draw vertical lines where you think the mean, mode and median are on each of your sketches.

You have just read three statistical reports which quote values for the mean, mode and median. You only have these values to go by. The first report shows them to have the same value. In the second the mean has a greater value than the median and in the third the median is greater than the mean. Decide which data set is positively skewed, which one is negatively skewed and which one is symmetric about the centre.

What would a graph look like where the mean = median but there is no mode?

Percentiles

Percentiles are a slightly different concept to the previous measures of location and basically provide information about how the data is spread over the range. In this sense they are similar to the 'measures of spread' talked about in the next section. However, they are classed as measures of location because one percentile by itself gives an indication of the location of an individual data point. They are most useful for data sets that do not contain lots of repeated values.

You can take any percentile between 0 and 100 (e.g. the 10th, the 35th, the 76th, etc.). The *p*th percentile is the value which divides the data set in such a way that at least *p*% of the observations are *either less than or equal to* that value, and at least (100 − *p*)% of the observations are *greater than or equal to* that value.

You find percentiles all over the place. One common one you might have come across already concerns your academic performance at school or otherwise. For example, if your score in an exam corresponds to the 80th percentile, this means that around 80% of the students scored lower than you, and 20% higher. Well done!

If you want to compute a given *p*th percentile by hand (which is rarely done), you must first arrange the data in ascending order (like for the median), and you can use the following formula first to compute an index *i*:

$$i = \left(\frac{p}{100} \right) n$$

where *p* is the percentile you want and *n* is (as usual) the sample size.

If *i* is not a whole number, then you must round up, and then the next whole number greater than *i* is the position in the data set of the *p*th percentile. If *i* is a whole number, then the *p*th percentile is the average of the values in positions *i* and *i* + 1 in the data set. In other words, you count along the data set to get position *i* and then one more to get *i* + 1. Then average these values.

think it over 4.15

In an exam you scored 80% and were in the 20th percentile. What does this statement tell you about your performance in relation to the rest of the people who took the same exam? Can you make any conclusions from this about the exam and/or the people who took the same exam? Explain the difference between a percentage and a percentile. Why do they both begin with 'percent'?

Quartiles

Quartiles are really special cases of percentiles, and they divide the data into four parts, each part containing around a quarter of the data, or 25%. So it should not be a surprise for you to know that the quartiles are defined as:

Q_1 = The first quartile, the 25th percentile

Q_2 = The second quartile, the 50th percentile (which is also the median)

Q_3 = The third quartile, the 75th percentile

Of course, the top 25% of the data are above the third quartile.

You already have the skills to compute all of the quartiles. Q_1 and Q_3 are computed just as any other percentile. And Q_2 is the median.

To cement the idea of computing percentiles and quartiles, let's work through the computation of the third quartile (i.e. the 75th percentile) of the data set below, regarding the test scores of 12 quantitative students:

23 25 45 54 55 58 59 62 65 67 71 90

To compute Q_3 we use the following equation to compute *i* first:

$$i = \left(\frac{75}{100} \right) 12$$

which equals nine. Now because $i = 9$, a whole number, we must take the average of the 9th and 10th values of the data set for the third quartile. Counting along the data set, the 9th value is 65, and the 10th is 67. So the average is $(65 + 67)/2$, which is 66.

One thing to remember, though, is that sometimes quartiles are computed slightly differently, and therefore you might see them reported as slightly different answers across various software packages. Even so, the basic objective of dividing the data into four equal parts is always the same.

 think it over 4.16

Think of an example of when you would use quartiles.

Measures of Spread

Measures of spread, also called measures of variability or dispersion, are aimed at giving an indication of how wide the range of a variable is. This is important because measures of central location like the mean or median for two variables can be the same, even though the values of each variable can be wildly different.

For example, imagine you run a business. Something which would be important to you would be how long it took your clients to pay their invoices from you. The two data sets below are the number of days it took two clients to pay their last 10 of your invoices:

Client 1: 7 7 8 9 9 9 11 11 12 16

Client 2: 9 9 10 10 10 10 10 10 10 12

The mean of both these variables is 10, but it is clear that client 2 is much more reliable at paying its invoices after 10 days. For client 1, sometimes it pays earlier, sometimes later. In fact, client 1 has not paid any of its invoices on 10 days. At times, it is important to know the variability of things such as this, since widely divergent values of things such as delivery dates or payments can really hurt long-term plans. Just looking at the mean or median would not show this at all.

The Range and the Interquartile Range

The simplest measure of variability is the range, which is just the largest value minus the smallest.

For client 1 above, the range is therefore 9, and for client 2 it is 3.

Of course, the range is rarely the only thing we compute in this regard, because it is highly influenced by extreme values. For example, client 1's range is heavily influenced by one single value at the high end. For this reason, the interquartile range is commonly used. This of course relies on the quartiles you learnt about above, and is the range for the middle 50% of the data. Therefore, the interquartile range (IQR) is $Q_3 - Q_1$.

Variance

The variance is slightly more complex in concept and is based on the idea of how much each value x_i of a variable differs from the mean of that variable (i.e. $\bar{x}$ for a sample and μ for a population). More technically, this is called a variable's *deviation about the mean*. For example, within a sample, the deviation of x_i from the mean of a sample is written as $(x_i - \bar{x})$. It is also important to know that these deviations are *squared*, to stop the values above and below the mean cancelling each other out to zero.

The formula for the population variance is:

$$\sigma^2 = \frac{\sum (x_i - \mu)^2}{N}$$

and the formula for the sample variance s^2 is:

$$s^2 = \frac{\sum (x_i - \bar{x})^2}{n-1}$$

We are usually interested in the sample variance, since we usually have a sample, not a population. As you will see when you get to the chapters about statistical inference, you are usually interested in using the sample variance to estimate the population variance. While it is beyond the scope of this text to go into detail, it can be shown that if you divide the sum of the deviations about the mean by $n - 1$, not n, the resulting s^2 is an unbiased estimate of the population variance.

think it over 4.17

The $n - 1$ is derived from what is known as degrees of freedom. These are basically the number of free options we have when dealing with data. In engineering the term degrees of freedom is used in a similar way to statistics. For example, if a robot arm has 3 degrees of freedom, it can move up/down, left/right and in/out (i.e. three ways). What if I decide to fix the movement in one direction? I have decided the robot arm does not need to move in/out. How many degrees of freedom are left? Answer, 2. If n was the number of degrees of freedom my original robot arm had, it now has $n - 1$, because I am not allowing one movement to change (in/out). It is the same with statistics: think of the population as the original robot arm and the sample as the restricted one. Since I am using statistics rather than parameters, I am imposing a restriction on the data. This restriction is that I am assuming the sample mean is the same as the population mean, in other words I am 'fixing' one parameter. So, say I had 10 values from my population and I calculate the mean of this sample. I fix this value, which means the other 9 can vary as much as they like as long as the mean is still 10.

While we do not often calculate the variance by hand, it might help you get some more confidence with equations if you do. Table 4.10 gives the relevant working using client 1's data above.

If you plug this into the formula you will get 66.9/9 = 7.43.

Table 4.10   Computation of the variance for client 1

Days to pay invoice	Mean days ($\bar{x}$)	Deviation about the mean ($x_i - \bar{x}$)	Squared deviation about the mean ($x_i - \bar{x}$)^2
7	9.9	−2.9	8.41
7	9.9	−2.9	8.41
8	9.9	−1.9	3.61
9	9.9	−0.9	0.81
9	9.9	−0.9	0.81
9	9.9	−0.9	0.81
11	9.9	1.1	1.21
11	9.9	1.1	1.21
12	9.9	2.1	4.41
16	9.9	6.1	37.21
Totals		**0**	**66.9**

You might also now understand more clearly why we need to square the deviations, because without doing so you can see they cancel to zero. One other thing to note is that interpreting the actual number itself can be quite hard in isolation. This is because it is squared, so it can often appear very large compared with the actual values of the data. Thus, it is usually best to use the variance to compare different variables – the one with the largest variance has the most variability.

Standard Deviation

The standard deviation is a manipulation of the variance, defined as the *positive square root* of the variance. The sample standard deviation (also termed SD) is denoted as s and the population as σ. Note they are the same as the variance with the absence of the superscript. So the sample standard deviation is:

$$s = \sqrt{s^2}$$

Thus, the standard deviation for client 1's data is $\sqrt{7.43} = 2.73$.

The point of converting a variance to a standard deviation is clear. Remember that I mentioned above that the variance was hard to interpret because it was squared? Well, by taking the square root I convert the units of the standard deviation back to the same root as my original variable, and this makes it much easier to compare with the mean and other statistics.

 think it over 4.18

I have conducted an experiment on how fast business students can down a pint of beer. The values were: 4, 9, 2, 2, 1, 8, 7 and 7 s. I also calculated the mean to be 5 s. I would like to know if the mean is a good model of my data. I have calculated the variance and it came out to be zero, which tells me it is a good model. But looking at the data I am not convinced because of the range of values. Where have I gone wrong? What should I have done?

The Five-Number Summary and the Box Plot

The five-number summary is a term for a combination of the numbers and measures already mentioned, which gives a very useful quick description of a single variable. The box plot is a pictorial representation of the five-number summary. The summary consists of the following five numbers:

- The smallest value.
- The first quartile.
- The median (i.e. the second quartile).
- The third quartile.
- The largest value.

You can see that all the skills you learnt above can be used to develop the five-number summary. From here you can pretty easily draw a box plot, which is sometimes called a 'box-and-whisker plot', for reasons which will become apparent soon. The top panel of Figure 4.15 shows a box plot exactly as it would appear as output from SPSS, and the bottom panel contains some annotations to help explain the various parts.

To draw a box plot by hand, start with a five-number summary of your data. You then need a horizontal axis for your chart, which is numbered using the range of values in your data (usually extending beyond the actual range of your data). Importantly, if you look at Figure 4.15, you'll see that SPSS has

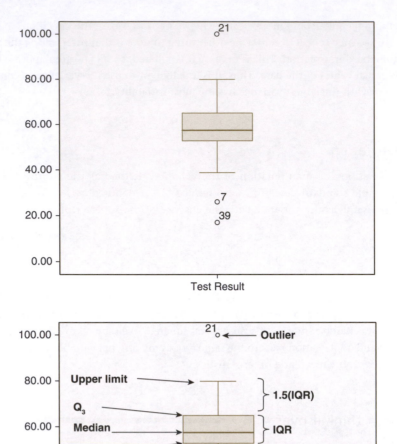

Figure 4.15
Box Plot
Using SPSS

made this the vertical axis, which is not really correct. So the one you will draw will be look like it's been rotated 90 degrees from the one in Figure 4.15. Hopefully that's not too confusing. Anyway, once you've drawn your horizontal axis as described:

- Draw a box, with the ends located at the first and third quartiles (as they are located on the horizontal axis). In other words, this box represents the middle 50% of the data – the interquartile range.
- Draw a vertical line in the box located at the median.
- You now need to locate the *limits* of the plot. You do this by multiplying the interquartile range by 1.5. The lower limit is 1.5 times the interquartile range below Q_1, and the upper limit is 1.5 times the interquartile range above Q_3. You indicate

them with vertical lines. Note that these limits are rarely the same as the highest and lowest values in the actual data set. They are used because we consider that any data outside the limits is an outlier (i.e. an extreme value).

- Then draw dashed horizontal lines called whiskers. The whiskers are drawn from each end of the box to the smallest and largest values of the data which are *inside the limits*.
- Each value of the data which appears *outside the limits* is indicated by an asterisk, to show the outliers.

You might not see the actual lines for the limits on a box plot output from certain different programs. But they are always computed to show outliers. Getting a box plot in SPSS is simple: follow the steps that you used to compute a stem-and-leaf plot and, instead of it, make sure one of the radio buttons in the 'Boxplot' section is selected.

Looking in More Depth

For the last few pages, you have been learning about numbers to demonstrate location and variability of data. But before then, I showed you some ways of looking at the distribution of a variable, in chart and table form. These kinds of things allow us to get a basic idea of what our data looks like, but we cannot draw too many hard conclusions because they really rely on our judgement.

Instead, we can develop numerical measures of the shape of a distribution which are then directly comparable across different sets of data, and have less room for judgement in their interpretation (usually this is considered a good thing in quantitative analysis).

Skewness

One important measure of the shape of a distribution is called skewness. It measures basically how symmetrically the data is distributed around the mean. Think back to Figure 4.8, which showed various differently skewed variables. Instead of just looking at them and estimating whether or not they are skewed, we can use the formula for skewness to work it out numerically, which is:

$$\frac{n}{(n-1)(n-2)} \sum \left(\frac{x_i - \bar{x}}{s} \right)^3$$

Do not worry, I will not be asking you to do that by hand – although, to be honest, you have all the skills already. Remember: you learnt what the symbols represent, with s being the standard deviation and the like. So I bet you *could* do it on a simple data set yourself, like the data in Table 4.10 above – if you wanted to of course.[2] But normally, we get a statistical package like SPSS to do it for us, which will be explained later.

The output of the skewness is a number which is either positive or negative. The larger the number, the higher the skewness. Negative skewness represents a skew to the left (i.e. the tail extends to the left), and positive skewness is to the right. If you think about it, no skewness means the mean and the median are the same, whereas usually a negative skew means that the mean is less than the median. The reverse is usually true for a positive skew. Thus, the higher the skewness, the more useful the median is compared with the mean as a measure of central tendency.

The z-score

At this point, I am going to introduce something which I will return to repeatedly through the rest of the book. It is a critical part of statistical inference and is in turn a vital component of learning about quantitative analysis for business. The z-score is a measure of each data point's *relative location*, compared with the mean. For example, is a particular value close to the mean, or far away? Understanding this concept is, as I already said, a vital part of statistical inference, and it is simple to work out using the standard deviation and the mean of any variable.

Let's recap our usual assumptions at this point. Remember that we have a sample of n observations, and each data value in that sample is denoted using our usual notation of $x_1, x_2, ..., x_n$. We can compute

---

[2] Why don't you have a go? Go on, you know you want to...

the mean and the sample standard deviation as normal. Each value of x (remember, we use the general term of x_i) has a z-score, which represents how far away it is from the mean. The z-score is computed by:

$$z_i = \frac{x_i - \bar{x}}{s}$$

You should already know what x_i, $\bar{x}$ and s represent; z_i represents the z-score for x_i.

The z-score is sometimes termed the standardized value. It represents how far x_i is from the mean. So a z-score of 1.2 would mean that the x was 1.2 standard deviations greater than the mean, while −1.2 would mean that it was 1.2 standard deviations below the mean. Of course, $z = 0$ means that x is equal to the mean. It is pretty simple to compute a z-score for any data value as long as you have the mean and standard deviation. Table 4.11 shows the z-score computations for the client 1 data used above.

Table 4.11   Computation of the z-scores for client 1

Days to pay invoice	Mean days	Deviation about the mean	z-score $z_i = \dfrac{x_i - \bar{x}}{s}$
7	9.9	−2.9	−1.06227
7	9.9	−2.9	−1.06227
8	9.9	−1.9	−0.69597
9	9.9	−0.9	−0.32967
9	9.9	−0.9	−0.32967
9	9.9	−0.9	−0.32967
11	9.9	1.1	0.40293
11	9.9	1.1	0.40293
12	9.9	2.1	0.769231
16	9.9	6.1	2.234432

While z-scores are useful on many occasions, as you will see through the book, at this stage you can use them to detect outliers more accurately than the box plot method shown above. Specifically, it is generally considered that z-scores greater than ±3 indicate extreme values which need investigation. This is because (as you will discover when I talk more about distributions in later chapters) almost all of the data values will usually appear within three standard deviations above or below the mean. Thus data points with z-scores greater than this should be reviewed. However, be aware that you should not always remove outliers from your data. Sometimes, outliers certainly indicate data that has been incorrectly recorded into the data set (which you might have seen when you tabulated the frequency earlier in the chapter), but they can also represent genuine data, albeit unusual, and thus should normally be retained unless there is a good reason for removing the data.

 think it over 4.19

Your dear old Gran has left you some money. You, being an astute business student, would like to invest some of it. You are given some statistical information about two investment instruments. The information on the first instrument states the mean return on investment is 50 with a standard deviation of 5. The second one has a mean of 80 and standard deviation of 10. You decide to invest £60000 (your Gran was a lovely person!) and still have money left for a Porsche 911.

How could you find out which one should give you the best return? Can you make, say, comparisons of the respective means? Or standard deviations? If not, why not?

Getting These Numbers from SPSS

The easiest way to get these different measures in your own data is to use SPSS to perform some descriptive analysis. Normally, we would never calculate any of this by hand, usually because we are dealing with much larger data sets, which would take a long time to analyse by hand. To get the various numerical measures just discussed using SPSS, select Analyze → Descriptive Statistics → Descriptives, which will bring up a dialog box as shown in Figure 4.16. You can do this in Excel also, but it is more complicated and I will show you how in another exercise in Chapter 7.

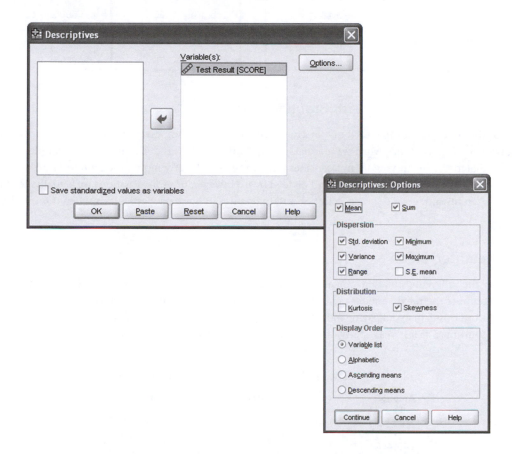

Descriptive Statistics

	N	Range	Minimum	Maximum	Sum	Mean	Std. Deviation	Variance	Skewness	
	Statistic	Statistic	Statistic	Statistic	Statistic	Statistic	Statistic	Statistic	Statistic	Std. Error
Test Result	50	83.00	17.00	100.00	2937.00	58.7400	13.39785	179.502	-.162	.337
Valid N (listwise)	50									

Figure 4.16
Descriptive
Statistics
Using SPSS

Again, you can see I moved the variable from left to right. Then select Options to bring up the next dialog box as shown. I have checked a number of options you have already read about here. Then Continue and OK, and you will get some output in the Output Viewer. To get the median and quartiles, you need instead to select Analyze → Descriptive Statistics → Frequencies which will bring up a similar dialog box. In this one, select Statistics, which will bring up the dialog box shown in Figure 4.17. Note you can also click on 'Charts' which will give you some options to create histograms, bar charts and pie charts similar to what you did before. Anyway, make sure you have the Quartiles and Median options checked, and I have also checked Mode. Select Continue, then OK, and you will get output in the Output Viewer like that in Figure 4.17. You might also get a bunch of other stuff too, depending on the various options selected.

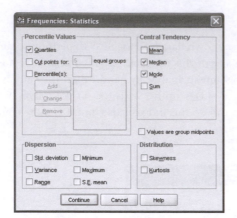

Statistics

Test Result

N	Valid	50.0000
	Missing	.0000
Median		57.5000
Mode		54.0000
Percentiles	25	53.0000
	50	57.5000
	75	65.2500

Figure 4.17
More
Descriptive
Statistics
Using SPSS

Weighting and Working with Grouped Data

Most of the time, we consider each of our data points to be just as important as any other, and thus all are given equal importance when we are making calculations – as was done above. For example, when you calculated the mean you did not consider any of the xs to be any more or less important than the other, so you just added them together and divided by n. However, in some situations we actually need to *weight* different values of x to take account of certain features in our data, particularly when it is grouped.

The Weighted Mean

Consider the following situation. You are organizing the office Christmas party, and your boss has asked you to compute the mean amount per litre that the alcohol for last year's Christmas party cost the company, so your boss can avoid paying more this year if possible. Table 4.12 shows the five different types of alcohol consumed at last year's party, the cost per litre and the amount of litres purchased.

Table 4.12 Data for Christmas party alcohol consumption

Alcohol	£/litre	Amount
Beer	3.35	45
Babycham	5.15	25
Vodka	14.99	7
Gin	16.99	5
Wine	4.5	15

If you were just to take the mean cost per litre from the second column, the answer would be misleading, because considerably more litres of beer were drunk than vodka, for example. So we need to *weight* the different costs by the amount purchased (the third column). The formula for the weighted sample mean is a little more complex than the standard mean, but it is still quite simple really:

$$\bar{x} = \frac{\sum w_i x_i}{\sum w_i}$$

Of course by now you know what x_i means (see above if you need to recap), and w_i represents the weight for each observation i. Also, remember that, for a population, the symbol μ is used instead of $\bar{x}$.

In this case, it is easy to choose the weight for each value of x. Each cost per litre must be weighted by the amount of litres purchased. This would result in the following working within the formula:

$$\bar{x} = \frac{45(3.35) + 25(5.15) + 7(14.99) + 5(16.99) + 15(4.5)}{45 + 25 + 7 + 5 + 15}$$

Thus, the weighted mean is 5.53. However, in some situations, you do not have such obvious weightings. Then, you must choose some weight that is appropriate to the purpose of the analysis. Most of the time, unless you have a specific reason in mind, it is best to stick to unweighted means in that situation.

Grouped Data

Think back to earlier in this chapter, when we developed class limits to form a frequency distribution about glasses of wine. If we wanted to look at the mean and variance of such data, we would really need to go back to the raw data, before the data was put into classes. But what if we did not have the raw data? Maybe we just have the frequency distribution, as secondary data. Or maybe we only got the classes in the first place. Either way, we can use the weighted mean formula developed above to get approximate means, variances and standard deviations from grouped data like this.

The basic principle is to treat the midpoint of the class as representative of all the values in that class, with M_i denoting the midpoint and f_i denoting the frequency of class i. Thus, the weighted mean formula can be used, with slightly different notation to make clear that this is a grouped data mean:

$$\bar{x} = \frac{\sum f_i M_i}{n}$$

Remember, this is a formula for a sample mean. Of course, n is the sum of the frequencies of each class – which is the same as the sample size. We can return to the glasses of wine data for an illustration, in Table 4.13, where the working required to calculate the grouped mean is shown. Most important to note is how the midpoint is computed from that data: you just sum the $f_i M_i$ column (which is 98) and divide by n (which is 20), to get 4.9.

Table 4.13   Computation of the grouped mean for wine consumption

Glasses p/wk	Frequency (f_i)	Class midpoint (M_i)	Product ($f_i M_i$)
0-3	10	1.5	15
4-6	3	5	15
7-9	4	8	32
10-12	2	11	22
13-15	1	14	14

Computing the variance of grouped data is done using a similar process, with the midpoint of the class taken to represent each of the x_i values in the class. Remember, you will need to calculate the mean first, though. It is made slightly more complex by the need to weight each value by the frequency of the class f_i. Also, do not forget that we use $n - 1$ as the denominator for the variance calculation, not n. The formula for the sample variance is:

$$s^2 = \frac{\sum f_i (M_i - \bar{x})^2}{n - 1}$$

Again using the wine data, the working to calculate the sample variance is shown in Table 4.14. You can see from the table that you simply sum up the $f_i(M_i - \bar{x})^2$ column (which is 311.3) and then divide by $n - 1$ (19) to get 4.36. Also, remember that the sample standard deviation is simply the square root of the sample variance, which in this case would be 2.09.

Table 4.14 Computation of the grouped variance for wine consumption

Glasses p/wk	Frequency (f_i)	Class midpoint (M_i)	Deviation ($M_i - \bar{x}$)	Squared deviation ($M_i - \bar{x}$)²	Product $f_i(M_i - \bar{x})^2$
0-3	10	1.5	−3.4	11.56	115.6
4-6	3	5	0.1	0.01	0.03
7-9	4	8	3.1	9.61	38.44
10-12	2	11	6.1	37.21	74.42
13-15	1	14	9.1	82.81	82.81

Finally, for the sake of completeness, and to reinforce the point that the sample and population are different, the formula for the population mean for grouped data is:

$$\mu = \frac{\sum f_i M_i}{N}$$

while the formula for the population variance is:

$$\sigma^2 = \frac{\sum f_i (M_i - \mu)^2}{N}$$

SUMMARY

Wow! That was a lot of information was it not? But it was important stuff for many reasons. Most importantly, we need really to understand our data before we commit to doing any fancy analysis on it. This is because the characteristics of the data might influence the conclusions we can draw from it for one thing. Also, it helps us check for any mistakes in our data, and make sure we have done everything right so far.

Also, this kind of stuff is actually a gentle introduction to coming to grips with your data, and beginning to gain some confidence in working with numbers. The formulae given here are very simple most of the time, and it is possible for you actually to perform the calculations by hand for small data sets. Therefore, where possible I have tried to show this to you. As a result, I hope that you are becoming more comfortable with manipulating numbers, and also with the attention to detail needed to get the correct answer.

If you can go through the things shown here, both by hand and using the software, you will be in a great position to go further – so let's get on with it!

 final checklist

You should have covered and understood the following basic content in this chapter:

☑ Why descriptive analysis is important.
☑ What frequency distributions are and how to create them.
☑ How to display frequencies graphically in various forms.
☑ How to create a stem-and-leaf display.

☑ What cross-tabulations are and how to create them.

☑ How to describe your data with numbers, including measures of locations (e.g. mean, median, mode) and spread (e.g. range, variance, percentiles, quartiles).

☑ How to use these descriptive numbers to create a five-number summary and, from that, a box plot.

☑ What skewness and z-scores are.

☑ How to generate descriptive statistics and charts in SPSS.

☑ How to weight data to describe it more accurately with numbers.

☑ How to deal with grouped data when describing it.

EXERCISES

1. You have been asked to perform a study on business students concerning their stress levels before an exam. The commissioners of the research would like to know relative stress levels starting 12 hours prior to the exam.

   a. Decide on the variables and variable types.
   b. How would you measure stress levels?
   c. How would you display the data?
   d. What conclusions, if any, could you draw from the study?

2. Targets are the mother of invention. But few surpass the creative zeal exposed in May by the Police Federation. The target was to solve more crimes. Hence a child in Kent arrested for throwing a cream bun at a bus; a man in Cheshire 'found in possession of an egg with intent to throw'; and, best of all, a child accused of keeping £700 raised as sponsorship for Comic Relief, leading to interviews of every sponsor. The result: not one crime, but 542, the Federation said, and all solved. (From *The Times*, 22 December 2007.)

   a. What do you think was the purpose of collecting the above data?
   b. Do you agree with the conclusion (i.e. more solved crimes)?
   c. If the result was presented as 'Police solve more crimes' and only the fact that 542 crimes were solved but the type of crime not described, would your reaction be different?

3. You are negotiating pay deals for your fellow players. Table 4.15 gives the salaries of people in your team. You need to prove to the manager the salaries are unfair.

   a. Which measure of central tendency would you use? Explain your choice.
   b. Calculate the mean and median of the data set. Using these two values, what can you say about the 'skewness' of the data set?

Table 4.15

Player	Salary
Flintstone	3500
Rubble	4000
Mouse	12300
Batman	15500
Robin	14600
Spidey	25000
Joker	65000
Puzzler	60000
Pluto	80000
Minnie	90000

4. The town you live in is reported to be in the 90th percentile in terms of crime rate compared with towns of a similar size. What does this mean and is it a good thing?

5. You take an entrance exam for two different universities. The exams are totally different with different numbers of questions as well. You score 60 in exam A. You are told that the mean of the results, for all students, was 50 and the standard deviation was 5. For exam B you score 90 and the mean is 80 and the SD is 10. Both sets of results are normally distributed. In which exam did you do best compared with the other candidates? How can you find out?

6. Table 4.16 gives the measures of variability of three data sets.

Table 4.16

Variability measures

	Variance	Standard deviation	Range	Interquartile range	Semi-interquartile range	Mean deviation
Data set 1	38.5	6.2	20	11	5.5	5.3
Data set 2	22	4.7	20	4	2	3.2
Data set 3	11.6	3.4	20	2	1	1.7

Note: Mean = 10.

a. From the numbers given for each data set, what can you say about the data they represent?
b. The table summarizes the data obtained from three independent random samples of people who were asked how much money they would be prepared to spend on a bottle of wine. Data set 1 was a group of business studies lecturers, data set 2 a group of lawyers and data set 3 a group of accountants. By analysing the summary data, which group would you say thought that £10.00 was a reasonable price?

7. The bar chart shown in Figure 4.18 indicates the disposable incomes of five different age groups per month.

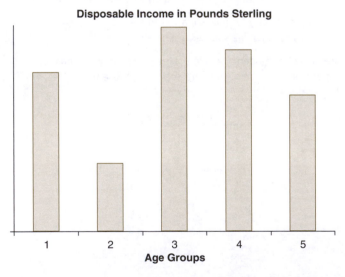

Disposable Income in Pounds Sterling

Figure 4.18

Age Groups

a. Looking at Figure 4.18, which age group would you say had significantly less disposable income than the others?
b. Looking at Figure 4.19, is there a significant difference between the disposable incomes between the age groups?
c. Comparing the two bar charts, what factor(s), if any, affected your answer to part (a) and part (b)?

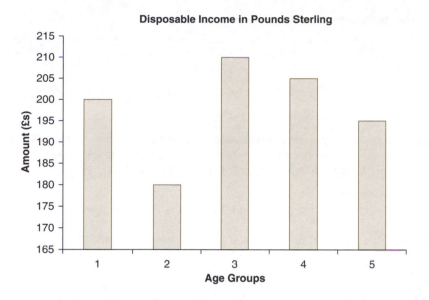

Figure 4.19

8. Figure 4.20 shows the dividends paid out on a yearly basis.

   a. What information can you obtain from the graph?
   b. From the graph, can you say what the dividend would be after 18 months?
   c. Could you make a prediction from the graph for the payout in year 10?

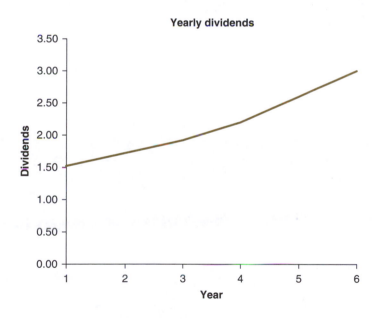

Figure 4.20

9. Table 4.17 shows the number of minutes that 30 employees were late on one day.

   a. Organize the data into five classes of equal size.
   b. Construct a frequency distribution for the data using the class size determined in part (a).
   c. Can you deduce any information regarding the lateness of the employees from the frequency distribution?

Table 4.17 Minutes late for 30 employees in one week

10	14	15	13	17	9	15	11	13	11
16	12	14	11	13	12	10	17	16	12
15	18	9	14	14	11	16	12	14	15

10. You are the manager of a retail outlet and you want to know the mean profit margin of five products. You know that the profit margin for product A is 3.5%, B is 5%, C is 2.1%, D is 8.4% and E is 6.5%. You sell £12000 of product A, £8000 of B, £15000 of C, £5000 of D and £6000 of E.

   a. Calculate the mean profit margin.
   b. Will the individual profit margins along with the sales figure have an effect on the mean profit margin?
   c. If you answered yes to part (b), how should you have calculated the mean profit margin?

To access additional online resources please visit: **https://study.sagepub.com/leepeters**

The Ballad of Eddie the Easily Distracted: Part 5

Eddie was busy, although as usual this busyness was not caused by doing his pre-reading for QUAN101. This week's lecture was on probability, and Eddie really couldn't make head nor tail of the book chapter, and besides it was 'soooo' boring. No, Eddie was busy preparing his flat for a weekend party which he was having with his flatmates. There wasn't much of an occasion, but his flatmates did like to throw a party, that much was certain. They'd gone to the supermarket to buy some food, and they'd spent quite a while working out the chances of different numbers of people coming; in the end they'd given up and just gone off to get sausages and beer, since that was cheaper, in case lots of people turned up. Eddie was just putting up a rather awkward piece of decoration when his mobile phone rang. 'Jeez, what are the odds of that?' thought Eddie, as he tried to get the phone without dropping the decoration or falling off the step ladder. Just as he got the phone out, it stopped ringing – 'Of course,' he thought ruefully, 'that was certain to happen.' Later, at the party, his flatmates were a little dismayed to see that they could have bought rather less sausages and beer, as rather fewer than 100 people turned up (Eddie had thought that this estimate was rather optimistic in the first place). However, Eddie was surprised to see Esha turn up with her friends: 'Hmm, what are the chances of that?' he thought.

Esha's Story: Part 5

Esha was quite surprised when she turned up with her friends at the party in Flat 5, Charles Darwin House, only to find it was Eddie's flat. They'd got on improbably well as PC Workshop partners in QUAN101, or at least as well as Esha would expect considering he was such a slacker. That said, the flat looked nice, although Esha didn't expect Eddie to have done much of the decoration – he'd probably organized the awful food! And no one had considered the chances of a vegetarian turning up now, had they? Fortunately Esha had already eaten – she'd expected it. Anyway, the party was fun, she'd said hello to Eddie, but he had spent most of the evening poking around on his computer, which was playing the music. The next day, Esha took out her QUAN101 textbook, to look at the chapter on probability for the coming week's lecture. There was a lot of information there, and she found it all rather boring and pointless, although it wasn't that hard to follow if you took your time. That said, Esha rather appreciated the examples, which had given her plenty of ammunition the next time she told off her Mum for wasting money on lottery tickets. Even so, when Esha got to the end she was pleased to have worked through the material – quite proud of herself in fact – and she was beginning to understand that most of the time when you did quantitative analysis, you were really trying to estimate the probability of something happening in the future, or perhaps somewhere else. With that in mind, probability seemed kind of important.

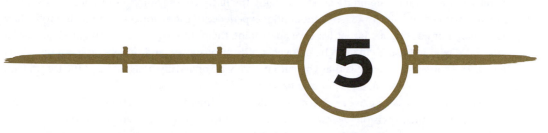

INTRODUCTION TO PROBABILITY

CONTENTS

 learning objectives

Here are the learning objectives for this chapter:

- ☑ Understand the probability of an event as the likelihood of the occurrence of that event, expressed by a number between 0 (no chance) and 1 (certain).
- ☑ Understand the difference between theoretical and empirical probability.
- ☑ Learn what a probability experiment, a sample space, an outcome and an event are.
- ☑ See how a tree diagram can represent multiple step experiments and how the counting rule can be used to determine the total number of outcomes.
- ☑ Understand how the counting rules regarding permutations and combinations can be used to determine how many permutations and combinations are possible from any given set.
- ☑ Learn how to assign a probability to an outcome using classical, relative frequency and subjective methods.
- ☑ Learn the relationship between the probability of an event and its complement, and the addition law.
- ☑ Begin to understand conditional probability, joint probability, marginal probability and the multiplication law.
- ☑ Learn about basic Bayesian concepts and Bayes' Theorem.

Probability is a concept that often baffles people; certainly I remember struggling with it as a student, and even as a lecturer when I first started teaching statistics. But it really does not have to be a mystery. Think about your day-to-day life: you are dealing with probability on an almost constant basis whether you know it or not. Cognitive psychology aside, every time you cross the road you automatically judge the likely probability of making it successfully. In fact, every time you make a choice of whether or not to act in a situation, you have somehow judged the probability of the outcomes. You might call it 'instinct', but it is really a rough probability judgement. While many scientists have explored failures in our ability to judge, in a general sense we humans are pretty good at judging the likely consequences of our actions – well, at least compared with other animals – even without prior experience of the action. Of course, our probability judgements may not be accurate, but at least we are making them. In fact, some say the most successful people are those who judge inaccurately, being over-confident of success and under-confident of failure. But I digress. The point I am making is that you automatically do on a daily basis many of the things I am about to introduce. All we need to do is put numbers on them.

In the business world, of course, we are often interested in putting numbers on probabilities. This helps decision makers with their decisions. Perhaps more importantly it helps them justify to their superiors exactly *why* they made a certain decision – especially if it is wrong. In the past, management has often been characterized as being largely 'gut feeling' – or instinctual probability judgements. However, in today's environment the ability to understand and work with probability figures is far more valuable in the main, allowing us to make good decisions clearly and consistently. Probability is also indispensable to statistics, as you will see in a few chapters. Basically, we cannot do any statistical testing without relying on an underlying base of probability,[1] because we are trying to *estimate* the chances of certain things happening in the real world, but using only a sample of data, like sampling a wine.

BASIC CONCEPTS IN PROBABILITY THEORY

Probability values are always indicated by a number between 0 and 1, with a value near 0 indicating a small likelihood and near 1 a large likelihood. Sometimes in other settings you can see this number represented in other ways, like a percentage or a ratio (e.g. 2:1, as in betting odds), but these are not formal representations of probability, and they can always be easily converted into a value between 0 and 1.

The simple rule to remember is that *as the number gets closer to 1, the event is more likely to happen*, and at 1 it is certain to happen.

There are two ways in which we can estimate this probability number. We can use logic to make a judgement if we want. For example, if you are into complicated fantasy games like some of my friends, you might have great experience with many-sided dice. You can estimate the probability of obtaining a particular value here easily. If the die is fair, the probability is always 1/the number of sides of the die. So for six sides the probability of getting a '5' is 0.167 (1/6), and for a 12-sided die (called a D12 by those 'in the know'), the probability of getting a 9 is 0.0833. This is called theoretical probability, and is what we usually roughly estimate automatically, without even knowing it. However, more often in a quantitative analysis situation we work with empirical probability, which is where we estimate the probability of an event based on past observations.

A probability experiment is a process which generates some kind of outcome, which we can use to estimate empirical probability. Rolling a die is a probability experiment, with the outcomes being each possible number on the die, but almost anything can be defined in this way, as long as it has discrete, definable outcomes (i.e. only one of the outcomes can occur at any one time). The sample space is the set of all possible outcomes for the experiment. Thinking about this as a *set* will be of considerable use to you as you move on through the book, so Back to Basics Box 5.1 introduces very basic set theory and terminology.

---

[1] Technically, I'm being over-simplistic here, because I'm ignoring the entire field of Bayesian statistics. However, this is far beyond the scope of this book in the main, and I encourage you later in your studies to find out more about this fascinating approach.

 back to basics

Box 5.1   Fundamentals of Set Theory

Imagine we are playing a game of 'truth or dare' around a table at a party. There are six of us, and we each have a number. We can roll a six-sided die for a more random selection method than spinning an empty bottle. When your number comes up, it is truth or dare time!

Now, think about all the possible outcomes of the roll of a six-sided die. This is pretty obvious: they are 1, 2, 3, 4, 5, 6. Are you with me? Set theory begins with the relationship between a single *object* and a single *set*. If an object is a member of a set, we say that it is an element of the set. Consider the possible outcomes of the die roll as objects and the collection of all possible outcomes of the die roll as a set. The individual outcomes are thus elements of the set of all possible outcomes.

If an object o is an element of a set A we can use specific terminology to show this:

$$o \in A$$

The basic relationship between two sets is the subset, or set inclusion. For example, if all the members of set B are also members of set A, then B is a subset of A. The way to show this is:

$$B \subset A$$

Moving back to the die example, if set A is the possible die roll outcomes – which we can show enclosed in curly brackets like this: {1, 2, 3, 4, 5, 6} – and B is the set of possible outcomes from a four-sided die roll {1, 2, 3, 4}, then:

$$B \subset A$$

There are lots of other common set operations which will be of use to you later in this chapter, and in the book.

The union of the sets A and B is the set which contains all members of at least one of either A or B. This is denoted:

$$A \cup B$$

For example, if A = {1, 2, 3, 4, 5, 6} and B = {9, 10}, then:

$$A \cup B = \{1, 2, 3, 4, 5, 6, 9, 10\}$$

The intersection of sets A and B is the set which contains all members of both A and B. This is denoted:

$$A \cap B$$

For example, if A = {1, 2, 3, 4, 5, 6}, and B = {5, 6, 7} then:

$$A \cap B = \{5, 6\}$$

The complement of set A relative to set U is denoted as A^c. It means all the members of set U which are not members of set A. We use a set called U not B in this case, because complements are most often used when U refers to what is called a universal set. Different types of set theories have different universal sets, but for probability theory the universal set is all the possible events that could happen – which you might know as the sample space! So the complement of set A = {1, 2, 7} relative to a set U of the sample space of a six-sided die experiment = {1, 2, 3, 4, 5, 6} is {7}.

There are many other operations on sets, which may be introduced later on, but those above are the basics. You might also remember set theory being expressed in terms of diagrams of overlapping circles – called Venn diagrams. Don't worry, these will appear later on!

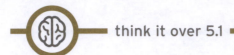

think it over 5.1

The word 'set' sounds a bit intimidating. One straightforward way to think of a set is to go shopping. You have two bags to carry the shopping home. Since you are a very organized person, you put all the freezer stuff in one bag and all the alcoholic drinks in another. The freezer bag contains ice cream, chicken balti ready meal, beef curry ready meal and pizza. The alcohol bag contains four cans of lager, four cans of cider, four cans of bitter and a bottle of whisky. In mathematical notation, let F be the set of frozen items and A be the set of alcoholic items:

F = {ice cream, chicken balti ready meal, beef curry ready meal, pizza}

A = {4 cans of lager, 4 cans of cider, 4 cans of bitter, 1 bottle of whisky}

U = all possible items you could have purchased

How would you write mathematically that pizza belonged to set F?

What does $A \cap F$ mean and does it have any members?

What does $A \cup F$ mean and does it have any members?

think it over 5.2

Consider the following.

Suppose there is a town with just one male barber and that every man in the town keeps himself clean-shaven, some by shaving themselves, some by going to the barber. It seems reasonable to imagine that the barber obeys the following rule: He shaves all and only those men in town who do not shave themselves.

Under this scenario, we can ask the following question: Does the barber shave himself? Or in mathematical language: Which set does the barber belong to? (Men who shave themselves or men who are shaved by the barber.)

The different possible outcomes in the sample space are called sample points. In the sample space for the six-sided die roll experiment used already, there are six sample points. However, it is not always easy to count up all the possible experimental outcomes. In some cases we have rules that can help us, which will be discussed below.

Multiple Step Experiments and Tree Diagrams

Imagine the common practice of measuring defects in production. The simplest check is whether a product which is produced has a defect or not. So, every time a product was finished, and rolled off the production line, we could employ a quality assessor to check it for any defects. A product check would be an experiment with two possible outcomes – defect or no defect. If defect was denoted D and no defect was denoted N, we could describe the sample space like this:

$$S = \{D, N\}$$

To illustrate the idea of multiple step experiments, imagine if we were producing a total of two products, so our experiment would consist of two product checks (i.e. a two-step experiment). The sample space for this two-step experiment would be a little larger than the single-step example above:

$$S = \{(D, D), (D, N), (N, D), (N, N)\}$$

To make this clearer, there are four elements here – each enclosed in normal brackets – and the elements are all enclosed in curly brackets. The first element of (D, D) indicates that there was a defect on the first check and a defect on the second. So in this case, it was easy to list all of the possible outcomes. But in many more complex situations it is not so simple. Fortunately, the *counting rule for multiple step experiments* allows us to figure out the number of experimental outcomes without listing them all out as above.

 box 5.1

The Counting Rule for Multi-step Experiments

If we can describe any multi-step experiment as a sequence of k steps with n_1 possible outcomes for the first step, n_2 possible outcomes on the second step, up to n_k possible outcomes at the kth step, the total number of experimental outcomes is:

$$n_1 \times n_2 \times \ ..... \times n_k$$

Thus, even if we could not have listed the two-step quality-check experiment above, it is easy to work out the possible outcomes by considering the first quality check ($n_1 = 2$), followed by the second check ($n_2 = 2$). The counting rule tells us that the total number of outcomes is $2 \times 2 = 4$. If we were to check three products, the total number of outcomes would be $2 \times 2 \times 2 = 8$. And so on.

Another way of doing this, which is often used when we want to look at the differences between the individual outcomes as well as count the possible number of them, is to use a tree diagram. This diagram is a way of graphically representing a multiple step experiment, and it shows each possible combination of outcomes, which can help us understand the range of possible outcomes from a multiple step experiment.

As an example, let's consider the following situation, which will be used in various places throughout this chapter. Imagine you have an assignment to plan for your course. You can split it into two stages: research and writing. The stages are sequential in this instance, because you want to complete all your research before beginning to write. However, you cannot predict the exact time each of those stages will take. Even so, your prior experience in the past suggests that you can take anywhere from 10 to 21 days to do your research, and anywhere from 5 to 14 days to write it all up. You have a deadline in 4 weeks (28 days), and you need to be done by then. For simplicity's sake at this point, you can set this up as a two-stage experiment, each with three possible outcomes corresponding to the shortest and longest times, as well as a time in the middle. Thus, the first stage (research) could take 10, 16 or 21 days, and the second (writing) could take 5, 10 or 14 days.

Applying the counting rule above is simple and shows there is a total of $3 \times 3 = 9$ possible outcomes, and we can describe them numerically as well. For example, the outcome (10, 5) would indicate that the research stage took 10 days and the writing took 5, which would be a total of 15 days for the project – well within the deadline! Figure 5.1 shows a tree diagram which sets out all the possible outcomes.

The tree diagram allows you to create the sample space quite easily – from the sample point column. From the diagram you can see that the completion time for the assignment ranges from 15 to 35 days, and six of the nine possible outcomes result in a completion time under 28 days. Of course, we have no

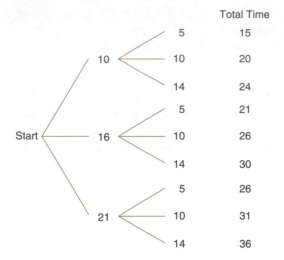

Figure 5.1
Tree Diagram
for the
Assignment

idea at this point of the actual probability of any of these particular outcomes, so right now we do not know if they are equally likely to occur. As a result, we would need more information before assessing the likelihood of the assignment being completed in under 28 days.[2]

Permutations and Combinations

When I was a first-year undergrad, one of my proper genius friends (hi Todd!) was already doing a second-year maths paper called 'permutations and combinations'. I thought it sounded really difficult, but, really, it is all about counting the possible number of outcomes or objects – which you might think is pretty useful right now. We have already worked out a simple counting rule, but what do we do in more complex situations? Imagine you were an auditor checking company records for accuracy. As already mentioned in Chapter 1, most of the time auditors check a smaller sample of records, not the whole lot. So if you had a set of six bi-monthly expense reports from salespeople, and you could check only three of them, how many possible different combinations of three records could be selected from the set of six? To work this out we need the counting rule for combinations.

 box 5.2

The Counting Rule for Combinations

The number of possible combinations of k taken from a set of N objects is given by:

$$C(N, k) = {}_N C_k = {}^N C_k = \binom{N}{k} = \frac{N!}{k!(N - k)!}$$

OK, I know that looks complex, but it really just shows different ways it can be notated. The actual formula is on the right hand side, the fraction with the exclamation marks.

One important term you might not have come across is the factorial, which is indicated by the exclamation mark ! in the formula. Factorials are really quite simple, and just mean that for any non-negative

---

[2] In fact, rather than spending time working this out, you'd probably be better off just getting on with doing the assignment!

integer *n* (i.e. any whole number from zero to infinity inclusive) the factorial is the product of all the positive integers less than or equal to *n*. What does this mean? Well...:

$$4! = 4 \times 3 \times 2 \times 1 = 24$$

By the way, you might be wondering what 0! is? Well, it is one. Look, it just is, OK? Oh, go on then – if you want an explanation, check Above and Beyond Box 5.1 (I haven't done one of these for a while).

 above and beyond

Box 5.1   Why 0! = 1

Factorial 0! = 1 because it represents zero multiplied by nothing; the result of multiplying no numbers is called the empty product and has a numerical value of 1. Why is this? Well, there are lots of different definitions and justifications of why this is the case, but I am going to show you only one of them. Imagine the multiplication of $3 \times 5 \times 5$, which can be represented by:

$$\text{prod}((3 \times 5 \times 5)) = \text{prod}((3 \times 5)) \times 5 = \text{prod}((3)) \times 5 \times 5 = \text{prod}(()) \times 3 \times 5 \times 5$$

Now of course, the only logical thing which can be in those brackets is a one, making:

$$1 \times 3 \times 5 \times 5$$

If a zero was in there, the equation would all of a sudden fall apart and equal zero.

It kind of makes sense if you think about it.

Moving on to our combinations problem, remember that we have six expense reports, and can select three. Thus, $N = 6$ and $k = 3$. So inputting these into the counting rule for combinations results in:

$$C(6,3) = \frac{6 \times 5 \times 4 \times 3 \times 2 \times 1}{(3 \times 2 \times 1) \times (3 \times 2 \times 1)} = \frac{720}{36} = 20$$

So there are 20 possible outcomes of the experiment of selecting three reports from a group of six. You will find that the numbers quickly get extremely large. For example, if you think about a lottery – say the first one introduced in New Zealand when I was a kid, which had 6 balls being selected from 40 – the possible combinations of 6 balls from 40 would equal 3838380 – cunningly just more than the population of New Zealand at the time of its introduction (not an accident I imagine). So you had nearly a 1 in 4 million chance of winning the top prize at that time. Add a few more balls to the total, increase it to 45 for example, and the possible combinations leap to over 8 million, and at 50 balls the number is nearly 16 million!

 think it over 5.3

Which is the best strategy for improving the probability of winning the lottery?

Strategy 1 – stick with the same numbers.

Strategy 2 – use different numbers each time.

If the probability of winning the UK National Lottery is approximately 1 in 14 million and the population is roughly 60 million, why are there not four winners per draw?

Now, imagine you are interested not just in a particular combination, but also in the *order* that the combination was selected in. So the same set of *k* objects is a different outcome when it is selected in a different order (unlike the combinations situation above).

box 5.3

The Counting Rule for Permutations

The number of possible permutations of *k* taken from a set of *N* objects is given by:

$$P(N, k) = {}^{N}P_{k} = k! \binom{N}{k} = \frac{N!}{(N-k)!}$$

You should be able to see that the denominator of the permutations formula (the bottom part of the fraction) is less than that for the combinations formula, therefore the number of permutations for a given number of objects will be greater. This makes sense, since every selection of *k* objects can have *k*! different orders.

Let's stick with the auditing example, where you need to select three expense reports from six to check. If you are concerned with the order of selection you will want to use the permutations rule, not the combinations one:

$$P(N, K) = \frac{6!}{(6-)3!} = \frac{6!}{3!} = 120$$

So 120 outcomes are possible for the experiment of randomly selecting three expense reports from a group of six, when the order matters. As you can see, the numbers here will quickly get huge. In the New Zealand lottery example, if you have to get the correct exact order of the 6 numbers from the 40, your chances of winning are now 1 in 2763633600. Yes, that is nearly 1 in 3 billion.

Assigning Probabilities to Outcomes

Up until now, we have been working purely within a somewhat abstract theoretical framework, so let's come back to the real world. A key question we would probably be interested in is how we assign probabilities to experimental outcomes in the real world. This is the problem we had with the assignment example earlier – the tree diagram was interesting, but almost useless as a decision tool without some probabilities assigned to the outcomes. Even so, before we can even start assigning probabilities, we need to consider two fundamental conditions:

- The probability of *any given outcome* must be between 0 and 1 inclusive. This makes sense, because if you remember I said earlier that 0 can represent no chance of an outcome and 1 could represent certainty. So every possible probability must range between these extremes (no possible outcome can have less chance than none, or more chance than certainty, surely?!).

- The sum of the probabilities of *all possible outcomes* must equal 1. This makes sense, because if the set contains all possible outcomes, then there must be a certain chance of one of them happening, no matter how small the chance of any individual one is.

There are three main approaches used to assign probabilities, and each is appropriate in different situations. The simplest method is the classical method, which is the best one to use if you are sure that all of the outcomes are equally likely. In this case, if *n* represents the number of outcomes that are possible, then the probability of each individual outcome is simple 1/n. The bonus here is that the two conditions above are automatically fulfilled. A very simple example is the die roll already discussed. There are six possible outcomes for a roll of a six-sided die, and if the die is fair each outcome is equally likely. The probability of any outcome is therefore 1/6, or 0.167.

The classical method used above was a theoretical method. In other words, I did not need to roll the die to estimate the probabilities, I had a theory which told me that there were six outcomes, each of which was equally likely. In that case, this was justifiable, but of course it is not often that we are certain about such things. In many cases, we have data from prior experience or research which suggests the possible probabilities. In such cases you can use the relative frequency method. This is an *empirical* method, since it relies on data from the real world to estimate probability.

Table 5.1   Data for errors in first-year test

Student name	Number of errors in paper
Dagmar Baggins	8
Carole Reddy	2
John Cardigan	8
Rowena Yates	4
Jon Fall	3
Anne Surgeon	0
Max Power	7
Brylie Russ	3
Laura MacKenzie	0
Annamarie Green	6
Geert van Damme	1
Carl Old	4
Jack Junior	0
Lucy Textor	1
Caroline Rider	2
Keesje Stars	7
Huw Brewer	3
Charlie Danger	6
John Radd	2
Trecia Painter	5

Take the data in Table 5.1, for example, which shows the data from a quick study of error rates in the first quantitative analysis test of the year. You can see that out of the sample of 20 tests that I checked, there were no errors in three of them, ranging to eight errors in two of them. 'Not bad' you might think. But then I might tell you that there were only 10 questions. Anyway, we can use this data with the relative frequency method to calculate probabilities very easily. For example, the chance of getting no errors can be assigned a probability of 3/20, or 0.15, and that of getting eight errors is 2/20 or 0.1. Again, this is pretty simple (if you have the data) and automatically satisfies the two conditions above.

I teach a similar group with the same number of students. Can I use the above data to predict precisely the number of students who will make no errors in this new group? Give a reason for your answer.

Things get more complex if we have little good data, or if we cannot assume equal probabilities for outcomes. Unfortunately, this is quite common in reality, and means the previous two methods are of no use to us. In such cases we must assign probabilities by using the subjective method. If this sounds a little to you like 'make it up' then you would be right. The subjective method is basically the use of any available information, including prior experience, others' experiences and even your own assumptions, opinions or intuitions. Of course, everyone's subjective estimates might be different, so two different people might decide on different probabilities for the same event. In fact, this is what the gambling industry depends on – I might judge the odds of my favourite football team winning more generously than the bookmaker. If I am correct then I make money, but bookmakers depend on the assumption that they will be more correct more often, over the course of many bets by many people, and thus they will come out ahead.

With this in mind, consider the following example. I am a big cricket fan, and I enjoy the regular contests for the 'Ashes' between England and Australia. Now, being born in Wales and living in New Zealand for a long time, I really do not want Australia to win, but I know plenty of Australians who do rather enjoy an Australian victory and are not shy of letting the world know about it. Imagine if, in 2009, I bet one of them £10 that England would win the Ashes. Two outcomes are possible – England win and regain the Ashes so traumatically lost in 2006–7 (designated O_1), or Australia win and retain the Ashes (designated O_2). Before the beginning of the series, I believed the chances of an England win to be 0.6, and thus I set $P(O_1) = 0.6$ and $P(O_2) = 0.4$. On the other hand, my betting buddy, being an Aussie, might set $P(O_1) = 0.1$ and $P(O_2) = 0.9$. Thus, he is very optimistic about Australia's chances. This is clearly a situation where at least one of us is letting their allegiances cloud their judgement – or perhaps both of us are?

Either way, it can be seen that in this case we have both assigned probabilities that adhere to the two fundamental conditions for assigning probabilities. This is important to keep in mind, because even when using subjective assignment, it is logically impossible to set probabilities which do not have a value between 0 and 1 inclusive, and where the sum of all outcomes does not equal 1.

As a final note, the methods above are not mutually exclusive. Instead, one can combine empirical data with subjective experiences and intuitions to estimate probabilities, or combine classical estimates with subjective probabilities. Doing so may make use of all the possible information, and result in more accurate estimates.

THE PROBABILITY OF EVENTS

You probably think you know what an 'event' is, right? *Wrong!* For the purposes of probability theory, an event has a specific definition. First, remember that a sample point is an outcome of a probability experiment. An event is simply a collection of sample points. Why talk about events? Events are useful because in many cases we are more interested in the probability of a set of sample points than any single one, as you will soon realize. For example, if you have an assignment due in 28 days, you are more interested in the probability of the set of sample points representing 28 days or less for assignment completion than any particular amount of days (e.g. 27, 26, 15 and so on). If you refer back to the example in Figure 5.1 you can see that six of the nine sample points give us a hand-in time less than

28 days away. These points are: (10, 5), (10, 10), (10, 14), (16, 5), (16, 10), and (21, 5). So, we use C to indicate the event that the assignment is completed in less than 28 days, shown by:

$$C = \{(10, 5), (10, 10), (10, 14), (16, 5), (16, 10), (21, 5)\}$$

Thus event C occurs if any single one of those sample points occurs. It is pretty easy to calculate the probability of an event. It is simply *the sum of the probabilities of the individual sample points in the event*. Of course, this means you have to define probabilities first for each sample point (which has not been done for this example). How you do this is a key decision, and the different methods were given above, but once you have done this, it is quite simple to define the event and sum the individual probabilities of the sample points.

Or perhaps I spoke too soon. Above it was easy, but what if you have hundreds of sample points? In principle it would still be simple, but in practice this would be a bit of a pain. So, we have a set of really helpful principles which can be used to work out the probability of an event, even if we do not have all the individual sample point probabilities. And it is at this point that your earlier digression into set theory will come in handy – but this time there will be pictures!

The Complement of an Event

The simplest situation to start with is the complement of an event A, which is defined as all of the sample points which are not in A. The complement of A is denoted by $\bar{A}$, and I can most easily show it with a Venn diagram, which is another way of looking at sets. You might have first come across Venn diagrams at school; they are made up essentially of circles and boxes with shading, to represent sets. Figure 5.2 shows the complement nicely. The shaded box is the entire sample space for the experiment, and the white circle represents event A. Thus, the complement $\bar{A}$ is all of the sample points not in A, meaning it is the complement of A.

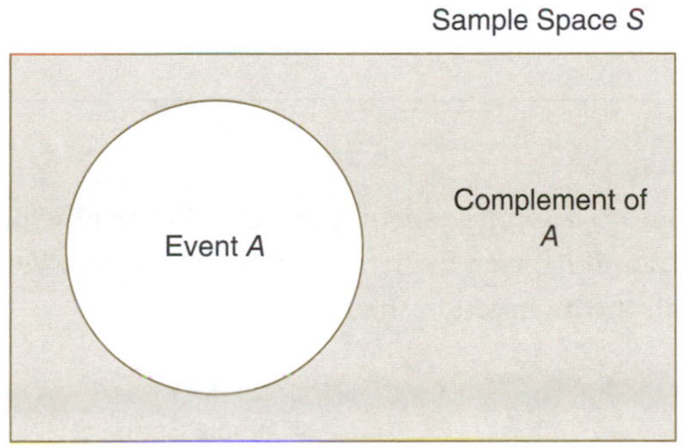

Sample Space S

Event A

Complement of A

Figure 5.2
The Complement of A (shaded)

If you think about it, it is always true that in any probability situation, either event A or its complement must occur, and therefore:

$$P(A) + P(\bar{A}) = 1$$

So, if you solve this equation for $P(A)$ you get:

$$P(A) = 1 - P(\bar{A})$$

Thus, getting the probability of any event is simple, if you know the probability of the complement of an event. In fact, if you know one, you must know the other. But when would this situation actually occur in reality? It is not as uncommon as you might think. Imagine you are trying to compute the probability of a customer making a purchase once he or she walks into your store. Your records show that 60% of those who enter the store make a purchase. You can use A to represent the event of a sale and $\bar{A}$ to represent the no-sale event. In the absence of any other information, you must set the probability of a sale event at 0.6, thus $P(A) = 0.6$. Using the equation above you can easily see that the event of no sale has a probability of $1 - 0.6$, and therefore $P(\bar{A}) = 0.4$.

The Addition Law

Before moving to the addition law, I want to recap some more key set theory concepts which are relevant, and transfer them to Venn diagrams. First, remember that an event is simply a special type of set, so for now I am going to stop talking about sets and use the word event, and, instead of elements, I am going to use the term sample point. If you get confused with how this relates to the content of Back to Basics Box 5.1, just swap the terms around for a while. Now, remember that the *union* of any two events is the event which contains all sample points of both events, so given two events A and B, the union of A and B is all sample points in A and B, and is given by $A \cup B$. In the Venn diagram in Figure 5.3 the union is shaded. You can see the circles overlap, and this means that there are some sample points in both A and B, but this is not a necessary condition for a union.

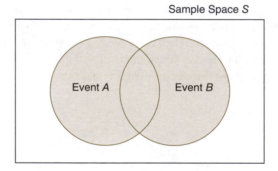

Figure 5.3
The Union
of *A* and *B*
(shaded)

Now, recall the intersection idea. The *intersection* of A and B is the event which contains only the sample points which belong to *both* A and B, given by $A \cap B$. Figure 5.4 shows a Venn diagram representing the intersection relationship, with the intersection shaded.

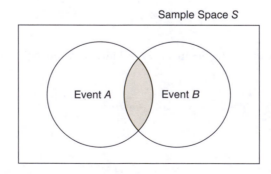

Figure 5.4
The
Intersection
of *A* and *B*
(shaded)

To understand the addition law, you need to understand the concept of union and intersection. But first, the addition law itself, as follows.

box 5.4

The Addition Law

$$P(A \cup B) = P(A) + P(B) - P(A \cap B)$$

think it over 5.5

If events A and B did not have any sample points in common, how would you write the formula in Box 5.4? Draw a Venn diagram to illustrate the situation where there are no sample points in common. What is the statistical term used to define this situation?

This makes sense intuitively because we need to account for the sample points which are in both A and B. If we just add A and B together we will double count all those sample points in both (if there are any). So to account for this we must subtract the intersection $A \cap B$ to ensure those points are only counted once.

Let's work through this in an example. Imagine you are a sales manager with 10 sales representatives out in the field. At the end of the month, four of your reps fell short of the target, three of them did not complete their reports properly, and two fell short of the target and also didn't complete their reports properly. Let:

A = the event of falling short of target

B = the event of not completing the reports properly

Looking at the relative frequencies we can determine the following probabilities:

$$P(A) = \frac{4}{10} = 0.3$$

$$P(B) = \frac{3}{10} = 0.4$$

$$P(A \cap B) = \frac{2}{10} = 0.2$$

Your management style is such that you consider that both missing your target and not filing your reports properly are worthy of a poor rating, so you are interested in the probability of $A \cup B$, which is the probability of getting a poor performance rating. To work out this probability we can use the addition law as shown above:

$$P(A \cup B) = P(A) + P(B) - P(A \cap B)$$

You can easily substitute the probabilities above into this as follows:

$$P(A \cup B) = 0.3 + 0.4 - 0.2 = 0.5$$

This tells us that if we were to select a sales rep randomly from your team, there would be a 0.5% chance that the rep would have received a poor rating.

Conditional Probability

I often tell stories of when I first became a lecturer and had to teach introductory quantitative analysis. Writing this chapter reminds me of the exact time when I realized that I had a lot of work to do to get up to speed: it was when I picked up the notes for the lecture on conditional probability. I remember thinking 'this is really tough', and I am hoping that I can explain it in such a way that you will find it much easier than I did.

Conditional probability is based on the idea that, in some cases, the probability of an event is based on whether some other related event has already occurred. In this case, if we are interested in an event A which has a probability $P(A)$, and if we know that some related event B has occurred, then we can use this information to calculate a new probability for A, called a conditional probability, and shown as $P(A|B)$. The vertical line | means that we are thinking about the probability of event A given that B has already occurred.

I would like to work this through with an interesting example drawn from my research. One of the things I am interested in is the decisions managers make about whether or not they should punish unethical employees. There are lots of interesting things which could influence this decision, but to avoid any heated arguments about what they might be, I am going to look only at the past performance history of the employee in this example. It is often thought that managers are reluctant to punish high-performing employees for unethical behaviour, whereas they are much quicker to punish low performers. Conditional probabilities could be used to analyse this situation quite nicely. Imagine we had data for 1000 unethical employees. Let:

H = the event that the employee is a high performer

L = the event that the employee is a low performer

P = the event that the employee is punished for an unethical action

$\bar{P}$ = the event that the employee is not punished for an unethical action

Table 5.2 Employee punishment data

	High performer	Low performer	Total
Punished	530	210	740
Not punished	190	70	260
Total	720	280	1000

Using this data, you can define the following probabilities using the skills you have already learnt. If you get confused, look carefully at the symbols and go back to the relevant section. First, the probability that a randomly selected employee is a high performer and is punished is the intersection of the high-performer and punish events, clearly seen in the relevant cell of Table 5.2, namely the number 530:

$$P(H \cap P) = \frac{530}{1000} = 0.53$$

Note especially that the non-punish event is actually the complement of the punish event, denoted of course as $\bar{P}$. So the probability that a randomly selected employee is a high performer and not punished is:

$$P(H \cap \bar{P}) = \frac{190}{1000} = 0.19$$

The probability of a randomly selected employee being a low performer and punished is:

$$P(L \cap P) = \frac{210}{1000} = 0.21$$

The probability of a randomly selected employee being a low performer and not being punished is:

$$P(L \cap \overline{P}) = \frac{70}{1000} = 0.07$$

Each one of these probabilities is an intersection of two specific events, and is called a joint probability. However, this information alone is not enough to work out the conditional probability. In fact, superficially it looks likely that being a high performer makes you more likely to be punished. But, similar to Simpson's paradox in Chapter 4, this might be misleading because what we are really interested in is the conditional probability. Table 5.3 summarizes this information and provides crucial information to work out the conditional probability. The values in the main body are the joint probabilities. The values in the row and column marked 'total' are called marginal probabilities (because some consider the outside row and column to be the 'margins' of the table) and represent the probabilities of each separate event, and are found by summing up the joint probabilities in the relevant row or column.

Table 5.3 Joint probability table for employee punishment

	High performer	Low performer	Total
Punished	0.53	0.21	0.74
Not punished	0.19	0.07	0.26
Total	0.72	0.28	1.00

To calculate the conditional probability of an employee being punished given that he or she is a high performer, namely $P(P|H)$, we recall that we are dealing only with the probability of punishment for the high performers. There were 720 high performers, and 530 of them were punished for unethical behaviour. It is simple to work out the conditional probability in this situation: $P(P|H) = 530/720 = 0.74$. So, given that an employee is a high performer who commits an unethical action, there is a 74% chance of their being punished for it.

That was easy, because I had the frequency data in Table 5.2 to work with. But now I am going to show you how to work it out with only the event probabilities to work with. First I will show you the basic principle. If $P(P|H) = 530/720 = 0.74$, try dividing both the numerator and denominator of the fraction by the total number of employees in the sample (1000):

$$P(P|H) = \frac{530}{720} = \frac{530/1000}{720/1000} = \frac{0.53}{0.72} = 0.74$$

So the conditional probability $P(P|H)$ can also be computed as 0.53/0.72, and if you look at the joint probability table (Table 5.3) you will see that 0.53 is the joint probability of P and H, namely $P(P \cap H)$, and 0.72 is the marginal probability that a random employee is a high performer, $P(H)$. So in other words the conditional probability $P(P|H)$ can also be computed as the ratio of the joint probability $P(P \cap H)$ to the marginal probability $P(H)$, or:

$$P(P|H) = \frac{P(P \cap H)}{P(H)} = \frac{0.53}{0.72} = 0.74$$

This leads us to a general formula for conditional probability, which I bet you could work out for yourself anyway.

box 5.5

Conditional Probability

$$P(A \mid B) = \frac{P(A \cap B)}{P(B)}$$

think it over 5.6

How could you show the conditional probability $P(A|B)$ with a Venn diagram?

So, moving back to the problem in hand, the marginal probability of being punished is 0.74, whether or not the employee is a high or low performer. The issue is whether or not you are more likely to be punished if you are a low or high performer. Thus the key is to compare the conditional probabilities $P(P|H)$ and $P(P|L)$. In other words, what is the probability of punishment given the employee is a high performer, and what is the probability of punishment given the employee is a low performer? If the two conditional probabilities are equal, there is no evidence for any bias of managers towards high performers, and a difference would indicate some bias.

Of course, you already worked out $P(P|H)$ as 0.74, so why not use the conditional probability formula to work out $P(P|L)$? Let's do so:

$$P(P \mid L) = \frac{P(P \cap L)}{P(L)} = \frac{0.21}{0.28} = 0.75$$

What conclusion should you draw? Well, even though the probability of punishment is higher if you are a low performer than a high performer, this difference is very small indeed. You would be on safer ground determining that there was probably no real difference. This result might raise one or two questions for you, for example how big does a difference have to be before we can conclude there is a difference? Indeed, this question has vexed the minds of many mathematical experts over the years, and is the foundation of *statistical inference*, which I will discuss later in the course of this book.

One final point to make about conditional probability is that not all events are dependent on others. Above, we were making the assumption that the probability of the punishment event (event P) is influenced by whether or not the employee was a high performer. If we find that the conditional probability of one event A given another B has occurred is different from the overall probability of A – expressed as $P(A \mid B) \neq P(A)$ – we say that A and B are dependent events. However, if this is not the case, and the probability of event A is not changed by the prior occurrence of event B, we say that A and B are independent events. In this case $P(A \mid B) = P(A)$.

The Multiplication Law

Previously, you saw that you could use the addition law to discover the probability of the union of two events. Here, I will show you how the multiplication law can be used to find the probability of the *intersection* of two events. The multiplication law is founded on conditional probabilities, which can be quite easily seen if you look at the conditional probability equation in Box 5.5. More specifically, if you multiply both sides of the equation in Box 5.5 by $P(B)$, you would get the following.

box 5.6

The Multiplication Law

$$P(A \cap B) = P(B)P(A \mid B)$$

which is the same as:

$$P(A \cap B) = P(A)P(B \mid A)$$

The multiplication law expresses that the probability of one event depends on the occurrence of the other. Thus the probability of both events occurring is dependent on the probability of one or the other occurring as well. So, in other words, the probability of A and B both occurring (i.e. $A \cap B$) is the probability of B multiplied by the probability of A given that B has occurred.

Strictly speaking, though, the multiplication law above only applies to dependent events. When events are independent we do not need to worry about conditional probabilities because $P(A \mid B) = P(A)$ or $P(B \mid A) = P(B)$. Thus, you could easily substitute these into the equation above to get the multiplication law for independent events, which is $P(A \cap B) = P(A)P(B)$.

Some of you might be wondering why we need the multiplication law to find the intersection, since previously we used the data (as presented in Tables 5.2 and 5.3) to get the intersections. Well, in many cases we do not have that information, but instead we have probability information instead, so we can use the multiplication law.

BAYES' THEOREM AND BAYESIAN CONCEPTS

Well, that conditional probability was not so hard, was it? What I am going to introduce briefly now as the final section of this introduction to probability is Bayes' Theorem. It was about this point in my early lecturing career that I really got completely lost. It really took some serious efforts to begin to understand it. But, persevere I did, and hopefully now you'll reap the benefit of that![3]

Remember, one of the key concepts of conditional probability is that we can revise probabilities of a given event if we know about an earlier event happening. This concept is extended in the Bayesian approach. Oftentimes in the real world, we begin our probability analysis with a given estimate of probability – which we can call the prior probability estimate. Subsequently, it is common to receive additional information, like maybe a new report, or a piece of research we conduct or stumble upon. We can use this new information to *revise* our prior probabilities, to what are called posterior probabilities. We use Bayes' Theorem to calculate the posterior probabilities using the new information.

Using Bayes' Theorem can get quite complex and unwieldy, so I am going to go through it in a step-by-step manner, using an example. Imagine you are a human resources manager in a big international investment bank called Metrobank, with offices in the UK and the USA. In all, 42% of your staff work in London and 58% work in New York. Thus, if I was to select an employee at random, I would assign prior probabilities in the following manner: the probability of the employee being from London as $P(A_1) = 0.42$ and the probability of the employee being from New York as $P(A_2) = 0.58$. Now, imagine that the number

---

[3] Interestingly, concepts based on Bayes' Theorem – or what are now called 'Bayesian' approaches – have been influential in many ways since 1900 (including cracking the Enigma code in the Second World War), and there is now a real rise in Bayesian analysis in management and business research. It is well beyond the scope of this book to cover Bayesian analysis, but you might be interested in reading further on this as you move on in your career.

of employees who get their huge bonus for making the bank massive amounts of money differs across each location, with 12% of London employees making the bonus and 17% of New York employees making the bonus. If event B is the event that an employee makes a bonus, and N the event that an employee does not, we can work out the following conditional probabilities:

$$P(N \mid A_1) = 0.88 \qquad P(B \mid A_1) = 0.12$$

$$P(N \mid A_2) = 0.83 \qquad P(B \mid A_2) = 0.17$$

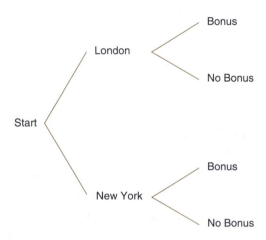

Figure 5.5
Tree Diagram for the Human Resource Example

Figure 5.5 shows a tree diagram for the process of your pulling an employee file at random, discovering whether it referred to a New York or London employee, and then seeing whether or not the employee made the bonus or not. This process can be represented as a two-step experiment with four outcomes (two bonus and two non-bonus). Each of the four outcomes is the intersection of two events, and this means the multiplication rule you learnt earlier should come in very handy, right? For example:

$$P(A_1, N) = P(A_1 \cap N) = P(A_1)P(N \mid A_1)$$

Figure 5.6 shows a probability tree incorporating this information and can help us work through the key issues. The probabilities shown at the first stage are the priors, and at the second stage the conditional probabilities are shown. Finding the probability of each individual outcome is simply a case of multiplying out the probabilities along the relevant branch.

Now, imagine you are at a bar having a drink (mine's a single malt if you're asking), and you are talking to a stockbroker who says she's from Metrobank. She looks pretty rich, and after buying your drink she says she just made her bonus for the year. So, given the information that the employee made the bonus (and also assuming that her accent is acceptably mid-Atlantic), what is the probability that this employee is from London, and what is the probability that she is from New York? This information is important for your prediction of how events for the evening may unfold...

Fortunately, you can use Bayes' Theorem to work this out. Let B be the event that the employee got the bonus; then what you are really looking for is the posterior probabilities $P(A_1 \mid B)$ and $P(A_2 \mid B)$. Looking back to the law of conditional probability, you already know that:

$$P(A_1 \mid B) = \frac{P(A_1 \cap B)}{P(B)}$$

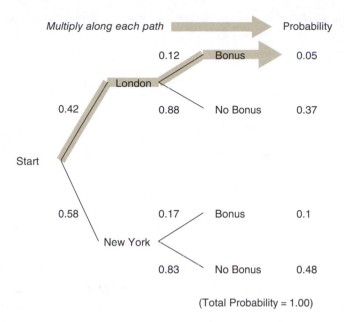

Multiply along each path   Probability

0.12   Bonus   0.05

London

0.42   0.88   No Bonus   0.37

Start

0.58   0.17   Bonus   0.1

New York

0.83   No Bonus   0.48

(Total Probability = 1.00)

Figure 5.6
Probability Tree for the Human Resource Example

Looking at Figure 5.6, you can also see that:

$$P(A_1 \cap B) = P(A_1)P(B \mid A_1)$$

and to find $P(B)$ you need to consider that it can only happen in two possible ways, either $(A_1 \cap B)$ or $(A_2 \cap B)$, and this means that we can work out that:

$$P(B) = P(A_1 \cap B) + P(A_2 \cap B)$$

Thinking back to the multiplication law, this means that $P(B)$ must also equal:

$$P(A_1)P(B \mid A_1) + P(A_2)P(B \mid A_2)$$

So, if we substitute the multiplication law equations into the conditional probability equation, we get Bayes' Theorem, and we can do the same for $P(A_2 \mid B)$ to get Bayes' Theorem for a two-event case, as shown in Box 5.7.

 box 5.7

Bayes' Theorem for Two Events

$$P(A_1 \mid B) = \frac{P(A_1)P(B \mid A_1)}{P(A_1)\,P(B \mid A_1) + P(A_2)\,P(B \mid A_2)}$$

and:

$$P(A_2 \mid B) = \frac{P(A_2)P(B \mid A_2)}{P(A_1)\,P(B \mid A_1) + P(A_2)\,P(B \mid A_2)}$$

OK, so let's do it! Using the first equation in Box 5.7, and the probabilities already provided, we get:

$$P(A_1 \mid B) = \frac{P(A_1)P(B \mid A_1)}{P(A_1)P(B \mid A_1) + P(A_2)P(B \mid A_2)}$$

$$= \frac{0.42 \times 0.12}{0.42 \times 0.12 + 0.58 \times 0.17} = \frac{0.0504}{0.0504 + 0.0986}$$

$$= \frac{0.0504}{0.149} = 0.338$$

Then, using the second equation in Box 5.7, we can get:

$$P(A_2 \mid B) = \frac{P(A_2)P(B \mid A_2)}{P(A_1)P(B \mid A_1) + P(A_2)P(B \mid A_2)}$$

$$= \frac{0.58 \times 0.17}{0.42 \times 0.12 + 0.58 \times 0.17} = \frac{0.0986}{0.0516 + 0.0986}$$

$$= \frac{0.0986}{0.1498} = 0.6582$$

Nice work! Now, remember that we started with a probability of 0.58 that the stockbroker was from New York, but given the later information that she got a bonus, the probability can be adjusted to 0.66, with a corresponding 0.34 probability that she is from London. These are our *posterior probabilities*. You can make a joke here about posteriors if you want. I wouldn't of course…

Bayes' Theorem can be used when the events for which we are considering computing posteriors are mutually exclusive (i.e. only one can happen), and the union of the events is all the possible outcomes (i.e. the entire sample space). If this is the case, we are not restricted to two events either, Bayes' Theorem can be extended to any number of posteriors, as shown below in Box 5.8. All you need are the relevant prior probabilities and the conditional probabilities.

box 5.8

Bayes' Theorem

$$P(A_i \mid B) = \frac{P(A_i)P(B \mid A_i)}{P(A_1) P(B \mid A_1) + P(A_2) P(B \mid A_2) + \ldots + P(A_n) P(B \mid A_n)}$$

Now remember that the subscript i refers to any given event (e.g. event 1 or 2 or 3, or whatever), and n refers to the total number of events we are working with (i.e. A_1, A_2, A_3), all the way up to A_n. Go back to Chapter 1 if you are a bit unsure here.

think it over 5.7

Misuse of Conditional Probability

Prosecutor's Fallacy

A murder has been committed. DNA taken from the scene is found to match that of a man's stored sometime earlier in a national database. The man is arrested and charged with the murder. At the trial the prosecution state that the probability is 1 in 1 million that the two samples could have matched by chance. They then go on to claim that therefore the probability that the man is innocent in 1 in 1 million.

This is a false claim.

Let E be the evidence and let I be the event 'the accused is innocent'. Then we are given that $P(E \mid I) = 0.0000001$. But what we want is $P(I \mid E)$.

Defender's Fallacy

In response to the above, the defence might argue that there are 60 million samples in the database, so we would expect on the order of 60 matches. Hence there is a 59 in 60 chance that the accused is innocent. Again though, this is ignoring other evidence, although the exact nature of the fallacy is less clear cut than the prosecutor's example above.

---

 think it over 5.8

False probabilistic reasoning

A judge tells a condemned prisoner that he will be hanged at noon on one weekday in the following week but that the execution will be a surprise to the prisoner. He will not know the day of the hanging until the executioner knocks on his cell door at noon that day. Having reflected on his sentence, the prisoner draws the conclusion that he will escape from the hanging. His reasoning is in several parts. He begins by concluding that the 'surprise hanging' cannot be on a Friday, because if he has not been hanged by Thursday, there is only one day left – and so it will not be a surprise if he is hanged on a Friday. Since the judge's sentence stipulated that the hanging would be a surprise to him, he concludes that it cannot occur on Friday. He then reasons that the surprise hanging cannot be on Thursday either, because Friday has already been eliminated and if he has not been hanged by Wednesday night, the hanging must occur on Thursday, making a Thursday hanging not a surprise either. By similar reasoning he concludes that the hanging can also not occur on Wednesday, Tuesday or Monday. Joyfully he retires to his cell confident that the hanging will not occur at all. The next week, the executioner knocks on the prisoner's door at noon on Wednesday – which, despite all the above, will still be an utter surprise to him. Everything the judge said has come true.

Serious point: You must be very careful when using conditional probability or Bayes' Theorem to make sure you are asking the right question (assigning the probabilities the right way around). For example, you can do some independent research about the case of Sally Clark, who was wrongly convicted on faulty probabilistic reasoning, to see what disastrous effects can occur.

SUMMARY

As I mentioned earlier in this chapter, probability is one of the things I found most difficult to understand when I was first teaching. Some of you I guess will have also found this chapter pretty difficult to get a handle on, but I hope that many of you will have followed along in a step-by-step fashion. If not, perhaps you could go back and try to do this – I promise that doing things step by step is much easier than just rushing through, or, even worse, dipping in and out in a non-sequential fashion.

However, whether or not you followed the techniques and equations, I imagine that many of you will still be wondering 'so what?' Why did I go to all this trouble to introduce probabilities, and where does it fit in with the rest of the material you will learn? Well, the answer to this question is sometimes not too self-evident. After all, I did give you some examples, but is this kind of thing really likely to happen in the real world? Well, actually, yes as you might have seen if you did the independent research suggested earlier about Sally Clark (and she was by no means the only person to be harmed by faulty understanding of probability in the courts). But, in day-to-day life, sometimes it can be hard to see how probability can help you.

So why waste time here? In fact, the concept of probability is the foundation stone of almost all of the later techniques you will learn – whether you will focus on statistical analysis, financial modelling, quality assurance, or virtually any other quantitative analysis technique. Understanding the basic concepts of probability will prove to be essential to understanding later parts of this book. Without it, you will not really make the critical connections about what it is you are actually trying to do with these more advanced techniques.

So it turns out that it is kind of important. Even more so, it offers a very important example to you of things which may not seem that relevant at the time, turning out to be important concepts for later work. If you want to understand how to use quantitative tools correctly, you pretty much have to understand probability. In that respect it is a little like algebra – without it you cannot do many more interesting things, but at the time it seems a little abstract and pointless.

 **final checklist**

You should have covered and understood the following basic content in this chapter:

☑ The probability of an event as the likelihood of the occurrence of that event, expressed by a number between 0 (no chance) and 1 (certain).

☑ The difference between theoretical and empirical probability.

☑ What a probability experiment, a sample space, an outcome and an event are.

☑ How a tree diagram can represent multiple step experiments, and how the counting rule can be used to determine the total number of outcomes.

☑ How the counting rules regarding permutations and combinations can be used

to determine how many permutations and combinations are possible from any given set.

☑ How to assign a probability to an outcome using classical, relative frequency and subjective methods.

☑ The relationship between the probability of an event and its complement, and the addition law.

☑ Conditional probability, joint probability, marginal probability and the multiplication law.

☑ Basic Bayesian concepts, and Bayes' Theorem.

EXERCISES

1. You are playing a game which involves tossing a coin. In statistical language the coin is said to be fair (i.e. there is an equal likelihood of a head or a tail). You toss the coin four times and each time it comes up heads.

   a. What is the probability of this occurring?
   b. What is the probability of the next toss coming up tails?

2. You, being an astute business student, can see a way of making money out of this game. You play the game again with a friend but this time after a run of five heads, you ask her to place a bet on whether the next toss would be heads or tails. She bets tails.

   a. Is the following statement true: after a run of heads the chances of a tail must improve?
   b. What is the likelihood of her winning?
   c. What is the probability of the next toss coming up heads?

3. Suppose you are on a game show and you are given the choice of three doors, red, green and blue, from which to choose, one of which has a prize hidden behind it. Suppose you choose the red door. The presenter, who knows where the prize is (and will not choose that door to open), opens the blue door and reveals that there is no prize behind it. He then asks if you wish to change your choice from your initial selection of red.

   a. Will changing your mind at this point improve our chances of winning the prize?
   b. What probability method could you use to determine whether it is worth changing your initial selection?

4. It is lunchtime and you cannot decide what to have. Your friend, who loves stats, buys six cheese sandwiches (which you hate), four ham sandwiches and five egg sandwiches and puts them in a box. You have to put your hand in without being able to see, and pick one. What are the chances of your ending up with:

    a. A cheese sandwich
    b. A ham sandwich
    c. An egg sandwich
    d. Not a cheese sandwich
    e. A cheese or a ham sandwich?

5. Which of the following sets are equal: {1,3,5}, {5,1,3,3}, {1,5,3,1}, {1,3,5,5}?

6. A universal set $U = \{1,2,3,4,5,6,7,8,9\}$ and the sets $A = \{1,2,3,4,5\}$, $B = \{4,5,6,7\}$ and $C = \{5,6,7,8,9\}$. Find:

    a. $A \cup B$
    b. $A \cap B$
    c. $A \cup B$
    d. $A \cap B$

7. Using the same sets as in question 6 find:

    a. $(A \cup B \cap C)$
    b. $C \cup (A \cup B)$
    c. $(C \cup A) \cap (C \cup B)$

8. Use Venn diagrams to illustrate the following:

    a. $A \cup B$
    b. $A \cap \bar{B}$

9. A universal set $U = \{1,2,3,4,5,6,7,8,9\}$ and the sets $A = \{1,2,3,4,5\}$, $B = \{4,5,6,7\}$ and $C = \{5,6,7,8,9\}$. Use Venn diagrams to illustrate the following:

    a. $A \cup B$
    b. $A \cap B$

10. Two events A and B are such that $P(A) = 0.6$ and $P(B) = 0.4$ and $P(A \mid B) = 0.2$.

    a. Using a Venn diagram, determine the probability that neither A nor B occurs. [0.2]
    b. Are the events independent? Give a reason for your answer.
    c. Calculate $P(A \cap B)$

 To access additional online resources please visit: **https://study.sagepub.com/leepeters**

The Ballad of Eddie the Easily Distracted: Part 6

Another lecture on probability was leaving Eddie completely cold again. He kind of got the picture of the last lecture, but this one was getting really heavy, with all of the talk about infinity and stuff. But he was glad he had spent a bit of time talking about last week's stuff with Esha in the computer lab – there'd not been much to cover last week, so Eddie took the opportunity to ask a few questions after they'd whizzed through the exercises. Looking at some of the formulas (or 'formulae' as Esha had said, which Eddie thought was a little pretentious to be honest), he was glad he'd paid attention.

Probably the most important part, Eddie thought, was to understand the idea of the continuous distributions, and especially how to use the area under a graph to compute probability. He had a strange tingle of remembrance here, something to do with his calculus classes at school, but he ignored it as he did with most strange tingles.

In fact, after his talk with Esha, Eddie was feeling quite confident about the calculations required. Esha had shown him how, even though they looked intimidating when you looked at the whole thing, they were much easier to do if you broke them down into small parts, based on things you already knew. So the trick seemed to be to learn the earlier steps before trying the later ones.

'It might be boring,' thought Eddie ruefully, 'but the chances of my success approach zero if I don't…'

Esha's Story: Part 6

Esha had a strange feeling about Eddie after the computer lab but couldn't quite locate it somehow. What was it? Oh yes, she was slightly *impressed* that he'd asked her to work through the probability calculations with him after going through the computer lab exercise. In fact, she'd also been somewhat impressed that he'd helped her to do the PC exercise so quickly. Certainly, when he was motivated he could do things pretty quickly! Esha stored that observation away for future reference.

In fact, explaining it had helped Esha too, and she was glad of this because the next part of the course on probability distributions needed some pretty serious thinking. The calculations were reasonably simple, if a little intimidating now and then, but they really were only based on stuff she'd done earlier. The idea of infinity, and continuous distributions where a variable could not take on a single value but only be considered in terms of a range, was hard to get her head around.

She resolved to read the textbook more carefully. On doing so, things became clearer. 'Well,' she thought, 'I suppose infinity is, well, infinite.' Slightly embarrassed by that observation, she continued to think: 'So, every time I think of one number, I can split it into two more, and then two more, and so on, but the key is that I keep doing that *for ever*.' It was beginning to click: 'So then, I could never ever stop splitting, so it is *impossible* to stop at one actual number – there's always a smaller division.' Now she was getting excited, it was starting to make sense, and she knew that once she got this idea under her belt, the rest of it made more sense too. She got up and made a coffee, as she liked to do when she was pleased with her thinking, and then got back to the chapter.

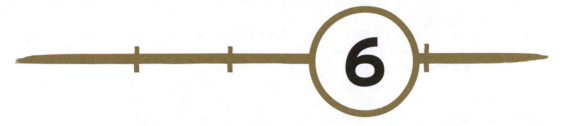

RANDOM VARIABLES AND PROBABILITY DISTRIBUTIONS

CONTENTS

 learning objectives

Compared with the previous chapter, these learning objectives are short and (hopefully) sweet, but no less important:

☑ Understand the concepts of discrete and continuous random variables.

☑ Learn the idea of a probability function and its associated distribution.

☑ Understand discrete probability distributions, the binomial, Poisson and hypergeometric, and their characteristics and uses.

☑ Understand the concept of a continuous distribution.

☑ Learn how to use the area under a graph as a measure of probability.

☑ Learn about the normal distribution and its relationship to probability.

☑ Learn how to use the standard normal distribution to compute probabilities for real-world events.

This chapter follows on from the previous one in setting the foundations for all of your later learning about quantitative analysis. Without gaining a grip on the idea of probability distributions, and especially the normal distribution, you will never truly understand statistical inference, which is *completely fundamental* to almost all of the rest of your quantitative analysis career.

The concepts of probability distributions and random variables introduced in this chapter are not quite as basic to our day-to-day thinking as the concepts in the previous chapter were, but as you will see as you move through the chapter, you will find a great many business applications of these concepts. In fact, a number of tools used here could have direct application to many of your future jobs – I am quite pleased with some of the examples!

A word of warning, however. By the end of the chapter, I will be asking you to think about some pretty complex things, and right from the beginning there are some reasonably complex formulae. The reason that I have spent so long building up the basic concepts in this book is so that you can do these calculations quite easily, in a step-by-step process. If you cannot do something here, do not give up and move on. In fact, go *back* to the earlier chapters, and deal with the individual components before trying to do it all together. If you do this, then by the end of the chapter you will be doing things that may even surprise you.

RANDOM VARIABLES

If you refer back to the last chapter, I introduced the concept of the probability experiment, which had a set of outcomes. For example, the coin toss experiment has two possible outcomes – a head or a tail. However, for most situations that you might be interested in from the perspective of quantitative analysis, words like 'heads' or 'tails' are not that useful. It would be more helpful to give a number to each of these possible outcomes. A random variable is a numerical value which describes the outcome of an experiment. The random variable gives a number to each possible experimental outcome, depending on the outcome of the experiment. For example, we might give '1' to heads and '2' to tails in the example above.

think it over 6.1

What do the words 'random variable' imply?

Discrete and Continuous Random Variables

A random variable can be either *discrete* or *continuous*. Discrete random variables are those which can be either a finite number of possible values, or one of an infinite series such as 0, 1, 2, 3... to infinity. The single coin toss experiment example above must be assigned a discrete random variable because only the outcomes 'heads' and 'tails' (1 and 2 above) are possible, thus the random variable $x = 1, 2$. Another example could be a study of store traffic in which you are to count the number of customers who enter the store between 1 and 2 p.m. on Tuesday afternoon. Thus, the random variable x = the number of customers, and the possible values of x are the integer number sequence 0, 1, 2, 3.... Technically, this is an infinite sequence, but of course we know in practice there are not an infinite number of people who can enter a shop in one hour! So, one random variable was a finite set of values (the coin toss) and the other was an infinite sequence (the store traffic study). Note the other important difference here: for the coin toss example, we assigned numbers ourselves to the qualitative outcomes of 'head' or 'tail'. However, for the store traffic example the outcomes were naturally described as numerical values (e.g. one customer, two customers and so on).

On the other hand, a continuous random variable is one that can be any value in a given interval. The concept of 'continuous' in this context can be quite hard to grasp, though. Imagine an interval of say 0–5. A continuous variable can assume any value in this interval, and I do not mean any value of 0, 1, 2, 3, 4,

5 – I mean *any* value. That means 1.1, 2.22228 and even π. Continuous random variables often refer to measurements like time, weight, speed, distance and the like, where the scale can theoretically vary to any point. Imagine a variant of the store traffic example above, where instead of counting the number of customers, you have to measure the amount of time the first customer to enter after 1 p.m. stays in the store. Theoretically, the random variable x in this case could take on any value between 0 and 4 hours (assuming a 5 p.m. closing time). But x is not 0, 1, 2, 3, 4. Of course, it is perfectly possible that the amount of time the customer spends in the store is not exactly a complete hour. In fact, it is possible for any value greater than 0 and up to 4 hours to occur – as fine as you can measure in fact. We designate this as $0 < x \leq 4$ hours. In other words, 'the random variable x can assume any value greater than 0 hours, but less than or equal to 4 hours'. Why greater than 0 and not greater than or equal to 0? Well, it is impossible for someone to leave at exactly the same time as they enter, so there must be *some* time spent in the store, even an infinitesimally small amount. Keep that in mind – the idea of really, really, really, tiny amounts – because it will come in handy later on when we look at continuous variables and distributions.

 think it over 6.2

What is the smallest number between 0 and 1?

BASIC CONCEPTS OF PROBABILITY DISTRIBUTIONS

Like random variables, probability distributions can be either discrete or continuous. A probability distribution for a given random variable is a description of the probabilities of each value of a random variable. In other words, it shows the chances of each experimental outcome happening. An understanding of the concept of probability distributions is critical for many quantitative applications, particularly statistical inference, and I am going to build it up piece by piece in this chapter. Let me begin with the now familiar coin toss example. Labelling a 'head' as 1 and 'tail' as 2, we can define the discrete random variable of the coin toss outcome as $x = 1, 2$. Using the correct probability function notation, $p(1)$ is the probability of a head and $p(2)$ the probability of a tail. For a fair coin, we know that there is a 0.5 probability of a head and a 0.5 probability of a tail.

We can also describe this probability distribution with a formula that gives $p(x)$ for every value of x. The coin toss is an example of the very simplest one, called the discrete uniform probability function, which applies whenever there is an equal probability of each outcome. This is the case in the coin toss, as well as in other things like a fair die roll. Box 6.1 gives the function. Of course, the uniform function is kind of simple, but the concept is important. I will be dealing with more complex functions later in this chapter.

 box 6.1

Discrete Uniform Probability Function

$$p(x) = \frac{1}{n}$$

where n is the number of values that the random variable can assume (e.g. in the coin toss $n = 2$ because the only two values the outcome can assume are 'head' and 'tail').

Let's build on this a small amount. Imagine a coin toss experiment where we toss the coin three times and are interested in how many heads we get as a result of these three tosses. There are eight possible events for this experiment. In other words, there are eight possibilities for the result, which can range from no heads (i.e. three tails) to three heads (i.e. no tails). Write each event down if you like. For example, the first possible event is TTT (i.e. three tails and no heads). If you do so, you will see that there is one possible event where there are no heads, three possible results where there is one head, three possible results where there are two heads, and one possible result where there are three heads. Table 6.1 shows the probability distribution for this example, and Figure 6.1 is a graphical representation of it – pretty simple, right?

Table 6.1 Probability distribution for the coin toss

No. of heads	Probability
0	0.125
1	0.375
2	0.375
3	0.125

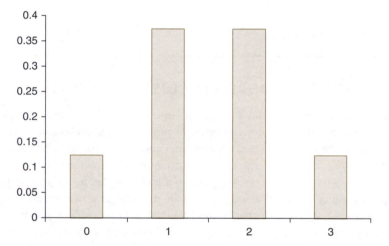

Figure 6.1
Probability
Distribution
for Three-Toss
Coin Experiment

The coin toss example was a useful starting point, but it does not really show you how probability distributions can be useful, so let me move on a step. Consider the situation where you are in charge of making decisions on whether or not to invest in a certain stock in the financial markets each day. In this case, you would have a lot of historical data to work from to help you in the decision. Let's simplify it to a single variable of interest – the percentage the stock price rises or falls in a single day – and let's keep the range to plus or minus 3% each day (it is a simplification, certainly, but for ease of calculation, you could justify rounding to the nearest per cent). In the last year (365 days), the stock price dropped 3% 32 times, 2% 63 times, 1% 70 times, stayed the same (0%) 20 times, rose 1% 80 times, rose 2% 65 times and rose 3% 35 times. That totals 365 times you measured the rise or fall, one each day. We could set up a probability experiment of selecting a day at random and define our random variable of interest x as the % movement in the stock price that day. The data we have suggests that x can be considered a discrete random variable which could take the values of –3, –2, –1, 0, 1, 2 or 3. As you should remember, $p(-3)$ provides the probability of the price dropping 3%, $p(-2)$ the probability of a 2% drop and so on. Our data shows that there were 32 days out of the 365 measured in which the stock price dropped 3%, which means we assign a value of $32/365 = 0.088$ to $p(-3)$, which means the probability of seeing a stock price drop of 3% is 0.088. You can quite easily continue for all the values of the random variable as shown in Table 6.2, which is the probability distribution random variable x. The distribution can also be graphed, as shown in Figure 6.2. You can also check in Table 6.2 that the conditions for a discrete probability distribution are satisfied: the probability of any single event is greater than 0, and together all the probabilities add to 1. Go back to the previous chapter if you have forgotten this.

Table 6.2 Probability distribution for stock price change

Per cent change	No. of days	x.p(x)
−3	32	−0.2630
−2	63	−0.3452
−1	70	−0.1918
0	20	0.0000
1	80	0.2192
2	65	0.3562
3	35	0.2877
	365	**0.0630**
		Expected value

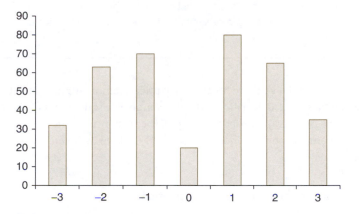

Figure 6.2 Probability Distribution for Stock Price Change

You will also see an extra column in Table 6.2 which did not appear on Table 6.1 – this is used to calculate the expected value of x. The expected value for a random variable is basically the mean of that variable. It can be calculated with the formula in Box 6.2.

 box 6.2

Expected Value for a Discrete Random Variable

$$E(x) = \mu = \sum x.p(x)$$

Note that the expected value $E(x)$ is also notated as μ. This equation basically says you must multiply each value of the random variable x by its probability $p(x)$ and then sum these products.

 think it over 6.3

Convert the equation in Box 6.2 into plain English.

Looking at the extra column in Table 6.2, you can see that I have calculated the products in the $x.p(x)$ column, and then summed them to make the total of 0.063, which is the expected value. So even though a change of plus or minus 3% is possible on any given day, you can anticipate an average change of 0.063.

You can also use this information to calculate the variance of the random variable, which is exactly the same concept as was introduced earlier in this book to summarize the variability in data. The formula is a tad more complex, but pretty simple if you work it through, as in Box 6.3.

 **box 6.3**

Variance of a Discrete Random Variable

$$Var(x) = \sigma^2 = \sum(x - \mu)^2 p(x)$$

Note again that $Var(x)$ is also notated as σ^2 because σ represents the standard deviation of x, and you should remember that the standard deviation is simply the square root of the variance.

The key to this formula is the $x - \mu$ part, which expresses how far any given value of x is from the expected value. It is then weighted by the probability of that x value, and we sum it all together. So you should recognize this concept as being very similar to the variance formula for grouped data, with its weightings and the like.

The working for calculating the variance for the stock price example is given in Table 6.3, resulting in a variance of 3.462 and a standard deviation (which is simply the square root of the variance) of 1.861. The standard deviation is generally easier to interpret, because it is in the same units as the original random variable. By contrast, the variance is in squared units, which can make it hard to work out exactly what it means.

Table 6.3 Variance and standard deviation calculations

Per cent change	No. of days	$x - \mu$	$(x - \mu)^2$	$(x - \mu)^2 p(x)$	
−3	32	−3.063	9.382	0.8225	
−2	63	−2.063	4.256	0.7346	
−1	70	−1.063	1.130	0.2167	
0	20	−0.063	0.004	0.0002	
1	80	0.937	0.878	0.1924	
2	65	1.937	3.752	0.6682	
3	35	2.937	8.626	0.8271	
	365			3.4618	Variance
				1.8606	Std dev.

THE BINOMIAL PROBABILITY DISTRIBUTION

From here, I am going to move on to talk about a few specific types of probability distributions, which can help us solve problems. If you think back to the beginning of the previous section, I introduced the uniform distribution, which had a specific form (each outcome was equally likely). The next distribution was the stock price one, and it did not really have a specific form but was created from historical data. Therefore we could not really describe it with a function, which meant we needed actual data to make any forecasts.

But what if we *knew* that a particular experiment's outcomes (i.e. the random variable) would be distributed with a certain form, like the coin toss, for example? Then we would not need data to predict what would happen. This is the basic concept I will be explaining in the balance of this chapter. In fact, we know that certain types of experiments will result in probability distributions of certain specific forms, as long as the experiment exhibits certain properties. The first one of interest is the binomial distribution, and it is associated with a specific type of experiment called the binomial experiment, somewhat obviously. The properties of a binomial experiment are as follows:

- The experiment consists of n trials which are identical.
- Each trial has only two possible outcomes, a *success* and a *failure*.
- The probability of success is denoted π and cannot change over repeated trials.
- Thus, the probability of failure is $1 - \pi$ and also does not change.
- The trials are independent (in other words, the outcome of one trial does not depend on the previous ones).

think it over 6.4

What does the word binomial mean? How does this meaning relate to the binomial distribution?

You should notice that the coin toss example is an example of a binomial experiment (assuming we denote one outcome as success and the other as failure). So why not use the uniform function? Well we could, if we wanted to work out the chances of success or failure on any single toss of a fair coin. However, the interest of the binomial experiment is on the number of successes occurring in n trials, not the outcome of any single trial – such as the three-toss experiment introduced before the stock price example (indeed, I could have used the binomial distribution there too). Furthermore, the binomial distribution is not restricted to dealing with experiments where the chances of success and failure are equal. But remember: in order to be a binomial experiment, *all five conditions must be satisfied*. Often, the fourth and fifth are confused and considered the same, so do make sure to think carefully about it.

If you can be sure you are dealing with a binomial experiment, you are in the happy situation of being able to use the binomial probability function to compute the probability of x successes in n trials – where x in this case is the number of successes you are interested in (not an individual outcome). The binomial function is superficially a little intimidating, but if you work through it with me in the following example you should be fine.

Would You Like a Career in Selling Menu Boards?

Before I became an academic, I spent a depressing two weeks as a salesman for a company which drew and sold those chalk menu boards you sometimes see in cafés or bars – you know, the ones with fancy writing and little pictures of food and stuff on them? Unfortunately, I was not very good at it, but we will not dwell on that (I sold a round total of zero!) But let's imagine that I was OK at it, and I did sell some, and from there we can set the scene. First, consider that for every visit I make to a potential customer, a sale is a success denoted S and a no sale is a failure denoted F. Let's estimate my probability of making a sale in any given visit as 0.15, so I sell 15% of the time. Imagine then that I make in total five visits per day to potential customers, and my boss wants to know the probability that I sell two boards a day. You could set this up as a tree diagram if you wanted (if you want to, go back to the previous chapter and work through it), but this is time consuming and the whole point of this is to begin to work without the security blanket of diagrams – I want you to get confident with working through formulae since the benefit of them is that you do not have to draw the diagrams.

Anyway, I can set this up as an experiment where S denotes a successful sale and F denotes no sale, and I am interested in the experimental outcomes that result in two sales from the five calls. Before we get started, we better check that it is a binomial experiment, which will involve making some assumptions too:

- The experiment is a sequence of five identical trials, one for each time I make a sales call.
- There are two outcomes possible for each trial, either success as I make a sale or failure if I do not.
- We assume the probability of success (0.15) for each call is the same.
- We also assume the probability of failure (1 – 0.15 = 0.85) is the same, for each call. This assumes my level of skill and/or enthusiasm does not drop as the day goes on, and I run the same routine for each call.
- We assume that each sales call I make is independent, and the purchase decision made by each customer is independent of the other people I have visited. This assumes that the customers for example do not call each other and warn them I am coming, or conversely contact other customers to say how great the product is, or something like that.

 think it over 6.5

What are assumptions? Are they based on past experience, educated guesses (whatever they are!) or are they just guesses?

In these sort of situations, I like to think of Spock in *Star Trek* when he is asked to calculate the trajectory of the *Enterprise* to sling-shot around our Sun to enable them to get home. He was told to 'guess' one of the variables, much to his horror!

If we can make those assumptions, we have a binomial experiment. In real life, you usually need to make educated judgements in this kind of thing, rather than expect to know for a fact. In real life I would probably question whether the assumptions are really justifiable, but for this example let's assume they are OK.

The first thing we need to know is the number of possible experimental outcomes which will result in exactly *x* successes in *n* trials (two in five in this case). To get this number, you could draw a tree diagram, but as I said this would take a while. Instead, you can use a formula you have already seen in Chapter 5 – the *counting rule for combinations*. See, I told you it would be useful! Just to recap, the counting rule for combinations, which also provides the number of *x* successes in *n* experimental outcomes, is:

$$\binom{n}{x} = \frac{n!}{x!(n-x)!}$$

There is no need to recap the details here, just go back to Chapter 5 if you need to. So let's use this rule to work out how to determine the number of experimental outcomes which result in two sales, or more formally the number of ways to obtain *x* = 2 successes in *n* = 5 trials. Working from the equation we get:

$$\binom{n}{x} = \binom{5}{2} = \frac{5!}{2!(5-2)!} = \frac{120}{2 \times 6} = 10$$

So there are 10 possible outcomes of the five calls which result in two sales. But to work out the probability of *x* successes in *n* trials we need to know the probability of each of these outcomes of course. Fortunately, because the trials are independent in the binomial situation, we can just multiply out the probabilities of each outcome to find the probability of any given sequence of success and/or failure.

For example, consider the sequence where I sell boards to the first two customers of the day, and fail with the final three; this sequence would be (*S, S, F, F, F*). Happy at the start, pretty depressed at the end! Using the notation for the binomial experiment probabilities given above, you can write the formula:

$$\pi.\pi.(1-\pi).(1-\pi).(1-\pi)$$

Since the probability of success π is 0.15, it is relatively simple to multiply out the formula:

$$0.15 \times 0.15 \times 0.85 \times 0.85 \times 0.85 = 0.014$$

What is useful about the binomial case is that the probability of *any* sequence of trial outcomes with x successes in n trials is the same. So the sequence of (F, F, F, S, S) also has a probability of 0.014.

We can formalize this by creating a formula to work out the probability of a given sequence of trials resulting in x successes in n trials as follows:

$$\pi^x(1 - \pi)^{(n-x)}$$

which is basically a general version of the more convoluted working we just did.

think it over 6.6

Before going any further, prove to yourself that the formula:

$$\pi^x(1 - \pi)^{(n-x)}$$

is correct (use the example given above to start with). You should adopt this practice for any new equation you come across – do not accept anything as fact without questioning it!

Now, we can do something extremely clever here and combine the equation which gave us the number of outcomes resulting in x successes from n trials with the equation which gives the probability for each sequence of x successes into the full binomial probability function, as seen in Box 6.4.

box 6.4

Binomial Probability Function

$$p(x) = \binom{n}{x} \pi^x (1 - \pi)^{(n-x)}$$

where $p(x)$ is the probability of x successes in n trials:

$$\binom{n}{x} = \frac{n!}{x!(n-x)!}$$

and π is the probability of success for any one trial, with $1 - \pi$ the probability of failure.

So we can compute this for any number of successful sales calls per day if we wished. For example, we already have the numbers for two successes:

$$p(x) = \binom{n}{x} \pi^2 (1 - \pi)^{(n-x)} = 10 \times 0.014 = 0.17$$

which means there is a 0.14 probability that I will make two sales on any given day. If you do not know where those numbers came from, just go back to the start of the exercise and try to pick them out. You could also run the function for all the different values of *x* possible (e.g. 0 sales, 1 sale and so on up to 5 sales), and plot a chart of them if you wanted. You can apply the binomial function to any situation that adheres to the conditions of a binomial experiment, and this makes it very handy in the right circumstances.

think it over 6.7

You work for the same company but the boss wants to know the probability of your selling three boards a day. You have the same probability of making a sale (0.15) and visit the same number of customers. Your calculations show, using the binomial distribution, that the probability of your sell- ing three boards is 0.0024. This seems to you a huge difference; Nick had a 14% chance of selling two boards yet you only have a 0.2% chance of selling three boards. Where have you gone wrong in your calculation?

Of course, in most situations you would not use the formula, which can become cumbersome with large numbers especially. Often you will use a table of binomial probabilities, to read off the answer. To use these tables, you must know the values of *n*, *x* and π, and you can then read the answer from the appro- priate place. Unfortunately, it is impossible to have a table with all possible combinations, and in the case where you do not, you would need to use the function. You can also use IBM SPSS Statistics Software (SPSS) or Excel to work out binomial probabilities, and I will show you how to do that later on.

Finally, in the binomial case with a known number of trials *n* and a known success probability π, it is simple to calculate the expected value and variance:

$$E(x) = \mu = n\pi$$

$$Var(x) = \sigma^2 = n\pi(1 - \pi)$$

think it over 6.8

Calculate the expected value for the example above. What does it tell you?

OTHER DISCRETE PROBABILITY DISTRIBUTIONS

I spent a long time on the binomial distribution because it is an excellent example of how such things work, but it is not the only one. Two other useful ones which I will cover in a little less depth are the Poisson and hypergeometric probability distributions which each have their own particular use.

The Poisson Distribution

The Poisson distribution is particularly useful when we want to estimate the number of occurrences of an event in a specific *interval* of time or space (e.g. distance and the like). For example, the number of cus- tomers entering a store in an hour, or the number of potholes in the 6 mile (10 km) distance to my office from home (a subject close to my heart). However, like the binomial case, to describe an experiment in terms of the Poisson[1] distribution, a number of conditions must be satisfied:

- The probability of an occurrence is the same for any two intervals of the same length.
- Whether or not an event occurs or does not occur in any interval is independent of whether or not an event does or does not occur in any other interval.

As well as this, you should note that the actual number of occurrences of the event in the interval has no upper limit – thus it is an infinite sequence. So, if the two conditions above are satisfied, the random variable of interest can be described by the Poisson probability distribution as shown in Box 6.5.

 box 6.5

The Poisson Probability Distribution

$$p(x) = \frac{\mu^x e^{-\mu}}{x!}$$

where:

$p(x)$ = the probability of x occurrences in an interval

μ = the expected value of the number of occurrences in an interval

e = 2.71828

You should consider two things here: first, that you will need somehow to find the expected value; and, secondly, that e is a mathematical constant, a critical number in maths that has specific properties. You will remember e from Chapter 1, where it was discussed in terms of the natural logarithm.

A simple example can be created from another aspect of my past. When I was younger I dreamed of owning a record store (records are those circular things which contain music, you used to buy them rather than download them). Unfortunately, given the type of music I enjoy, it probably would not have sold many records so it is lucky I never went into business. Anyway, let me set up a Poisson experiment from this premise. What I am interested in is the number of customers who visit the shop in one hour. First I must make the assumptions that the probability of a customer entering the shop is the same for any two time periods of the same length (i.e. an hour) and also that the entry or non-entry of a customer is independent of the entry or non-entry in any other time period. It is kind of hard to work out whether or not you should consider these assumptions as satisfied in many real-life cases, but in the absence of any other information or obvious reasons not to accept them, let's go with them.

Imagine that before I set up my own record store I do some research (this is a good idea, incidentally) and look at how many customers visit similar types of record stores in an hour. The average number of customers who visit such stores per hour is, according to my research, 11. This is the expected value of x. So we can insert this into the function and get the following equation:

$$p(x) = \frac{11^x e^{-11}}{x!}$$

[1] If you are wondering why it is that the word Poisson is capitalized, it's because the Poisson distribution is named after its discoverer – the French scholar Simeon Poisson (1781–1840), who made many other major contributions to science. I suspect that in fact the 1980s hair metal band 'Poison' may have been named in tribute to him, with a cunning misspelling to throw people off.

Of course, the random variable x is the number of customers arriving in an hour. Now suppose I do some profit calculations about the chances of customers purchasing once they arrive[2] and decide that in order to stay afloat I need only nine customers to enter the store per hour, so in this case x = 9. It is easy to put that into the formula:

$$p(9) = \frac{11^9 e^{-11}}{9!} = 0.109$$

It is pretty simple to compute this, using a decent calculator. An easier way to do it would be to use a table of the Poisson distribution, which is organized by the values of x and μ. You just read off the right value from the tables. If you were to do that, you would see that my calculations were correct (I just checked…).

Interestingly, one of the properties of the Poisson distribution is that the mean/expected value is the same as the variance. If you use a Poisson distribution, this is just a fact, and quite a handy one at that. So, the expected value is 11, and therefore so is the variance, with the standard deviation being the square root of 11 or 3.32.

 think it over 6.9

You are the new business director of a national coffee shop chain. You have received an application from a couple in Birmingham who would like to open a coffee shop using your company's name. In front of you is a map of the city and it appears to you that existing coffee shops are randomly distributed. You decide to test this using the Poisson distribution but unfortunately the result does not make sense. Where have you gone wrong?

The Hypergeometric Probability Distribution

Apart from sounding super-impressive and sci-fi, the final discrete distribution I will talk about – the hypergeometric probability distribution – is extremely handy. It is closely related to the binomial distribution, but its usefulness relates to the fact that it relaxes two of the key assumptions of the binomial distribution. Specifically, the hypergeometric probability distribution does not require the trials to be independent, and the probability of success changes across trials.

The hypergeometric probability distribution is used to find the probability that in a random selection of a certain number of elements denoted n, which are selected without replacement, we will get x elements labelled success and n – x elements labelled failure. For example, imagine you had a bag of 20 ping-pong balls, some white and some black. You select five balls from the bag at random, without replacing them back in the bag after looking. You are interested in the probability of selecting two black balls. So in this case n = 5, x = 2 and n – x = 3. As well as this, r denotes the number of elements in the population of size N which are labelled success. So if there are 8 black balls among the 20 balls in the bag, r = 8 and N = 20. N – r denotes the number of failures in the population, which in this case is 12. So for the outcome of interest to occur (two black balls in five selected), you must obtain x successes from the total of r successes in the population (i.e. in this case, two from eight). In order to work out the probability p(x) of this event, you can use the hypergeometric probability distribution presented in Box 6.6.

---

[2] Hey, I could use the binomial function here as well for that task! In fact, you might notice that in many cases you could use the binomial distribution to examine the experiment probabilities as well, and the binomial is actually more precise. So why use Poisson? Well, as the number of trials gets larger, the binomial starts to look like the Poisson distribution, and the Poisson is much easier to work with – as you can see from the functional forms given.

box 6.6

The Hypergeometric Probability Distribution

$$p(x) = \frac{\binom{r}{x}\binom{N-r}{n-x}}{\binom{N}{n}}$$

This formula looks rather complex, but it is actually not too difficult, because you know that all you are really doing is computing multiple instances of the counting rule for combinations, given in Chapter 5 (and also touched on earlier in this chapter). So for example to compute:

$$\binom{r}{x}$$

all you need to do is work out:

$$\frac{r!}{x!(r-x)!}$$

and so on. Of course it takes a bit of work to do so with a calculator, but you should not be confused about what to do, just take it step by step.

A classic example of where the hypergeometric probability distribution is useful is in quality control. It is often the case that inspectors select a sample of products from a box, or a day's production, or suchlike, and count the defects. Imagine that you are an inspector of shoes in a factory in Milan, and you have a box of pairs to inspect for defects. There are 10 pairs in each box, and there are 3 defective pairs in the box; if you randomly select 2 pairs from each box, what is the chance you will find one of the defective pairs? For this problem, $n = 2$, $N = 10$, $r = 3$, and the probability of finding $x = 1$ defective pair is:

$$p(1) = \frac{\binom{3}{1}\binom{10-3}{2-1}}{\binom{10}{2}} = \frac{\binom{3}{1}\binom{7}{1}}{\binom{10}{2}} = \frac{\frac{3!}{1!2!}\frac{7!}{1!6!}}{\frac{10!}{2!8!}} = \frac{3\times7}{45} = 0.47$$

To determine the expected value and the variance for the hypergeometric probability distribution, the formulae are a little more complex than the other two distributions, but they still follow the same basic principles. I will work through them with the same example of shoe quality control, remembering that $n = 2$, $N = 10$ and $r = 3$. First, the expected value:

$$E(x) = \mu = n\left(\frac{r}{N}\right) = 2\left(\frac{3}{10}\right) = 2\times0.3 = 0.6$$

Note in this case that the things in the brackets are simple fractional divisions, not the combination rule functions you used to find the probability above – so remember to take care to work out what you are doing before you do it. The variance is a bit long-winded, but simple enough if you take your time:

$$Var(x) = \sigma^2 = n\left(\frac{r}{N}\right)\left(1-\frac{r}{N}\right)\left(\frac{N-n}{N-1}\right) = 2\left(\frac{3}{10}\right)\left(1-\frac{3}{10}\right)\left(\frac{10-2}{10-1}\right) = 0.37$$

Of course, the standard deviation is simply the square root of this, which is 0.61.

You might be thinking that this example is a bit unrealistic (why would we check if we knew there were three defective pairs of shoes already?), but actually it is not so far-fetched. You could use the basic ideas here to work out an idea of how many defective shoes were in an average box, over the course of many checks, or you could work out how many shoes to tell your inspectors to check, based on the likelihood of finding a defective pair, or things like that. In other words, you could try the formula many times, with different values of x, r, N and n.

DISCRETE PROBABILITY DISTRIBUTIONS USING SPSS AND EXCEL

You have not read much about computers for a while, because you have been getting pretty good at hand calculations. But at this point you can use software to get a lot of information of use to you in real-life applications. In particular, software is great when you need to do many calculations as in the situation I just outlined above of trying out lots of different values to make decisions.

Using SPSS

Let's use the binomial experiment described in the menu board sales example which I discussed earlier, to show how SPSS can compute discrete probabilities. Remember that the number of trials $n = 5$ and the probability of success $\pi = 0.15$. This is pretty easy to set up in SPSS, but first you have to enter some data. In a blank SPSS Data View, enter the trials in the leftmost column by entering the values 0, 1, 2, 3, 4, 5, which will automatically be labelled VAR001 by SPSS. You can go to the Variable View and change this to something like 'x', and, in doing so, your data entry sheet will then look like Figure 6.3.

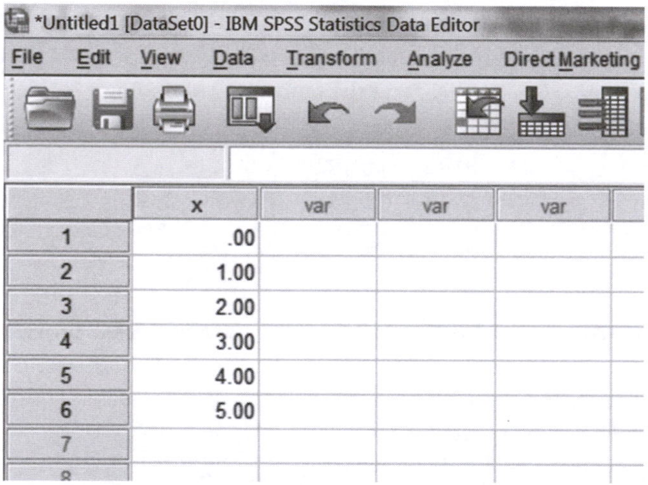

Figure 6.3

Now follow the sequence, beginning with <u>Transform</u> → <u>Compute Variable</u> which will bring up the Compute window. Enter a variable name such as 'px' to represent the probability of x in the Target Variable box, then look to the right and you will see two white boxes. The upper one is labelled Function Group, and in here you need to select PDF & Noncentral PDF which will change the things in the lower box entitled Functions and Special Variables; you need to select Pdf.Binom in this box. You can see both are highlighted in Figure 6.4. Click on the Pdf.Binom function, then click the small 'up' arrow to the right, which will move it up to the Numeric Expression box at the top. You should see something like PDF.BINOM(?,?,?), where the '?' represents an *argument* for the function, which needs to be changed. The first argument should be the data used to make the distribution, x, the second represents n which is 5 for us, and the third is π which is 0.15. When you are done (you can type in the box to replace the question marks), it should look like the top part of Figure 6.4. Then click on OK, and the Data View should show a new variable called px being created, which gives the binomial probabilities for each number of successes in five trials, from 0 successes to 5 successes.

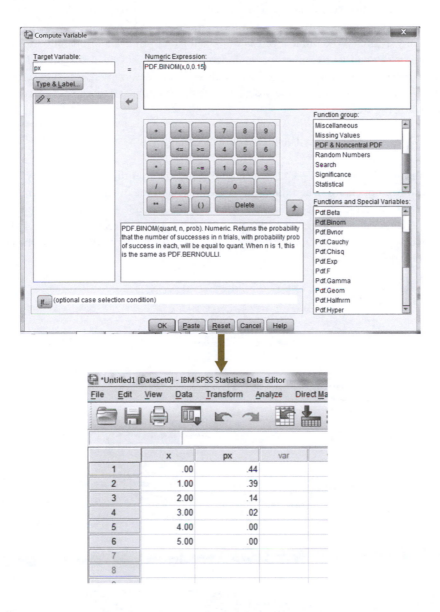

Figure 6.4

SPSS will allow you to use many other distributions, including the Poisson and hypergeometric ones. The principles are basically the same, but you will need to make sure you read the instructions which appear in the Compute Variable window when you select the various functions; these show you what to enter as the arguments.

Using Excel

Using Excel to do the working is slightly more complex, but on the upside it helps us to cement a number of key Excel concepts already discussed in Chapter 3 about formulae, cell values, etc. So this should be a good exercise to follow along with. Let's repeat the same example as in the SPSS exercise. The Excel function is called BINOMDIST and it has four arguments: x = the number of successes, n = the number of trials, π = the probability of success, and *cumulative* is something you will not have come across before. If we enter FALSE for this argument, we tell Excel we want the probability of x successes, and if we enter TRUE we tell Excel that we would like the cumulative probability of x *or fewer* successes.

Figure 6.5 shows the basic worksheet we will use, and we can set it up so it can be used for many different probability experiments, with changes in the numbers. So pay attention as it may be very handy later on. Basically, I entered the number of trials into cell B1 = 5, then the probability of success (0.15) into B2. These are our consistent values for the function. Then in cells B6–B11 I entered the values for the random variable x representing the possible number of successes in my five-trial experiment, which are of course 0–5. In order to compute the probability for the example of 0 successes I enter the following formula by typing it into C6:

$$=BINOMDIST(B6,\$B\$1,\$B\$2,FALSE)$$

Then I copy this formula to cells C7–C11. You should remember that the cell addresses with the $ signs are *absolute* and will not change when the formula is copied, and the others are *relative* and will change. This means that the formula can change to reference the right x variable each time it is copied (B6 above), but still use the same values for n and px which you placed in B1 and B2 each time. If you look at the top part of Figure 6.5, you can see the formulae as they are correctly copied to the cells. In the bottom part you can see the values.

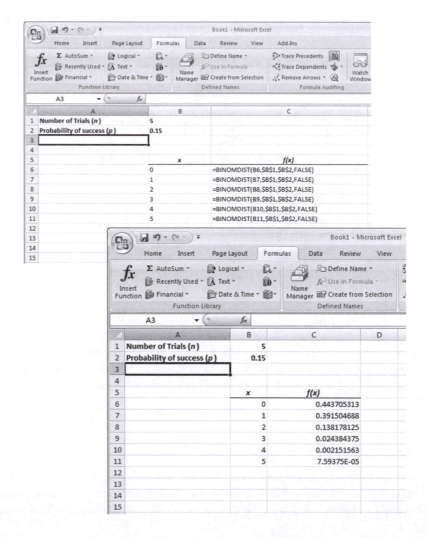

Figure 6.5

Just like SPSS, Excel can also use many different distributions, including the Poisson and hypergeometric, and can also give you useful help on inserting the right arguments.

CONTINUOUS PROBABILITY DISTRIBUTIONS

Getting your head around the idea of continuous probability distributions is a critical part of understanding statistical inference. Thus, you reach here a real watershed moment in your quantitative analysis career. Without getting a handle on these ideas, you will always struggle to understand statistical inference – a huge part of quantitative analysis in business.

Perhaps the hardest part to understand is the most fundamental: the *continuous* nature of the distribution. If you think back to the early part of this chapter, a *discrete* distribution was one in which the random variable could take on a particular value, for example a 'head' or a 'tail' for the coin toss. There is no overlap between a head or a tail, therefore they are discrete values or outcomes of a probability experiment.

To explain a continuous distribution, think back to what a probability distribution really is, namely a special case of a frequency distribution. More specifically, if you do not have a theory about the probability of an event occurring (such as you do with a fair coin toss, for example, where you know there is a 0.5 probability of each event), the only way to create a probability distribution is to do lots of trials and record the outcome of each trial. You then can create the distribution, such as was the situation with some of the examples earlier in this chapter (e.g. the stock price). So let me create an example. Imagine you are interested in the time taken to get from my house to my office in the morning. You could create an empirical probability distribution by measuring the time it took every day for 100 days. Probably, you would measure the time in minutes, which would likely be as accurate as you thought you needed. So if this were the case, you would have a distribution which ranged between a lower and upper bound, and contained values for each minute. For example, on 20 occasions it may have taken 29 minutes, on 25 it may have taken 30 minutes and so on.

You could either tabulate or graph the values, and what you would have is an empirical probability distribution, which is discrete. It is discrete because there is no overlap between the values, say 29 and 30 minutes. So if you graphed it, you would have some bars representing each separate value of time, and their height would represent how many times that value was observed. To understand a continuous distribution I want you to imagine two things. First of all, imagine you did not measure in minutes, but in seconds, so there are many more values that the time variable can take. Then imagine you used a stopwatch and measured in hundredths of a second. Then imagine you measured in microseconds, and then try to keep imagining that you make the measure of time more and more and more fine-grained; in fact, make it *infinitely* fine-grained. Then, imagine that instead of 100 measurements, you take 1000, or 10000, and keep going until you take an *infinite* number of measurements on an *infinitely* fine-grained measuring device. If you were to graph this, the bars would ultimately merge together, and there would be no gap between any one value and the next. All of a sudden, you have a continuous probability distribution.

Of course, this is a purely theoretical idea, since we could never do it in practice. But that is neither here nor there – the fact is that we can think about it. If we do so, we come up with some interesting ideas. First of all, we can come up with the idea that we can never know how often a single value occurs, because there are an infinite number of them. This kind of makes sense when you think about it, and it is to do with the nature of infinity. Basically, any value you can think of can be divided into more than one smaller value, no matter how small you go (remember, infinity), so the idea of a single value of a variable in this case is not relevant.

Instead, what we are interested in is an *interval between two values*. So instead of a probability distribution (which we have in the discrete case), we have what is called a probability density function, or $f(x)$, which corresponds to the probability that the continuous random variable x will take on some value within a given interval. We often think about probability density functions in terms of their graphs, which you will be seeing a few of from here on in. The probability of a continuous random variable x assuming any value within a given interval is given by the area under that graph corresponding to that interval. Of course, since we can never know how often a single discrete value occurs, the area under the graph for a single value is zero, which means a quirk of the continuous probability distribution is that the probability of any single value occurring is 0. Which is why we talk of intervals.

The most important continuous probability distribution is the normal distribution, which is indispensable to statistical theory. However, to introduce and explain the above concepts more clearly, I will start by explaining the case of the uniform probability distribution. At the end of that section, you should have the major concepts nicely under your belt.

THE UNIFORM PROBABILITY DISTRIBUTION

The best way to get everything nice and clear is to work through an example, so let me move back to the situation where I am interested in how long it takes to get from my house to my office in the morning. Through long and (sometimes) painful experience, I know that the time ranges from a best-case scenario of 19 minutes (if I fracture a few laws, the traffic is quiet, there are no roadworks, etc.) up to a realistic maximum of 45 minutes. Now, despite the fact that we divide time up into units like seconds and minutes, this is merely a human construction (like creating grouped frequencies as in earlier chapters of this book), because time is really a continuous variable. So, the random variable x represents my commute time and is a continuous random variable which can assume any value between 19 and 45 minutes. But we can divide that continuous random variable up into 26 one-minute *intervals*, and try to work out the probability that my commute time will be within any one of the intervals.

Now, given that I have no information on any given morning to work out how long the journey will take, I must assume that the probability of a commute time within any given one-minute interval is the same as the probability of its being within any other one-minute interval, as long as the minute interval is contained within the larger interval between 19 and 45 minutes. Because I am making the assumption that every one-minute interval is equally likely, the random variable x can be considered to have a uniform probability distribution. We represent the probability density function that defines the uniform probability distribution for this particular situation as follows:

$$f(x) = \begin{cases} 1/26 & \text{for } 19 \leq x \leq 45 \\ 0 & \text{elsewhere} \end{cases}$$

What does this mean? Well it is basically an instruction that tells you that the probability of x is 1/26 (or 0.038) for any one-minute interval between 19 and 45. You can tell it is a minute interval because the larger interval is divided up into 26 smaller intervals – one per minute. The function also tells you the probability is 0 of getting a time outside the interval between 19 and 45. The most useful thing I can do with this probability function is plot it on a graph so you can see it, which is done in Figure 6.6a.

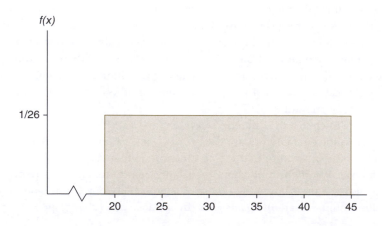

Figure 6.6a
Uniform Probability Density Function for Commute Time

You can see in the figure that the probability of x falling in a given interval is always 1/26 (as shown on the y axis, which represents $f(x)$), as long as the value is a one-minute interval between 19 and 45, and outside that range it is 0. But we can also use this to calculate the probability of the commute time being within any other interval between 19 and 45 minutes. This is easy because the distribution is uniform. So we could work out the probability of the time being between 19 and 25 minutes if we wanted, which we would express as $P(19 \leq x \leq 25)$. We could do this by simply adding up the probabilities of the individual minutes. So there are six minute intervals between 19 and 25, and we know the probability of each minute interval is 1/26 or 0.038. So we just add them up, which means $P(19 \leq x \leq 25) = 6/26 = 0.23$. Simple?

Before I move on to the really important concept, let me just show you the general form of the uniform probability, in Box 6.7.

box 6.7

The Uniform Probability Density Function

$$f(x) = \begin{cases} \dfrac{1}{b-a} & \text{for } a \leq x \leq b \\ 0 & \text{elsewhere} \end{cases}$$

Using Area as a Measure of Probability

This is the vital piece in the puzzle: the use of area in a graph as an indication of the probability of an interval. Look at Figure 6.6b, which is just Figure 6.6a with some added detail. I have shaded now only the area between 19 and 25 under the graph. How large is this area? Well it is quite easy to work out the area of a rectangle, which is the width multiplied by the height. The width of the shaded bit (let's call it the interval) is $25 - 19 = 6$. The height in this case is equal to the probability density function, $f(x)$, which is 1/26. So the area $= 6 \times 1/26 = 6/26 = 0.23$.

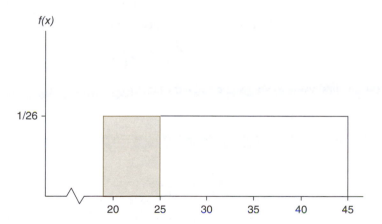

Figure 6.6b
Probability of Commute Time between 19 and 25 Minutes

The sharper eyed among you will have just worked out that the area under the graph is exactly the same as the probability we worked out together above! In fact, this is the case for all continuous random variables: if you know the probability density function $f(x)$ for the random variable x, you can always work out the probability that x takes a value between a lower bound x_1 and an upper bound x_2 (i.e. an interval), by computing the area under the graph of $f(x)$ for the interval x_1 to x_2.

The amazing thing about this is that we can now answer a huge number of questions about my commute time. It would be simple to work out the probability of a commute time of between 39 and 41 minutes. The interval is 41 − 39 = 2. We know that the uniform height of $f(x)$ is 1/26, and therefore $P(39 \leq x \leq 41) = 2 \times 1/26 = 0.077$.

Importantly, $P(19 \leq x \leq 44) = 26 \times 1/26 = 1$. In other words, the total area under the graph equals one. This is a critical property, and it is the same for all continuous probability distributions. It is the same basic idea that the sum of all probabilities must equal 1 for a discrete probability distribution. Also, the probability for all possible intervals must be greater than 0, or, more formally, $f(x) \geq 0$ for all values of x. This is the same principle that all probabilities must be greater than 0 for a discrete probability distribution.

Just to recap, Back to Basics Box 6.1 restates the two critical differences between discrete and continuous probability concepts.

back to basics

Box 6.1

Recall the following two points about continuous probability distributions, and you should be OK:

1. Stop thinking about random variables taking a single value, and instead start thinking about them taking a value within a particular interval. In other words, we are interested in the probability of x assuming a value within a given interval.
2. The probability of x taking a value between an interval x_1 to x_2 can be shown to be the area under the graph of the relevant probability density function between x_1 and x_2.

Of course, condition 2 means that the probability of any single value of x is 0, because the area under one single point of the graph of a continuous distribution is zero.

Just to finish off the discussion of the uniform probability distribution, I will show you how to calculate the expected value:

$$E(x) = \frac{a+b}{2}$$

and the variance (of which the standard deviation is the square root):

$$Var(x) = \frac{(b-a)^2}{12}$$

where a equals the smallest value x can assume and b the largest.

think it over 6.10

Have a go at working out the formula for the mean of the uniform probability function. Now do it for the median. What do you notice about the formulae for $E(x)$, the mean and the median?

THE NORMAL DISTRIBUTION

The most important continuous probability distribution is the normal probability distribution. In fact, this section is probably the most important part of the last two chapters. I guess you could say the whole of the previous discussion has been building up step by step to this section so you can understand it. So do pay attention, and do not waste all of the effort you made in working through the last stuff.

The normal distribution is critically important for many practical applications, since it describes quite well many random variables which occur in nature, and also in business applications. For example, the results of any situation where you take imprecise measurements of many examples of the same object or property – such as test scores, or characteristics of things on an assembly line – can be approximated by the normal distribution. Thus it is vital for situations like quality control or educational testing, for example. It is also used almost constantly in statistical inference, which is what most of the rest of this book is about. Above and Beyond Box 6.1 gives a little bit of background on the normal distribution for those who are interested.

 —— **above and beyond** ■——————————————

Box 6.1   The Normal Distribution

The normal distribution describes a random variable that tends to cluster around the mean, which is around the middle of the range of the variable. For example, take height. The mean height of adult females in England is 5.3 feet, or 162 centimetres. Which is weird because they all seem taller than me, and I am 171 centimetres. Is it the shoes? But I digress. Most women have a height close to the mean (either a bit above or below), and fewer have a height further away from the mean; even fewer have a height which is very far from the mean. So if we were to collect height data on many female subjects, and chart it, we would see a distribution shaped like the one in Figure 6.7a.

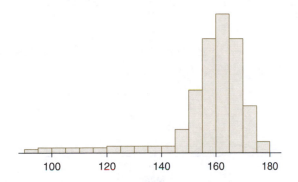

Figure 6.7a

This is a histogram, with height on the x axis, and the height of each bar represents how many subjects of that height there are. You can see that most subjects cluster around the mean, with much fewer further away. This approximates what is called a bell curve, and the more subjects we measure (and the more exact the measurements we use), the closer it gets to the bell curve, an example of which is shown in Figure 6.7b.

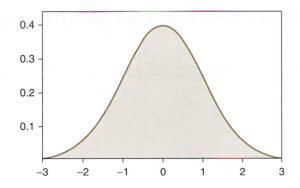

Figure 6.7b

This situation is exactly the same as the example I gave above of the move from discrete to continuous distributions. The normal distribution approximates the occurrence of many variables in nature and science, and is thus used as a very useful model of natural and scientific phenomena.

(Continued)

(Continued)

The normal distribution was first articulated in the 1700s, and is sometimes known as a Gaussian distribution after the great scientist and mathematician Johann Carl Friedrich Gauss (1777–1855), who used it in his early nineteenth-century work on least squares (which you will learn about soon). The terms bell curve and normal distribution go back to around the 1870s, and were simultaneously coined by various scientists and mathematicians, so let's not get into any arguments here.

As a final note, just remember that the normal distribution is a critical part of quantitative analysis and the fields that depend on it, and in this book I can only scratch the surface of the applications and characteristics of it – there is far more depth you could go into if you wanted to.

A typical approximation of the normal distribution is shown in Above and Beyond Box 6.1, but a more accurate one is shown in Figure 6.8. The main difference is that this is a general one (the mean and standard deviation are not specified), but also you will note that the line representing the distribution (the curve) never touches the *x* axis. This is one of the key features of a normal distribution, and basically implies that the random variable *x* that is described by the normal distribution can take on an infinite range around the mean. This is the first thing which should tip you off to the idea that a normal distribution is an *approximation* of many real random variables, but not exactly the same. How close an approximation varies, and whether or not it is close enough, depend on what you need to do.

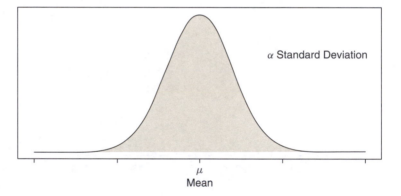

α Standard Deviation

μ
Mean

Figure 6.8
Normal
Distribution

The probability density function for the normal distribution as shown in Box 6.8 is quite a bit more complex than the ones you have seen before, but do not worry too much about it – you will find the calculations you have to do later on pretty simple.

 **box 6.8**

The Normal Probability Density Function

$$f(x) = \frac{1}{\sigma\sqrt{2\pi}}\, e^{-\frac{(x-\mu)^2}{2\sigma^2}}$$

where:

μ = the mean

σ = the standard deviation

$\pi \approx 3.14159$ (i.e. this is pi)

$e \approx 2.71828$ (the exponential function, as mentioned earlier)

The characteristics of the normal distribution are worth noting. First of all, the basic shape of the normal distribution is always the bell-like shape you have just seen, and it has the following constant features:

- The mean is always the highest point of it, and always exactly in the middle, which means it is also the median and mode.

- It is always symmetrical. In other words, the side to the left of the mean is the mirror of the side to the right. Because it is symmetrical, its skewness is zero.

However, the mean and standard deviation can change, and these two values determine the exact shape, as follows:

- The mean can take on any value, positive or negative. This simply means the distribution moves along the *x* axis as appropriate.
- The standard deviation determines how high and pointy or flat and wide the distribution is.

The larger the standard deviation, the flatter the distribution. Figure 6.9 shows three examples of various standard deviations of a normal distribution.

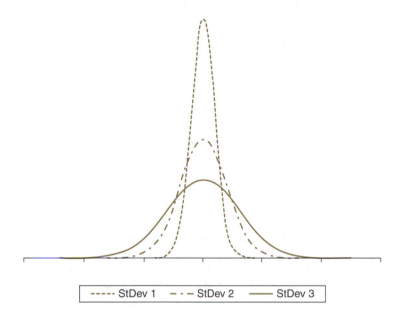

----- StDev 1   – – StDev 2   —— StDev 3

**Figure 6.9
Various
Normal
Distributions**

 think it over 6.11

Thinking about the relationship between the mean and the standard deviation, if the value for the standard deviation is much less than the mean, what does this tell you about the shape of the standard deviation curve? Many textbooks on statistics will tell you that the value for the standard deviation should be much less than the value for the mean. Is there an ideal ratio of standard deviation to the mean?

Probability and the Normal Distribution

The critical reason why I am talking about the normal distribution here is its relationship to probability. Remember: the normal distribution is just like any other continuous probability distribution, in that we can determine the probability of a random variable *x* falling within a specified interval by taking the area under the graph for that interval, just like you did with the uniform distribution above. Since you know the total area under the graph is one, and that the normal probability distribution is symmetrical, you also know that the area under the curve to the left and right of the mean is 0.5. But, because of the specific features of the normal distribution, we also know the area under a number of other very useful intervals:[3]

- 68.3% of the area under the curve of a normal distribution is between one and minus one standard deviation of the mean;

- 95.5% of the area is between two and minus two standard deviations of the mean;
- 99.7% of the area is between three and minus three standard deviations of the mean.

Figure 6.10 shows these percentages graphically. But what does it mean? Think about it for a while: if 68.3% of the area is between plus or minus one standard deviation of the mean, then this means that there is a 0.683 probability that a value of a normally distributed random variable x will fall between plus or minus one standard deviation of the mean. So if we know that the mean female height in the UK is 162 centimetres, we know there is a 0.683 chance that any female I meet will have a height which is between plus or minus one standard deviation of the mean of 162. All I need to know is the standard deviation of height in this case, and I can work out the actual height values corresponding to plus or minus one standard deviation. That is potentially very handy in situations like this.

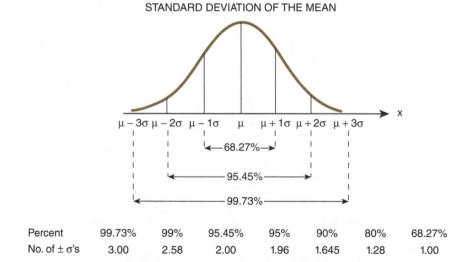

STANDARD DEVIATION OF THE MEAN

Figure 6.10 Percentage of Area Under the Normal Distribution

Percent	99.73%	99%	95.45%	95%	90%	80%	68.27%
No. of ± σ's	3.00	2.58	2.00	1.96	1.645	1.28	1.00

The Standard Normal Distribution

Above, I discussed the normal distribution in general terms, but now I want to be more specific. A random variable with a normal distribution, a mean of 0 and a standard deviation of 1 is considered to have a standard normal distribution. In such a situation, the random variable is usually no longer called x, it is called z. It looks just like the usual bell curve, with a standard deviation of 1, but because of its mean of 0 we can simplify the density function to what is called the standard normal density function, as below:[4]

$$f(z) = \frac{1}{\sqrt{2\pi}} e^{\frac{-z^2}{2}}$$

---

[3] In fact, it's easy to work out the area under the curve for any interval, as you'll do later, but for now let's focus on a few key ones.

[4] If you're wondering how I got this, try replacing the mean and standard deviation in the normal probability density function above with 0 and 1 respectively. You'll find the mean terms σ disappear, and the standard deviation terms, being 1, also cancel out. Try it and see.

Of course, everything else I have discussed so far is the same, so we still compute probabilities by taking the area under the curve for the relevant interval. The advantage of using a standard normal probability distribution is that there are tables of probabilities already computed, which you can use if you have the relevant interval. Let me give you a few examples.

First, consider the situation where you want to find the probability that the random variable z will take a value between 0 and 1, which in the case of the standard normal deviation is the mean and one standard deviation above the mean, or more formally $P(0.00 \leq z \leq 1.00)$. In this case, you should already know the easiest way to get a good answer.

If you do not, look at Figure 6.10 where I show how big the area is under the normal distribution between plus or minus one standard deviations.

Worked it out yet? Well, if 68.3% of the area is between plus or minus one standard deviation of the mean, this means that the area between the mean and one standard deviation is half that, or 34.15,[5] which means that there is a 0.3415 probability of getting a z between the 0 and 1, because 0 is the mean and 1 is the standard deviation for the standard normal distribution.

The table of standard normal probabilities simply shows the area under the graph between the mean and the relevant upper bound of the interval (in this case 1). Since the normal distribution is symmetrical we do not need to worry about whether the interval is above or below the mean. Table 6.4 presents a section of a standard normal distribution table. To find the relevant value for $z = 1.00$, simply read down the left column to get to the first digit (1), and then look for the other digits by reading across the top row (in this case .00). You can see that the exact value for $P(0.00 \leq z \leq 1.00)$ is highlighted, namely 0.3413. So the above value was slightly out, which, as already mentioned in the footnote in the last paragraph, is a rounding error. Using the same idea, you can find any probability value which is in the table, so try finding $P(0.00 \leq z \leq 1.12)$. You should get 0.3686.

Table 6.4 **Section of Normal Distribution Table**

	0.00	0.01	0.02	0.03	0.04	0.05	0.06	0.07	0.08	0.09
0.0	0.0000	0.0040	0.0080	0.0120	0.0160	0.0199	0.0239	0.0279	0.0319	0.0359
0.1	0.0398	0.0438	0.0478	0.0517	0.0557	0.0596	0.0636	0.0675	0.0714	0.0753
0.2	0.0793	0.0832	0.0871	0.0910	0.0948	0.0987	0.1026	0.1064	0.1103	0.1141
0.3	0.1179	0.1217	0.1255	0.1293	0.1331	0.1368	0.1406	0.1443	0.1480	0.1517
0.4	0.1554	0.1591	0.1628	0.1664	0.1700	0.1736	0.1772	0.1808	0.1844	0.1879
0.5	0.1915	0.1950	0.1985	0.2019	0.2054	0.2088	0.2123	0.2157	0.2190	0.2224
0.6	0.2257	0.2291	0.2324	0.2357	0.2389	0.2422	0.2454	0.2486	0.2517	0.2549
0.7	0.2580	0.2611	0.2642	0.2673	0.2704	0.2734	0.2764	0.2794	0.2823	0.2852
0.8	0.2881	0.2910	0.2939	0.2967	0.2995	0.3023	0.3051	0.3078	0.3106	0.3133
0.9	0.3159	0.3186	0.3212	0.3238	0.3264	0.3289	0.3315	0.3340	0.3365	0.3389
1.0	0.3413	0.3438	0.3461	0.3485	0.3508	0.3531	0.3554	0.3577	0.3599	0.3621
1.1	0.3643	0.3665	0.3686	0.3708	0.3729	0.3749	0.3770	0.3790	0.3810	0.3830
1.2	0.3849	0.3869	0.3888	0.3907	0.3925	0.3944	0.3962	0.3980	0.3997	0.4015
1.3	0.4032	0.4049	0.4066	0.4082	0.4099	0.4115	0.4131	0.4147	0.4162	0.4177
1.4	0.4192	0.4207	0.4222	0.4236	0.4251	0.4265	0.4279	0.4292	0.4306	0.4319
1.5	0.4332	0.4345	0.4357	0.4370	0.4382	0.4394	0.4406	0.4418	0.4429	0.4441

---

[5] Note that this is actually a rounded value, and you'll see the more accurate answer soon...

To get the probabilities of the occurrence of z for intervals which span the mean, such as $P(-1.00 \leq z \leq 1.00)$, you simply use your knowledge that the normal distribution is symmetrical. So, all you need to do is double the probability of $P(0.00 \leq z \leq 1.00)$, which gets you 0.6826. You could try this for $P(-1.12 \leq z \leq 1.12)$ as well; what do you get?[6]

The next thing is to learn about how to find z values of at least a certain value, say 1.65, which would be notated $P(z \geq 1.65)$. You can easily find this by looking at the left row of the standard normal distribution table (look for one in the appendix to this book) to find the 1.6 row, and across the top row to find the 0.05 column, and then find the value that corresponds to the intersection of that row and column – which is 0.4505. Again, remember that 0.5 of the area under the normal distribution curve is to the left of the mean of 0, and 0.5 to the right. If 0.4505 is the amount of area between the mean 0 and $z = 1.65$, then it makes sense that the area under that interval of the curve *greater than* 1.65 must be $0.5 - 0.4505 = 0.0495$. Figure 6.11 shows this graphically, to help you confirm what is going on.

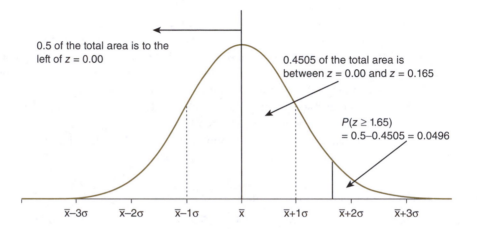

Figure 6.11
Calculating Area Under the Distribution

You can use this kind of knowledge to compute all kinds of probabilities for z intervals. For example, imagine that you want to compute the probability of a z value between 1.12 and 1.65, or $P(1.12 \leq z \leq 1.65)$. Now, you know that there is a 0.3686 probability of a z between 0 and 1.12, and a 0.4505 probability of a z between 0 and 1.65 (they were computed above, remember?) So, there must be a probability of $0.4505 - 0.3686 = 0.0819$ of obtaining a z value between 1.12 and 1.65. This situation is illustrated in Figure 6.12.

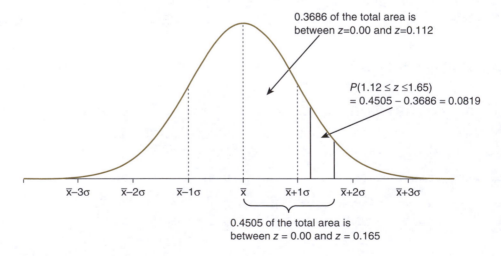

Figure 6.12
Calculating Intervals of Area Under the Distribution

---

[6] The answer is 0.7372 by the way.

As one final example, how about if someone asked you to find a *z* so that the probability of finding a larger *z* was 0.05? If you want to see that in a picture, check out Figure 6.13. Now, this problem is essentially the opposite of what you have been doing so far, where you were given a *z* and asked to compute the area (i.e. the probability). Here, you need to use a table of standard normal probabilities, but differently. Check out Table 6.5, which is another section of the standard normal probability table.

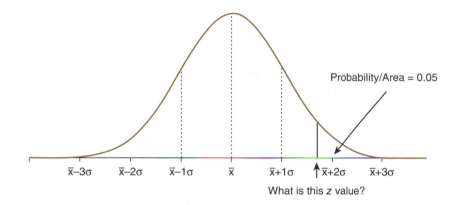

Probability/Area = 0.05

x̄−3σ   x̄−2σ   x̄−1σ   x̄   x̄+1σ   ↑x̄+2σ   x̄+3σ

What is this *z* value?

Figure 6.13
Calculating
z for a Given
Probability

Table 6.5   Segment of standard normal distribution table

z	.	0.4	0.5	0.6
.				
.				
1.4		0.4251	0.4265	0.4279
1.5		0.4382	0.4394	0.4406
1.6		0.4495	0.4505	0.4515
1.7		0.4591	0.4599	0.4608
1.8		0.4671	0.4678	0.4685
.				
.				

Two areas are equally close to 0.4500,
so take the average

Remember that the values in the main body of the table give you the area under the curve of the graph, between the mean (0) and a given value for *z*. So normally we read the *z* off the left column and top row, and get the probability. But here we have already been given the probability value (0.05). The way to work this out is as follows. First, remember that you know that 0.5 of the area under the curve is to the right of the mean (and the left of course). This is an unarguable fact. Second, recall that you are interested in the value for *z* such that the area under the curve to the *right of z* is 0.05. Look at Figure 6.13 again if you are confused. So the area under the graph between the mean and *z* must be 0.5 − 0.05 = 0.45. Looking at the body of the table, you will find that there is no exact 0.45 in there – the closest values are 0.4495 (for *z* of 1.64) and 0.4505 (for *z* of 1.65). Remember, we find the *z* values by reading the left column and the top row. Now, because the value of *z* we were looking for (0.45) falls exactly between the two values we have obtained (i.e. 0.4495 and 0.4505), we can also interpolate the *z* value to the same extent – using exactly halfway between 1.64 and 1.65. Thus, the *z* we are looking for is 1.645, since this is the *z* such that the probability of finding a larger one is 0.05. If you cannot find an exact answer like we have done here, either in the chart or by taking the average of two values, just use the closest one to the exact value.

So, we have learnt quite a bit about the standard normal distribution. One tip, if you are confused at any point with a problem of finding out the area under the curve, is to sketch it out as done in the figures above. As long as you remember that the probability each side of the mean is 0.05, you can always work out a procedure of subtraction and addition to compute the area under any interval of the standard normal distribution.

Using the Standard Normal Distribution

You might be wondering why I spend so long on the standard normal distribution, when clearly it is only one example of the many different normal distributions you could have, with different means and standard deviations, and all of that (remember Figure 6.9). Well, the trick is that we use the standard normal distribution to compute probabilities for *all other normal distributions*. We do this by converting them. In other words, whatever the mean μ or standard deviation σ is for the specific normal distribution we are working with, we answer any questions about probability by first converting it to a standard normal distribution with a mean of 0 and a standard deviation of 1. Then, a table of standard normal probabilities can be used. There is a very simple formula to convert any normally distributed random variable x with a mean μ and standard deviation σ to a standard normal distribution, namely:

$$z = \frac{x - \mu}{\sigma}$$

That is, you convert the normally distributed variable x you are working with to a standard normally distributed variable z. As I already mentioned, doing this allows you to compute probabilities much easier than using the original values of x.

How does this work? Well, imagine you had a random variable x that was normally distributed with $\mu = 15$ and $\sigma = 5$. What is the probability that x falls between 15 and 17? Using the conversion equation above, this is a simple problem. First, see that when $x = 15$, $z = (x - \mu)/\sigma = (15 - 15)/5 = 0$, and when $x = 17$, $z = (x - \mu)/\sigma = (17 - 15)/5 = 0.4$. So, the answer to the question of the probability of x being between 15 and 17 is exactly equivalent to the answer to the question of the probability of z being between 0 and 0.4 on the standard normal distribution. Or another way of expressing it is that the probability you are looking for is the probability that x is between the mean and 0.4 standard deviations greater than the mean.

This can be easily found in a standard normal distribution table, using $z = 0.4$. If you were to do that, you would find the probability is 0.1554. So, the probability that x falls between 15 and 17 is 0.1554.

 **think it over 6.12**

You were shown above how to convert your raw data into standardized data. This involves another calculation step, so why bother with the extra work?

Let's try to cement all of this stuff with an example.

Service Quality at Happy Burger

I like burgers and fast food of all types. When I order a burger, I want it quickly. Happy Burger is also concerned with this issue, and it wishes to develop an advertising campaign that promises that your meal is free if it does not arrive within a certain time frame. However, in order to do this, the management of Happy Burger need to know some probability information about how long it really takes to serve a typical Happy Burger meal. They certainly do not want to set a time so short that it means everyone gets a free meal! Right?

So what Happy Burger does is some research. The management do a two-week study of a sample of its 'restaurants' in different locations (I will talk about sampling later on in the book) and find the mean time it takes for a customer to get a meal is $\mu = 64$ seconds, with a standard deviation of $\sigma = 7$ seconds. Furthermore, the data indicates that it is a fair assumption to assume that the time variable is normally distributed.

The first question we could ask is what is the probability that a meal will take longer than 70 seconds to serve to a customer? Figure 6.14 shows what we are trying to do here. First, let's do the maths. For $x = 70$:

$$z = \frac{x - \mu}{\sigma} = \frac{70 - 64}{7} = \frac{6}{7} = 0.86$$

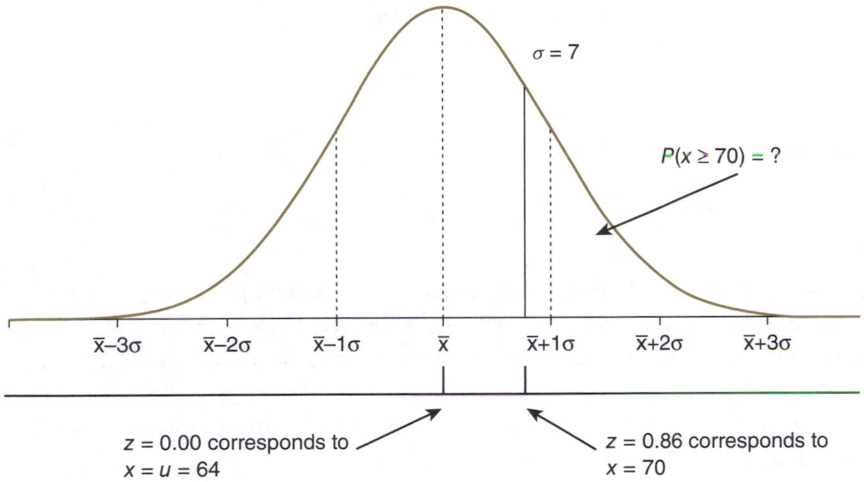

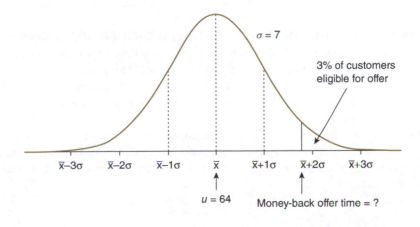

Figure 6.14
Happy Burger Serving Time Distribution

This means that a value of $x = 70$ corresponds to a value of $z = 0.86$ on the standard normal distribution. In other words, 0.86 standard deviations above the mean. This is expressed at the bottom of Figure 6.11. Looking at a table of standard normal probabilities, you can see that the area under the curve between the mean and $z = 0.86$ is 0.3051 – which you can see in Figure 6.11 is the same as the difference between the mean of x and $x = 70$. So, using what you know about the area under the curve of each side of the normal distribution (i.e. there is 0.5 under each side), you just work out $0.500 - 0.3051 = 0.1949$, and conclude that there is about a 19.5% chance that a meal will take longer than 70 seconds to be served.

Imagine that Happy Burger wants to offer a money-back scheme set at a time which means that no more than 3% of meals are refunded. What this means is that we need to find out the time which is far enough from the mean $x = 64$ seconds that there is only a 3% chance of a time greater than this being observed. You can see this graphically in Figure 6.15.

Figure 6.15
Happy Burger Money-off Offer

In essence, this means that 47% of the area under the curve must be between the mean and the – currently unknown – money-back offer time. If you go to the standard normal probability table, looking up 0.4700, you can see that this area is at 1.88 standard deviations from the mean. Well, in fact the area for this is 0.4699, but the difference is so small as to be irrelevant. In other words, $z = 1.88$ is the value of the standard normal random variable which corresponds to the right number of seconds on the Happy Burger time normal distribution. To determine the value of x which corresponds to $z = 1.88$, we just do some simple manipulation of the formula as shown below:

$$z = \frac{x - \mu}{\sigma} = 1.88$$

$$x - \mu = 1.88\sigma$$

$$x = \mu + 1.88\sigma$$

Since we know that $\mu = 64$ and $\sigma = 7$, then:

$$x = 64 + (1.88 \times 7) = 77.16$$

Therefore, if Happy Burger publicizes its money-back offer by saying that any customer whose meal takes longer than 77.16 seconds to be served gets it for free, then approximately 3% of customers will be eligible. Of course, Happy Burger would probably choose a nice round number here, and if you were the Happy Burger management, you would check out the probabilities for $x > 75$ seconds and $x > 80$ seconds too, because these numbers are indeed nice and round. But, as you know now, the exact answer is 77.16.

So, with this example, you can see the critical role that knowledge of a probability distribution can have in giving you information to make a decision. I would like to think that fast-food companies use this kind of method to determine their guarantee, but I wonder if they do (get in touch if you work at one and know they do – I would love to find out). You can imagine how bad things could get if you made the wrong decision based on a gut feeling. Imagine if you set the time at 60 seconds! Well, more than half of customers would get their meals free since 60 is not even the mean!

CONTINUOUS PROBABILITY DISTRIBUTIONS USING SPSS

In this section I will show you how to compute the relevant probability distributions for the Happy Burger example using SPSS. Remember that the time taken for a customer to get a meal was described by a normal distribution with $\mu = 64$ seconds and $\sigma = 7$ seconds. We asked a number of questions about this, including the probability that a meal will take longer than 70 seconds to get served, and this question lends itself nicely to being used as an example of using SPSS.

SPSS uses cumulative probabilities in this case, which means that it gives the probability that the random variable you are interested in will take a value equal to or less than a constant which you specify. In this case, for the Happy Burger question, it is very simple to get SPSS to give us the cumulative probability that the time taken to serve a customer will be equal to or less than 70 seconds (our specified constant is therefore 70). Of course, to get the probability that the time taken to serve the customer is *over* 70 seconds, simply subtract this number from one.

First, SPSS needs some data to work with. Open a blank data sheet, and enter the constant of interest in the top left hand cell (70). SPSS will automatically label this variable VAR001, so you can go into the Variable View and change this to 'x' or whatever makes you happy. After you have done that, your SPSS sheet should look like Figure 6.16.

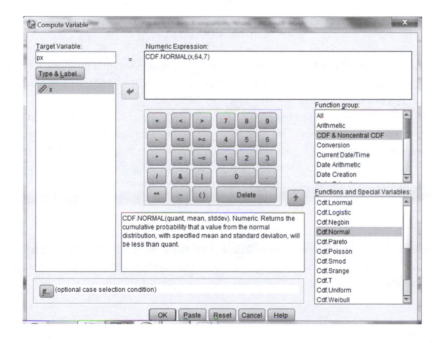

Figure 6.16

The next thing you need to do is give SPSS some commands in order to do the sums for you. This is essentially the same as the discrete example, but let's go through it step by step one more time to make sure you are happy with the process. Select Transform → Compute Variable and the Compute window will come up. Now pay attention to the next bit because it could be rather complex. First, give your new variable a name, like 'px' (indicating that it is the probability of 'x') in the top left hand Target Variable box. Then, look to the right and you will see a white box entitled Function Group. Click on the CDF & Noncentral CDF words, and you will see the things in the box below, entitled Functions and Special Variables, change. If you move down that box, you'll see Cdf.Normal; click on this, and its description will appear to the left in the box. Then click on the arrow to shift the function up into the Compute window at the top, and you will see something like CDF.NORMAL(?,?,?) appear in the box. This signifies that the Cdf.Normal function has three arguments, each represented by a '?' symbol.

The first argument needs to be the variable x (which you entered as '70' earlier), so replace the first '?' with 'x'. Replace the second with the mean of your distribution, 64, and the third with the standard deviation, 7. It should look like Figure 6.17 when you have done that. Then click on OK and the answer should appear.

Figure 6.17

As you can see, a new variable px gets created with the answer of 0.80. Subtract this from 1 and you get 0.2, which is the same as the answer you created by hand, rounded.

SPSS can of course also compute inverse probabilities, which would match the main question in the Happy Burger example, which is the time that Happy Burger should set its money-back offer to ensure that no more than 3% of customers get refunded. In this case, rather than enter the mean in the top left cell, you enter the desired probability. Here, the desired probability is 97%, because we are asking SPSS to give us the number of seconds *below which* 97% of customers will get served, which means that 3% of customers will not be served in this time. Make sure the variable name is 'x', and select Transform → Compute Variable to bring up the Compute window again. This time, select Inverse DF from the Function Group box, and then Idf.Normal. Again this has three arguments; make sure that 'x' is the first argument, 64 the second and 7 the third. After clicking on OK you should see the answer appear, 77.17, again the same as your hand-worked answer within rounding differences.

Also, SPSS can compute the results using lots of other continuous probability distributions, so it is just a case of finding the right function and using the right arguments in place.

CONTINUOUS PROBABILITY DISTRIBUTIONS USING EXCEL

Excel can also compute probabilities in a similar (although in my opinion slightly less intuitive) fashion. So to show the differences, let's do a similar normal distribution problem as above using Excel. The procedure for using other distributions is pretty much the same.

Recall the Happy Burger problem, where the time taken for a customer to get a meal was described by a normal distribution with $\mu = 64$ seconds and $\sigma = 7$ seconds. Now imagine I am interested in the probability that the time for a customer to get a meal will exceed 70 seconds. We can use the NORMDIST function to compute this very easily. To do this we need to insert a function, as explained in Chapter 3. You can do this most easily by clicking inside a cell bar and typing. The general form of this function is NORMDIST(x, μ, σ, cumulative). You can see there are four arguments here, rather than the three in SPSS. The fourth argument tells Excel whether you want cumulative probabilities, and can take the value of TRUE, or FALSE. So to get the cumulative probability that the time taken to serve the customer will exceed 70 seconds, enter the following in any cell of an Excel worksheet:

$$=\text{NORMDIST}(70,64,7,\text{TRUE})$$

You will get the result 0.804317 (depending on your decimal settings). Remember: this is the probability that the meal's serving time will be less than or equal to 70 seconds. If we subtract this from 1 we get the probability that it will exceed 70 seconds, which equals 0.195683.

We can use the NORMINV function to compute the inverse of this (i.e. the x which is associated with a given cumulative probability), just as in the SPSS example. So imagine again you want to find the number of seconds above which only 3% of customers are eligible for the free meal. Remember that this is the same as asking the question of what the number of seconds is below which 97% of customers get served. So to do this, you enter the following in any cell of an Excel worksheet:

$$=\text{NORMINV}(0.97,64,7)$$

Note that there are only three arguments here. You will get the answer of 77.16556, which as you know is the right answer, the amount of time in which only 3% of customers are served their meal, and are thus eligible for a free meal.

SUMMARY

If you have done things in the way I told you to – step by step and carefully – you should have reached the end of this chapter feeling that you have a handle on these concepts. The last two chapters did contain a lot of information, I must admit. But remember: try to think about it as applying formal concepts to the things you do every day, and the things that you will need to do later in life.

In fact, you could look at it like this: the person who best judges the probability of events is going to be the most successful. Much of your life is really about judging probabilities of occurrences. Most of the time we do this by instinct, very quickly. However, as the stakes increase, for example in business, we need to formalize our decisions and base them on information and analysis. You can clearly see this in the Happy Burger example. Imagine how much money you could cost the company if you got that badly wrong!

So with all this in mind, the next chapter will discuss sampling in more detail, and also introduce the idea of estimating intervals and point values from data. These concepts complete the 'toolbox' you will need to begin learning about quantitative analysis methods which are based on statistical inference – the subject of the second part of this book.

 final checklist

You should have covered and understood the following basic content in this chapter:

- ☑ The nature of discrete and continuous random variables.
- ☑ The concept of a probability function, and its associated distribution.
- ☑ Discrete probability distributions, the binomial, Poisson and hypergeometric, and their characteristics and uses.
- ☑ The concept of a continuous distribution.
- ☑ The use of area under a graph as a measure of probability.
- ☑ The normal distribution and its relationship to probability.
- ☑ How to use the standard normal distribution to compute probabilities for real-world events.

EXERCISES

1. You have been invited to play in a game of chance where you could win various amounts of money. In this game of dice you would win £20 if you get a 2, £40 if you get a 4, but you lose £30 if you throw a 6; any other number you do not win or lose.

   Let x be the random variable giving the amount of money won on any toss. The possible winnings when you throw a 1, 2, ..., 6 are $x_1, x_2, ..., x_6 x_1, x_2, ..., x_6$ respectively, while the probabilities of these are $p(x_1)$, $p(x_2), ..., p(x_6) p(x_1), p(x_2), ..., p(x_6)$.
   Calculate how much money you can expect to win.

2. You are working as a marketing analyst for a large company. The company wants to know if a product it is developing, which is aimed at families with at least one boy out of four children, could be a commercial success.

   a. Find the probability that a family with four children has at least one boy.
   b. The company is also interested if the same families have at least one boy and one girl. Find the probability of the same families having at least one boy and one girl.
   c. Would you recommend the company to go ahead with developing the new product?

3. A pharmaceutical company has asked you to determine if a probability of 0.001 is realistic that someone could suffer a bad reaction to one of its new drugs being developed. You have been told to base your calculations on a population size of 2000 people. Assume a Poisson distribution.

   a. Calculate if exactly three people will suffer a bad reaction.
   b. Calculate that more than two people will suffer a bad reaction.

4. You have been asked to check if a quality control procedure for checking saucepans used by a local company is effective. The saucepans are collected into batches of 12 ready for packaging. Suppose an inspector randomly selects 3 of the 12 saucepans in a batch for testing. If the batch contains five defective saucepans, what is the probability that the inspector will find exactly one of the three saucepans defective?

5. The mean contents of a fizzy drink bottle out of a sample of 200 bottles is 0.502 L and the standard deviation is 0.005 L. The company loses money if the contents are not within a tolerance of 0.496 to 0.508 L.

    a. Determine the percentage of loss-making bottles assuming the contents are normally distributed.
    b. In your opinion, is the percentage of loss-making bottles acceptable?
    c. If you answered no to part (b) what should or could be done to improve profitability?

6. You have been engaged by a train company to calculate a probability distribution of the number of passengers arriving at a station during a 15-minute interval. In a previous study, the mean was found to be 10.

    a. State any assumptions you can make.
    b. Select an appropriate probability distribution.
    c. Using Excel, calculate the probability of 0 up to 20 arrivals.
    d. Plot your results.

7. The Happy Burger company is running a promotional campaign. The slogan is: 'Fed up waiting to be FED? Get fed in 2 mins at Happy Burger.'

    a. Using Excel and the normal distribution function, determine if the company is justified in making this statement.
    b. Can the company guarantee to get every order to customers within two minutes?

8. Repeat question 5 using SPSS.

9. Repeat question 6 using SPSS.

 To access additional online resources please visit: **https://study.sagepub.com/leepeters**

The Ballad of Eddie the Easily Distracted: Part 7

Eddie was having a drink at the Student Union bar again, as he liked to do on a Wednesday night, to watch the football, or any excuse really. In fact, this time he was trying to drown his sorrows at his complete misunderstanding of his QUAN101 lecture on sampling. He had struggled with the idea of 'randomness' in particular and how to work out whether something was really 'random' or not. And what was the 'population' anyway?

Eddie finished his pint and had an odd thought: 'I wonder how long the average person takes to drink a pint?' He had the idea that he could time various people in the Union as they drank their pints. But would this be an accurate estimate? How should he select the people to time? He couldn't time all of them – that would be impossible. He thought back to the lecture this week, and considered that he could use a random number generator as he was taught in class. But would this be a random sample? Eddie was warming to his task and began to think that it definitely wouldn't be a random sample of the general population, because the people who came to the Union were (a) students and (b) in the Union – which made them more likely to drink at a different rate than other members of the general population. It would also probably not be a random sample of 'pub-goers' because again the student nature of the patrons was likely to make them different to others in the general population. Eddie remembered a term from class: 'This makes them not *independent*,' he thought. But they *would* possibly be a random sample of Student Union bar customers, on a Wednesday night.

Eddie was quite pleased with his thinking there, so pleased he thought he deserved another pint. He ordered one and, as he did, his friends walked in, late as usual. As they got to the bar to order their drinks ('Unlucky to miss out on a round,' Eddie thought slyly), he noticed a bunch of girls, including Esha, walk in. She waved at Eddie as she noticed him. 'Hmm, random,' thought Eddie.

Esha's Story: Part 7

After Esha got home from her quick drink at the Union bar (she'd seen Eddie, who appeared to be somewhat the worse for wear as usual, although perhaps it was just his scruffy outfit – 'the boy really needed cleaning up!' thought Esha) she sat down to work through this confusing stuff on confidence intervals from this week's QUAN101 lecture. She remembered it from school, but it didn't make it easier! The basic idea seemed to be that you needed to allow for the fact that when you took a sample, any numbers you get from it (like a sample mean) might not be the same value as the same thing (e.g. the mean) in the population. In fact, remembering that idea of infinity from last week, the chance of the sample mean being *exactly* the same as the population mean was probably zero! Esha thought she was quite clever there.

Anyway, so you had to give some kind of 'interval' which could tell you the range of values which the population mean (or whatever) was likely to fall into. This reminded Esha of those political polls in last year's election, where they talked about a 'margin for error' of something like plus or minus 5% of the figure they gave for a party's popularity. 'Hang on a minute,' thought Esha with a flash of inspiration, 'that was not right at all! They should have given the level of confidence for that margin of error. Was there a 95% confidence that the population figure was plus or minus 5%? A 90% level? Or something else?' The pollsters could have used any confidence level – and this might change how the results of the poll 'looked' to viewers. All of a sudden, Esha began to realise the truth of the statement about 'lies, damn lies, and statistics'.[1] It was probably time for another coffee.

---

[1] This is a paraphrase of a famous quote which is usually attributed to the British Prime Minister Benjamin Disraeli, who is also famous for inspiring the name of the excellent album by Cream, 'Disraeli Gears' (via a roadie's misunderstanding of the name for gears on racing bikes). The original quote is: 'There are three kinds of lies: lies, damned lies, and statistics.' However, this phrase cannot be found in any of Disraeli's works, and in fact was not popular until after his death! Mark Twain attributed it to Disraeli, but current thinking seems to agree that Sir Charles Dike is the most likely originator.

7

SAMPLING AND INTERVALS

CONTENTS

 learning objectives

The objectives for this chapter are:

- ☑ Learn why we sample, and understand what a sample is.
- ☑ Understand the difference between statistics and parameters.
- ☑ Understand the nature of the simple random sample and how to take one.
- ☑ Learn about the point estimator of a parameter.
- ☑ Understand sampling distributions, and learn how to use them to indicate the probability that a statistic is within a given range of the population parameter.
- ☑ Understand how the sample size relates to the standard error.
- ☑ Learn how to estimate confidence intervals for the sample mean and proportion.
- ☑ Learn how to estimate required sample sizes for given confidence levels for both the sample mean and proportion.

Imagine the situation where you work for a company that makes motorcycle helmets. I know, it is an odd way to start a conversation, and I can guarantee that it is not a great pick-up line either. But anyway, bear with me. So, what do you think the most important characteristic of a motorcycle helmet is? Apart from having a cool design, like flames or skulls or something, on the side, I guess the critical feature is how protective the helmet is. If you fall off your motorcycle, your helmet should protect you, right? So how do we know if a new helmet design is protective or not? We better test it by seeing how much force it takes to break it.

But we cannot do that for every helmet that comes off the line, because that would involve us breaking all our helmets. Now while that is a funny sentence, it is pretty poor business practice, isn't it? So, how about we take a small number of helmets and test *those* to breaking point? That would certainly solve one problem, but are we 'allowed' to say anything about *all* our helmets if we only test *some* of them? To help answer that, let's recap some of the ideas I talked about earlier:

Remember, a population is the set of all the elements of interest to your study, and a sample is a defined subset of that population. So looking at the example above, we are testing a sample of motorcycle helmets. Motorcycle helmet standards are based on the amount of force that the head experiences from a given impact. So, the mean force transmitted to the head of the entire population of helmets is termed a parameter – in fact a parameter is the name given to all numerical characteristics of a population, such as the mean and standard deviation (i.e. the mean of the population is one of many possible parameters).

The main purpose of statistical inference, which is the subject of the second part of this book, and probably lots of your quantitative methods training from now on, is either to estimate the value of, or to test ideas and beliefs (called hypotheses) about, population parameters by using information from a sample. So bringing this back to the helmet example, we could take a smaller sample of helmets, test the mean force transmitted to the head in the sample, and use this sample mean to estimate the value of the corresponding parameter (i.e. the mean) in the population.

The motorcycle helmet example is an obvious one where we need to use a sample, because we would destroy the entire population – and sampling is commonly done in such applications. But there are many other reasons for using a sample. For example, the population may simply be too large and expensive to collect data from, as is the case when we use opinion polls before a political election instead of surveying the whole population. But you need to remember that a sample estimate is just that, an *estimate* of the population. There may be more or less error in this estimate, because we are unable to take data from the whole population. However, if we use rigorous sampling methods, we can provide good estimates of the error.

This chapter will discuss the most basic form of sampling, namely simple random sampling, and also explore how to estimate population parameters from the sample. I will also present the concept of the sampling distribution and how it can be used to judge the accuracy of our sample estimates. Finally, I will show you how to compute intervals around your sample estimates, which allows us to show more accurately how close we think the sample estimate is to the population parameter.

THE SIMPLE RANDOM SAMPLE

I am going to begin by describing a situation which might be quite common in an organizational situation, for example in human resource management. The supplementary data file SALES.sav is an SPSS data file (also in Excel format called SALES.xls) which contains 500 personal profiles of salespeople. It is based on real data I collected, although it is not the exact data. Figure 7.1 is a screenshot of how it looks in IBM SPSS Statistics Software (SPSS).

The data shows three variables, ID, AGE and GEN. The latter two refer to the age of the sales rep and his or her gender (with 1 being male and 2 being female). The 'ID' variable is there to help us deal with the data, which you will see is very handy later on. Briefly, the mean age is 38.2 years, with a variance of 115.7 and a standard deviation of 10.76. The proportion of males in the population is 0.71. You could use the formulae already presented in this book (see Chapter 4), but I just used SPSS, since it would be a major hassle to do this for 500 cases!

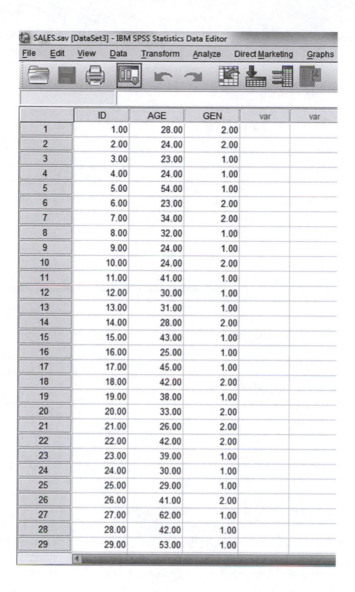

**Figure 7.1
Sales Data
in SPSS**

However, you would be a lucky human resource manager if all of that information on all your salespeople was just sitting on a database. So what if you had to go and collect that data? Getting data on all your salespeople would be pretty difficult – even if it was possible, it would be expensive and probably time consuming. What would be excellent is if we could get an estimate of these population parameters with only a sample of the full sales force. But how confident could the HR manager be with a sample of only, say, 25 salespeople out of the full 500? Furthermore, how best to take the sample?

I will answer these questions over the course of this chapter, beginning with taking the sample itself. The simple random sample is the most basic method of sampling from a population. That said, you should remember that there are many methods of sampling, and you will probably cover those in some depth in later courses, more specialized to your business area (e.g. market research, business psychology, etc.). Sampling is mainly a data collection issue, not an analysis one. However, if we have a simple random sample, we are justified in using all of the techniques in this book, which is not always the case with other samples.[2]

---

[2] Again, this is a data collection issue, so outside the scope of this book. However, please do make sure you pay attention when you learn about it in other courses. For a simple introduction, check out, *Doing Business Research* (yes, yes, I know I'm always plugging it, but it's good! Honest!).

Now, the nature of the simple random sample, and the method for taking it, differs between finite and infinite populations. In the sales force example, we have a finite population – we consider the 500-person sales force to be the population, so let me begin with this example.

Taking a Simple Random Sample from a Finite Population

The most basic definition of a simple random sample of size n from a finite population of size N is that it is a sample selected in such a way that *each possible sample of size n has an equal probability of being selected*. Sometimes, it is easier to understand this as *each element of the population has an equal non-zero probability of being selected*. It basically amounts to the same thing. This definition is quite important and can lead to some misunderstandings about random sampling. Back to Basics Box 7.1 provides some discussion of this, to help those who might be a little confused.

 back to basics

Box 7.1   When Is 'Random' Not Random?

Many people tend to misunderstand the nature of random when it comes to sampling. It seems that we as humans have a kind of woolly idea of what random means. But the mathematical and scientific definition of random is much more strict.

A common misunderstanding about random sampling is that 'choosing a sample element for no particular reason' is random. For example, I have quite commonly spoken to students who say they took a random sample by standing on the street and just selecting people 'at random' (their words) who walk past.

This is not random for many reasons. The most obvious ones revolve around our innate human biases. We may think we are selecting people at random, but we almost never are. We always implicitly bias our choices, either towards people we find attractive or at least not intimidating, or, if we realize we might do that, away from them. So that is definitely not random.

But even if we could get away from that (say we select a random number x and choose every xth person who walks by), it is still not random. This is because in order to fulfil the definition of random, every sample element must have an equal non-zero chance of being selected. If you stand on the street corner, trying to take a random sample of customers, or citizens, then those who do not walk past you at that time have a zero chance of being selected, compared with those that do, who have a much higher one. You could theoretically define your population as 'only those people who were on street x at time y', but then you run into some problems with why you would define the population in that way, and you still would have problems with the implicit bias issue above. But at least that would be an improvement.

In order to select a true random sample from a finite population, we must have two things: first, a list of all elements of the population; and secondly some unbiased way of selecting a sample from this list. In the present case, we do have such a list, the data set of 500 salespeople. There are many ways to select an unbiased random sample from such a list. Perhaps the easiest one is to use random numbers.

You will remember that each salesperson has an ID variable, the leftmost variable on the data sheet in Figure 7.1. You will also remember that I said it would be very useful later on. I was right, and we can use this variable with a random number table, or you could use a random number generator on your calculator, computer or some such. Table 7.1 is a random number table. Each digit has an equal chance of appearing, and you can see that the numbers are in groups of five for ease of reading. It is pretty simple to use this table to select our sample of 25 salespeople. The key thing to remember is that the population size

Table 7.1 Random number table

93900	30880	46497	26203	87086	77878	78946	75741	85355	56515	69592	83477
15262	66792	65319	96295	76809	82150	66128	14194	69996	29148	25135	90291
68264	07785	89223	71469	98172	18062	84950	84286	59719	59978	12317	28743
52906	06976	44765	04840	51174	85614	08853	86018	81082	69333	04581	98836
42629	11249	31948	43293	35816	58247	90954	92831	34084	36884	55042	00567
63992	20603	50770	13385	25539	62519	78137	57842	18726	09517	10585	07381
16994	88154	74673	88559	46902	98431	70401	01377	08449	13790	97768	45834
01636	60787	30216	21930	99904	39425	20862	03108	29812	49702	16589	15926
91359	65060	17399	60383								

N is 500, which has three digits. So we should use groups of three numbers to select our sample. Because it is a random number table, we can start anywhere, and I have chosen to start on the second line of the table, at the third grouping of 6 digits from the left, and move left to right, just because I am contrary. So, moving across that line, the first 10 random three-digit numbers are

$$653\ \ 199\ \ 629\ \ 576\ \ 809\ \ 821\ \ 506\ \ 612\ \ 814\ \ 194$$

These numbers are equally likely to occur, because all the digits are also equally likely. Using these numbers will allow us to select a truly random sample, as long as we have a numbered population list. The first number is 653, but that's above 500, so we don't use it. The next number is 199, so we select salesperson 199 in the data set. The next seven numbers, 629, 576, 809, 821, 506, 612, and 814, are above 500, so we do not use them and we move on, to 194, and so on. We continue to do this until we have our sample of 25.

So what happens if a number appears twice? Well, this depends on our method. Most of the time we are using a method called sampling without replacement, which means that an element cannot be selected twice, so we skip over that number to the next one. We do this so that certain sample elements (any ones selected more than once) do not influence our results. However, in some situations we may wish to sample with replacement, which means that we *could* select elements more than once. However, this is rarely used, and if you are using it, you will know why. So let's assume from now on that all simple random samples in this book (unless mentioned otherwise) are taken by sampling without replacement.

So that is it! Of course, we could also use SPSS and Excel to do this for us, which I will show you later on. But, if you do this, you are relying on the software to use a truly random method. It is not always the case that you can rely on this, as there have been some controversies about how 'random' some software methods are. This may seem pointless nit-picking to you, but when your decisions influence millions of people (e.g. politics) or billions of dollars (e.g. economics and business) then it is not so trivial.

But what about the case of an infinite population? In many cases, it is impossible to get a finite list of the population, because it is either too big or constantly increasing, such as for example the motorcycle helmets coming off the production line, or customers entering a shop. How do we select a random sample without a defined population list? For the case of the infinite sample, a simple random sample is defined as one in which (a) *each element comes from the population* and (b) *each element is selected independently*.

This makes our task a little easier in some ways. However, the trick is the second condition – that each element is independently selected. This makes it hard to justify selecting, say, every fifth person, since the selection of one customer influences the selection of the next (although it probably would not be too bad). An even worse situation is where you have no criteria, and then you are almost always going to fall prey to implicit biases, even if you try not to. You could of course use a random number generator to select which customer to choose; for example, you could use single digits from the above sequence, which would tell you to pick the first customer, then the second after, then the fifth after that, and so on. That would be quite good. There are many ways of doing this, but you must be careful to avoid potential bias as much as possible.

POINT ESTIMATION

So, I have taken a sample of 25 salespeople, from my finite population, and the data set is shown in Table 7.2, which includes the age and gender of my sample. Each sample element is denoted with an x, so x_1 indicates the first salesperson and so on. We can use the data from our sample to estimate the value of the population parameter very simply. For example, if we want to estimate the population mean, we take the sample mean, which is called a sample statistic; similarly, if we want to estimate the population standard deviation, we take the sample standard deviation. Chapter 4 gave you the formulae to do that, and you could go through it with the data from Table 7.2 if you wanted. If you did, you would get the following answers for salesperson age:

The sample mean $\bar{x} = 37.64$ years

The sample standard deviation $s = 11.8$ years

To estimate the population proportion of salesmen is relatively simple: we just take the sample proportion, which will give you an answer of 0.76.

 think it over 7.1

Earlier in this chapter it was stated the proportion of salesmen within the population was 0.71. In the preceding paragraph it was stated that the proportion of salesmen within the sample was 0.76. Explain why these two values are different.

What you are doing above is computing what are known as point estimators of population parameters. Point estimators are statistics which correspond to parameters in the population. As you can see, the point estimates of each population parameter are slightly different from the population value, but frankly they are not too far away. For example, you can see that the population mean was 38.2, while the point estimator from the sample was 37.64. Of course, you should not expect exactly the same values here, because you are using a sample, not the whole population.

Of course, in most cases, we do not have the population parameter to compare the point estimate with – if we did, why waste our time with the sample, other than to demonstrate the concept as I just did above? So if I do not have the population parameter, how do I know whether the point estimator from my sample is close? It is to this task we now turn, and the rest of this chapter will build up the knowledge you need to make this judgement, as a way of putting a capstone on the introductory part of this book.

SAMPLING DISTRIBUTIONS

So, you should be fairly comfortable with the idea of the sample statistics being point estimators of the population parameters. Just to recap, for the sample of 25 salespeople shown in Table 7.2, the sample mean $\bar{x}$ was 37.64. I could take *another* random sample from the 500 salespeople and get something different. In fact, let me do just that; the answer is:

Sample mean $\bar{x} = 38.21$

This one is different, and incidentally much closer to the population parameter of 38.2. We should expect this because a *different sample* will provide a *different estimate*. Now, just extrapolate for a minute. Imagine

Table 7.2 Sample of 25 salespeople

	AGE	GEN
X_1	30	1
X_2	33	2
X_3	55	1
X_4	26	1
X_5	54	1
X_6	56	1
X_7	22	1
X_8	24	2
X_9	23	1
X_{10}	42	1
X_{11}	33	2
X_{12}	44	1
X_{13}	26	1
X_{14}	27	2
X_{15}	45	2
X_{16}	54	1
X_{17}	33	1
X_{18}	31	1
X_{19}	39	1
X_{20}	54	1
X_{21}	22	1
X_{22}	39	1
X_{23}	53	1
X_{24}	45	1
X_{25}	31	2

Note: For gender, '1' = male and '2' = female.

that I took not just one sample of 25 salespeople from the population of 500, but 500. So I would get 500 different values for the sample mean.

Before we go further, let me just make it clear that each time you take a sample from the population, you take it from the entire population, not the part that is left from the first sample. So after I take my first sample of 25 from 500, I take the second sample from the same 500.

think it over 7.2

Why should subsequent samples be taken from the entire population rather than from the remainder after taking a sample?

I could of course tabulate the results of my 500 samples, each time taking the sample mean. Table 7.3 presents a segment of this. From there, I could create a frequency distribution, and relative frequency distribution (Table 7.4), of how often each value of the sample statistic occurred, and then I could graph that relative frequency distribution (Figure 7.2), which I have done for you to make a point. Figure 7.2 should look at least somewhat familiar to you, but I will come back to that later.

Table 7.3 Partial table of sample mean ages from 500 random samples of 25 salespeople

Sample number	Sample mean
1	40.4
2	32.1
3	37.3
4	39.8
5	38.1
.	.
.	.
.	.
500	38.9

Table 7.4 Frequency distribution of sample mean ages for 500 random samples of 25 salespeople

Mean age	Frequency	Relative frequency
21-25	3	0.006
26-30	57	0.114
31-35	105	0.21
36-40	119	0.238
41-45	107	0.214
46-50	60	0.12
51-55	32	0.064
56-60	15	0.03
61-65	2	0.004
66-70	0	0

Let me try to explain all of this in terms which I have already used in this book. Remember in Chapter 6 that I defined a random variable as a numerical value which describes the outcome of an experiment? Well, how about we consider the task of selecting a simple random sample as an experiment? Then, the sample mean is a description of the outcome of that experiment. Thus, the sample mean is a random variable, which means it has an expected value (which could be called its mean), a standard deviation and a probability distribution. However, in this case, we call the probability distribution of the sample means the sampling distribution of $\bar{x}$. The sampling distribution is quite handy, because, if we know this, we will know how close a given sample mean is to the population mean.

Figure 7.2 is an approximation of the sampling distribution of $\bar{x}$. To get the actual sampling distribution you would need to take every single possible sample of 25, which is a lot, but the distribution of the 500 samples I did take gives a good idea of it. You can clearly see that it is a bell-shaped curve, which is very similar to a normal distribution, and the largest proportion of the sample means observed were close to the population mean, with far less either a lot higher or lower.

You can of course do exactly the same thing for the sample proportion p, and if you did you would also get a similar bell-shaped curve.

But remember that, in the real world, you only take 1 sample, not 500. So we do not compute the sampling distribution each time. I simply did this to show you, as an example, that you can take many

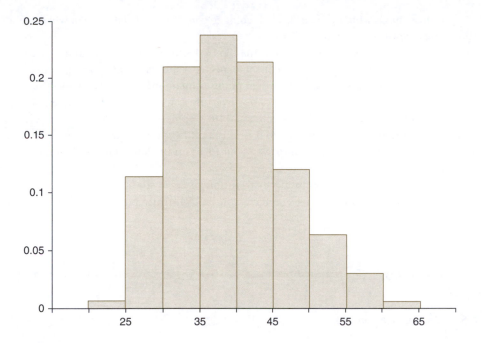

Figure 7.2
Relative
Frequency
Histogram of
Sample Mean
Ages from
500 Random
Samples
of 25
Salespeople

samples, and that each sample will give you a different set of point estimates/statistics. From here on in, I am going to describe the sampling distribution of $\bar{x}$ in some detail, and your ability to understand the rest of this book will greatly depend on how much you understand the rest of this chapter. So maybe you should take some time here.

THE SAMPLING DISTRIBUTION OF $\bar{x}$

OK, so we have established that the sample mean $\bar{x}$ is a random variable, and that we should use the term 'sampling distribution of $\bar{x}$' to refer to its probability distribution. You should remember that if it is a probability function, it has an expected value (which is also the mean), a standard deviation and a particular shape.

Let's begin with the expected value. Think back to Table 7.3, which showed the value of $\bar{x}$ for 500 samples. Of course, those 500 sample means could also have their *own* mean. The mean of the means is the expected value of $\bar{x}$. One interesting thing you may want to remember is that in the case of simple random sampling, the expected value of $\bar{x}$ equals the population mean μ. We would express this mathematically as in Box 7.1.

 box 7.1

The Expected Value of $\bar{x}$

$$E(\bar{x}) = \mu$$

where:

$E(\bar{x})$ = the expected value of $\bar{x}$

μ = the mean of the population

This is one of those things which you just know is going to come in handy later on, or will somehow help other things make sense, so just retain it for now.

Another interesting morsel of information is that Box 7.1 shows that $E(\bar{x})$ is an unbiased estimator of μ. An unbiased estimator is one for which the expected value is equal to the population parameter. It basically means that, while any individual point estimate may not be equal to the population parameter, these errors will cancel themselves out over the course of many estimates, and thus the mean of all the individual point estimates will equal the population parameter. One could say quite a lot about biased and unbiased estimators, but that is a bit beyond the scope of even an Above and Beyond box at this point, and I want you to keep your focus on the key issues. So let's move on to the standard deviation.

The standard deviation of the sampling distribution of $\bar{x}$ is slightly more involved, although not much – it just depends on whether you have a finite or infinite population. Box 7.2 gives both formulae.

 box 7.2

The Standard Deviation of $\bar{x}$

Finite population   Infinite population

$$\sigma_{\bar{x}} = \sqrt{\frac{N-n}{N-1}}\left(\frac{\sigma}{\sqrt{n}}\right) \qquad \sigma_{\bar{x}} = \left(\frac{\sigma}{\sqrt{n}}\right)$$

where:

$\sigma_{\bar{x}}$ = the standard deviation of $\bar{x}$

σ = the standard deviation of the population

n = the sample size

N = the population size

You will note that the finite population formula is slightly more complex, because it contains an extra square root bit. This part:

$$\sqrt{\frac{N-n}{N-1}}$$

is called the finite population correction factor. However, if you have a large finite population and a comparatively small sample, you will find that the result of this is very close to one, which renders it essentially meaningless in terms of its influence on the result. In other words, the result is very close to the result from the infinite population formula. In practical terms, *any time the sample is less than 5% of the finite population size*, you can use the infinite standard deviation formula, and that is what I will be doing in this book (unless I specifically say otherwise).

 think it over 7.3

If I calculated a finite population factor of 1.23, would this be sensible? Explain your answer.

think it over 7.4

A colleague tells you that she has calculated a finite population factor of one. What does this tell you about the size of her sample?

You should also notice that to compute $\sigma_{\bar{x}}$ you will need to know the population standard deviation. Sometimes, we can get confused over the terminology, so generally the sample standard deviation $\sigma_{\bar{x}}$ is termed the standard error of the mean rather than the sample standard deviation. In terms of its usage, you will see soon that it is very useful in working out how far our sample mean is from the population mean.

Finally, let's take a look at the form of the sampling distribution, or in other words what shape the distribution is. While the tools presented above for the expected value and standard deviation work for any population, when we consider the form of the sampling distribution we need to consider whether the population has a normal distribution or not.

If the population has a normal distribution, then the sampling distribution of $\bar{x}$ is also normally distributed, whatever the sample size. When the population does *not* have a normal distribution then we need some more information to help us out. Most important is something called the Central Limit Theorem, which used to give me nightmares when I was a student, but in hindsight is actually quite simple.

The Central Limit Theorem states that, whatever the shape of the population distribution, the sampling distribution of $\bar{x}$ is approximated by a normal distribution as the sample size n becomes large. The key question of course is how large is large? The simple answer to this is that n should be *over 30* for you to safely use the Central Limit Theorem in practice. You should also note that the theorem is only provable with independent observations in the sample. You will note that this is always true for infinite populations, and also for sampling *with replacement* from finite populations. But, in practice, we usually apply the Central Limit Theorem to situations where we have sampled without replacement (as done in the sales example above), as long as the sample size is large. In this case, a *sample size of 25* is close enough for us to assume the theorem holds.

think it over 7.5

If you had a V-shaped distribution and took many samples and then calculated the value of the mean for each sample, you would find that the resulting distribution would become increasing symmetrical (i.e. resemble the normal distribution) about the mean of the original population. This behaviour is the Central Limit Theorem. The constraints are that the random variables must be independent and the samples must come from the same distributions.

above and beyond

Box 7.1 The 'King' of Probability Theory

While it is not necessary for a working knowledge of probability and statistical testing to know anything more about the Central Limit Theorem (CLT) than presented in the main body of the text, it is quite interesting, and some of you may be inspired to dig deeper.

(Continued)

(Continued)

In particular, many of you (as did I) may wonder *why* the distributions of so many measurements of natural variables (e.g. height, exam grades, etc.) and various other things take the form of a normal distribution. In fact, the CLT tells us to expect this. A more general definition of the CLT states that 'the mean of a large number of independent random variables with finite mean and variance will be approximately normally distributed'. The definition you read in the text was a special case of this definition, applied to the context of interest.

So, take a variable like exam grades. Your exam grade is a score, which could be considered as a measurement. That score is actually caused by a large number of other factors, from your ability in the subject of the test, your past behaviour (studying time, etc.), right up to conditions on the day (whether the exam room was too cold or hot, etc.). While you could quibble with how independent some of these are of each other (e.g. is study time dependent on ability?) we can generally consider your exam score as the weighted average of many different, independent, small influences. The CLT therefore tells us to expect that this would usually be approximately normally distributed.

Of course, I could go into more detail about this, and show you how the CLT generalizes to this result, but that is really beyond the scope here. However, as a general rule, the more that your variable of interest is like the average of a lot of small influences with approximately equal effect, the more likely that the distribution of that variable will approach normality.

Using the Sampling Distribution of $\bar{x}$

The brilliant thing about the sampling distribution of $\bar{x}$ is that it allows us to get information about the difference between our sample mean and population mean. As you now know that we can justify considering the sampling distribution of $\bar{x}$ to be normally distributed, you should begin to get an inkling of what kind of information we are interested in, namely *probability information*.

Let's return to the salesperson study above. Imagine that the head of HR wants you to guarantee that the sample mean age is within 2 years of the actual population mean. You know you cannot guarantee this, because you saw in Tables 7.3 and 7.4 that some of the sample means will be much further from the population mean than 2 years. So rather than being able to 'guarantee' a result, we have to rephrase the request into the terms of probability. In other words, what the head of HR is really interested in is *what is the probability that the mean of a simple random sample of 25 salespeople is within 2 years of the population mean?*

It is actually quite simple to answer this question, because you already know the properties of the sampling distribution of $\bar{x}$. In essence, if you look at Figure 7.3 you will see what you are trying to do, and also that it is *almost* exactly the same as what you have already done in Chapter 6. So let's take it step by step.

First, you need to convert the numbers into *z*-scores, to use a standard normal distribution table, so do that as follows:

$$z = \frac{36.2 - 38.2}{2.152} = -0.92$$

It is really important that you know where these numbers came from to get the answer. The one you might not remember is the bottom line of the equation, which was referred to above as the standard error of the mean. Go back up there to work out how to calculate it. Remember, you can use the population standard deviation (10.76) and the sample size (25) to calculate it, and if you are doing the exercises as we go, you have already done it![3]

---

[3] Note, we haven't used the finite population correction factor here, as the sample size of 25 is 5% of the population size of 500. As such, using the FPCF would be virtually meaningless. You can calculate it if you want, though.

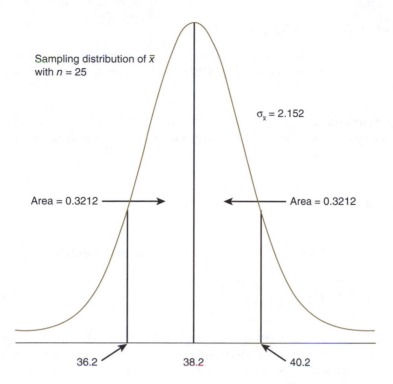

Area = 0.3212 ⟶   ⟵ Area = 0.3212

Sampling distribution of $\bar{x}$ with $n = 25$

$\sigma_{\bar{x}} = 2.152$

36.2   38.2   40.2

Figure 7.3
Sampling Distribution for $\bar{x}$ for a Simple Random Sample of 25 Salespeople and the Probability of $\bar{x}$ Being Within 2 Years of the Population Mean

Anyway, moving on, go to a standard normal distribution table, and you will see that the area under the distribution between $z = 0$ and $z = -0.92 = 0.3212$. We could then do the same calculation for a sample mean 2 years *above* the population mean if we wanted. However, you should remember that the normal distribution is symmetrical, so you will get the same area of 0.3212.

If you add these probabilities together you will get 0.6424, meaning the probability of getting a sample mean within 2 years of the population mean is 0.6424, or 64.24%. Conversely, this also means there is a 0.3576 chance of getting a sample mean outside this range. Are we happy with this? Of course it depends on the importance of accuracy in this estimate. If we are not happy with this chance, we need to reconsider our method.

The first thing we could consider was taking a bigger sample. But what would this change? Think about it for a while. You know that the expected value of the sample mean always equals the population mean whatever the sample size, so that would not change. But what about the standard error of the mean? That is a different story. In fact, as the sample size increases then the standard error of the mean will *decrease*. This is not too difficult to visualize if you look at the place where the sample size appears in the standard error formula:

$$\sigma_{\bar{x}} = \left(\frac{\sigma}{\sqrt{n}} \right)$$

You can see that (and the same applies with the finite population correction factor) as the sample size gets bigger, the denominator of the formula will also increase, which will decrease the size of the standard error. Try it with a sample size of 100 and see for yourself. In other words, larger sample sizes reduce the standard error and increase the probability that our sample statistics are within a given distance from the mean. We could say that we were *more confident* that our statistics were within a given distance from the mean as well, and this terminology will be discussed later in this chapter.

You will also notice that we used the population mean and standard deviation in our calculations. But what if we do not know them? This would seem likely, would it not? In fact it is very common that we do not know these things, and another thing to be discussed later is how we can substitute the sample mean and standard deviation in the formulae.

THE SAMPLING DISTRIBUTION OF p

I am not going to spend much time here, because a lot of the stuff concerning the sampling distribution of the sample proportion p is the same as above in the case of the sample mean. However, there are some important differences.

But first, the similarities. The sample proportion p is a random variable, and the probability distribution of p is called the sampling distribution of p, just as in the case of $\bar{x}$. The expected value of p is denoted $E(p)$ and it equals the population proportion π according to the following formula:

$$E(p) = \pi$$

The standard deviation of p, like that of $\bar{x}$, requires consideration of whether the population is finite or infinite, as follows:

Finite population   Infinite population

$$\sigma_p = \sqrt{\frac{N-n}{N-1}}\sqrt{\frac{\pi(1-\pi)}{n}} \qquad\qquad \sigma_p = \sqrt{\frac{\pi(1-\pi)}{n}}$$

Just like $\bar{x}$ the finite population correction factor need only be used if the sample is greater than 5% of the finite population. In the case of our sales sample, we have 25 salespeople from a population of 500, which is 5%, so we don't really need to use it. However, just to practice, let's use it anyway. In doing so, you can see that it has a negligible influence, being very close to one anyway. Since I made you work through the sample mean formula yourself, I am going to work through this one with you, as follows:

$$\sigma_p = \sqrt{\frac{N-n}{N-1}}\sqrt{\frac{\pi(1-\pi)}{n}} = \sqrt{\frac{500-25}{500-1}}\sqrt{\frac{0.71(1-0.71)}{25}} = 0.086$$

Now, let's look at the differences, and in particular at the form (although it really is not that different). But to do this, let's recap how to find the sample proportion p, remember that:

$$p = \frac{m}{n}$$

where m is the number of elements in the sample that have the property of interest (in this case, being male) and n is the sample size. To talk more formally, if we take a simple random sample from a large population, then the sample proportion m is a binomially distributed random variable, the value of which indicates the number of sample elements with the property of interest to us (e.g. being male in this case).

A handy fact is that the sample size n is a constant value, which means that the binomial probability of m is the same as the probability of m/n, and therefore that the sampling distribution of p (which equals m/n, remember) is a discrete probability distribution.

The next handy fact is that we know that a binomial distribution approximates a normal distribution, if the sample size is large enough. As long as the sample satisfies the following conditions:

$$n\pi \geq 5 \text{ and } n(1-\pi) \geq 5$$

If the sample size is large enough to satisfy the conditions, we can use a normal distribution to approximate the sampling distribution of p, which is handy since we already know how to use a normal distribution to compute the probability of getting a sample value within a certain range.

How does our salesperson problem fare with the conditions above? Well, remember that the population proportion π is 0.71 and our sample is 25. Using the formulae above, $n\pi = 25 \times 0.71 = 17.75$, and $n(1 - \pi) = 25 \times 0.29 = 7.25$, so we are in business and are OK to use the normal approximation of the binomial distribution (phew!).

So let's work through a problem to cement this, and also to reinforce the previous section (since the working is the same). Imagine my HR manager wants to know the probability of getting a sample proportion p which is within 0.1 of the population value of 0.71. Or, in other words, what the probability is of getting a sample proportion between 0.61 and 0.81. We can work through just the same formulae as we did with the sample mean case. But, first, remember that we already worked out the standard error of the sample proportion σ_p above, getting 0.086. We need this for the formulae. First, we need to convert to a z-score:

$$z = \frac{0.61 - 0.71}{0.086} = -1.162$$

Looking at a standard normal distribution table, we see that the area under the distribution between the mean and −1.162 is around 0.377, which is of course the same as we would find if we looked at the area between the standard normal distribution mean and $z = 1.162$, which we would find if we converted the distance between the population proportion 0.71 and the maximum allowed sample proportion of 0.81. So the probability of getting a sample proportion within 0.1 of the population proportion is 0.377 + 0.377 = 0.754.

And just to remind you, the effect of increasing the sample size in this case is just the same as for the sample mean above – it decreases the standard error, increasing the probability of getting a sample proportion within any given interval when compared with a smaller sample.

RANDOM SAMPLING USING EXCEL AND SPSS

There is not much in the earlier part of this chapter where software can help you significantly, apart from doing calculations for things like the mean, but you know how to do that already. One thing that software does do well, though, is selecting random samples, which we saw above could be a bit laborious to do by hand.

Using Excel makes things pretty simple as long as you have a list of the population as an Excel spreadsheet. If you look at the SALES.xls file you will see that there are three columns, labelled ID, AGE and GEN. It is easy to select a random sample from such a file, by creating a new column and filling it with random numbers, which can be created by Excel's handy =RAND() function. In the sales data set you would simply add another column to the right of the data (column D), give it a heading such as RANDOM in cell D1, and then in cell D2 you would type =RAND(), then copy the cell all the way down the column. To select the sample, you simply sort the data set using that column. So in the present case you select a cell in column D, and click Sort & filter, which will then give you the option of selecting Sort smallest to largest. This is the same as the sort ascending option in previous versions of Excel. This will order the data so the smallest random numbers appear at the top of the file. You can then select a simple random sample by counting the number of rows you need and selecting this number of rows from the top of the spreadsheet. So if you want to take 20, you use the first 20 elements of the sorted population.

Using SPSS, things are actually simpler in my opinion. Again, using the sales data in the file SALES.sav, you have three columns of data. From the Data View select Data → Select Cases which will bring up the window at the top of Figure 7.4. Then select the radio button next to Random sample of cases as shown. Then click Sample... which will bring up the next dialog box as shown in the bottom panel of Figure 7.4. To get a sample of 25 from the population of 500, simply specify this in the dialog as is done in the figure. You can delete all of the other cases, filter them out or save a new file, by clicking the relevant radio buttons in Select Cases. I tend to save a new file, not delete.

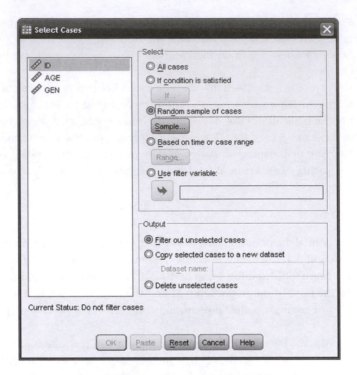

Figure 7.4
SPSS
Steps for
Random
Sampling

ESTIMATING CONFIDENCE INTERVALS

What we are about to do is kind of the inverse of what we just did. Previously, I showed you how to use knowledge of the sample distribution and things like that to estimate the probability of getting a point estimate within a given distance of the population parameter. But surely, what would be more useful would be to tell the boss how close any given estimate was likely to be to the population parameter. A confidence interval is the term we use to indicate the margin of error above and below a point estimate within which we are confident the population parameter lies. This is also known as taking an interval estimate. In doing so we of course need to compute a point estimate, and also to determine the *level of confidence* we want to achieve. I will discuss these points as we move through the chapter, and they will also come up a lot in later chapters, so do pay attention.

The first thing to note is that the way of doing this changes slightly, dependent on whether you know the population standard deviation beforehand. Now, in the real world it is rare to know the real population parameter if you are interested in working out sample statistics. So why worry about this case? For two reasons: first, it is the easiest way for you to learn about the basic concepts; but, as well as this, there are situations where historical or other data can be used to estimate the population standard deviation. In these cases, we consider the population standard deviation as known.

Confidence Intervals for the Sample Mean

Let's begin with the case where you know the population standard deviation and want to estimate a confidence interval for the sample mean. I will continue to work with the salesperson example. An advantage of this is also that we are clearly in a situation where we know the population standard deviation. So let me just recap the information of relevance you already know:

- The population standard deviation is 10.76 years.
- We take a sample of 25 and then calculate a standard error of 2.152 (remember, no need to use the finite population correction factor for this case).
- The sampling distribution is normal (we either consider the population to be normally distributed, or rely on the CLT and a 'largeish' sample to assume the sampling distribution is approximately normal).
- Because we have a simple random sample of the population, we know that the expected value of the sample mean is the population mean.

So, summing this up, all possible values of the sample mean are normally distributed about the population mean. Following on from this, you could use the table of areas below the standard normal distribution to find that 95% of the possible values of any normally distributed random variables are within +1.96 and −1.96 standard deviations of the mean. Using this information we can work out how wide the interval has to be to include 95% of all the sample means. How can we do this? It requires a little manipulation of something you already know: the formula to compute z-scores from intervals in the previous couple of sections. In this case we have the z-score we want (±1.96) but we need to find the interval. A simple manipulation of the formula will show you that the interval:

$$= \pm 1.96 \times \sigma_{\bar{x}} = \pm 1.96 \times 2.152 = \pm 4.218$$

So, this shows that 95% of all of the sample means from samples of 25 will fall between ±4.218 of the sample mean. Figure 7.5 expresses this, and also shows a number of other points which will be addressed subsequently.

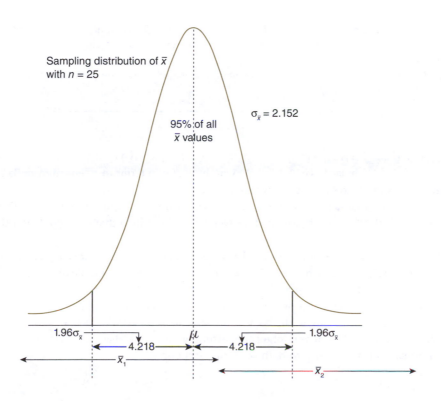

Figure 7.5
Theoretical Sampling Distribution for $\bar{x}$ Simple Random Samples of 25 Salespeople

So how should we use this interval? Figure 7.5 shows that for any sample of 25 from this population, any sample mean $\bar{x}$ within the marked area (between the solid lines on the distribution) will provide an interval of $\bar{x} \pm 4.218$ which contains the population mean. Note that $\bar{x}_1$ does provide such an interval, while $\bar{x}_2$ does not. Therefore, 95% of all sample means fall in this area, and again therefore 95% of all possible intervals of $\bar{x} \pm 4.218$ will include the population mean. Think back to the first sample mean we took from the salesperson population. We got a point estimate of 37.64 if you remember. We can therefore append our interval to this point estimate to get 37.64 ± 4.218, which says we are 95% confident that the population mean falls within 4.218 of 37.64.

Another way of expressing this is by using the upper and lower bounds of the interval. The lower bound is $37.64 - 4.218 = 33.42$ and the upper bound is $37.64 + 4.218 = 41.86$. We can therefore say that we are 95% confident that the population mean is contained within the interval 33.42 to 41.86. To use the 'official' terminology, the interval 33.42 to 41.86 is called the confidence interval, and 0.95 is the confidence coefficient which refers to a confidence level of 95%.

We can put this in a more general form by developing a formula which can be used in any situation where we know the population standard deviation, as in Box 7.3. However, you will notice that the right-most part of the formula in Box 7.3, the standard error of the mean ($\sigma/\sqrt{n}$) does not include the finite population correction factor, which sometimes you will want to include. This is to simplify the formula for the present purpose. If you need to use the finite population factor to construct the standard error, then you will need to do so to construct the confidence interval as well – so do take care.

 box 7.3

Formula for an Interval Estimate Where σ Is Known

$$\bar{x} \pm z_{\frac{\alpha}{2}} \frac{\sigma}{\sqrt{n}}$$

You find α by first deciding on your confidence coefficient (e.g. 0.95 as in the example), and then computing $(1 - \alpha)$, the confidence coefficient. $z_{\alpha/2}$ is the z-score which provides an area of $\alpha/2$ in the upper tail of the standard normal distribution.

Important: This formula assumes that the finite population correction factor is not necessary to compute the standard error $\sigma/\sqrt{n}$.

The description in Box 7.3 is actually quite complex, even though it is a relatively simple formula. In fact you already met that formula above. But to help you think of it in terms of a general formula I will work through another example to show you how simple it is.

Above, we used our first sample mean of 37.64, so let's continue with that figure to show the differences in working with the general formula. However, let's now assume that our population size is 1000 not 500.

Assuming we want to use a 95% confidence level, our confidence coefficient is 0.95, and we find α by working out that $0.95 = (1 - \alpha)$, which makes $\alpha = 0.05$. We now turn to our table of the standard normal distribution, to work out the area for a value of $\alpha/2 = 0.05/2 = 0.025$. So what we want to do is use the table to determine the z-score that provides an area under the graph in the upper tail of the distribution of 0.025. If you do this by looking in the body of the table for $0.5 - 0.025 = 0.475$ you will find that the table shows a z of 1.96 for this. If you forgot the reasoning for this, go back to Chapter 6 where I introduced the normal distribution, and work through that section.

So, using $z = 1.96$, $\bar{x} = 37.64$, $\alpha = 10.76$ and $n = 25$, we would calculate:

$$37.64 \pm 1.96 \frac{10.76}{\sqrt{25}} = 37.64 \pm 4.22$$

You could change various values in this formula to see what happens to the interval. For example, try changing α or the sample size – but remember to consider the finite population issue. In fact, some of you might be able to see why we use the finite population correction factor (FPCF) now. Simply put, the FPCF corrects our results to take account of the fact that the sample is a higher proportion of the population, therefore we are more confident that it can give us an accurate estimate. Logically speaking, this should result in a smaller standard error, and therefore a narrower confidence interval.

When You Do Not Know the Population Standard Deviation

In the situation – usually the case – where you do not know the population standard deviation σ, you are unable to use the standard normal distribution to compute the margin and interval estimate. Instead, you must approximate σ by using the sample standard deviation s, and instead of using the standard normal distribution, you must use something called the t-distribution, which is somewhat similar but with a couple of important differences. Using the t-distribution assumes that the population is normally distributed, and, in fact, it is a family of distributions, not one single distribution.

Each different t-distribution is different depending on its degrees of freedom. Degrees of freedom are a common concept in statistics, which you will come across again and again (as a little exercise, maybe you can find the other times degrees of freedom are talked about in this book...?). In each situation they mean something slightly different. In this case, the higher the degrees of freedom, the closer the t-distribution is to a standard normal distribution, and for the t-distribution the degrees of freedom depend on the sample size – the larger the sample size, the higher the degrees of freedom and the closer to the standard normal distribution until you get to an infinite sample size and the distributions are identical.

You use the t-distribution similarly to the standard normal one, by using tables as before. However, where $z_{0.025}$ indicated the z-score which gave an area of 0.025 in the upper tail of a standard normal distribution (1.96), in the case of the t-distribution we would use $t_{0.025}$. A further difference is that the t-distribution table shows values for the different degrees of freedom. Each row in the table shows the values for a specific t-distribution with given degrees of freedom (noted down the left side). Along the top of the table are the relevant areas under the upper tail. So using a t table is actually easier than a z table for the standard normal distribution!

For example, to find $t_{0.025}$ for five degrees of freedom, we simply go down the left to find 5, and then read across to the 0.025 column, to get 2.571. The same case with 20 degrees of freedom would be 2.086, and you should already know the answer for infinite degrees of freedom: 1.96, the same as a standard normal distribution. In fact, we usually use infinite degrees of freedom for any case where the degrees of freedom are over 100 – although this is admittedly only an approximation.

Interestingly, sometimes the t-distribution is called 'Student's t'. When I was in fact a student, I assumed that this implied it was somehow the simple version, and when I was no longer a student I would have to learn more complex things. Kind of like training wheels on a bike. When I later found out that it was named after its creator, I felt this was a very strange coincidence – that he should be called Student – until much later I found out that the real name of 'Student' was in fact William Sealy Gosset, writing under a fake name.

Anyway, we use the t-distribution almost exactly the same as the standard normal one to compute an interval estimate for the case where the population standard deviation σ is unknown. We simply replace the relevant terms in the formula in Box 7.3, to get the one in Box 7.4.

box 7.4

Formula for an Interval Estimate Where σ Is Unknown

$$\bar{x} \pm t_{\frac{\alpha}{2}} \frac{s}{\sqrt{n}}$$

where s is the sample standard deviation, and you find α by first deciding on your confidence coefficient (e.g. 0.95 as in the example) and then computing $(1 - \alpha)$ as the confidence coefficient. $t_{\alpha/2}$ is the z-score which provides an area of $\alpha/2$ in the upper tail of the t-distribution with $n - 1$ degrees of freedom.

Note that degrees of freedom are $n - 1$. Back to Basics Box 7.2 explains a little more about degrees of freedom, which is a concept that can be baffling to students.

back to basics

Box 7.2 'They May Take Our Lives, But They Will Never Take Our [Degrees of] Freedom!'[4]

Degrees of freedom are an interesting concept, and you will see them again and again in this book. Unfortunately, they are devilishly hard to explain to someone without assuming a certain level of mathematical knowledge, which I am going to try to avoid. One reason that degrees of freedom can be confusing is that the concept is spoken about in two ways which mean the same basic thing: (a) the number of independent pieces of information which are used in the computation of an estimate; and (b) the number of values in the sample which are free to vary in any statistical situation.

First, think about beer, as it sometimes helps you firm up complex concepts...

Anyway, imagine you want to estimate your mean beer consumption in pints over a year. Right now, if you took a sample of any five days, theoretically the values could be anything. But once you begin to use this sample for something, you immediately begin restricting the freedom those values have to vary. So, say you take a sample of one day per week for five weeks, and come up with 0, 7, 10, 3, 5. Because you do not know the population mean, you want to use the sample mean as an estimate in order to calculate the standard deviation of the population. The sample mean is in this case 5, therefore we assume the population mean is also 5. This population parameter must be assumed correct and therefore is fixed at a value of 5. The fact that you have now specified a parameter as constant means that not all of the sample values are independent, or able to vary freely. For example, if you changed four of the sample to 2, 6, 4 and 10, then to maintain the constant mean parameter of 5, the final value *would have to be* 15. So in other words, only $n - 1$ of the sample values are free to vary if we hold one parameter constant, because the remaining value can be determined exactly by using the condition that the mean must equal 5.

This is implemented in the case of the t-distribution, because of the use of the standard deviation for the sample s. If you go back to the formula for this in Chapter 4, you will see that it includes the sum of squares:

$$\sum(x_i - \bar{x})^2$$

which always equals zero, and therefore if this parameter is held constant at zero, only $n - 1$ of the sample values are free to vary, which is why we divide by $(n - 1)$ in the formula and why the number of degrees of freedom for t always equals $n - 1$.

For different types of statistics, degrees of freedom are calculated in a different way, but the same basic principle always applies.

---

[4] What may have occurred if William Wallace (as portrayed in *Braveheart* at least) had been a mathematician.

It is relatively easy to do the calculations required to compute the interval estimate for using a *t*-distribution, as long as you can do the *z*-distribution calculations already detailed. The only real difference is the change to how you get the *t* value, using the degrees of freedom as already shown.

One thing you need to take into account is the sample size, and with this the shape of the population distribution. The basic rule of thumb is that if you are confident the population is normally distributed, the interval provided by the formula in Box 7.4 is exact for any sample size. However, if you cannot assume the population is normally distributed, the interval is only an approximation, and the accuracy of it depends on a couple of factors, namely the shape of the population distribution and the size of the sample. If you have a sample of 30 or more, you can be pretty confident in the normal approximation. However, if you think the population is likely to be very skewed, or contain lots of outliers (remember, these are extreme values, far from the mean), then you should really try to use a sample of more than 50. On the other hand, if you are confident that the sample is pretty symmetrical, then sample sizes as small as 15 can be OK. Anything smaller, and you really need to be confident in your assumption that the population is normal.

Enquiring minds such as yours will doubtless be wondering how you can gain any information about the population from the sample – because in most cases you have none (this is why you use the *t*-distribution mostly). What you can do is look at the sample distribution, by checking it out descriptively. Are there outliers in the sample? Is it highly skewed? If not, then perhaps you have evidence to say the population might be OK and you can use a sample a little less than 30, but only if you are absolutely confident in the normality assumption should you drop below 15.

think it over 7.6

The normal distribution is used a lot in economics, but beware of the unpredictability of the financial markets. If the normal distribution were a perfect or even a good model then financial crashes (e.g. 2008) would be predictable. The message is: be careful with outliers; they may actually mean something!

back to basics

Box 7.3   Making a Decision on What Procedure to Use

So, in your locker you now have two basic ways of determining confidence intervals for a population mean, but how should you decide which to use?

The first question to ask is whether or not you know the population standard deviation. If yes, then use the *z*-distribution as shown in Box 7.3 and be done with it.

If not, then you must use the sample standard deviation and the *t*-test. But then you must think about how large a sample you need. If you are very confident that the population is normal, you can use a sample smaller than 15. If you are not confident that the sample is normal, but that it is reasonably symmetrical and does not contain a lot of outliers, then more than 15 but less than 30 is OK. If you suspect that the population is not symmetrical and/or contains outliers, you really must use a sample of 50 or more.

However, remember, as a general rule a larger sample is better whatever the situation.

SAMPLE SIZE DETERMINATION FOR A SPECIFIC MARGIN OF ERROR

If you read carefully above, you would be aware that the sample size can have an impact on how accurate an estimate is, and therefore how large the margin of error is. Up until now we have not really taken this into account other than in a general sense. But if we were being clever, we could actually use the formulae we already have to work out how large the sample must be to give us a certain margin of error. All we need to do is some simple algebraic manipulation of the formula, and therefore this exercise also allows you to practise that.

First, recall the formula from Box 7.3:

$$\bar{x} \pm z_{\frac{\alpha}{2}} \frac{\sigma}{\sqrt{n}}$$

The margin of error is given by the latter term in this expression, and of course you can easily see how the sample size helps determine the margin. In order to create the formula used to compute the required sample size n we do the following, with E representing the margin for error:

$$E = z_{\frac{\alpha}{2}} \frac{\sigma}{\sqrt{n}}$$

We then solve for $\sqrt{n}$ (see Back to Basics Box 7.4) which gives:

$$\sqrt{n} \pm \frac{z_{\frac{\alpha}{2}} \sigma}{E}$$

To get n you then square both sides of that equation to get:

$$n = \frac{\left(z_{\frac{\alpha}{2}}\right)^2 \sigma^2}{E^2}$$

 back to basics

Box 7.4   Recap of Algebraic Manipulation

I remember having trouble remembering how basic algebraic manipulation worked as I moved through my early years of quantitative methods at university (in fact, even up until now I need to check up on it regularly). So here I will go through the steps I used above in some more detail, with a particular focus on the idea of 'solving for...'. However, the first critical aspect of algebra to remember is that whatever you do to one side of an equation must be done to the other side as well.

'Solving for' something basically means manipulating the formula so that something (say 'x') becomes the term on the left hand side, which the formula on the right gives the answer to. It is a basic term in algebra. Consider the basic equation:

$$2x = 10$$

'Solving for x' would involve simply dividing both sides by 2, to give:

$$x = 5$$

It is the same principle above. Solving for $\sqrt{n}$ means manipulating the equation so that $\sqrt{n}$ is on the left hand side. This takes a couple of steps in the present example, so I will go through it step by step. We begin with:

$$E = z_{\frac{\alpha}{2}} \frac{\sigma}{\sqrt{n}}$$

To get $\sqrt{n}$ on the left hand side we first multiple both sides by $\sqrt{n}$ as follows:

$$E\sqrt{n} = z_{\frac{\alpha}{2}}\sigma$$

Then we divide everything by E to get:

$$\sqrt{n} = \frac{z_{\frac{\alpha}{2}}\sigma}{E}$$

Simple! To solve for n you need to square both sides of the equation. This involves squaring every term on the right hand side separately as follows:

$$n = \frac{\left(z_{\frac{\alpha}{2}}\right)^2\sigma^2}{E^2}$$

Once you know the formula, it is a simple procedure to input the values into the formula to come up with a value for n. Remember: first you need to select a confidence coefficient $1 - \alpha$ to determine what $z_{\frac{\alpha}{2}}$ should be (go back to the relevant section in this chapter to work out how to determine z). Usually, we use a 95% confidence level, which works out to a z of 1.96. Then you need to specify the relevant margin of error. The population standard deviation is then used, but what if you do not have it? In practice, we hardly ever have the population standard deviation, but it can be approximated in a number of ways. You could use a pilot study to take a standard deviation, you could use the data from previous studies to compute a value, or you could use 'judgement', which basically translates as a guess. This guess could be based on an estimate provided from the sample data. For example, the range of the population (difference between largest and smallest values in the population) divided by 4.

Working with the Population Proportion

Up until now, I have focused on methods for computing interval estimates and the like for the population mean, but we can do the same thing for the population proportion as well. As is the case with the mean, the population proportion π can be estimated by the sample proportion p plus or minus a margin of error. Again, the sampling distribution of p is critical here, and, remember, it was previously stated that the sampling distribution of p can be approximated by a normal distribution if $n\pi \geq 5$ and $n(1 - \pi) \geq 5$. If this is the case, then you should remember that the mean of the sampling distribution p is in fact the population proportion π, and the standard error of p is:

$$\sigma_p = \sqrt{\frac{\pi(1-\pi)}{n}}$$

If we assume the sampling distribution of p is normal, we can use z to estimate the margin of error in a similar way as before, with the margin of error equal to:

$$z_{\frac{\alpha}{2}}\sigma_p$$

If this is the case, then you should remember that $100(1 - \alpha)\%$ of the intervals generated will actually contain the true population parameter (go back to the beginning of this chapter if you do not understand why; you need to internalize this information before moving to the next chapter).

Unfortunately, some of you would already have realized that you cannot use σ_p because you do not know π. Instead, we substitute p into the formula for margin of error, and we can therefore derive the expression in Box 7.5 for an interval estimate for the population proportion:

box 7.5

Formula for an Interval Estimate of a Population Proportion

$$p \pm z_{\frac{\alpha}{2}}\sqrt{\frac{p(1-p)}{n}}$$

You find α by first deciding on your confidence coefficient (e.g. 0.95 as in the example) and then computing $(1 - \alpha)$ as the confidence coefficient. $z_{\frac{\alpha}{2}}$ is the z-score which provides an area of $\frac{\alpha}{2}$ in the upper tail of the standard normal distribution.

If you can compute the mean interval examples above, you can easily transfer those skills to the proportion formula. It is a similar case to determine the sample size necessary for a given interval size. Essentially all the same logic as used for the mean interval example applies. Begin with the formula for a population proportion interval and let E = the specified margin of error:

$$E = z_{\frac{\alpha}{2}}\sqrt{\frac{p(1-p)}{n}}$$

We can condense some of the steps used in the mean example above (see Back to Basics Box 7.4) and solve for n to get a formula which will provide the sample size necessary for a given margin of error E:

$$n = \frac{\left(z_{\frac{\alpha}{2}}\right)^2 p(1-p)}{E^2}$$

Of course, the flaw in this logic is that we do not know p until we have already selected the sample! Instead, similar to the situation where we do not know the population standard deviation needed to compute the sample size for the margin of error for the mean above, we use an estimate – sometimes called a planning value. There are at least four possible ways of determining the planning value for p, which can be denoted by p^*:

- Use data from a previous sample of the same sort of thing to compute a proportion.
- Use a pilot study for a preliminary sample, and use the proportion from there.
- Use an estimate, or 'educated guess'.
- If all else fails, use a planning value of 0.5.

While using 0.5 for p^* seems on the surface to be completely arbitrary, it actually makes sense. In essence, this will provide the largest possible required sample size for a given margin of error, which guarantees that the sample size will be big enough whatever the actual sample proportion. You can test this by running the formula with various different values for p^*, and comparing the sample size results with that obtained by using 0.5 for p^*.

INTERVAL ESTIMATION USING EXCEL

Excel is actually quite powerful when it comes to this kind of basic statistics, arguably more than SPSS, but it is also a little more complex to use in this case, which is why I have waited until now to demonstrate. So let me use an example. SALESSAMP.xlsx is a sample of 25 salespeople taken from the salesperson data, with only the age variable. Let's assume that we do not know the population standard deviation, which is more common in practice. In estimating the interval, we will compute a number of other statistics by using the descriptive statistics tool. First, select Data → Analysis which should be on the right hand side. A small dialog box will appear in which you can highlight Descriptive Statistics. The whole process will look like the screenshot in the top part of Figure 7.6. When you click on OK you will be brought to another dialog box where you need to specify the data to be used in the Input Range box – in this case use A1:A26, make sure you click the Grouped by Columns button, and tick the check-box Labels in first row. Then specify C1 for the output range, which tells Excel to begin the results in cell C1. Tick Summary statistics, and make sure you tell Excel to give you the required Confidence Level for Mean, in this case 95%. It should look exactly like the bottom part of Figure 7.6.

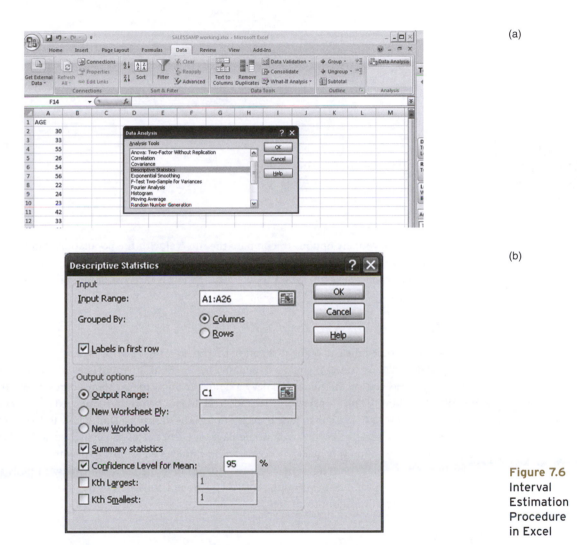

(a)

(b)

Figure 7.6
Interval
Estimation
Procedure
in Excel

Figure 7.7 shows the results of this process. You can see that the mean is 37.64 and the margin of error is ±4.86.

However, if we do know the population standard deviation σ (which is 10.76 for the age variable in this case), and we want to compute a confidence interval for the mean, we do something slightly different. In fact, you can do everything we already did, but once you have the descriptive results, select a cell below and enter the Excel formula =CONFIDENCE(0.05,10.76,25) where the first parameter is $\alpha - 1$, the second is the known population mean, and the third is the sample size. If you do so you will get a result of 4.22, which is the margin of error you can append to the sample mean computed already.

	A	B	C	D	E
1	AGE			AGE	
2	30				
3	33		Mean	37.64	
4	55		Standard Error	2.357173449	
5	26		Median	33	
6	54		Mode	33	
7	56		Standard Deviation	11.78586724	
8	22		Sample Variance	138.9066667	
9	24		Kurtosis	-1.358564741	
10	23		Skewness	0.285123402	
11	42		Range	34	
12	33		Minimum	22	
13	44		Maximum	56	
14	26		Sum	941	
15	27		Count	25	
16	45		Confidence Level(95.0%)	4.864966856	
17	54				
18	33				
19	31				
20	39				
21	54				
22	22				
23	39				
24	53				
25	45				
26	31				

Figure 7.7
Interval
Estimation
Results From
Excel

SPSS does not give you any options to compute the interval with the population standard deviation known. However, it does allow you to compute a confidence interval where it is unknown, when you use the *t*-test function. I will be teaching you this later on, so there is no sense doubling up here.

SUMMARY

OK. So you have reached the end of the first part of this book – as have I![5] Consider this part 1 to be like a set of very basic tools and concepts you need to master before doing anything else. Kind of like in order to play 'Stairway to Heaven' on the guitar, you need to know first how to play some chords, then how to play some scales, then how to link the parts together and so on. In fact, before then you need to know even more basic things like how to hold a guitar, how to pick a note, how to strum a chord, how to keep a rhythm. If you tried to learn the tune before then, you would have no chance at all of playing it, and would probably have given up in frustration very quickly – no matter how much you wanted to play the song.

From here on, we start learning more advanced quantitative methods, starting with basic statistical inference. But, again, I cannot stress enough that if you are not confident in the things in this first part, you need to keep rereading it until you are!

 final checklist

You should have covered and understood the following basic content in this chapter:

- ☑ Why we sample, and what a sample is.
- ☑ The difference between statistics and parameters.
- ☑ The simple random sample, and how to take one.

---

[5] Let me tell you – it took longer than I thought. Phew!

☑ The concept of the point estimator of a parameter.

☑ Sampling distributions, and how to use them to indicate the probability that a statistic is within a given range of the population parameter.

☑ How the sample size relates to the standard error.

☑ How to estimate confidence intervals for the sample mean and proportion.

☑ How to estimate required sample sizes for given confidence levels for both the sample mean and proportion.

EXERCISES

1. Figure 7.8 shows a graph of the results of taking a single observation on a random variable having a continuous uniform distribution.

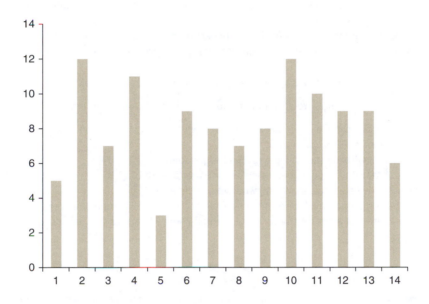

Figure 7.8

What sort of distribution would you expect if we continued to take more samples from the same population and then calculated the mean of the means from each sample?

2. A university business school decides to experiment with a new way of teaching statistics. A class of 99 students is selected where 50 students will be taught with the new way and the remaining 49 taught in the standard way. In the past a test has been administered to similar groups of students and the standard deviation is known to be 15.

    At the end of the trial both groups are given the same test used with previous years. The mean for the group taught in the new way was calculated to be 116 and in the other class it was calculated to be 113.1.

    a. Write down the assumptions you would make.
    b. The head of school has asked you to evaluate the outcome. You need to decide, given the above statistics, if there is sufficient evidence to justify the school investing in the new way of teaching.

3. Eddie and Esha are arguing about the quantity of beer served in the two bars on campus. Eddie says, in his experience, that the Mad Marketeer bar fills the glass to the top whereas the Acid Accountant serves short measures. Esha says the reverse. To show he is right, Eddie decides to do some stats. He assumes the population variances are equal.

a. Write down the hypotheses H_0 and H_1.
b. Use different significance levels to decide who is right.

4. The head of the business school has asked you to determine the living expenses of typical business students. He wants to be 95% confident that the sample mean has a margin of error of £25.00. A similar study has been conducted in previous years and indicates that the standard deviation is approximately £250.

a. Calculate the number of students required.
b. If the margin of error is reduced to £20.00, how many students are now required?

5. The university's computer department are concerned that students are using the same password for all computer access. The department conducted a survey and found that 43% of students were in fact using the same password for everything.

a. In order to be 95% confident in this result, how many students should they interview given a margin of error of 3%?
b. They decided to break down the result into departments. The business school has 350 first-year students. Calculate if there are enough students to allow a margin of error of ±0.05.

6. Using the file SALES.xls, create a spreadsheet containing a random sample of 50 salespeople.

7. Repeat question 6 using SPSS. You can either import the Excel spreadsheet or use the file SALES.sav.

8. a. Using Excel and a sample of 25 sales personal from SALES.xls, create an interval estimation with a confidence level of 99%.
b. Repeat part (a) with another sample of 25 sales personnel.
c. Repeat part (a) with the combined samples for parts (a) and (b).
d. Are the summary statistics in part (c) what you would expect?
e. Look at the confidence level for each analysis and compare the margin of errors. What do you notice about the margin of error for the combined sample? And what does this tell you about using a larger sample?

 To access additional online resources please visit: **https://study.sagepub.com/leepeters**

The Ballad of Eddie the Easily Distracted: Part 8

Eddie was still thinking about how long the average person took to drink a pint. He was beginning to find that if he could translate the ideas from QUAN101 from dry old numbers into things he liked, like beer, he was able to grasp them a bit easier. It wasn't that his mind couldn't handle the concepts, but more that it was easier to get a handle on them if they related to real things he was dealing with right now. Sure, it was interesting to think about business problems he might deal with in the future, but, really, to think about things like production quotas and error rates when he was just starting Uni? Please…

Anyway, Eddie was getting quite interested in this problem of beer, and found he enjoyed watching other people's behaviours and so forth. He even surprised himself with that thought. That evening, he was in the Union bar again. Was the music getting worse each week? Either way, Eddie started to subtly watch how long his friends took to drink their pints. There was Steve, Eddie's flatmate. He liked to show how much of an experienced drinker he was, so took about 5 minutes to drink his first pint and about 25 to drink the next! Fred, on the other hand, was always complaining about money, so he would take around 40 minutes per pint – if he was buying it. Vincent styled himself as some kind of Victorian-era dandy, so refused to drink anything other than single malt whisky. Eddie himself tended to drink a pint in around 20 minutes.

Thinking back to last week's QUAN101 lecture, Eddie realized that his odd group of friends was in no way any kind of useful sample of the normal population. However, it was helpful information all the same. He began to formulate a hypothesis: that the average length of time it took a student to drink a pint – no, a *male* student (he had no information on females, he thought sourly) – was around 20 minutes. But how to test this? And how many pint-drinkers would he have to observe in order to be confident he'd got the right answer? These questions consumed Eddie for the rest of the evening; he even tripped over the kerb on his way home. 'I hope no-one saw that,' he thought sheepishly.

Esha's Story: Part 8

Esha was confused. She'd just returned from a nice night out with her friends in the city, and for some reason she couldn't get to sleep. She was trying to work out the stuff she had to learn for QUAN101 tomorrow. The confidence intervals from last week had been pretty simple once she broke the ideas down, but this week's material on statistical significance was just so much to remember. The formulae were getting tougher too. She found it frustrating to keep forgetting things, but reasoned she'd just have to work harder to get things right. She was also thinking about Eddie, strangely. She'd seen him across the street as she got out of the taxi home, but he totally ignored her. He seemed deep in thought, but as if that was going to be the case! Who knows what was going on there?

One of the things she was finding tough was this idea of statistical power. To her, it seemed to depend on so many different things together! She found that confusing, as she liked things to be cut and dried. As she mulled over the problem, she began to think that the best way to deal with it was to think about the 'worst case' scenario –how far out were you willing to go? So, if you took this worst case as your base, you could work out the rest of the details from there. That seemed most obvious in the description of how to work out the appropriate sample size – it was the experience of the people involved in the situation which helped to make the right decisions. 'Wow, yet again,' Esha thought – nothing is as certain as it seems with statistics, since human judgement again can influence the conclusions! But why didn't more people know that? It seems that as soon as a number was presented, everyone just trusted it to be 'right'! She resolved to be more careful every time she saw some 'statistics' in the newspaper or on the TV.

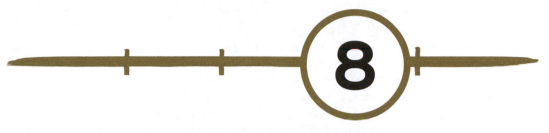

STATISTICAL HYPOTHESIS TESTING

CONTENTS

 learning objectives

Below are the key learning objectives for this chapter:

☑ Understand the relationship between a hypothesis test and a confidence interval.

☑ Learn what null and alternative hypotheses are, and how hypotheses are used in practice.

☑ Learn about what statistical significance testing is, and the key concepts of Type I and Type II errors, as well as the difference between one- and two-tailed testing.

☑ Learn how to test hypotheses about the population mean, whether or not you know the population standard deviation.

☑ Learn the critical value and p-value approaches to testing hypotheses.

(Continued)

(Continued)

☑ Learn how to test hypotheses about the population proportion.

☑ Understand the importance of statistical power and the likelihood of Type II error when using hypothesis tests in the real world.

☑ Understand the relationship between the significance level, the likelihood of Type II error, and the sample size, as well as how to use this relationship to calculate the appropriate sample size for a given level of power.

So here we are at the start of the 'real stuff' at last, right? I suppose some of you have your eyes wide open thinking 'What? I thought that other stuff was the real stuff – it was hard enough!' To some extent you would be right. The previous chapters of the book were indeed vital and important, but they formed a foundation for the things that an analyst usually wants to do in the real world. Certainly, a lot of that information was useful, and a large part of it even finds use on a day-to-day basis in many contexts, but it is usually considered as basic knowledge, which we build on to conduct many interesting analysis tasks.

This chapter shows how we move from the basic description of a sample and how it relates to a population – which was the most advanced thing we did – to how we build up assumptions about what we might find in a sample, and then test those assumptions. Our ideas and assumptions are called hypotheses, and testing hypotheses is the building block of modern scientific research, as well as the quantitative analysis tools you will learn here.[1] I will begin with a discussion of what makes a hypothesis, and ensure to make the differences between a hypothesis and what was done in Chapter 7 clear, because they are very different things – even though the actual method is very similar.

MOVING FROM A CONFIDENCE INTERVAL TO A HYPOTHESIS TEST

Chapter 7 finished with a look in some detail at how to develop confidence intervals for sample statistics. In essence, when you create a confidence interval, you are making a statement about the chances of the population value being within a certain range of values. To take the example of using a sample of 50 to create a 95% confidence interval around the sample mean, you are saying something like 'hey, I took this sample of 50, and there's a 95% probability that the population mean falls within this range'. And what we did was simply look at the data – we did not have any pre-existing ideas about the population. In the real world, this sort of thing is purely *descriptive*. While it can sometimes be useful when the objective of our work is to describe a situation, we are usually concerned with testing *predictions* about the population. In order to do this, we need to make those predictions *before* we collect and analyse the data – but I will deal with this later on.

At its most basic level, a hypothesis is a prediction that something exists in the population. This 'something' can be a particular parameter value like the mean, proportion or variance as will be dealt with in this chapter. Or it can be a prediction that one variable has a certain association with another, as will be covered in many different ways in other chapters. Whatever the case, the hypothesis will then be *tested* by collecting data and then analysing it. We then look at the results of the analysis and see whether or not they support our initial prediction.

In fact, we have done most of the 'technical' things already – we collected data and we learnt some analysis tools such as the confidence interval. But what we did not do is the critical pre-data phase – the hypothesis creation.

---

[1] If you want to know more about how science is done, then I can of course recommend *Doing Business Research*.

So, let me give you some examples of hypotheses which might start you off – though one is a bit of a trick:

- Increased exercise is associated with increased fitness.
- Drinking single-malt whisky is related to the level of intoxication.
- Loud music is related to the level of hearing loss.
- Smoking causes cancer.

You can see that these are basically predictions you are making about the world. First let me deal with the 'trick'. The final hypothesis 'Smoking causes cancer' is a little bit controversial – because of the use of the word 'causes'. It is a good example of where common sense interpretations can differ from more scientific analysis. Using the word causes in this instance might actually be a problem. For instance – what does 'cause' mean? Does it mean that everyone who smokes gets cancer? Virtually everyone in the world can think of someone who smoked and did not get cancer. Furthermore, many people have smoked in the past and stopped – they of course hope that they will not get cancer. But the hypothesis basically states that any smoking will cause cancer. So in that case, once you start, why stop? When we create hypotheses we need to stay away from this type of language, because it leads us to arguments we do not want to have – such as above, about the nature of causality, which is more of a philosophical question than a technical one.

Instead, in most cases, a hypothesis should be simply a *prediction* about something that is occurring in the population. The first three examples express this well. Note that they only talk about whether two variables are related or associated. This sort of question is easily answered with data alone. However, data can never answer the question of whether one variable *causes* another by itself. I will discuss more specific practical applications of hypotheses in the next part of this section, but before I do, I need to cover one final idea, which does tend to cause confusion.

If a hypothesis is a prediction that one variable will have an effect on another, the null hypothesis is the reverse: that *no association or relationship between the two variables exists in the population*. Every hypothesis has a null hypothesis attached to it, although it is not normally stated. For example, the first three examples above have the following null hypotheses associated with them:

- Increased exercise is not associated with increased fitness.
- Drinking single-malt whisky is not related to the level of intoxication.
- Loud music is not related to hearing loss.

The null hypothesis can be a confusing concept for many, but it is based on the scientific principle of falsification and the notion that we can never prove anything beyond doubt. Instead, scientific procedure suggests that we should try to *disprove* our hypotheses, and that if we fail to do so, we have some evidence that they may be correct. So for each prediction, there are really two hypotheses: one is called the null and the other is called either the experimental or alternative hypothesis. Sometimes the alternative is just called the 'hypothesis', but this is not strictly correct. The next section will discuss three specific uses of hypotheses, and this will hopefully clarify a little more about the difference between null and alternative hypotheses.

 think it over 8.1

Hypotheses in real life are rarely as straightforward as the ones shown in textbooks. When I do a hypothesis test, I write my hypotheses out in English. I then refine them until I am left with a concise, unambiguous statement which can be translated into mathematical form. This process can take some time, but will make your life easier when you come to justifying your test results.

USING HYPOTHESES

In many cases, we use hypothesis testing approaches to test whether or not a claim made by someone else is trustworthy, or valid. My favourite example of this is to recall the situation of when I used to walk to school every day (in the snow; uphill both ways; for miles!), I passed a sweet shop that sold acid drops, my favourite. One could buy a bag, using one's lunch money. Short-termism ruled then, so I was never worried about what to eat for lunch. Anyway, the shopkeeper might claim that there was an average of 20 acid drops per bag. In this kind of case, we normally make the assumption that the claim is true unless evidence suggests otherwise. We could test the claim by taking a sample of bags and counting the number of sweets in each bag. We can set up the hypotheses as follows:

The null hypothesis H_0: $\mu = 20$

The alternative hypothesis H_1: $\mu \neq 20$

In other words, we are saying that the mean may be above or below 20 to disprove the null hypothesis. If we were primarily interested in whether the mean was *only* either above *or* below 20, we could change the alternative hypothesis. For example, if I was mainly concerned with whether I was getting stiffed by the shopkeeper who was putting less than 20 in the bag, and I was pretty certain that there would not be *more* than 20 on average, I might restructure the alternative to:

$$H_1: \mu < 20$$

Equally, if I was instead quite sure that the shopkeeper was overfilling the bags, rather than underfilling them, I might restructure my alternative hypothesis to:

$$H_1: \mu > 20$$

This has some important implications for the testing process, which we will come to in the near future. But for now all you need to know is that it is possible.

The thing to remember is that the reason for the hypothesis tests tends to influence how we use them. Above, we were testing the validity of someone's claim about a population parameter. In this case, as you saw, we assumed the claim was true, and therefore the null hypothesis was that the sample evidence was not different from the population parameter. However, in other situations, we assume something else in the first instance.

For example, if we want to do research in a scientific manner we must formulate things differently. Take the idea that we are interested in a new drug which is supposed to reduce the amount of time that an individual has the influenza virus. In order to test this claim we need to do some pretty robust research to make sure we do not get it wrong. If it takes an average of seven days for the patient to recover under normal circumstances, to be of any clinical use the new drug has to reduce this time. In this case we would structure our hypotheses as follows:

$$H_0: \mu \geq 7$$

$$H_1: \mu < 7$$

If your sample does not show that the null can be rejected, you cannot say that the new drug has the required effect. You might need to do more research, or just conclude that the drug is not very good, and move on to other ideas. The difference between this research situation and the claim testing situation is that the rejection of the null hypothesis supports the research *conclusion*, whereas in the validity testing situation acceptance of the null supports the *original claim*. However, both situations are fundamentally the same, in that the null hypothesis essentially represents the status quo,[2] and the alternative requires us to take some action.

think it over 8.2

Translate the following statistical statements into English:

$$H_0: \mu = 20$$

$$H_1: \mu > 20$$

Sometimes, though, we can use hypothesis testing to decide on one action over another. For example, if we were in the motorcycle helmet testing situation outlined at the start of Chapter 7, we would be interested in the mean force transmitted to the head of the wearer at a given impact. So our null hypothesis would be the testing standard force, and we would test an alternative hypothesis of whether or not the force experienced was above or below this.

Why not just test whether the force was less than standard? Certainly, if our helmet fails the standard (i.e. handles less force) we are concerned. However, if we are a smart business we are also concerned very often if we exceed the standard. This is based on the assumption that it costs money to increase the strength, and if we exceed the standard we are spending money we do not have to. So, the results of our test help us to make a decision. If the null hypothesis is supported, we can release the helmets to market. However, if the null is rejected, we have more to think about. Certainly if the sample value is lower, then we need to reject these helmets and rethink our methods. However, if we exceed the standard then we also need to rethink our process because we may be spending too much to produce the helmets. So in this case we take action whether or not the hypothesis is rejected or accepted.

box 8.1

Forms of Hypotheses

There are three basic forms of hypothesis pairs (a pair is a null and alternative), as shown below. Let μ_0 represent the hypothesized value in each case:

$$H_0: \mu = \mu_0$$

$$H_1: \mu \neq \mu_0$$

This expresses that the alternative is a value other than the null, but there is no preference regarding whether it is greater or lesser:

$$H_0: \mu \geq \mu_0 \quad \text{and} \quad H_0: \mu \leq \mu_0$$

$$H_1: \mu < \mu_0 \qquad\qquad H_1: \mu > \mu_0$$

(Continued)

---

[2] Note that I don't mean the actual band Status Quo, as they are getting a little too old for hypothesis testing.

(Continued)

These express that the alternative is specifically either greater or lesser than the null.

The first form is known as a two-tailed test, while the second and third are both known as one-tailed tests. I will explain what the difference is in a short while, but for now just keep these terms in mind.

think it over 8.3

Another way of perhaps remembering the difference between the null and alternative hypotheses is to consider a court of law. In law a defendant is considered innocent until proven guilty. In much the same way the null hypothesis is considered 'true' unless evidence suggests otherwise.

TYPE I AND TYPE II ERRORS IN HYPOTHESIS TESTING

Before moving on, you should stop to think about, and really cement in your mind, the idea that hypotheses are simply *statements about the population*. Either the null *or* the alternative hypothesis can be true, but it is impossible for both to be true. Take a look back at some of the pairs of hypotheses already shown to confirm this to yourself. So to recap the basic testing process: you develop the hypotheses about the population, collect a sample of that population, then analyse the sample to test which hypothesis is supported and which is not. Ideally, this testing of the hypothesis using a sample should lead to the correct conclusion about the population – in other words, if H_0 is accepted then it should be true in the population, and the same goes for H_1. However, if you are thinking carefully, you should realize that this is not always going to be the case. There are plenty of technical issues as to why this is the case, but in the most basic terms it depends on how likely it is that our results from a sample (which we used to test the hypotheses) can be transferred back to the larger population (which is what we are really interested in). There are many factors that can influence this likelihood, but all we need to know right now is that it is never 100% certain that the sample statistics relate directly to the population parameters – so of course this means that we can never be totally certain that our hypothesis test results on the sample would be mirrored in the population. Back to Basics Box 8.1 provides some more information.

back to basics

Box 8.1   Errors of Inference in Hypothesis Testing

Type I and Type II errors are termed errors of inference because this name refers to the main task of the hypothesis test: to infer what is happening in the population from a sample. Remember always: the hypothesis refers to the population, but the test is done on a sample. So, there are two main ways you can get this wrong. Either you can accept H_0 when in the population it is not true, or you could accept H_1 when in the population it is not true. Table 8.1 sets out these different error situations.

If you look back to the earlier examples of hypothesis testing, you can see that such errors can have more or less serious consequences, depending on the circumstances. But I will come to this in due course.

How is it possible to get things wrong? Well, by completely ripping off the great Ronald Fisher, who basically invented this idea, I can explain things to you. Fisher seemed to have a liking for cups of tea,

Table 8.1

		In the population	
		H_0 is true	H_1 is true
Hypothesis test result	**Accept H_0**	Correct!	Type II error
	Reject H_0	Type I error	Correct!

but I prefer beer, so let me go with that. Imagine I claim to you that I can tell whether a pint of beer was from a bottle or a can, just by tasting it. You probably would not believe me to be honest – many people do not. You could test my fanciful claim by giving me some pints of beer, some from bottles and some from cans, and see how many times I get the source right. If you give me one pint, and ask me to identify whether it is from a bottle or can, then I have a 50% chance of getting it right, even if I just guessed. Therefore, even if I got it right, you would not be that confident that I knew what I was doing, would you? However, the more pints you get me to test, the less chance I have of getting it completely right.

Again, to steal from Fisher,[3] what if you gave me six pints? If I know that there are an equal number of bottled and canned pints, and you ask me which are which, there are 20 possible combinations in which those six pints can be arranged. Therefore, I would only guess the right arrangement 1 time out of 20 – a 5% chance of getting it right if I was just guessing. So if I *did* get it right, you have two choices of opinion. Either you think I got lucky (5% chance type of lucky, so pretty lucky), or you accept that I really can tell the difference between canned and bottled beer. And also that I can drink six pints relatively quickly and still stand up!

Fisher suggested exactly this (not the thing about my drinking), and said that only when you are 95% certain that your findings are genuine should you accept them. We continue (not without controversy) to use this concept in statistical inference to this very day, with the concept of *statistical significance*. However, the key point to take from here is that it is *impossible* to be 100% sure that your sample results are true in the population, no matter how rigorous your testing process is. Whenever we are testing a hypothesis, we are always making a compromise between the likelihood of its being true in the population and the chance that we may get this wrong in our sample.

The Level of Significance

Intertwined with the idea of Type I and Type II error is the concept of the level of significance, which is sometimes called statistical significance. To talk definitions, the definition of the level of significance is *the probability of making a Type I error*. This is a very important concept which will be returned to over and over again for the rest of this book, so you might as well get it under control now.

First, look back at Back to Basics Box 8.1 and the beer example. With the six-pint arrangement (three bottled, three canned), there is a 1/20 chance of making a Type I error. In other words, the null hypothesis would be that I cannot tell the difference between bottled and canned beer. However, there is a 1/20 chance that I could simply guess the right order, and therefore you might conclude from the experiment that I could tell the difference even if I was just guessing. So there is a 1/20, or 5%, chance of this occurring. The key thing to remember is that if I do get the right answer, *you can never know whether I got the right order because I guessed correctly through luck, or because I really can tell the difference*. This is pretty much the same as any data analysis situation – you cannot go to a data spreadsheet full of numbers and say 'now come on guys, be honest – do you *really* represent a population result, or are you just guessing?' So we have to work with probabilities. In the six-pint beer example, if I get it right, there is a 95% chance I get it right because I know, and a 5% chance I get it right because I guessed. In other words, a 5% chance of a Type I error. Back to Basics Box 8.2 states the logic behind this in simpler words, just to make sure you get it.

---

[3] For more information see Andy Field and Graham Hole (2003) *How to Design and Report Experiment*. London: SAGE.

 **back to basics**

Box 8.2   Significance Testing Logic

Let's return to the six-pint beer example (which is making me thirsty) for a couple of minutes and restate the decision process you must go through:

1. You set up the six-pint experiment, knowing that if I get it right, then you have two choices – either you accept I can tell the difference, or you say that I got it right by chance (i.e. that I guessed).
2. You test me and I get it right.[4]
3. Now, you know that you *observed* me getting it right, but you are trying to draw a conclusion back to something you cannot actually see – my ability. This is the same as using sample data and analysis (observed) to draw conclusions in a population (you cannot see the population).
4. You know there is a 95% chance of my being right indicating that I can tell the difference (my ability), but a 5% chance of me just being lucky. You know this simply because of the characteristics of the experiment – there are 20 possible orders and I have to guess 1 – therefore there is a 1/20 chance that I would guess correctly purely by chance. Of course, if I *can* tell the difference, then I will not need to guess.
5. You are confident that your experiment was conducted correctly, therefore you are confident that the observation is correct.
6. Should you pick the 95% chance or the 5% chance?

Placed in this context, it seems quite simple that you should choose the highest probability – and conclude that I have the skills to pick between bottled and canned beer. But recall above that I made a point of saying you have to be confident that you conducted your experiment and analysis correctly! If not, then your probabilities are not accurate at all and cannot be trusted!

This is the basic decision process for all hypothesis tests, even though the data collection and analysis can get much more complex. Essentially, you are trying to judge whether to accept that your observed results from your sample, which you can see right in front of you, are likely to be the case in the population, which is impossible to observe directly. You must remember that you are trading off probabilities and that your research must be done correctly or else those probabilities are meaningless.

The level of significance is traditionally denoted by the symbol alpha, or α, which also denotes a number of other things in quantitative analysis, which is a pain. As you might have worked out, 5% is very typically used as α, and you might wonder why. Well, it all goes back to Fisher. In fact, who knows what level he would have come up with if he had been in a different mood? In reality, the researcher specifies the α level for the purposes of the research (although usually 5% is used). In essence, by changing the level of significance you are looking for, you change the probability of making a Type I error. It makes sense that the lower the harm inherent in making a Type I error, the higher the value of α that can be used. However, it is crucial to remember that *you must always choose your significance level before doing your analysis*. Otherwise, you can bias your results. Box 8.2 explains this in more depth.[5]

---

[4] However, note that the logical process given here doesn't really transfer to the example where I get it *wrong*. This is much more controversial, and I will address it as the chapter moves on.

[5] However, it's important that you realize that this basic approach has been subject to criticism for many years from many different scholars. It's a bit complex to go into here, but the essence is that there is no practical difference between, say, only just *passing* a 5% test and only just *failing* it. So why do we set this arbitrary pass/fail level? Similar criticism has been levelled at a number of the ideas that will appear in the next few pages, but this doesn't change the fact that significance testing is a fundamental concept in this context, and you need to understand it before looking at any disagreements with it.

box 8.2

Bias and Significance Tests

It is very important that you understand why you must always make your hypotheses and decide on your significance levels before you conduct your analysis, and thus why you should never change them after looking at the results.

To put it most simply, changing after analysis is cheating and invalidates the entire process of testing hypotheses. Imagine that you decided to test a hypothesis that the population mean was equal to 10, but your analysis and hypothesis test showed that it was not. However, if you *changed* the hypothesis to one of expecting the population mean to be 15, the hypothesis test may support this.[6] Even if you do not understand anything about statistics, you can see this is cheating.

Why? Basically, you are changing your opinion based on a small sample of the data – and you already know that data can be unreliable because sometimes it does not represent the population. This is exactly like picking a winner in a horse race *after the race has finished*! I watched a great film that had a scene about a betting scam involving this, set in a time before mobile phones of course! I wish I could remember what it was called. Send me an email if you know!

If you change the level of significance after your analysis, you change the probability of making a Type I error, and in doing so you make the chance of rejecting the null hypothesis incorrectly greater. However, again you are using the data to *change* your opinion rather than *test* it. This is kind of like the reverse of the horse racing example above. If you place a bet on a horse on the Monday before a race on Saturday, imagine if the betting shop was allowed to change the odds on your bet if it found out all the other horses were feeling sick on Saturday morning. That would be unfair!

In essence, both changing your hypotheses and changing your significance levels after analysis are a dangerous game. It seduces you into believing that you are getting more 'significant' results, but what you are really doing is increasing your chances of getting 'false positives' or, in other words, finding results that are present in the sample but not the population.

This is A Bad Thing.

think it over 8.4

I have been commissioned by a company to produce some statistical data for it to use in an advertising campaign to promote one of its products over a similar product from a rival manufacturer. I have to decide what significance level I should set to ensure the alternative hypothesis (the product being promoted is better than the rival one) and I have come to you for advice. What level would you recommend to ensure I obtain the result I want?

Statistical health warning: Always check the significance level before believing any claims made using statistics!

But what about Type II error? This type of error is basically *the chance of accepting the null hypothesis when it is in fact not true in the population*, and is denoted by the Greek letter beta, β. In practice, most people ignore Type II error, which means that if you accept the null hypothesis, you are not really sure of how confident you can be. Researchers tend to ignore Type II error because it is more complex to establish than Type I error, and also that in many situations where significance testing was established, it was more

---

[6] At this point, if you don't understand how this could happen statistically, it will actually help you get the point of the example.

important to determine the chances of a 'false positive' (Type I error) than a 'false negative' (Type II). Why is this? In most cases, a negative result for a hypothesis test means 'take no action', which leaves you in the current situation. However, a positive result often means 'do something' or 'conclude something', which means take action to change the situation. Many of the contexts in which statistical testing was developed (e.g. medical and psychological research) have the mantra 'do no harm', which means that it makes sense that practitioners would be more cautious about acting than not acting.

Even so, if we do not consider Type II error, we should really never say we accept H_0, because you do not know the chance that you are doing this incorrectly. Instead, you should say you *do not reject H_0*. This basically means: 'hold off judging it, because I don't know the chances I got this wrong'. Of course, this still means you reject H_1. So in actual practice, most people think the outcome is the same.

Type II error is directly associated with the idea of statistical power, which would not be my choice of super-power if I had one. Statistical power is basically the ability your statistical tests have to correctly reject the null hypothesis (i.e. reject it if it is false in the population), and is defined as $1 - \beta$. Power is also an under-appreciated concept in statistics, and one can often detect problems in this regard in published research, even in the best research journals. However, later in this chapter I will explain how to determine the chances of Type II error, and therefore how to determine statistical power.

ONE- AND TWO-TAILED HYPOTHESIS TESTS

Apart from Type I and II error, in my experience the other key concept which trips up many people (from students to established academic researchers) is the idea of one- and two-tailed testing. I will be covering this in more statistical terms throughout the chapter, but I think it would be helpful to bring the main concepts into the open before this. First, remember that when you are using statistical testing methods, you are testing specific predictions about a population (i.e. about the real world), by using a sample of data. In other words, you might test a hypothesis that 'listening to heavy metal music makes an individual more attractive to the opposite sex'. In that case, you have an expectation of what will happen. Equally, if you expected some difference in attractiveness, but you did not know whether that would be an increased or decreased level of attractiveness, you could test the hypothesis that 'listening to heavy metal music could make an individual more or less attractive to the opposite sex'.

The first example is what is called a directional hypothesis in that it predicts a direction of the effect of heavy metal on attractiveness. In this case, we predicted a positive direction, but equally we could predict a negative direction, in which case the hypothesis would read 'listening to heavy metal music makes an individual less attractive to the opposite sex' (more likely in my experience). The second hypothesis in the previous paragraph is known as a non-directional hypothesis because it states that we expect some change in the dependent variable (attractiveness) in response to the independent variable (listening to heavy metal music), but it does not state whether this will be an increase or decrease.

Testing directional hypotheses is done by using what is called a one-tailed test, and testing non-directional hypotheses is done with a two-tailed test. In fact, the calculations are essentially the same, but the interpretations are different. To illustrate this in a very basic form, I am going to set up a very simple experiment to show how it could be used to test these hypotheses. So, imagine that I have two randomly selected groups of male experimental subjects. The first group is told to listen to at least one hour of heavy metal music per day for one week, and the second control group is told to not listen to any heavy metal music at all for that week. Subsequently, we set up a kind of speed-dating situation, where each subject gets two minutes to speak with the same female. At the end of the process, the female writes down a rating from 1 to 10 as to how attractive each male subject was.

There are three basic outcomes possible for this experiment. We could find that the female rater finds the heavy metal listeners more attractive, which is a positive relationship. Secondly, we could find that the female rater finds the heavy metal listeners less attractive, which is a negative relationship. Finally, we could find no difference between the ratings across both groups. The last option is the null hypothesis, but the other two results are determined by the direction of our test statistic, which in this case would be either a positive or negative difference in the mean attractiveness of each group (i.e. the mean for heavy metal listeners minus the mean for non-listeners).

Now, let's look at the interpretation of these outcomes in light of the one-tailed or two-tailed choice. Imagine that your hypothesis is the one-tailed 'listening to heavy metal makes you more attractive'. If there is a positive difference in reality, then we should observe a positive test statistic (i.e. a positive difference between the means). However, as you already know, a positive test statistic does not always mean the hypothesis is supported – remember, you can get it wrong – and we need to take account of possible error. Usually, we use a figure of 0.05 as an amount of Type I error that we are happy with, as already discussed. So how big does our positive test statistic have to be to achieve this? Well, there are plenty of things I will teach you soon to get to this figure in each situation, but, for now, just imagine that your test statistic has to reach a level greater than 1.65 to give you this level of confidence. So if the test statistic is greater than or equal to 1.65, you conclude that you will support your one-tailed hypothesis that listening to heavy metal makes you more attractive. But what if the statistic is actually –2? Of course, you would reject the hypothesis because –2 is not greater than 1.65. However, it is smaller, and it might actually represent the idea that, in the real world, listening to heavy metal makes you *less* attractive! However, because you *already formulated and tested* a one-tailed hypothesis test before collecting the data, you would simply have to accept your null hypothesis, rather than all of a sudden conclude that there may be a negative relationship in the population, despite the data indicating this possibility. Remember, you cannot change things later on.

In order to avoid this, in situations where we are unsure of the direction of relationships in the population (e.g. we are not sure whether listening to heavy metal makes you more or less attractive), we look at both sides of the story, and therefore can take account of both positive and negative test statistics. This is a two-tailed test. However, there is a price to pay. In order to keep the criterion of 0.05 we have to split this across both 'directions'. I will show why this is the case using a normal distribution later on, with some more examples, but for now what you need to know is that the practical upshot of this is that our required test statistic is no longer '1.65' but will be *plus or minus some value greater than 1.65*. For example, if we spread the 0.05 out over both positive and negative ends of possibility, we may end up with ±2 as our required test statistic.

If that was a bit confusing, all you need to remember is that, if you make a specific prediction of direction, and use a one-tailed test, you *always* need a smaller test statistic to find a significant result at the same level as a non-directional test and to support your hypothesis. On the other hand, you have the disadvantage that possible effects in the other direction may be missed. However, recall Box 8.2 – you cannot change your hypotheses after you do your analysis! So if you want to change a one-tailed to a two-tailed test in order to accommodate your results, you should not!

TESTING HYPOTHESES IF THE POPULATION STANDARD DEVIATION IS KNOWN

I will begin by explaining situations where the population standard deviation σ is known, because they are a good basis for all the other things I need to teach you. While it may seem unrealistic for you to know this value, remember that perhaps we can have historical data or other information which helps us ascertain σ, so it is not completely off the wall to think we may know it. It is also important that you realize that the following methods will only return exact answers if the sample is randomly selected from a normally distributed sample, although you can still use them if you have a large enough sample.

 think it over 8.5

What does 'knowing the population standard deviation' mean?

The One-Tailed Situation

To begin with the case where you make a directional prediction in your hypothesis, recall the earlier situation where you might be interested in whether a shopkeeper gives you enough acid drops. The shopkeeper fills the bag using a scoop and claims that a bag contains 20 acid drops. Now, the shopkeeper also claims that given how busy she is, she cannot count the sweets exactly each time. So as long as the population mean number of acid drops in each bag is at least 20, the shopkeeper is legally entitled to claim there are 20 per bag. This claim is easy to check using a one-tailed hypothesis test, focusing on the *lower tail* of the distribution.

First of all, what are the null and alternative hypotheses? If the shopkeeper is right, then the mean number of acid drops in the bag is at least 20 – which is the null hypothesis. If the population mean is less than 20 per bag, then her claim is incorrect. Thus, the hypotheses are:

$$H_0: \mu \geq 20$$

$$H_1: \mu < 20$$

In order to test these hypotheses, we must collect a sample of bags of acid drops and compute the sample mean $\bar{x}$ as an estimate of the population mean μ. If the sample mean is less than 20, then we can doubt the claim of the shopkeeper that the population mean is 20. However, the important question is *how much less than 20* does the sample mean have to be before we have evidence to reject the null hypothesis? Remember that there is always the chance of drawing an incorrect conclusion from the sample and incorrectly rejecting the null hypothesis. In doing so we are committing a Type I error – falsely accusing the shopkeeper of incorrectly labelling her bags of acid drops.[7]

It is our choice to specify α, or the significance level, as the probability of making a Type I error by falsely rejecting the null hypothesis, before we collect the data and do the analysis. In order to judge what level of significance we need, we need to think about the cost of making a Type I error – with higher costs meaning that smaller levels of significance should be chosen. Imagine that if the data suggests the shopkeeper is underfilling her bags, she might get a big fine, or even go to jail! In this case you would probably think 'if the shopkeeper is actually meeting expectations of a $\mu = 20$, then I want a 95% chance of not taking any action'. In doing so, you must accept a 5% chance that you make an error and incorrectly reject H_0, leading to punishment for the shopkeeper.[8] So, in this situation, your $\alpha = 0.05$, and you need to design a hypothesis test where the probability of making a Type 1 error when $\mu = 20$ is 0.05.

 **think it over 8.6**

Going back to the null hypothesis, $H_0: \mu \geq 20$, give an alternative English interpretation.

The above two steps – developing the hypotheses and specifying the significance level – are needed for all hypothesis tests. However, from here, the researcher has to go and carry out the hypothesis test, and this is where things differ according to the situation and method that the research is using. Most importantly,

---

[7] This is a nice example that shows why there has historically been more concern for Type I error than Type II – false accusation (incorrect rejection of the null) is probably more harmful than missing out on a few acid drops (incorrect acceptance of the null).

[8] Remember, you can never have a 100% certainty of getting it right, and if you don't know why, you need to reread the previous two chapters until you do.

the test statistic to be used will be different in each type of test situation. For the present situation we can use the z-test.

In this situation, previous studies of this shop have shown the population standard deviation is known and has a value of $\sigma = 0.5$. Further, we are confident that the population of filling numbers has a normal distribution. Thus, from our prior work in Chapter 7 we know that if the population is normally distributed, then the sampling distribution of $\bar{x}$ will also be normally distributed.

To test our hypothesis, we can take a sample of 25 bags of acid drops and take the mean number of acid drops per bag, $\bar{x}$. We know that the population standard deviation is $\sigma = 2$, and the sample size is 25. We can therefore construct the standard error of the mean as follows:

$$\sigma_{\bar{x}} = \frac{\sigma}{\sqrt{n}} = \frac{2}{\sqrt{25}} = 0.4$$

think it over 8.7

What does this equation tell you about the relationship between the standard error of the mean, the population standard deviation and the sample size?

Following on from this, because the sampling distribution of $\bar{x}$ is normally distributed, we can determine the sampling distribution of our test statistic z as a standard normal distribution:

$$z = \frac{\bar{x} - \mu_0}{\sigma_{\bar{x}}} = \frac{\bar{x} - 20}{0.4}$$

The question you may ask now is why do I place 20 in that formula? Well, the simple answer is that in constructing sampling distributions for hypothesis tests, we assume that the null hypothesis H_0 is satisfied as an equality. In other words, that it takes the exact number we are interested in (in this case the mean needs to be 20), not a range of values such as 'below 20'.

The two steps above can be combined into one handy formula to compute the test statistic z:

$$z = \frac{\bar{x} - \mu_0}{\dfrac{\sigma}{\sqrt{n}}}$$

So, converting to a standard normal distribution makes life easy for us, as you should recall from Chapter 7. To recap, if z for example is -2, this means that the value of $\bar{x}$ is two standard deviations below the mean. This allows us to use a standard normal distribution table to find the lower-tail probability of any z-value. The probability of getting a z two or more standard errors below the mean is $0.5 - 0.4772 = 0.023$. This appears to be highly unlikely if the null hypothesis really is true in the population.

So just to recap the above – which was very detailed in order to lead you carefully through the logic – for hypothesis tests about the population mean, when σ is known, we use the standard normal random variable z as a test statistic to determine whether the sample mean $\bar{x}$ deviates from the hypothesized population mean (expressed as an equality, e.g. $\mu = 20$) enough to justify rejecting H_0.

Of course, the critical question you might ask is: how small must z be to reject H_0? There are a number of different ways to approach that question. The traditional approach is called the critical value approach. However, with the decline of hand calculation and rise of computer software, the p-value approach has become the dominant one in practice. Of course I will deal with both, beginning with the critical value method.

The Critical Value Method

The critical value method is applicable to any test, but in this case we are using a lower-tail test. Therefore, the critical value is that value of the test statistic which corresponds to the level of α in the lower tail of the sampling distribution of that test statistic. A rather wordy way of saying something simple is: *the critical value is the largest value the test statistic can take and still allow rejection of the null hypothesis.*

 **think it over 8.8**

Sketch a normal distribution curve and mark on it where a critical value of 1.645 (assuming a normalized normal distribution) compared with the mean would be. Shade the critical region.

Traditionally, you would be taught the critical value approach in school, using just such an example as we have here with the acid drops, so let me continue with the example. We know that, where σ is known, the sampling distribution for the test statistic z is a standard normal one. We can use the tables of normal distribution values to find this quite easily. To recap our hypothesis development process, we wanted an α of 0.05 because we wanted to be 95% sure that, if we rejected H_0, that we would be right. So, the critical value for z in this case corresponds to an area of $\alpha = 0.05$ in the lower tail. Going to the standard normal table, we look in the body of the table to find this value. Remember, though, that what you need to look for is the value of z which corresponds to $0.5 - 0.05 = 0.450$. You will find if you do this that the closest numbers to 0.450 that you can find are 0.4495, which corresponds to a z of 1.64, and 0.4505, which corresponds to a z of 1.65. Equally between these z-values is the value which you want, $z = 1.645$. Now it is important to remember that you are dealing here with a *lower-tail* test, and therefore you are looking for a z-score *below* the mean, so in fact your critical value for z is −1.645.

To sum this up, for a lower-tail test with α of 0.05, z must be exactly −1.645 or less to reject H_0. Take a look at Figure 8.1 for a representation of this.

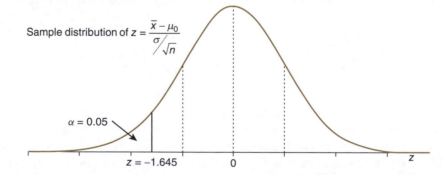

Figure 8.1 Critical Value Approach; α = 0.05

Sample distribution of $z = \dfrac{\bar{x} - \mu_0}{\sigma / \sqrt{n}}$

$\alpha = 0.05$

$z = -1.645$ 0 z

Returning to the acid drops example, if $\bar{x}$ = 19, z = −2.5. Try working through the formula above to get this. Because $z = -2.5 < -1.645$, you can reject H_0 at the 95% level of confidence (or 0.05 level of significance) and conclude that the sweet seller is not filling the bags with enough acid drops to make her claim that a bag contains 20. However, if z does not reach the critical value, this *does not* mean that you automatically *accept* the null, but instead that you have to reserve judgement on this matter. I will deal with this in some more detail in the next section, and later.

Of course, this logic applies to any level of α; it is just the critical value which changes according to what level you set for α.

The *p*-value Method

The critical value method is cool, but is kind of old fashioned now, which as you get older seems to describe more and more things! It is particularly useful for hand calculations, but most of the time you will be working with statistical software, which uses a different approach to giving you the same answer: the *p*-value approach. A *p*-value is a probability value which is computed using the test statistic. It is commonly considered to measure directly the support or lack of support for the null hypothesis, and it is easy to see why this perception could occur. However, it does not really do this at all – at least in the conclusive fashion noted in most texts. In fact, a *p*-value is just one type of evidence that can be used in making a decision about a null hypothesis – as I will show in due course. Either way, it is still a key part of your statistical education, and is the way in which most software calculates significance, so let's learn about how to use it.

The *p*-value is considered as a probability, ranging from 0 to 1. Small *p*-values represent support for the rejection of H_0 and the corresponding acceptance of H_1. On the other hand, larger *p*-values suggest that one should *reserve judgement* regarding the hypotheses – although most statistics texts and statistics users actually mistakenly assume that this means one should automatically accept H_0. Anyway, all will become clear in due course, but for now: how do you calculate a *p*-value? First, you must calculate a test statistic just as in the critical value approach. Using this, you can compute a *p*-value, and then you must interpret the meaning of the *p*-value. The computation of the *p*-value depends on whether you are doing an upper, lower or two-tailed test, as will be shown later. From here, you have to decide whether that *p*-value suggests that you reject the null hypothesis or not. Traditionally, we do this by comparing it with our pre-specified level of significance.

Let me work through the acid drops example using the *p*-value approach, using the same numbers as above in the critical value example. Remember that we took a sample of 25 bags of acid drops and found a sample mean $\bar{x}$ of 19. We know that $\sigma = 2$ as well, and this means we can easily compute z as -2.5.

The *p*-value is the probability that $z \leq -2.5$ in the one-tailed case – which translates as the area under the standard normal distribution to the left of the test statistic.

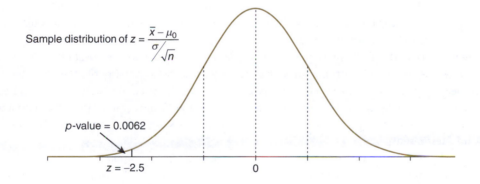

Sample distribution of $z = \dfrac{\bar{x} - \mu_0}{\sigma / \sqrt{n}}$

p-value = 0.0062

$z = -2.5$ 0

Figure 8.2
***p*-value**
Approach;
Acid Drops
Example

Of course, by now you should know that we can find just this probability from the standard normal distribution table. In doing so, you will find that the area between the mean and $z = -2.5$ is 0.4938. The *p*-value is $0.5 - 0.4938 = 0.0062$. Take a look at Figure 8.2 to get this under control.

think it over 8.9

Why is the *p*-value, in this case, calculated as $0.5 - 0.4938$?

A probability of 0.0062, or 0.62%, is rather small, don't you think? What this is saying is that if the population mean really *was* 20 (with $\sigma = 2$), there would be a 0.62% chance of drawing a sample of 25 and getting a mean of 19 in that sample. Right now, this does not give us much confidence that the population mean really is 20, does it?

The traditional hypothesis testing approach then suggests that you should interpret this *p*-value in light of your already-decided level of significance. It was noted above that you selected a value of $\alpha = 0.05$, meaning you are willing to accept a 5% probability of rejecting the null hypothesis incorrectly if it was true as an equality in the population (i.e. $\mu_0 = 20$). The *p*-value you got was 0.0062, much less than your α of 0.05. Thus, you would conclude that, because your *p*-value is less than the pre-selected α, you should reject the null hypothesis. Box 8.3 sums this up in a rule.

 box 8.3

The Rejection Rule for Using *p*-values

Reject H_0 if *p*-value $\leq \alpha$

In this way, the *p*-value approach is similar to the critical value approach in that it relies on a decision rule. Even so, this rule-based approach is not the only way to use a *p*-value. You could simply say that because there was a 0.62% probability of observing $\bar{x} = 19$ if the population mean really was 20, you should conclude this is highly unlikely and prosecute the shopkeeper, without worrying about a significance level.

In fact, while you must be clear that the significance testing approach is the standard way things are done, it has been regularly criticized, with good reason. Towards the end of this section I will introduce the criticisms, but for now just remember that this significance testing logic is entrenched in statistical analysis and unlikely to go away, so please learn to interpret it logically. One thing I will say (again) is that using the 'set values' for α as I have shown seems to me to be pretty much the same as using a critical value. For example, if α is 0.05 and $p = 0.0499$, you reject the null hypothesis, but if $p = 0.501$ you do not reject it. Does this really make sense? To me, not really, because the practical difference between these two *p*-values is virtually nothing, they give virtually the same probability of observing the sample mean if the null were true, yet in each case we make a completely different decision. Personally, I tend to recommend a more 'nuanced' interpretation of *p*-values and significance, rather than the hard and fast 'cut-off' values approach that is standard. I tend to report *p*-values or test statistics in my own work, not significance test results.

However, just remember that rule-based significance testing logic is standard in most situations. But also, be aware that it has developed because people really like 'rules' to make decisions with, rather than necessarily because it is the most useful or informative approach.

Upper and Two-Tailed Tests

Remember, a one-tailed test can be either upper or lower tailed. If you want to do an upper-tail test, the approach is the same as the lower-tail test to compute *z*. However, if you use the critical value approach, you reject H_0 if *z* is greater than or equal to the critical value. If you use the *p*-value approach, you must consider the *p*-value to represent the probability of finding a test statistic as large or larger than the sample value. Thus, to obtain the *p*-value for the upper-tail case, you find the area under the normal curve to the *right* of the *z*-value.

Moving on to two-tailed tests, recall that the basic idea of them is simply that the alternative hypothesis states that the sample mean is *not the same as* the null hypothesis mean; it can be above or below it. More formally:

$$H_0: \mu = \mu_0$$

$$H_1: \mu \neq \mu_0$$

A two-tailed situation can be used either when you have no pre-existing knowledge or expectation of how the alternative hypothesis may differ from the null (just that it will be different), or instead if you actually expect that it really could be above or below. For example, consider the wonderful game of cricket, or if you are confused about it, think of baseball, soccer[9] or almost any ball sport. Anyway, in any ball sport, there are important regulations regarding how large the ball can be. A cricket ball must be 9 inches or 230 millimetres in circumference. So imagine a cricket ball manufacturer, like 'Dukes' or 'Kookaburra', who wants to make sure it is adhering to the laws of the game, and that therefore its balls (ahem) can still be used in official matches. Of course, it might be the case that for a top-level international match there is a measuring device to make sure that the ball is the right size and shape. Indeed, my friend who is a cricket umpire assures me there is such a device. However, if the companies want to sell their balls to the general public and advertise them as 'test-match standard', they must be able to be confident that their balls are typically neither too small nor too large, without relying on a professional umpire being there to check each ball when it comes out of the packet!

This is a classic two-tail quality control situation. As a quality control engineer for Dukes, you could take a sample of 25 balls intended for the market each week, and use two-tailed hypothesis testing to see whether or not the manufacturing controls are still working to produce balls of the right size. The hypotheses are reasonably clear:

$$H_0: \mu = 230$$

$$H_1: \mu \neq 230$$

So, if the sample mean $\bar{x}$ deviates from 230 – either being significantly above or below to cause the rejection of H_0 – then we need to readjust the equipment. On the other hand, if it does not, then we have no evidence to reject the null. Again, to use the significance testing approach, you need to select a level of significance. In this case, I am again willing to accept a 5% chance of Type I error (i.e. a chance of rejecting the null when it is in fact true in the population). So my $\alpha = 0.05$. Again, in this case we know the population standard deviation from many prior tests, which has a value of $\sigma = 8$. So, with a sample of 25 balls, the standard error of $\bar{x}$ can be calculated as:

$$\sigma_{\bar{x}} = \frac{\sigma}{\sqrt{n}} = \frac{8}{\sqrt{25}} = 1.6$$

In this case, we do not know whether or not the population distribution of the ball circumferences is normally distributed. However, we have a large enough sample that the CLT allows us to assume that the sampling distribution of $\bar{x}$ is approximately normal.

If we select a sample of 25 cricket balls, and the sample mean is $\bar{x} = 227$ millimetres, then what conclusion can we draw regarding whether or not the population mean is different from 230 millimetres? We can again use the critical value or *p*-value approach to make this decision.

---

[9] Some of you may think I'm pandering to the US market by using this word instead of 'football'. Not so! In fact, the word soccer is an abbreviation of 'Association Football', as opposed to 'Rugby Football'. So, in fact, 'soccer' is the more traditional name. So there.

The Critical Value Method

The first thing to remember here is that in a two-tailed case, the critical value can occur in both tails of the distribution, upper and lower. In other words, a deviation either above *or* below the null hypothesis could be considered significant, and we do not prefer one over the other. Figure 8.3 shows this visually; note how it is different from Figure 8.1, even though α is the same at 0.05.

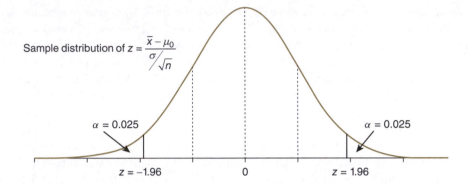

Figure 8.3
Critical Value
Approach;
Two-Tailed
$\alpha = 0.05$

The important thing to note here is that, in order to conduct a two-tailed test, we need to divide α by 2 to get the critical value. More specifically, if $\alpha = 0.05$, then the area in the upper *and* lower tails of the distribution beyond the upper and lower critical values is $\alpha/2 = 0.05/2 = 0.025$. You can go to the normal distribution table to find this, but remember that you need to look for the z-value which corresponds to $0.5 - 0.025 = 0.475$. If you do this, you will see that the relevant z-value is 1.96. Therefore, the critical value for the lower part of the two-tailed test is $-z_{0.025} = -1.96$, and for the upper part it is $z_{0.025} = 1.96$. Therefore, you can reject the null hypothesis if:

$$1.96 \leq z \leq -1.96$$

Thus, if our test statistic is outside the critical values here, we can conclude that we may reject the null hypothesis. So, remembering our sample mean of 227 millimetres, let us calculate z and find out:

$$z = \frac{\bar{x} - \mu_0}{\dfrac{\sigma}{\sqrt{n}}} = \frac{227 - 230}{\dfrac{8}{\sqrt{25}}} = -1.875$$

As you can see, because $z = -1.875$, which is not less than, more than or equal to either -1.96 or 1.96, the statistical evidence suggests that we do not reject the null hypothesis at the 0.05 level of significance, and continue happily making cricket balls.

The *p*-value Method

Using the *p*-value method can also give us insight into the problem, as you might expect. Remember that in the two-tailed situation the test statistic can indicate lack of support for the null hypothesis in either direction – above or below. So for the two-tailed case, the *p*-value can be considered to be the probability of getting a test statistic at least as unlikely as the one our sample did provide. It can be a little confusing to follow this, however, compared with the simpler one-tailed test. So, step by step:

1. Calculate z.
2. If $z > 0$ (i.e. positive), this means that the test statistic is in the upper tail. Therefore, use the normal distribution tables to determine the area under the normal curve to the right of z.

If $z < 0$ (i.e. negative), then it is in the lower tail. Therefore find the area under the curve of the normal distribution to the left of z.

3. Double the area under the tail which you determined in step 2, and this is the p-value.

So, let's do this in practice, using the cricket balls example. We calculate z just as above, and come up with -1.875. So to compute the p-value we need to work out the probability of getting a test statistic at least as unlikely as -1.875. You should by now have no trouble with understanding the area under the normal curve as a probability, and therefore that the further I get away from the mean, the less likely that z is to occur if the null is true in the population. Therefore, it is obvious that all values of $z \leq -1.875$ would be at least as unlikely. However, in the two-tailed situation, values of $z \geq 1.875$ are also at least as unlikely. Figure 8.4 shows this.

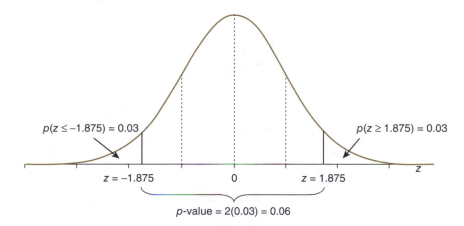

Figure 8.4 p-value Approach; Acid Drops Example – Two-tailed

Figure 8.4 shows that the p-value in the two-tailed case is given by finding the area under the normal curve corresponding to $z \leq -1.875$ and $z \leq 1.875$. It is simple enough to do this because the normal curve is symmetrical. So, you just find the area under the curve corresponding to $z = 1.875$ and double it. Going to the normal distribution table, we find that the area between the mean and 1.875 is 0.4696, and thus the area under the curve to the left (or right) of the test statistic is $0.5 - 0.4696 = 0.03$. If you double this, you will find that the two-tailed p-value is 0.06. Comparing this with $\alpha = 0.05$, we can see that we should not reject H_0 because $0.06 > 0.05$.

However, an alternative perspective could be that this p-value is rather close to the point where we would reject H_0. We could therefore consider that there was some evidence for concern here. Perhaps we should conduct more research? But even so, in this quality control context, we have not achieved the level of confidence to reject H_0.

Summary of Basic Hypothesis Testing

OK, that was a lot of information to take in, so perhaps a summary would help. The basic hypothesis testing procedure is as follows, and – remember – this applies to *all* hypothesis testing situations, not just the basic hypotheses outlined above; the only things that change later in the book are the specific test statistic methods.

First, and always first, you must develop your null and alternative hypotheses for all the tests you want to conduct. From here, you specify the level of significance. *Only now* should you collect data, and then compute the test statistic. Once you have the data, you must decide whether to use the p-value or critical value approach. If you take the p-value approach, use the test statistic to compute the p-value,[10] and from

---

[10] In fact, often a computer package such as Excel or SPSS will do this for you.

there reject H_0 if the p-value is less than or equal to your predetermined level of significance (see Box 8.1 for the formalized rule). If you take the critical value approach, you must use the level of significance to determine the critical value and the rejection rule. From there, use the value of the test statistic and rejection rule to determine whether to reject H_0. If you are one of those people who prefer such information in pictures – like me – you will appreciate the restatement of this paragraph in Figure 8.5 as a cool flowchart. And because I am convinced of the beauty and utility of flowcharts, Figure 8.6 provides all the decision rules for one- and two-tailed hypotheses in such a form too. You will find Figure 8.6 super-useful in future, so maybe you could copy it out and put it on the ceiling of your bedroom or something, so you can stare up at it each night?

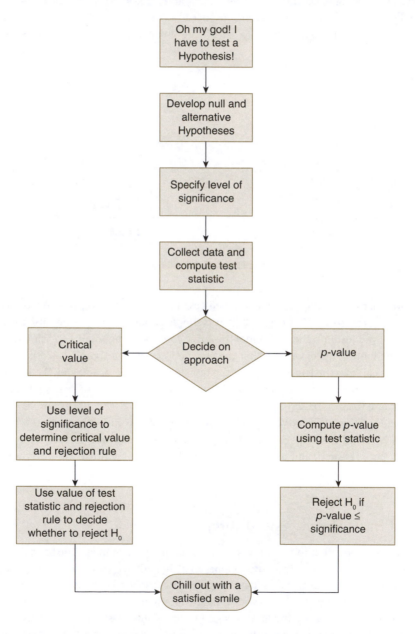

Figure 8.5
Hypothesis
Testing
Flowchart

A final note at this point concerns sample size. The same basic rules apply here as I have already discussed in previous places – such as Chapter 7 when I gave some ideas about sample size regarding intervals. To recap, usually a sample size of 30 or more is enough for this sort of thing. However, if you have less than 30 (e.g. in the acid drops and cricket balls examples above), you need to think about the

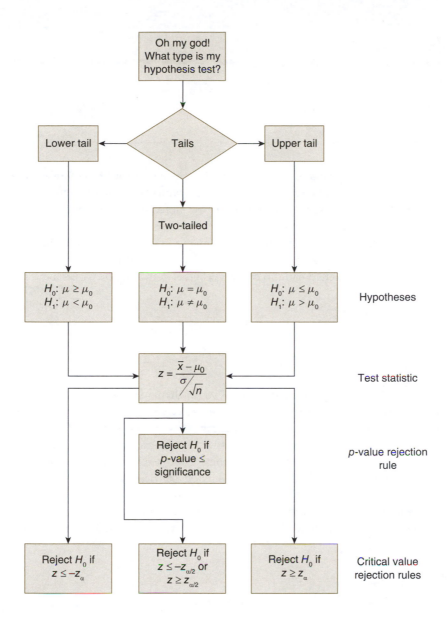

Figure 8.6
Decision Rule Flowchart

population. In essence, if you are convinced the population is normally distributed, you are fine with any sample size – or as we say in the statistics bars and clubs I frequent, 'the procedure is exact'. However, if the population is not normally distributed, you can get away with samples of 15 or more as long as you can argue that the population is pretty much symmetrical around the mean. Smaller than this and you are on shaky ground. You should only use the methods here if you can convince yourself (and anyone else important) that the population is at least somewhat normally distributed.

TESTING HYPOTHESES IF THE POPULATION STANDARD DEVIATION IS UNKNOWN

It is relatively common to find ourselves in the situation where there is no knowledge available of the population standard deviation σ. In such cases, the sample standard deviation σ has to be used to estimate σ and the sample mean to estimate μ.

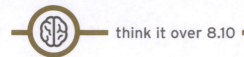

If the population standard deviation is not known, how can we be confident of how good a model the mean is?

All the basic steps from the previous σ-known case apply here, but of course because σ is unknown the calculation of the test statistic and p-value are different. It is particularly important to note that the sampling distribution of the test statistic is more variable in the σ-unknown case, while in the σ-known case it is a standard normal distribution. This is because, for σ-unknown cases, we have to use the sample to estimate σ and μ. In fact, just as in the interval estimation examples in the previous chapter, hypothesis tests for the σ-unknown situation are based on the t-distribution, and this distribution has $n - 1$ degrees of freedom. The test statistic therefore in this case is t, whereas in the σ-known case above it was z:

$$t = \frac{\bar{x} - \mu_0}{\frac{s}{\sqrt{n}}}$$

One-Tailed Tests

As an example, think about the student evaluation forms you might have to hand in at the end of every course, where you rate how great (or otherwise) your lecturers are. We lecturers hate them, let me tell you, but that's a story for another day. Anyway, imagine you were taking my class on 'Philosophy and Really Hard Statistics', and my colleague Laura's class on 'Cool Things About Advertising (With Free Chocolate)'. Now, at the end of the year, you rate how good the class was from 0 (meaning rubbish) to 10 (meaning awesome). We each have to get an average rating of 8 in order not to get a telling-off from our Head of Department, John the Ruthless.

So, we survey 25 members of the class (i.e. we take a sample, not the entire population), and Laura returns a sample mean of $\bar{x} = 9.2$, with a sample standard deviation of $s = 2.3$. So what we need to do is work out whether Laura's population mean score would be higher than 8. Therefore, what we need is an upper-tail test with:

$$H_0: \mu \leq 8$$

$$H_1: \mu > 8$$

and we can use a significance level of $\alpha = 0.05$.

Thus, it is quite easy to run the numbers here – just use the t equation above, as follows:

$$t = \frac{\bar{x} - \mu_0}{\frac{s}{\sqrt{n}}} = \frac{9.2 - 8}{\frac{2.3}{\sqrt{25}}} = 2.61$$

So what do we do now? Unlike with the z-test we do not have a constant value of the test statistic which always corresponds to a given level of significance (e.g. $z = 1.96$). This is because for the t-test we have to take account of the degrees of freedom, which are $n - 1$. Because our sample size $n = 25$, the degrees of freedom here are 24. What we need to do to find the p-value here is use tables. And what we are looking for is the area under the curve of the t-distribution to the right of $t = 2.61$.

Looking at a section of the t table, as shown in Table 8.2, one can see there is no exact p-value for a t of 2.61. It seems to fall between the values of 2.492 and 2.797. These values correspond to p-values of 0.01 and 0.005 respectively. This is enough information to reject the null hypotheses, because whatever the exact p-value is, we know it is less than 0.05 for sure.

Table 8.2 Table segment for the *t*-distribution

Degrees of freedom	Area in upper tail					
	.20	.10	.05	.025	.01	.005
.						
.						
.						
23	.858	1.319	1.708	2.069	2.500	2.807
24	.857	1.318	1.711	2.064	2.492	2.797
.						
.						

So, the conclusion is that Laura is a great lecturer and will not get into trouble with John the Ruthless. As for me, well, that's another story…

Two-Tailed Tests

A more typical business situation can be used to illustrate how to conduct a two-tailed test regarding the population mean when σ is unknown. A sales manager for a company which sells high-tech components to hundreds of electronics manufacturers has a new product on its product list this year. The sales manager needs to know at what level to set the sales target for the upcoming quarter, to motivate her salespeople to sell this new product. Yet she has no way of knowing what the demand for this product should be. If she sets the target too high, the salespeople might be demotivated by the impossible task. Yet if the target is too low, the company will have to pay out too many bonuses to the salespeople. Her hunch is that the typical customer will order around 50 of these per quarter, but she is far from certain. Thus, the sales manager decides to do a quick survey of a sample of potential customers to gather more insight. She calls 30 purchasing managers from her customer list, discusses the new product with them, and then asks how many they think they might order in a typical quarter. From here, it is a relatively simple two-tailed hypothesis test as follows:

$$H_0: \mu = 50$$

$$H_1: \mu \neq 50$$

Remember, μ is the population mean quarterly order per customer. If the sales manager cannot reject H_0 then she will set the quarterly target based on her original hunch. However, if H_0 can be rejected, she can rethink her sales target based on the new information.

The sample of 30 customers provides a sample mean $\bar{x}$ of 53.8 and a sample standard deviation $\sigma = 18.4$. Remember, because we have no information on the population parameters, we must estimate them using sample statistics. Also, recall that you should be confident that the population distribution is pretty much normal before using the *t*-test. In this case, a histogram of the sample data shows nothing out of the ordinary (e.g. skewness, outliers and so forth), so we can therefore move on with a *t*-test, with $n - 1 = 29$ degrees of freedom. We can compute *t* as follows:

$$t = \frac{\bar{x} - \mu_0}{\frac{s}{\sqrt{n}}} = \frac{53.8 - 50}{\frac{18.4}{\sqrt{30}}} = 1.13$$

We can then take this value to the trusty old *t* tables, remembering that because we have a two-tailed test, the appropriate *p*-value is *two times* the area under the curve of the *t*-distribution to the right of $t = 1.13$.

The section of the t table in table 8.3 shows that $t = 1.13$ falls somewhere between 0.854 and 1.311. The upper-tail area value for $t = 1.13$ therefore falls somewhere between 0.20 and 0.1. Doubling this for the two-tailed case means our p-value must be between 0.4 and 0.2. Given that our significance level $\alpha = 0.05$, we know we do not have enough evidence to reject H_0. Thus, the sales target should remain at 50 units at least for this first quarter.

Table 8.3 Table segment for the t-distribution

Degrees of freedom	Area in upper tail					
	.20	.10	.05	.025	.01	.005
.						
.						
.						
28	.855	1.313	1.701	2.048	2.467	2.763
29	.854	1.311	1.699	2.045	2.462	2.756
.						
.						

As a side note, t tables tend to have values only in the upper tail. This is because the distribution is symmetrical. So if we end up with a negative t value, just use the same positive value of t when you are using the tables.

Recap

Figure 8.7 contains a basic pictorial summary of the procedures I have just described. You can see it looks remarkably similar to Figure 8.6, but note that the formulae have changed, because we are dealing with t-tests, not z-tests.

In terms of sample size, the advice given for z-tests is similar, but not exactly the same. Remember, because we have no population standard deviation, we have less information and so must be more cautious. If we know the population is normally distributed, then these tests are exact for any sample size. However, this is of course unlikely, and whenever the population is not normally distributed, the t-test is just an approximation. In this case, you should really have a sample greater than 50. That said, as long as the sample distribution is 'OK' – by which I mean it is not very skewed and does not contain outliers – sample sizes of 15 and above can be acceptable. However, the onus is on you as the analyst to understand these issues and do the right thing.

TESTING HYPOTHESES ABOUT THE POPULATION PROPORTION

In situations where we are interested in the population proportion, we refer to it as π. If π_0 denotes the proportion, we have three different types of hypothesis test, which should begin to look very familiar by now:

$$H_0: \pi \geq \pi_0 \qquad\qquad H_0: \pi \leq \pi_0 \qquad\qquad H_0: \pi = \pi_0$$

$$H_1: \pi < \pi_0 \qquad\qquad H_1: \pi > \pi_0 \qquad\qquad H_1: \pi \neq \pi_0$$

You should also be able to work out which of those is two-tailed, lower tailed or upper tailed, so I will not even tell you (if you are unsure, check the bottom of the page).[11]

---

[11] The lower tailed is the left, upper tailed in the middle, and two-tailed to the right.

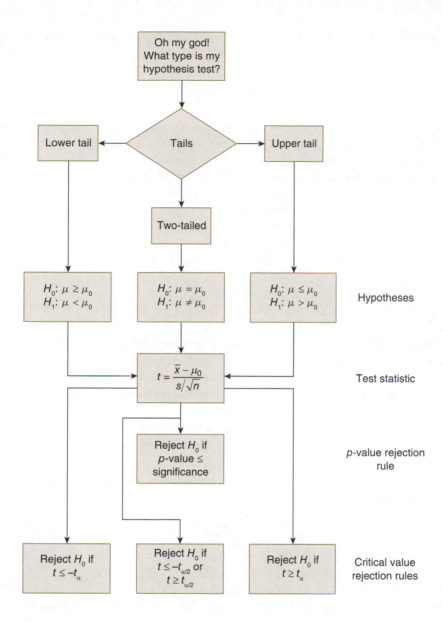

Figure 8.7
t-test
Decision Rule Flowchart

The method to conduct hypothesis tests about population proportions is similar to those I have just covered for the means. However, there is some additional complication, and the equations can look somewhat intimidating. That said, they are simple when you get to know them better. The main difference is that we use the sample proportion p (of course), and the standard error, to compute the test statistic. Using this test statistic, we can use either the p-value or critical value approach to test the hypothesis. I will present the p-value approach, because the critical value is just another (less popular) way of doing the same thing.

As an example, let's consider the situation of a beer brand manager. This manager is in charge of the brand 'Old Musty', and the vice-president of marketing has decided that the brand should start being a bit 'cooler', appealing to a younger audience of 20–35 year olds, rather than its traditional over-50s market. Because currently only 10% of 'Old Musty' customers are 20–35 (a proportion of 0.1), this is a pretty unforgiving assignment really, but our brand manager tries his best and puts together an advertising campaign and so forth, to try to increase the proportion of 20–35 year olds who drink 'Old Musty'. After six months of this programme, the VP of marketing asks for a piece of market research to determine whether the brand manager has been successful.

This situation is an upper-tailed test with H_1: $\pi > 0.1$, making the null and alternative hypotheses:

$$H_0: \pi \leq 0.1$$

$$H_1: \pi > 0.1$$

Rejecting the null hypothesis will support the idea that the brand manager has been successful and increase the proportion of 20–35 year olds in the customer base for 'Old Musty'. We can use $\alpha = 0.05$ for the significance level, and our next task is to collect a good sample and compute the test statistic.

The computation of the test statistic in this case is, as I said above, a bit more complex. What we need to do is to use the sampling distribution of p. The sample proportion p is the point estimator of the population proportion π, and we use the sampling distribution of p to compute the test statistic.

Recalling some of the concepts from earlier in this book, if the null hypothesis is true as an equality, the expected value of the sample proportion p must be the same as the hypothesized value of π_0, or in mathematical terms $E(p) = \pi_0$. In this case, the standard error of p is calculated as:

$$\sigma_p = \sqrt{\frac{\pi_0(1-\pi_0)}{n}}$$

Now, recall from Chapter 7 that we can use the standard normal distribution to approximate the sampling distribution of p only in situations where $n\pi \geq 5$ and $n(1 - \pi) \geq 5$. Fortunately, this is usually the case. If it is not, things become more complicated, because the sampling distribution of p is then actually the discrete binomial distribution. If we can use the normal approximation, we can use a z-test. We find z with the following equation:

$$z = \frac{p - \pi_0}{\sigma_p}$$

Substituting in the equation for σ_p will give you the equation below, which is the test statistic for hypotheses regarding the population proportion:

$$z = \frac{p - \pi_0}{\sqrt{\frac{\pi_0(1-\pi_0)}{n}}}$$

Using this, we can deal with the 'Old Musty' case. Let's say we draw a sample of 500 random 'Old Musty' drinkers somehow. Imagine we find that 65 are between 20 and 35 years old. This makes the proportion of 20–35 year olds in our sample $p = 65/500 = 0.13$. We can now plug the numbers into our equation:

$$z = \frac{p - \pi_0}{\sqrt{\frac{\pi_0(1-\pi_0)}{n}}} = \frac{0.13 - 0.1}{\sqrt{\frac{0.1(1-0.1)}{300}}} = \frac{0.03}{0.017} = 1.76$$

Our hypothesis is upper tailed, so the p-value is the area under the standard normal distribution curve to the right of $z = 1.76$. A standard normal table will show that the area between $z = 0$ and $z = 1.76$ is 0.4608. Our p-value is thus $0.5 - 0.4608 = 0.0392$.

Given that the VP for marketing has set $\alpha = 0.05$, it is clear that our p-value is less than α, meaning that we have statistical support for a decision to reject the null. So, well done brand manager! We could of course also use the critical value approach. We would already know that we can reject H_0 if $z \geq 1.645$ for an upper-tail test. In this case $z = 1.76$, meaning that we reject H_0. So, again, the critical value and p-value approach give us the same information.

Recap

As you can see, these hypothesis testing procedures for means and proportions are broadly similar in logic and technique – with just some differences in the equations to worry about. To cement this, Figure 8.8 shows a similar setup to 8.6 and 8.7, referring to proportion testing.

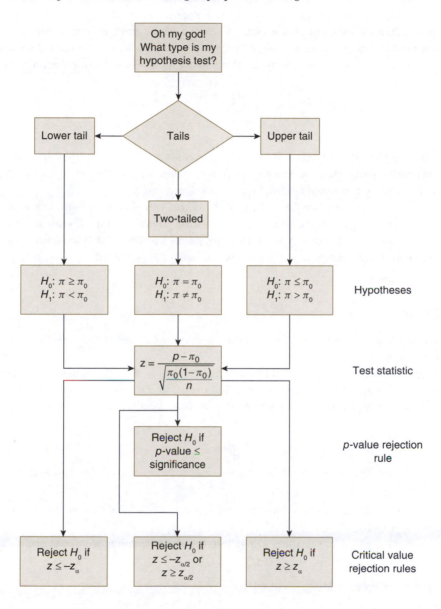

Figure 8.8
Testing
Differences
in
Proportions
Decision
Rule
Flowchart

USING HYPOTHESIS TESTS IN THE REAL WORLD

So far, the techniques I have taught you have mainly had application in cases where you are looking to test a scientific research hypothesis, or to test the validity of some claim being made about the population. Both these situations require us to take some action if H_0 is rejected, but to take no action if H_0 is not rejected. In such cases, we have naturally been concerned with Type I error – that is, the chance of making an error by rejecting H_0 when it is true in the population. We control Type I error by setting the significance level α. In situations where action is taken only if H_0 is rejected, Type I error is very important.

However, in many real-world business decision-making situations, we may take action both when H_0 is rejected and if it is accepted. For example, imagine you are a purchasing manager in a big industrial manufacturing company. You have a shipment of resistors that are components of your next major new product. You need to test a sample of these to determine whether they perform according to design. The resistance should be 10 ohms, and anything significantly less than this will cause problems. It is impossible to test thousands of these individually of course. Therefore, for each shipment, before accepting it, you draw a sample of 20 resistors to test their resistance. This is a simple and typical manufacturing problem. Basically, you need to test the mean resistance in ohms of your sample, and estimate the probability of this being true in the population. So, μ is the mean resistance in ohms for the shipment of resistors and:

$$H_0: \mu \geq 10$$

$$H_1: \mu < 10$$

If your analysis suggests the rejection of H_0, the situation is simple: you return the shipment to the supplier, probably with a nasty letter too, threatening finding a new supplier. However, if you accept H_0 you must still make a decision to accept the shipment – so action is taken.

Yet, up till now you have not considered the probability that you got this decision to accept H_0 wrong, only whether or not you got the decision to reject H_0 wrong. Therefore, Type II error is not controlled. Importantly, we must remember that Type II error is not simply the inverse of Type I error. So, when some action is taken even if H_0 is accepted, we should take account of Type II error.

Type II Error

To learn how to calculate Type II error, I will use the resistor case detailed above. So refresh your memory by rereading the details.

OK, back now? Good. Let's take our usual level of significance, $\sigma = 0.05$. We know how to calculate the test statistic z whether or not the population standard deviation σ is known, so let's assume it is known for simplicity's sake, with $\sigma = 1$. With the information we have already:

$$z = \frac{\bar{x} - \mu_0}{\frac{\sigma}{\sqrt{n}}} = \frac{\bar{x} - 10}{\frac{1}{\sqrt{20}}}$$

Because it is a one-tailed test, we know the critical value of $z_{0.05} = 1.645$ and that we should reject the null hypothesis if $z \leq -1.645$.

This means that if we were to substitute -1.645 into the above equation, we would get:

$$-1.645 = \frac{\bar{x} - \mu_0}{\frac{\sigma}{\sqrt{n}}} = \frac{\bar{x} - 10}{\frac{1}{\sqrt{20}}}$$

All we have missing here is the sample mean. However, we could rearrange the equation to solve for the sample mean as follows:

$$\bar{x} = 10 - 1.645 \left(\frac{1}{\sqrt{20}} \right) = 9.63$$

So, we reject H_0 when the sample mean is less than or equal to 9.63, sending the shipment back. But we keep the shipment of resistors when the sample mean is greater than 9.63. With this information, you can compute the probability of Type II error in making the latter decision. It is a pretty simple process, but it is rather step by step. So do pay attention. However, if you are a little baffled by how I rearranged the formula just now, check out Back to Basics Box 8.3

 back to basics

Box 8.3   Recap of Algebraic Manipulation

They *told* you it was going to be useful at school, didn't they? But did you pay attention? Anyway, I feel the time is right for a brief recap on algebraic manipulation. I did this in the last chapter too, so this is the last time! Make sure to pay attention!

Recall that I started with:

$$z = \frac{(\bar{x}-\mu_0)}{\frac{\sigma}{\sqrt{n}}} = \frac{(\bar{x}-10)}{\frac{1}{\sqrt{20}}}$$

Let's just work with the one with our numbers in it:

$$-1.645 = \frac{(\bar{x}-10)}{\frac{1}{\sqrt{20}}}$$

How do we move $\bar{x}$ to the left? I will do it step by step. Remember: the key rule is to *do the same operation on both sides of the equation*. Do this and you will be fine.

First, multiply both sides by $\frac{1}{\sqrt{20}}$ to get:

$$-1.645\left(\frac{1}{\sqrt{20}}\right) = \bar{x}-10$$

Beginning to make sense yet? I hope so. Anyway, from here, simply add 10 to both sides to get:

$$10 - 1.645\left(\frac{1}{\sqrt{20}}\right) = \bar{x}$$

which is the same thing of course as:

$$\bar{x} = 10 - 1.645\left(\frac{1}{\sqrt{20}}\right)$$

See how that works?

Now, remember that you will make a Type II error any time you accept H_0: $\mu \geq 10$, when the true population mean of the shipment of resistors is actually less than 10 ohms. To work out the probability of Type II error, we have to work it out for a given value of $\mu < 10$. This is slightly different from the more general things we have been doing so far, so just take it slowly from now on.

Imagine that your production manager would consider the shipment to be poor quality if the population mean $\mu = 9$ ohms. So, if the shipment really does have a mean of 9 ohms, what is the probability of accepting H_0: $\mu \geq 10$ and therefore committing a Type II error? In other words, what is the probability that you find a sample mean of 9.63, if the population mean is 9?

This is a relatively simple task of substituting numbers into the formula. In this case, our sample mean would be 9.63 and μ_0 would correspond to our hypothetical population mean of 9:

$$z = \frac{\bar{x} - \mu_0}{\frac{\sigma}{\sqrt{n}}} = \frac{9.63 - 9}{\frac{1}{\sqrt{20}}} = 2.82$$

We can then find the probability of observing a sample mean of 9.63 when the true population mean is 9 by using a standard normal distribution table as you have already done plenty of times before. With $z = 2.82$, the area in the upper tail of the distribution is $0.5 - 0.4976 = 0.0024$. Therefore, 0.0024 is the probability of making a Type II error when the real population mean $\mu = 9$. The probability of making a Type II error is denoted as 'beta', or β, so when $\mu = 9$, $\beta = 0.0024$.

To find Type II errors for other values of μ, we need to repeat the calculations, and each time we do so, we will find a different value for β. In fact, Table 8.3 shows a number of different probabilities for various values of $\mu < 10$. As you can see, as we get closer to $\mu = 10$, the probability of making a Type II error increases. This should not be surprising when you think about it. When the true population mean is close to our null hypothesis value of 10, then we would be very likely to reject the null hypothesis, despite the true value of μ not being exactly 10. However, the consequences of this error are likely to be small – after all, the difference between 9.9979 and 10 is pretty insignificant.

Table 8.4 Probability of making a Type II error for the resistor acceptance hypothesis test

$$z = \frac{9.63 - \mu}{\frac{1}{\sqrt{20}}}$$

μ	z	Probability of Type II error β	Power $(1 - \beta)$
9	2.82	0.002	0.9976
9.2	1.92	0.027	0.9726
9.5	0.58	0.281	0.7190
9.63	0.00	0.500	0.5000
9.8	−0.76	0.745	0.2546
9.85	−0.98	0.837	0.1635
9.9	−1.21	0.887	0.1131
9.9979	−1.645	0.950	0.0500

Or is it? In some contexts it could actually be very important – say, in engineering where tolerances can be very low, or in medicine where small dosage differences can be life and death issues. What do we do here? Well, as we will see later, Type II error also depends on the sample size – the smaller the differences we need to detect between the true population mean and our null hypothesis, the larger our sample must be. But let's save that discussion for now.

Moving back to Type II error, we can use this to define something called the statistical power of a test. Power is the probability of correctly rejecting H_0 when it is actually false, and is calculated for any given value of μ as $1 - \beta$. Table 8.4 also shows the power calculations, and one could conceivably graph these as a power curve, which sounds way cooler than it is. See Figure 8.9. You can easily read off from the power curve the probability of correctly rejecting the null hypothesis, as it is indicated by the height of the curve at the given value of μ on the x axis.

OK, so that was rather a lot of things to remember, wasn't it? To make things easier, Box 8.3 provides a step-by-step list, without the formulae.

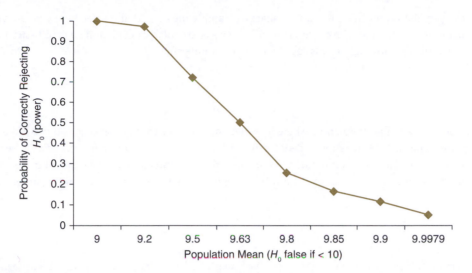

Figure 8.9
Power
Curve for
Resistor Lot-
acceptance
Hypothesis
Test; a
Sample Mean
9.63 and
Sample Size
20 (Sample
Standard
Deviation 1).

 box 8.3

How to Compute the Probability of Making a Type II Error

1. Decide on your null and alternative hypotheses.
2. Use α (level of significance) and the critical value associated with that value of α to determine the relevant critical value and rejection rule for the test statistic.
3. Use this rejection rule to solve the equation for the value of the sample mean $\bar{x}$ associated with the critical value of the test statistic.
4. Use the results from the last step to decide the values of $\bar{x}$ which correspond to acceptance of H_0.
5. Use the sampling distribution of the test statistic z for a value of μ which would correspond to the alternative hypothesis, and the acceptance value results from step 4 above, to work out the probability that $\bar{x}$ will be in the region of acceptance. This probability is the Type II error probability for the given value of μ.

Now, if this is a little complicated, go back through the section and relate each step above to the working given – it will make more sense that way.

DETERMINING THE SAMPLE SIZE FOR A HYPOTHESIS TEST

You should remember from the previous section that I briefly mentioned that power also depended on sample size. In this section, I will show you how to use sample size to control the probability of making a Type II error, and therefore the power. Once you have gone through this section, you can begin to think of β as another factor that the researcher has control over – just like α, the Type I error probability (which is of course controlled by setting the significance level). Of course, computer programs can do this kind of calculation for you, but you will never understand the logic behind it without actually going through it yourself.

Let's stay with our resistor problem to work through the issues. Forgetting the specific numbers for a while, in a general sense we have a simple lower-tail hypothesis test about the population mean as follows:

$$H_0 = \mu \geq \mu_0$$

$$H_1 = \mu < \mu_0$$

As you should remember, the critical value of the test statistic is denoted $-z_\alpha$ for a lower-tail test. You should also remember that for any given value of population standard deviation σ, sample size n and null hypothesis population mean μ_0, we can calculate the sample mean $\bar{x}$ that we need to be below or equal to in order to reject the null hypothesis. This formula was particularly detailed in Back to Basics Box 8.3, and is shown below (although in this case there are no numbers):

$$\bar{x} = \mu_0 - z_\alpha \left(\frac{\sigma}{\sqrt{n}} \right)$$

Now, consider the alternative situation, where H_1 is true, and therefore the population mean μ_1 is less than the null hypothesis mean μ_0. As we know, β denotes the probability of a Type II error, which occurs if we were to accept the null hypothesis if it was not true in the population. We can calculate the required $\bar{x}$ here as well, using almost the same formula as above, but with z_β representing the z-value corresponding to a given β:

$$\bar{x} = \mu_1 + z_\beta \left(\frac{\sigma}{\sqrt{n}} \right)$$

The task at hand is to select the value of $\bar{x}$ so that when you reject H_0, accepting H_1, the probability of Type I error is equal to α and the probability of Type II error is equal to β. This means of course that both those values of $\bar{x}$ must be equal! This means in turn that the following equation is also true:

$$\mu_0 - z_\alpha \left(\frac{\sigma}{\sqrt{n}} \right) = \mu_1 + z_\beta \left(\frac{\sigma}{\sqrt{n}} \right)$$

Of course, what we really want to know in this case is the sample size, so a little bit of algebraic manipulation is required here to solve this equation for $\sqrt{n}$, as below:

$$\mu_0 - \mu_1 = z_\alpha \left(\frac{\sigma}{\sqrt{n}} \right) + z_\beta \left(\frac{\sigma}{\sqrt{n}} \right) = \frac{(z_\alpha + z_\beta)\sigma}{\sqrt{n}}$$

Now it is just a case of multiplying both sides by $\sqrt{n}$:

$$\sqrt{n}(\mu_0 - \mu_1) = (z_\alpha + z_\beta)\sigma$$

and then dividing both sides by $(\mu_0 - \mu_1)$:

$$\sqrt{n} = \frac{(z_\alpha + z_\beta)\sigma}{(\mu_0 - \mu_1)}$$

Personally, I would leave it at that, and square the answer at the end to get n. However, some other approaches square both sides of the equation to get an answer for n directly. I feel that is overcomplicated. I would much rather square a single number at the end to get n than mess around squaring all the other stuff on the other side of the equation.

Either way, the equation works for any one-tailed test regarding a population mean. If you want to run a two-tailed test, you need to remember that you should use $z_{\alpha/2}$ instead of z_α.

OK. So, let's go back to the task at hand – how to deal with the shipment of resistors. Remember, our resistance has to be 10 ohms, and we reject shipments where H_0: $\mu \geq 10$ is rejected. The production manager has decided that she wants an $\alpha = 0.05$, or, in other words, a 0.05 probability of rejecting a shipment if $\mu = 10$. This is our allowable Type I error for this case. On the other hand, if the mean resistance is 0.5 ohms under specification ($\mu = 9.5$), the production manager is willing to risk a $\beta = 0.1$, which is a 0.1 probability of accepting a faulty shipment – our Type II error chance.

Of course, these error chances are simply based on the judgement of an individual manager, who should have some knowledge of the situation at hand. Different people in different situations may or may not come up with different answers. But, either way, we need to have some specification of the Type I and II errors allowed, and this is as good as any other right now.

So, given $\alpha = 0.05$ and $\beta = 0.1$, we can use the standard normal probability distribution tables to work out $z_{0.05} = 1.645$ and $z_{0.1} = 1.28$. We also know that $\mu_0 = 10$ and $\mu_1 = 9.5$. Remember, we also know the population standard deviation $\sigma = 1$. So we have all the information necessary to use our formula as follows:

$$\sqrt{n} = \frac{\left(z_\alpha + z_\beta\right)\sigma}{\left(\mu_0 - \mu_1\right)} = \frac{(1.645 + 1.28)1}{(10 - 9.5)} = 5.85$$

Squaring the answer and rounding gives us an answer of 34. This is the sample size we need to be confident. At this point, because we are confident we have some control over both Type I and II errors, we are also confident in either rejecting or accepting the null hypothesis.

This should lead us to the idea that there must be some relationship between α, β and n, meaning that once we have two of these values, we can calculate the other. Also, given a sample size n, if you decrease α, you increase β, and vice versa. Finally, given a significance level α, increasing n will decrease β.

One important final point which comes from this is that, given a specific n, one should not just be concerned with lowering α. In fact, only if one does not care at all about incorrectly accepting the null hypothesis is the concern for the lowest α the only concern. This is often a mistake made by newbies to the hypothesis testing game. Most of the time, we need to compromise between α and β.

 think it over 8.11

Many professional statisticians consider significance at the 5% level as being an indicator that more sampling should be done. Why do you think they have this opinion?

USING SPSS FOR HYPOTHESIS TESTING

IBM SPSS Statistics Software (SPSS) does not have a direct way for performing z-tests, but this does not matter since, as your sample size n gets larger (in maths-speak, approaches infinity) the t-test works just like the z-test.

There are two ways in which you can test your statistics using SPSS. The first way I am going to show you is really intended as a way of exploring or checking your data to ensure it meets the assumptions of hypothesis testing.

We are going to use the data from the test scores.sav file. Load this file into SPSS. Once the data is loaded, select Analyze → Descriptive Statistics → Explore. You should have the same as in Figure 8.10. Select Statistics and you should then have in front of you the boxes shown in Figure 8.11.

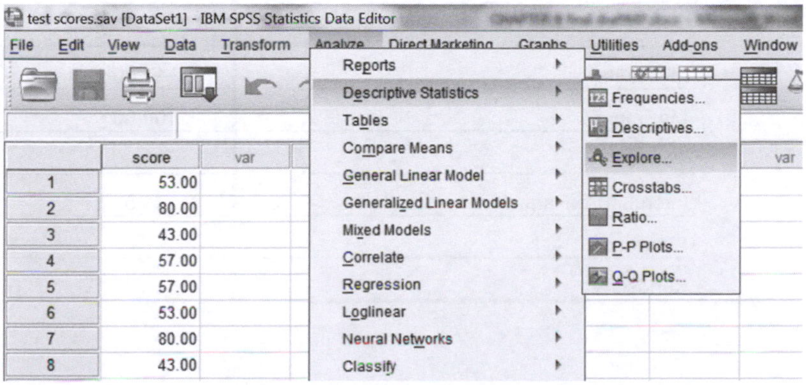

Figure 8.10
SPSS Explore function

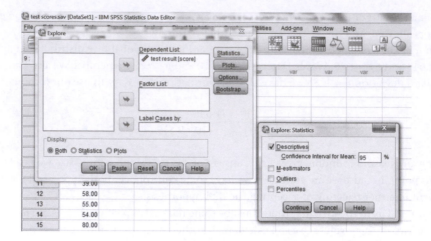

Figure 8.11

You may have noticed that you can also choose various ways to plot your data by clicking on the Plots button (I always like to have a visual representation of my data so I get a 'feel' for it). Select Explore → Statistics, make sure Descriptives is checked and you have set your confidence interval for the mean (the default is 95%). Select Continue then OK. Figure 8.12 shows the output. The tables give a lot of information, but the bits we are interested in are the values for the mean and the lower and upper bounds.

Case Processing Summary

	Cases					
	Valid		Missing		Total	
	N	Percent	N	Percent	N	Percent
test result	50	100.0%	0	0.0%	50	100.0%

Descriptives

			Statistic	Std. Error
test result	Mean		59.4000	1.83392
	95% Confidence Interval for Mean	Lower Bound	55.7146	
		Upper Bound	63.0854	
	5% Trimmed Mean		59.4111	
	Median		57.0000	
	Variance		168.163	
	Std. Deviation		12.96778	
	Minimum		17.00	
	Maximum		100.00	
	Range		83.00	
	Interquartile Range		11.50	
	Skewness		.062	.337
	Kurtosis		2.759	.662

Figure 8.12

think it over 8.12

Looking at Figure 8.12, what do you think is the purpose of the rest of the information given? For example, what do the skewness and kurtosis values tell you? Compare the values of the mean and median; what information can you get from these values? Similarly, compare the value of the standard deviation with the mean; again, what does this information tell you?

The other approach to using SPSS for hypothesis testing is to use the one-sample *t*-test. We will use the same data, but this time perform a one-sample *t*-test.

Our null hypothesis is that the mean score is 59 and the alternative hypothesis is that the mean score is not equal to 59.

This time select Analyze → Compare Means → One Sample T-Test. You should see the same as Figure 8.13.

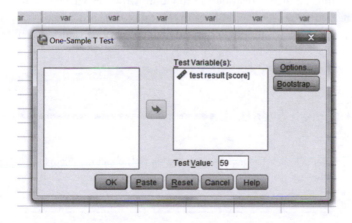

Figure 8.13

Notice the Test Value box in Figure 8.14. This box is where you put the null hypothesis value for the mean. In this example I have entered a value of 59 as shown.

Figure 8.14

Now select <u>Options</u> and set your Confidence Interval Percentage (again the default is 95%). Click <u>Continue</u> then <u>OK</u>.

Figure 8.15 shows the results from SPSS performing the analysis.

One-Sample Test

					95% Confidence Interval of the Difference	
			Test Value = 59			
	t	df	Sig. (2-tailed)	Mean Difference	Lower	Upper
test result	.218	49	.828	.40000	-3.2854	4.0854

Figure 8.15

 think it over 8.13

Referring to Figure 8.15, you are given a value for the t statistics and a value for the Sig. (2-tailed). By comparing these values, what can you say about your null hypothesis that the mean height was 59?

HYPOTHESIS TESTING USING EXCEL

Hypothesis testing can be done using Excel; it is a bit fiddly, but fun. It is also a good way to clarify the interpretation of *p*-values. We are going to use the wine data.xlsx spreadsheet and then play with hypothesized values for the mean. Open Excel, load up the spreadsheet and copy the formulae shown in Figure.8.16 One formula that you may not be familiar with is the formula T.DIST(E10,E11,TRUE) found in the statistics drop-down list under more functions. Figure 8.17 shows the formula and the information required to use it. The formula T.DIST(x,deg_freedom,cumulative) requires three bits of information: x is the value of the test statistic t, deg_freedom is the number of degrees of freedom, and cumulative if set to 'true' will give the cumulative distribution function, which is what we want. If you enter a value of 5 for the hypothesized value, you should have in front of you a spreadsheet that is the same as Figure 8.18. Now for the fun bit: change the hypothesized value to various values and note what happens to the *p*-values.

 think it over 8.14

In the Excel spreadsheet change the hypothesized value to the same value as the sample mean. What is now the value of the test statistic t? Is this a result you would expect? Give an explanation for the value of the test statistic.

	A	B	C	D	E
1	ID	Glasses			
2	1	0			
3	2	3	sample size		=COUNT(B2:B21)
4	3	7	sample mean		=AVERAGE(B2:B21)
5	4	15	sample SD		=STDEV.S(B2:B21)
6	5	2			
7	6	1	hypothesised value		5
8	7	0			
9	8	0	standard error		=E5/SQRT(E3)
10	9	10	test statistic t		=(E4-E7)/E9
11	10	3	degrees of freedom		=E3-1
12	11	4			
13	12	8	p-value (lower tail)		=T.DIST(E10,E11,TRUE)
14	13	1	p-value (upper tail)		=1-E13
15	14	7	p-value (2 tail)		=2*MIN(E13,E14)
16	15	7			
17	16	4			
18	17	4			

Figure 8.16

	B	C	D
1	Glasses		
2	0		
3	3	sample size	=COUNT(B2:B21)
4	7	sample mean	=AVERAGE(B2:B21)
5	15	sample SD	=STDEV.S(B2:B21)
6	2		
7	1	hypothesised value	4.3
8	0		
9	0	standard error	=D5/SQRT(D3)
10	10	test statistic t	=(D4-D7)/D9
11	3	degrees of freedom	=D3-1
12	4		
13	8	p-value (lower tail)	=T.DIST(D10,D11,TRUE)
14	1	p-value (upper tail)	=1-D13
15	7	p-value (2 tail)	=2*MIN(D13,D14)
16	7		

Figure 8.17

	A	B	C	D	E	F
1	ID	Glasses				
2	1.00	0.00				
3	2.00	3.00		sample size		20.0000
4	3.00	7.00		sample mean		4.4000
5	4.00	15.00		sample SD		4.1346
6	5.00	2.00				
7	6.00	1.00		hypothesised value		5.0000
8	7.00	0.00				
9	8.00	0.00		standard error		0.9245
10	9.00	10.00		test statistic t		-0.6490
11	10.00	3.00		degrees of freedom		19.0000
12	11.00	4.00				
13	12.00	8.00		p-value (lower tail)		0.2621
14	13.00	1.00		p-value (upper tail)		0.7379
15	14.00	7.00		p-value (2 tail)		0.5241
16	15.00	7.00				
17	16.00	4.00				

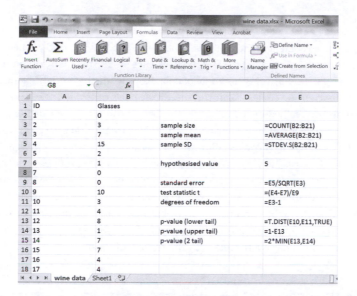

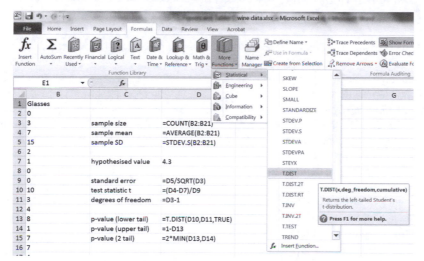

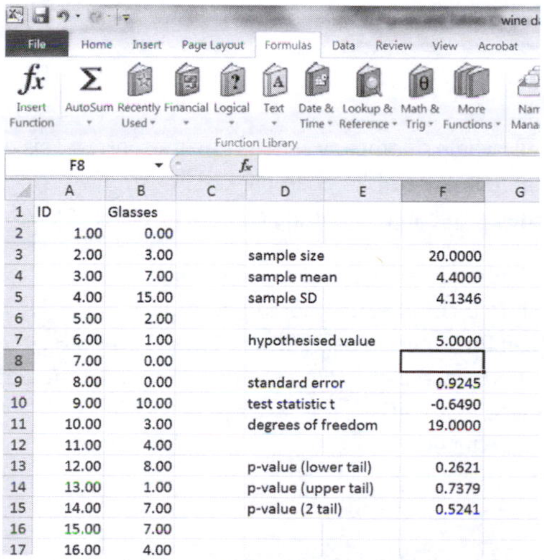

Figure 8.18

SUMMARY

Wow! That was some serious content, right? Well, remember, you only have to read it. I had to write it! Multiple times. What you got through in this chapter was the very essence of statistics in my opinion: the idea of testing some idea about the population by using a sample of data. Now, while there might be plenty of controversy in statistical and other scientific circles about the specific *methods* of testing, the basic idea of hypothesis testing is fundamental. You really do need to master this before you can go on further in this course.

Unfortunately, very few people ever master all of this material, even those who go on to careers in research like me. For example, I was having a conversation with a friend of mine who works in another department, after we had just played football. He told me that when he was forced to produce for his PhD the statistical power calculations that I showed you at the end of this chapter, he had to cope with a stream of colleagues (many much more senior than him) coming to his office asking him to teach them how to do it!

So, just remember that if you are finding this stuff hard, you are not the first or the last to have difficulties. However, also remember that it is really important that you *do* persevere and get to the bottom of this stuff, or you are going to have trouble with the rest of this book.

 final checklist

You should have covered and understood the following basic content in this chapter:

- ☑ The relation between a hypothesis test and a confidence interval.
- ☑ What null and alternative hypotheses are, and how hypotheses are used in practice.
- ☑ What statistical significance testing is, and the key concepts of Type I and Type II errors, as well as the difference between one- and two-tailed testing.
- ☑ How to test hypotheses about the population mean, whether or not you know the population standard deviation.
- ☑ The critical value and *p*-value approaches to testing hypotheses.

- ☑ How to test hypotheses about the population proportion.
- ☑ The importance of statistical power and the likelihood of Type II error when using hypothesis tests in the real world.
- ☑ The relationship between the significance level, the likelihood of Type II error and the sample size, as well as how to use this relationship to calculate the appropriate sample size for a given level of power.

EXERCISES

1. You have been commissioned to help a company with its quality control. This company has received a number of complaints concerning the contents of its crisp packets. Customers are complaining that there are not enough crisps in a packet. The packet states that the contents weigh 50 g. You decide to do a hypothesis test.

    a. Write down the null and alternative hypotheses in English.
    b. Refine your statement into a concise, unambiguous form.
    c. Write down the statistical formulation using the notation H_0 and H_1.
    d. State any assumptions you make concerning the distribution of the population.
    e. Determine the appropriate test statistic.
    f. Determine the significance level.

2. You now have to decide how close the weight of the contents should be compared with the stated weight.

    a. Outline the procedure you would follow to obtain the necessary data in order to perform your hypothesis test.
    b. You calculate a value of 49.45 g for the mean with a standard deviation of 5 g from 100 samples. Calculate the value of the test statistic.

   c. Determine the outcome of the test using a significance level of 5%.

   d. Interpret the result.

3. The company is thinking of upgrading the crisp production facilities. One consideration is the avoidance of wastage (i.e. not having too many crisps in a packet). In order to make a decision the production manager wants to know what the difference between the 90% confidence limits and the 98% confidence limits would be for the production line.

   a. Calculate the confidence limits at 98% and 90%.

   b. Interpret the results from part (a) and advise the production manager on the appropriateness of using these statistics.

4. You have been commissioned by a hospital to find out if waiting times to see a doctor have changed. In a previous study the mean waiting time was 11 minutes with a population standard deviation of 3 minutes. You observe the waiting room for a day and record that 40 patients visited the doctor and the mean waiting time was 12 minutes. You have chosen to use a 5% significance level.

   a. Determine the p-value.

   b. Interpret the result.

   c. What does the result not tell you?

5. What type of error would you have made if, in question 2, you decided to reject the null hypothesis?

6. If you were reviewing a hypothesis test made by a colleague and you suspected a Type II error, what would you advise your colleague to do?

7. The level of significance α can be interpreted as the probability of committing a Type I error, and β, the probability of committing a Type II error. A pharmaceutical company is developing a lifesaving drug and it is therefore important that the company does not commit a Type II error. The company wants to be confident of its results at a 5% significance level. It will accept a 5% risk of committing a Type II error. The data the company has received indicates a null hypothesis mean of 23 and an alternative hypothesis mean of 22.6.

   a. Calculate the minimum sample size the company should use to fit its stated Type I and Type II error requirements.

   b. The cost of running trials works out at £1000 per experiment. The cost to the company of your recommendation would work out at £271000. It is now prepared to adjust its risk assessment in order to reduce costs. You have been given a target budget of £170000 per trial. Calculate the sample size and hence any changes that need to be made to the risk of rejecting the null hypothesis when it is in fact true, and the risk of not rejecting the null hypothesis when it is actually false.

   c. The null hypothesis states: this new drug works faster than currently available medications to reduce the risk of a heart attack; and the alternative hypothesis states: this drug has no effect. Comment on your proposed alterations and the effect of the company's decision.

8. Use SPSS to compute the p-values for the wine data referred to in the Excel tutorial above (Testing Hypotheses Using Excel) with an hypothesized value of 5. Do the same with an Excel worksheet and compare the results; they should be the same for the two-tailed test.

9. Repeat question 8 for different values.

 To access additional online resources please visit: **https://study.sagepub.com/leepeters**

The Ballad of Eddie the Easily Distracted: Part 9

Eddie was having confusing feelings. In fact, he's just shocked himself so much that he needed to stop by the Union Bar for a drink. And this time he thought he might try that whisky that Vincent seemed to like so much, since he felt he needed something rather stronger than his usual ale.

As he nursed his whisky (which he had to admit was an odd flavour, not immediately pleasant, somewhat medicinal in fact – like iodine!), Eddie thought about his last QUAN101 tutorial. He was working with Esha on trying to work out what had been called 'goodness of fit' tests. But Eddie couldn't concentrate this time – he kept looking at Esha and feeling odd inside. Eddie was beginning to worry about it, because he didn't want to end up falling for her, of all the possible options. I mean, how different could two people be? She was such a bookworm! She didn't seem to like anything Eddie did, and they shared pretty much nothing in common at all. As if she would be interested in a guy like him!

Eddie was lost in thought for a while. Against his better judgement, he was thinking about the chances of Esha feeling anything for him. All of a sudden he had a surprising insight into goodness of fit. Eddie had not understood the concept at all, but suddenly the basic idea began to make sense. In essence, if Esha *did* like him, then Eddie guessed she would behave in a certain way. That was like the *expected distribution* for the goodness of fit test. Then, all Eddie had to do was observe her actual behaviour – like the *observed distribution* for a goodness of fit test. Compare the two, and get your answer! Of course, he thought, this did rather depend on how much he could rely on his expected distribution, and how close the observed data was to it. Eddie was pleased with this insight on a number of levels. He finished his drink and got up to go. On a whim, he thought, 'Why not one more?'

Esha's Story: Part 9

'Just what was Eddie's problem?' thought Esha. He'd been mooching around the QUAN101 tutorial like a sad little puppy, and here he was in the Union drinking whisky by himself! Esha guessed that it was about some girl. It usually was for boys. She wondered why boys felt the need to mope around about such things; why not just get it over with and sort it out?

That was her attitude at least, or so she liked to think. She walked out of the Union Bar. She had more important things to think about than boys, like the upcoming QUAN101 test. The latest material on goodness of fit and independence was getting more complex, but with a bit of work she could do it. The concepts were pretty simple, but at times the calculations could get a little complex. The trick was to take them step by step. Sometimes, even making up spreadsheets on her computer to do the calculation steps helped her understand.

In fact, Esha thought later on, when she had finished studying the material, the key to everything was the idea of comparing what your hypothesis said you should expect to see in the data with what you really did see. When testing independence, the contingency table was a really helpful concept, because it helped her to understand this difference. It could get pretty complex at times, but Esha thought it was probably better to keep things simple for now.

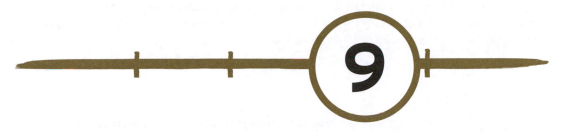

9

FIRST STEPS IN TESTING RELATIONSHIPS – GOODNESS OF FIT AND INDEPENDENCE TESTS

CONTENTS

learning objectives

There are only four objectives for this chapter, but they are critical ones, so bear them in mind as you study:

☑ Understand the idea of an expected distribution of data, for a given null hypothesis.

☑ Understand the concept of comparing your observed distribution of data with the expected distribution, and learn how to use the chi-square statistical test to determine how close they match each other as a hypothesis test.

☑ Learn how to use the chi-square statistic to test goodness of fit for hypotheses concerning multinomial, Poisson and normal distributions.

☑ Learn how to use the chi-square statistic to test independence.

In the previous chapter, you learned that we could statistically test whether or not a sample statistic was likely to be different to a population parameter. This is called *univariate* analysis. In other words, we were only looking at a single variable – say, the mean of some variable like the number of acid drops in a bag. It is also common that we might want to look at the *relationship between two variables*, which would be called *bivariate* analysis. For example, are higher levels of advertising associated with higher levels of sales for a product? There are many ways we can test for such relationships, and I will show you a lot of them later in this book. We can even test for relationships between more than two variables! If you work hard, and pay attention, I promise you will be able to do all this magical stuff by the end of the book.

In this chapter, I am going to help you take your first steps into testing for relationships in your data, beginning by introducing the idea of goodness of fit tests.

BASIC CONCEPTS

I will begin by explaining the idea of goodness of fit in more detail, In fact, while goodness of fit is presented here as one of the first things you will learn, the basic ideas I am teaching are relevant to even some of the most advanced statistical analysis methods available right now. I use goodness of fit tests all the time in my own work, using what is called structural equation modelling, for example. It is the same test as you will learn here, applied to a more complex set of statistical tools. It's a good example of how paying attention to even things you might think are unimportant can help you later on!

A goodness of fit test basically compares your sample data with how it would look if the null hypothesis was true in the population. The latter is called the *expected* values of your data, and your sample data is called the *observed* values. Simply put, if the expected and observed values are close, we cannot reject the null hypothesis. The trick, as always, is working out 'how close is close?'

The basic process of goodness of fit testing involves first defining some particular goodness of fit test statistic to use, based on the characteristics of your data and the task at hand. This test statistic will measure the 'distance' between the observed data you have and the data you would expect to get under some hypothesized model. For example, our usual null hypothesis in such situations is that there are no relationships in the data. If this null hypothesis were true in the population, we could expect a certain distribution of the data to be observed. Our task is to compare the real data we *did* observe in our sample with that expected if the 'no relationships' null were true in the population.

For example, consider the distribution of gender in the population. We may assume that the distribution of males and females in the general population is essentially equal. If we draw a random sample of say 50 people from a certain profession, we can use goodness of fit testing to get some information about whether the distribution of males and females in that population is equal. Imagine your sample included 10 females and 40 males. If the gender distribution in the population was equal you would *expect* 25 females and 25 males. Now, of course, in this case you can eyeball it and make a pretty solid guess that the observed sample data is so far away from this expected distribution that you can be pretty confident that, as long as the sample was random, the population is not equally distributed in terms of gender.

But what about if your sample was 22 females and 28 males? Can you *now* be so confident? Of course not. It is here we need a goodness of fit test. The choice of goodness of fit test is determined by the data you are dealing with, and I will show you a number of different ones in the course of the chapter. However, the most common test by far is sometimes termed the chi-square test, which relies on the chi-square distribution. Of course, chi-square is also referred to by the Greek letter χ^2 – so please do bear this in mind.

However, it is a little misleading for me simply to refer to the chi-square, or χ^2, test. Rather, it is more correct to say that, in most cases, the test statistic for the goodness of fit test has a chi-squared distribution. Sometimes, people like me who use statistical tests for a living simply refer to the 'chi-square test', when we really should say 'chi-square goodness of fit test'. I actually have a funny story about χ^2 that I might get into later. Well, I say funny, but someone ended up in tears at the end. Let's hope that does not happen here.

USING CHI-SQUARE TO TEST GOODNESS OF FIT FOR A MULTINOMIAL POPULATION

For our first foray into the use of the chi-square goodness of fit test, we will take the case of a multinomial population. The basic idea here can be extended to most any population, with some modifications, but it is best to start with the simplest case. A multinomial population is one in which every element is a member of one and only one category, out of several possible categories. Some examples of this are your country of birth, your choice of a single product from a number of competitors, and your choice of a candidate to vote for in an election. The multinomial population is a generalization of the binomial population (which only has two classes) to any number of classes above two. For each 'trial' (e.g. product choice, birth or vote), only one of the possible outcomes can occur. Each trial should be assumed independent of the others (e.g. you do not come out of the booth and tell the next person who you voted for), and the probabilities of each possible outcome are the same for each trial.

Right now, I am in a hotel room in Houston, Texas, where I am visiting the University of Houston for a month on sabbatical (Go Cougars!), and there is a lot of talk about the upcoming US election, like who the candidate for the Republicans is going to be. As we say in the UK, they are a pretty rum bunch, but it does give me a good idea for an example here – although I am not going to use any real names (the legal teams seem like velociraptors[1] over here!).

Let's say we have three candidates for the Republican nomination for the US Presidency. The average approval rating over the last six months for Candidate A is 15%, for Candidate B 40% and for Candidate C 45%. Candidate A has recently produced some new policy, and done well in the candidates' debates, while Candidates B and C have become embroiled in some unfortunate scandals from their past. So, Candidate A has asked you as a professional 'pollster' to work out whether this recent success (and the problems of the other candidates) will change their share of the approval rating.

Here, we clearly have a multinomial population, but let's check the features. First, there are at least three categories/classes. Secondly, each voter can only select one of the candidates for approval. Thirdly, we have to assume that (a) voters must not tell others what their choice was (independence) and (b) we have no reason to expect any individual voter to prefer one or another of the candidates (equal probability of success). Yep, definitely multinomial, as some people might say.

You might recognize this problem as one about proportions, which I introduced in the previous chapter. So, we can use the notation below for the three possible proportions:

$$\pi_A = \text{share of approval for Candidate A}$$

$$\pi_B = \text{share of approval for Candidate B}$$

$$\pi_C = \text{share of approval for Candidate C}$$

Since it is a test for proportions, why could we not use the techniques of the last chapter? Well, those techniques relied on a binomial distribution (i.e. only two possible proportions), which really reduces to only one, since the other is dependent on the value of the first.[2] Incidentally, you might now realize that my gender example at the start was overly simplistic. This is correct, but I only used it so I could guarantee everyone would get me quickly. So we're cool, OK?

So, moving along, you can conduct a survey of a random sample of potential voters and work out the proportion of the sample who said they approve each candidate. We can easily set up a hypothesis test for this. If we can reject the null hypothesis, we can give evidence to Candidate A that his or her ratings have improved in the population.

---

[1] Note: the velociraptors in the *Jurassic Park* movies are nothing like what archaeologists believe the real ones were like. Plus, I guess I don't mean lawyers really are literally like that, it's a simile.

[2] For example, if in a binomial distribution the proportion in one group is 0.4, the other has to be 0.6.

If we assume that recent events have not altered the approval ratings of Candidate A in the population, the hypotheses are:

$$H_0: \pi_A = 0.15, \pi_B = 0.40, \pi_C = 0.45$$

H_1: The population proportions are not $\pi_A = 0.15$, $\pi_B = 0.40$, $\pi_C = 0.45$

Assume that you have a voter panel of 500 potential voters, randomly selected across the relevant geographic area (e.g. the nation or state where the upcoming election is taking place). If each person in the panel must select one of the candidates for their approval, this basically works out to be a multinomial experiment with 500 trials.

So, in our case, let's say that Candidate A is chosen by 95 of the voters, Candidate B by 180 of the voters and Candidate C by 225. Using this data, we can relatively easily perform a goodness of fit test using the chi-square statistic, to see whether our observed results are consistent with our null hypothesis. The test works by comparing your observed results with those which would be expected if the null hypothesis really were true in the population. We have the observed results already, but what we need to do now is work out the expected candidate preferences for the 500-voter sample, assuming that the null hypothesis of $\pi_A = 0.15$, $\pi_B = 0.40$, $\pi_C = 0.45$ was true in the population.

This is a simple expected frequency problem: just multiply the sample size by the hypothesized proportion for each candidate. More specifically, if the expected proportion of Candidate A's votes is 0.15, we simply multiply our sample size by 0.15, to get an expected frequency of 500(0.15) = 75. In turn, the expected frequency for Candidate B is 500(0.40) = 200 and for Candidate C, 500(0.45) = 225.

So now we have a set of observed frequencies, and a set of expected frequencies, which is all we need for the goodness of fit test. We can see that the observed and expected frequencies are certainly different, but, again, the trick is *how different*? It is the chi-square test statistic that can tell us this, found in Box 9.1.

box 9.1

Chi-square Test Statistic for Goodness of Fit

$$\chi^2 = \sum_{i=1}^{k} \frac{(f_i - e_i)^2}{e_i}$$

where:
  f_i = observed frequency for category i
  e_i = expected frequency for category i
  k = number of categories

Important note: The test statistic has a chi-square distribution with $k - 1$ degrees of freedom *only if* expected frequencies are greater than or equal to five for *all categories*.

think it over 9.1

As I have suggested previously when a new equation has been introduced, explain the equation given in Box 9.1 to a colleague or, better still, to someone unfamiliar with statistics.

OK, so that formula looks somewhat intimidating,[3] but actually it is rather simple, as long as you take a systematic approach to working through it. If you are confused about what the formula means, go back to earlier sections of this book and work through the examples of basic formulae. Remember, the Greek letter 'sigma' signifies you add up stuff. Here, it is saying, for every category (denoted i), create the expression on the right and then add them all together. I will show you how to do it below – all you need is a working table, where you can create the numbers for each category. Table 9.1 shows this clearly, with chi-square coming out at 7.33.

Table 9.1 Computations for chi-square test statistic for the politician example

	Hypothesized proportion	Observed frequency (f_i)	Expected frequency (e_i)	Difference $(f_i - e_i)$	Squared difference $(f_i - e_i)^2$	Squared difference divided by expected frequency $(f_i - e_i)^2/e_i$
Candidate A	0.15	95	75	20	400	5.33
Candidate B	0.4	180	200	−20	400	2.00
Candidate C	0.45	225	225	0	0	0.00
Totals		500	500			
Chi-square						7.33

You can reject the null hypothesis if the difference between observed and expected frequencies is large enough to result in a large chi-square value. This means in practice that we are always dealing with a one-tailed (upper-tail to be specific) test. We can determine 'how large is large enough' in two ways as usual; the p-value and the critical value methods of deciding whether or not to reject the null hypothesis.

 think it over 9.2

What chi-square value would you expect if the observed frequency and expected frequency values were identical? Use this to remember that a high chi-square value is required to reject the null hypothesis which states the difference between the observed and expected frequencies is large.

Let's begin with the p-value method. First, we decide our level of significance, and as is usual we will use a level of significance $\alpha = 0.05$. Then, we need to know the degrees of freedom. For the chi-square test, degrees of freedom are the number of categories (k) minus one. In this case $k - 1 = 3 - 1 = 2$

---

[3] So, I said I would tell you a story about chi-square. Well, when I was a young, long-haired and good-looking grad student, a very good friend of mine was confused about a specific statistical technique which used the chi-square test. She basically needed to know what the chi-square number meant. I guess, in hindsight, what she really wanted to know was how to go from a chi-square number to a hypothesis test conclusion. Unfortunately, at that point I was not smart enough to help, so she went to the office of one of the course tutors, now a very good friend of mine, expecting a 10-minute explanation. Three hours later, she came out in tears, having had the entire chi-square test explained in minute detail from go to whoa, and I can only imagine all kinds of other statistical concepts as well. Great learning experience, but kind of overwhelming at the time. I remember her tearful words: 'I don't even remember what I wanted to know in the first place.' Or something like that at least.

degrees of freedom. In order to make our decision, we use a chi-squared distribution table. To do this, you find the degrees of freedom on the left hand side of the chi-square table – here it is 2. Then, you try to locate your chi-square value in this row of the table. You can see that our chi-square of 7.33 falls somewhere between the two values of 5.991 and 7.378. These values represent p-values of 0.05 and 0.025 respectively. Thus, even though we do not know our exact p-value from the table, we know that it is definitely less than 0.05.

As such, we can reject the null hypothesis and conclude the following: that the population proportions are not $\pi_A = 0.15$, $\pi_B = 0.40$, $\pi_C = 0.45$. Note, that is *all* we can conclude. We can*not* say specifically that Candidate A's share of vote has increased with these results. All we know is that the observed proportions were significantly different from the expected ones. However, is it that Candidate B or C's proportions have changed? Looking at the observed values, it does seem likely that the significant result has been driven by Candidate A increasing, and B decreasing, but you cannot 'prove' that this is the sole driver.

As a couple of final notes, it is rare to run the chi-square test by hand, despite my story in the footnote above. We normally use Excel or IBM SPSS Statistics Software (SPSS) to analyse the data, particularly in larger data sets with more categories and so forth. Also, we could use a critical value approach rather than a p-value one. This is simple to do. We can see from the chi-square distribution table for $\alpha = 0.05$ and 2 degrees of freedom that the critical value for the chi-square test statistic is $\chi^2 = 5.991$. So, the rejection rule in this upper-tail case is:

$$\text{Reject } H_0 \text{ if } \chi^2 \geq 5.991$$

OK, that was not so hard ,was it? I could have saved my friend some tears back in the day if I had known all that (Hint: always read the footnotes). So, make sure you paid attention, it could make you a knight in shining statistical armour (probably).

USING CHI-SQUARE TO TEST INDEPENDENCE

While the above application of the chi-square distribution was an excellent starting point, we can use it in a lot of other situations where we have an expected and observed set of values. Probably the most common use of the chi-square distribution is to examine the possible relationship between two variables.

Technically, this is called a test for independence of two variables – in other words, whether one variable's values are independent of another. However, you could look at it from the other perspective, as a way of getting evidence of a possible dependence between two variables. Statistically speaking, we are testing for independence, but in practice most situations where this is used are where the researcher is actually interested in whether or not there is a dependence. Statistics can only give us a reason either to accept or reject the hypothesis of independence, but often our theories concern dependence. It is two sides of the same coin, and I will explain it as we go through our example.

 **think it over 9.3**

Fred can do two things: sit down or run a marathon. Are these two events independent or mutually exclusive? Explain your choice.

Fred decides to run a marathon and his time is 4 hours 35 minutes. Prior to the event he was told that he has a very high level of fitness. Is the relationship between his fitness level and the time he took to run the race mutually exclusive, independent or dependent? Explain your answer.

In this case, let's stay with the political example I introduced earlier, but add a layer of complexity. Imagine that the campaign team for Candidate A also wants to know whether the preferences for its candidate differ across males and females. The implications of these findings are clear. For example, if the team finds voter preferences for Candidate A are not independent of gender, then perhaps Candidate A should modify his or her campaign – maybe focusing on issues that appeal more to one gender than another, to raise his or her approval in that gender. Our chi-square testing skills can be applied to this problem, and many others of the same nature. For example, do product preferences depend on gender or other categorical variables such as country of birth and so forth? It is a highly useful test, and one used very often in many research contexts, especially market research. In this particular case, our hypotheses are:

H_0: Candidate approval is independent of voter gender

H_1: Candidate approval is not independent of voter gender

In order to do this test, we need to extend some of our skills. Remember above how we used a table to help our working? Well, in this situation, tables are vital, and we will create a number of them. In fact, what we will create is a set of contingency tables. These tables are an extremely useful tool, and are often used in many situations where we are interested in the possible associations between two (or sometimes more) variables. In fact, they are so important to this test that it is sometimes even called a contingency table test. Also, you may see these sorts of tables referred to as cross-tabulations (or crosstabs for short), or in some situations pivot tables. So do not get confused.

A contingency table is created by crossing one variable against another, and tabulating the results of a given data set. As you can see in Table 9.2, every sample element contains two characteristics, a gender and a candidate preference. As such, it can only appear in one of the six possible cells. If you are a male who prefers Candidate A, you will fall into cell (1,1), while if you are a female who prefers Candidate C, you will fall into cell (2,3). You can only appear in one cell, and every sample element must appear somewhere. In other words, a table should be exhaustive (contain all possible values of the variables) and mutually exclusive (each sample element must appear in one and only one cell).

Table 9.2 Contingency table for candidate preference according to gender

		Candidate preference		
		A	B	C
Gender	Male	Cell (1,1)	Cell (1,2)	Cell (1,3)
	Female	Cell (2,1)	Cell (2,2)	Cell (2,3)

If we go back to our sample data from the last example, recall that we had a 500-person sample. Imagine that sample consisted of 250 males and 250 females, and we recorded that data as well as the candidate preferences. Table 9.3 shows this data.

Table 9.3 Sample data for candidate preference according to gender

		Preference			
		Candidate A	Candidate B	Candidate C	Total
Gender	Male	35	120	95	250
	Female	60	60	130	250
	Total	95	180	225	

However, getting the observed frequencies is only part of the story – we still need the expected frequencies. Getting these is a little more complex in the independence testing situation than it was for the previous goodness of fit context. In fact, it is not immediately obvious where these would come from. Sometimes, our hypotheses give them to us. For example, we could set up a set of expected frequencies which were completely even across the entire table. Such a set of frequencies would imply that our null hypothesis was one of no difference in preference across either the candidates or the genders. That would in fact be the simplest answer to the problem.

However, this is not actually our current null hypothesis. Instead, we are interested only in whether there is independence between gender and preference. So, in fact, we are not so much concerned with the observed differences in candidate preferences, but only with whether they are different across the genders. Thus, let's take our observed voter preferences as given, and think what this would mean if they were independent of gender. Remember: for our sample of 500, 95 preferred Candidate A, 180 preferred Candidate B and 225 preferred Candidate C. This means that 95/500 preferred Candidate A, 180/500 preferred Candidate B and 225/500 preferred Candidate C. If the independence assumption were valid, these fractions would be the same for both males and females. We can therefore apply them to the female and male sample sizes to get our expected frequency table as shown in Table 9.4.

Table 9.4 Expected frequencies if candidate preference is independent of gender

		Preference			
		Candidate A	Candidate B	Candidate C	Total
Gender	Male	47.5	90	112.5	250
	Female	47.5	90	112.5	250
	Total	95	180	225	

Working through one of the values in this table should help you understand how things work, and allow us to come up with a generalization to find all the values in every situation. Let's take the female preference for Candidate A.

First, let e_{ij} denote the frequency for the contingency table in row i and column j. Recalling the fractional method above, we have:

$$e_{21} = \left(\frac{95}{500}\right)250 = 47.5$$

But we could rewrite this in a more easily generalizable form, as follows:

$$e_{21} = \left(\frac{95}{500}\right)250 = \frac{250 \times 95}{500} 47.5$$

So, you should immediately see that 95 is the total number of the sample who preferred Candidate A, which is the total of the first column, and 250 is the total number of females, which is the total of the second row. Therefore, this can easily be generalized to the following expression to get the expected frequencies for any contingency table in a test of independence – in the absence of any more specific hypotheses:

$$e_{ij} = \frac{(\text{row } i \text{ total})(\text{column } j \text{ total})}{\text{sample size}}$$

Note that the brackets are just a more elegant way of expressing the multiplication of the two numbers.

From this, you should also note that the fact that the expected frequencies are the same for males and females for each candidate is merely an artefact of our sample of equal numbers of males and females. This would not be the case otherwise – there is no necessity that any or all column frequencies should be the same.

Using the chi-square to compare the observed (Table 9.3) with the expected (Table 9.4) frequencies is broadly similar to the goodness of fit testing method outlined in Box 9.1, with one important difference. See Box 9.2 for details.

 box 9.2

Chi-square Test Statistic for Independence

$$\chi^2 = \sum_i \sum_j \frac{(f_{ij} - e_{ij})^2}{e_{ij}}$$

where:

f_{ij} = observed frequency for category in row i and column j

e_{ij} = expected frequency for category in row i and column j assuming independence

Important note: The test statistic has a chi-square distribution with $(n - 1)(m - 1)$ degrees of freedom (where there are n rows and m columns), *only if* expected frequencies are greater than or equal to five in *all cells*. If this is not the case, sometimes you can solve the problem by combining some categories together.

Also, if you are confused about the double summation (double sigma) in the equation, it just means that you have to make the calculation for all cells (i.e. all rows and columns), not just one or the other. If that confuses you, keep going until you see the working below, then it should start to make sense.

 think it over 9.4

Explain the following calculation in plain English and perform the calculation:

$$\sum_{y=1}^{5} \sum_{x=1}^{4} x + y$$

Let's go through the working of this step by step. If you can do the goodness of fit example, this is a simple extension. First, we check whether our expected frequencies are all more than five. This is the case, so we can move on. Following this, we set our significance level, which for this case we will set at $\alpha = 0.05$. Now we can get on with our calculations, and they are shown in Table 9.5, which is a simple extension of the earlier working in Table 9.1, to capture a contingency table's extra cells. You can see that the chi-square test statistic works out as $\chi^2 = 32.02$, which at first glance seems very large.

Of course, we need to interpret any value of chi-square in light of degrees of freedom. In this case, we have two rows and three columns, so according to our formula the degrees of freedom are $(2 - 1)(3 - 1) = 2$. The test for independence rejects the null hypothesis of independence H_0 if the chi-square statistic resulting from the differences between observed and expected frequencies is large enough. Again, this is a one-tailed upper-tail test, and the chi-square distribution will enable us to work out the significance. Looking at the distribution for 2 degrees of freedom, we can see that the highest value of chi-square for 2 degrees of freedom is 10.597 for an $\alpha = 0.005$. *It is therefore clear that our p-value is less than $\alpha = 0.05$*, and we can reject the null hypothesis that candidate preference is independent of gender. Of course, these days, we would usually do this using Excel or SPSS.

Table 9.5 Chi-square calculation for test of whether candidate preference is independent of gender

Gender	Candidate preference	Observed frequency (f_{ij})	Expected frequency (e_{ij})	Difference $(f_{ij} - e_{ij})$	Squared difference $(f_{ij} - e_{ij})^2$	Squared difference divided by expected frequency $(f_{ij} - e_{ij})^2/e_{ij}$
Male	Candidate A	35	47.5	−12.5	156.25	3.29
Male	Candidate B	120	90	30	900	10
Male	Candidate C	95	112.5	−17.5	306.25	2.72
Female	Candidate A	60	47.5	12.5	156.25	3.29
Female	Candidate B	60	90	−30	900	10
Female	Candidate C	130	112.5	17.5	306.25	2.72
	Totals	500	500			
	Chi-square					**32.02**

Again, though, we cannot draw any other formal conclusions here. In other words, we cannot justify a conclusion of 'females like Candidate A more than Candidate B' and so forth. All we can say formally is that our analysis suggests that gender and candidate preference do not appear to be independent. Of course, we are likely to provide informally some deeper level of analysis looking at the observed frequencies, but you should be careful not to give the wrong impression from such analysis – you are not dealing with 'facts' here, nor even statistical conclusions about the individual candidates. It is tempting for the analyst to go too far here, so do be careful.

USING THE GOODNESS OF FIT TEST FOR A POISSON DISTRIBUTION

The previous example used a multinomial population as its base. However, we can extend our knowledge to situations where we hypothesize the population in other ways to take account of other potential situations we may find ourselves in. Let me begin with the example of a Poisson distribution. You should remember the Poisson distribution from earlier in the book, but, as a recap, recall that the Poisson distribution can be used to describe the probability that a given number of events will occur in a given fixed period of time (and/or space), if we know the average rate of occurrence and can assume that the events occur independently of the time since the last event (i.e. the probability of an event in one fixed period is independent of the probability of an event in any other period).

 think it over 9.5

Probability distributions are used a lot in statistics. How do you know which one to use? Briefly explain the criteria you would use to decide whether a binomial, normal or Poisson distribution is appropriate. Give an example of each.

Let me move from our political example earlier to one concerning a statistics-themed fast-food restaurant called 'Taco Bell Curve' (I'm still in the USA). The manager of the fast-food chain has just employed you as a hot-shot service strategist for the firm, and you have some ideas about how to modify the staffing patterns for the drive-in service. However, your theory will only work if you can analyse the data on the queuing for drive-in customers in each time period based on the assumption that it follows a Poisson distribution. So before we get into anything like modifying strategies and so forth, we need to test whether you can assume that the drive-in arrivals follow a Poisson distribution within reasonable limits. Before we go further, we have to specify more clearly what we mean by drive-in arrivals.

Let's do this for our purposes as the number of cars that join the drive-in line in a given 10-minute time interval. This leads to the following hypotheses about the distribution :

H_0: The number of cars joining the drive-in line during 10-minute intervals has a
Poisson distribution

H_1: The number of cars joining the drive-in line during 10-minute intervals does not
have a Poisson distribution

So, if we cannot reject H_0 with our data, we can move on with our clever new staffing strategy. Thus, this amounts to a goodness of fit test, comparing our observed data with that expected if a Poisson distribution were the case in the population. In essence, you should immediately start to think that the main task here (apart from collecting data) is to create the expected distribution for the test.

First, the data. Let's divide up the working day into 10-minute intervals and randomly select a sample of $n = 100$ of these intervals from a two-week period of trading for Taco Bell Curve. For each 10-minute period, we get a research assistant to count how many cars join the drive-in line and to produce a summary frequency distribution. This is presented in Table 9.6.

Table 9.6   Observed frequency of drive-in customers at Taco Bell Curve for a sample of 100 10-minute periods

Number of cars	Observed frequency
0	2
1	3
2	5
3	6
4	7
5	10
6	13
7	15
8	17
9	10
10	7
11	4
12	1
Total	100

You can see that two periods have 0 cars arriving, and the maximum number of cars arriving was 12, which occurred once. This is our observed frequency distribution. From here, we need to compute the expected frequencies for each of the 13 categories if the assumption of a Poisson distribution in the population were true. You should remember the Poisson probability function from Chapter 6, restated below:

$$p(x) = \frac{\mu^x e^{-\mu}}{x!}$$

Again, while looking intimidating, it is simple if you unpack it a little and take it step by step. First, x represents the random variable of the number of cars arriving during a given period, μ is the expected number of cars arriving each period, and $p(x)$ is the probability that x cars will arrive in any specific period. I really hope you can remember that e refers to the exponential. Apart from that, the first thing which may baffle you is how to get μ, since it is not really evident unless you think about it. Simply put, μ is the sample mean for our sample data from Table 9.6 (i.e. the mean number of cars during any single period), and of course the best estimate of the expected number of cars during a period is the sample mean. This is easy enough to compute from the data, and is 6.44. With this in hand, we can insert it into the function above and end up with the observed distribution in Table 9.7. To create the expected frequency column, simply multiply the relevant Poisson probability by the number of periods in your sample (100 in this case). Also, you might see a new category down the bottom of '13 or more'. Why do we need this? Well, you should know that the probability of any single event

Table 9.7 Expected frequency of Taco Bell Curve drive-in arrivals, assuming a Poisson distribution with $\mu = 6.44$

Number of cars	Poisson probability $p(x)$	Expected number of 10-minute periods with x car arrivals, $100p(x)$
0	0.002	0.160
1	0.010	1.028
2	0.033	3.310
3	0.071	7.106
4	0.114	11.441
5	0.147	14.736
6	0.158	15.817
7	0.146	14.552
8	0.117	11.714
9	0.084	8.382
10	0.054	5.398
11	0.032	3.160
12	0.017	1.696
13 or more	0.015	1.498
Totals	1.000	100

happening is 1. In other words, *something* has to happen (i.e. some number of cars has to be observed from zero to infinity). Now just because we only observed 12 cars or fewer in any single period, does this completely discount the chances of 13 or more cars being observed in any other period we *might have* observed? No, of course not. So, we need to add this category. In order to get $p(x)$ for that catch-all category, you simply subtract the total Poisson probabilities for all the other categories in your observed distribution (in this case 0–12) from 1.

Now we can get on with calculating the chi-square, can't we? Well, before you rush off and do so, remember that one of the key assumptions of chi-square is that all categories must have expected frequencies of five or more. You can see that six categories in Table 9.6 violate this condition: the first and last three. But this is no real hardship, because we can just combine them to avoid the problem. So, we create a new category of '0–2', and one of '11 or more', and we are fine. Or are we? See, the '0–2' category is *still* less than five, so we will combine it with the next category and create a '0–3' category. Table 9.8 shows the new observed and expected frequencies, along with the chi-squared calculations. As you can see, $\chi^2 = 8.89$ here.

Table 9.8 Computation of chi-square test for Taco Bell Curve drive-in arrivals

Number of cars (x)	Observed frequency (p$_i$)	Expected frequency (e$_i$)	Difference (p$_i$ – e$_i$)	Squared difference (p$_i$ – e$_i$)^2	Squared difference divided by expected frequency (p$_i$ – e$_i$)^2/e$_i$
0–3	16	11.61	4.39	19.27	1.66
4	7	11.44	–4.44	19.71	1.72
5	10	14.74	–4.74	22.47	1.52
6	13	15.82	–2.82	7.95	0.50
7	15	14.55	0.45	0.20	0.01
8	17	11.71	5.29	27.98	2.39
9	10	8.38	1.62	2.62	0.31
10	7	5.4	1.6	2.56	0.47
11 or more	5	6.35	–1.35	1.82	0.29
	100	100		Chi-sq. =	**8.89**

What is needed now is the degrees of freedom in this case. The general rule here is that the chi-square goodness of fit test has $k - p - 1$ degrees of freedom, with k equal to the number of categories and p equal to the number of parameters estimated from the sample. Looking at Table 9.7, we can see nine categories. As for the parameters, well, you used the sample data to estimate the *population mean*, remember? So that is one parameter. We therefore end up with $9 - 1 - 1 = 7$ degrees of freedom.

All we have to do now is use this information to test our null hypothesis that the probability distribution for car arrivals at the drive-in is of Poisson form. Our null hypothesis is that the population distribution is Poisson, with $\alpha = 0.05$. To test this, we need to find the p-value for $\chi^2 = 8.89$, by finding the area in the upper tail of a chi-square distribution with 7 degrees of freedom. Using the standard chi-square table, you can see that $\chi^2 = 8.89$ gives an area in the upper tail of more than 0.1 and therefore, given that $p > \alpha = 0.05$, we have no grounds to reject H_0, and no grounds to reject the assumption of a Poisson distribution for the car arrivals.

think it over 9.6

If it turned out that our calculation implied we should reject the null hypothesis, what would this mean?

USING THE GOODNESS OF FIT TEST FOR A NORMAL DISTRIBUTION

It should not be too much of a stretch now for you to imagine that, just as we can base a goodness of fit test around the assumption of a Poisson distribution, we can do the same for a normal distribution. Of course, given that you should by now understand how central the normal distribution is for statistical testing, you should also be thinking that it would be very useful to have a way of testing an assumption about whether a population has a normal distribution. For example, we could then test an observed frequency distribution to see whether we were able to have confidence in the assumption that the observed sample came from a normally distributed population.

That said, the fact that the normal distribution is continuous does present a few complications as to how we define categories and compute expected frequencies. As such, it will be best to work through an example. Consider a typical large-scale staff training situation. Say I have a call centre of 500 employees, each tasked with calling prospective customers and trying to sell them a new financial services product. Everyone loves those guys. To be most effective, my callers need a good level of knowledge about the new product, so I put all 500 through an online training course, which they have to complete in their own time (i.e. when they are not working), and then I test them all. Yes, this really does happen. Often, they have to pay for their own training too. Welcome to the real world.

Anyway, the director of sales has just got an MBA and wants to know whether the population of test scores can be assumed to conform to a normal distribution. She suggests that knowing this would help in the interpretation of individual scores.

As a budding quantitative expert, you know that this is a situation where you are testing the null hypothesis that the population is normally distributed. The first thing to do is to take a sample of the 500 tests, to use for the test. Therefore, you take a simple random sample of 50 test scores. You do not need to see the exact data in this instance, just imagine that it is there. The first thing to do is to calculate estimates of the mean and standard deviation of the normal distribution. You should by now realize that we use the sample mean and standard deviation for this purpose. In this case, the test score had a maximum of 100, and the values are:

$$\bar{x} = 54$$

$$s = 14.3$$

So, you can now define your hypotheses formally:

H_0: The population of test scores is normally distributed with a mean of 54 and a standard deviation of 14.3

H_1: The population of test scores is not normally distributed with a mean of 54 and a standard deviation of 14.3

The next task is to compute expected values. However, some of you might have already begun to suspect there may be a problem here. More specifically, what categories should you define? For a discrete distribution like Poisson, this was no problem – they were predefined, such as '0–2' cars visiting the drive-in during a defined period. However, the normal distribution is continuous, and you therefore need to spend some time defining your own categories, in order to ensure the test makes sense.

The first thing to remember is the important rule for expected frequencies – that there must be five or more in each category. So, if there are 50 in your sample, you can satisfy this by dividing the normal distribution into 10 equally probable categories. This would lead to the same expected frequency in each category, namely five. Of course, the more categories there are, the closer you get to an accurate representation of a continuous probability distribution like the normal distribution. In this case, satisfying the expected frequency rule means 10 is the most categories you can have. If you had a smaller sample you would have to create fewer categories, and if you had more you could create more. In any case, though, 10 is a good number.

With this number of categories, you can define the boundaries for each category quite easily. This is simply a case of 'slicing up' the normal distribution into 10 parts, where each part is equally probable. Remember: the area under the normal distribution graph corresponds to the probability of a value occurring, so what you are really doing is slicing up the distribution into 10 parts of equal area under the graph. This can easily be done mathematically, using a normal distribution table. For example, the lowest 10% of the distribution corresponds to a $z = -1.28$. How do I know this? Well, look at the normal distribution table in the Appendix. You should remember that the table shows the area under the graph between the mean and the z-score you choose. The value for $z = 1.28$ corresponds to 0.3997. Remember that the distribution is symmetrical, so it is the same for $z = -1.28$. This means there is 10.03% of the probability distribution below $z = -1.28$. We usually round this to 10%. We can do the same for the lowest 20%. Here we would look for a z-score corresponding to 0.300, which can be found to be $z = -0.84$, which is again slightly rounded.

 think it over 9.7

In the text it stated that 10.03% of the normal probability distribution is below a corresponding z-value of –1.28. Explain why this is the case.

To convert these z-scores into the cut-off points for the expected test score distribution, simply multiply them by the sample standard deviation and subtract them from the sample mean for the bottom half of the distribution, or add them to the sample mean for the top half. The working for each category boundary is:

Lower 10%: 54 – 1.28(14.3) = 35.67

Lower 20%: 54 – 0.84(14.3) = 41.99

Lower 30%: 54 – 0.52(14.3) = 46.56

Lower 40%: 54 – 0.25(14.3) = 50.43

Mean: 54

Upper 40%: 54 + 0.25(14.3) = 57.58

Upper 30%: 54 + 0.52(14.3) = 61.44

Upper 20%: 54 + 0.84(14.3) = 66.01

Upper 10%: 54 + 1.28(14.3) = 72.30

So now you know the categories, and the expected frequencies (remember, five in each category), you can compute Table 9.9, the working and results for the test. However, note that you would need to have the data in front of you to count up the observed frequencies. For now, you will just have to trust that I counted correctly.

Table 9.9 Observed and expected frequencies for call-centre test scores and chi-square calculation

Test score	Observed frequency (p_i)	Expected frequency (e_i)	Difference ($p_i - e_i$)	Squared difference ($p_i - e_i$)^2	Squared difference divided by expected frequency ($p_i - e_i$)^2/e_i
Less than 35.67	3	5	−2	4	0.8
35.67 to 41.99	4	5	−1	1	0.2
41.99 to 46.56	5	5	0	0	0
46.56 to 50.43	7	5	2	4	0.8
50.43 to 54	8	5	3	9	1.8
54 to 57.58	8	5	3	9	1.8
57.58 to 61.44	6	5	1	1	0.2
61.44 to 66.01	3	5	−2	4	0.8
66.01 to 72.30	2	5	−3	9	1.8
Over 72.3	4	5	−1	1	0.2
Totals	50	50		Chi-sq. =	8.4

You should now be able to see quite easily how I get to the chi-square test statistic, which is $\chi^2 = 8.4$. From here, you need to go to the appropriate chi-square distribution table to determine whether 8.4 is a large enough chi-square to reject the null hypothesis. Remember: the rule for computing degrees of freedom is $k - p - 1 = 10 - 2 - 1 = 7$ degrees of freedom. There are $k = 10$ categories and $p = 2$ parameters estimated from the sample data (standard deviation and mean).

The null hypothesis H_0 is that the distribution of the test scores is normal. If you use a 0.05 level of significance, meaning you need to recover the p-value for $\chi^2 = 8.4$ by looking at the area in the upper tail of a chi-square distribution with 7 degrees of freedom. You can see that the area in the upper tail of the chi-square distribution with 7 degrees of freedom for $p = 0.05$ is more than 8.4. As such, the null hypothesis that the product knowledge test scores are normally distributed cannot be rejected.

 **think it over 9.8**

Who really wants to be normal? Do we really need to worry about being normally distributed? Recall the CLT (Central Limit Theorem). *If you applied a goodness of fit test to the average distribution, what would it tell you?*

INDEPENDENCE TESTING WITH EXCEL

We can use Excel to perform independence testing. We will use the politician example shown earlier (refer to Table 9.1). Figure 9.1 shows the data arranged in two columns. It also shows where to find the chi-square within the pull-down menu system. Figure 9.2 shows the formula which will be used in cell D5. You may have noticed by now that if Excel is using a column of data, it separates the start and end points with a colon. The different inputs required are separated by a comma.

Figure 9.3 shows the result of the calculation. This value for the statistic is from the chi-square distribution and can be seen to be much lower than the 0.05 alpha value used as the significance level when we calculated the result by hand. Remember that the numbers act as a guide, so, as before, we use the value of the test statistic to recommend rejection of the null hypothesis.

In other words, the 0.026 p-value calculated by Excel is less than 0.05, therefore we reject the null hypothesis on the grounds that there is a 2.6% probability of getting this result due to chance.

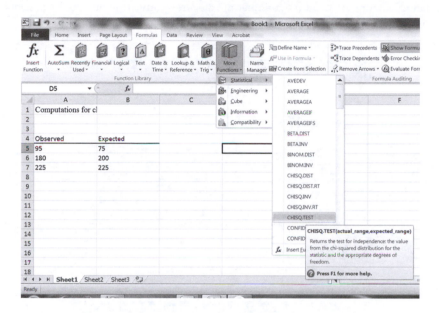

Figure 9.1

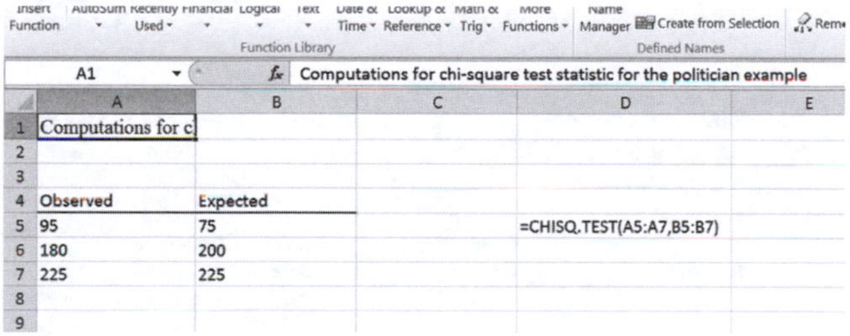

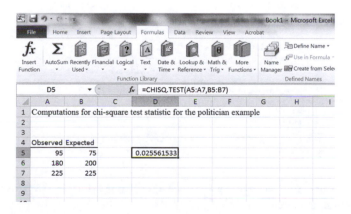

Figure 9.2

Figure 9.3

GOODNESS OF FIT TESTS USING EXCEL

Since you will probably being using data which is supposedly from a normal distribution, we will use the data given in Table 9.9. Unfortunately, Excel does not give a formula for directly calculating the statistic, so we will use the formulae we are familiar with and enter these into the cells of the spreadsheet.

Figure 9.4 shows the layout of the spreadsheet. You should adjust the cell references according to where you put your data. Notice that the degrees of freedom had to be adjusted according to the formula we used when calculating by hand (i.e. number of categories minus the number of parameters minus one). The number of categories was also entered by hand.

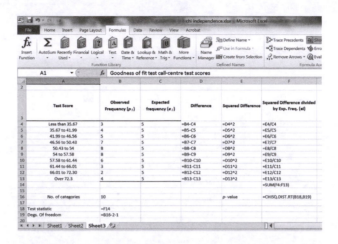

Figure 9.4

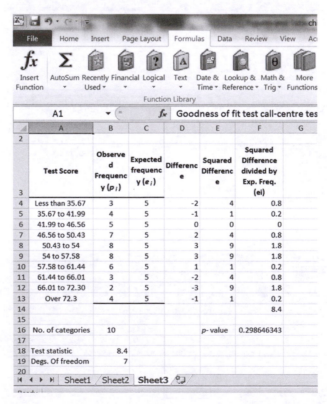

Figure 9.5

Figure 9.5 shows the result of the calculation giving a p-value of approximately 0.3. This means we cannot reject the null hypothesis as before.

INDEPENDENCE TESTING WITH SPSS

In order to use SPSS for testing independence, it has to be told to 'weight' the data in favour of the frequency count. We will use the politician example used above with Excel. Figure 9.6 shows how this is done. If you select Data then Weight Cases a pop-up window will appear. In this case we are going to choose observed frequencies as the data to be weighted. Click on OK.

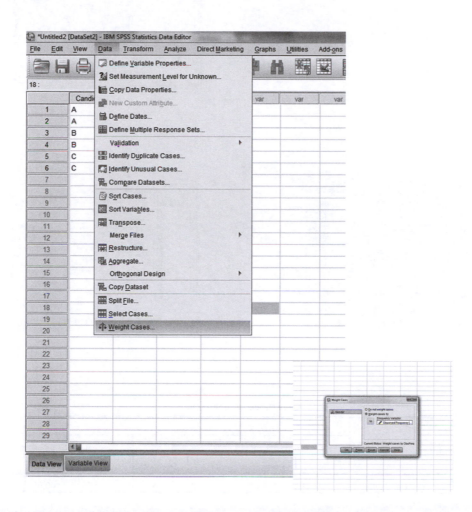

Figure 9.6

Select Analyze → Descriptive Statistics → Crosstabs. This will bring up the pop-ups shown in Figure 9.7.

Transfer Gender into the rows box and Candidate into the columns box. To specify the test, select Statistics and the pop-up Crosstabs Statistics will be shown. Check the Chi-square box and then Continue which will return you to the main pop-up. Select Cells and Crosstabs: Cell Display will appear. Check Observed and Expected frequencies then Continue. Click on OK and SPSS will run the test.

Figure 9.8 shows the Output Viewer from SPSS. The first box confirms the data used in the test. It is always worth looking at this box just to confirm you are analysing the correct data!

The second box looks like the crosstabs tables you created earlier. Again, check this table to make sure you are using the correct data. The final table gives you the value of the test statistic, which in our case is the Pearson Chi-Square. You can see that SPSS returns a value of 32.023, which is what you should have got when you calculated the value by hand. Using SPSS means you do not have to use tables to check if you could reject the null hypothesis, since it gives you the significance value. In this case it is so small that SPSS returns a value of 0.

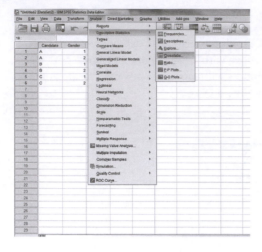

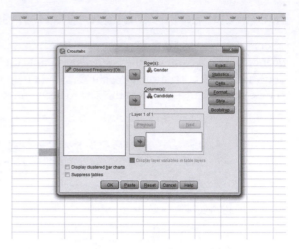

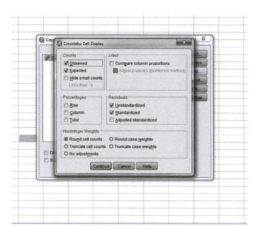

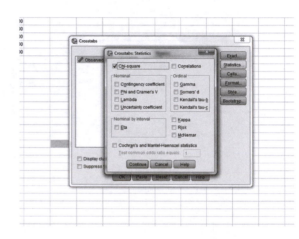

Figure 9.7

Case Processing Summary

	Cases					
	Valid		Missing		Total	
	N	Percent	N	Percent	N	Percent
Gender * Candidate	500	100.0%	0	0.0%	500	100.0%

Gender * Candidate Crosstabulation

			Candidate			Total
			A	B	C	
Gender	Male	Count	35	120	95	250
		Expected Count	47.5	90.0	112.5	250.0
		Residual	-12.5	30.0	-17.5	
		Std. Residual	-1.8	3.2	-1.6	
	Female	Count	60	60	130	250
		Expected Count	47.5	90.0	112.5	250.0
		Residual	12.5	-30.0	17.5	
		Std. Residual	1.8	-3.2	1.6	
Total		Count	95	180	225	500
		Expected Count	95.0	180.0	225.0	500.0

Chi-Square Tests

	Value	df	Asymp. Sig. (2-sided)
Pearson Chi-Square	32.023[a]	2	.000
Likelihood Ratio	32.512	2	.000
N of Valid Cases	500		

a. 0 cells (0.0%) have expected count less than 5. The minimum expected count is 47.50.

Figure 9.8

GOODNESS OF FIT TESTING WITH SPSS

In order to be able to compare calculating goodness of fit tests in Excel and SPSS, we will use the same data which is given in Table 9.9. To use SPSS we need to put the data into a form SPSS can work with. If you look at Figure 9.9, you will see that the data has been coded in the Values column.

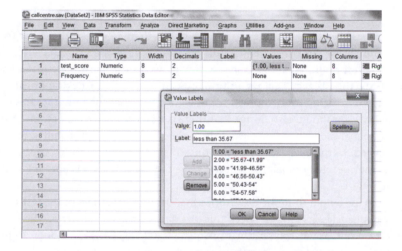

Figure 9.9

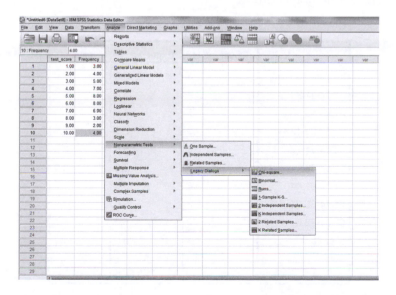

Figure 9.10

Figure 9.11

You can see that 1 has been used to represent a score of less than 35.67. All the other test scores have been coded in a similar way. In effect we will now be using non-parametric data since we are using a value to represent a test result. Figure 9.10 shows how to access the Chi-square test. First of all, go to Nonparametric Tests, then Legacy Dialogs and finally Chi-square test. Clicking on this will bring up the dialog box shown in Figure 9.11. You will see in Figure 9.11 that the test score has been moved to the Test Variable List. You should also notice that there is a box for expected values. In this case leave the All Categories equal radio button checked since there is an equal probability of any of the test scores being achieved. In the exercises below, in question 12 you will need to check the other radio button and enter the expected probabilities in the same order as the data is entered. Click on OK and SPSS will run the test.

Figure 9.12 shows the output from the test. Notice that the original ranges of the test scores are shown along with their frequencies. As always, check that the data displayed is correct. The second box, Test Statistics, shows the result. As you can see, the Chi-Square result is 8.4, the number of degrees of freedom is 9 and the significance is 0.494. As before, this result tells us that the null hypothesis cannot be rejected and that the data is normally distributed.

test_score			
	Observed N	Expected N	Residual
less than 35.67	3	5.0	-2.0
35.67-41.99	4	5.0	-1.0
41.99-46.56	5	5.0	.0
46.56-50.43	7	5.0	2.0
50.43-54	8	5.0	3.0
54-57.58	8	5.0	3.0
57.58-61.44	6	5.0	1.0
61.44-66.01	3	5.0	-2.0
66.01-72.3	2	5.0	-3.0
over 72.3	4	5.0	-1.0
Total	50		

Test Statistics

	test_score
Chi-Square	8.400[a]
df	9
Asymp. Sig.	.494

a. 0 cells (0.0%) have expected frequencies less than 5. The minimum expected cell frequency is 5.0.

Figure 9.12

think it over 9.9

Compare the degrees of freedom used in the 'hand' calculation and Excel with the reported value in SPSS. Why is there a difference? Could this potentially cause a problem?

SUMMARY

That was quite a lot of effort to get across only one main concept and only a few specific techniques. We are building directly on the previous chapter about statistical hypothesis testing, but applying it to more complex situations, which gives us much more flexibility in the sort of questions we can ask of our data. There are a lot of interesting and useful things you can do even with just the techniques we have learnt already, but there are wonders to come!

However, if you are having trouble, remember that you are not the only person to get confused at this point. In fact, a lot of people do get confused here, and I was one of them when I was at your stage of learning. The trick is to persevere, and to take it step by step. Also, do not worry about the complexity of the chi-square statistical formula itself – just create a spreadsheet to help you understand the working at each step. Remember: it does not take 'brains' to master this stuff, it takes work. And work is something we can all do!

final checklist

You should have covered and understood the following basic content in this chapter:

- ☑ The idea of an expected distribution of data, for a given null hypothesis.
- ☑ The concept of comparing your observed distribution of data with the expected distribution, and using the chi-square statistical test to determine how close they match each other as a hypothesis test.
- ☑ How to use the chi-square statistic to test goodness of fit for hypotheses concerning multinomial, Poisson and normal distributions.
- ☑ How to use the chi-square statistic to test independence.

EXERCISES

1. What does $p < 0.05$ mean in terms of interpreting the result from a χ^2 test?
2. When occurrences are said to be mutually exclusive, what do we mean?
3. Complete the following calculation using the values shown in Table 9.10:

$$\sum_{j=1}^{5}\sum_{i=1}^{4}x_{ij} = \sum_{j=1}^{5}(x_{1j} + x_{2j} + x_{3j} + \ldots)$$

Table 9.10

x_{ij} **Values**

i/j	1	2	3	4
1	2	4	5	7
2	3	0	1	5
3	6	4	2	8
4	3	5	1	8
5	5	9	0	2

4. If in Table 9.10 the *i* variable represented four different people, the *j* variable represented five different hotels and the x_{ij} values how the people rated the accommodation on a scale of 0 to 10 (where 10 is excellent), what rating did person 3 who stayed at hotel 5 think of it?

5. What two conditions should be met before the X^2 test can be used?

6. You are helping a colleague who works in flower genetics. Established theory says that if you cross sweet peas with red flowers with sweet peas with blue flowers, the next generation of sweet peas have red, blue and purple flowers in the proportions 0.25, 0.25 and 0.5, respectively. Her observed results are: 84 with red flowers, 92 with blue flowers and 157 with purple flowers. Determine whether these results support the theory.

7. Explain in your own words what is meant by 'goodness of fit'.

8. The 2 × 2 contingency table in Table 9.11 shows the result of a survey to find out the best student bar close to the university.

Table 9.11

	Student bar		
Favourite	**Plate of Spuds**	**Bucket of Frogs**	**Total**
Yes	163	154	317
No	64	108	172
Total	227	262	489

Test whether there is a difference in the preference of the students for a choice of bar.

9. Table 9.12 shows only the totals from a survey. Explain how you would find the number of degrees of freedom.

Table 9.12

	Participant 1	**Participant 2**	**Participant 3**	**Total**
Like				150
Dislike				30
Total	55	63	62	180

10. In a further study of student preferences for a bar, the students were asked for the primary reason for not using a particular bar.

Table 9.13

Primary reason	Bar			Total
	Plate of Spuds	Bucket of Frogs	Dish of Olives	
Cost of drinks	23	7	37	67
Location	39	13	8	60
State of the bar	13	5	13	31
Other	13	8	8	29
Total	88	33	66	187

Table 9.13 shows the result of the survey. Test the hypothesis that there is no relationship between the primary reason for not using a bar and the bar.

11. Table 9.14 shows the data you have collected concerning the heights of students who attend your statistics class. In order to do some analysis you would like the data to be normally distributed.

   a. Fit a normal curve to the data.
   b. Test the goodness of fit of the data.

Table 9.14

Heights of students in statistics class

Height (cm)	Number of students
152–157	5
158–163	18
164–169	42
170–175	27
176–181	8
Total	100

12. Repeat questions 6, 8, 10 and 11 using Excel and SPSS. Note that, for question 6, with SPSS you will need to put in the proportions. To do this, when you click on Chi-square Test and the dialog box comes up, enter the proportions in the same order as your variables as shown in Figure 9.13, then click on OK.

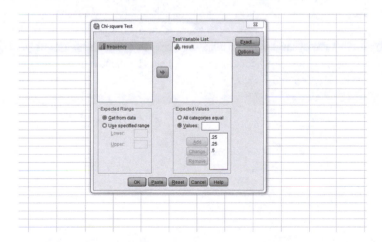

Figure 9.13

To access additional online resources please visit: **https://study.sagepub.com/leepeters**

The Ballad of Eddie the Easily Distracted: Part 10

Eddie was arguing with Vincent again. Well, Vincent called it 'debating', but to Eddie it usually felt like Vincent was simply arguing for the sake of it. They were discussing issues that had come up in Eddie's QUAN101 lecture, which was odd in itself since Vincent tended to think he was above such mortal concerns. More specifically, the topic of discussion was causality. Eddie had spent a long time trying to get his head around the difference between causality and correlation, and ended up thinking himself into a corner, as Vincent put it rather eloquently (or pretentiously, depending on your point of view).

Eddie just couldn't work out the difference between the two, and he was very surprised to find himself enjoying the thinking. 'But surely,' he said, 'it doesn't matter if we can never really see a cause-and-effect relationship – it's just so *obvious* when one thing causes another.' 'Really, is it *really*?' replied Vincent. 'Let's talk about that girl you like,' he continued, to Eddie's quite evident shock. 'You have a theory about the way she might behave, which in your mind is caused by her liking you. You know, things like giving you extra help, smiling at you, and so forth,' Vincent continued. 'But those behaviours could be caused by all kinds of things really, anything from her just being a nice person, to thinking you are a total idiot and therefore feeling sorry for you, to even just mild indigestion.' Eddie was still totally shocked by this turn in the conversation, but he was just managing to follow the logic: 'So, you mean that just observing the behaviours I have predicted is not enough to uncover the causes of them?' Vincent was warming to the subject, and finished with 'yes, exactly – in fact, you'll *never* be able to truly observe the causal mechanisms of the Universe around us, in my opinion.' Eddie didn't like the sound of that; he thought that even if this was true, we couldn't be sure – after all, it wasn't too long ago we were sure that the Earth was flat. His mood wasn't improved when Vincent patted both his pockets and indicated with his usual shrug that Eddie would be paying for breakfast.

Esha's Story: Part 10

It was another late night of study for Esha, and by this point of the year she really felt she needed a break. Unfortunately, most of her courses were just getting a little more difficult now, and if anything she had to work harder. She was annoyed by this, but she was not one to give up, so she kept going. Even so, she thought it would be nice to have some company and distractions from all the work sometimes. She didn't see a lot of her friends at the moment, what with study pressures and also with many of them all 'loved up', she thought cynically. She found her thoughts being drawn to Eddie, whom she'd seen on her morning run; he'd been arguing with that long-haired idiot friend of his at some greasy café, probably over football or something like that. Even so, it was odd to see him looking thoughtful and, dare she say it, passionate about something. Esha shook her head and cleared her mind. What an odd thing to think about – not helpful at all. Even if Eddie wasn't such a …, she searched for the word, '*boy*', she hardly had time for that kind of thing. She focused again on the last part of the QUAN101 material for the week: the diagnostics and assumptions of multiple regression. Although she was naturally conscientious, even she was sick of all of the tests and things that she needed to do to make sure her results were trustworthy. On the other hand, she thought it was really important to make sure that all of the assumptions of a given test were satisfied, or else the conclusions one could draw could be inaccurate and misleading.

That, Esha thought, would be a real shame.

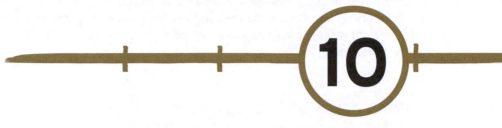

10

CORRELATION AND REGRESSION

CONTENTS

learning objectives

There are a few more objectives here than in the previous chapter, but then again there was a lot more content! Try to achieve the following objectives in your study of this chapter:

- ☑ Understand the concept of covariation between two variables.
- ☑ See the usefulness of standardizing the covariance, to make a correlation.
- ☑ Understand the difference between correlation and causation.
- ☑ Learn how to extend the concept of covariance to incorporate notions of predictor and outcome variables, leading to simple linear regression.
- ☑ Learn how to calculate and evaluate a simple linear regression model.
- ☑ Learn how to extend simple linear regression to multiple linear regression.
- ☑ Learn how to evaluate a multiple regression model, in terms of how well the model explains the data.
- ☑ Learn how to assess critical diagnostics for multiple regression.
- ☑ Learn how to test the important assumptions of a multiple regression model.

In the previous chapter, we introduced the idea of relationships between two variables by testing the goodness of fit. Well, to be totally accurate, we actually explored this idea by testing the *independence* of two variables by using the chi-square test applied to contingency tables. Of course, if two variables are not independent, they are somehow related.

In this chapter, we will extend this idea by directly exploring the *association* between two variables. An association can also be called a *relationship* between two variables, and the terms are often used interchangeably in various books and so forth. This is not a big issue, but, to my mind, if you really want to be strict with yourself, and keep your thinking disciplined, association is the correct word to use when talking about correlation in statistical terms. To me, the word relationship seems to imply some extra meaning (like one variable causes the other), which is impossible to prove using correlations alone. I will address these key concepts in the following section.

COVARIANCE, CORRELATION AND CAUSATION

The simplest way to begin to understand the association between two variables is to explore the idea of *covariation*. Consider the following situation. I might be interested in whether lecture attendance has any association with exam performance for my statistics class. So, I could easily measure how many lectures my students attend, and then record their exam performance. It could be that those who attended more lectures also tended to score higher on their exams, in which case we would say there might be a *positive association* between lecture attendance and exam performance. This makes me look good. Alternatively, those who attended more lectures might tend to score lower on the exam. In this case, we have a *negative association* between the lectures. Which makes me look bad. Suppose I take a random sample of five students and record how many lectures they attended, and also their exam scores. This data is shown in Table 10.1.

Table 10.1 Exam result data

Student	1	2	3	4	5	Mean	s
Lectures attended	4	6	8	7	9	6.8	1.92
Exam score (%)	42	64	70	67	82	65	14.56

Understanding covariance starts with understanding variance. Remember that Chapter 4 introduced variance and the standard deviation. To recap, the formula for variance (which is the squared standard deviation) is:

$$s^2 = \frac{\sum(x_i - \bar{x})^2}{n-1} = \frac{\sum(x_i - \bar{x})(x_i - \bar{x})}{n-1}$$

where the mean of the sample data is denoted $\bar{x}$, x_i represents any given data point, and of course n is the sample size.

If you are interested in the association between two variables then any change in one variable should appear at the same time as a change in the other. To look at it another way, if one variable deviates from the mean then you would expect the other to deviate from the mean as well. The manner of this deviation depends on whether you expect a positive or negative association. Specifically, for a positive association, if for any given individual one variable is greater than the mean, you would expect for the same individual the other variable also to be greater than the mean, and vice versa. For a negative association, you would expect deviations above the mean in one variable to be associated with deviations below the mean for the other, and again vice versa.

We can look at the data in Table 10.1 to get a feel for this. Students 1 and 2 attended fewer lectures than the mean of 6.8, and student 1 scored well below the mean, while student 2 scored close to the mean, but still below. The same picture is evident for those who attended more lectures than the mean – their exam scores are all higher than the mean score. Looking at the data, I am confident we will find an association.

However, the above is just 'eyeballing' the data, and our intuition can often be wrong. So how do we compute an exact figure that would express the association between number of lectures and exam score? The first way of doing this is to compute the covariance. The covariance formula is very similar to the variance formula above. However, in this case we are dealing with two variables. As such, we multiply the difference for one variable by the difference for the other, rather than squaring the differences. The results of these multiplications are the cross-product deviations, which, as well as sounding cool, allow us to compute the covariance. In order to help you understand this, I will work through the example, beginning with the formula for the covariance. In this case, x will represent the lectures attended for each individual and y will represent the exam score for each individual:

$$
\begin{aligned}
\mathrm{cov}(x,y) &= \frac{\sum(x_i - \bar{x})(y_i - \bar{y})}{n-1} \\
&= \frac{(-2.8)(-23) + (-.8)(-1) + (1.2)(5) + (.2)(2) + (2.2)(17)}{4} \\
&= \frac{64.4 + .8 + 6 + .4 + 37.4}{4} \\
&= \frac{109.4}{4} = 27.25
\end{aligned}
$$

This is kind of neat, but what does it mean? Well, there's the rub with covariance. You see, a covariance greater than 0 indicates a positive association, which means that as one variable deviates from the mean, the other deviates in the same direction. A covariance below 0 indicates a negative association, meaning that as one variable deviates from the mean, the other deviates in the opposite direction. But how do we know how 'strong' the association is? The problem with covariation is that it depends on the scale of measurement used. So, for example, the exam mark is expressed in percentage terms. However, if I had marked out of 10, or 200, the covariance would have been different. Thus it is not possible to compare two covariances and say whether one is bigger than the other objectively, unless the same measurement scales are used.

Correlation

The solution to our thorny problem with covariance is to standardize it – or in other words to convert it somehow into a standard unit. In fact, you've already done this when you converted various data sets into z-score data. The principle is the same here. Remember: the standard deviation can be used to convert any distance from the mean, in whatever scale you have, into standard deviation units. What you do is divide the deviation from the mean for any individual data point by the standard deviation, and you get the deviation from the mean in standard units, rather than the units of the original scale.

Take an example from Table 10.1. Student 3 scored 70 on the exam, which had a mean score of 65. This means the deviation from the mean in the original units is 5. The standard deviation is 14.56, so divide 5 by 14.56 and you get 0.34. So we can see that the deviation from the mean for student 3 is 0.34 standard deviations. Of course, this logic applies to the covariance as a whole. In this case, because there are two variables, we divide the covariance by the product of the standard deviations for each variable. This standardized covariance is called the correlation coefficient, and the formula is:

$$
r = \frac{\mathrm{cov}_{xy}}{s_x s_y}
$$

where s_x and s_y represent the standard deviations of each of the two variables. There are various different formulae for correlation coefficients. This particular one is called the *Pearson product moment correlation coefficient*, or just the Pearson correlation for short, and is denoted by r. This is why sometimes you will note the more expert, or perhaps the more pretentious, statistician referring to it as *Pearson's rho*. Calculating r for our existing example is simple: $s_x = 1.92$ and $s_y = 14.56$, so $s_x s_y = 27.96$. The covariance $cov_{xy} = 27.25$, and dividing this by 27.96 gives us $r = 0.97$.

It is important to note that a correlation can only range between –1 and +1. This allows correlations across various situations to be compared, unlike covariances. A correlation of +1 indicates what we call a *perfect positive association* between two variables. This means that as one variable increases, the other increases by a fixed proportionate amount. For a *perfect negative correlation*, as one variable increases, the other decreases by a proportionate amount. Often, the size of the correlation is used to indicate the strength of the association between the two variables. It is commonly considered that a correlation of ±0.1 is weak, ±0.3 is moderate and anything over ±0.5 is strong. There is not much else a correlation alone can tell us, and it is especially problematic when people make the mistake of interpreting a correlation as an indication of *how much* change in y is associated with a change in x. As we will see later in this chapter, that is a serious mistake. For example, it is a common misunderstanding that our correlation above of 0.97 means that for every increase of 1 in our x (i.e. lectures attended), we would get an increase of 0.97 in y (i.e. exam score). This is simply impossible to say from a correlation alone; a correlation simply tells you how closely two variables are associated. We will deal with such things later in this chapter, when regression is introduced.

However, you can slightly extend the interpretation of the correlation coefficient by squaring it. More specifically, R^2 – which is also called the coefficient of determination – measures the amount of variation in one variable that is accounted for by the other. Consider our earlier example. Exam performance for any given individual student clearly depends on attending lectures, but also on a host of other factors (e.g. prior knowledge of the subject, time spent studying and so forth). In a simplistic way, R^2 for our bivariate correlation of lecture attendance and exam score would tell us how much variability in exam score was accounted for by lecture attendance. Given the correlation of 0.97 between lecture attendance and exam score, $(0.97)^2 = 0.94$. It is standard practice to convert this into a percentage by multiplying by 100, giving us the ability to say that 94% of the variability in exam score is accounted for by lecture attendance. This makes me look like the greatest lecturer on the planet. However, for those of you who have attended my lectures and might now be a little suspicious, this is a great example of why it is important to think about the nature of causality and correlation.

Causality and Correlation

It is important to make it crystal clear that finding strong correlations in a data set does *not* provide proof of causality. In other words, an association between two variables does not mean one causes the other. Just because there is a high correlation between lecture attendance and exam performance does not prove that attending lectures causes an increase in exam performance. A full understanding of this would require a long discussion of what exactly a *cause* is, or could be, and this is well beyond the scope of this book. In fact, you might be surprised that even today philosophers argue about what causes are, or even whether there is such a thing as a cause. If you are interested in this, Above and Beyond Box 10.1 introduces the area.

However, if you are not philosophically inclined, that is no problem, because in practical terms it is easy to understand why a correlation between two variables can never prove that one causes the other. First of all, because a bivariate correlation can only ever take into account two variables at a time, we are unable to investigate the potential for a third variable to be the source of the correlation. Consider again the lecture attendance–exam performance correlation. It is quite easy to imagine that there could be a third variable like a student's 'conscientiousness', which would increase both lecture attendance and exam performance. For example, students who were more conscientious would likely attend more lectures, and they would also perform better in their exams because they would put time in to study the material. But, if we never measured conscientiousness, we would never be able to find this out. The problem is that there might be many of these possible variables, and if they are not measured we are never able to determine how important they are. This is a strong reason for planning very clearly what data to collect before you do it.

above and beyond

Box 10.1   What Is Causality?

Causality is one of the major problems in the philosophy of science, and it is particularly problematic because the issues involved seem so counterintuitive to us in day-to-day life that it seems like a silly philosophical argument over nothing. More specifically, every day we create causal theories of the world around us, imagining that one thing causes the occurrence of another. In fact, this is really how we predict the world around us and the consequences of our actions. How else would we be able to make a decision on what action to take?

But causality itself is not as simple as we think. The basic problem is that you can never *see* a cause. All you can see is one event, followed by another (in simple terms). The cause–effect relationship is a layer of theory that we as humans place on observed events. But what could a cause really be? It is commonly thought that if a cause occurs, the effect must then occur. But this *deterministic* view is almost never born out in any real-world causal situations. Consider the very well-accepted causal link between smoking and cancer. If causality were deterministic, would not everyone who smoked get cancer? But this is patently not the case. How then can smoking *cause* cancer? One could argue that in order to support the causal nature of this link, we need to have perfect knowledge of the *causal mechanism* by which smoking causes cancer. In other words, can we trace the effect of smoking through from the act of smoking to the cancer formation? Perhaps there are many hundreds of *intervening variables* which need to be taken into account, and if they do not happen, smoking does not cause cancer. This is of course a highly difficult – if not impossible – task.

In fact, the deterministic notion of causality has gradually been eroded since the early twentieth century, as physicists moved away from classical Newtonian physics (based on determinism) and developed quantum mechanics. Because we could no longer rely on deterministic predictions, many philosophers of science began to consider that causality should be considered to be *probabilistic*. This is complex to explain in full, but in very simple terms, causes are considered as increasing the chances of occurrence of effects. However, this description is very counterintuitive to most people, and even some of the greatest physicists of all time found it uncomfortable – including Einstein (who thought that 'God does not play dice with the Universe').

There is no question, though, that *thinking* causally is a clear advantage, and likely to be a major factor in our survival – as such it is probably an evolved capability in humans. But this does not *necessarily* mean that the Universe works this way. In fact, some questions you might want to think about are: Do animals perceive causality? Or more interestingly, do we think causally because that is the way the Universe works, or do we think the Universe works causally because that is the way we have evolved to think?

Spooky, huh?

The other problem with correlation is that it cannot tell you the direction of any possible causal relationship. In other words, you cannot tell which of the two variables causes the other. Sometimes, this problem can be tentatively solved with theory – for example, it seems illogical that your exam performance could cause your lecture attendance, since lecture attendance comes first (this time-ordering property is a very important concept when discussing causality). But it is important to remember that there is no statistical evidence provided by the correlation, especially if the data on the two variables is collected at the same time. To illustrate the problem further, consider the correlation between job satisfaction and work performance. One theory suggests that if you are satisfied with your job, you will perform better.

However, another equally plausible one suggests that if you perform well, you will be more satisfied with your job. It is impossible to unpack this conundrum with a simple bivariate correlation.

think it over 10.1

Is money a strong motivator?

A fast-food company wanted to motivate its staff to perform better. To this end it decided to give every employee a 20% pay rise. To measure the effect of this the company calculated the correlation coefficient between wages and performance. Initially $r = 0.95$ but after three months when the correlation coefficient was recalculated it came out at $r = 0$.

a   How would you interpret these results?
b   What conclusions can you make about the relationship between wages and performance?

Partial Correlation

One way of beginning to take account of the problems of bivariate correlations as discussed above is to include additional variables in our analysis. There are many ways of doing this, but a first step in understanding them is the idea of partial correlation. Again, let's return to the lecture attendance–exam performance situation. Recall that I suggested that student 'conscientiousness' might be a third variable of interest to us, because it might influence both lecture attendance and exam performance. If we have data on all three variables, partial correlation can help us to unpack the unique and shared parts of the correlations.

Remember: the R^2 for the association between lecture attendance and exam performance was 0.85, and as such lecture attendance accounts for 85% of the variance in exam performance. Now, imagine that there is an R^2 of 0.2 for the association between conscientiousness and exam performance, and an R^2 of 0.5 between conscientiousness and lecture attendance. So, each variable shares some variance with the other two. It is likely that all three share some variance, and that there is also some shared variance which is unique to each pair of variables. Figure 10.1 shows this graphically.

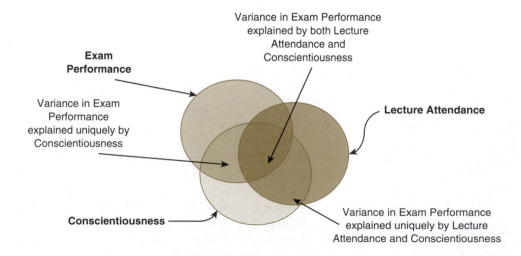

Figure 10.1
Basic Principles of Partial Correlation

Partial correlation is a way of determining the size of the unique parts of the shared variance in Figure 10.1. For example, a partial correlation would allow us to see the unique association between exam performance and lecture attendance. This basic idea is called *controlling* for the effect of conscientiousness, or sometimes called *partialling out* the influence of conscientiousness. Of course, we could also control for the effect of lecture attendance on the association between exam performance and conscientiousness, and so on. The idea of controlling the influence of additional variables is a critical one in quantitative model building, and I will return to it later – this is just a taster to get you warmed up.

 think it over 10.2

Cold weather causes people in the UK to spend more in shops compared with when it is hot. Can you think of another reason which might influence this apparent correlation? [Hint: think about the time of year when it is cold in the UK.]

SIMPLE LINEAR REGRESSION

The idea of regression moves things on a step. Specifically, while correlation simply concerned how closely two variables were related, simple linear regression analysis develops an equation which allows the value of one variable to be used to predict the other. Just like correlation, simple linear regression assumes the relationship between variables can be described by a straight line (hence the term linear). However, unlike correlation, using simple linear regression automatically makes you think about which variable is being predicted, and which is predicting it. The simplest way of thinking about this is to introduce the idea of predictor and outcome variables.[1] The outcome variable is being predicted by values of the predictor variable. It is always the case in regression that x denotes the predictor variable and y denotes the outcome. The simplest type of regression is called simple linear regression; it only contains one predictor x variable, and the relationship between x and y is assumed to take the form of a straight line. In the next chapter, multiple x variables will be introduced, in what is called multiple regression.

Simple linear regression is an example of a *model* which we as quantitative analysts assume will explain our observed data. In the case of linear regression, the model is assumed to take the form of a straight line, and our task is to determine the straight line which 'best' fits the data. In order to do this, we use a specific method called the *method of least squares*.

 think it over 10.3

Models can refer to aeroplanes or men and women walking down a catwalk, so what on Earth is a statistical model? Explain what we mean by a statistical model.

---

[1] Note that sometimes the predictor is referred to as the *independent* and the outcome as the *dependent*. This isn't really correct, as those terms come from experimental methods, and imply a level of control over the independent that most data sets analysed with regression never achieve. As such, I prefer predictor and outcome. Also, the outcome is sometimes called the *criterion* variable, but I prefer outcome as it's easier to understand at this level. Really hardcore modellers also sometimes use the term *exogenous* to refer to the predictor and *endogenous* for the outcome. Again, I'm going to avoid using these because they just add a layer of confusion at this point. But you will see them in other books.

It is important to understand that a model is always a simplification of the real world, but it is useful to us insofar as it is able to do what we want. In this case, we want to be able either (a) to *explain* the reasons behind the occurrence of our outcome variable, or (b) to *predict* future values of the outcome, given values of the independent. Note that, being able to predict *y* may not always be the same as being able to explain why it occurs. Think back to Above and Beyond Box 10.1, and consider that there is a lot of data showing that murder rates in US cities are predicted strongly by ice cream sales. Now, a regression model based on this data would be a good predictive model, but it would be a poor explanatory model. It does not explain *why* there is a strong prediction between ice cream sales and murder rates. What is needed for explanation is a strong theory, and probably more data (additional predictor variables in particular – such as temperature data perhaps). This becomes clearer when you consider that there are similar predictive models which can be built for ice cream consumption and boating accidents, shark attacks and drowning. Think about it...

The difference between a purely predictive aim and an explanatory one will be covered again as we move through different regression concepts, but for now let's put it aside and start to build up a real example. At my university, there is a bar which I used to frequent as a PhD student, and this bar was also popular with the undergraduates – although these two things were entirely causally unrelated. I used to notice quite severe fluctuations in the number of undergraduates attending this bar across different nights of the year (there were always the same number of PhD students there). At some point, I came up with the idea that the weekly sales of the bar (the outcome variable *y*) was negatively related to the number of assignments that were due across the various undergraduate programmes at the university (the predictor variable *x*). In other words, the more assignments due for the undergrads, the less time they spent drinking and living it up.

The Regression Equation

First, assume that the population in our student bar example consists of all the weeks of a single year (we will make an, ahem, 'simplifying assumption' that each lecturer simply repeats the same course material they used last year). So, for every week of the year, there is a value of *x* (undergrad assignments due) and *y* (weekly sales). The regression equation is the model which describes how *y* is related to *x* and looks like this:

$$y = \beta_0 + \beta_1 x + \varepsilon$$

The two β terms (Greek beta) are called *parameters* of the model, and the ε (Greek epsilon, sometimes simplified to *e*) is called the *error term*, which is a random variable representing all the variance in *y* which is not accounted for by *x*. Obviously, smaller ε values mean *x* is a better predictor of *y*.

Together, the parameters perfectly describe a straight line, which can be plotted on a graph. The first parameter, β_0, is the intercept, and the second parameter, β_1, is the gradient, also called the slope of the line. In a regression context, the parameters are specifically referred to as *regression coefficients*, and Figure 10.2 presents three possible regression lines, each with the same intercept, to show how we can describe straight lines with just two coefficients. The gradient describes whether the slope of the line is positive or negative, and this in turn describes the relationship between the two variables *x* and *y*. Lines that slope upwards from left to right have positive gradients and thus describe positive relationships. Conversely, lines that slope downwards from left to right have negative gradients and describe negative relationships. The intercept describes the point where the line cuts the vertical *y* axis. With the intercept in hand, we can easily then use the gradient to calculate a second point of the line, and draw it.

think it over 10.4

The regression equation is given by:

$$y = \beta_0 + \beta_1 x + \varepsilon$$

a   Plot the curve of the regression equation, $y = 3 - 2x$ where $\varepsilon = 0$ for x values between 0 and 20.
b   Explain what the regression equation tells you about the relationship between the x variable and the y variable.

think it over 10.5

The regression equation $y = \beta_0 + \beta_1 x + \varepsilon$ is known as a linear equation. In Think it Over 10.4 (a) you plotted values between 0 and 20 based on a linear relationship. If you used your regression equation to predict a y value at x = 50, how certain could you be that it would be accurate. List any assumptions that you have made to justify your prediction.

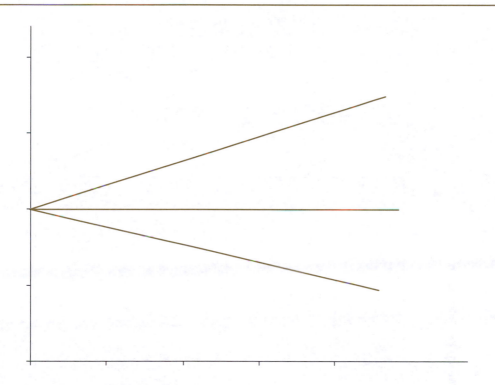

Figure 10.2 Example Regression Lines

The Method of Least Squares

The method of least squares is the method by which we determine the line that best fits the data, or, in other words, to come up with the parameters for our regression equation. This concept can be illustrated nicely by continuing with our student bar example. Table 10.2 presents the data collected from a sample of 10 weeks out of the possible 52 in a given year. Strictly, β_0 and β_1 represent population parameters. Because we are now working with a sample, we must change our notation to b_0 and b_1 respectively. Also, we are predicting an estimate of y, which is denoted as $\hat{y}$, which math types often call 'y-hat', if that helps. Our estimated regression equation therefore becomes:

$$\hat{y} = b_0 + b_1 x$$

with the error term ignored for the purposes of estimating a given value of $\hat{y}$.

Moving back to the data, for the ith observation in the sample, the predictor variable x_i is the number of undergraduate assignments due that week, while the outcome variable y_i is the weekly sales of the bar. Figure 10.3 is a scatterplot of the same data, with the number of undergraduate assignments due, x, on the horizontal, and the weekly sales, y, on the vertical. The outcome variable is always on the vertical axis on regression diagrams.

Table 10.2 Student bar data

Week	UG assignments due	Weekly bar sales (£000)
1	2	45
2	4	41
3	4	43
4	5	37
5	5	32
6	6	34
7	7	28
8	8	20
9	8	22
10	12	15

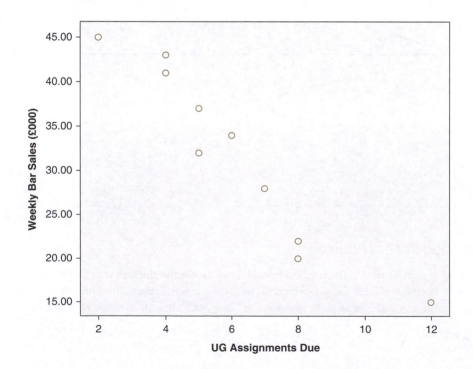

Figure 10.3
Scatterplot

Just from looking at the scatterplot, you can get a fair idea that there are fewer bar sales in weeks with more assignments due, and that it looks possible that we could approximate this relationship with a straight line.

However, we cannot just draw a line through the data and be done with it – how do we know that it is the best line, or in other words the line which best represents the relationship? If you imagine any straight line through the data, you will clearly see that not all of the points would fall on that line, if any. In other words, there are differences between the values of y predicted by the line and those which we actually observed in the data. Because we are trying to predict values of y from x, we are especially interested in the vertical distances. In this regard, imagining your straight line, you would see some values above the line and some below. We call these differences residuals, some of which are negative (for points below the line, meaning the line overestimates their real value) and some positive (for points above the line, meaning the line underestimates their real value). As you should remember from previous sections of this book, adding up positive and negative differences will cancel each other, so we square them. The smaller the sum of the squared differences (which is shortened to SS), the better the line fits the data. The method of least squares is a method of finding the line which has the smallest SS, based on differential calculus. The formal criterion for the least squares method is:

$$\text{Min} \sum (y_i - \hat{y}_i)^2$$

where y_i refers to the observed value of the outcome variable y for the ith observation and $\hat{y}_i$ refers to the estimated value of the outcome variable y for the ith observation (i.e. the value predicted by the line).

The equations in Box 10.1 can be proved via differential calculus to result in a regression line which minimizes the criterion above. It is well beyond the scope of this book to do the proofs for you, and, in fact, few of you will ever need to actually perform the calculations in Box 10.1 by hand. However, I do think it is a useful exercise to see how things work, and it is reasonably simple for this small student bar data set. Further, you may actually find yourself on a desert island without access to software to do it for you, and desperately need to calculate a regression line by hand to escape. Then you will thank me.

Table 10.3   Least squares calculations

Week i	x_i	y_i	$x_i - \bar{x}$	$y_i - \bar{y}$	$(x_i - \bar{x})(y_i - \bar{y})$	$(x_i - \bar{x})^2$
1	2	45	−4.1	13.3	−54.53	16.81
2	4	41	−2.1	9.3	−19.53	4.41
3	4	43	−2.1	11.3	−23.73	4.41
4	5	37	−1.1	5.3	−5.83	1.21
5	5	32	−1.1	0.3	−0.33	1.21
6	6	34	−0.1	2.3	−0.23	0.01
7	7	28	0.9	−3.7	−3.33	0.81
8	8	20	1.9	−11.7	−22.23	3.61
9	8	22	1.9	−9.7	−18.43	3.61
10	12	15	5.9	−16.7	−98.53	34.81
Totals	61	317			−246.7	70.9

box 10.1

Calculation of a Regression Line

$$b_1 = \frac{\sum(x_i - \bar{x})(y_i - \bar{y})}{\sum(x_i - \bar{x})^2}$$

$$b_0 = \bar{y} - b_1\bar{x}$$

where:

x_i = value of the predictor variable for the *ith* observation

y_i = value of the outcome variable for the *ith* observation

$\bar{x}$ = mean value for the outcome variable

$\bar{y}$ = mean value for the outcome variable

It is quite easy if you take your time to do the working on the student bar example to get the regression equation for the line that best fits the data. A lot of the basic work is given in Table 10.3, and from there you can use the equations in Box 10.1. Of course, you will also need the means $\bar{x}$ and $\bar{y}$. By now you should be able to compute these from the data in Table 10.3 to be 6.1 and 31.7 respectively.

From here, we compute the slope b_1 as follows:

$$b_1 = \frac{\sum(x_i - \bar{x})(y_i - \bar{y})}{\sum(x_i - \bar{x})^2}$$

$$= \frac{-246.7}{70.9}$$

$$= -3.48$$

and the intercept b_0 as:

$$b_0 = \bar{y} - b_1\bar{x}$$
$$= 31.7 - (-3.48)(6.1)$$
$$= 52.93$$

and thus our regression equation is:

$$\hat{y} = 52.93 - 3.48x$$

The slope of the regression equation is negative, which implies that as the number of undergraduate assignments due in a given week increases, bar sales for that week decrease. If we are happy with this equation, we can use it to predict bar sales for any given week where we know the number of assignments due that week. In fact, one could make weekly sales projections for the bar, if one were in possession of the details of how many undergraduate assignments were due that week.

Calculating the Goodness of Fit Using r^2

Of course, just because we can calculate a regression model does not mean it is necessarily a good model. Even though it is a 'line of best fit', that best fit of a linear model may still be a bad fit in absolute terms. We measure how well the model fits the data by calculating the coefficient of determination, or r^2. It can be a little hard to understand this, but, basically, what we do is compare the fit of our regression model with the fit of what is called a *naive model*, which is a term used to describe the simplest model available in any given situation. For example, if there are two possible outcomes to a non-random decision (e.g. buy/don't buy), a naive model would predict a 50% probability of each outcome, which would probably not be a completely accurate prediction of the outcome of any non-random decision. However, we could use some variables (say price and quality) to predict whether a customer would be more likely to buy or not buy. If we still predicted the outcome with the same accuracy as the naive model, then what was the point of the more complex model? This is the basic gist.[2]

To get r^2 we first need to decide on what naive model we will use. For linear regression, the simplest model we could use was to try to predict y by using the mean value of y. In other words, for whatever value of x we have, we predict the mean value of y will be the outcome. Next, we need to remember this basic formula, which we will use repeatedly to calculate quantities:

$$\text{deviation} = \Sigma(\text{observed} - \text{model})^2$$
$$\text{sum of squares of residuals} = \Sigma(y_i - \hat{y})^2$$

The ith residual is the difference between the observed value of y_i and the value of the dependent variable predicted by the model $\hat{y}_i$. The sum of squares of these residuals is what we minimized above using the least squares model to find the best fit line. When we minimize it by calculating a best fit line, this quantity is known as the *sum of squares due to error*, or SSE. Although it is very rare that you will ever have to do this by hand, Table 10.4 gives the basic working for doing so. You can see that you use the regression equation to calculate the values in the third column from the right, and then these values are used to calculate the two columns to the right of that. From the table, SSE = 89.7 (with rounding).

Table 10.4 Calculating SSE

Week i	UG assignments due x_i	Weekly sales y_i	Predicted sales (from regression line)	Error: $y_i -$ predicted sales	Squared error
1	2	45	45.97	−0.97	0.9409
2	4	41	39.01	1.99	3.9601
3	4	43	39.01	3.99	15.9201
4	5	37	35.53	1.47	2.1609
5	5	32	35.53	−3.53	12.4609
6	6	34	32.05	1.95	3.8025
7	7	28	28.57	−0.57	0.3249
8	8	20	25.09	−5.09	25.9081
9	8	22	25.09	−3.09	9.5481
10	12	15	11.17	3.83	14.6689
				SSE =	89.6954

---

[2] In fact, the example I just gave was of *logistic regression*, which will be covered in a later chapter. But the principle is the same, and it's a clearer example to use a dichotomous outcome variable.

However, we could also use the naive model (the sample mean of y) to predict the estimated values of y for each x. This would of course give us new values for the residuals, and the resulting sum of squares would then be called the *total sum of squares*, or SST. Table 10.5 shows the calculations for this, using a sample mean $\bar{y} = 31.7$, which results in SST = 948.1.

Table 10.5 Calculating SST

Week i	UG assignments due x_i	Weekly sales y_i	Error $y_i - \bar{y}$	Squared error $(y_i - \bar{y})^2$
1	2	45	13.3	176.89
2	4	41	9.3	86.49
3	4	43	11.3	127.69
4	5	37	5.3	28.09
5	5	32	0.3	0.09
6	6	34	2.3	5.29
7	7	28	−3.7	13.69
8	8	20	−11.7	136.89
9	8	22	−9.7	94.09
10	12	15	−16.7	278.89
			SST =	948.1

If SSE were much lower than SST (which it is in this case), we would be more confident that our model was a good predictor. So, we could calculate the reduction in inaccuracy which is due to us using our model over the naive model. In fact, that is just what we do. We calculate the *model sum of squares* SSM by calculating SST – SSE, which in this case is 948.1 – 89.7 = 858.4. The larger the SSM value, then the greater the improvement that our model provides over the naive model. Of course, the absolute value of SSM is not comparable across different studies. As such, we can calculate r^2 as the proportion of improvement in our predictions due to the use of our model over the naive one:

$$r^2 = \frac{\text{SSM}}{\text{SST}}$$

$$= \frac{858.4}{948.1}$$

$$= 0.905$$

You might remember r^2 from earlier in the chapter, and you would be quite right to. Therefore, we can easily calculate a Pearson correlation coefficient r by simply taking the square root of the r^2 we have just calculated, which would result in $r = 0.951$.

think it over 10.6

If the SSE had a value of 0, what would that tell you about your regression equation?

TESTING THE SIGNIFICANCE OF THE MODEL

Once you have r^2, you have an indication of whether the model can explain variance in your outcome variable. However, we have no indication of the statistical significance of this result yet (please go back to the previous chapters in this book if you are not following the idea of significance). There are a number of specific tests to help you assess significance, but they depend on some key assumptions about the regression error term ε. Now, listen very carefully: regression depends on many assumptions, and we can test for most of them. In fact, I am going to spend a long time later in this chapter showing the tests for each assumption all in one section. Right now, I am simply going to explain briefly the specific assumptions which relate to the significance test, because it is just not right to talk about significance testing without first stressing that the very possibility of doing it depends on assumptions. So do not get confused when this comes up again later.

Of course, you should already be aware of one assumption: that of a *linear relationship* between x and y. However, there are a number of other assumptions we need to make before we can test for statistical significance of our regression model. First, we have to assume that the error term ε is a normally distributed random variable with a mean of 0. This basically means in practice that the differences between the model-predicted value $\hat{y}_i$ and the actual observed value y_i are generally small or zero, and large deviations are rare. Note that this does not mean that predictors must be normally distributed; this is a trap many fall into (including me in the past). Secondly, the errors in prediction for any two observations must be uncorrelated (also called independent). If they are correlated (non-independent) then this is termed autocorrelation, which I think is a cool word. There are simple tests for this, which I will detail later in this chapter. Finally, and this is often the most confusing one, there is the assumption of homoscedasticity. What this means is the residuals (errors in prediction) at each level of the predictor variable x should have the same variance. An absence of this is termed heteroscedasticity. This is a rather difficult concept to explain, and even more difficult to show what it really means. However, it is not really necessary for you to understand it at this level – only that you need to test for it, and how to test for it. Of course, I will show you this in due course.

Estimating σ^2

OK, once you have tested for these assumptions (which will be discussed later), you are ready to assess the significance of your regression model. The first thing needed is an estimate of σ^2, or the variance of ε. We use something called the mean square error or MSE to estimate this, which is simply SSE divided by the degrees of freedom. If you think back to earlier chapters, I discussed degrees of freedom and noted that, in each different statistical situation, a different way of calculating degrees of freedom is used. In the case of SSE, degrees of freedom are calculated as $n - 2$, because we must estimate the two regression coefficients using your sample data (which has n data points). As such the estimate of σ^2, which is denoted s^2 because it is an estimate, is given by the formula:

$$s^2 = \text{MSE} = \frac{\text{SSE}}{n-2}$$
$$= \frac{89.7}{8}$$
$$= 11.21$$

Using this, we can compute some very useful tests of significance of our model, and the coefficients. Furthermore, we can easily compute what is called the standard error of the estimate, or s, as:

$$s = \sqrt{\text{MSE}} = \sqrt{\frac{\text{SSE}}{n-2}}$$
$$= \sqrt{11.21}$$
$$= 3.35$$

think it over 10.7

Convert the following statement into a mathematical expression: 'the variance of the error is equal to the unexplained portion of the total of the squared deviation using the mean as a model, divided by the number of degrees of freedom'.

think it over 10.8

Which model below is more appropriate?

You have been asked to check how good a model the regression equation for a chain of 12 restaurants is. The only data you have is that the total sales per week amount to £852 and the regression equation is $45 + 4x$.

a   Plot the graph of the regression equation and superimpose the graph of the mean sales per month.
b   From looking at the graphs, what can you say about using the mean weekly sales figure as a model?

The *F*-test

The *F*-test will be referred to in much more depth later in this book, when ANOVA is introduced, but here it performs a very similar function. In fact, it helps link ANOVA and regression together, and later I will show how they are basically the same thing. The *F*-test is based on the *F*-distribution, and it is a way to test the significance of the entire model. The logic behind the *F*-test is simple. First, remember MSE described above. This was argued to be an estimate of σ^2. Another estimate of σ^2 could be provided by dividing SSM by its degrees of freedom, which is called the mean square due to model or MSM. The degrees of freedom in this case are the number of predictor variables, and thus the formula is:

$$MSM = \frac{SSM}{\text{Number of predictor variables}}$$

Of course, in this case, there is only one predictor variable in a simple regression, so MSM = SSM = 858.4. The *F*-test works by comparing these two mean square estimates of σ^2. More specifically, if H_0 is true, $\beta_1 = 0$ in the population. If so, then MSE and MSM are independent estimates of σ^2 and should be pretty much the same value. However, if H_0 is not true, then $\beta_1 \neq 0$ and MSM should overestimate σ^2. Another simpler way of looking at this is to think of MSM as relating to the improvement in prediction accuracy due to our regression model, and MSE as the difference between the data and the regression model. A good regression model should have a high improvement in accuracy over the naive model (i.e. a high MSM) and a low difference between the observed data and the regression model (i.e. a low MSM). So, look at the formula for calculating *F* with this in mind:

$$F = \frac{MSM}{MSE}$$

$$= \frac{858.4}{11.21}$$

$$= 76.57$$

You should be able to predict that as the regression model improves, so *F* gets larger. As such, larger values of *F* lead us to reject the null hypothesis and conclude that there is a statistically significant relationship between the predictor(s) and outcome. Again, it is fairly easy to calculate *F*, and many authors suggest that an F greater than 1 generally indicates a significant relationship. However, this is not really correct. Strictly speaking, you should determine the significance of F by looking at an F table as you have already done with chi-square. You need to use the degrees of freedom in the numerator (number of predictor variables) and the denominator ($n - 2$) of the F formula to determine significance. It is convention that the numerator comes first and the denominator second. It is usual that, in the table, the columns are numerator degrees of freedom and the rows are denominator, but make sure you always check. Further, there are multiple F tables, corresponding to different areas in the upper tail. If you were to do this, you would see that for a numerator of 1 and a denominator of $n - 2 = 8$, you can see that $F = 11.26$ provides an area of 0.01 in the upper tail, while $F = 5.32$ provides an area of 0.05 in the upper tail. Therefore, the area in the upper tail for our $F = 76.57$ must be much less than 0.01, and we can conclude that the p-value has to be less than 0.01. As such, we reject H_0 and conclude that our regression model is significant.

The t-test

The F-test above is used to gain an indication of the significance of the regression model as a whole. By contrast, the t-test is used to test the significance of the individual predictor variable (or variables if you have a multiple regression model, as shown later on). In a simple regression model, there is only one predictor, so the conclusions you get from the F- and t-tests are the same. However, when you begin to use more than one predictor (which is coming soon, I promise), the t- and F-tests provide different functions.

You have come across the t-test before, and it is the same basic principle here. The t-test for regression coefficients is based on the idea that if the regression model fits the data, then it must be the case that $\beta_1 \neq 0$. Our regression coefficient b_1 is an estimate of the population parameter β_1 and is thus an estimate of the change in the outcome variable y associated with a unit change in the predictor variable x. Think back to our naive model that we used to calculate SST. That model was essentially a flat line, because it used the mean value of y, so that every level of x resulted in the same predicted value of y. As such, a change in x did not result in any change in y at all, and the gradient of that regression line would be zero. So, it follows that any regression line which does predict an outcome y cannot have a gradient of zero. The t statistic tests the null hypothesis that the value of a given $\beta = 0$ in the population. If we reject this null hypothesis, then we are saying the evidence suggests that the predictor variable does contribute significantly to the ability to estimate the outcome.

A problem with using the t-test in this context is that the magnitude of any b coefficient depends on the units of measurement for the relevant x variable. As such, we need to use the standard error. Again, the standard error is a concept you should be familiar with from earlier chapters, so review it if you are not sure. In brief, the standard error is the term we use for the standard deviation of the sampling distribution of the b we are performing the t-test on, in this case b_1. It represents how different the different estimates of b_1 would be if we took a lot of different samples and computed the regression line for each.

If the standard error is small, than the various values of b_1 we would get from many samples would be similar, and if the standard error is large, then the b_1 estimates would vary widely across samples. As such, the larger the standard error, the larger the b_1 value has to be before we conclude it is significant (i.e. unlikely to be due to random chance).

To calculate the estimated standard deviation of b_1, which I just called the standard error, we need to use the s we calculated earlier as the square root of MSE. With this in mind, the estimated standard deviation of b_1 is:

$$S_{b_1} = \frac{s}{\sqrt{\sum(x_i - \bar{x})^2}}$$

In fact, you should remember how to get the bottom line of this equation from your calculation of the least squares line – the working is already done in Table 10.3. So it would be trivial to calculate this if you wanted to, as follows:

$$S_{b_1} = \frac{3.35}{\sqrt{70.9}}$$

$$= \frac{3.35}{8.41}$$

$$= 0.4$$

We calculate the t statistic using the principle that it should capture the difference between the observed b_1 coefficient and the β_1 parameter that would be expected in the population if the null hypothesis were true. The statistic follows a t-distribution with $n - 2$ degrees of freedom (which again you should remember from prior chapters). As such, the full formula is:

$$t = \frac{b_1 - \beta_1}{S_{b_1}}$$

Of course, our null hypothesis is that $\beta_1 = 0$. Thus, the formula reduces to:

$$t = \frac{b_1}{S_{b_1}}$$

$$= \frac{-3.48}{0.4}$$

$$= -8.7$$

We use a t-distribution table to test the significance of this, using $n - 2 = 8$ degrees of freedom. First, do not worry about the negative sign – the principle is just the same as with a positive t value. You can see that for 8 degrees of freedom, $t = 2.31$ provides an area of 0.025 in the upper tail, and as the distribution is symmetrical, the area is just the same in the lower tail. So with our $t = -8.7$, we can see that the area in the lower tail must be less than 0.025. Also, remember that this is a two-tailed test, as we did not predict a direction for our relationship. So we double the p-value and conclude that the p-value for $t = -8.7$ with 8 degrees of freedom must be less than $2(0.025) = 0.05$. This means at an alpha of 0.05, two-tailed, we can reject H_0 and conclude that β_1 does not equal 0. Thus, there is a significant relationship between number of undergraduate assignments due and weekly bar sales.

think it over 10.9

Why is this test a two-tailed test? You should refer to the null and alternative hypotheses.

USING THE ESTIMATED REGRESSION EQUATION

You have the regression coefficients, you did your significance testing and you are pleased with the results of your efforts. So what now? You might be in a situation where your boss has actually asked you to do something useful, like predict the weekly bar sales based on the number of undergraduate assignments due that week. If this is the case, you cannot stop just yet. First, you need to remember that you have not found a *causal* relationship here, but we already discussed that at the beginning of the chapter.

Secondly, remember that the assumption of the regression model is of a *linear* relationship between x and y. However, a significant regression model does not 'prove' this. In fact, even a curved (termed curvilinear) relationship might be explained by a linear model, to more or less extent, depending on how curved the true relationship is. So, all a significant linear regression model shows is that a linear model provides a good approximation of your data.

Further, it could be the case that your model becomes non-linear at values of x outside the range you have data on. Perhaps, as x gets very large, the relationship between x and y becomes very non-linear, for example. So, really, the further outside the range of x that you have in your data, the less confident you can be that the results given by your model will hold. Few people ever really give this genuine thought.

With those points in mind, we can move on to using a regression model for the two purposes of *estimation* and *prediction*.

Using a Regression Model for Point Estimation

Let's return to our estimated regression equation for the bar sales example:

$$\hat{y} = 52.93 - 3.48x$$

This model estimates the relationship between the number of undergraduate assignments due, x, and the weekly bar sales, y. It is very simple to use this to create a point estimate of weekly sales, as long as you know a figure for undergraduate assignments that week. All you need to do is plug the number of undergraduate assignments into the equation in place of x. So, imagine a week where there were 10 assignments due, and thus x = 10. This is what you would do:

$$\hat{y} = 52.93 - 3.48x$$
$$= 52.93 - 3.48(10)$$
$$= 52.93 - 34.8$$
$$= 18.13$$

Thus our bar sales (in £000) are 18.13. In fact, this value is the mean estimate for all weeks in which there are 10 undergraduate assignments due. The difference between a point estimate of sales for a given week with 10 assignments due and the mean value of sales for all weeks with 10 assignments due therefore appears trivial. However, when we begin to talk about interval estimation, the difference suddenly becomes important, as you will see below.

Using a Regression Model for Interval Estimation

Point estimates are cool, and in fact they are as far as many people ever go. However, they do not provide any information on how precise the estimate is. In other words, how confident can you be that your estimate of 18.13 is actually accurate? In order to gain some indication of this, you need to incorporate some information about the variance of the predicted y. Moreover, the process is different depending on whether we are dealing with an estimate of the mean value of y or an individual value of y. For the former case, we use a confidence interval, and for the latter we use a prediction interval. The difference is that prediction intervals are wider, because we are dealing with a single estimate, not a mean. Either way, you are about to learn how to do both...

Let's begin with confidence intervals. We start with the point estimate we calculated earlier. However, now there is some new(ish) notation to introduce:

x_p = the given value of the predictor x
y_p = the value of the outcome y corresponding to x_p
$E(y_p)$ = the mean or expected value of the outcome y corresponding to x_p
$\hat{y}_p = b_0 + b_1 x_p$ = point estimate of $E(y_p)$ when $x = x_p$

Going back to our point example above, using this notation for the estimation of the mean bar sales for all weeks where there were 10 undergraduate assignments due gives us $x_p = 10$. $E(y_p)$ itself is not known, as it is the mean value of bar sales for all weeks where there are 10 undergraduate assignments due. However, the point estimate of $E(y_p)$ is 18.13. Remember, you have already calculated this.

However, you cannot expect your estimated value to be exactly equal to $E(y_p)$. Rather, you need to make some statistical inference about how close the estimate is to $E(y_p)$. In order to do that, you need to estimate the variance of your point estimate. This is given by the equation:

$$S_{\hat{y}_p}^2 = S^2 \left[\frac{1}{n} + \frac{(x_p - \bar{x})^2}{\sum (x_i - \bar{x})^2} \right]$$

This looks kind of complex, but it is not really, and neither is the formula for the confidence interval for $E(y_p)$ which follows:

$$\hat{y}_p = \pm t \alpha/2\, s \sqrt{\frac{1}{n} + \frac{(x_p - \bar{x})^2}{\sum (x_i - \bar{x})^2}}$$

where the confidence coefficient is $1 - \alpha$ and using a t-distribution with $n - 2$ degrees of freedom.

I think in this case it *is* actually quite helpful to work through this formula and calculate your own confidence intervals. In fact, analysts who rely on software seem rarely to use confidence intervals for their estimates, so I think it is a good exercise to help your actual conceptual thinking. So, let's use the formula for the confidence interval above to calculate a 95% confidence interval for the mean weekly bar sales for all weeks where there are 10 undergraduate assignments due. You might want to refresh your knowledge of confidence intervals from previous chapters, as I am going to assume that you know the basics.

First, we need a value of t for $\alpha/2 = 0.025$, and $n - 2 = 8$. You find this value by using a t-distribution table, and you will know you did it right if you get the same answer as me, which is $t_{0.025} = 2.306$. So, with our estimate of $E(y_p) = 18.13$, and $x_p = 10$, we can use the values we already calculated earlier to calculate the 95% confidence interval as follows:

$$\hat{y}_p \pm t_{\frac{\alpha}{2}} s \sqrt{\frac{1}{n} + \frac{(x_p - \bar{x})^2}{\sum (x_i - \bar{x})^2}}$$

$$= 18.13 \pm 2.31 \times 3.35 \sqrt{\frac{1}{10} + \frac{(10 - 6.1)^2}{70.9}}$$

$$= 18.13 \pm 2.31 \times 1.878$$

$$= 18.13 \pm 4.34$$

So, to recap, the 95% confidence interval for the *mean weekly bar sales* for all weeks where there are 10 undergraduate assignments due is £18130 ± £4340, which means the confidence interval is £13790 to £22470. When you look at it like that, it is kind of a wide interval, right? Well, in fact, the estimated standard deviation $\hat{y}_p$ is smallest when $x_p = \bar{x}$, and therefore $x_p - \bar{x} = 0$, which means that the estimate for the standard deviation of $\hat{y}_p$ changes from:

$$s \sqrt{\frac{1}{n} + \frac{(x_p - \bar{x})^2}{\sum (x_i - \bar{x})^2}}$$

to:

$$s \sqrt{\frac{1}{n}}$$

Do you see why? If $x_p - \bar{x} = 0$, having a zero as the numerator means that the value of any simple fraction is also 0. So that part of the equation disappears. This means that the value of the estimated standard deviation is at its minimum when $x_p - \bar{x} = 0$, and therefore the estimate is at its most precise and thus the confidence interval is at its smallest. As x_p gets further away from $\bar{x}$, the confidence intervals will get wider.

think it over 10.10

In the above bar example, you calculated the 95% confidence interval for weekly bar sales against student assignments. The result was £18130 ± £4340.

a   Your manager needs to have this result in the form of a percentage of mean weekly bar sales. Calculate this percentage and give an explanation using language your manager can understand (he's never studied statistics).

b   How does the percentage calculated for part (a) relate to the 95% confidence interval?

OK, let me now move on to prediction intervals. In this case, rather than looking to estimate the mean value of weekly bar sales for all weeks with 10 undergraduate assignments due, we are looking to estimate the sales for a specific individual week with 10 assignments due. The point estimate is the same, at 18.13, but there is a different procedure for calculating the prediction interval – which essentially takes into account that you are trying to be more 'exact', which means you can be less confident, and thus the interval is wider. In technical terms, you need to calculate the variance of $\hat{y}_p$ as an estimate of the individual value of y_p when $x = x_p$, and not as a mean estimate. Doing so requires two things.

First, we use s^2 as the variance of individual y values around $E(y_p)$, which is the mean expected value of y_p.

Second, we need to estimate the variance associated with $\hat{y}_p$ as an estimate of $E(y_p)$, which you will recall as:

$$S^2_{\hat{y}_p} = S^2 \left[\frac{1}{n} + \frac{(x_p - \bar{x})^2}{\sum(x_i - \bar{x})^2} \right]$$

We combine these components in the formula to estimate the variance of an individual y_p as follows:

$$S^2 + S^2_{\hat{y}_p} = s^2 + s^2 \left[\frac{1}{n} + \frac{(x_p - \bar{x})^2}{\sum(x_i - \bar{x})^2} \right]$$

$$= s^2 \left[1 + \frac{1}{n} + \frac{(x_p - \bar{x})^2}{\sum(x_i - \bar{x})^2} \right]$$

So, we can now create a general formula to calculate a prediction interval as:

$$\hat{y}_p \pm t_{\alpha/2} s \sqrt{1 + \frac{1}{n} + \frac{(x_p - \bar{x})^2}{\sum(x_i - \bar{x})^2}}$$

If you can calculate confidence intervals, it is trivial to calculate prediction intervals. I am not going to dwell on it, but for a single week with 10 undergraduate assignments due, the prediction interval for weekly bar sales is:

$$\hat{y}_p \pm t_{\frac{\alpha}{2}} s \sqrt{1 + \frac{1}{n} + \frac{(x_p - \bar{x})^2}{\sum(x_i - \bar{x})^2}}$$

$$= 18.13 \pm 2.31 \times 3.35 \sqrt{1 + \frac{1}{10} + \frac{(10 - 6.1)^2}{70.9}}$$

$$= 18.13 \pm 2.31 \times 4.4$$

$$= 18.13 \pm 10.164$$

You can therefore see that this prediction interval of £18130 ± £10164 or £7970 to £28290 is much wider than the confidence interval. Again, this is because we can estimate mean values of y much more accurately than individual values. Furthermore, just like a confidence interval, a prediction interval is more accurate as x_p approaches $\bar{x}$.

MULTIPLE REGRESSION

Simple linear regression is all very well, but it is a very rare situation where you will use it in practice. That is because, in the real world, there are very few situations where you only have one predictor variable that you are interested in. Far more likely is the situation where you have two or more predictors. Think back to the example about exam scores when we only had one predictor and we ran a serious risk of missing out some other important predictor (we thought it might be 'conscientiousness', for example) and as a result getting misleading results. Because the business and social worlds are complex, it is very likely that your theories will involve multiple predictors. In order to model this situation, we can very easily extend the techniques of simple regression to cope with multiple predictors. If we do so, we create a multiple regression model. A multiple regression equation is of the same basic form as a simple regression equation, but in this case we add a new β coefficient for each new predictor variable as follows:

$$y = \beta_0 + \beta_1 x_1 + \beta_2 x_2 + \ldots + \beta_n x_n + \varepsilon$$

Again, the β terms in the above equation represent parameters. However, we have to estimate these from sample data, and as such in practice they become estimates, denoted b rather than β. Further, as in the estimated simple regression equation, we ignore the ε term when estimating the model. As such, the estimated regression equation for the model we talk about from now on is:

$$\hat{y} = b_0 + b_1 x_1 + b_2 x_2 + \ldots + b_n x_n$$

An Example of Multiple Regression

While earlier in this chapter you went through the calculations by hand, the approach here is different. That said, the basic approach is the same, and we still use the least squares method to come up with the estimated regression equation. However, we are not going to go through the calculations, because they involve matrix algebra, and that is beyond the scope of an introductory quantitative text. Also, in practical terms, no one ever does it by hand these days. As such, most benefit can come from going through a typical worked example, using IBM SPSS Statistics Software (SPSS).

Consider a typical sales force management situation. Salespeople in the field have to visit a number of people each day, making calls on existing customers and potential new customers. Sales calls are very expensive, and a leading bicycle manufacturer is interested in reducing costs. The managers at BikeCo believe that fuel costs are a major area where they could make savings. It was immediately obvious to them that the distance a salesperson drives per week should have a major impact on fuel consumption. However, during a meeting, the sales director also suggested that the proportion of calls the salesperson makes inside large cities versus outside large cities also makes a difference. More specifically, driving in urban areas uses much more fuel than motorway mileage, so the higher the proportion of city driving the salesperson does, the more fuel is used. Thus our theoretical multiple regression model is:

$$\text{fuel spend}_i = \beta_0 + \beta_1 \text{mileage}_i + \beta_2 \text{proportion of city driving}_i + \varepsilon_i$$

which translates to our estimated regression model of:

$$\hat{y} = b_0 + b_1 x_1 + b_2 x_2$$

There is some data for this model in the file SP_FUEL.sav, and you can run the models yourself if you like (instructions on how to run multiple regression in SPSS come later), as well as go through the various other analysis checks shown later. Running a multiple regression model with weekly fuel spend as the outcome, and weekly mileage and proportion of city driving as predictors, results in the output shown in part in Figure 10.4. You should recognize some of the terms used in the output.

Before moving on, it is worth thinking about how to interpret coefficients in a multiple regression, as opposed to a simple regression. In fact, if you were to use the data in SP_FUEL.sav to run a simple regression with mileage as the single predictor, and fuel spend as the outcome, you would see the b_1 value change from the value of 0.358 that it takes in the multiple regression output in Figure 10.4. How is this possible?

Well, in a simple linear regression, where by definition there is only a single predictor, b_1 is an estimate of the change in the outcome y for a one-unit change in the predictor x. However, in a multiple

Model Summary[b]

Model	R	R Square	Adjusted R Square	Std. Error of the Estimate
1	.910[a]	.829	.816	20.93171

a. Predictors: (Constant), Proportion of City Driving, Weekly Mileage
b. Dependent Variable: Weekly Fuel Cost (£)

ANOVA[b]

Model		Sum of Squares	df	Mean Square	F	Sig.
1	Regression	57347.518	2	28673.759	65.445	.000[a]
	Residual	11829.682	27	438.136		
	Total	69177.200	29			

a. Predictors: (Constant), Proportion of City Driving, Weekly Mileage
b. Dependent Variable: Weekly Fuel Cost (£)

Coefficients[a]

Model		Unstandardized Coefficients		Standardized Coefficients	t	Sig.
		B	Std. Error	Beta		
1	(Constant)	-52.506	16.753		-3.134	.004
	Weekly Mileage	.358	.053	.724	6.712	.000
	Proportion of City Driving	45.688	19.844	.248	2.302	.029

a. Dependent Variable: Weekly Fuel Cost (£)

Figure 10.4 Partial Regression Output from SPSS

regression, where there are multiple predictors, the interpretation of b_1 is not the same. Specifically, in a multiple regression, b_1 represents an estimate of the change in y corresponding to a one-unit change in x when all other predictors are held constant.

 **think it over 10.11**

Simple linear regression uses only one predictor whereas multiple regression models involve more than one predictor. Which one of these models would be more sensitive to the assumptions you make when setting up the model? Explain your answer.

Overall Model Fit

In the simple regression example, we calculated F, r^2 and r manually, by using the various sums of squares, which we also calculated manually. Doing this for a multiple regression model is more difficult in terms of computation, so in this case we rely on the computer package. We can easily calculate r^2 if we want to (termed 'R Square' in SPSS), but using the sum of squares values on the ANOVA table, which are given in a column. The one thing you might notice is that SPSS uses some different terms than we have used. In the SPSS ANOVA table, the *Regression* is the SSM, the *Residual* is SSE and the *Total* is SST. Using these values, you could easily calculate the r^2 of 0.829 as SSM/SST = Regression/Residual = 57347.518/11829.682.

You will also notice an r value of 0.910 (termed 'R' in SPSS). This is what is called a multiple correlation coefficient, or Multiple R, which is the correlation between the observed values of y in your data and the values of y that are predicted by the regression model. Of course, higher values of multiple R represent better correlation between the model and the data. As such, the interpretation of r^2 in a multiple regression is just the same as in a simple regression: the amount of variance in the outcome accounted for by the predictors.

Further, there is a value of 0.816 given for something called the Adjusted R Square. To calculate this value we use a method to adjust for the number of predictors included in the model. This is supposed to avoid the chance of overestimating the impact of adding more predictor variables, and therefore takes into account the number of predictors p and sample size n in the following formula:

$$\text{adjusted } R^2 = 1 - (1 - R^2)\frac{n-1}{n-p-1}$$

The general convention, at least in my experience, is to report adjusted R^2 in most cases when using multiple regression.

TESTING THE SIGNIFICANCE OF THE MODEL

A lot of the following techniques for testing the significance of a multiple regression model are essentially identical to the case of simple regression. As such, it seems silly to repeat them. So what we will do is explain them in relation to a multiple regression situation and refer you back to the simple regression discussion for details where it seems gratuitous to repeat ourselves.

First things first, remember that you are dealing with a model that assumes *linear* relationships. This is pretty easy to visualize for a simple regression, since it is just a line on a two-dimensional graph. For a multiple regression, it can be more difficult, if not impossible, actually to visualize the relationships between your variables. Figure 10.5 is an attempt to visualize the multiple regression model from the salesperson fuel example above. Weekly mileage and proportion of driving in cities are represented on the two horizontal (bottom) axes (labelled 'mileage' and 'city'), and the outcome variable of fuel is represented on the vertical. As such, it is a reasonably easy to follow three-dimensional graphs. Of course, add more predictors and things get rather nasty. But the principle is the same. One thing you might also find useful is that, sometimes, this kind of graph is called a response surface, because it presents as a surface. Kind of cool.

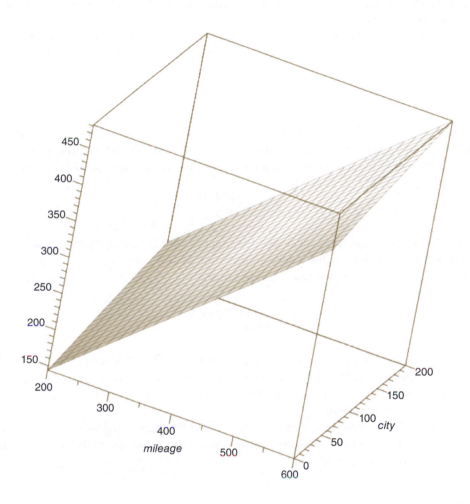

Figure 10.5 Visualization of Multiple Regression

Moving on, just like simple regression the use of a multiple regression model also depends on the same assumptions about the error term. Recapping, we must assume: (a) that the error term ε is a normally distributed random variable with a mean of 0; (b) that there is no autocorrelation; and (c) that there is no heteroscedasticity. Check back to the simple regression section for more details.

Now, technically, we should check these assumptions before doing anything else. But doing this is actually quite a bit of work. As such, what is more usual is that we check whether our model is of any use to us first – in other words, we first check goodness of fit, significance of the overall model, and also significance of the individual estimates. If the model is looking good, then we check the assumptions behind the error term and other diagnostics that I am going to show you. However, many analysts actually 'forget' to test assumptions and diagnostics, which is *very bad practice*. You must check the assumptions, because it is critical to the confidence anyone can have in your model, as you will find when I demonstrate it. For now, let's focus on whether our model is *worth* the extra effort of checking assumptions – in other words, is it significant?

The *F*-test

The *F*-test was used in the simple regression example above, but, really, in simple regression it provides the same conclusion as the *t*-test. This is because the *F*-test is used to answer the question of whether there is a significant relationship between the outcome variable *y* and the entire set of predictors. In a simple regression, there was only one predictor, so if the *F*-test was significant, so was the *t*-test. However, in a multiple regression context, there are multiple predictors, so the *F*-test can be significant when not all of the *t*-test results are significant.

Because of this, the *F*-test is called a test for overall significance of the model. If the *F*-test shows overall significance, you then move on to the *t*-tests for each *b* estimate. The null hypothesis for the *F*-test is that all the model parameters are zero, which basically looks like this:

$$H_0: \beta_1 = \beta_2 = ... = \beta_p = 0$$

The alternative hypothesis is H_1: at least one of the parameters does not equal zero. Rejecting the null hypothesis gives us evidence that the overall relationship between the predictors and outcome is significant. The details on how to calculate the *F* value are given earlier in the chapter, but to recap the formula:

$$F = \frac{MSM}{MSE}$$

We get these values from the regression output if we want to do it by hand (of course, SPSS has already done it for you). MSM is given by the number in the 'Mean Square' column for 'Regression' and MSE is given by the number below, for 'Residual'. This gives us an *F* of:

$$F = \frac{28673.759}{438.136} = 65.445$$

SPSS has also helpfully given us a significance of the *F* as equal to 0.000. Many people mistake this for meaning a significance of '0', but really it just means that rounding to three decimal places gives you 0, and of course, as you know, significance could *never* be exactly 0. If you are unsure, take a look back at the chapters on statistical inference.[3]

So, if we use $\alpha = 0.05$, then the *p*-value of 0.000 given by SPSS shows that we can reject H_0, because $p < \alpha$. Therefore, we can conclude that our regression model shows a significant relationship between the outcome and the overall set of predictors.

 think it over 10.12

The alternative hypothesis for the *F*-test for a multiple regression states 'at least one of the parameters does not equal zero'. If you had four predictors, draw a table to show all the possible combinations of parameters that might not be zero.

The *t*-test

Once we have observed a significant *F*-test result, we use the *t*-test results to show us which of the individual predictors is significant. Again, our SPSS output provides us with the results, and the means to

---

[3] I'm not going to tell you how to check this by hand, since it is somewhat pointless. First, the procedure is exactly the same as for the simple regression *F*. Secondly, if you've used a software package to calculate everything else you will never be using an *F* table to calculate significance. I don't want to keep repeating this for later examples – just take it as read.

calculate our own tests by hand if we wish. Remember: the t-test for regression coefficients is based on the idea that if a predictor x_i is significant, then $\beta_i \neq 0$. As such, the t-test formula simplifies to:

$$t = \frac{b_i}{S_{b_i}}$$

The output gives us the b_i values, and the values for the bottom line, which are the estimates of the standard deviations of b_i. As such it is simple to calculate a t for each estimate. Even though SPSS did it for us, let's check it for b_2:

$$t = \frac{b_2}{S_{b_2}}$$

$$= \frac{45.688}{19.844}$$

$$= 2.302$$

One thing which might confuse you is that SPSS uses the capital 'B' to indicate what we have called b so far. You will also see 'beta' in that output, but I will come to this in due course, so ignore it for now.

Like the F-test, SPSS gives us handy p-values. For b_1, $p = 0.029$. So using $\alpha = 0.05$, we see that $p < \alpha$ and therefore we conclude that we can reject H_0 that $\beta_i = 0$. You could check SPSS's working by hand if you want, by using a t table as shown earlier, but I am pretty confident that it is OK.

 think it over 10.13

The t-test shows which of the individual predictors is significant. Does this mean that we can just ignore the other predictors of lesser significance and revert back to a simple regression model? Explain your answer.

CHECKING DIAGNOSTICS

The next thing we should do is to check what are called the diagnostics of the model. What we are doing here is checking whether the model is a good representation of our observed data, or whether it is influenced mainly by a small number of extreme observations. There are two types of extreme observation, the outlier and the influential case, which are subtly different. An outlier is a data point that is way off the estimated regression line, and as such it exerts an influence on the regression model in some way. On the other hand, an influential case is a data point which is also extreme when compared with the others, and it exerts a major influence on the model. But in contrast to an outlier, an influential case is actually explained well by the estimated model. So, I guess, outliers are a special category of influential cases. Figure 10.6a (upper panel) shows an outlier and Figure 10.6b (lower panel) shows an influential case. You can see that the solid lines represent the estimated line with the extreme observation included, whereas the dashed lines represent the regression lines that would result with the extreme observations removed. In a purely statistical sense, extreme observations are considered to bias the model and should be removed. However, the critical issue of concern is how much influence the extreme observation has over the model. For example, an observation which can be classed as an outlier might not have much influence over the model. Its influence is something we need to be concerned with, as you will see.

Of course, it is reasonably simple in the simple examples given in the figures to actually see the problematic data points. However, in real life it is rarely that easy; for one thing there are usually many more data points, and the extreme observations are rarely quite as extreme as in the examples here. So, rather than using our (unreliable) human judgement, we instead use numerical methods, and more specifically

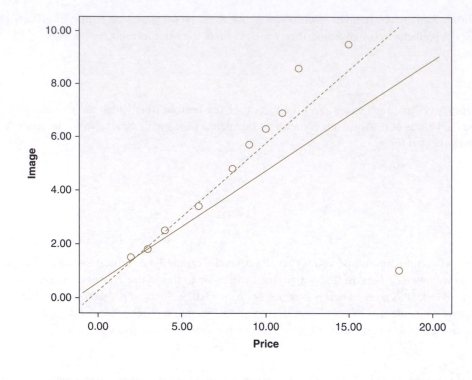

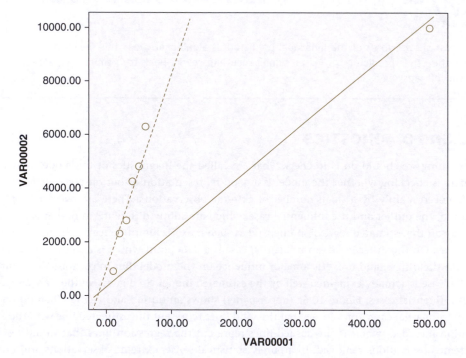

Figure 10.6a and b
Outliers and Influential Cases

the standardized residuals for each case. For the simple regression case, it is possible to compute these values by hand if you like, but for multiple regression it is just too complex. Fortunately, our analytic software of choice will give us residuals if we ask nicely, or even if we just ask. Table 10.6 shows the predicted values, unstandardized residual and standardized residuals from 10 cases of the 30 in the SP_FUEL. sav data set with the highest standardized residuals, to give you a feel for things.

Table 10.6 Diagnostic data for SP_FUEL

SP	DIST	CITY	FUEL	PRE_1	RES_1	ZRE_1
16.00	593.00	.94	259.00	202.72345	56.27655	2.68858
7.00	621.00	.72	254.00	202.69545	51.30455	2.45104
10.00	212.00	.10	53.00	27.95442	25.04558	1.19654
26.00	301.00	.34	88.00	70.77995	17.22005	.82268
28.00	311.00	.64	103.00	88.06630	14.93370	.71345
5.00	271.00	.32	74.00	59.12675	14.87325	.71056
2.00	316.00	.12	80.00	66.09820	13.90180	.66415
13.00	302.00	.32	81.00	70.22416	10.77584	.51481
25.00	250.00	.0	44.00	36.98884	7.01116	.33495
18.00	302.00	.05	64.00	57.88827	6.11173	.29198

PRE_1 = Predicted value of y
RES_1 = Unstandardized residual
ZRE_1 = Standardized residual

think it over 10.14

Outliers tend to be viewed as a nuisance to creating a regression model. Before testing for the impact of outliers, there are some other non-mathematical checks that can be made. Write down two checks that you would make before doing any mathematics.

Checking for Outliers Using Residuals

We can use the residuals to check for outliers. There are a number of different basic ways of doing this. First, remember that standardized residuals are essentially a form of z-score. In other words, they should adhere to certain probabilities. For example, in a normally distributed sample, 95% of the z-scores should be between +1.96 and −1.96, while 99.9% of the z-scores should lie between +3.29 and −3.29. These basic properties are used to devise some criteria for standardized residuals. First, any standardized residual greater than +3 or less than −3 is cause for concern by itself, as it is very unlikely that they should occur by chance. Secondly, any standardized residual greater than +2 or less than −2 is worthy of more investigation. More investigation means checking the other diagnostic measures discussed later on. If more of our diagnostics indicate that the observation may be problematic, then there is a case for removal. So, as an example of how to go about this process, let's look at salesperson 16 (using the term SP16), whose data returns the highest standardized residual of 2.69 (check Table 10.4 to confirm this if you like).

First, it is greater than 2, so we know there is something to think about, but it is less than 3, so we know the residual by itself is not necessarily a reason to consider SP16 an outlier. Rather, we should assess it in light of other diagnostics. Next, we can check the studentized residuals. These residuals cope with the problem where, as more outliers occur in a data set, the standard error of an estimate s increases. This means that (because s is in the denominator of the standardized residual formula), sometimes, large residuals can actually fail to result in large enough standardized residuals to indicate an outlier. Studentized residuals correct for this potential problem by calculating the residual for an item i using the data set with i deleted. If i is an outlier, this will correct any potential problems. As such, studentized residuals are sometimes called studentized deleted residuals. That is kind of a complicated explanation, but all you need to know is that (a) studentized residuals are larger than standardized residuals and (b) your analysis software will do the calculations for you.

The studentized deleted residual (which can be seen in Table 10.7) for SP16 is 2.99. However, we do not just use the raw number. Rather, we need to check its significance using a t table just like a t-test.[4] To do so, we need degrees of freedom. In this case, with the sample size $n = 30$ and number of predictors $p = 2$, the degrees of freedom needed are $(n - 1) - p - 1 = 29 - 2 - 1 = 26$. The procedure is just like the two-tailed t-test described earlier in this chapter for the regression estimates. With $\alpha = 0.05$, looking at the t table shows that for 29 degrees of freedom, $t_{0.025} = 2.05$. As such, the studentized residual we are evaluating must be either less than -2.05 or greater than $+2.05$ to give us cause for concern. We can see that for SP16, there is a potential problem. As such, SP16 may be an outlier. We could be within our rights to delete this case and rerun our analysis, but let's hold off for a minute and try a different approach.

Checking for Influential Cases

As well as the residuals, there are all kinds of other diagnostic numbers we can use. In this section, we will explain the most commonly used ones, and then use them to evaluate the data set. Remember, from the discussion above, that the critical thing we need to worry about for any extreme observation is whether it has a large enough influence on the regression model to be of concern. As such, even though we may find an 'outlier' according to the strict definitions of residual analysis, this outlier may not exert much influence. At the same time, a very influential case may not be exposed as an outlier (check the lower panel of Figure 10.6 for an example). When looking at the residuals, we found that SP16 was an outlier, but let's delve deeper to see whether it, or any other observation, is really that influential on our model, and thus justifies a decision on whether to remove it or not. Table 10.7 shows the various diagnostics we will discuss (as well as the studentized residual, for your interest), for the same 10 cases as in Table 10.6.

Table 10.7 Diagnostics for SP_FUEL

SP	DIST	CITY	FUEL	SRE_1	MAH_1	COO_1	LEV_1
16.00	593.00	.94	259.00	2.98806	4.55511	.69996	.15707
7.00	621.00	.72	254.00	2.80409	5.87607	.80943	.20262
10.00	212.00	.10	53.00	1.29683	3.34529	.09791	.11535
26.00	301.00	.34	88.00	.85124	.94696	.01706	.03265
28.00	311.00	.64	103.00	.77896	3.70617	.03835	.12780
5.00	271.00	.32	74.00	.74621	1.73790	.01909	.05993
2.00	316.00	.12	80.00	.69463	1.52262	.01510	.05250
13.00	302.00	.32	81.00	.53197	.87373	.00639	.03013
25.00	250.00	.0	44.00	.36055	3.00476	.00638	.10361
18.00	302.00	.05	64.00	.30967	2.25151	.00399	.07764

SRE_1 = Studentized residuals
MAH_1 = Mahalanobis distance
COO_1 = Cook's distance
LEV_1 = Leverage

The first thing to discuss is leverage. One can discuss leverage in great detail, but, really, what you need to know is that leverage is a measure that gauges the influence of a given observed outcome value for a particular data point, on the regression-predicted values. Leverage can range from 0 to 1, with higher

---

[4] You should now know why it is called 'studentized' – think back to the t-test discussion in earlier chapters.

values indicating that an observed data point has a greater influence over the predicted values. We use the calculated leverage value in conjunction with the average leverage, computed as:

$$\frac{(p+1)}{n}$$

where, as you should remember, p is number of predictors and n is sample size. We would expect a data set without influential observations to return leverage values for each case that were close to the average. As such, it is often said that leverage values greater than two or three times the average are causes for concern. With that in mind, the average leverage for our SP_FUEL data set is $(2 + 1)/30 = 0.1$. So we would be looking for leverage values in our data of 0.3 to be really concerned, and 0.2 to give us pause for thought and further reflection. We can see from the sample of data in Table 10.5 that one value is just over 0.2, but that is the highest (if you look at the full data set, you will see that there are no other high leverage values that I am hiding from you!). Interestingly, the data we previously considered as an outlier is not seen to be influential here.

However, the leverage values can be misleading, because they focus on the predicted values of y, not the estimated model coefficients. As such, a data point can have high leverage but not actually be influential on the model as a whole. To solve this problem, Cook's distance uses the leverage value for observation i along with the residual for i. In essence, Cook's distance measures the effect on the model of deleting observation i and recalculating the model. If the estimates change by a large amount, we can say that observation i had a large impact on the model, and as such is a candidate for an influential case. Like leverage, we tend to use a decision rule to decide whether Cook's distance for an individual data point is a problem. Specifically, Cook's distances above 1 are usually considered to be a cause for concern. Looking at Table 10.7, the highest Cook's distance is 0.81, for the same case that had the high leverage value. So, Cook's distance does not give us any cause for concern.

Finally, we can look at the Mahalanobis distance for each data point. Similar to Cook's distance, the Mahalanobis distance is related to the leverage. It is somewhat more complex to explain fully the details of the Mahalanobis distance, but the basic principle is that it measures the distance of a given data point from the mean of the predictor variable(s). As such, higher Mahalanobis distances indicate likely influential cases. However, it is less easy to define a decision rule for the Mahalanobis distance, because it depends on both the sample size and number of predictors in a given model. There are tables available, however, which show the critical values for Mahalanobis distance depending on sample size and number of predictors, which you can consult to get an estimate of the Mahalanobis distance you should be concerned about.[5] Looking at these, we can see that with $n = 30$ and $p = 2$, as in our SP_FUEL data set, Mahalanobis distances greater than 11 are causes for concern. The data set (again see Table 10.7) gives us no cause for concern in this regard.

Interpreting Diagnostics

Before moving on, it is important to look at the idea of diagnostics holistically, to try to get an overall feel for what should be done. While there are lots of diagnostics available, which can help us substantially in dealing with our model, it is easy to get seduced by them, which in this case would not be good. What I mean is that diagnostics should never be used as a way to justify removing some data point without good reason. Consider that removing any data point which has a high residual will always make your data fit better. As such, sometimes, removing these values can make a failing model (e.g. poor overall fit, non-significant b estimates) into a statistically significant one. If a data point really is an outlier, then removing it is justifiable. However, take a look at the two data points that turned up concerning values on our diagnostics in the SP_FUEL example. We could have deleted both of them, on diagnostic grounds. But would this have been a good decision?

In my view, the decision should be made to keep both those values in the data set. First, they are not hugely outside the critical values for our diagnostics, and also there seems no reason to consider these

---

[5] For more information see Vic Barnett and Toby Lewis (1978) 'Outliers in Statistical Data', *Psychological Bulletin*, 95(2): 334–344.

data points to be completely outside the parameters of our theory. If we delete those data points, our model does not have any predictive power in situations that those two data points describe (very high fuel use), and therefore we would have to bound the conclusions we could draw. Further, consider the situation the managers would be most interested in – surely this would likely be high-fuel-use situations? Worse, there would be the situation where our model was non-significant until we removed those two points. If we removed them, and got a significant model, it would only have explanatory power on the lower-fuel-use situations described by the data used to create the model. However, many analysts conveniently forget to 'bound' their conclusions when removing outliers like this, and as such imply the model explains 'all' situations. This is not correct, and is in fact misleading. Worse, as explained above, it is probably precisely the high-fuel-use situations that the managers are interested in and that the model does not explain.

So, diagnostics as explained above should be used as inputs into decisions, but not as hard-and-fast rules – especially when their calculated values are close to the critical values for each diagnostic, or when different diagnostics suggest different courses of action for the same data point.

 think it over 10.15

You have carried out diagnostic testing on a particular data point and found that it has a significant influence on the regression model. Explain the course of action you would follow in this case.

CHECKING ASSUMPTIONS

Now we have a model that we are generally pleased with, in that it seems to explain the sample data well and gives us significant results, we normally check the assumptions of our model. Remember, before the significance test discussion above, some assumptions were detailed which those significance tests rest on. At last, we are going to test to see if those are acceptable. In fact, as I alluded to earlier, it is more logical to do this first because I think it is dangerous to do it later on. What I mean is that by now you are probably quite happy with your model, and therefore you can be tempted to ignore problems that turn up at this stage, especially since so few analysts really check assumptions thoroughly. If I wrote statistical software, I would pop these results up first, and you would have to click on a button before getting the model test results. But I do not, so here we are. Besides, I guess I am being overly harsh here. To look at it another way, these assumptions are only necessary when we are looking to generalize the model from the sample to the population. If all you are doing is describing the data set, then such issues are not that important. But, in most cases, we *are* trying to generalize, so the issues I am going to talk about are very important.

Anyway, recall the set of assumptions that the *F*- and *t*-tests rest on, regarding the error term, which are in brief that:[6]

- the error term ε is a normally distributed random variable with a mean of 0;
- there is no autocorrelation;
- there is no heteroscedasticity.

Now we are going to test them. Again, we use the standardized residuals in the main, and by now you should be relatively comfortable with what they represent. However, in this case, much of our work is done with plots of the standardized residuals.

---

[6] For more depth, return to the section earlier in this chapter on simple linear regression.

Plotting the Standardized Residual Against the Predicted Value

In a multiple regression, it is very useful to plot the standardized residuals against the predicted value of the outcome variable $\hat{y}$. In a simple regression, the plot of standardized residuals against the predictor variable will give the same outcome, but with a multiple regression this is not possible (as there are multiple predictors).

If our assumption about heteroscedasticity holds, then what we should see in the plot is basically a 'cloud' of points, which do not exhibit a pattern and are essentially evenly dispersed around zero. Make sure you check the axes of the graph for where zero lies when drawing this conclusion. Figure 10.7 is the relevant plot for the SP_FUEL data.

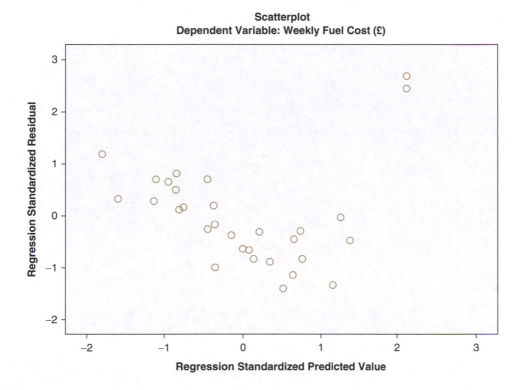

Scatterplot
Dependent Variable: Weekly Fuel Cost (£)

Figure 10.7
Residual Plot for SP_FUEL Data

As you can see, the plot looks slightly odd. It should describe a cloud around zero, but there are a couple of features that would concern us. First, there are two clear data points that are way outside the rest. Obviously, the smart money is on those being the two that we have already been concerned about. Perhaps this is more evidence to remove them? Secondly, while there is no obvious heteroscedasticity, or non-linear pattern, the data does not exactly show a cloud around zero. This is not a disaster by any means, but it is certainly not perfect. That said, there is nothing here that by itself would cause us to panic, although if our other tests are also worrying, we would have to make some tough decisions.

By way of comparison, Figure 10.8 shows more worrying patterns (bear in mind these are idealized examples, not actual output). The upper panel in Figure 10.8 shows a classic 'funnel' pattern, where the cloud appears to open out from left to right. This is the typical indication of heteroscedasticity. The lower panel in Figure 10.8 is a pattern which indicates a non-linear relationship of some kind. If you see this kind of plot, you should consider modelling a non-linear relationship in your data (although this is beyond the scope of this chapter). Of course, it is perfectly possible that the plot can be a mix of both of these patterns, in which case you have two problems to consider. You might note that Figure 10.7 bears at least some resemblance to the non-linear example in Figure 10.8, so that would be worth thinking about if you were really conducting the SP_FUEL analysis.

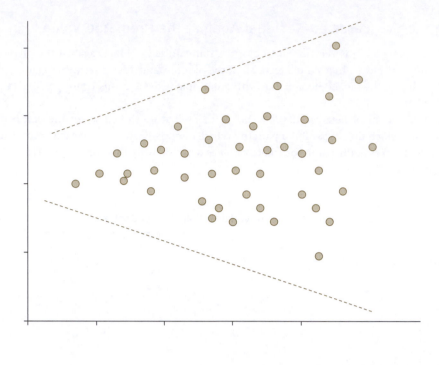

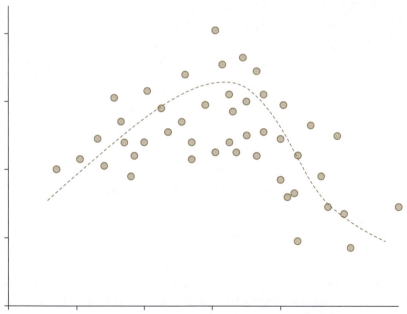

**Figure 10.8a
and b
Bad Residual
Plots**

Residual Histogram and Normal Probability Plot

The next tests that can be done deal with the assumption that the error term is normal. We can look at this in two different ways. Looking at the histogram of the standardized residual provides our first indication. If the residuals are normally distributed, the histogram should look roughly like a normal distribution. Figure 10.9 shows the SP_FUEL example.

Here, with a sigh of relief, we can conclude that this is generally OK, bearing in mind that we do not have a huge amount of data. Sure, it is not perfect, but there is nothing wrong about this, such as all the data being skewed to one side, or most of the data at the extremes and so forth.

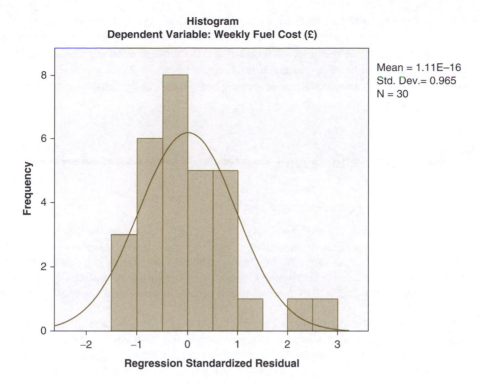

Figure 10.9
Residual
Histogram
For SP_FUEL
Data

The next thing we would do is look at what is called the normal probability plot, sometimes also called the normal P–P plot. This is slightly complex to explain, but, in essence, the diagonal line represents a perfect normal distribution, and the points are the standardized residuals. The closer the observed residuals follow the straight line, the closer to normality they are. Figure 10.10 shows the

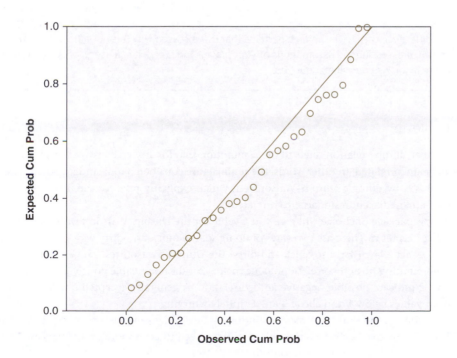

Figure 10.10
Normal P-P
Plot for SP_
FUEL Data

SP_FUEL normal P–P plot, and this looks pretty reasonable to me. Again, if you look closely, you will see those two extreme values, but they do not look so bad here. I would be relatively pleased with this. The further away from that line the observed residuals get, the more worried you should be. Of course, the assessment procedure for both the residual histogram and normal P–P plot was based on judgement. Above and Beyond Box 10.1 provides a way of moving beyond this potentially open-to-abuse reliance on subjective judgement.

above and beyond

Box 10.1   Using a Kolmogorov–Smirnov Test

One thing that always confused me when I was learning regression is why we rely on judgement when testing whether our residuals are normal. It seems possible that researchers could come to different conclusions about the same plot or histogram, leading to different conclusions about the model. Worse, pressure to use a model might lead researchers either deliberately to ignore this subjective evidence, or to convince themselves that it is 'OK'. And do you know what? I have seen it happen...

This seems unnecessary when there is in fact a rather well-established way of testing whether a variable is normally distributed, one that is very often used in describing data. It is called a **Kolmogorov–Smirnov** test, and it basically tests whether or not a variable is distributed normally. The null hypothesis for the K–S test (as it is often known) is that the distribution of the variable in question does not differ from a normal one. Thus, if we *reject* this null hypothesis, we conclude that the variable is non-normal.

So, it baffles me that the K–S test is not used as a rule when describing residuals to assess assumptions of regression. If we are going to all the trouble of plotting them, we can easily run a K–S test on the standardized residuals. If the null hypothesis is rejected, we have evidence that the residuals are not normally distributed. In fact, I think analysis packages should do this as a rule, whenever we request a normal histogram or normal P–P plot. Why they do not is a mystery to me.

Of course, the use of the K–S test in this context has the same caveats as any other, namely that with large sample sizes, the test is very often significant. In other words, large samples make it very powerful and more likely to find small differences as significant. This could lead to over-rejection of models, when the differences are trivial. In fact, perhaps that is the reason why it is not a default. However, it is another way of assessing the assumptions of your model, and I think it is a useful one, when used in an informed manner. As you will no doubt do.

Autocorrelation

If you remember, autocorrelation refers to the assumption that for any given two observations, the residuals should be uncorrelated. In other words, the residuals are considered to be independent. The simplest way to test this is by doing a Durbin–Watson test, which explicitly tests for serial correlation between errors (i.e. whether adjacent residuals are correlated).

Your analysis package of choice will give you a value for the Durbin–Watson test if you ask for it, and the task is to interpret it. There are two ways of doing so: the quick-and-dirty way, or the more involved and accurate 'exact' way. First, the quick-and-dirty: the Durbin–Watson test ranges from 0 to 4, with a value of 2 representing no autocorrelation. Values below 2 indicate possible positive autocorrelation, and values above 2 indicate possible negative autocorrelation. A generally accepted quick-and-dirty rule of thumb is that values below 1 and above 3 are definitely worrying.

If we take a look at the Durbin–Watson result for our SP_FUEL example, however, we come up with a value of 1.05. To me, that is a *potential* problem, and we need to get a more exact analysis. To do so, we need to refer to the tables developed by Durbin and Watson.

The Durbin–Watson tables are available in the appendices, and need to be used in conjunction with the number of predictor variables and sample size. In this case, we have 2 predictors and a sample size of 30. The first thing to do is decide on a level of significance, which in this case will be 0.05. Now the Durbin–Watson tables are one-tailed.[7] However, we have no reason to predict either negative or positive autocorrelation, and so we should be doing a two-tailed test. As such, we need to double the level of significance. In other words, if you want to do a two-tailed test with a significance of 0.5, you need to use the Durbin–Watson tables for a significance of 0.025 (which is one-tailed).

For each number of predictors, and sample size, the tables give us two values, an upper bound d_U and a lower bound d_L. If we take our Durbin–Watson test result as d then the following rules apply for a two-tailed Durbin–Watson test:

If $d_U < d < 4 - d_U$ then there is no autocorrelation in the data.

If $d_L < d < d_U$ or $4 - d_U < d < 4 - d_L$ then the test is inconclusive.

If $d < d_L$ or $d > 4 - d_L$ then there is autocorrelation present in the data.

You can tell of course whether it is negative or positive autocorrelation by whether the number is below or above 2.

So, looking at the Durbin–Watson table for 2 predictors, a sample size of 30 and significance of 0.025, $d_L = 1.18$ and $d_U = 1.46$. Looking at our Durbin–Watson test result of 1.05, we can clearly see cause for concern and an indication of possible negative autocorrelation.

So what do we do? Well, remedies for autocorrelation are some way outside this introductory book. In most cases, autocorrelation is caused by time series data; in other words, the outcome variable is measured at multiple ongoing time periods (common in economic research). In such cases, you can investigate whether you have omitted an important predictor which may have a time-dependent effect on the outcome. If so, and you have the data, you can include it. If not, another option is to include a new variable as a predictor that simply measures the time order of each data point. In this case, though, our data is not measured over time, so it is more of a problem. In such cases, we can transform the predictor or outcome variables, which sometimes works. However, we are in a thorny problem here, no doubt about it. Most analysts would be tempted to return to the 'quick-and-dirty' method, which we just scrape a pass in. Or even to ignore the Durbin–Watson results. Personally, I would want to investigate things much more closely before making any decisions.

Multicollinearity

The final assumption to be discussed is the one that, if analysts only know about one assumption, this is the one they know about. Multicollinearity is a term which refers to the correlations between the predictor variables. When we are talking about only two predictors, then, strictly speaking, we should use the term collinearity. In most cases, predictors are correlated in some way, either as a result of their being correlated in the real world (where most things are correlated to some degree) or as random statistical chance.

The simplest way to check for collinearity between any two predictors is to test the correlation(s) between the predictors. In the SP_FUEL example, the correlation between weekly miles driven and proportion of city driving is 0.675. Now, as a rule of thumb, I was always told that you should not worry too much until correlations got around 0.8, or even 0.9. But I never trusted such advice too much. Remember: rules of thumb are ripe for abuse. So we need more thought here.

First, let's think why collinearity might be a problem. Well, consider what would happen if the correlation between the two variables was perfect (i.e. a correlation coefficient of 1). In this case, there is no way to obtain unique estimates of b for either of the variables – there are an infinite variety of possible b coefficients that would work. In other words, in such a situation the estimates are interchangeable, and we

---

[7] The reason for this is that economists normally test for positive autocorrelation, as it is very unusual to see negative autocorrelation in economic data.

cannot identify the unique effects of each predictor on the outcome. The closer the correlation gets to 1, the more serious this problem is. In practical terms, higher collinearity makes the b estimates untrustworthy. It is harder to determine how important each predictor is, and also the estimates in the regression model become unstable (i.e. they will differ from sample to sample). Finally, multicollinearity reduces the size of R^2 as well, because the multiple predictors share a large proportion of variance.

So, this problem looks too serious to be trusted to some old rules of thumb I got told in the last century (really). The most common way that collinearity is assessed is with the variance inflation factor or VIF. The formula for the VIF is:

$$VIF(x_j) = \frac{1}{1 - R_j^2}$$

The term on the bottom line of the equation is basically the coefficient of determination that is calculated when a given predictor x_j is regressed on all the other predictors in the model. So each x_j has its own VIF. If x_j is not correlated with the other predictors, then the coefficient of determination will approach 0, and this will in the end give a VIF close to 1. The more correlation that exists between x_j and the other predictors, the higher the VIF gets. Normally, an individual VIF that is above 10 is cause for concern as regards that predictor. VIFs can easily be obtained from analysis packages, and in the SP_FUEL example the VIFs for both predictors are the same, at 1.84. Of course, with only two predictors the VIFs are symmetrical for each predictor.

A related way of assessing multicollinearity is the tolerance, which is simply 1/VIF (i.e. the reciprocal of VIF). Naturally, then, tolerance values below 0.1 are of concern. Just like the VIFs, the tolerances for the predictors in the SP_FUEL example are symmetrical and fine, at 0.54. There are various other, more complex ways of judging multicollinearity, but they are beyond the scope of this particular book.

 think it over 10.16

We are constantly told that the more data we have, the better our model will be. Can the same be said about the number of predictors? Explain your answer.

NOTES ON USE AND INTERPRETATION OF MULTIPLE REGRESSION

Before wrapping up what has turned out to be an epic achievement of a chapter, on a par with Marcel Proust's *A la recherche du temps perdu*,[8] at the very least, there are a few final things to consider about how we might use the multiple regression coefficients in practice.

If you remember, earlier in the chapter we discussed how to calculate confidence and prediction intervals for the b coefficient. The concepts are exactly the same here. Specifically, the first step of the procedure – calculating a point value – is completely identical, and simply involves substituting in the values of interest for the predictor variables.

Calculating the prediction or confidence intervals involves a process which is basically the same as for a simple regression. However, the actual calculations are rather more difficult, and again beyond our scope. Instead, the software package you use will provide you with confidence and prediction intervals if you want to use them.

As a final note, sample size is worth discussing. There is a pervasive rule of thumb (another one?!) out there that simply says that to be confident in a regression model, you should have 10 or 15 data points for

---

[8] Classy, right?

every predictor. So, in our case, with 2 predictors, we had 30 cases, and are fine. However, this is a gross simplification. In particular, the sample size you need also depends on the effect size you are intending to find, and in simple terms the more data you have, the better.

This is because the R value is also influenced by the number of predictors p and the sample size n. It might surprise you to find out that the expected value of R for random data is:

$$\frac{p}{n-1}$$

which means that the smaller the sample size, the more likely you are to get an R which suggests a strong effect. Of course, you would hope for random data (where we would expect to find no effect, and $R = 0$), but let's calculate the expected R for our SP_FUEL example, with 2 predictors and 30 data points. In fact, it is $2/29 = 0.069$. This is OK, pretty close to zero. But try increasing p, and quite quickly you will be getting into R values which would normally indicate moderate effect sizes, with a sample of 30. This should help you to understand the importance of sample size and the model-building strategy you use. In other words, throwing many variables into a regression equation, with little reason behind them, is rarely a clever strategy – especially with smaller sample sizes. However, that is exactly what a lot of analysts do, and it serves as an excellent closing point for this chapter, because it is just what we are going to talk about in the next chapter.

Using Excel for Covariance, Correlation and All That Jazz

It is always a good idea to plot your data before you start going down the road of correlation and regression. As was stated at the start of this chapter, it is very easy to convince ourselves that there is a relationship between our variables when in fact none exists (length of skirts and the price of coal). The best way is to plot your data in a scatterplot. This is straightforward with Excel. Take a look at Figure 10.11 where the data from the investigation into whether there was a correlation between exam scores and attendance is shown.

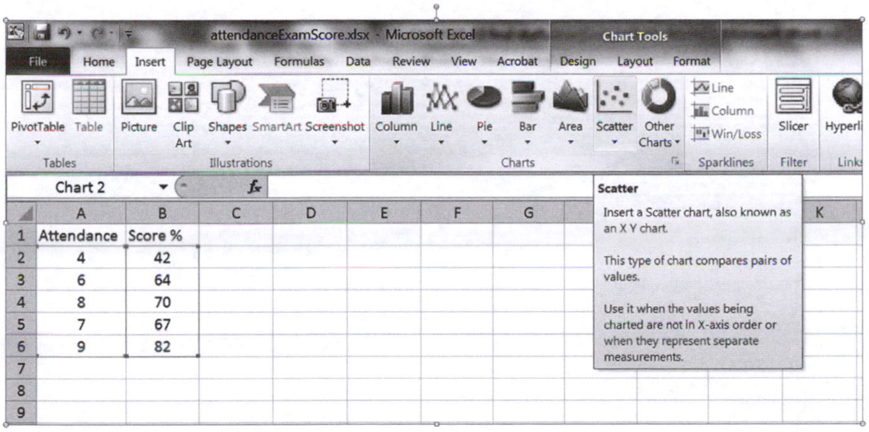

Figure 10.11

The data is put into two columns, not forgetting to label them. Once you have entered your data, select both columns, but not the titles, then select Insert → Scatter. Figure 10.12 shows the result of this operation with titles added.

By looking at the scatterplot we can see that we could probably draw a line of best fit (this is a straight line where the data points are at similar distances from the line) between the points, indicating there could be a relationship between the data. We could then with some confidence start the statistical investigation.

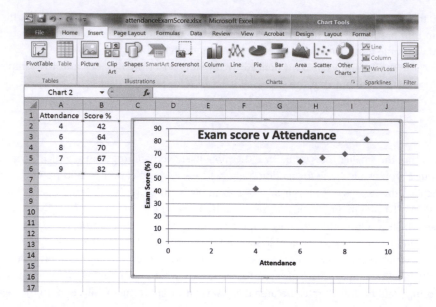

Figure 10.12

Using the same data, we can now investigate the covariance using Excel. Using the same spreadsheet, click on a cell where you want the result displayed (I have used cell E6), select <u>Formulas</u> → <u>More</u> <u>Functions</u> → <u>Statistical</u> and then <u>Covariances</u> (see Figure 10.13).

think it over 10.17

Why did we choose to use covariances.s rather than covariances.p? What do you think the s and the p stand for?

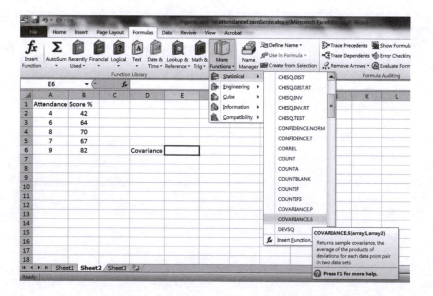

Figure 10.13

Once you have made your selection, a pop-up box will appear where you enter the column references for the data. Figure 10.14 shows the result, which, as you can see, gives the same answer as when it was calculated at the start of this chapter.

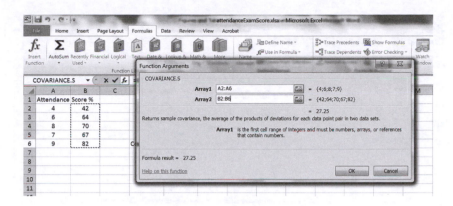

Figure 10.14

Figures 10.15 to 10.17 show you how to use Excel to calculate the correlation coefficient. The result is shown in Figure 10.18, where *r* is the same value as calculated earlier in the text.

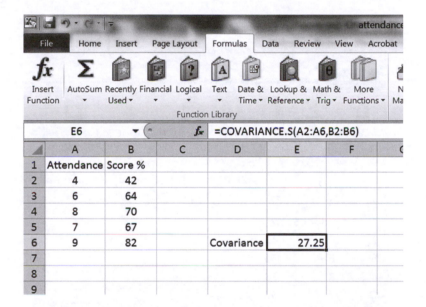

Figure 10.15

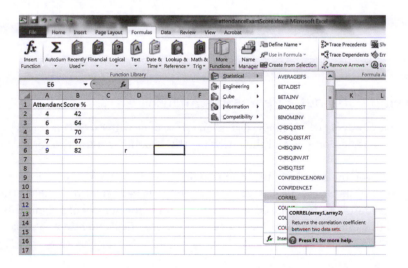

Figure 10.16

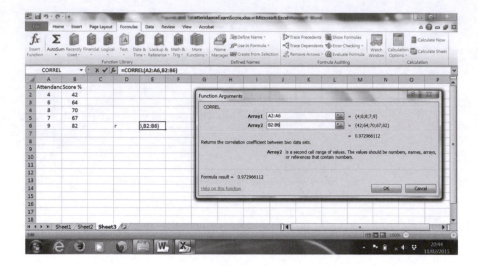

Figure 10.17

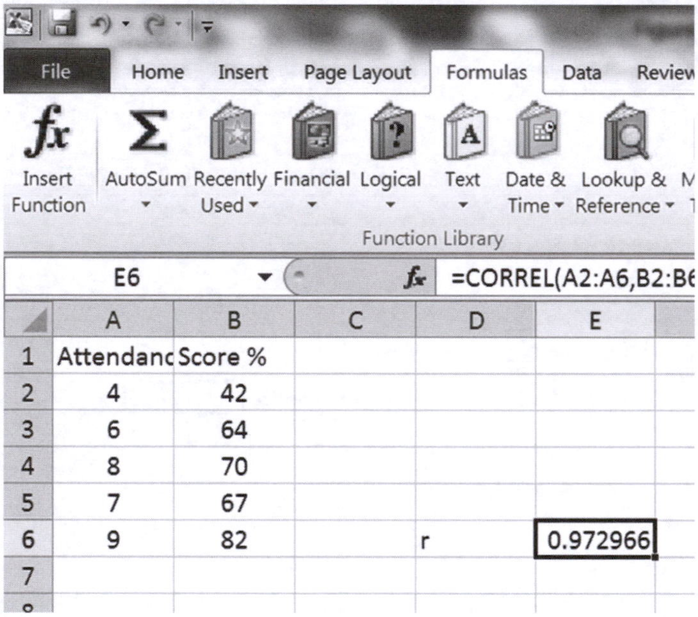

Figure 10.18

Using Excel to Carry out a Regression Analysis

There are a couple of ways in which simple regression can be done with Excel. One way is just to calculate the gradient of the regression line and the intercept. This is done by using two formulae: 'Trend' and 'Linest'.

'Linest' will give you the gradient of the regression line. Figure 10.19 shows you where to find this formula and Figure 10.20 shows you the dialog box in which you have to enter your values. The weekly sales data goes into the 'known y's' field (the dependent variable) and the number of assignments goes into the 'known x's' field (the independent variable). Click on the 'Const' field and read what it says (by the way,

Excel has this useful feature for all of its formulae). In this case we want the value of the intercept, the *b* value, to be taken into account, so enter 'TRUE'. Enter 'TRUE' in the 'Stats' field. Click 'OK'. You should get an answer of –3.48. If you do not, check that you have entered the data in the right fields.

	A	B
2	2	45
3	4	41
4	4	43
5	5	37
6	5	32
7	6	34
8	7	28
9	8	20
10	8	22
11	12	15

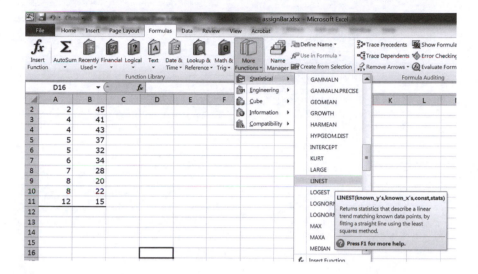

Figure 10.19

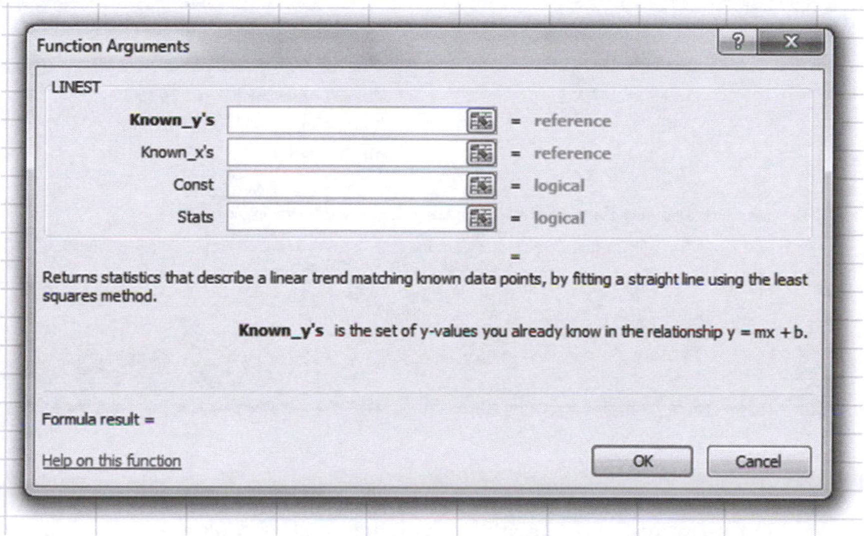

Figure 10.20

'Trend' will give you the value (the dependent value) for a particular value (the independent variable). In order to use this formula you have to think back to the meaning of the regression equation (also known in mathematics as the equation of a straight line). Ask yourself, at what value of the independent variable does the regression line (trend line) cross the independent variable axis? The answer is 0.

Look at Figure 10.21. This shows you how to find the 'Trend' formula. Figure 10.22 shows the pop-up window where you enter the function arguments. This box is similar to the 'Linest' box except for the third field 'New x's'. This is where the 0 is entered to obtain the intercept value. Click on 'OK' to activate the function. You should have a value of 52.93.

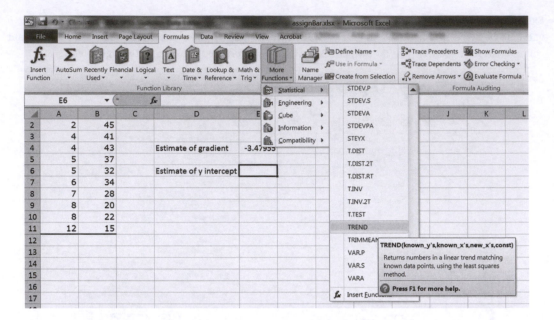

Figure 10.21

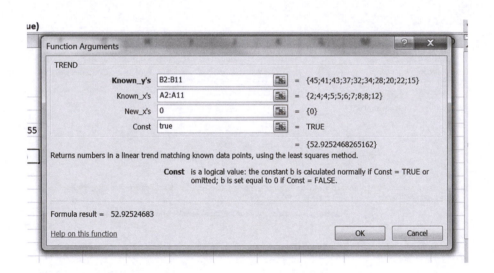

Figure 10.22

The other way to perform regression is using the in-built data analysis tools that come with later versions of Excel. Select Data and then click on the 'Data Analysis' function, found at the far right of the screen. Figure 10.23 shows the <u>Data</u> Analysis tool selection window. Scroll down to 'Regression' and click 'OK' (it is also worth exploring some of the other functions available). This will then take you to another screen to select the output you want, also shown in Figure 10.23.

You will notice that you can choose to have all sorts of output. Enter your data in the appropriate fields. Once you have entered your data, you can make various selections. By default Excel will calculate the 95% confidence level and will always display it in the output tables. If you want, say, a 99% confidence level, enter it here. The output range expects the cell reference for the top left corner of where you want the output table displayed. You also have the option to select residuals, etc. It is worth ticking all the boxes so that you can then relate the output to the theory you have learned (always play and investigate!). Click 'OK' and you should see an output similar to Figure 10.24.

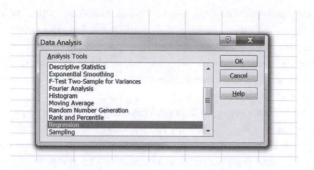

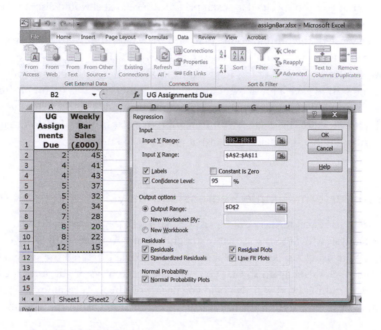

Figure 10.23

Figure 10.24

To make the output shown in Figure 10.24 look less cluttered, I have reduced the number of decimal places to three. It shows three output tables. The first table 'Regression Statistics' gives you the information you would expect but with different names in some cases. Multiple R is the square root of the coefficient of determination or, easier to remember, the Pearson correlation coefficient. The R Square value is the coefficient of determination or how good a fit the model is to the data. The next is the Adjusted R Square value and then the Standard Error. This is the value for *s* the estimated value for σ.

The ANOVA table gives the analysis of variance information (covered in detail in the next chapter). It gives information on the three sources of variance: regression, residuals and total; *df* are the degrees of freedom, *SS* is the sum of squares, *MS* is the mean square value. The *F* value is also given along with the *significance F* which is the associated *p*-value.

The table of most interest for this chapter is the last one. This one gives the intercept value and the gradient, called 'X Variable 1' under the heading *Coefficients*. The standard error, in this table, is the estimate for the standard error for *b* (note that this is different from the standard error given in the Regression Statistics box). You are also given the *t Stat* and the *p-value*. Excel will always give the 95% upper and lower confidence level limits, but if you also specified for example a 99% level, Excel would also display the upper and lower limits for this confidence level alongside the 95% levels.

In order to make sense of the output, compare it with the values that were calculated by hand in the text. This will help you to get used to the different terms used in Excel.

You have now seen two ways of doing regression in Excel. The first method only gave very basic information and the second gave a lot of extra information. Sometimes it is useful just to have the basic information to get a 'sort of feel' for the analysis. The second method is quicker, since you only enter the data once, and it also provides the diagnostic information to assist in your decision making. As always, the method you choose to use is dependent on what you want to know.

Using SPSS to Perform Simple Regression Analysis

You have seen how to use Excel to carry out regression. Now let's look at using SPSS.

To perform the analysis with SPSS is reasonably straightforward. As usual, with SPSS you have to specify the type of data you are using, unlike Excel where all numeric data is treated the same.

We will use the bar sales data again so that you will have three ways of checking the analysis and be able to compare the terminology. It will also help you decide on the 'best tool' for the job.

Figure 10.25 shows you how to find the linear regression function within the SPSS menu system.

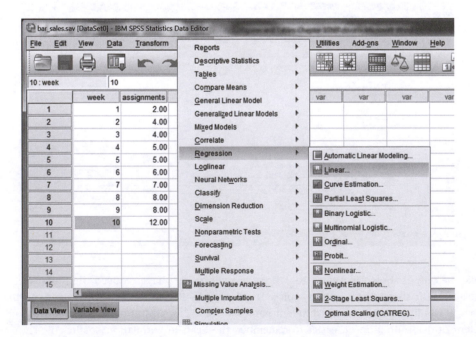

Figure 10.25

Figure 10.26 shows the result of selecting the linear regression function. It is important, as it was with Excel, to make sure you put the correct data in the appropriate field. Since weekly bar sales are dependent upon the assignments due, it is the dependent variable and assignments due is the independent variable. Once you have entered your variables, click on 'Statistics'. This will give you access to the available regression options and the residual diagnostics. Click on 'Continue'. You can now choose to plot the residual data. Diagrams help me to visualize things, so I tend to select the normal probability plot so I can see how close the observed data is to the expected data due to my regression model.

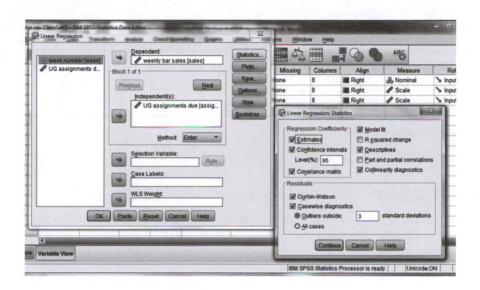

Figure 10.26

The output from SPSS is shown in Figure 10.27. As you can see, it gives the same information as Excel but in more familiar terms.

Model Summary[b]

Model	R	R Square	Adjusted R Square	Std. Error of the Estimate
1	.952[a]	.905	.894	3.34842

a. Predictors: (Constant), UG assignments due

b. Dependent Variable: weekly bar sales

Figure 10.27a

ANOVA[a]

Model		Sum of Squares	df	Mean Square	F	Sig.
1	Regression	858.405	1	858.405	76.562	.000[b]
	Residual	89.695	8	11.212		
	Total	948.100	9			

a. Dependent Variable: weekly bar sales

b. Predictors: (Constant), UG assignments due

Figure 10.27b

Coefficients[a]

Model		Unstandardized Coefficients		Standardized Coefficients	t	Sig.	95.0% Confidence Interval for B	
		B	Std. Error	Beta			Lower Bound	Upper Bound
1	(Constant)	52.925	2.647		19.996	.000	46.822	59.029
	UG assignments due	-3.480	.398	-.952	-8.750	.000	-4.397	-2.563

Figure 10.27c   a. Dependent Variable: weekly bar sales

	Minimum	Maximum	Mean	Std. Deviation	N
Residual	-5.08886	3.99295	.00000	3.15692	10
Std. Predicted Value	-2.102	1.461	.000	1.000	10
Std. Residual	-1.520	1.192	.000	.943	10

Figure 10.27d   a. Dependent Variable: weekly bar sales

Multiple Regression with Excel

To perform multiple regression with Excel is very similar to doing simple regression. The only difference is that you select all of the predictor data. If you look at Figure 10.28 you will see that the 'Input X Range' encompasses cells B2 to C31 (i.e. both columns of the independent variables). The original data can be found in SP FUEL.xlsx.

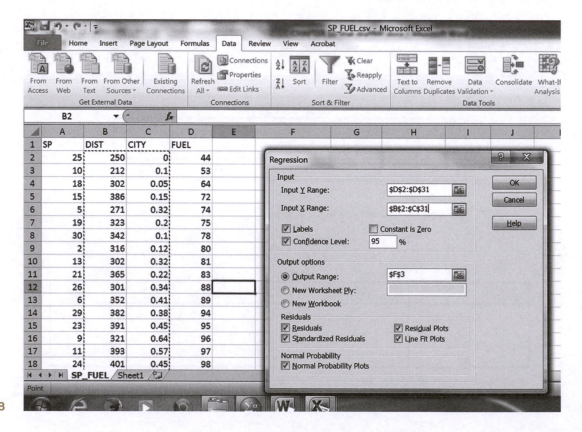

Figure 10.28

Figure 10.29 shows the output once you have clicked 'OK'.

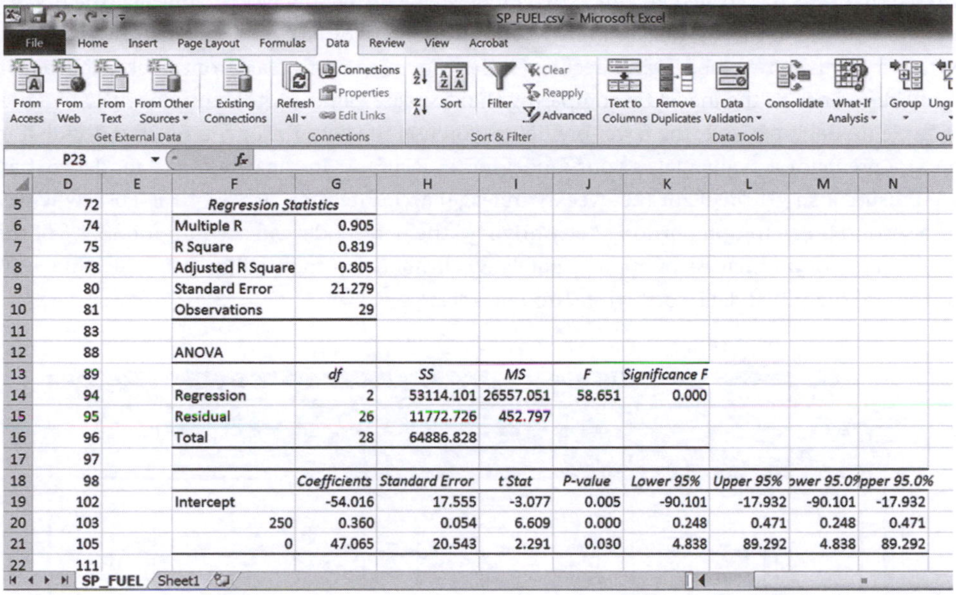

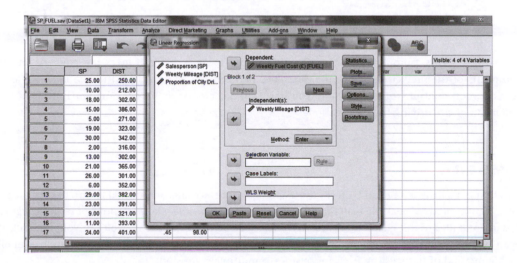

Figure 10.29

Multiple Regression with SPSS

We will use the data from SP_FUEL.sav so the results can be compared with the ones given in the text and the output from Excel (SP FUEL.xlsx contained the same data).

Performing multiple regression with SPSS is very similar to carrying out simple regression. Once you have entered your data, select <u>Analyze</u> → <u>Regression</u> and then <u>Linear</u>. To perform multiple regression analysis we need to be able to enter more than one predictor. To do this with SPSS, put the variable most likely to influence the model in the independent window. In order to enter more than one, click on 'Next' (which is just above the window, see Figure 10.30) and transfer the next most likely variable to influence the regression analysis. As before, you can request various statistics and plots. Once you have made your selections, click 'OK'.

Figure 10.30

As before, SPSS will display a lot of information which we have already covered, and you can see much of it in Figure 10.31. One of the interesting tables is the 'Model Summary' table. If you look beneath it you will see that SPSS has created, in effect, two models, one using only weekly mileage (the first variable entered) and the second using weekly mileage and proportion of city driving. This useful feature now allows you to compare two models and decide if in fact any predictors apart from weekly mileage make a significant difference to the model by comparing the R Square values. A golden rule with any analysis is 'use a simple model if possible: the fewer predictors you use, the better'. So, you need to decide if including an extra predictor actually makes your model more 'accurate'. In the case of the model we have just produced, using a single predictor (i.e. weekly mileage) accounted for 79.5% of the cost, whereas if we include a second predictor (proportion of city driving), the new model can account for 82.9% of the cost. The question is: for an increase of approximately 3% in model accountability, was the time and effort used to acquire the initial data worthwhile? You decide!

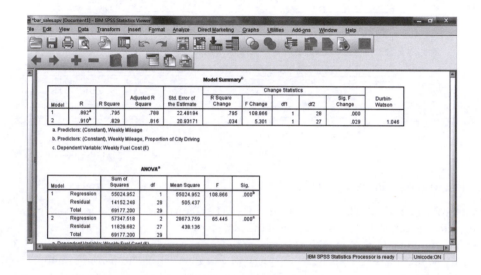

Figure 10.31

Figure 10.31 shows a proportion of the 'Coefficients' table. As expected it gives the gradient and the coefficients of the predictors. Notice the difference between the 'B' values for the two models. Reread the section on multiple regression before you start thinking along the lines of how much influence the proportion of city driving had on the model.

SUMMARY

Well, that got a little out of hand. I feel I must apologise for the rather substantial length of this chapter. However, it is hard to break the material up and keep what I consider a helpful 'flow' of ideas going. The fundamental idea of this chapter was that of *relationships* between specific variables in your data set. We began with the simple idea of covariance and ended up by detailing arguably the most powerful and flexible method of statistical analysis for business – multiple regression.

Regression analysis is what I consider the wellspring for pretty much all other types of statistical analysis that are popular in business, finance and economics. Many of the techniques you will learn later are special cases, techniques and applications of the seminal concepts you have learned here. Even what many consider the 'other' main form of statistical analysis in business – ANOVA (you will learn this in Chapter 14) – can be explained as a particular case of regression, and if we do this (which we will) it is much easier to get across.

So, in terms of actual practical value for your later statistical career, this is probably the most important chapter to really understand. And of course, you cannot understand it without getting to grips with the earlier material in the book. Hopefully, it is all beginning to come together, but if it is not, just go back and work through some of the more basic ideas again.

 think it over 10.18

'I'm going to collect my data and then I'm going to construct my model ... or should I?'

This chapter has shown the statistical techniques we can employ to check the validity and accuracy of a model. What process would you follow before constructing a complex statistical model to ensure the time and effort of doing all these calculations is worthwhile?

 final checklist

You should have covered and understood the following basic content in this chapter:

☑ The concept of covariation between two variables.

☑ The usefulness of standardizing the covariance, to make a correlation.

☑ The difference between correlation and causation.

☑ How to extend the concept of covariance to incorporate notions of predictor and outcome variables, leading to simple linear regression.

☑ How to calculate and evaluate a simple linear regression model.

☑ How to extend simple linear regression to multiple linear regression.

☑ How to evaluate a multiple regression model, in terms of how well the model explains the data.

☑ How to assess critical diagnostics for multiple regression.

☑ How to test the important assumptions of a multiple regression model.

☑ Where your nearest coffee supply is...

EXERCISES

1. The formula for variance is given by:

$$s^2 = \frac{\sum (x_i - \bar{x})^2}{n-1}$$

Show how this is equal to:

$$s^2 = \frac{\sum (x_i - \bar{x})(x_i - \bar{x})}{n-1}$$

2. Figure 10.32 shows a scatterplot of data for the number of customers visiting a shop (horizontal axis) and the sales volume (vertical axis).

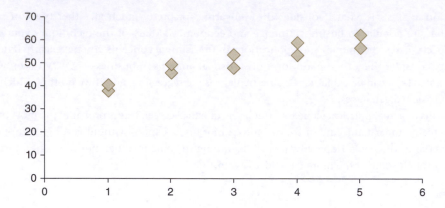

Figure 10.32

a. By looking at Figure 10.32, decide if the covariance will be positive, negative or zero.
b. Using Table 10.8, calculate the covariance and explain what your result means.

Table 10.8

No. customers	Sales
2	50
5	57
1	41
3	54
4	54
1	38
5	63
3	48

3. Figure 10.33 shows a scatterplot of temperature (vertical) and sales of ice cream (horizontal).

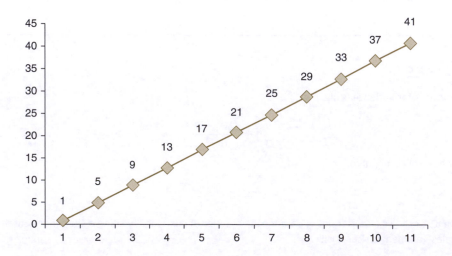

Figure 10.33

a. How would you describe the relationship between the temperature and ice cream sales?
b. Delete as appropriate: 'There is a negative/positive/zero correlation between temperature and ice cream sales.'
c. By using the appropriate equations, demonstrate why the correlation coefficient can never be greater than 1.

4. What calculation would you use to see how well your model fits your data?

5. Figure 10.34 shows the actual data (diamonds), the regression equation (squares) and the mean value (triangles) of a chain of ice cream parlours.

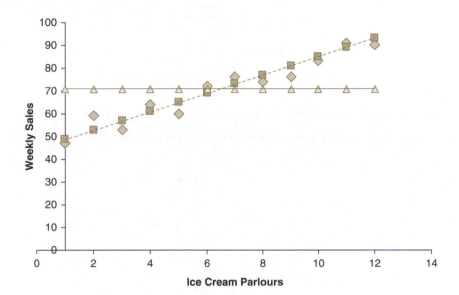

Ice Cream Parlours

Figure 10.34

a. In your opinion, which is the best model of the actual data?
b. Verify your answer by calculating SST. Table 10.9 shows the weekly sales and the values predicted by the regression equation.

Table 10.9

Parlour	Weekly sales	Predicted sales
1	47	49
2	59	53
3	53	57
4	64	61
5	60	65
6	72	69
7	76	73
8	74	77
9	76	81
10	83	85
11	91	89
12	90	93

c. Explain the equation SST = SSM + SSE.

6. In estimating σ^2 the degrees of freedom for a regression equation were equal to $n - 2$. The example calculation in the text was:

$$\sigma^2 = \frac{SSE}{n - 2}$$

Give an explanation as to why the degrees of freedom value is equal to the number of data points, minus the number of parameters, in this case β_0 and β_1.

7. With the F-test:

$$MSM = \frac{SSM}{\text{Number of predictor variables}}$$

Convert this equation into an English statement.

8. If the value of the squared error due to the model (MSM) is 10 times as large as the mean of squared error (MSE), what F value would you expect?

9. Use the relationship between MSM and MSE to describe a good regression model.

10. Figure 10.35 shows observed data, the mean and the deviations about the estimated regression line.

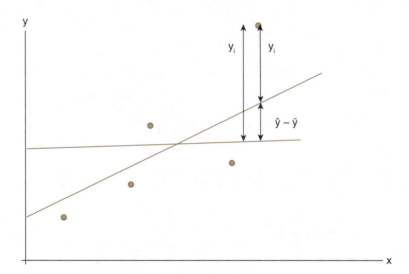

Figure 10.35

Indicate on the diagram the observed data, the mean and the regression line.

11. Can you deduce from the F-test that if the null hypothesis is rejected, which parameters, if any, are equal to zero?

Table 10.10

Weight (kg)	29.09	32.27	24.09	30.45	25.00	26.36	35.00	25.91	25.45	23.18	34.55	30.91
Height (m)	1.45	1.50	1.24	1.57	1.30	1.27	1.40	1.22	1.32	1.07	1.55	1.45
Age (yrs)	8	10	6	11	8	7	10	9	10	6	12	9

12. Table 10.10 shows the weights in kilograms, heights in metres and ages in years of 12 boys.

    a. Using Excel construct the regression equation.
    b. What does this equation tell you about the relationship between the variables?

   c.   Estimate the weight of a boy who is 9 years old and 54 inches tall.

   d.   Convert the height in part (c) to metres and redo the estimate.

13.

   a.   Using the data from Table 10.10, calculate the estimated weights of the boys using the regression equation (use Excel to produce the new table).

   b.   Use the formula

$$s = \sqrt{\frac{\sum (z - z_{est})^2}{n}}$$

to calculate the standard error (z is the observed weights, z_{est} is the estimated weights from the regression equation and n is the sample size).

   c.   Calculate the percentage of points that fall within ±1 SE.

   d.   In theory, you should have calculated a value of approximately 67%. Does this value remind you of another statistical measure? [Hint: look at dispersion statistics.]

   e.   What conclusions can you draw from calculating the value of the standard error of estimate?

   f.   Rather than perform the tedious calculation, SPSS gives a value for the standard error of the predicted values. Locate this value from the SPSS output table and recalculate the percentage of points that lie within 1 standard error of the estimate.

   g.   If the sample size were larger, what would you predict about the value of the standard error of the estimate given by SPSS?

 To access additional online resources please visit: **https://study.sagepub.com/leepeters**

The Ballad of Eddie the Easily Distracted: Part 11

Eddie and Esha were working together on their tutorial exercise for QUAN101. The tutor had slipped out to 'go to the bathroom', or so he said. Everyone knew he snuck out the back for a cigarette while they were working. While Eddie had usually taken that opportunity to relax and muse on something important, like whether the Smashing Pumpkins would ever reform properly, over the last few weeks he had found himself continuing to work with Esha on the tutorial problems. This week's lecture on 'dummy variables' had both amused and confused Eddie: 'At least that's better than just being confused,' he thought wryly.

Anyway, apart from the grin he got from the use of the word 'dummy', Eddie thought that some of the material was actually quite simple. It wasn't too hard for him to get his head around using the dummies, but it *was* confusing learning how to interpret the results. It seemed very easy to misrepresent what the numbers meant, especially if you had messed up your dummy coding. Eddie resolved to try to be careful here, and repeated the mantra 'don't be a dummy about dummy variables' over and over in his head. He was brought back to Earth with a bump when Esha poked him in the ribs. 'Come on Eddie, *concentrate*!' she said. 'But, but, I was, honestly,' said Eddie. 'Whatever,' sighed Esha.

Esha's Story: Part 11

That Eddie was utterly infuriating at times! Esha had found herself wandering around the lake on campus on her way home. She'd taken the long way back to her room after class, annoyed about how the tutorial had gone. By the time the tutor had come in after his 'toilet break', they hadn't quite finished the exercises, and, worse, they'd been asked to explain the answers. Eddie had completely clammed up, leaving Esha to report back to the class. It was so hard to keep his attention on the work in hand, which was especially annoying since, when he set his mind to it, he could usually work it out quite quickly. It was getting close to the end of term now, exams were coming up, and Esha really couldn't afford to be messing around nursemaiding this guy through the tutorials.

'On the other hand,' she thought, 'it does help me really get to grips with things when I have to explain them to Eddie,' and it was quite pleasing to see how far he'd come during the year they'd been tutorial partners. He was quite smart really, but Esha couldn't understand why he was more interested in computer games and music than getting good grades. She shook her head to clear her mind; now was not the time to get distracted. She'd actually enjoyed this week's work on logistic regression. Although the calculations looked complex, and they were, a slow and steady approach really paid off when thinking about them. It turned out that the basic principles were relatively simple – it was all about probabilities, and that helped to recall the earlier material from the course too! That was a brainwave she was quite proud of. She resolved to mention it to Eddie next time she saw him at the tutorial.

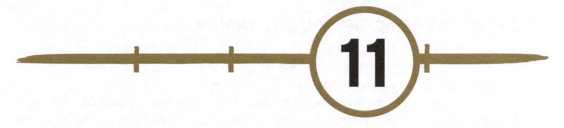

REGRESSION SPECIAL TOPICS

CONTENTS

 learning objectives

The important learning objectives for this chapter are:

- ☑ Understand what a categorical predictor is, and how to incorporate them into a regression context by using dummy variables.
- ☑ Learn how to interpret the results of a dummy variable regression.
- ☑ Learn how to incorporate a categorical outcome into a regression by using logistic regression.
- ☑ Learn how to interpret the output of a logistic regression.

- ☑ Learn how to explore non-linear relationships in regression, including interactions.
- ☑ Understand key issues in transforming predictor and outcome variables for use in regression.
- ☑ Understand the important concepts to consider when choosing which method to use for entering variables into a multiple regression model.

If you thought that you had seen the back of regression analysis after the previous chapter, then think again! In fact, regression is an extremely powerful technique and can go well beyond what was covered in Chapter 10. Here we will extend it to deal with categorical predictor and outcome variables, as well as begin to touch on more complex types of relationship such as non-linear models. Finally, we will cover techniques of actually 'building' your regression model, and touch on the differences between a traditionally 'scientific' approach and the methods that may be more common in commercial business research contexts. So, to quote Shakespeare (things have got rather literary lately, haven't they?), 'screw your courage to the sticking place, and we'll not fail'![1]

On we go...

CATEGORICAL PREDICTORS: DUMMY VARIABLES

Dummy variables are one of those regression topics that has given me more pleasure, and less understanding, than almost any other. Pleasure, because the name always makes me smile,[2] and lack of understanding because I have always struggled to really 'get' them sorted in my head.

So far, all the variables you have worked with have been quantitative, such as miles driven, number of assessments due and so forth. However, a lot of variables we might want to use as predictors are not quantitative. Instead, they are categorical, which is sometimes called qualitative, although I think using the latter term is confusing so let's avoid it from now on and just use categorical. Categorical variables are things such as gender (i.e. male or female), which has two categories, or nationality, which can have many more. To illustrate the use of categorical predictors, we can extend the student bar example.

Table 11.1 Student bar data with sports

	WEEK	SPORT	UG	SALES
1	1.00	Cricket	5	32.00
2	2.00	Football	4	43.00
3	3.00	Football	2	45.00
4	4.00	Football	4	41.00
5	5.00	Football	5	37.00
6	6.00	Football	6	34.00
7	7.00	Cricket	7	28.00
8	8.00	Cricket	12	15.00
9	9.00	Cricket	8	20.00
10	10.00	Cricket	8	22.00

Table 11.1 shows the student bar data, with an extra predictor. Specifically, we may theorize that the type of sport shown on the television at the bar may have an impact on bar sales. In this case, we suspect that when football is shown, students drink more than when cricket is shown, as well as drinking less when

---

[1] I always thought this was kind of a weird statement from someone who was supposed to be a great writer. However, on further research, I've discovered that experts think that Shakespeare was actually alluding to 'screwing up' a musical instrument tuning peg, or something like that, until it sticks. In other words, then, the quote is kind of 'screw up your courage until it gets to the sticking place'. Makes more sense now. See, it's amazing what you can learn if you look at the footnotes, isn't it?

[2] Seriously, I'm still grinning while reading this over, two weeks before my 40th birthday! Apparently my sense of humour is 'immature'...

a greater number of assignments are due. You should recall that the estimated simple linear regression equation for the student bar example is:

$$\hat{y} = b_0 + b_1 x$$

and this is estimated as:

$$\hat{y} = 52.93 - 3.48x$$

But how do we incorporate the categorical sport variable into this analysis? The first thing to do is to define what the sport predictor x_2 should look like. Let's use:

$$x_2 = 0 \text{ if the sport is football}$$

$$x_2 = 1 \text{ if the sport is cricket}$$

This makes x_2 into a dummy variable, which is a powerful and flexible method for incorporating categorical predictors into regression models. It also has major overlaps with the methods that will be discussed in the next chapter, comparing two means. But let's leave that for now. Recoding the data set in this way results in Table 11.2.

Table 11.2   Dummy-coded student bar data with sports

	WEEK	SPORT	UG	SALES
1	1.00	1.00	5	32.00
2	2.00	.0	4	43.00
3	3.00	.0	2	45.00
4	4.00	.0	4	41.00
5	5.00	.0	5	37.00
6	6.00	.0	6	34.00
7	7.00	1.00	7	28.00
8	8.00	1.00	12	15.00
9	9.00	1.00	8	20.00
10	10.00	1.00	8	22.00

With the dummy variable, the estimated equation becomes:

$$\hat{y} = b_0 + b_1 x_1 + b_2 x_2$$

As a basic multiple regression model, we can run this in IBM SPSS Statistics Software (SPSS) and get the following estimated equation:

$$\hat{y} = 46.47 - 1.62x_1 - 11.75x_2$$

Figure 11.1 shows the basic SPSS output of the model. From this you can see that the F-test is significant at a 0.05 level, as are the t-tests for each estimate. Both R^2 and adjusted R^2 suggest that the regression equation is a good fit to the data.

Variables Entered/Removed[b]

Model	Variables Entered	Variables Removed	Method
1	SPORT, WEEK[a]	.	Enter

a. All requested variables entered.

b. Dependent Variable: Weekly Bar Sales (£000)

Model Summary

Model	R	R Square	Adjusted R Square	Std. Error of the Estimate
1	.944[a]	.892	.861	3.82442

a. Predictors: (Constant), SPORT, WEEK

ANOVA[b]

Model		Sum of Squares	df	Mean Square	F	Sig.
1	Regression	845.717	2	422.858	28.911	.000[a]
	Residual	102.383	7	14.626		
	Total	948.100	9			

a. Predictors: (Constant), SPORT, WEEK

b. Dependent Variable: Weekly Bar Sales (£000)

Coefficients[a]

Model		Unstandardized Coefficients		Standardized Coefficients	t	Sig.
		B	Std. Error	Beta		
1	(Constant)	46.467	2.613		17.786	.000
	WEEK	-1.617	.494	-.477	-3.274	.014
	SPORT	-11.750	2.836	-.603	-4.143	.004

a. Dependent Variable: Weekly Bar Sales (£000)

Figure 11.1
Basic Dummy Variable Regression Output

Interpreting Dummy Variable Estimates

It is all very well getting an estimate for our dummy variable x_2 but the real trick is to know how to interpret it. Understanding dummy variables hinges on the idea that they represent group membership. In this case, we have two groups of data, one representing football weeks ($x_2 = 0$) and one representing cricket weeks ($x_2 = 1$). Let's use the notation $E(y \mid \text{football})$ to show the mean (or expected value of) weekly bar sales for football weeks. As such, we have the following equation for football weeks:

$$E(y \mid \text{football}) = b_0 + b_1 x_1 + b_2(0) = b_0 + b_1 x_1$$

For cricket weeks we have:

$$E(y \mid \text{cricket}) = b_0 + b_1 x_1 + b_2(1) = b_0 + b_1 x_1 + b_2$$

which simplifies nicely to:

$$E(y \mid \text{cricket}) = (b_0 + b_2) + b_1 x_1$$

Compare the equations for cricket and football weeks and you may come to a startling conclusion. First, the weekly bar sales is a linear function of x_1 in both cases, with a slope of –1.62 in both cases. However, the intercept for football weeks is simply $b_0 = 46.47$, whereas it is $b_0 + b_2 = 46.47 - 11.75 = 34.72$. So, the interpretation of b_2 is that it shows the difference between the mean weekly bar sales for football weeks and the mean weekly bar sales for cricket weeks. Note of course that a negative value for b_2 indicates that the mean sales for cricket weeks is less than football, whereas the reverse would be true if b_2 were positive.

This might be clearer if you see the full estimated regression equations for both cases. For football weeks, when $x_2 = 0$:

$$\hat{y} = 46.47 - 1.62x_1$$

and for cricket weeks, when $x_2 = 1$:

$$\hat{y} = 34.72 - 1.62x_1$$

So in essence what is happening here is that the dummy variable method results in two regression equations, each with a different intercept but with the same gradient. Further, since $b_2 = -11.47$, we can conclude that, on average, cricket weeks result in bar takings of £11470 less than football weeks.

Dummy Variables for More Than Two Categories

I am slightly ashamed to admit that the dummy variable concepts introduced above are a lot simpler than I remember them being, so I hope that you won't find them too confusing. In my defence, though, I suspect it was the idea of creating dummy variables for more than two categories that actually confused me. So, I'm going to try extra hard to explain this…

Above, you will note that there were only two categories for the dummy variable, cricket and football. But what if the bar wanted to include a third sport, say, rugby? A dummy variable can only take on two values, 0 and 1. But with three or more categories, this is not enough, so how do you deal with it? One thing you do *not* do is add categories to the single dummy – for example, using values of 0, 1 and 2 to represent three groups. If you do this, the variable is no longer a dummy one and in fact represents an ordered quantitative variable, making the coefficients uninterpretable for the categorical case. If you do not quite get this, check out Back to Basics Box 11.1.

 back to basics

Box 11.1 Categorical and Quantitative Variables

Dummy variables are an absolutely classic example of how numerical analysis must be aligned to the 'real-world' concepts you are dealing with. In this case, the real-world categorical variable does not have a linear quantitative order (which is why we must create dummies to represent categories). Using a dummy variable with 0 and 1 allows us to interpret the coefficient as representing the difference between two categories. But, remember, we only get one *b* estimate for each *x* variable. A single beta cannot be used to differentiate between more than two qualitative unordered categories. If you tried to use a dummy variable with three or more values, you would still only get a single *b*. You would misinterpret this estimate as meaning that there is the same difference between each category. This would then imply that the categories are not in fact unordered, but instead had an

(Continued)

(Continued)

equal linear interval between them. For example (assuming bar sales was the outcome), if 0 = football, 1 = cricket, 2 = rugby, the assumption in regression would be that rugby was associated with more (or fewer) sales than cricket, which was in turn associated with more (or fewer) sales than football. Can you see the difference in assumptions here? Your predictor is no longer a dummy, but instead a classical linear predictor. Which is absolutely not what your real-world variable is. The real-world variable is just a set of unordered categories.

Try rereading the section on 'scales of measurement' earlier in the book if you are still a bit baffled. Unordered categories are *nominal*, and the three-value variable (0, 1, 2) I used above was by nature *interval*. Try to see the difference, and always remember that the variables you use in your analysis *must* match the real-world characteristics of the things you are dealing with.

And, if you do not yet fully understand, keep trying. But always remember the rule presented below in the meantime.

So, with that out of the way, how do we deal with categorical variables which can take on more than two values? Again, it is pretty simple, but just requires a little thought in the design and interpretation. The basic rule is:

If the categorical variable has *k* categories, you must create *k* – 1 dummy variables.

Each of the dummies is coded either 0 or 1, and the combination of these values gives the category membership for each case. Take the bar sales example again. We have three possible sports categories, so we need 3 – 1 = 2 dummies to represent this situation. Let's go back to the original equation for weekly bar sales:

$$\hat{y} = b_0 + b_1 x$$

Recall that you added a dummy to this, which was represented as x_2 and could take the values of 0 or 1 to represent football or cricket. Because we now have three categories, we need two dummies, each of which can be coded as 0 or 1:

$$x_2 = 1 \text{ if sport is cricket}$$

$$= 0 \text{ otherwise}$$

$$x_3 = 1 \text{ if sport is rugby}$$

$$= 0 \text{ otherwise}$$

If both dummies take the value of 0 then by definition the sport must be football. So, just to make it crystal clear, if you had an observation (i.e. a week) where the sport on TV at the bar was football, you would code it as $x_2 = 0$, $x_3 = 0$; for a cricket week you would code $x_2 = 1$, $x_3 = 0$; and for a rugby week you would code $x_2 = 0$, $x_3 = 1$. The regression equation would then be estimated as:

$$\hat{y} = b_0 + b_1 x_1 + b_2 x_2 + b_3 x_3$$

Interpreting the estimates is broadly the same as for a single dummy, using:

$$E(y \mid \text{football}) = b_0 + b_1 x_1 + b_2(0) + b_3(0) = b_0 + b_1 x_1$$

$$E(y \mid \text{cricket}) = b_0 + b_1 x_1 + b_2(1) + b_3(0) = b_0 + b_1 x_1 + b_2$$

$$E(y \mid \text{rugby}) = b_0 + b_1 x_1 + b_2(0) + b_3(1) = b_0 + b_1 x_1 + b_3$$

As such, just like the single-dummy case, we can simplify the expressions to get three separate regression equations. Each equation has the same gradient, but different intercepts, as follows:

$$E(y \mid \text{football}) = b_0 + b_1 x_1$$

$$E(y \mid \text{cricket}) = b_0 + b_1 x_1 + b_2 = (b_0 + b_2) + b_1 x_1$$

$$E(y \mid \text{rugby}) = b_0 + b_1 x_1 + b_3 = (b_0 + b_3) + b_1 x_1$$

So, the different intercepts can be interpreted as the differences in mean weekly bar sales. More specifically, b_2 is the difference between mean weekly bar sales for cricket weeks and football weeks, whereas b_3 is the difference between mean weekly bar sales for rugby weeks and football weeks.

 think it over 11.1

Sketch plots of the three regression equations and explain the relationship between them.

As a final note, it is important to understand that the allocation of dummy variable values to categories is entirely arbitrary in numerical terms, but can have important implications for testing when there is more than one dummy. In other words, in this case football weeks were represented by $x_2 = 0$, $x_3 = 0$, but the regression model would have worked just as well if it had been $x_2 = 1$, $x_3 = 0$, with cricket weeks being $x_2 = 0$, $x_3 = 1$ and rugby as $x_2 = 0$, $x_3 = 0$. However, the choice of the category that is represented by 0 values for all the dummies can be interpreted as a *baseline* value, because all other categories are compared with it. In an experiment, you would usually choose your *control group* as the baseline. But in other situations, it is important you decide what the baseline for comparison is. In this case, we chose football weeks as the baseline, but there may be theoretical or testing reasons to choose one of the others. So do make sure you think about this. Often, if there is no other, more obvious theoretical reason, researchers choose the largest category.

 think it over 11.2

When we were developing the regression equations comparing bar sales for football weeks and cricket weeks, the following was stated:

'since $b_2 = -11.47$, we can conclude that, on average, cricket weeks result in bar takings of £11470 less than football weeks'.

What can you conclude from this statement regarding the control group?

CATEGORICAL OUTCOMES: LOGISTIC REGRESSION

So far, every application of regression has involved an outcome that was essentially quantitative and continuous. However, plenty of important situations involve categorical outcomes, and a large proportion of these are outcomes that can take only one of two discrete values. For example, a classic purchase decision model may have an outcome variable that can take only two values, purchase or no purchase. We could code the outcome variable y in this case as $y = 0$ for no purchase and $y = 1$ as purchase. However, none of the existing regression techniques covered so far are of use here. What we need to use instead is something called logistic regression.

Interestingly, logistic regression is not as common as other forms of regression, and in my own experience I have very rarely seen it used in research.[3] It is also seldom seen in introductory textbooks like this one, which is rather tragic as it can be very useful indeed. Lots and lots of key business-relevant outcomes are best expressed as dichotomies (i.e. two discrete outcome values). Perhaps the reason that logistic regression is rarely covered is that it is somewhat hard to get one's head around, and the equations can seem somewhat terrifying. But that is no reason to avoid a useful method, as I am hoping you are beginning to understand. So, while a full exposition of logistic regression is beyond the scope of this book, a basic introduction is well worth the effort, and I bet that it will come in very handy as you move through your career. So, let's begin.

Let's go back to the sales mileage example from the previous chapter and make some modifications. In this case, the company is not so much interested in the fuel consumption, but in whether or not the salesperson makes their weekly quota.[4] As such the dependent variable is coded as $y = 1$ if the salesperson makes the quota, and $y = 0$ if they do not. You do not have to code them as '0' and '1', technically, but it does help a lot in later interpretation, so I would advise you continuing to do so – indeed that is what I am going to assume from now on.

Logistic regression can be used to estimate the probability that a salesperson makes the quota, given the values of a set of predictors. In this example, the firm thinks that whether or not a salesperson makes the quota can be predicted by the number of miles they drive, but also whether or not they use a new customer relationship management (CRM) system called SNAP which helps them organize their customer and competitor information. In our data set, values are coded '1' if the salesperson uses the system, and '0' if not. Table 11.3 shows a sample of the data from our 30 salespeople. Of course, because the data contains a dichotomous outcome variable, we must use logistic regression to test the model if we want to use a regression method.[5]

Table 11.3 Salesperson distance, CRM use and quota success

Salesperson	Distance	SNAP use	Quota
10	212	0	0
25	250	1	0
5	271	0	0
26	301	1	1
18	302	1	1
13	302	0	0
28	311	1	1

Estimating the Logistic Regression Equation

Logistic regression shares many things with 'regular' regression, so let's recap the ordinary multiple regression equation, with an outcome predicted by multiple predictors:

$$\hat{y} = b_0 + b_1 x_1 + b_2 x_2 + \dots + b_i x_i$$

However, in logistic regression, instead of predicting specific values of y from the predictors, as we have done many times before, what we do is predict the *probability that y will occur* given known values of the

---

[3] Of course, this is at least partly to do with the kind of research I commonly look at, and in other fields logistic regression and similar techniques are much more common.

[4] In most firms, a salesperson would more likely have a yearly, quarterly or perhaps monthly quota to hit rather than a weekly one, but let's just go with this example as it is.

[5] As another footnote, you might think that the company's model is rather simplistic in that there may be many non-sales-related reasons for a salesperson to drive around a lot. Indeed, I agree – but you would be surprised also at how accurately very basic behaviours can be used to predict sales performance.

predictor variables. There are a number of ways of arranging the logistic regression equation, but the one I think is simplest is as follows:

$$P(y) = \frac{1}{1 + e^{-(b_0 + b_1 x_1 + b_2 x_2 + \dots + b_i x_i)}}$$

think it over 11.3

If you performed a calculation to find the value of $P(y)$ and the answer came out as 1, what does this tell you about your calculation?

You might notice that the bit inside the brackets is in fact just the same as the regular multiple regression equation. The term e refers to the natural logarithm, which you met all the way back in Chapter 1. Go back there if you cannot remember it.

While for ordinary least squares methods, such as those used before in simple and multiple regression, computation of the estimates is at least feasible by hand (although multiple regression does go a bit beyond), things are different for logistic regression. More specifically, the logistic regression equation is in a non-linear form, and as such computing it by hand is well beyond the scope of this book, and my sanity. As such, our trusty computer friend will do the heavy lifting for us and provide estimates.

If our dummy is coded as 0 for non-use, and 1 for use of the system (as we suggested earlier), then the value of $\hat{y}$ from our estimated regression equation can be interpreted as the probability that $y = 1$ (i.e. the salesperson uses the system). As such the equation can be more formally represented as:

$$\hat{y} = P(y = 1 \mid x_1, x_2, \dots, x_i) = \frac{1}{1 + e^{-(b_0 + b_1 x_1 + b_2 x_2 + \dots + b_i x_i)}}$$

think it over 11.4

If $b_0 + b_1 + b_2 = 0$, what would the value of $\hat{y}$ be?

This basically says we are calculating an estimate of the probability that $y = 1$, given a set of predictor variables. Just the same as in multiple linear regression, each predictor has an associated coefficient which is estimated by fitting various different models to the observed data set. The model coefficients we end up with are the ones which result in values of y closest to the observed values in the data. While in multiple linear regression we used a least squares method to calculate these coefficients, for logistic regression SPSS uses a maximum likelihood method, which is a little beyond our present scope to consider in detail here.

So let's recap the variables we are working with. Our outcome variable y is whether or not the salesperson makes the quota, with $y = 1$ if the salesperson makes the quota, and $y = 0$ if they do not. Our first predictor x_1 is the weekly distance driven by the salesperson. Our second predictor x_2 is whether the salesperson uses the SNAP CRM system, with $x_2 = 0$ if they do not, and $x_2 = 1$ if they do. We can use SPSS to compute the estimates for us, and Figure 11.2 shows some of the output, specifically referring to the coefficients, with SNAP referring to the dummy variable of CRM usage. However, before using them to do some calculations, we first want to know if our model is significant (just like any other regression situation).

Variables in the Equation

		B	S.E.	Wald	df	Sig.	Exp(B)	95% C.I.for EXP(B) Lower	Upper
Step 1[a]	DIST	.017	.008	4.632	1	.031	1.017	1.001	1.032
	SNAP(1)	-2.373	1.126	4.442	1	.035	.093	.010	.847
	Constant	-4.267	2.642	2.608	1	.106	.014		

a. Variable(s) entered on step 1: DIST, SNAP.

Figure 11.2 Logistic Regression Coefficients

think it over 11.5

Think back to when we looked at probability and in particular the minimum and maximum values. With logistic regression we are calculating the probability of y occurring given certain predictor values. With these two facts in mind, in theory, what are the minimum and maximum values that $P(y)$ can have? Now think about the logistic equation simplified to:

$$\hat{y} = \frac{1}{1 + e^{-x}}$$

Can this ever reach 0 or 1?

Significance of the Logistic Regression Model

In the previous chapter we discussed all kinds of ways to evaluate whether the regression model was significant as a whole, and of course in logistic regression we can use similar ideas. However, the equations for the various indicators of significance are considerably more complex for logistic regression, so please do not panic when you see the equations; the important thing is that you follow the logic in the text.

In essence, logistic regression predicts the probability that some dichotomous outcome will occur for a given case (e.g. a salesperson), based on observations of whether or not that outcome did actually occur. So, for any case, the actual value of the outcome y must equal either 0 (did not occur) or 1 (did occur), and the predicted value of y, denoted as either $P(y)$ or $\hat{y}$, depending on your preference, will lie somewhere between 0 (no chance of the outcome occurring) and 1 (outcome will certainly occur). As such, it would be a useful indicator of how well the model works if we could compare these observed and predicted values – just as we demonstrated in a multiple regression context. The log-likelihood is the measure used in logistic regression, and the formula for this is shown below. However, do not panic if this is hard to understand. All you need to know is that it is based around the idea of summing (the sigma symbol, remember?) the probabilities of the predicted and actual outcomes, and it is essentially comparable with the residual sum of squares from the previous chapter. I am really only including it here to pacify the secret statistical police who have been known to haul off unsuspecting statistics book writers if they do not include all the required equations.[6] The equation is:

$$\text{log- likelihood} = \sum_{i-1}^{N}\{y_i \ln(P(y_i)) + (1 - y_i)\ln[1 - P(y_i)]\}$$

Larger log-likelihood values indicate worse-fitting models. That said, an obvious question is 'how large is large?' Which is a little like 'how soon is now?', not because it is the title of a song by The Smiths, but because it is rather impossible to answer. As such, the best way to use a log-likelihood is to compare the value for your model with some baseline model. Most statistical software therefore calculates by default a baseline model that does not include any predictors, only a constant, and then compares this with subsequent models with predictors added. Now you have a baseline and a new model, you (or, rather, your computer pal) can compute the improvement in the model caused by including the predictors as follows:

$$x^2 = 2[\text{log-likelihood(new)} - \text{log-likelihood(baseline)}]$$

The cool thing to note is that if you multiply the result of the subtraction by 2 the result will be a chi-square (i.e. χ^2, remember?) distribution, which allows you to calculate the significance of the change using the degrees of freedom calculated as:

$$df = k_{new} - k_{baseline}$$

---

[6] Is that a knock at my door? Hmm, let me go check...

where k represents the number of parameters in each model. For the baseline model this is always 1 (i.e. the constant), and for the new model, k = the number of predictors + 1.

You might also remember that in the previous chapter we used something called R^2 to give us an indication of how 'good' the model was. Unfortunately, in logistic regression, it is not quite as simple as that. While we have a few things that are called R^2 for logistic regression, they are not strictly the same thing, and they do not relate to the thing that is called R in logistic regression, which confuses things even more. As such, we are going to hold off looking at R until the next section, and talk about different forms R^2 here, since they are concerned with the model as a whole, whereas R is only relevant to individual predictors.

There are a number of different types of R^2 which can be calculated in logistic regression. SPSS gives us two of them. The first is Cox and Snell's R^2_{CS}, which is calculated using the equation (note that 'LL' refers to log-likelihood):

$$R^2_{CS} = 1 - e^{\left[-\frac{2}{n}(\text{LL(new)} - \text{LL(baseline)}) \right]}$$

We also get a modification of this equation called Nagelkerke's, R^2_N which is calculated as follows:

$$R^2_N = \frac{R^2_{CS}}{1 - e^{\left[\frac{2(\text{LL(baseline)})}{n} \right]}}$$

Both give different answers, but their basic interpretation is the same: the higher they are, the better the model explains the outcome variable.

Assessing the Individual Predictors

Once we are happy that our model has some good predictive power, we can look at the contribution of the individual predictors. Figure 11.2 showed the relevant output for this part of the process from SPSS. For linear regression, we used a b coefficient and a t statistic to assess whether a predictor was significant, and in logistic regression we have a similar situation.

Specifically, each predictor in logistic regression has a b coefficient and a standard error, both of which are used to calculate the Wald statistic, analogous to the t in linear regression. The Wald statistic is calculated by:

$$\text{Wald} = \frac{b}{\text{SE}_b}$$

It has a chi-square distribution and as such it is simple to test for significance. If the Wald statistic is significantly different from zero, just as in any other test we have done, we assume that the predictor makes a significant contribution to the prediction of the outcome. Unfortunately, the Wald statistic can be unreliable, because, as the b coefficient increases, the standard error becomes inflated, in turn leading to underestimation of the Wald statistic. This may lead to some Type II error situations (if you cannot remember Type II error, go back to the relevant chapter in this book and reread the sections).

We can also use the Wald statistic (subject to the caution above) to calculate a value analogous to R in multiple regression, which indicates how much the predictor contributes to the overall model. This is calculated as follows:

$$R = \pm \sqrt{\left(\frac{\text{Wald} - (2 \times df)}{-2\text{LL(original)}} \right)}$$

Where −2LL(original) refers to the −2 log-likelihood of the model without predictors (remember, we multiply the log-likelihood by −2 to make it chi-square distributed), and the degrees of freedom are read from the SPSS output (you can see them in Figure 11.2 for each predictor; remember, you calculate an R for each predictor).

The final, and most important, thing to look at is the 'Exp(B)' value for each predictor. This value indicates the change in odds (i.e. probability) resulting from a unit change in each predictor variable. It is far more useful than the b coefficient in interpreting a logistic regression. The odds of an event happening are formally defined as the probability of an event happening, divided by the probability of that event not happening.[7] Or in equation form:

$$odds = \frac{P(\text{event})}{P(\text{no event})}$$

You should remember that the probability for an event is given by the formula earlier, and then it is simple to work out that the probability for no event is 1 – the probability for an event, or more specifically:

$$P(y) = \frac{1}{1 + e^{-(b_0 + b_1 x_1 + b_2 x_2 + \dots + b_i x_i)}}$$
$$P(\text{no } y) = 1 - P(y)$$

In order to calculate the change in odds, you first calculate the odds of the event happening given a certain set of values for the predictors, using the above equation. You then calculate the odds of the event happening given a single unit change in the value of the predictors, and then use these values to calculate the proportionate change in odds as follows:

$$\Delta odds = \frac{\text{odds after a unit change in the predictor}}{\text{original odds}}$$

This will make more sense as we go through an example, but in the meantime note that what you need to calculate the answer are the coefficients given as the output of your logistic regression analysis, and also values for the predictor variables. The proportionate change in odds is the Exp(B) value given in the SPSS output, and it is very useful in interpretation. A value of Exp(B) greater than 1 means that as the predictor increases, the odds of the outcome y occurring also increase, and vice versa if the value is less than 1.

Interpreting Logistic Regression Output

It can be challenging to interpret the output from logistic regression, and also to explain it, because the various outputs you get change depending on the way you tell the program to work. In this section, the assumption is that you have done things in the most typical way, using a simultaneous entry method for all of your predictors at the same time (different methods will be discussed towards the end of this chapter, and they apply to all regression model types, including logistic regression). Of course, different packages give you different outputs, but understanding the SPSS output is a good base here.

SPSS first gives you a set of results for what it calls Block 0, which is the equation with only the constant in it, and no predictors; this is what we called the baseline model above. There is not much to do with this output to be honest, and it would be more helpful in my opinion if you at least got the –2LL for Block 0, but you do not. Anyway, one thing you can do is look at the *classification table*, which is quite handy and presented in Figure 11.3.

---

[7] Don't get this confused with the common usage of the word 'odds', which seems to mean simply the probability of an event happening.

Classification Table[a,b]

Observed			Predicted		
			Made quota or not		Percentage Correct
			.00	1.00	
Step 0	Made quota or not	.00	0	12	.0
		1.00	0	18	100.0
	Overall Percentage				60.0

a. Constant is included in the model.

b. The cut value is .500

Figure 11.3
Block 0
Classification
Table

This basically shows how good your model is at predicting the outcome variable, which boils down to how good it is at classifying the cases into the two groups. Without any predictors, the best this baseline model can do is to classify all the cases into one of the two groups. Because our model is trying at all stages to maximize the accuracy of prediction, it always chooses the group containing most of the observed data.[8] In this case, you can see that is the 'Made quota' group (i.e. with a value of '1'). This gives it 18 correct classifications out of the 30 salespeople, or 60%, which is the accuracy of classification. This is the baseline figure, or naive model as we termed it in the previous chapter. Our hope is to increase this accuracy by including relevant predictors.

Omnibus Tests of Model Coefficients

		Chi-square	df	Sig.
Step 1	Step	13.380	2	.001
	Block	13.380	2	.001
	Model	13.380	2	.001

Model Summary

Step	-2 Log likelihood	Cox & Snell R Square	Nagelkerke R Square
1	27.000[a]	.360	.486

a. Estimation terminated at iteration number 6 because parameter estimates changed by less than .001.

Hosmer and Lemeshow Test

Step	Chi-square	df	Sig.
1	11.278	8	.186

Classification Table[a]

Observed			Predicted		
			Made quota or not		Percentage Correct
			.00	1.00	
Step 1	Made quota or not	.00	10	2	83.3
		1.00	3	15	83.3
	Overall Percentage				83.3

a. The cut value is .500

Figure 11.4
Basic Block
1 Logistic
Regression
Output

We can then see in Figure 11.4 the basic output for Block 1, which gives us the results if we include the predictors in our logistic regression model. Looking at the classification table, you can see that the new model classifies 83.3% of cases correctly, which is clearly a big improvement. The two R Square values both seem OK, and the −2LL looks OK. Or does it? In fact, just one value of −2LL does not say much by itself (remember, it is meant to be compared with another one), and smaller values are better. However, because SPSS does not give us a −2LL for the baseline Block 0 model, we can use the *model chi-square* given in the output to assess this. In fact, in a general sense, the −2LL added to the model chi-square should give us the −2LL for the baseline model. We can of course calculate the significance of the change

---

[8] Just like using the mean as a baseline value in linear regression.

in −2LL across the model by using the chi-square distribution, which SPSS has helpfully done and given us a significance value of 0.001. This clearly suggests that the new model with predictors significantly outperforms the baseline model.

You will also see something called a Hosmer and Lemeshow Test in there, which is another type of R^2 which is turned out by SPSS if you ask for it. This basically tests a hypothesis that the observed values of the outcome variable are different from the ones predicted by the model. So in this case you want a non-significant result. As you can see, the significance of 0.186 is fine.

Figure 11.5
Logistic
Regression
Coefficients
Recap

Variables in the Equation

		B	S.E.	Wald	df	Sig.	Exp(B)	95% C.I.for EXP(B) Lower	Upper
Step 1[a]	DIST	.017	.008	4.632	1	.031	1.017	1.001	1.032
	SNAP(1)	-2.373	1.126	4.442	1	.035	.093	.010	.847
	Constant	-4.267	2.642	2.608	1	.106	.014		

a. Variable(s) entered on step 1: DIST, SNAP.

Figure 11.5 is a recap of Figure 11.2, which presented the coefficients and related results for the individual predictors. It is easy to see the B coefficients, standard errors, the Wald statistic, the significance of B and those all-important Exp(B) values. You could easily use these numbers to calculate R for each predictor as well, if you like. You should note from the Exp(B) values that the distance driven seems to increase the likelihood of making the quota, while the use of CRM seems to decrease it. This does bear closer analysis. First, let's look at the confidence intervals. Because none of them include 1 (which would indicate no effect), we can be reasonably confident our predictors have some effect on the odds ratio.

Before going further, one must understand that the Exp(B) value refers to the individual predictor, holding all other predictor(s) in the model constant, just as a B coefficient does. Let's explore this result a bit more, by calculating some odds ratios for particular types of salespeople by hand. As an example, we calculate the probability that a salesperson makes the quota (i.e. event y occurs) if they drive the mean number of miles per week, which is in fact 392.4 miles (i.e. $x_1 = 392.4$), and does not use SNAP (i.e. $x_2 = 0$). In order to do this we simply substitute in the relevant values and coefficients as follows:

$$P(y) = \frac{1}{1+e^{-(b_0+b_1x_1+b_2x_2)}}$$

$$= \frac{1}{1+e^{-(-4.267+(0.017\times392.4)+(-2.372\times0))}}$$

$$= 0.917$$

$$P(\text{no } y) = 1 - P(y)$$

$$= 1 - 0.917$$

$$= 0.083$$

$$\text{odds} = \frac{0.917}{0.083}$$

$$= 11.05$$

And we then calculate the odds of the same thing happening (i.e. a salesperson drives 392.4 miles per week and makes the quota); when they do use SNAP CRM (i.e. $x_2 = 1$), as follows:

$$P(y) = \frac{1}{1+e^{-(b_0+b_1x_1+b_2x_2)}}$$

$$= \frac{1}{1+e^{-(-4.267+(0.017\times392.4)+(-2.372\times1))}}$$

$$= 0.51$$

$$P(\text{no } y) = 1 - P(y)$$

$$= 1 - 0.51$$

$$= 0.49$$

$$\text{odds} = \frac{0.51}{0.49}$$

$$= 1.04$$

Since we now know the odds,[9] we can calculate the proportionate change in odds as shown earlier:

$$\Delta \text{odds} = \frac{\text{odds after a unit change in the predictor}}{\text{original odds}}$$

$$= \frac{1.04}{11.05}$$

$$= 0.094$$

You should note that this is essentially the figure for Exp(B) given in the SPSS output (the differences are due to rounding). You can calculate this same figure using a different weekly mileage and you should find the same result (subject to rounding error of course). It shows relatively clearly that, in general, if SNAP is used, the chances of making the quota are lower than if SNAP is not used.

A similar, and perhaps more useful in a business context, way of using this calculation is simply to use the probability values which were calculated above. For example, one could say that a salesperson who drives 392.4 miles per week and does not use SNAP has a 0.917 chance of making the quota, while if they drive the same distance and do use SNAP, they have a 0.49 chance of making the quota. These probabilities will differ based on the different values of the predictors that are entered into the equation.

One clever way of using these probabilities would be to calculate them based on different values of weekly mileage, to see whether they changed depending on whether the salesperson drove more or fewer miles. This would give you a finer-grained analysis than just using the mean mileage to give a basic overview. It might uncover for example that salespeople who drive more miles derive greater benefit from CRM than those who drove fewer.

As a final note on using logistic regression results, we can demonstrate another clever way of using the odds ratios given by Exp(B). Recall that Exp(B) shows the odds ratio for a one-unit change in the predictor. For a dichotomous predictor such as whether or not the salesperson used CRM, this is all we need to know (indeed, all we can know). However, for a predictor such as weekly mileage, it is only half the story. For example, Exp(B) for weekly mileage is 1.017, showing that the odds in favour of making the quota for a salesperson who drives 500 miles per week are 1.017 greater than if they drive 499 miles. But what if we wanted to compare a salesperson who drove 600 versus one who drove 400 miles per week? In other words, what if we wanted to compare changes of greater than one unit in a predictor? Exp(B) as reported in SPSS does not help us here.

However, a little knowledge of the relationship between Exp(B) and the coefficient for a predictor can help us here. Specifically, Exp(B) is in fact the exponentiation of the coefficient. Or in other words:

$$\text{Exp(B)} = e^{b_i}$$

You can test this yourself, with the odds ratios given in Figure 11.5.

We can use this knowledge to investigate odds ratio changes for more or less than one-unit changes in a predictor. For example, if we want to investigate the change in odds ratio for a salesperson who drives 600 miles versus 400 miles (holding use of SNAP constant of course), this is a change of 200 units, and we can calculate the change in odds ratio as follows:

$$e^{200(b_i)} = e^{200(0.017)} = e^{3.4} = 29.96$$

So the estimated odds of making the quota for a salesperson who drives 600 miles per week increase by 29.96 over one who drives 400. The odds ratio increase for an increase of 200 miles per week is 29.96.

---

[9] Of course, these calculations should always be used with the caveat that, according to Han Solo in the (original and best) *Star Wars* movies, one should 'never tell me the odds'.

EXTENDING LINEAR REGRESSION: BASIC CONCEPTS

In the previous section, you saw the first example of using regression to explore a *non-linear* relationship, although you might not have realized it. In fact, the whole reason we had to use a logistic regression model is because the binary dependent variable necessitates a non-linear relationship between the predictor(s) and outcome, and linear regression, of course, can only handle linear relationships.

However, for continuous outcomes, we have other methods of exploring non-linear relationships which allow us to continue using the basic multiple linear regression model. The key is in *transforming* either the predictor or outcome variables, to enable the linear regression model to work properly. There are three situations where we might want to do this: (a) when we predict a non-linear relationship between the predictor and outcome; (b) when we predict an interaction between two (or more) predictors; and (c) when our residual analysis suggests we have certain problems.

In this section, we will explain the basic idea behind each type of transformation, but you should remember that full explanations of these issues are well beyond the scope of an introductory statistics textbook like this, and there are entire books written on regression in general and these specific transformations in particular. So treat this section as an introduction to what *can* be done with regression, to help you understand the possibilities.

Before we begin, let's recap the basic multiple linear regression model:

$$y = \beta_0 + \beta_1 x_1 + \beta_2 x_2 + \ldots + \beta_n x_n + \varepsilon$$

and the estimated model:

$$\hat{y} = b_0 + b_1 x_1 + b_2 x_2 + \ldots + b_n x_n$$

This model can also be called a first-order model, which will help differentiate it from some of the other models coming up.

An Introduction to Non-linear Relationships

Recall in the previous chapter that we discussed checking residual plots and so forth? You should remember Figure 10.8b being described as an indicator of a possible non-linear relationship, and in fact in passing we mentioned that Figure 10.7 could also be seen as kind of similar. Indeed, there are ways of dealing with this. If you interpret Figure 11.6 as a scatterplot of weekly sales versus miles driven per week, then it clearly indicates a possible non-linear relationship: sales increase with higher amounts of miles per week up to a point where the increase seems to tail off, and then becomes a decrease. There could be all kinds of reasons for this sort of relationship, but what it means for us in analytic terms is that our assumption of a linear relationship does not hold. If we try to model this with a simple first-order linear regression model, we might find a non-significant model, even though there is clearly some relationship here.

 think it over 11.6

We have been using the terms linear and non-linear quite a lot. How would you explain these terms mathematically?

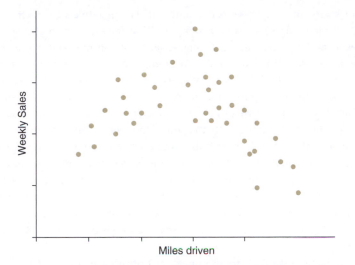

Figure 11.6
Possible
Non-linear
Scatterplot

However, there is a simple way of accounting for this in our model. More specifically, to model a non-linear relationship between a predictor and outcome we add another term to our first-order model. The exact term we use depends on the form of the non-linear relationship, though. Figure 11.6 suggests what is known as a quadratic relationship, which is basically shaped like an inverted 'U', or more formally has one change in direction (also known as an inflexion point), and goes from up towards (but not always completely to) down; an inverse quadratic is like a regular 'U', going from down towards up. These two forms are most commonly used and can explain many different forms of non-linear relationship, The other, most common form of non-linear relationship is a cubic, which has two inflexion points and basically can be thought of as an 'S' shape.

So, for the quadratic form shown in Figure 11.6 we would start with a simple first-order model:

$$\hat{y} = b_0 + b_1 x_1$$

where the outcome variable is sales and the predictor is miles driven. To account for a non-linear relationship, we must add in another predictor term, of a specific form for each type of non-linear relationship. For a classic quadratic like we have here, we need to add a *squared* term to the equation, as follows:

$$\hat{y} = b_0 + b_1 x_1 + b_2 x_1^2$$

Can you see what has happened here? In practice, we have squared the miles driven variable and added it to the model, so we now have two b coefficients. This model is still considered to have one predictor technically – because the two variables are essentially representing the same thing. The squared term accounts for the quadratic non-linear relationship. This is termed a second-order model.

This basic technique gives us some pretty sensational levels of flexibility, simply by using different terms for the non-linear relationship. For an inverse quadratic we would use a negative squared term, and for a cubic we would use a cube term. These terms are often referred to as power terms or even polynomials by some.

Interactions

Consider the following highly relevant situation in many organizations: an HR manager is interested in predicting the level of turnover of managers in the firm (i.e. how many leave the firm). He has information on the length of service of managers and also the results of a staff survey that measured the 'motivation' of the managers. A first-order multiple regression model might look like this:

$$\hat{y} = b_0 - b_1 x_1 + b_2 x_2$$

where x_1 represents salary and x_2 represents commitment. The negative signs in the equation represent the theory of the HR manager, who has an assumption that managers of higher length of service will be less likely to leave, and also managers with higher levels of commitment will be less likely to leave. However, the data did not seem to fit the model. By doing some more research in the firm, the HR manager was able to come up with the idea that managers with a longer length of service were usually at a higher level in the organization, and therefore more attractive to competitors. As such, they got many more job offers than those on lower salaries. So, for a manager with less length of service, commitment might be a strong predictor of staying with the firm. However, because managers on higher salaries received many more job offers, their level of commitment was a less powerful predictor.

This is an example of an interaction relationship. More specifically, the value of one predictor influences the relationship between another predictor and the outcome. In this case, our idea suggests that level of salary influences the relationship between commitment and turnover, making it weaker at higher levels of salary. When there is an interaction effect, it is incorrect to examine the effect of each predictor on the outcome independently – so, in other words, the values of the b coefficients in the first-order model are meaningless.

We account for interactions similarly to non-linear relationships, by introducing additional terms into the model. In the case of interactions, we introduce what is called a multiplicative term. For the theory of the HR manager above, the equation with the interaction term would look like:

$$\hat{y} = b_0 - b_1 x_1 - b_2 x_2 + b_3 x_1 x_2 + e$$

You can see that we introduce a new variable into the model, which is the two interacting predictors multiplied. This is now known as a two-way interaction model. We can also have three- and more-way interactions, although these can be very hard to think about. Figure 11.7 shows a 3D representation of such a model,[10] which is kind of analogous to Figure 10.5 in the previous chapter. Compare the two figures and see how they are different.

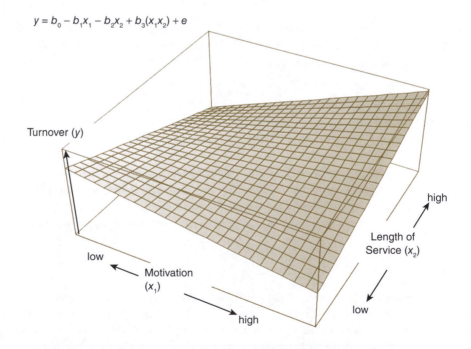

Figure 11.7 Example 3D Plot of a Regression Interaction Model

---

[10] Many thanks to my mentor and great friend, the legendary Professor John W. Cadogan, for letting me use one of his cool pictures.

above and beyond

Box 11.1   Cautionary Notes on Transformation

Before moving on to discuss transforming the outcome variable, it is worth making a few notes on the above methods of transforming predictor variables. Perhaps most importantly is the need for you as the analyst to be clear on what you are trying to do and why. It is my own personal view that we should have ideas in mind of what kinds of non-linear or interactive relationships are to be modelled before analysis – and in fact before collecting data if possible. This is important, because if you allow yourself to be guided by the data too much, you can end up being data-driven. What you are doing in that case is chasing after what are likely to be chance results in your data set, not generalizable features of the real population 'out there'. Of course, as my old friend and first mentor Professor Geoff Durden used to say, 'research is a dirty business', and in the real world of data analysis we can often rethink our ideas partway through research, sometimes after inspiration from our analysis. It is impossible to deny that this happens, and even though we should then collect new data to test these new ideas, this is rarely done. So what I am saying is: be careful when messing around with non-linear and interaction terms – you can end up tying yourself in knots.

A further issue with both non-linear and interactive terms is multicollinearity. You will remember this from the previous chapter, and it is a big issue here. Specifically, if you are creating some power term, or multiplicative interaction, your new variables will almost always be highly correlated with the predictors used to create them. This makes sense. For example, if you square a variable, the result *must* be very highly correlated with the original source variable. It is usually the same if you multiply two variables to create a third. We all know by now that multicollinearity is a problem for regression, as explained in Chapter 10. The concern in this case is that nobody really knows how to solve the problem – at least in my opinion. For many years, it was generally thought that you should mean-centre the variables, but more recent work has shown mathematically that this does not work – although in practice for some reason it does seem to help. Other techniques include using the residual of the interaction term – called residual centring – or even ignoring the problem. However, nobody really seems to have come up with a practical way of solving the problem. I have read articles which simply show how the various centring methods do not work, and then say something like 'just design your research better' or 'use experiments'. Thanks for that, but it does not solve the problem. Unfortunately, all I can say here is that you should really spend some time investigating the issue of multicollinearity in non-linear and interaction models before rushing off to do it. In my own experience, I have used mean and residual centring methods quite successfully, but one cannot argue with the mathematical reasoning behind the criticisms of these techniques.

Transforming the Outcome Variable

While the above discussion was focused on transforming the predictor(s), it is often handy to transform the outcome, and it is very useful at least to be introduced to it now. This is because it is quite common to see people struggling with these concepts later on in their analysis careers. A typical situation where you might want to transform the outcome is where the residuals indicate heteroscedasticity. If you see this pattern in your diagnostic tests (recall the previous chapter), you have a problem, and you cannot really justify drawing conclusions from the regression model.

While it is not guaranteed, in many cases transforming the outcome in some way can work wonders. A classic transformation that is often applied in cases of heteroscedasticity is the logarithmic transformation, which has the result of compressing the values of the outcome, which can diminish the effect of non-constant variance.

There are two types of logarithmic transformation of use in these cases, the base 10 (common logarithm) or base e (natural logarithm), and it is relatively simple to transform your outcome in this way in a package like SPSS. If you use for example a natural logarithm transformation your regression model would look something like the following:

$$\log_e \hat{y} = b_0 + b_1 x_1$$

for a case with one predictor.

The trick is in interpreting the results of such a model. Remember, your outcome is now expressed as a natural logarithm in this case, not in the original scale of the predictor. So, any answer for a predicted value of the outcome you get from using the estimated regression equation (as you have already done in many cases in the last two chapters) must in turn be transformed back to the original scale to be meaningful. How you transform it depends on your method of transforming the outcome. In this case, you must raise e to the power of the outcome value from the equation. So if in the following example the answer to the equation is 2.5:

$$\log_e \hat{y} = b_0 + b_1 x_1$$

$$\log_e \hat{y} = 2.5$$

$$\hat{y} = e^{2.5}$$

Hopefully, that follows logically.

Of course, there is an infinite variety of possible transformations to your outcome variable. The most common ones are the logarithmic transformations detailed here, and also something called a reciprocal transformation, which uses $1/y$ as the outcome, not y. Unfortunately, there is generally no way of telling whether reciprocal or logarithmic transformations will work better, before trying them out. So in this case, I do recommend testing both, depending on what your diagnostics suggest.

VARIABLE ENTRY METHODS

The final topic of substantive importance in our regression-based odyssey is that of how you enter your variables in the regression model. If you have more than one predictor, you automatically have some choice over how you want to enter them. For example, do you want to shove them all in at the same time, or one by one? Or use some other method? There are a number of standard methods available in most analysis packages, including SPSS, and it is important to understand them all. They can be usefully split into 'theory-driven' and 'data-driven' methods, and this is how they will be discussed here.

Theory-Driven Entry Methods

The simplest type of method is called forced entry, where you simply add all the predictors at the same time. This is implicitly the method used in almost all cases so far in the previous two chapters. There is not much to say about this method, other than it should be considered the 'default' method, and you should only deviate from it for specific reasons.

The next method is termed hierarchical or sometimes block entry. In this case, you define the order in which predictors are entered into the model, for theoretical reasons. Usually, you want to compare one model with another. A great example was the binary logistic example given in this chapter. In that case, you compared the model with predictors with the model with only a constant. Other common uses of this are when non-linear or interaction terms are used. In that case, you compare the model without the non-linear or interaction terms with a model with those terms added to see whether the non-linear or interaction terms improve the model. You can use things like R^2 and so forth to compare the models. This sort of regression was often referred to as hierarchical regression in the past, but in more recent times this has fallen out of favour.

I would advocate in almost all cases to use one of these two theory-driven model-building methods. In other words, each predictor should be in the model for a reason, and not simply because the data says it should be there. The more you let the data decide for you, the more likely you are to end up with a model that explains the data well, but is very unlikely to replicate in the population.

Data-Driven Entry Methods

The most common term for this collection of methods is stepwise regression. They all rely in various ways on selecting which variables are entered into the model automatically, by using some criteria, usually to do with the correlation or partial correlation with the outcome. In forward entry methods, the computer begins with a baseline model, containing only the constant, and then searches for the predictor that best predicts the outcome. The user defines the set of predictors to work from. Usually, the computer uses the simple correlations to determine the best predictor: if that predictor improves the model, it is entered in, and the computer begins again until there are no predictors in the set that improve the model. After the first predictor, the computer uses the semi-partial correlation to determine what variable to enter. Some variations on this method (including the one in SPSS) test at each stage whether any of the existing predictors in the model have become redundant with the addition of new ones.

Backward methods are of course the opposite of forward. In this case, the computer block-enters all the predictors and then begins a process of removing the non-useful ones according to some criteria. For example, it could be whether the b was significant at 0.05 or not. In this case the computer would remove the non-significant predictors, re-estimate the model and begin the process again. It is usually considered that if one *must* use stepwise methods, backward methods are best, because they are less susceptible to the Type II errors which can be caused by suppressor effects (where a variable has a significant effect on the outcome, but only when another is held constant).

Selecting a Method

As I have already mentioned, many researchers argue against stepwise methods, because they rely solely on mathematical rather than theoretical criteria for entering variables in a model. This takes important decisions away from you as a researcher, and can lead to data-driven models that are not generalizable (i.e. they are dependent on random sampling variation, not real features of the population). Most scientists argue that theory should decide what variables should be included in a model. Furthermore, they often argue that the simplest explanation is the best, and therefore the minimum number of variables should be used to explain the outcome.

However, in commercial research, things are often very different. Modern research techniques often rely on what are known as data mining methods, which are often founded on stepwise regression-type models. The idea goes that if you have a completely massive data set, you should 'interrogate' it and see what comes out. If you have hundreds of possible predictors, and hundreds of thousands (maybe millions) of data points – which is quite possible these days for companies like Google – it is possible to ignore the concept of statistical generalizability and take advantage of the raw power of your data set. This sort of idea basically argues that it does not matter 'why' things happen, only that we can associate some variables with important outcomes. In fact, Google uses these sorts of data mining methods to drive its advertising placement models, and their use across many companies is growing very quickly. When you have the amount of data coming in that Google does, it can be a justifiable technique. That said, I remain convinced that theory-driven models are in most cases preferable.

Excel and Logistic Regression

All I will say about running logistic regression in Excel is that it is not for the faint-hearted! It can be done, technically speaking, but, in my opinion, using a program like SPSS is much better, so we will not be using Excel in this instance.

SPSS and Logistic Regression

We will use the data from the example in the text about the salespeople, their use of SNAP and mileage to investigate their sales performance. Load the file SP_QUOTA.sav.

The binary logistic analysis tool can be found by selecting <u>Analyze</u> → <u>Regression</u> → <u>Binary Logistic</u>, see Figure 11.8.

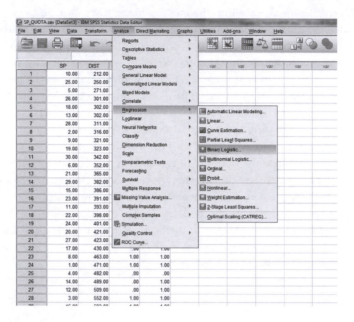

Figure 11.8

SPSS needs to be told which is the dependent variable and which are the covariates. It also needs to be informed which of the independent variables are of type categorical. Figure 11.9 shows the dialog box where this information is entered.

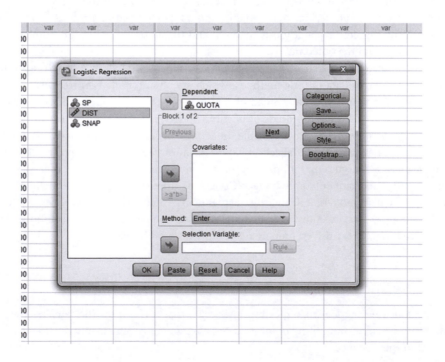

Figure 11.9

First, since we are interested in whether a sale was made or not, this is our dependent variable and goes into the Dependent text box. Distance and SNAP use are entered one at a time into the Covariates text box. Highlight DIST and click on the curly arrow pointing at the Covariates box. Click on 'Next' and do the same with SNAP as you did with DIST. SPSS also needs to know which of the dependent variables is of type categorical. You will see in the top right hand corner of the dialog box a button labelled 'Categorical'; click on this and transfer SNAP into the text box. Click on Continue and finally select the Options button. You can now select different options. In Figure 11.10 the Hosmer–Lemeshow goodness of fit has been selected along with the confidence interval (CI) for Exp(B).

Figure 11.10

Click on Continue, then, back at the main dialog box, click on OK. SPSS will now run your analysis.

SUMMARY

So, these last two chapters were an introduction to regression, contained in a mere 25000 words or so. In fact, if you understand all of these two chapters, you are considerably more advanced than many lecturers – and I would have had to include myself in that group at one stage. Regression is one of those topics that so many people 'think' they know enough about, but it is only when you delve into it that you realize that your knowledge was really shallow. This particular chapter focused particularly on things few people really master, and the material here actually extends the range of potential applications of regression massively. Specifically, now, we have a method which can handle categorical data as well, and can thus be used in a huge variety of potential situations. Personally, I think if you only have to master one technique, you should choose to focus on regression methods.

That said, in a later chapter we will introduce the other major foundational method of data analysis – the analysis of variance, or ANOVA. But even here we will see that it can be interpreted as regression in essence.

 final checklist

You should have covered and understood the following basic content in this chapter:

☑ What a categorical predictor is, and how to incorporate them into a regression context by using dummy variables.

☑ How to interpret the results of a dummy variable regression.

(Continued)

(Continued)

☑ How to incorporate a categorical outcome into a regression by using logistic regression.

☑ How to interpret the output of a logistic regression.

☑ How to explore non-linear relationships in regression, including interactions.

☑ Key issues in transforming predictor and outcome variables for use in regression.

☑ Important concepts to consider when choosing which method to use for entering variables into a multiple regression model.

EXERCISES

1. You have been asked by your marketing director to analyse the results from a recent trade fair, where 50 people visited your stall and some left contact details. Those who left their contact details were contacted either by email or telephone and, in some cases, by both methods.

    a. Using the data from FAIRSALES.sav perform an analysis to determine if contacting the people who left their contact details was beneficial in terms of increased sales.

    b. Using the results from your analysis, determine if the time and effort involved with following up visitors to your stall was worth it. Does your conclusion depend on what you were selling?

2. In the section 'SPSS and Logistic Regression' you used the data from SP_QUOTA.sav to see how to perform logistic regression with SPSS. Using the same data, perform a binary logistic regression.

    a. Compare the percentage correct figures found in each of the classification tables for Block 0, Block 1 and Block 2. What do you notice about the overall percentage figures?

    b. Explain the different models produced by SPSS for the different blocks.

    c. Referring to the three blocks, this time compare the Wald statistic. What does this tell you about the different models?

    d. The Exp(B) value is an important indicator of what? Compare the values given in each of the models.

    e. State your conclusions concerning the regression analysis and in particular discuss the final model in terms of fitting the supplied data and if it could be used as a reliable predictor of salesperson performance.

3. Your line manager has asked you to prepare a short report based on your analysis. She wants to know if (a) SNAP is worth investing in, in terms of staff training; (b) how reliable your analysis is; and (c) how she can report your analysis to the sales director who does not really trust statistics and prefers to go by his 'gut instinct'.

    Your task is to produce evidence to support your recommendation concerning SNAP and also to produce evidence from the output indicating how reliable the analysis is (you might want to look at some of the other 'options' offered by SPSS). In order to write a report for someone who does not trust statistics (quite a common challenge), you need to translate the numbers into plain language in such a way that you are both convincing and persuasive in your discussion. Non-statisticians love diagrams and pictures [Hint, hint], so you might like to think about how statistics are reported in magazines and newspapers.

To access additional online resources please visit: **https://study.sagepub.com/leepeters**

The Ballad of Eddie the Easily Distracted: Part 12

Eddie was unusually pleased with himself this week. He had been quite happy after his QUAN101 lecture, and he felt it was beginning to make sense a little. He figured that was because this week's material was quite close to material they'd covered earlier in the course. The repetition was really beginning to help him understand a few things at least. One thing Eddie had really found helpful was the switch to comparing populations, from the previous weeks' concentration on relationships between variables. For some reason, he found this a lot easier to understand.

It was kind of like comparing attitudes towards music between girls and boys, thought Eddie. He'd always had this theory when he was younger, when his sister used to talk about how 'sensitive' some singer was in some band, or how the 'lyrics were really meaningful'. That seemed to be something really important to girls, but Eddie had no real idea why – it just seemed like they were whining to him. What he and his school friends liked then, he recalled, was long-haired guys in makeup and tight trousers singing about… Well, he didn't really care what they were singing about mostly, as long as it was loud. In hindsight, Eddie thought, this was kind of weird really, but he pushed that thought back to where it had come from. He figured that he could go to a school and take two random samples (*independent* random samples, he thought smugly), one from boys and one from girls, and somehow measure their attitudes to music and lyrics, and then… His train of thought was broken as he tripped on a protruding paving stone, just managing to avoid falling flat on his face. He didn't manage to save his coffee, though. Eddie swore at himself as he turned to return to the coffee shop; he figured he'd have enough change for another.

Esha's Story: Part 12

Esha was surprised to see Eddie walk into the coffee shop on campus – Bernie's Corner – and stand in line looking annoyed, fishing around for small change in his pocket (at least that's what she hoped he was doing). She'd been having a cup of tea (Esha never drank coffee) with her best friend, Madeleine, earlier, but she'd had to go and meet some boy or something. Esha tried not to take too much interest in that kind of thing – it was exam time after all. After Madeleine left, Esha had thought it would be nice to look over her notes from QUAN101. It had been a relatively simple lecture this week, just a bit of an extension of the earlier stuff they'd done on statistical inference and the like.

One bit had caused her to think, though, namely the difference between independent samples of two populations, and what the lecturer called matched samples. This was kind of confusing thought Esha (and it didn't help that sometimes he'd called them paired samples, too). Basically, the matched sample idea was that you could take the same sample of the population and measure it at two different points in time – so each member of the sample returned two scores on your measure. The important thing to remember is that this approach needed its own special type of test. Esha made certain to underline that part of her notes, matched samples are different from independent samples, and resolved not to forget them. She looked up. Eddie had got his coffee and was fumbling around for change. It looked like he didn't have enough. 'Typical,' thought Esha, 'always act now think later.' It was therefore somewhat ironic that, on what must have been a pure whim, Esha got up, walked over and tapped Eddie on the shoulder: 'Do you need to borrow a pound, Eddie?' she said. Eddie gratefully (and awkwardly) said he did, so Esha paid for his coffee. There was a self-conscious silence. Esha broke it by saying 'Do you want to sit down?'

COMPARING TWO POPULATIONS

CONTENTS

 learning objectives

Keep the following learning objectives in mind when you are studying this chapter:

- ☑ Understand the basics of designing group comparison research.
- ☑ Learn how to calculate interval estimates of the difference between two population means when the population standard deviation is known and when it is unknown.
- ☑ Learn how to test hypotheses about the difference between two population means when the population standard deviation is known and when it is unknown.
- ☑ Understand what matched or paired samples are.

(Continued)

(Continued)

☑ Learn how to calculate intervals and test hypotheses about the difference between the means of paired/matched samples.

☑ Learn how to calculate interval estimates and test hypotheses about the difference between two population proportions.

In this chapter, we will introduce what many people have considered an alternative approach to looking at the world than that covered in the last few chapters. More specifically, the last few chapters have really concentrated on looking at *associations between variables*. In other words, we take some sample, make some measurements of important variables we are interested in, and use statistical analysis to give us an idea of how likely it is that our variables or interest are associated in the population.

However, a different approach focuses on looking at *differences between groups*. In other words, we collect samples from two (or more) groups, which differ in some important way (e.g. males versus females), and compare the groups on some key variable of interest. So, for example, perhaps we compare the sales made by male fashion retail salespeople versus female ones. This approach is often considered to have its roots in the experimental approach to research, which is fundamentally based on comparing groups, whereas the associations approach is often considered to have roots in economic or social-survey-based approaches.

In fact, there is something of a schism between the two approaches, to the extent that many people only have knowledge of one of these approaches. For example, I was mainly trained in the association-based approaches, and my knowledge of group-based analysis was very poor until later in my career, and for many others the reverse is true. However, this is not really smart, and to be a good researcher/analyst you really need to have solid knowledge of both. In fact, we will show you in this chapter and the next that a lot of these seemingly different analytic approaches really reduce to pretty much the same thing! Which does help bring it all together in my opinion.

BRIEF INTRODUCTION TO GROUP COMPARISON DESIGNS

Although this is not a research methods, or research design, book, it will help you get a feel for what this sort of analysis is all about if we introduce or recap some important research design ideas of relevance, and set them in context.[1] Imagine a situation where a food retailer wishes to understand why sales of organic vegetables are higher in one inner city retail location than another. The retail manager has an intuition that it has something to do with the sort of clientele that shop in each store. More specifically, store A is located in the heart of London's financial district, while store B is located on a busy shopping street. The retailer surmises that many customers of store A are affluent professionals who are in fact buying food to cook when they get home, whereas, in store B, customers buying produce to cook may tend to be less affluent (being retail workers) and thus more likely to choose the cheaper non-organic vegetables. What we have here could be called a *natural* or *quasi*-experiment, where there are two natural groups, possibly differing on a key variable of importance.

Similarly, a *true* experiment would be one where the researcher controlled the groups in some way. Take for example a classic medical research design. Perhaps a pharmaceutical company is interested in determining whether its latest potential blockbuster drug really does work to reduce headaches. We might randomly split 100 people into two groups. One group of 50 gets to take the new drug, and one group of people takes what is called a placebo (which is exactly the same in appearance, but should have no effect – normally a starch or sugar pill). Later we measure the incidence of headaches in some way. This is a classic experimental design.

---

[1] It's important that you accept that this is in no way a full discussion of experimental designs. If you need to know more, you should consult specialist research methods textbooks. You could even read *Doing Business Research*. And by 'read' I of course mean 'buy and then read'...

In both cases, we have two groups, and we want to compare them in some way. Figure 12.1 shows this diagrammatically. There are many ways we could compare the two groups, and we will begin by exploring the most common – comparing the difference between the mean value of some variable of interest.

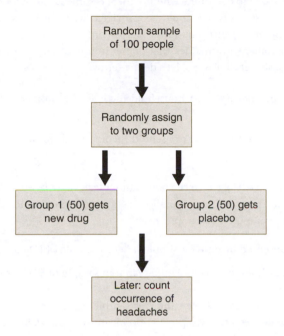

**Figure 12.1
Basic
Experiment
Example**

INFERENCES ABOUT DIFFERENCES IN POPULATION MEANS WHERE THE POPULATION STANDARD DEVIATIONS ARE KNOWN

So, whenever we have two groups – such as for example in the experimental designs above – we may be interested in comparing them. In order to set you up for what follows, let's get some terminology straight first. First and foremost, it is important to understand that here (unless we tell you specifically otherwise) you should think about it as if you are testing samples from two separate populations. These two samples are independent, and an element can only be a member of one of the samples (there is no overlap in the populations).

Moving on, let μ_1 denote the mean of population 1 and μ_2 denote the mean of population 2. What we are doing is using our sample data to make some inference about the difference between those two means, which we denote by the simple operation $\mu_1 - \mu_2$. To make inferences about the population mean difference, we need the aforementioned independent samples. As such, we need to take a simple random sample n_1 from the first population and another simple random sample n_2 from the second population. The samples are independent because they are taken separately and independently.

think it over 12.1

When we say the samples are independent, what does this imply regarding the relationship between the samples?

For the purposes of this first illustration, we assume that the standard deviations of each of the two populations are known, denoted σ_1 and σ_2. We begin by showing how to calculate an interval estimate and margin of error for the difference between the two population means, when the population standard deviations are known. Following this, we show how to test hypotheses about the difference in means.

To begin, imagine a situation like the retail example already mentioned. Management at the retailer decide to do a systematic study to determine whether there is some key difference in the customer demographics of each of the two stores which could be associated with the differences in organic vegetable sales. They consider testing intelligence, but decide it is too difficult, and controversial. Thus, they decide to focus on household income, with the idea that higher household incomes would be associated with higher purchasing of organic vegetables. So, let's define terms:

μ_1 = population 1 mean: that is, mean household income of customers who shop at the Financial District (FD) store.

μ_2 = population 2 mean: that is, mean household income of customers who shop at the Shopping Street (SS) store.

In order to estimate the difference between the population means $\mu_1 - \mu_2$, we need to select two independent simple random samples, one for each population, denoted (as you should remember) n_1 and n_2. From these samples, we need to compute two sample means:

$\bar{x}_1$ = sample mean household income for simple random sample of FD customers n_1.

$\bar{x}_2$ = sample mean household income for simple random sample of SS customers n_2.

We simply compute the difference between the two sample means as $\bar{x}_1 - \bar{x}_2$ and use this as a point estimate of the difference between the two population means. Of course, just like every other point estimator, this one has a standard error, which can be thought of as describing the variation in the sampling distribution of the estimator. If our assumption of two independent simple random samples is a safe one, the standard error of $\bar{x}_1 - \bar{x}_2$ is:

$$\sigma_{\bar{x}_1 - \bar{x}_2} = \sqrt{\frac{\sigma_1^2}{n_1} + \frac{\sigma_2^2}{n_2}}$$

Do not get confused with the notation here – it simply means that both σ_1 and σ_2 are squared within the expression. Get it?

If both the populations are normally distributed, or if your sample is large enough that you can apply the CLT to argue that the sampling distribution of the sample means approximates a normal distribution, then you can assume that $\bar{x}_1 - \bar{x}_2$ is normally distributed, with a mean of $\mu_1 - \mu_2$.

We can build an interval estimation of our population mean difference by using our point estimator ± some margin of error. If we are able to make the assumption that the sampling distribution of $\bar{x}_1 - \bar{x}_2$ is normal, as discussed above, then our margin of error is computed by using the standard error of $\bar{x}_1 - \bar{x}_2$, which was shown above, as follows:

$$\text{Margin of error} = z_{\frac{\alpha}{2}} \sigma_{\bar{x}_1 - \bar{x}_2} = z_{\frac{\alpha}{2}} \sqrt{\frac{\sigma_1^2}{n_1} + \frac{\sigma_2^2}{n_2}}$$

 think it over 12.2

The test statistic is taken as $z\alpha/2$. Why are we using $z\alpha/2$?

This basic procedure should look familiar to you by now, and it ends up with the expression for an interval estimate of the difference between two population means as follows:

$$(\bar{x}_1 - \bar{x}_2) \pm z_{\frac{\alpha}{2}} \sqrt{\frac{\sigma_1^2}{n_1} + \frac{\sigma_2^2}{n_2}}$$

OK, so now to work through the example with some numbers we can return to our retail managers. Let's imagine we are employed as researchers in this situation, and we collect two independent samples, one from each store. Our FD sample n_1 is of 44 people and has a mean annual income of £82000. Our SS sample n_2 is of 48 people and has a mean annual income of £58000. For ease of computation, let's divide these income figures by 1000, and if we do that we end up with $\bar{x}_1 = 82$ and $\bar{x}_2 = 58$. Helpfully, prior research has given us the population standard deviations, such that we know $\sigma_1 = 15$ and $\sigma_2 = 10$ (both divided by 1000, as are the sample means). Now we have all the information we need to provide an interval estimate of $\mu_1 - \mu_2$.

First, we calculate $\bar{x}_1 - \bar{x}_2$ which gives us 24, our point estimate. Then we use our margin of error expression to compute the margin of error and interval estimate, as follows:

$$(\bar{x}_1 - \bar{x}_2) \pm z_{\frac{\alpha}{2}} \sqrt{\frac{\sigma_1^2}{n_1} + \frac{\sigma_2^2}{n_2}} = (82 - 58) \pm 1.96 \sqrt{\frac{15^2}{44} + \frac{10^2}{48}} = 24 \pm 5.26$$

You should notice that we have used a 95% level of confidence, and therefore $z_{\alpha/2} = z_{0.025} = 1.96$. Using this, you can see that the margin of error is 5.26, and therefore the 95% confidence interval estimate of the difference between the two means is $24 - 5.26 = 18.74$ to $24 + 5.26 = 29.26$. Multiplying by 1000 to bring it back up to the original units gives us a 95% confidence interval for annual income of £18740 to £29260.

HYPOTHESIS TESTS ABOUT THE DIFFERENCE BETWEEN TWO MEANS WHEN THE POPULATION STANDARD DEVIATION IS KNOWN

Of course, a confidence interval is only one way of exploring the difference between means. Often, we have a hypothesis about the population difference that we want to test. In order to explain this, let's introduce the notation D_0 to denote the hypothesized difference between the two population means, $\mu_1 - \mu_2$. There are three different forms of hypothesis test about D_0 that we might be interested in, but it is by far most common that we hypothesize that $D_0 = 0$. If so, we are basically saying that our null hypothesis is that there is no difference between the means of the two populations, and rejecting H_0 allows us to draw the conclusion that there is some difference between μ_1 and μ_2. Of course, we could also hypothesize that there *was* some difference between the means in the two populations, so, for the sake of completeness, here are the three different types of hypothesis test we could use when considering the difference between two means:

$H_0: \mu_1 - \mu_2 \leq D_0$ $H_0: \mu_1 - \mu_2 = D_0$ $H_0: \mu_1 - \mu_2 \geq D_0$

$H_1: \mu_1 - \mu_2 > D_0$ $H_1: \mu_1 - \mu_2 \neq D_0$ $H_1: \mu_1 - \mu_2 < D_0$

think it over 12.3

Classify the above statements in terms of one-tailed or two-tailed tests.

The steps that were given for conducting hypothesis tests in earlier chapters are just as applicable here, so there is little need to dwell on them. In fact, you should already know them. But just in case, let's recap. First, choose a level of significance, then compute the test statistic and finally find the p-value of the test statistic to decide whether or not you should reject the null hypothesis.

The test statistic in this present case is z, as you might have predicted, and the expression to calculate z is similar to the interval estimate expression given earlier, so there seems little need to explain the terms again:

$$z = \frac{(\bar{x}_1 - \bar{x}_2) - D_0}{\sqrt{\frac{\sigma_1^2}{n_1} + \frac{\sigma_2^2}{n_2}}}$$

It would be simplest to demonstrate this with an extension of the retail example given above. In this case we might have some theory that leads us to expect a difference across the mean incomes for the two separate populations shopping at each branch. However, our null hypothesis always includes the idea that there is no difference, and we then interrogate the sample evidence to see if we have grounds to reject that null hypothesis and thus tentatively accept the alternative that there is some difference in the population means. As such, our hypotheses are:

$$H_0: \mu_1 - \mu_2 \leq 0$$

$$H_1: \mu_1 - \mu_2 > 0$$

think it over 12.4

If $\mu_1 - \mu_2 = 0$, what does this tell you about the average incomes of the respective groups?

You should note that the alternative hypothesis states that the mean difference should be *greater than zero*, rather than just 'not equal to' zero (where it could be greater than or less than zero). This is because our theory suggests that customers of the FD store should have on average greater annual incomes than those of the SS store – indeed that is the main point of our investigation. In such a case, it is more appropriate to hypothesize in this directional manner and thus use a one-tailed test.

So, using exactly the same sample results as before, when calculating the confidence interval, we can calculate the hypothesis test:

$$z = \frac{(\bar{x}_1 - \bar{x}_2) - D_0}{\sqrt{\frac{\sigma_1^2}{n_1} + \frac{\sigma_2^2}{n_2}}} = \frac{(82 - 58) - 0}{\sqrt{\frac{15^2}{44} + \frac{10^2}{48}}} = 8.95$$

Even though with your experience so far, you should already know that $z = 8.95$ is going to be significant at almost any level you could choose, let's go through the motions of checking it against the tables. We choose to use a 0.05 level of significance, and a one-tailed test, because we have hypothesized a directional difference between the two means (i.e. the mean for the FD store must be higher than the mean for the SS store to support our hypothesis). However, if you use almost any typical standard normal distribution table, you will see that the values for z stop well before 8.95. As such, we can easily conclude that our sample results give us sufficient evidence to reject the null hypothesis at a 0.05 level of significance.

Before moving on, just remember that even though we have used the *p*-value method for the hypothesis tests, there is nothing stopping you using the critical value method if you prefer. Furthermore, two-tailed tests are just as feasible as the one-tailed test we used here. There is nothing inherent to the test that stops you doing these things, and the procedures are just the same as explained in prior chapters on hypothesis testing.

INFERENCES ABOUT DIFFERENCES IN POPULATION MEANS WHERE THE POPULATION STANDARD DEVIATIONS ARE UNKNOWN

Of course, in most practical situations one does not have the luxury of knowing the population standard deviations, and as such the techniques shown below are far more common. The basic principle is to use the sample standard deviations s_1 and s_2 to fill in for (i.e. estimate) the unknown population standard deviations σ_1 and σ_2 respectively. We also need to switch from using the standard normal distribution to using the t-distribution for our interval estimation and inferences.

To begin again with an interval estimation situation (along with a margin of error), let's imagine a situation common in practice, where a sales manager might be interested in the time taken to receive payment for accounts in two separate parts of the country. The firm sells screws and other small parts to hardware stores and contractors across the entire country. It is interested in whether those customers in the south take longer to pay their accounts on average than those in the north. So the manager takes a random sample of 25 accounts from the south and 25 from the north, and records the average length of time in days it takes these accounts to pay their outstanding balances.

So, if we set out clearly the data we need for our calculations, our sample size for the north sample $n_1 = 25$, the same as our sample size n_2 for the south. Calculating the means for each sample gives us a mean time to pay of $\bar{x}_1 = 37$ days for the north accounts and $\bar{x}_2 = 46$ days for the south accounts. We do not have our population standard deviations, so we calculate the standard deviations for the sample, to get $s_1 = 3.5$ and $s_2 = 5.2$. Now we have all we need to calculate our interval estimate. In fact, the calculation is essentially the same as the one where the population standard deviations is known, but you just substitute for the sample standard deviations and use t instead of z, as follows:

$$(\bar{x}_1 - \bar{x}_2) \pm t_{\alpha/2} \sqrt{\frac{s_1^2}{n_1} + \frac{s_2^2}{n_2}}$$

However, those with better memories will probably note that this is not really the end of it, because in order to use the t-distribution we need to calculate a figure for the degrees of freedom to use. Of course, when you are using some statistical software, all the mathematical heavy lifting is taken care of, but that is no fun at all. If you need to calculate degrees of freedom for this test by hand, the formula is:

$$df = \frac{\left(\frac{s_1^2}{n_1} + \frac{s_2^2}{n_2}\right)^2}{\frac{1}{n_1 - 1}\left(\frac{s_1^2}{n_1}\right) + \frac{1}{n_2 - 1}\left(\frac{s_2^2}{n_2}\right)}$$

This is an impressive formula, but it is not too difficult to use if you just take it step by step – as stressed all through this book.

Anyway, to return to the accounts example, let's calculate a 95% confidence interval estimate for the difference between the two means. As motivational books always say you should do the most difficult stuff first, let's begin by calculating the degrees of freedom:

$$df = \frac{\left(\frac{s_1^2}{n_1} + \frac{s_2^2}{n_2}\right)^2}{\frac{1}{n_1 - 1}\left(\frac{s_1^2}{n_1}\right)^2 + \frac{1}{n_2 - 1}\left(\frac{s_2^2}{n_2}\right)^2} = \frac{\left(\frac{3.5^2}{25} + \frac{5.2^2}{25}\right)^2}{\frac{1}{25 - 1}\left(\frac{3.5^2}{25}\right)^2 + \frac{1}{25 - 1}\left(\frac{5.2^2}{25}\right)^2} = 42.04$$

When we get a non-integer[2] answer, we always round downwards to provide a more conservative estimate of the interval. This is because the smaller degrees of freedom gives a higher t value, and thus makes

---

[2] Remember: an integer is a whole number, like 1, 2, 3. Non-integers are numbers that are not whole, like 1.5.

the interval wider. If we have a 95% confidence interval, this means we need to look at the *t*-distribution tables for $t_{0.025}$, and with 42 degrees of freedom we find that $t_{0.025} = 2.018$. Now we have this, it is almost trivial to calculate the confidence interval:

$$(\bar{x}_1 - \bar{x}_2) \pm t_{0.025}\sqrt{\frac{S_1^2}{n_1} + \frac{S_2^2}{n_2}} = (37 - 46) \pm 2.018\sqrt{\frac{3.5^2}{25} + \frac{5.2^2}{25}} = -9 \pm 2.53$$

So, our point estimate of the difference in mean time to pay accounts between the north and south is –9 days, with a margin of error of 2.53 days. So, the 95% confidence interval is –9 – 2.53 = –11.53 days to –9 + 2.53 = –6.47 days.

think it over 12.5

The above calculation has come up with two values: –11.53 days and –6.47 days. What would you expect the outcome to be if you were calculating the difference between the mean values with reference to the south (i.e. $\bar{x}_2 - \bar{x}_1$)?

HYPOTHESIS TESTS ABOUT THE DIFFERENCE BETWEEN TWO MEANS WHEN THE POPULATION STANDARD DEVIATION IS UNKNOWN

If we look at testing hypotheses about the difference between two means in situations where we do not know the population standard deviations, most of the concepts are exactly the same as what you should already know by now. Basically, the underlying ideas are the same as when the population standard deviations are known, but again you use the *t*-distribution rather than the *z*.

The different hypotheses you could test are exactly the same as when the population standard deviations are known, so there seems no need to restate them here. However, if you remember that D_0 refers to the hypothesized difference between means, and in the population standard deviation unknown case, the test statistic is as follows:

$$t = \frac{(\bar{x}_1 - \bar{x}_2) - D_0}{\sqrt{\frac{S_1^2}{n_1} + \frac{S_2^2}{n_2}}}$$

Let's demonstrate this statistic by extending the same example as before – the sales manager looking at the difference in account payment times between accounts in the north and south. Our population means are:

$\mu_1 =$ mean time taken to settle accounts in days for the north.

$\mu_2 =$ mean time taken to settle accounts in days for the south.

Our sales manager has a theory that because of economic conditions in the south, customers will take longer to settle their accounts. As such the manager is expecting the data to exhibit longer mean times to pay for the south than the north, meaning that $\mu_1 - \mu_2$ should be less than zero, which is our alternative hypothesis. So our hypothesis test becomes:

$$H_0: \mu_1 - \mu_2 \geq 0$$

$$H_1: \mu_1 - \mu_2 < 0$$

think it over 12.6

Just a reminder about the interpretation of the above mathematical statements: when you see something like $\mu_1 - \mu_2 \geq 0$ it means that if the value of μ_1 is greater than μ_2 you will end up with a positive value. In this example, this means that the mean times to settle accounts in the north are greater compared with the ones in the south.

We will use 0.05 as the level of significance, and the sample statistics we have already used for the interval estimation. As such, things should be quite smooth for us, and the only new calculation we need to do is for the t statistic:

$$t = \frac{(\bar{x}_1 - \bar{x}_2) - D_0}{\sqrt{\dfrac{S_1^2}{n_1} + \dfrac{S_2^2}{n_2}}} = \frac{(37 - 46) - 0}{\sqrt{\dfrac{3.5^2}{25} + \dfrac{5.2^2}{25}}} = -7.18$$

We already know our degrees of freedom are 42, so we turn to the t-distribution table for 42 degrees of freedom. Again, similar to the situation when we used the z table for the population standard deviation known case, we can see that a t of -7.18 is far beyond what is given in the table.

A couple of notes might help you with this interpretation. First, remember that this is a lower-tail test technically, since we are looking for a negative difference in the means (i.e. the mean for population 2 is hypothesized to be higher than for population 1). While this might be a little harder to follow, it happens in reality, so best get used to it. In fact, it is really simple, since the procedure is just the same as if we were doing an upper-tail test. In fact, it is best when using the table to ignore it and pretend you are doing an upper-tail test (remember, the upper tail is symmetrical to the lower tail). So, in essence we do not need to worry about it.

Now, we simply go to the t table and read down until we find the line for 42 degrees of freedom. In most typical t tables, you will see that the table stops when you get to the value for an area in the upper tail of 0.005, which for 42 degrees of freedom is 2.698. Of course, this is exactly the same area as in the lower tail. So, we know our t of -7.18 must correspond to a p-value of less than 0.005, which means that we certainly have a p-value of less than $\alpha = 0.05$ and can therefore reject H_0. Thus our results support the idea that customers in the south take a longer mean time to pay their accounts.

SOME IMPORTANT NOTES ON MAKING INFERENCES ABOUT TWO POPULATION MEANS

Before moving on, it is worthwhile to make a couple of important points about the methods that have just been covered. First, concerning sample size for the z testing procedures, in most cases, simple random samples of 30 or more are fine. However, when one has a sample size of less than 30, it is important that the researcher is reasonably happy to assume that the population distributions are at least approximately normal.

When it comes to using the t testing procedures, we can be more flexible. In fact, they can be used with samples that are surprisingly small with good results. In particular, as long as the sample sizes are close to equal, and as long as the combined sample size is 20 or more, the t-test can be used with some confidence – even if the populations cannot be assumed normal. That said, if you think the population distributions are highly non-normal (e.g. very skewed, or have serious outliers), you really need to have larger sample sizes. Finally, Above and Beyond Box 12.1 gives another approach to making inferences about the difference in population means, which is sometimes used in software packages.

above and beyond

Box 12.1   Equal Variances Assumed?

In many statistical software packages, you will see something like 'equal variances assumed' as an option, or as a result when testing the difference between two population means when the population standard deviations are unknown. For example, in IBM SPSS Statistics Software (SPSS) you automatically get two sets of results, one with and one without equal variances assumed. But why? What does it mean? Well, basically, if you can assume that the two population standard deviations are equal (i.e. the variances are also equal, and if you do not understand why that is, go back and look at the relationship between the standard deviation and the variance), you can make our calculations simpler.

First, we can combine the two sample standard deviations to create what is called a 'pooled' sample variance, s^2, using the formula:

$$s^2 = \frac{(n_1-1)\,s_1^2 + (n_2-1)\,s_2^2}{n_1 + n_2 - 2}$$

This is neat, and it changes the formula for the t statistic to:

$$t = \frac{(\bar{x}_1 - \bar{x}_2) - D_0}{s\sqrt{\dfrac{1}{n_1} + \dfrac{1}{n_2}}}$$

But the real bonus comes when we discover that this new version of t has $n_1 + n_2 - 2$ degrees of freedom, rather than that beast of a formula you saw earlier.

All the basic procedures of interpretation and testing are just the same as you have already learned. Of course, the difficulty is that you have to assume the population standard deviations are the same, which is generally a pretty unsafe assumption and also hard to verify (if you could verify it, you would have the population standard deviations anyway!). Also, when the sample sizes are quite different, this method is not particularly good.

So all in all, it is best to use the equal variances *not* assumed methods already explained in this chapter.

But at least now you know, right?

USING PAIRED SAMPLES TO MAKE INFERENCES ABOUT THE DIFFERENCE BETWEEN TWO POPULATION MEANS

Up until now, we have explained situations where the researcher has taken two independent simple random samples and compared the means, in order to draw inferences about the population difference. However, imagine we have a research situation where we want to test the impact of some new migraine drug, designed to lessen the time it takes for people to recover from a migraine. What we could do is give the *same* people the old drug for one migraine attack and the new drug for another later attack. Then we compare the mean times for the migraine to disappear for each drug.

More formally, we would do it like this. First, select a simple random sample of regular migraine sufferers. Each sufferer takes one of the two drugs for their first migraine and the other drug for their second. We would assign the order of drug taking randomly, so some of the sufferers took the old drug first, and some the new. So each sufferer would provide a *pair* of data points: the time it took the migraine to disappear with the old drug, and the time it took with the new drug.

This is called a *matched* or *paired* sample design. However, those terms are analytical (i.e. they refer to the analysis method), and in research design books you will probably see them referred to as within-subjects designs (the two independent sample designs discussed in the first part of the chapter are often called between-subjects designs). Paired sample designs are usually considered more powerful, or in technical terms to have a smaller sampling error, than independent sample designs. This is because one of the biggest sources of variation is eliminated – that between the different subjects in the samples – because the same subjects are used in both samples. Of course, this sort of design is only feasible in some cases, and it has its own problems, but that discussion is really for a research design text, not an analysis one.

Anyway, let's look at our migraine drug example in more detail by way of illustrating the method. First, let's set up the null and alternative hypotheses, as usual:

$$H_0: \mu_1 - \mu_2 = 0$$

$$H_1: \mu_1 - \mu_2 \neq 0$$

Now, we select a simple random sample of five migraine sufferers – say we have a medical database we can access for such things.[3] Table 12.1 shows the data on the times it took the migraines to dissipate for each of the five subjects after taking each drug, in minutes, with Drug 1 as the old drug and Drug 2 as the new drug. Each subject therefore returns two values, one for each drug, and the final column is the difference in time for each subject d.

Table 12.1 Migraine data

Subject	Drug 1 time (min)	Drug 2 time (min)	Difference in times (d_i)
1	10	9	1
2	13	14	−1
3	15	15	0
4	8	7	1
5	11	10	1

The important thing to remember when doing a paired sample analysis is that it is the difference between the two means for each subject that are important, not the means themselves. Those are given in the rightmost column of Table 12.1. This means we can tweak our hypotheses a little to make things clearer:

$$H_0: \mu_d = 0$$

$$H_1: \mu_d \neq 0$$

where μ_d is the mean of the time differences for the population of migraine sufferers.

OK, so what is required now is to calculate the sample mean of the differences, which we denote $\bar{d}$, and the sample standard deviations s_d. These formulae are just the same as you have done previously, apart from the appearance of d sometimes:

$$\bar{d} = \frac{\sum d_i}{n} = \frac{2}{5} = 0.4$$

$$S_d = \sqrt{\frac{\sum (d_i - \bar{d})^2}{n-1}} = \sqrt{\frac{3.2}{4}} = 0.282$$

---

[3] We use five here only because we are going to calculate things by hand – otherwise, we would prefer a much larger sample size.

Just to recap, remember that sigma signifies the sum. So, for example, in the formula for s_d the summation means you take the difference score for subject 1, subtract the mean difference from it, then square the result. You sum all the results for each member of the sample and get your result.

So, moving on, remember that we have a small sample of five. This means we have to assume explicitly that the population of differences is normally distributed, in order to use the t-distribution. If we are safe in this assumption, then we can calculate a test statistic which has a t-distribution and $n - 1$ degrees of freedom:

$$t = \frac{\bar{d} - \mu_d}{\frac{S_d}{\sqrt{n}}}$$

We can use this equation to test our hypothesis above. Recall that H_0: $\mu_d = 0$ and H_1: $\mu_d \neq 0$. Let's as usual use $\alpha = 0.05$, and then all that is needed is to substitute in the equation for t the sample numbers we calculated earlier:

$$t = \frac{\bar{d} - \mu_d}{\frac{S_d}{\sqrt{n}}} = \frac{0.4 - 0}{\frac{0.282}{\sqrt{5}}} = 3.17$$

From here, we can compute the p-value. We already know it is in the upper tail, as it is greater than 0. So with this in mind, we look at the row in the t-distribution table for 4 degrees of freedom ($n - 1$). You will see that an area in the upper tail of the distribution of 3.17 falls somewhere between the area for $p = 0.025$ (which is 2.776) and $p = 0.01$ (which is 3.747). Now, the test in this case is two-tailed, because we have not formally specified a direction. As such, we need to double the values, to see that the p-value is therefore between 0.05 and 0.025. So, the p-value is below 0.05, which means we can reject the null hypothesis. This gives us evidence that our new drug has some effect, and we think it probably reduces the time taken for migraines to dissipate. However, with only five subjects, we cannot be very confident of this result.

It would be simple to extend this example to create a confidence interval. First, we decide what level of confidence we want to use. In this case we will use a level of confidence of 95%, which gives us $\alpha = 0.05$. The formula is as follows:

$$\bar{d} \pm t_{\frac{\alpha}{2}} \frac{S_d}{\sqrt{\sqrt{n}}}$$

So, substituting in the values we already have:

$$\bar{d} \pm t_{0.025} \frac{S_d}{\sqrt{n}} = 0.4 \pm 2.776 \left(\frac{0.282}{\sqrt{5}} \right) = 0.4 \pm 0.35$$

This means we have a 0.35 minute margin of error, and therefore the 95% confidence interval for the difference in population means of the two drugs is 0.05 to 0.75 minutes. Of course, these figures are not in seconds – so you need to convert these decimals into seconds (i.e. 0.05 minutes is 3 seconds) if you want to get really exact times.

MAKING INFERENCES ABOUT THE DIFFERENCE BETWEEN TWO POPULATION PROPORTIONS

Place yourself in the position of a quality manager for a large company making doughnuts of various types. You have oversight for two factories, each in different locations. What you want to know is: is the quality of the doughnuts in each factory the same? This is a situation where you would probably need to compare proportions in two populations. In fact, you can do this quite easily with an extension of the tools you have learnt so far in this chapter. Let's begin by showing how to develop an interval estimate of the difference between two population proportions and a corresponding margin of error.

To formalize terms, let:

π_1 = the proportion of bad doughnuts for population 1 (factory 1).

π_2 = the proportion of bad doughnuts for population 2 (factory 2).

Now, imagine we take a simple random sample of 200 doughnuts from factory 1 and the same from factory 2. Let:

p_1 = the sample proportion for the simple random sample from population 1.

p_2 = the sample proportion for the simple random sample from population 2.

The difference between the population proportions is $\pi_1 - \pi_2$, and the point estimate of this is of course given by $p_1 - p_2$.

By now, you might be comfortable with the idea that $p_1 - p_2$ has a sampling distribution that contains all possible values of $p_1 - p_2$ if you were to take an infinite number of two independent simple random samples from the two populations, and the mean of this distribution would be $\pi_1 - \pi_2$. However, we cannot automatically say that this sampling distribution approximates a normal one if the sample size is big enough (as we have been doing for prior sampling distributions regarding the difference between population means). Instead, we need to take account of the population proportions as well as the sample sizes. Specifically, if n_1 is the size of the sample from population 1, and n_2 the size of the sample from population 2, then all of $n_1\pi_1$, $n_1(1 - \pi_1)$, $n_2\pi_2$ and $n_2(1 - \pi_2)$ must be greater than or equal to five. If this is the case, then the normal distribution can be assumed to approximate the sampling distribution of $p_1 - p_2$ and to have a standard error of:

$$\sigma_{p_1 - p_2} = \sqrt{\frac{\pi_1(1-\pi_1)}{n_1} + \frac{\pi_2(1-\pi_2)}{n_2}}$$

We can use this formula to compute the margin of error needed for an interval estimate. Unfortunately, we cannot, because we do not have values of the population proportions π. As such, we use the sample proportions to approximate the population proportions (but you probably guessed that, right?). In doing so we can develop an equation to calculate the margin of error, similar to those you have already seen in this chapter:

$$\text{margin of error} = z_{\frac{\alpha}{2}}\sqrt{\frac{p_1(1-p_1)}{n_1} + \frac{p_2(1-p_2)}{n_2}}$$

Now, let's work through our doughnut quality example. As we know, both n_1 and $n_2 = 200$ (they do not have to be the same, they just are in this case). The number of 'bad' doughnuts for sample 1 is 18, and for sample 2 it is 15. This makes it easy to calculate the relevant sample proportions of bad doughnuts: $p_1 = 15/200 = 0.09$ and $p_2 = 0.075$. Our point estimate is therefore $0.09 - 0.075 = 0.015$.

 think it over 12.7

Explain p_1 and p_2 as a percentage in plain English.

So, let's use the tools introduced above to calculate an interval estimate of the difference between the two population proportions, using a 95% confidence interval, with $z_{\alpha/2} = z_{0.025} = 1.96$. The full formula for an interval estimate for the difference between two population proportions is:

$$(p_1 - p_2) \pm z_{\frac{\alpha}{2}}\sqrt{\frac{p_1(1-p_1)}{n_1} + \frac{p_2(1-p_2)}{n_2}}$$

Substituting in our sample values gives:

$$(0.09 - 0.075) \pm 1.96 \sqrt{\frac{0.09(1-0.09)}{200} + \frac{0.075(1-0.075)}{200}} = 0.015 \pm 0.054$$

Since the margin of error is 0.054, the 95% confidence interval is –0.039 to 0.069.

think it over 12.8

Explain in plain English what the above result means in terms of the original question.

Testing Hypotheses about the Differences in Population Proportions

Again, the basic concepts here are the same as in the rest of this chapter, so you should be able to link them easily together. The basic forms of hypotheses you can test in this regard should therefore look familiar:

$H_0: \pi_1 - \pi_2 \leq 0$ $H_0: \pi_1 - \pi_2 = 0$ $H_0: \pi_1 - \pi_2 \geq 0$

$H_1: \pi_1 - \pi_2 > 0$ $H_1: \pi_1 - \pi_2 \neq 0$ $H_1: \pi_1 - \pi_2 < 0$

If we assume that H_0 is true in the population, then $\pi_1 - \pi_2 = 0$, which is equivalent to $\pi_1 = \pi_2$, which is handy, as it allows us to do some rearranging of the standard error formula, on which we base the test statistic for this particular hypothesis test.

Recall the formula for the standard error of $p_1 - p_2$:

$$\sigma_{p_1 - p_2} = \sqrt{\frac{\pi_1(1-\pi_1)}{n_1} + \frac{\pi_2(1-\pi_2)}{n_2}}$$

Well, if we assume H_0 is true, then $\pi_1 = \pi_2 = \pi$, and therefore the formula can be rearranged as follows:

$$\sigma_{p_1 - p_2} = \sqrt{\frac{\pi_1(1-\pi_1)}{n_1} + \frac{\pi_2(1-\pi_2)}{n_2}} = \sqrt{\pi(1-\pi)\left(\frac{1}{n_1} + \frac{1}{n_2}\right)}$$

Of course, we do not know π, and therefore we combine the sample proportions to estimate a pooled estimator of the population proportion:

$$p = \frac{n_1 p_1 + n_2 p_2}{n_1 + n_2}$$

In light of all this, we substitute p into the standard error formula and divide our point estimator $p_1 - p_2$ by this new standard error to create the test statistic z for the difference between two population proportions:

$$z = \frac{(p_1 - p_2)}{\sqrt{\pi(1-\pi)\left(\frac{1}{n_1} + \frac{1}{n_2}\right)}}$$

However, it is important to remember that this test statistic is only usable in situations where we have a large enough sample to assume that $n_1\pi_1$, $n_1(1 - \pi_1)$, $n_2\pi_2$ and $n_2(1 - \pi_2)$ are greater than or equal to five.

OK, back to the doughnuts example. We have no particular theoretical or practical reason to expect one factory to have a lower/higher error rate than the other, so we have a two-tailed test, with null and alternative hypotheses of:

$$H_0: \pi_1 - \pi_2 = 0$$

$$H_1: \pi_1 - \pi_2 \neq 0$$

We use $\alpha = 0.05$ as the level of significance. Looking at our sample data from earlier, we can see that $n_1 = n_2 = 200$, $p_1 = 0.09$ and $p_2 = 0.075$. First, we compute our pooled π estimate:

$$p = \frac{n_1 p_1 + n_2 p_2}{n_1 + n_2} = \frac{200(0.00) + 200(0.075)}{200 + 200} = 0.0825$$

From there, we can calculate the test statistic:

$$z = \frac{(p_1 - p_2)}{\sqrt{\pi(1-\pi)\left(\frac{1}{n_1} + \frac{1}{n_2}\right)}} = \frac{(0.09 - 0.075)}{\sqrt{0.0825(1-0.0825)\left(\frac{1}{200} + \frac{1}{200}\right)}} = 0.0545$$

We now use this value for z to compute the p-value for the two-tailed test. Using $z = 0.0545$. we go to the standard normal distribution and find that $z = 0.0545$ corresponds to a value somewhere between 0.0199 and 0.0239, which we will estimate using the midpoint between the two values, that is 0.0219. Thus, the area in the upper tail is $0.5 - 0.0219 = 0.4781$. Doubling this because of the two-tailed nature of the test gives us a p-value of 0.9562. This p-value is greater than our $\alpha = 0.05$, and therefore we cannot reject H_0. So, our evidence suggests there is no reason to think the two factories produce doughnuts of differing quality.

Using Excel

Unfortunately Excel does not explicitly do the calculations shown in this chapter. But, as usual with a little creativity, the knowledge you have about statistical formulae and your skills with Excel will enable you to create spreadsheets to perform the calculations that you want.

First of all, let's look at how we can adapt Excel to compare means and assist in the decision-making process. Figure 12.2 shows the results for calculating the margin of error and the 95% confidence limits for a company that manufacture light switches in two factories. Figure 12.3 shows the formulae used to perform the calculations. This is the great thing about using Excel: you can get it to perform the calculations that you want without the loads of extra information that programs like SPSS churn out for a pastime. As long as you know the formulae for a specific calculation, you can use Excel to do all of the calculations.

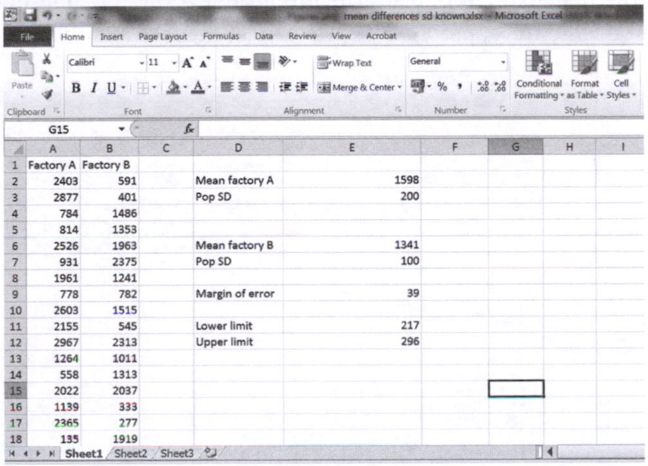

Figure 12.2

Figure 12.3

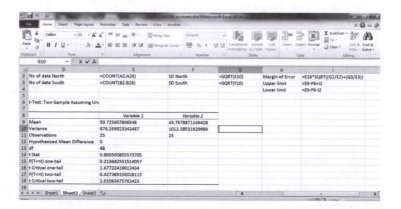

Figure 12.4

It is all well and good entering the formulae by hand, but to save time and effort we can also pro-duce a 'hybrid' model. If you have a go at calculating the number of degrees of freedom for the section on 'Inferences about Differences in Population Means Where the Population Standard Deviations Are Unknown', you will know what I mean! Take a look at Figure 12.4. This is similar to the example given in the text comparing two accounts and the time they took to pay invoices. The data for the two accounts are in columns A and B. Cells E2 and E3 give the amount of data collected, G2 and G3 calculate the standard deviation and, finally, Excel's built-in function 't-test: assuming unequal variances' was used to generate the mean, the variance and the test statistic.

Figure 12.5 shows the underlying formulae. The formulae used by the built-in function will not be displayed, but you can refer to the appropriate cells to extract the relevant data.

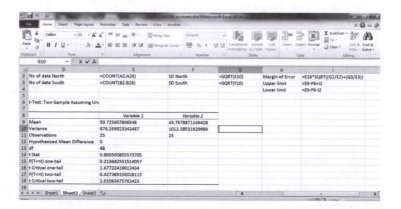

Figure 12.5

Using SPSS

Life is much easier using SPSS but the price you pay is less versatility. We will use data from two other factories that produce light switches. The data can be loaded from the file switches.sav. Figure 12.6 shows you how to find the procedure you need to perform a comparison of means and Figure 12.7 shows the output. As always, it is great fun analysing data but it still has to be interpreted. Looking at Figure 12.7, you can see that the correlation coefficient (Pearson's r) between the variables is low, namely 0.084, but more telling is the significance value which tells us the variables are not significantly correlated since $p > 0.05$ as a 95% confidence level was used. In the paired sample test you can see that the mean difference between the two factories is 335.066 and the standard deviation of the differences is 1018.005. The standard error of the mean is 143.968. So what does all this tell us? Basically, the standard error tells us there could be large differences between the sample means and the population mean. The significance tells us that the probability of this result due to chance alone is 2.4%. The lower and upper confidence limits tell us that the true value of the mean lies somewhere between 45.753 and 624.38, which is a large range.

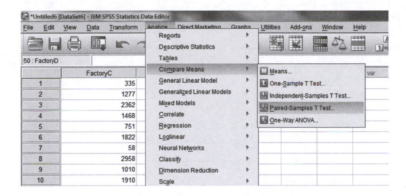

Figure 12.6

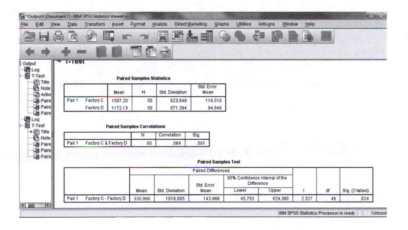

Figure 12.7

The conclusion is that the production processes at the two factories are not comparable and further investigation is warranted.

SUMMARY

Well, after the exertions of the last few chapters, this was hopefully a simpler and quicker exercise entirely. But that should not diminish its importance. The comparisons introduced in this chapter first help to reinforce the material you saw in earlier chapters (especially Chapters 7 and 8), as well as form the basis for understanding a critical part of research and analysis – how to compare populations. Along with the regression approach we have already covered, the group comparison approach is the major theme of social science, and therefore business research.

The next chapter will continue this theme, by extending our methods to allow us to examine population variances. Up until now, we have only looked at the slightly simpler concepts of population means and proportions. Variances require some special consideration, since they do not use the z- or t-distributions you have become so friendly with in this chapter. They also act as a nice introduction to the critical Chapter 14 on ANOVA.

final checklist

You should have covered and understood the following basic content in this chapter:

- ☑ The basics of designing group comparison research.
- ☑ How to calculate interval estimates of the difference between two population means when the population standard deviation is known and when it is unknown.
- ☑ How to test hypotheses about the difference between two population means when the population standard deviation is known and when it is unknown.

- ☑ What matched or paired samples are.
- ☑ How to calculate intervals and test hypotheses about the difference between the means of paired/matched samples.
- ☑ How to calculate interval estimates and test hypotheses about the difference between two population proportions.

EXERCISES

1. You have been commissioned by a British employment agency to compare average salaries between private sector nurses and UK National Health Service nurses. You select 40 private sector nurses and 50 NHS nurses at random and obtain the following results:

$$\text{NHS: } n_1 = 40, \bar{x}_1 = £\,24350, s_1 = £\,3500$$

$$\text{Private sector: } n_1 = 50, \bar{x}_2 = £\,25650, s_2 = £\,4400$$

   a. Formulate the hypotheses so that, if the null hypothesis is rejected, we can conclude that NHS nurses earn less than private sector nurses. Use $\alpha = 0.05$.
   b. Calculate the value of the test statistic.
   c. What is the p-value?
   d. State your conclusion.

2. A manufacturer produces switches at two different factories. The switches from factory A have a mean lifetime of 1524 hours with a population standard deviation of 200 hours. The switches from factory B have a mean lifetime of 1218 hours with a population standard deviation of 100 hours. As the quality manager, you collect random samples of 124 switches from each factory and test them. Using a 95% confidence level, calculate the margin of error between the means and find the confidence interval for the lifetime of the switches.

3. Using the data found in 'switch factory data.xslx', design a spreadsheet to answer question 1. You will need to enter the population standard deviations as fixed values. Compare the result from the spreadsheet with the one you calculated in question 1.

4. Using Excel's built-in random number generator, develop a hypothetical medical scenario where a pharmaceutical company is developing a new drug to combat liver disease. The company has one experiment where it is testing one formulation of the drug on 80 cultures, and another, more expensive formulation is also being tested on the same number of cultures. The reactions show that the range of successful 'attacks' by the first drug ranges from 0 to 50 and by the second drug from 0 to 100.

   a. Formulate your null and alternative hypotheses.
   b. Calculate the margin of error and, using a confidence interval of 99%, find the confidence interval.
   c. Interpret your results.

5. Repeat question 4 using SPSS. You can save time by importing the data from the Excel file.

 To access additional online resources please visit: **https://study.sagepub.com/leepeters**

The Ballad of Eddie the Easily Distracted: Part 13

Eddie was confused. This was not something entirely unusual for him, but in this instance the topic he was confused about was indeed unusual. While he had found the week's QUAN101 content confusing, this was entirely normal. No, Eddie was confused with Esha. He'd had a very pleasant cup of coffee with her last week. They'd started off talking about their QUAN101 assignments of course, but after a few minutes Eddie had for some reason mentioned his enjoyment of old cartoons, and Esha had burst out laughing: 'You're funny Eddie,' she'd giggled. 'Yes, um, funny,' he replied, making a mental note. Eddie had thought they'd got on surprisingly well, and Esha wasn't quite as boring as he'd thought originally. Maybe there was more to her than just work. But, he'd bumped into her again the next day, and she'd been totally weird, hardly saying anything to him and rushing off like she'd rather be anywhere else.

Just then, Eddie's thoughts turned to his impending QUAN101 tutorial, where of course he'd see Esha again. The subject was testing variances. Eddie smiled rather grimly. How appropriate – it was exactly this that he couldn't understand, either in statistical terms or human ones! On the other hand, at least he understood why variance was important. It didn't matter what the 'mean', or average, was at all really, since when was the average actually what you experienced at any single point? If there was a large variance, then people were just moody and you never knew what to expect – even if the 'mean' was some kind of normal behaviour. But if variance was low, people tended to be the same most of the time, Eddie thought that was kind of like him – pretty easy-going. Esha, on the other hand – well, Eddie just figured he'd have to accept he was more likely to understand statistics than he would ever understand her.

Esha's Story: Part 13

Esha was patiently trying to explain variances to Eddie in their QUAN101 tutorial, but for some reason she was finding this very hard. Part of it might have been because she was getting unusually frustrated with Eddie: 'Come on Eddie, try harder,' she'd said, an edge of exasperation in her voice. Eddie opened his mouth to say something but nothing came out, and Esha couldn't work out whether he'd thought better of it or been struck dumb. She felt something uncharitable forming in her mind, but refused to fully formulate the thought, and contented herself to wondering why he was being so weird. For some reason, Esha had rather engaged with the material this week, and found it quite easy to come to grips with. The problem was that the fairly simple concepts were hidden behind some equations that looked a bit more scary than those of the last few weeks, and Eddie seemed to be struggling with remembering how to do the calculations. That said, she was pleased to see he was working with the distribution tables almost without a second thought now, when he'd been completely baffled by them when he'd first seen them. In fact, Esha found herself feeling quite proud of him for showing such progress. She shook the thought out of her head. Why would she feel that? How weird. In fact, she reflected later as she took the teabag from her cup in her room, she couldn't work out quite how she felt about Eddie. That was an unexpected development.

POPULATION VARIANCES

CONTENTS

learning objectives

As you will see, this is quite a short chapter, although quite important – so there are not a lot of objectives here:

- ☑ Understand the concept of a population variance and why it might be important in research terms.
- ☑ Learn how to calculate interval estimates and test hypotheses about a single population variance using a sample.
- ☑ Learn how to test hypotheses about two population variances.

This chapter was not part of the original plan. In fact, if you want some advice on book writing (and I know you do), then I can tell you that adding an unplanned chapter is the single *worst* thing you can do when your wonderful and glamorous development editor is breathing gently down the back of your neck for the final manuscript.[1] For a long time, I'd hoped to squeeze the first part of this content into

---

[1] Little did she realize then that the book would take *another* two years to get finished.

Chapter 8 on hypothesis testing, and the second part into the previous chapter on testing differences between populations. It made sense, right up until I was writing those chapters. Try as I might, it just did not work. So, as the gentle encouragement to finish the book reached barely disguised threats of physical violence,[2] I bit the bullet and added another chapter to the list of 'things yet to do'.

In this chapter I will focus on the population variance – both on inferences about a single population variance and on the difference between two population variances. The importance of variance in many business decision-making situations cannot be overstated. For example, what about the situation where we have a machine filling bottles with 100 ml of sauce (I love condiments)? It is impossible to guarantee an exact 100 ml every time since there will be some amount under- or over-filled in every case. Even though the mean of 100 ml may be achieved across a sample of bottles, we are especially interested in the variance around that 100 ml mean. If it is small, we can continue our process, but if it is too large, some bottles will have much more, and some much less, and customers will complain.

You may think this situation hypothetical. However, on the very day of writing this I came across a real-life example of the problem, experienced by a very well-known sandwich chain which advertises its large size as 'footlong'. Someone had posted a photograph of one of these so-called 'footlong' sandwiches, which in fact measured 11 inches rather than the 12 inches so clearly implied as promised by the term 'footlong'. The company attempted to mitigate this bad press by explaining that the 'dough proving process' naturally led to some variation in length. Now, as a keen baker, I can vouch for the truth of that. However, the question is *how much variation* is acceptable to the firm and how much is acceptable to the consumer? Without knowing the variance of the population, the company cannot even begin to answer this question. As such, the firm experienced the effects of this lack of knowledge. Simply reading this chapter would have shown the firm how important it was to understand the variance of the processes. I hope this leads to a free sandwich![3]

INFERENCES ABOUT A SINGLE POPULATION VARIANCE

The first thing we need to know if we want to explore the variance of a population is generally the sample variance. This is of course if we do not know the population variance. But it should now be obvious at this point that if we knew the population variance, we would not be wasting our time trying to infer it now, would we?

Anyway, recall the sample variance:

$$s^2 = \frac{\sum(x_i - \bar{x})}{n-1}$$

The sample variance, as in the case of sample means and proportions, can function as a point estimator of the population variance σ^2, but in order to make inferences about the population variance beyond this, we need to know the sampling distribution. It is extremely complex to prove that the following quantity can be used in this regard, so you will just have to go along with me on this one. The quantity we need is:

$$\frac{(n-1)s^2}{\sigma^2}$$

---

[2] This is a joke! My wonderful editors have been nothing but supportive throughout this marathon process, and they remained so for the ensuing years – all of them.

[3] Update: so far not.

think it over 13.1

Can you explain why it is not possible to have a negative value for this distribution?

The sampling distribution of this quantity has a chi-squared distribution, with $n - 1$ degrees of freedom, and by now you should be getting more comfortable with dealing with such cases. Because of this helpful chi-square distribution, any time we have a simple random sample of n cases from a normal population, we can relatively easily develop interval estimates of the population variance. Remember, though, that the chi-square distribution changes across different degrees of freedom, and Figure 13.1 gives a classic comparison between three different values of degree of freedom.

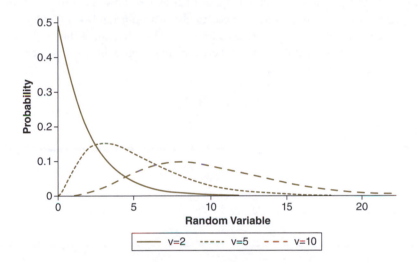

Figure 13.1
Examples of Chi-Square Distribution at Different Degrees of Freedom

Note: 'v' refers to degrees of freedom.

Interval Estimation of a Single Population Variance

Let me return to the touchy subject of length, or, more specifically, whether a firm should be allowed to call its sandwiches 'footlong'. While we would definitely be interested in the population mean of sandwich lengths in this case (see Chapter 8 for this), even if the mean length of a sandwich is 12 inches, the population variance is still important to whether consumers will think we are being truthful. More specifically, if the variance is large, many sandwiches will be much shorter than 12 inches, annoying many customers. Of course, many customers will be pleased with their extra-long sandwiches too. But we all know that complainers make more noise than satisfied customers in such situations.

So, let's take a sample of 30 sandwiches to test. Now, of course, in reality, if we had multiple branches, then we would normally have to test samples from each branch to be sure that the individual methods of each branch did not have an effect. But let's ignore that for now, and imagine we have only one shop to worry about.

We take our sample of 30 and find that the sample variance for the sandwich length is $s^2 = 0.4$ inches. Seems OK. Although, admittedly, it is hard really to know how much a sandwich company would really tolerate. As you know, this is not all we need to do – we need to calculate an interval estimate of this sample value.

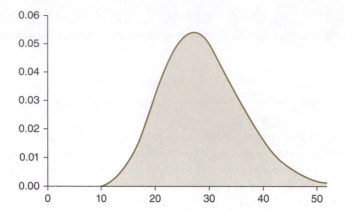

Figure 13.2
Chi-Square
Distribution
with 29
Degrees of
Freedom

To begin, let us use χ^2_α to represent the value of the chi-square distribution that gives us the probability of α to the right of the value of χ^2_α. Check out Figure 13.2, which shows a chi-square distribution with 29 degrees of freedom – which is the one we need to deal with our sandwich problem. If we want to determine a 95% confidence interval estimate, then we need to determine the $\chi^2_{0.025}$ and $\chi^2_{0.975}$ values, because 95% of the chi-square distribution falls between these two points. So, as such, there is a 95% probability of getting a χ^2 value such that:

$$\chi^2_{0.975} \leq \chi^2 \leq \chi^2_{0.025}$$

 think it over 13.2

Up until now, when we have used a z- or t-distribution with, typically, a confidence interval of 95%, we have used the critical value α divided by 2. We are not doing the same with this distribution; can you explain why?

You can look up in the chi-square table that, for a chi-square distribution with 29 degrees of freedom, $\chi^2_{0.025} = 45.722$ and $\chi^2_{0.975} = 16.047$. This means that 2.5% of the values in the chi-square distribution with 29 degrees of freedom are to the right of 45.722, and 97.5% of the values are to the right of 16.047.

Because $\dfrac{(n-1)s^2}{\sigma^2}$ follows the chi-square distribution, we substitute $\dfrac{(n-1)s^2}{\sigma^2}$ for χ^2 to get:

$$\chi^2_{0.975} \leq \frac{(n-1)s^2}{\sigma^2} \leq \chi^2_{0.025}$$

If you are getting a little lost, stop and consider what is really happening here. What the expression above does is provide an estimate such that 95% of all possible values of $\dfrac{(n-1)s^2}{\sigma^2}$ will be contained within the interval between, $\chi^2_{0.025}$ and $\chi^2_{0.975}$.

But how does this help us? Well, a little algebraic manipulation should clarify things:

$$\chi^2_{0.975} \leq \frac{(n-1)s^2}{\sigma^2}$$

so

$$\sigma^2 \chi^2_{0.975} \leq (n-1)s^2$$

or

$$\sigma^2 \leq \frac{(n-1)s^2}{\chi^2_{0.975}}$$

And, of course, if we do the same to the other side we can get to:

$$\frac{(n-1)s^2}{\chi^2_{0.025}} \leq \sigma^2$$

Then it is a simple matter of combining the last two expressions to get to:

$$\frac{(n-1)s^2}{\chi^2_{0.025}} \leq \sigma^2 \leq \frac{(n-1)s^2}{\chi^2_{0.975}}$$

Thus, we have an expression which can now give us the 95% confidence interval estimate for the population variance!

Now, it is just a simple case of substituting in the values we have already found for the sample variance, sample size and the values of $\chi^2_{0.025}$ and $\chi^2_{0.975}$ to get our interval estimate, as follows:

$$\frac{(29)(0.4)}{45.72} \leq \sigma^2 \leq \frac{(29)(0.4)}{16.05}$$

or

$$0.25 \leq \sigma^2 \leq 0.72$$

think it over 13.3

Translate the mathematical relationship $0.25 \leq \sigma^2 \leq 0.72$ into plain English.

Now, one thing that might catch you out in substituting values is the notation of s^2 and χ^2. Remember, these are the sample standard deviation and chi-square values respectively. There is no need to 'square' them when you substitute them in, as you can see in the example above.

So there you go, a bit of algebraic lifting required, but it is quite simple in the end to get the interval estimate. Importantly, just because I used an example of a 95% interval, this does not mean that you are restricted to 95% intervals. In fact, the expression can be generalized to any confidence level as shown below:

$$\frac{(n-1)s^2}{\chi^2_{\left(\frac{\alpha}{2}\right)}} \leq \sigma^2 \leq \frac{(n-1)s^2}{\chi^2_{\left(1-\frac{\alpha}{2}\right)}}$$

Testing Hypotheses about a Single Population Variance

The procedure for testing hypotheses about a single population variance relies on the same basic principles you already know, although it may take just a little effort for you to put them all together. Let's begin by presenting the different forms for hypothesis tests about a population variance, remembering that σ^2_0 represents the hypothesized population variance:

$$H_0 : \sigma^2 \leq \sigma^2_0 \qquad H_0 : \sigma^2 = \sigma^2_0 \qquad H_0 : \sigma^2 \geq \sigma^2_0$$
$$H_1 : \sigma^2 > \sigma^2_0 \qquad H_1 : \sigma^2 \neq \sigma^2_0 \qquad H_1 : \sigma^2 < \sigma^2_0$$

I am confident that you will recognize these forms from earlier chapters on hypothesis testing, but, if not, do go back and recap these.

The basic hypothesis testing process in this case relies on the chi-square, just as the interval estimation process does. In essence, we use the hypothesized population variance and the sample variance to compute a chi-square statistic:

$$\chi^2 = \frac{(n-1)s^2}{\sigma^2_0}$$

In order to use this statistic, one must assume the population is normally distributed, and once the statistic is computed, it can be used as normal to decide whether or not to reject the null hypothesis.

 think it over 13.4

Read the last paragraph again, particularly the assumption 'the population is normally distributed'. Which variables in the above equation refer to a normal distribution? Do they refer to the same normal distribution?

The best way to cement this in your brain is by an example. Let me use something that is very close to my heart – train times. In many countries, including the UK where I am living at present, passenger train operators are evaluated by way of how often their trains arrive on time. If they do not perform at a certain level, they can be penalized by the government. One way of doing this would simply be to calculate the ratio of trains arriving on time versus not. Another way would be to estimate the population variance by way of a sample. Doing so would reduce the burden on train operators to collect data on every train arrival time, and perhaps would be preferable.

Of course, train operators would like low variance in arrival times, so that their trains can be considered reliable.[4] The UK government can set a target of 2 for the variance in arrival times, where the time is measured in minutes, and this allows us to set up a simple hypothesis test:

$$H_0 : \sigma^2 \le 2$$
$$H_1 : \sigma^2 > 2$$

If we assume that the null hypothesis is true, we assume that the population variance for the train arrival times is within UK government guidelines, so the train operator will not receive a fine. Alternatively, H_0 is rejected if our sample evidence suggests that the population variance exceeds the guideline. We would of course expect that the train operator would take some remedial steps to solve the problem.

Before we begin, we need to specify a significance value, and we will use $\alpha = 0.05$. Let's take a sample of 30 train arrivals at Birmingham New Street (near my office), and calculate the sample variance, finding that $s^2 = 2.8$ in minutes. We must assume that the distribution of the population of arrival times is at least approximately normal, and then we can calculate the test statistic:

$$\chi^2 = \frac{(n-1)s^2}{\sigma_0^2} = \frac{(30-1)\_(2.8)}{2} = 40.6$$

In order to interpret this test statistic we must consult the chi-square table, looking for the distribution with $n - 1 = 29$ degrees of freedom. Also, we have to remember that this is an upper-tail test, which means that the area under the chi-square distribution curve to the right of the test statistic (40.6) is the p-value for the hypothesis test.

However, on consulting the table, you will find that there is not enough detail to determine the p-value exactly. Even so we can use the table to get a range for the p-value at least, and use that to make our decision. You should see that for a chi-square distribution with 29 degrees of freedom, the test statistic we have calculated (40.6) falls somewhere between the exact values for 0.1 in the upper tail (39.087) and 0.05 in the upper tail (42.557). As such, our calculated test statistic is less than 42.557,

---

[4] A train company would also typically estimate the mean arrival time (perhaps by way of measuring a sample of trains for how late or early they were) as well as the variance, but we will ignore that for this chapter as it has been covered elsewhere in the book.

which means that the area in the upper tail (i.e. the p-value) is more than 0.05. As such, $p > 0.05$, and we cannot reject H_0. So, our sample result suggests that the variance in arrival times in the population is not excessive. Of course, most of the time, one would use IBM SPSS Statistics Software (SPSS) or some other software package to calculate the exact p-value, but the decision would be the same.

You could also use the critical value method to test the hypotheses, and, to be honest, if you were doing this by hand you would probably prefer to do so. For $\alpha = 0.05$, $\chi^2_{0.025}$ gives the critical value for an upper-tail hypothesis test. Looking at the chi-square table, using 29 degrees of freedom, then it is simple enough to see that $\chi^2_{0.05} = 52.335$. Using this, the rejection rule for the hypothesis test in our train time example is then:

$$\text{Reject } H_0 \text{ if } \chi^2_{0.05} \geq 52.335$$

Because the test statistic is 40.6, you cannot reject the null hypothesis.

You might be wondering why I have been talking only about upper-tail hypotheses. It is a good question, and shows that you are starting to get to grips with this stuff. Well, in practice, it is much more common to encounter an upper-tail test in situations of inferences about population variances than anything else. Most usually, the situation is that a large variance in some value (e.g. departure times, sandwich lengths, engineering dimensions and the like) is a bad thing, so we often have some maximum allowable variance we can accept. As such, the upper-tail test works well, since some action will be taken to solve the problem if the hypothesis test rejects the null hypothesis. Of course, you could also conduct lower-tail tests, using the same concepts you already know.

But what about the two-tailed situation? Well, we can also develop a method for conducting a two-tailed test, and in this case we would be interested in determining whether the population variance was less *or* more than some hypothesized value. While it is not that easy to think intuitively of a situation where this might be useful, some careful consideration will turn up a few ideas. For example, imagine a typical testing situation. Most readers of this book will have already experienced many exams and tests. Imagine a national exam in maths for schoolchildren. Such a test will naturally have some variance in test scores. If the exam changes each year, it would stand to reason that for it to remain fair across different years, the variance should remain basically the same. Think about it: unless the mathematical ability of the population changes, then why should there be a difference in either the mean or variance of the test scores across the population? So, really we should make sure this is not a problem if we change the maths exam to a new one. In fact, this kind of debate happens all the time – at least once a year when school exams come up, and everyone complains about exams being different these days. Most of the time, people restrict their ill-informed complaints to the idea that the mean grades are increasing. But next time this happens, you will be able to show them how simplistic their arguments are by explaining that the variance is probably much more important.

So, say the population variance of the old maths exam was $\sigma^2 = 20$ points, and because the exam setting organization wants variance in scores for the new exam to remain at this level, the two-tailed hypothesis test is:

$$H_0: \sigma^2 = 20$$
$$H_1: \sigma^2 \neq 20$$

If we reject the null hypothesis, it signifies that something about the new exam might need changing to make sure it is consistent and fair. So, we take a sample of 20 students for our test and decide as usual on $\alpha = 0.05$ for our significance level. Our sample provides a sample variance $s^2 = 32$, and, as such, the chi-square test statistic can be calculated as follows:

$$\chi^2 = \frac{(n-1)s^2}{\sigma_0^2} = \frac{(20-1)(32)}{20} = 30.4$$

You will use the same procedure as before to get first a one-tailed p-value from the chi-square tables – remember to use 19 degrees of freedom. You can see that the test statistic of 30.4 falls somewhere between 0.05 and 0.025 in the upper tail of the chi-square distribution. So, doubling those values (because it is a two-tailed test, remember) means the two-tailed p-value must be between 0.1 and 0.05. Again, if you must, you could use SPSS or something similar to show the exact p-value.

Because the two-tailed p-value is greater than 0.05, we should accept H_0 and conclude that the new exam scores have a variance that is not different from the variance of the old exam scores.

Figure 13.3 gives a handy reference guide to the various tests and decision rules for testing hypotheses in this context. You might recognize it, as it is similar to those in Chapter 8. But it is just as useful, so do not ignore it.

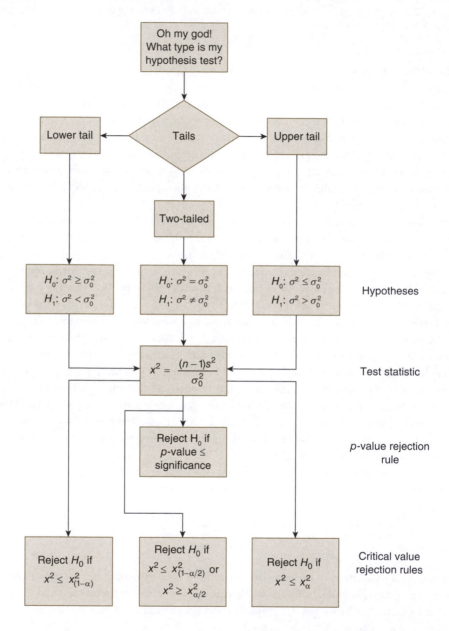

Figure 13.3
Decision Rules for Hypothesis Tests about a Single Population Variance

INFERENCES ABOUT TWO POPULATION VARIANCES

The most common situation in making inferences about population variances is in my experience covered above. However, there will be times when you are asked to make some inference about two population variances. Imagine for example you are the production manager for a large multi-site manufacturer of car parts. You might be interested in the variances of the diameter of driveshafts made by each production line, for example.

Of course, in order to make inferences about two population variances, you need data from two independent random samples. You can then use the sample variance from each population as the basis for inference. However, there are a few more steps to go through before you can do so in the case of two population variances, so perhaps a bit of terminology clarification will help:

The variance of population 1 is denoted as σ_1^2.

A simple random sample of population 1 is termed sample 1, and its variance is s_1^2.

The variance of population 2 is denoted as σ_2^2.

A simple random sample of population 2 is termed sample 2, and its variance is s_1^2.

We can draw inferences about the differences between the two population variances by thinking about what would happen if the two population variances were equal – or in other words when $\sigma_1^2 = \sigma_2^2$. In this case, we are in luck, because the sampling distribution of $\frac{s_1^2}{s_2^2}$ can be described with an *F*-distribution. This is set out in Box 13.1.

 box 13.1

Using the *F*-distribution in Inferences about Population Variances

If two independent simple random samples (sample 1 and sample 2) of n_1 and n_2 elements are drawn from two normal populations (population 1 and population 2) with equal variances, the sampling distribution of:

$$\frac{s_1^2}{s_2^2}$$

has an *F*-distribution, where the degrees of freedom for the numerator are equal to $n_1 - 1$ and the degrees of freedom for the denominator are equal to $n_2 - 1$.

The basic principles from here on are the same as you should already be used to. Like the chi-square, the *F*-distribution changes shape according to the degrees of freedom, but in this case there are two to take account of – in the numerator and denominator. It is simple enough to take account of this by reading the table carefully. Further, the *F* value can never be negative.[5]

The designation F_α can be used to denote the value of *F* that gives the probability of α in the upper tail of the distribution. As usual, you can find the specific value by referring to an *F*-distribution table and making sure to take account of the two different values for degrees of freedom that are needed. Of course, in practice, software is usually employed, but, again, it is useful to gain a basic appreciation of the steps required to do it by hand, as in many things in life.

So, let's get on with an example, shall we? Recall the brief driveshaft example from just above. Imagine you owned a large company, with two manufacturing sites, and your company made driveshafts for Jaguar. You would naturally be interested in whether the production processes at each plant produced driveshafts of equal dimensions – or as much as possible. You certainly would not want any systematic differences between the sites, such as shafts from one site being more variable than shafts from the other.

---

[5] Think about it: could you ever get a negative value on the denominator or numerator, given that they represent sample sizes? If you could, it would mean at least one of your sample sizes was zero or less! In that case, you'd have more to worry about than a negative *F* statistic.

This is a classic situation where you need to use the F-distribution to conduct a hypothesis test about whether the variances of the two populations are the same. This is how your hypotheses are stated:

$$H_0: \sigma_1^2 = \sigma_2^2$$
$$H_1: \sigma_1^2 \neq \sigma_2^2$$

Since the null hypothesis states that the two population variances are equal, rejecting it will allow you to draw the conclusion that they are not equal.

First, you need to draw two independent random samples, one from each population, and compute the sample variance from each. Now, there is an additional bit of terminology to remember:

Population 1 is always the population which provides the *larger sample variance*.

With that in mind, and assuming both populations are normally distributed, you can compute the F statistic as the ratio of the two sample variances:

$$F = \frac{s_1^2}{s_2^2}$$

It should eventually become apparent that, because the larger sample variance is the numerator (population 1, remember?), then the value of the test statistic will always be in the upper tail, which in turn allows F tables to provide only upper-tail areas. This is a nice simplification.

think it over 13.5

Looking at the equation for calculating the F statistic, what value would you get if both variances had the same value? How would you interpret this result?

So, let's return to the example where a company has two manufacturing sites. For the purposes of our example, site 1 is in London and site 2 is in Middlesbrough. Remember, the hypotheses are:

$$H_0: \sigma_1^2 = \sigma_2^2$$
$$H_1: \sigma_1^2 \neq \sigma_2^2$$

If we reject the null hypothesis, we conclude that the two manufacturing sites differ in the variance of their production, which is likely to be a problem for Jaguar. Because we are dealing with highly precise engineering here, we will use $\alpha = 0.1$ as our significance level. This is explained in a bit more detail in Above and Beyond Box 13.1.

above and beyond

Box 13.1   Error and Tolerance

In the present situation, Jaguar really needs the production processes across the manufacturing unit to be as close as possible. There is little margin for error here, because the parts are so important. As such, Jaguar will make a decision about which error it is most willing to accept.

Recall Chapter 8, where you learned about Type I and Type II errors. Well, Jaguar would much rather make a Type I error than a Type II error. In other words, Jaguar would rather reject the null hypothesis if it was true in the population than accept the null if the alternative was in fact true in the population.

Why is this so? Consider the two situations. If we commit a Type I error, we may unnecessarily take some corrective action at the two manufacturing sites. This may be unnecessarily expensive, but it is not likely to be detrimental. However, if we commit a Type II error here, we will incorrectly take no action, continuing to allow the two manufacturing plants to churn out different shafts. This is likely to be far more harmful than the alternative Type I error.

Think about this more carefully, by looking at what the test is trying to do. Remember that, in this case, accepting the null is what the company would like to do, and we are making it harder to do so by decreasing the chances of a Type II error.

In other cases, for example when we are hoping to detect differences between groups (e.g. whether a drug works), we might use significance values of 0.01, or even 0.001, to lower the chances of a Type I error.

It all depends on the potential harm of each of the two (accept or reject the null) conclusions.

OK, so with our significance level decided on, we need to go and get two samples. We take a sample of 26 driveshafts from the London site, and find a sample variance for the length of 3 millimetres, and 31 from the Middlesbrough site, which provides a sample variance for the length of 1.5 millimetres. Now, recalling our rule above, because the London site provided the largest sample variance, we denote that as population 1. With this in mind, it is simple to solve the equation to get the F- ratio:

$$F = \frac{s_1^2}{s_2^2} = \frac{3}{1.5} = 2$$

The F-distribution in this case has $n_1 - 1 = 25$ degrees of freedom in the numerator, and $n_2 - 1 = 30$ degrees of freedom in the denominator.

As usual, let's begin by using the p-value approach to test the hypothesis. Looking at the F tables, let's find the area in the upper tail for various p-values. If you do so, you will find that $F = 2$ falls somewhere between the F values for a p-value of 0.05 and 0.025.

However, because this is a two-tailed test, we need to double this, and as such our p-value is somewhere between 0.1 and 0.05. Because, in this case, our $\alpha = 0.1$, our p-value is less than $\alpha = 0.1$, and we must reject the null hypothesis. As such, we have to conclude that the two manufacturing sites do differ in the variance of driveshaft length.

Again, as usual, you would most often use SPSS or another software package to give an exact value for the two-tailed p-value for $F = 2$ and those degrees of freedom, but the basic conclusion would be the same.

Of course, you can also use the critical value approach to hypothesis testing here. For $\alpha = 0.1$ significance, you simply work out critical values for the area of $\alpha/2 = 0.1/2 = 0.05$ in each tail of the F distribution. Remember, though, that the F value you calculate is always in the upper tail, so you only need to find the upper-tail critical value. Thus, looking at the F-distribution for 25 degrees of freedom in the numerator, and 30 degrees of freedom in the denominator (from the above example), you will find that $F_{0.05} = 1.88$. Because of this, even though the test we want in this case is two-tailed, we can state our critical rejection rule as:

$$\text{Reject } H_0 \text{ if } F \geq 1.88$$

Of course, you should remember that $F = 2$ in the above example. As such, we reject the null hypothesis, just as we did when we used the p-value approach (of course).

It is also quite simple to do a one-tailed hypothesis test for two population variances. However, remember that it is always formulated as an upper-tail test, meaning that the p-value and critical value are always in the upper tail of the F-distribution, and you only need to compute upper-tail F values. This is how the hypothesis test looks:

$$H_0: \sigma_1^2 \leq \sigma_2^2$$
$$H_1: \sigma_1^2 > \sigma_2^2$$

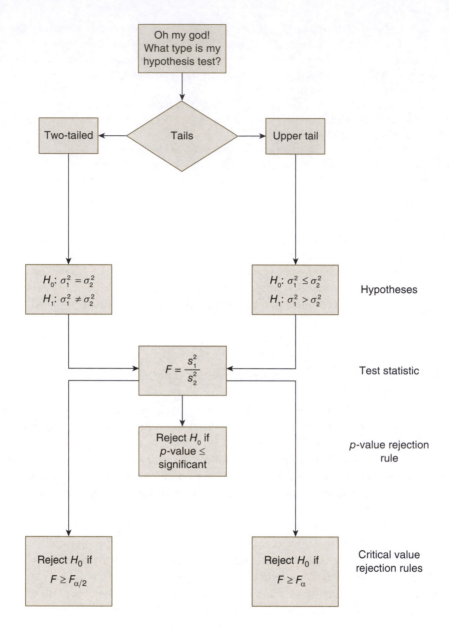

Figure 13.4
Decision
Rules for
Hypothesis
Tests
about Two
Population
Variances

Let's see an example. Imagine you are the sales director for a large pharmaceutical company. You might be interested in the variances in expense account usage between low- and high-performing salespeople – you suspect that the higher-performing salespeople are more creative and adaptive with the way they work with clients and solve problems, which should lead to more variability in their expense claims. On the other hand, you suspect low performers to have pretty consistent expense claim amounts.[6]

So, we will use a sample of 16 high performers and 11 low performers to test our hypothesis. More specifically, we want to test whether the sample data gives us evidence that high performers show greater variability in their expense claims than low performers. Because of the form of one-tailed hypothesis test, high performers will be denoted population 1 and low performers will be denoted population 2. As such, the hypothesis test is:

---

[6] Incidentally, you also suspect the mean expense claim value will be low for low performers, but this is not the subject of this particular test.

$$H_0: \sigma^2_{\text{high}} \leq \sigma^2_{\text{low}}$$
$$H_1: \sigma^2_{\text{high}} > \sigma^2_{\text{low}}$$

If we can reject the null hypothesis, we can conclude that high performers do show a higher variance on expense claims.

The sample variance for high performers is in the numerator and the sample variance for low performers is in the denominator. Therefore, the F-distribution will have $n-1 = 15$ degrees of freedom in the numerator and $n-1 = 10$ degrees of freedom in the denominator. The level of significant chosen for the test is $\alpha = 0.05$. The sample variance for high performers is 220 and for low performers 180. As such, the test statistic can be calculated as:

$$F = \frac{s_1^2}{s_2^2} = \frac{220}{180} = 1.22$$

We can then refer to an F table to find the distribution with 15 degrees of freedom in the numerator and 10 degrees of freedom in the denominator. In doing so, we will find that F for $\alpha = 0.1$ is 2.32. This means that because our calculated F of 1.22 is less than 2.32, then the area in the upper tail must be greater than 0.1. As such, our p-value is greater than $\alpha = 0.05$, and we cannot reject the null hypothesis. Our sample results do not support our hypothesis that high performers have higher variation than low performers on expense claims. Figure 13.4 shows what should be a now familiar decision process for hypothesis tests about two population variances.

USING EXCEL

Excel does have built-in functions for the χ^2_2 test but, for our purposes in this chapter, we will have to calculate the value for χ^2_2 and use the Excel function =CHISQ.DIST.RT to find the probabilities.

The file 'train times chi.xslx' contains the data for the difference between the time a train is supposed to arrive and the time it actually arrived. If you look at Figure 13.5 you will see the necessary calculations that need to be done first. Figure 13.6 shows where to find the procedure needed to calculate the probability. It also shows the result in cell D8.

Doing the F-test in Excel is reasonably straightforward. The thing to remember is that Excel will perform a two-tailed test and assume the variances are not significantly different. We will use the data in 'Ftest data.xslx' to demonstrate how to do an F-test with Excel. Staying with the theme of comparing actual train arrival times with the times they are supposed to arrive, we will compare two stations from the same company. In theory, there should not be any significant difference between the variances.

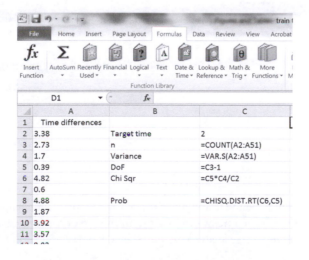

Figure 13.5

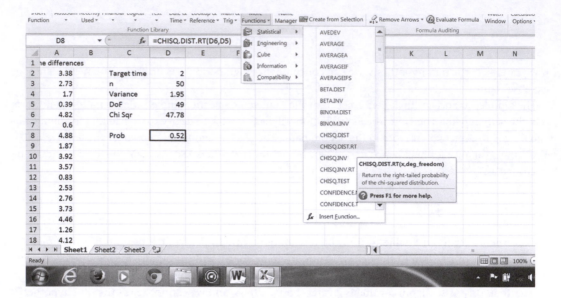

Figure 13.6

Figure 13.7 shows some of the data and where to find the *F*-test within Excel's menu system. Figure 13.8 shows the result of running the test. As you can see, the probability of there not being a difference between the variances is about 9%, which means there is a 91% chance they are different (in strict stats speak, we would say the probability of achieving an *F* value of 1.63 due to chance is about 9%). If you calculate the *F* value var_A/var_B (1.63) you will see it is greater than the value 1.53, found in a table, which means we reject the null hypothesis. In other words, one station is outperforming the other, but which one is best? Further investigation is required.

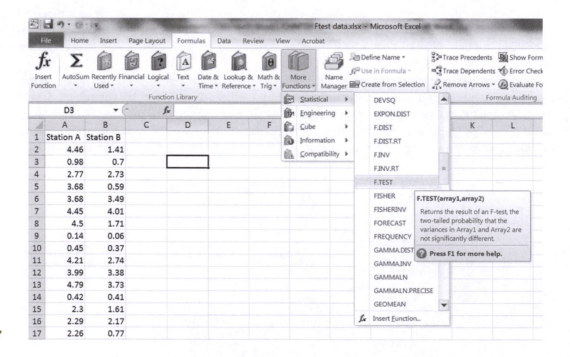

Figure 13.7

Unfortunately, SPSS does not have the facility to calculate the *F* statistic independently of more comprehensive tests such as ANOVA. Therefore, we will wait until the next chapter to deal with this statistic in the context of a more comprehensive analysis method (i.e. ANOVA).

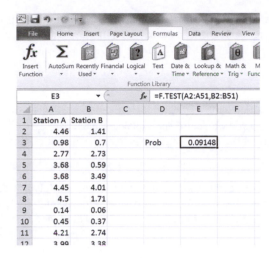

Figure 13.8

SUMMARY

So, that was kind of short and perhaps even sweet, but it is an important technique which I feel is quite underused. It does also recap some of the more important skills that you have learned so far in this book, such as confidence intervals, and using distributional tables. In this way, it is similar to the previous chapter, and by now you should be getting good at comparing groups, testing hypotheses and using distributional tables.

The next chapter will introduce the extremely valuable technique of ANOVA, which along with regression forms the basis of most statistical analysis tasks. Interestingly, I will show that ANOVA really can be thought of in terms of regression itself, which should help you gain a good grip of it.

 final checklist

You should have covered and understood the following basic content in this chapter:

☑ The concept of a population variance and why it might be important in research terms.

☑ How to calculate interval estimates and test hypotheses about a single population variance using a sample.

☑ How to test hypotheses about two population variances.

EXERCISES

1. You have been given a job where you have to investigate the manufacturing costs of a company which has two factories located within the UK and one in the USA. The company produces a range of fasteners for the aerospace industry and as such these are known as safety-critical components; in other words, people's lives depend upon your product doing its job properly. In addition to the safety-critical aspect of your products there is also the issue of limited space.

   a. Write down the features of your products which could be subjected to statistical analysis in terms of population variances.

   b. In whose best interest is it for your products to be produced within an acceptable tolerance?

2. Write down the hypothesis you would use to check if a production run of stainless steel bolts meets an agreed specification. The bolt has to be 54.35 ± 0.01 mm in length.

3. In one of the factories a sample taken from a production run of the bolts from question 2, has a mean length of 54.354 mm. In terms of quality control, would this production run be acceptable? Give reasons for your answer.

4. The two UK factories produce the same fasteners (bolts). You have been given the population variance from each factory.

   a. To compare the population variances, which test would you use?
   b. Write down the formula you would use and explain each element.
   c. Write down and interpret the possible outcomes of applying your chosen test.

5. You have decided that your null hypothesis is that there is no significant difference between the variances.

   a. Explain the significance of committing a Type I error within a safety-critical industry.
   b. Explain the significance of committing a Type II error within a safety-critical industry.
   c. Which, if any, would be preferable from the company's point of view? Give reasons for your answer.

 To access additional online resources please visit: **https://study.sagepub.com/leepeters**

The Ballad of Eddie the Easily Distracted: Part 14

Eddie was even more confused than usual. This week's QUAN101 work had been quite difficult, but what confused Eddie this time was that he almost 'got' it. In fact, the idea of ANOVA had seemed kind of clear(-ish) to him. After all, it was really just seeing if groups were different, and he could get that. It reminded him a lot of when he was at school. Certainly, he remembered that the sporty boys seemed to generally do worse at exams than the geeky kids, while the group of friends he belonged to, who mainly listened to music and played computer games (Eddie liked to refer to them as the 'nobodies') were somewhere in the middle. It was pretty easy for Eddie to transfer the ideas of ANOVA to this situation, and imagine doing a quick study of whether the exam scores really were different across the groups, or whether that was just what people expected to see.

Eddie also found the explanation of ANOVA easier to understand than he expected, because it was very much the same as the regression model he'd struggled so hard with earlier on. In fact, the thing that confused him the most was that this week it was Esha who was struggling a little to get it. He couldn't work this one out at all, but he was inordinately proud of himself for helping Esha even a little: 'look Esha, it's just like dummy variables in regression, isn't it?' he had said, which helped. Although it didn't help as much as when he said 'in fact, wasn't that what you called me once?'

Esha's Story: Part 14

This time, Esha was just as confused as Eddie. Which, in itself, was very confusing. Furthermore, this metaconfusion was not helping at all (although Esha was quite pleased with herself for thinking of that term, and wondered whether Philosophy 106 was in fact paying off). This was the first time she had had to struggle with the QUAN101 content, and it was all because Professor Smarty Pants had decided to teach ANOVA by treating it as a special case of regression, rather than in the way she'd learnt at school. Even though she'd done fine with regression ('Thank you very much' as she'd said irritably to Eddie when he'd tried to help), it was proving hard for her to forget some of the things from school. Even though they meant the same thing of course, everything was getting mixed up in her head. Esha supposed that this new approach to ANOVA was going to be worth it, because she could see it was simpler, but she was tremendously annoyed at the whole thing.

Still, she thought, it was good of Eddie to spend some time trying to help her, even though she'd been a bit embarrassed to accept his help after secretly thinking for most of the year that he was a bit dim. Perhaps he wasn't as dull as she'd thought. Certainly, he was a good teacher when he set his mind to it. He was very patient, and Esha could really see that he had a good way of explaining things, quite original. It was probably because he knew just what it was like to have no idea what was going on, she thought. Maybe that was something to mull over for future reference.

ANOVA

CONTENTS

 learning objectives

There is a lot of content in this chapter. However, it will help if you boil it down to some key objectives. Try to keep these in mind to avoid getting lost in all the information:

- ☑ Understand the key concepts of experimental design and, with them, the reasons behind an ANOVA approach.
- ☑ Learn how ANOVA can be understood in a regression context.
- ☑ Learn how to calculate sums of squares, mean squares and associated *F* statistics.
- ☑ Learn how to test for the significance of the overall effects in ANOVA.
- ☑ Learn how to use multiple comparison tests to interrogate ANOVA results in more detail.
- ☑ Learn how to include covariates in an ANCOVA analysis,
- ☑ Learn how to design a randomized block experiment and use ANOVA to analyse it.
- ☑ Learn how to design a two-factor factorial experiment and use two-way ANOVA to analyse it.

At this point, you have learned a lot. So you should be quite proud of yourself. This, to my mind at least, is the last chapter that deals with an 'essential' technique for all analysts in all fields. After this, the remaining chapters collect up more analytic methods which are more appropriate for specialized tasks. But enough about them (who knows what will happen in the future?). This chapter introduces the 'other' major analytic method, ANOVA, the acronym for ANalysis Of VAriance. I mentioned earlier that, along with regression, ANOVA was the key analytic tool for quantitative researchers, and also that different fields tend to be dominated by one or the other. Interestingly, in my opinion, business statistics and analysis are dominated by regression techniques, whereas the more psychological fields tend to be dominated by ANOVA techniques. For example, Andy Field's excellent *Discovering Statistics Using IBM SPSS Statistics* has six chapters on ANOVA and its various derivatives (e.g. MANOVA, ANCOVA and so forth), and somewhat less emphasis than this book on regression-based methods like time series models and forecasting – which are essential in a business context.

In fact, when I was a business student, I do not even remember studying ANOVA, and I think a lot of business statistics teachers are similarly regression focused. While this is understandable, because business research projects comparatively rarely use the experimental designs that are so common in fields like psychology and medicine, it is a real shame for two reasons. First, an understanding of experiments and how to analyse them has a lot to offer in creating good business research designs, but, secondly, ANOVA is actually almost the same as regression! In fact, it is a real misconception that ANOVA and regression are completely separate methods, since you will see here that ANOVA really reduces to a special case of regression, based on dummy variables – remember them?

I think that the approach to ANOVA presented here[1] has a lot to offer to business statistics education, and I really hope you can follow along and see how ANOVA really is quite simple. So, with this in mind, let us begin.

A BRIEF DIVERSION INTO EXPERIMENTAL DESIGN

In Chapter 12 I introduced the idea of experiments (and quasi-experiments), and I would like to revisit it in a little more depth here. Again, though, let me make the point that this is most definitely not a research design textbook – there are many other books out there for that. This is a book on data analysis, so I am going to talk about experiments in the service of data analysis. Now, this is kind of the wrong way around – the analysis should always be subservient to the experimental purpose – but here it makes sense. Specifically, you need to know in brief whether ANOVA suits your experimental purpose before you decide to use it.

So, with this in mind, let me explain the most basic experimental design, the true randomized experiment. An experiment is usually defined as a study in which at least one variable is somehow controlled in order to determine how it influences some consequence variable. Imagine a situation where you are the vice president of sales for a large photocopier manufacturer, and you want to test the most effective incentive (i.e. reward) plan for your salespeople. To this end, you want to compare three possible plans: Plan A where salespeople are paid only on commission; Plan B where there is only a salary paid; and Plan C which is a mix of both.

First, let us define the dependent variable as the variable that we are interested in seeing whether there are differences in, between the different groups in your experiment (e.g. is one group higher in this variable than the other(s)?). So in this case, it is sales performance. The dependent variable is also sometimes referred to as the response variable. The independent variable is the variable we suspect may have an impact on the dependent one. So in this case the independent variable is the incentive plan. When dealing with experimental studies, the independent variable is also often called the factor variable, and we

---

[1] It's only fair to say that I got the idea to do this from Andy Field's book above, and if you use ANOVA-type methods a lot in your later career, you'll benefit from taking a look at that book too.

consider the different values of the factor to be treatments; in the present case, the treatments are Plan A, Plan B and Plan C, which of course define the populations we are interested in. As such, this is what is known as a single-factor experiment, and the incentive plan factor is qualitative (i.e. categorical). Later, we will see multi-factor situations; it is also the case that factors can be quantitative (e.g. drug doses, etc.).

So, we could take a random sample of (for example) 15 salespeople, and then randomly assign one of the three incentive plans to each worker such that we now have three groups of five – each group is incentivized using one of the three plans. This is called a completely randomized design. The salespeople in the experiment are termed experimental units. We would measure their average sales performance (e.g. over two quarters), and there we have the data for our experiment. Figure 14.1 shows this diagrammatically, to help remind you of how it might work.

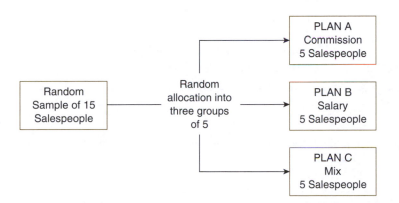

Figure 14.1
Incentive Experiment Design

I will continue this experimental example later on, and even further on I will explain some other experimental designs. But for now, let's move on to a discussion of the ANOVA method itself.

WHY USE ANOVA?

Earlier on in this book you learned how to use techniques like the *t*-test to compare two means, and we have explored quite a few other methods to compare two populations on various other things. But imagine the situation where you have *more than two groups* and you want to test the mean differences. What would you do then? Could you use multiple *t*-tests, for example? Well, imagine you had three groups. If you wanted to use *t*-tests you would have to use more than one, right? First, you would need to test the difference between the means of groups 1 and 2, then groups 1 and 3, and finally groups 2 and 3. Sounds simple enough, but the problem is that doing multiple tests like this increases our Type I error rate. While a lot of analysts simply stop asking questions at this point and accept this basic fact, if you want to know why, and by how much, error increases, check out Above and Beyond Box 14.1.

above and beyond

Box 14.1   Experimentwise Error

Imagine a three-group situation where you want to test for potential differences in the means across groups. As already shown, you would need to do three *t*-tests to compare the three groups fully. If we use a 0.05 level of significance, then as you should remember the probability of a Type I error (falsely

(Continued)

(Continued)

rejecting the null) is 5%. As such, the probability of no Type I error for each test is 0.95 (95%). We can assume each test is independent, and therefore we can multiply the probabilities to get the overall probability of no Type I error for the set of three tests: $(0.95)^3 = 0.95 \times 0.95 \times 0.95 = 0.857$. Subtract this from 1 (the maximum probability of anything) to get the probability of at least one Type I error in the set of tests: $1 - 0.857 = 0.143$. So, across the group of tests, the probability of making a Type I error has increased from 5% to 14.3%. Of course, this is far higher than your intended Type I error chance of 5%. This increase in the probability of Type I error is called experimentwise error (or familywise error). And the problem gets worse the more groups you have in your design. Once you get to five groups, you need 10 t-tests, and this blows the experimentwise error up to 40%! You can easily calculate the experimentwise error in this situation with the following equation:

$$1 - (1 - \alpha)^n$$

where of course n is the number of tests and $(1 - \alpha)$ is the probability of no Type I error for each independent test (i.e. 1 – the level of significance α).

---

 think it over 14.1

You have conducted an experiment involving three random samples from a population and plotted the distributions. The three distributions overlap in their tails but show separate means. Can you tell if, say, the dependent variable from sample 1 has an effect on the results from sample 2? Sketch three normally distributed samples with overlapping tails to clarify your thinking.

So, if we cannot use multiple t-tests, we have to have some other technique, and the answer to our conundrum is ANOVA. Think back to just above where I explained the sales incentive experiment and the data you would collect to test it. The data from the 15 salespeople can be used to test the null hypothesis that the mean sales performance for all three groups is the same. We can define population 1 as the salespeople on Plan A, population 2 as the salespeople on Plan B, and population 3 as the salespeople on Plan C. Therefore:

$$\mu_1 = \text{mean sales performance for population 1}$$

$$\mu_2 = \text{mean sales performance for population 2}$$

$$\mu_3 = \text{mean sales performance for population 3}$$

Of course, it is impossible to know the true population values, and so we use the sample results to test the hypotheses:

$$H_0: \mu_1 = \mu_2 = \mu_3$$

$$H_1: \text{the population means are not all equal}$$

ANOVA is the method of choice for this hypothesis test.

Now, it is not necessary that we have an experimental situation in order to use ANOVA. Any situation in which we can define groups can be analysed with an ANOVA method, as long as you can satisfy the assumptions of ANOVA (see Box 14.1). So, because of this potential for confusion, it will help if we settle on some common terminology. We mentioned these earlier, but let's recap. We define the dependent variable as the variable on which we are interested in determining the difference between the groups (remember, it is also sometimes referred to as the response variable). So in this case, it is sales performance. The independent variable is the variable we suspect may have an impact on the dependent one. So in this case the independent variable is the incentive plan. Remember: the independent variable is also sometimes called the factor variable. Sometimes, the different values of the independent variable are considered to be treatments, and in the present case the treatments are Plan A, Plan B and Plan C, which of course define the populations we are interested in.

 box 14.1

Assumptions of ANOVA

There are only three main assumptions required if you want to use ANOVA, and unless we have reason to believe otherwise, we usually assume they hold:

1. In each population, the dependent variable must be normally distributed.
2. The variance of the dependent variable must be the same for all populations (the assumption of equal variance).
3. The observations must be independent. In other words, the score for the independent variable (e.g. sales performance) for one salesperson must be independent of that for any other.

ANOVA as Regression

I have already alluded to the split between ANOVA and regression in terms of the different preferences of various groups of researchers over the years. It is outside our scope here to give you a history lesson, but suffice it to say the split has led to most people thinking ANOVA and regression are completely separate things, and as such need to be taught using separate concepts and in different ways. However, this is not really true at all, and regression can be used as the fundamental base to teach ANOVA very effectively. More so, I think it is especially important in the context of a business statistics course, because regression techniques are so fundamental to business analysis methods. There are many other benefits to teaching ANOVA within a regression framework – not least among them that for complex ANOVA designs the standard ways of explaining ANOVA get very unwieldy and complex – but there is little need to go into them here.[2]

At its core, ANOVA is simply a way of comparing the amount of systematic variance with unsystematic variance in an experimental study. However, as we said that the same concepts apply to both observational and experimental studies, a more general way to represent this idea is to say that it is a way of comparing the amount of variance in the dependent variable which is attributable to the independent variable(s) versus the amount of variance in the dependent variable that is not attributable to the independent variable(s). In an even more general way, it is a method to help us understand *whether the independent variable has an effect on the dependent one*. Now that is three ways of saying the very same thing, honestly, so please do try to take it in.

ANOVA does this comparison by way of the *F*-ratio – which, *of course*, you will recognize from Chapter 10 when you learnt about regression. For a regression model, the *F*-ratio shows how well the regression model predicts the dependent variable compared with the error in the model – which is *exactly the same* as saying that the *F*-ratio is the ratio of the amount of variance in the dependent variable which is

---

[2] That said, the fact that SPSS has moved towards using a regression model for ANOVA is also a compelling reason.

attributable to the independent variable(s) versus the amount of variance in the dependent variable that is not attributable to the independent variable(s). So, the F-ratio in ANOVA is just the same as an F-ratio for a regression model that contains only categorical predictors (which we called dummy variables in regression). So, to sum this up:

An ANOVA model can be represented by a multiple regression model in which the number of predictors is one less than the number of categories of the independent variable.

Let's move back to the sales performance experiment to show this. Remember that you are trying to discover which of three possible incentive plans is most effective: Plan A where salespeople are paid only on commission; Plan B where there is only a salary paid; and Plan C which is a mix of both. The dependent variable in this case is sales performance and the independent variable is the incentive plan (which has three treatment levels). In order to predict sales performance from the different incentive plans, you could use the general model:

$$\text{Outcome}_i = (\text{Model}_i) + \text{Error}_i$$

You can hopefully recognize this basic model from earlier in the book. If we assume our model is linear, then if we have only two groups (as in a t-test situation) we can simply replace the 'model' part of the equation with a categorical dummy variable with two possible values – 0 for one group and 1 for the other. If we have three groups, as in our incentive plan study, we use a multiple regression model with two dummy variables. We can extend this idea to as many groups as we want, with the rule being that the number of dummy variables needed is one less than the number of groups in the study – or in other words, one less than the number of categories of the independent variable (or in even more other words, one less than the number of treatment levels).

One key decision you may remember is that when you have more than two groups, you need to select a baseline group with which you compare the other groups. In many (but by no means all) experimental settings, we have a control group which is the natural base. But this is not always the case. For example, in our incentive study, which group should we choose as the baseline? Well, if one of the three plans is the one you already use, then this is the natural baseline. Otherwise, if there is no obvious choice, then just pick one that makes your hypotheses most meaningful – in other words, the one for which it makes most sense to compare the other groups with.

In this case, we decide Plan A is the baseline group, because the company already used a 100% commission plan. As such, we will be comparing the other two groups with the already standard plan for the company. So, we are therefore interested in comparing the 100% salary, and the salary/commission mix plan, with the 100% commission plan. Thus, if Plan A (100% commission plan) is the base, then we create two dummy variables, one of which represents each of the other two incentive plans. As such, one dummy variable is called 'Salary' and the other is called 'Mix'. The theoretical equation that results is:

$$\text{Sales Performance}_i = \beta_0 + \beta_1 \text{Salary}_i + \beta_2 \text{Mix}_i + \varepsilon_i$$

So, to predict an individual salesperson's performance, we simply need the model intercept (β_0 in the theoretical model, although of course, remembering Chapter 10, we recall that it will be estimated as b_0) and the group codes for the individual which indicate which group he or she belongs to (i.e. the values for the two dummy variables Salary and Mix). The simplest way to code the dummy variables is to give a value of 0 for the baseline (commission) in each case. So, if the salesperson were on a 100% salary incentive plan, they would receive a 1 for the Salary dummy and a 0 for the Mix dummy. If they were on a salary/commission plan, they would get a 0 for the Salary dummy and a 1 for the Mix dummy. If they were on the baseline 100% commission plan, they would score a 0 for both dummies. Table 14.1 shows this in a simple format.

Table 14.1 Dummy coding for the sales incentive experiment

Group	Dummy 1 (Salary)	Dummy 2 (Mix)
100% commission (base)	0	0
100% salary	1	0
Mix	0	1

So, let me explain the model for the baseline commission group, and hopefully things will start to make some sense. Remember, looking at Table 14.1, both dummies will be coded as 0 here, so ignoring the error term ε_1 we estimate:

$$\text{Sales Performance} = b_0 + (b_1 \times 0) + (b_2 \times 0)$$

$$\text{Sales Performance} = b_0$$

$$\bar{x}_{\text{Commission}} = b_0$$

What this means is that the 100% salary and mixed incentive groups are excluded, because of their 0 codes. As such, we are predicting sales performance when the two treatment levels of the independent variable are ignored, and the predicted value of sales performance will be the mean of the 100% commission group – the only group included in the model. So, it can be seen that the intercept b_0 is always the mean of the baseline category (for this case the 100% commission category).

Looking at the 100% salary group, the Salary dummy will be coded 1 and the Mix dummy will be coded 0, so substituting into the equation, we get:

$$\text{Sales Performance}_i = b_0 + (b_1 \times 1) + (b_2 \times 0)$$

$$\text{Sales Performance}_i = b_0 + b_1$$

Similarly, looking at the mixed salary and commission group, the Mix dummy variable is coded as 1, and the Salary as 0, so as such:

$$\text{Sales Performance}_i = b_0 + (b_1 \times 0) + (b_2 \times 1)$$

$$\text{Sales Performance}_i = b_0 + b_2$$

However, we can also discover something else from these equations. More specifically, looking first at the 100% salary group, the model should predict that the value for sales performance should equal the mean of the 100% salary group, in the same way as above where the predicted value of sales performance for the 100% commission group is the mean of that group. This can help us by changing the equation to:

$$\text{Sales Performance} = b_0 + b_1$$

$$\bar{x}_{\text{Salary}} = \bar{x}_{\text{Commission}} + b_1$$

$$b_1 = \bar{x}_{\text{Salary}} - \bar{x}_{\text{Commission}}$$

This means that b_1 represents the difference between the 100% salary group and the baseline 100% commission group.

The situation is just the same when considering the mixed incentive group:

$$\text{Sales Performance} = b_0 + b_2$$

$$\bar{x}_{\text{Mix}} = \bar{x}_{\text{Commission}} + b_2$$

$$b_2 = \bar{x}_{\text{Mix}} - \bar{x}_{\text{Commission}}$$

So, b_2 represents the difference between the means for the mixed incentive group and the baseline 100% commission group. It can be seen that this simple dummy coding scheme can be quite powerful and useful. Of course, there are others available, but this scheme is the best place to start.

think it over 14.2

The example showed how the relationship between the two independent variables affects the outcome. This is one reason why you will see the term model used since different scenarios can be tested using multiple regression equations.

Because of the interdependency between the variables, it is vital that any data you collect must be accurate and fit for purpose.

Before we move on, just remember that the example above was a simple three-group one. The basic approach can be extended to as many groups as you want. The key thing to remember is that you need one less dummy variable than the number of groups. You also need to remember to specify which of the groups is the baseline (in an experiment this will be the control group, but in other cases it may differ, as above).

THE *F*-RATIO

Ultimately, the basic purpose of ANOVA is to compare the means of a number of groups, and test whether they are different or not. In ANOVA, the *F*-ratio is used to test this overall hypothesis. You should remember the *F*-ratio from earlier in the book, when it was introduced as a way of testing the overall fit of a regression model to a set of data. Of course, now, the connection between ANOVA and regression should become even clearer, because, if ANOVA is treated as a special case of regression, this is exactly what the *F*-ratio is doing here too.

First, you must be clear that the null hypothesis for the *F*-test here is that the group means are the same across all groups in the study. If this were the case, then you would not expect to see any differences in the means of the groups in your sample. In other words, there should be no difference in the mean sales performance for the 100% commission group, the 100% salary group or the mixed incentive group. Of course, you should remember that in almost any case, pure random chance might lead to our observing some differences in the group means, so we need some method of working out whether we should judge that the differences in the group means we observe in our data are likely to be because the group means in the population really are different. This is what we use the *F*-ratio for.

Now, to put this basic premise into a more formalized statistical logic, recall that the b_1 and b_2 coefficients in the multiple regression model above were shown to represent the difference between the mean of the baseline 100% commission group and that of the 100% salary and mixed incentive groups respectively. If our null hypothesis of equal group means is true for the population, then we would expect the *b* coefficients to be zero, of course. In this case, the best model to fit our data set would be the overall mean – called the grand mean. This model, that one mean can represent all groups, is the simplest model, and the logic of using ANOVA relies on testing whether a model of different means for each group is a better fit to the data than the grand mean model. This is just the same basic logic as using a regression model, but dressed up with some different ways of spinning the same concepts.

So, remember that in a regression model, we calculate a straight line to model our data set. The slope of this line is described by the intercept and the regression coefficient. Of course, the bigger the coefficient, the steeper the line, which means that as the coefficient gets larger, there is a bigger difference between the grand mean and the regression line.

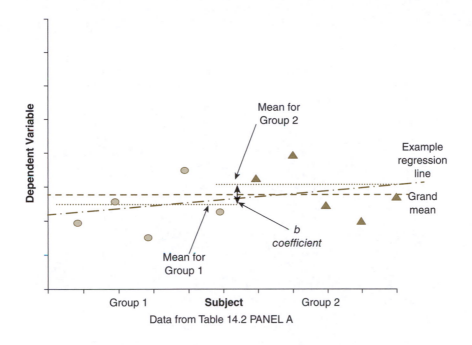

Data from Table 14.2 PANEL A

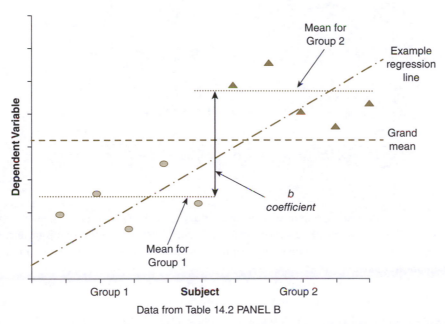

Data from Table 14.2 PANEL B

**Figure 14.2
Visualization
of Group
Data as
Regression**

Note: Group
1 data
represented by
circles, group
2 by triangles

Take a look at Figure 14.2, which shows this using a two-group example (it is much easier to draw it and visualize it with two groups). Table 14.2 shows a representation of the two data sets that could create these two panels (note, the data is not exact, because the Figure is stylized to make it easier to follow, but the basic principles are sound). You can see both in the data (Table 14.2 PANEL A) and in the upper panel of Figure 14.2 that the two group means are close, meaning that the grand mean and regression line are rather close. The grand mean is a reasonable model here. However, in both the data (Table 14.2 PANEL B) and the lower panel of Figure 14.2, the group means are very different, meaning that also the grand mean and regression line are very different. The grand mean is a poor model here. You can also see that the b coefficient represents the difference between the group means, and as it gets larger, the difference between the grand mean and regression line increases.

Table 14.2

PANEL A

Subject	Group 1	Group 2
1	2.2	3.3
2	2.99	4.05
3	1.9	2.85
4	3.9	2.2
5	2.8	3
Means	2.758	3.08
Grand Mean = 2.919		

PANEL B

Subject	Group 1	Group 2
1	2.1	6
2	2.95	6.4
3	1.8	5
4	3.7	4.6
5	2.3	5.5
Means	2.57	5.5
Grand Mean = 4.035		

If the differences between the group means are large enough, then the regression line will be a better fit than the grand mean, which will be shown by a significant difference in the group means. We can determine this in a general sense by comparing the improvement in fit due to the regression model rather than the grand mean model.

What this means is that when we use the grand mean model, there is an amount of error in the model (i.e. the grand mean model will explain some of the variation in the data, but not all). The regression model will also explain some of the variation in the model, but not all. So, we use the F-ratio to compare the ratio of explained with unexplained variation in the data. And we do this by using variations of one very simple equation:

$$\text{deviation} = \Sigma(\text{observed} - \text{model})^2$$

This equation expresses how much the data deviates from the model. In ANOVA, we use differences in how we define the 'model' and 'observed' data parts of the equation to create variations which express various important concepts for our task. We build our F-ratio from these equations, as you will see, beginning with the total sum of squares.[3]

---

[3] Remember: much of this is already covered in depth in the chapter on regression, so you can recap there if you like.

Table 14.3 Example sales incentive data

	100% Commission	100% Salary	Mixed
	124	105	162
	155	93	109
	243	126	280
	101	99	140
	85	115	70
$\bar{x}$	141.6	107.6	152.2
s	62.5	13.1	79.4
s^2	3905.8	171.8	6300.2
	Grand mean = 133.8 Grand SD = 57.9 Grand variance = 3352.9		

In order to illustrate the calculation simply, Table 14.3 gives a small data set for the incentive scheme problem already examined. In this case there are only five data points for each group – this will help us do the calculations by hand.

Just to recap, if you do not know what the 'grand mean' is, it is simply the mean of the entire data set, whereas the individual group means $\bar{x}$ refer to (of course) the individual groups. It is the same principle for the grand variance and grand standard deviation.

Calculating the Three Sums of Squares: SS_T, SS_M and SS_R

In order to get to the F-ratio, we need first to do some preliminary calculations to get the numbers to create the ratio. These numbers are referred to as the total sum of squares, the model sum of squares, and the residual sum of squares. Below is an explanation of each one and the simple calculations required to get each one. Of course, in reality, you would normally use a computer package to do the heavy lifting, but here you are going to do it by hand to illustrate the points.

The total sum of squares (which from now on will be referred to as SS_T) is a way of measuring the total amount of variation in our data set. It is calculated by taking the difference between each data point and the grand mean, squaring each difference and then summing:

$$SS_T = \sum \left(x_i - \bar{x}_{grand} \right)^2$$

It is relatively easy to calculate SS_T this way, but, you know, those summing operations can be a hassle – especially if you have loads of data. Fortunately, a simpler way of calculating SS_T relies on the fact that the variance and the sum of squares are related. In fact, $s^2 = SS(N - 1)$ where N is the number of observations. Rearranging this formula by multiplying both sides by $(N - 1)$ gives us $s^2(N - 1) = SS$, which of course is exactly the same as $SS = s^2(N - 1)$. This means we can calculate SS_T using the grand variance of our data set, and by counting the number of observations N, which is 15. Let's do so:

$$SS_T = s^2_{grand} \left(n - 1 \right)$$

$$= 3352.9 \, (15{-}1)$$

$$= 3352.9 \times 4$$

$$= 46940.6$$

Thus, the total amount of variation in the data is 46940.6. Incidentally, do not worry about the large numbers here – they are just a function of the fact that the values of our data are quite large; the 'number' itself does not mean anything, it is only when we compare this number with other sums of square numbers that we get any insight. So, with that in mind, we still need to know the amount of variation that is explained by the model. To find this, we calculate the model sum of squares (SS_M). The ANOVA model is essentially concerned with differences between the means of the groups, and therefore SS_M refers to the amount of total variation in the data that can be explained by the model, and remember that the 'model' is basically that different data points come from different groups (the number of groups is determined by your model). So, in an experimental context, the model is the effect of the experimental treatment, while in a non-experimental context, the model is the effect of the grouping variable.

Calculating SS_M is a little more involved than calculating SS_T, because it involves comparing the group means with the grand mean. Remember that, for ANOVA, the model is trying to predict the group means, and therefore for each individual the value that the model predicts is the group mean for the group that the individual belongs to. For example, in our incentive study, the performance value predicted for the 100% commission group is 141.6, for the 100% salary group 107.6 and for the mixed incentive group 152.2. So, to calculate SS_M, we calculate the differences between the predicted value of each participant and the grand mean. Then, these differences are squared and added.[4] Because we know that the predicted value for the members of each group is the group mean, we can simplify the calculation by only calculating the difference between the mean of each group and the grand mean, squaring it, and then multiplying it by the number of participants in each group (denoted as n_k). Then we simply add those group values together. This formula is expressed as:

$$SS_M = \sum n_k \left(\bar{x}_k - \bar{x}_{\text{grand}} \right)^2$$

Perhaps working through the incentive data will help cement this:

$$SS_M = 5(141.6 - 133.8)^2 + 5(107.6 - 133.8)^2 + 5(152.2 - 133.8)^2$$

$$= 5(7.8)^2 + 5(-26.2)^2 + 5(18.4)^2$$

$$= 304.2 + 3432.2 + 1692.8$$

$$= 5429.2$$

What this means is that we had 46940.6 units of variation in the data (SS_T) and our model can explain 5429.2 of them (SS_M). That does not seem like much really, but let's reserve our judgement and make no assumptions until we calculate the residual sum of squares (SS_R). SS_R tells us how much of the total variation cannot be explained by the model. We interpret this amount of variation as being caused by extraneous variables not included in our model – such as unmeasured individual differences. In the case of the incentive study, this could be things like personality, differences in selling ability and so forth. In fact, we should have thought about what these things might be before doing our study, and if any were likely to be very strong influences, we should somehow have measured them and included them in the model (which would have required a more complex analysis).

Somewhat obviously, the easiest way to calculate SS_R is simply as $SS_T - SS_M$. However, this is not really helpful in terms of learning about what is really going on. Also, if you messed up your earlier sum of square calculations somehow, you would also get the wrong answer here! So let's go about things in a more detailed way.[5] First, recall that SS_R represents the difference between what the model predicts and

---

[4] If you don't remember why we square them, go and reread the regression chapter.

[5] As such, this also provides a neat way of reassuring yourself that you calculated the other sums of squares properly.

what was actually observed. Also, recall that the ANOVA model predicts that for any given individual, his or her score should be the group mean. So, following this logic, we can also calculate SS_R by taking the difference between each individual's score and the mean of the group to which the individual belongs. This is summarized in the following equation:

$$SS_R = \sum \left(x_{ik} - \bar{x}_k \right)^2$$

That looks kind of tedious to calculate, because we would have to do it for each data point, and the more data we have, the more cumbersome it gets. But, we are saved this task by knowing that the sum of squares for each group is the sum of squared differences between each individual in that group's score and the group mean. Which is what we want to do anyway, right? Thus, we could get to SS_R by calculating $SS_R = SS_{group1} + SS_{group2} + SS_{group3} + \ldots + SS_{groupk}$ with of course k representing the number of groups in your study. Because we know the relationship between the variance and the sums of squares, our task is simplified further, and we can calculate SS_R as:

$$SS_R = \sum s_k^2 (n_k - 1)$$

This is really sweet, and just means that we take the variance from each group and multiply it by one less than the number of people in each group. Then we add them up. So, for our incentive data:

$$SS_R = s^2_{group1}(n_1 - 1) + s^2_{group2}(n_2 - 1) + s^2_{group3}(n_3 - 1)$$

$$= (3905.8)(5–1) + (171.8)(5–1) + (6300.2)(5–1)$$

$$= (3905.8*4)) + (171.8*4) + (6300.2*4)$$

$$= 15623.2 + 687.2 + 25200.8$$

$$= 41511.2$$

Mean Squares and the *F*-ratio

Now, we have the raw materials, but we are still not quite ready to get the *F*-ratio. Let's recap what we just calculated and what it means:

- SS_T is the total amount of variation in the data.
- SS_M is the amount of variation the model explains.
- SS_R is the amount of variation that is due to extraneous factors.

While these three numbers are all very useful and wonderful, they come with some problems. More specifically, because they are summed, their magnitude is influenced by the number of scores that were summed to get them. For example, SS_M is the sum of only 3 values (the group means), while the other two are sums of 14 different values in the end. This means they are not yet directly comparable. As such, we need somehow to remove the bias, and we do this by calculating the average of each sum of squares – which is called the *mean sum of squares*, or MS (as opposed to SS). This is calculated by dividing each SS by its number of degrees of freedom (which I have not shown you yet, hold your horses...).

The number of degrees of freedom for SS_M is the number of groups minus one (i.e. $k - 1$). The number of degrees of freedom for SS_R is the total degrees of freedom minus the model degrees of freedom, which, to put it another way, is the sample size minus the number of groups, or $N - k$. So, with this in hand, it is easy enough to calculate the mean squares we need as follows:

$$MS_M = \frac{SS_M}{df_M} = \frac{5429.2}{2} = 2714.6$$

$$MS_R = \frac{SS_R}{df_R} = \frac{41511.2}{12} = 3459.27$$

OK, now, at last, we are ready to calculate the F-ratio, which is the ratio of variation explained by the model versus variation explained by extraneous factors. Simply, it is the mean square model divided by the mean square residual:

$$F = \frac{MS_M}{MS_R}$$

Thinking about this logically, since the F-ratio is the ratio of systematic variation (i.e. that caused by your independent variable) to unsystematic variation (i.e. that caused by non-specific extraneous factors), if the value of F is less than one, then we must be dealing with a non-significant effect. If $F < 1$ then the mean square residual is larger than the mean square model. This means that there is more unsystematic than systematic variation. For our incentive study, the F-ratio is calculated as:

$$F = \frac{MS_M}{MS_R} = \frac{2714.6}{3459.27} = 0.78$$

You can see that here $F < 1$, as 0.78. This indicates that our independent variable (incentive plan) did not have any effect over and above natural differences in performance. At this point, we can stop thinking about it and conclude our study has not shown any evidence for an effect of incentive plan.

 think it over 14.3

Looking at the above calculation for the F-ratio, first notice that there are no units. The calculation provides a way of comparing two values. Interpreting the calculation allows us to determine if the proposed model makes a significant difference. We have three scenarios: the value of F could be less than one, equal to one or greater than one. Think about the meaning of the following values of F: $F = 0.002$, $F = 1$, $F = 50$.

However, just finding an F-ratio greater than one does not guarantee a significant effect. No, once $F > 1$ we then need to see whether it is large enough to give us confidence that it is not a chance result – just as in all the other significance testing situations we have seen so far. We do this by using the F-distribution table to compare the calculated value of F with the critical value for the given degrees of freedom.

In order to do so, you use the procedure you should now be familiar with. First, you decide on the required significance level, and then you look up the critical value for that significance level, given the degrees of freedom, and discover your critical value. Then you compare your calculated F with this critical value.

In the present incentive study case, $df_M = 2$ and $df_R = 14$, and looking at the F-distribution table, you can see that the critical value for $p = 0.05$ is 3.89, and for $p = 0.01$ it is 6.93. So, our calculated F-ratio would have to be greater than 3.89 in this case for us to reject the null hypothesis at a 95% level of significance, or 6.93 to reject the null hypothesis at a 99% level of significance. Thus, even without our 'F-ratio < 1' rule, we can still reject the null hypothesis using the critical value approach.

Before we move on, it is worth summarizing the general F-ratio approach to testing the significance of an ANOVA model. First, the hypotheses are as follows:

$$H_o: \mu_1 = \mu_2 = \ldots = u_k$$

H_I: Not all population means are equal

As you should surely remember, the test statistic is:

$$F = \frac{\text{MS}_M}{\text{MS}_R}$$

Once we have the F-ratio, we use the F-distribution table in conjunction with the relevant degrees of freedom to determine the p-value for our value of F. We reject H_0 if $p \leq \alpha$. As demonstrated above, though, you can also use the critical value approach, in which case you reject H_0 if $F \geq F_\alpha$ and you determine F_α by again using the F-distribution with the relevant degrees of freedom.

MULTIPLE COMPARISON PROCEDURES FOR ANOVA

Some of you will have already thought about the subject of this next section. More specifically, the ANOVA approach detailed above tests whether the means of k populations are equal. As such, rejection of the null hypothesis only allows us to conclude that the populations are not all equal. What is wrong with that? Well, sometimes that is all we need, sure. However, in many cases, we would also like to know something more specific; in other words, we might want to know *where* the differences between the means are. What I mean is that there could be a big difference between group 1 and 3, but not much difference between group 1 and 2, for example. A significant F-ratio test does not tell us anything about this.

There are plenty of different ways to do this, but they can be collected into two main groups: *post-hoc tests* and *planned comparisons*. Planned comparisons (also known as planned contrasts) are where you plan beforehand which groups you want to compare, and then test specifically those groups. This approach is commonly used in an experimental situation, where you develop specific hypotheses about how groups will differ. Post-hoc testing is when you do not decide before collecting your data, but instead decide which groups to compare after you have done the ANOVA (even sometimes comparing each group with all the others).

It is important to remember that the difference between planned and post-hoc comparisons is not a technical one about whether or not you compare all the groups, but is actually an important conceptual difference. In other words, if you plan before your research which groups to compare and then do that – and only that – you are doing a planned comparison. However, if you look at the results of your ANOVA and *then* decide to make comparisons, you are doing post-hoc testing, and this is the case even if you only compare two groups (because in deciding which groups to compare, you implicitly looked at all of them first).

Planned comparisons are more powerful but rarer, because you have to know exactly what you are going to do before doing your research. So, let me focus for now on post-hoc testing, since it is quite a common situation in practical business research (whereas planned comparisons should be more common in scientific research). Furthermore, there is more that can go wrong with post-hoc testing, even though in a technical sense it is easier to do and understand.

Using Fisher's LSD

If you have a significant F-ratio, indicating that you should reject the null hypothesis of equal population means, then you can use Fisher's least significant differences (LSD) procedure to get an idea of where the differences between population means occur. Now, it is important to realize that Fisher's LSD is only one of the many post-hoc tests you could conduct using software such as IBM SPSS Statistics Software (SPSS). However, it is a reasonable baseline technique to learn, since it helps to demonstrate the basic procedure of post-hoc testing and the key things you should be aware of.

The first thing to be sure of is that you have a significant F-ratio result for the overall ANOVA model. Without that, you cannot go any further with Fisher's LSD. Well, actually that is not entirely true. If you use the significant F-ratio as a criterion for using Fisher's LSD, you are doing what is called *protected* testing. However, technically speaking, you do not absolutely have to do this, and most software will allow you to do *unprotected* Fisher's LSD testing, where you do not require a significant F-ratio. I will discuss this in more depth soon, but for now let's assume we are using a protected Fisher's LSD method.

So, looking back at our incentive scheme data, the non-significant F we calculated means that we cannot use Fisher's LSD. That was a bit of poor planning on my part, although it does nicely demonstrate the point. We therefore need some new data, which can be seen in Table 14.4. This table shows the results of a study where we tested the hourly production rates for three different car assembly plants, in different countries.

Table 14.4 Car assembly data

	Serbia	Moldova	Montenegro
	12	3	10
	15	4	9
	20	2	12
	18	5	3
	17	7	5
$\bar{x}$	16.4	4.2	7.8
s	3.05	1.92	3.7
s^2	9.3	3.7	13.8
	Grand mean = 9.5 Grand SD = 5.97 Grand variance = 35.7		

Without going into detail, the F-ratio here is significant at $F = 22.075$ and with $p < 0.05$ (you can calculate this using SPSS very quickly using this data to check, if you want). So we can now go and examine where the differences are. In other words, the significant F-ratio gives us a belief that the plants differ in terms of production per hour, but we do not know where those differences are. In other words, does the Serbia plant differ from the Moldova plant, or rather does the Serbia plant differ from the Montenegro plant? Or does the Montenegro plant differ from the Moldova plant?

The basic principles of Fisher's LSD are identical to the t-test method of testing the difference between two means, with a modification made to the population variance estimate. However, you should always be careful when using LSD.[6] This is because it does *not* correct for multiple comparisons. In other words, you can get into trouble with your experimentwise error rate (as mentioned earlier in this chapter). As such, you need to be aware of this when you interpret the findings. This is the reason that it is sometimes considered essential to use the protected Fisher's LSD test. Some analysts consider that using the protected method compensates in some way for the lack of correction for multiple comparisons. However, other analysts disagree and think that this assumption is dangerous. I have some sympathy with this viewpoint actually, because there is not really any way that simply requiring a significant F-test can correct for the potential problems of experimentwise error inflation.

The basic hypotheses for Fisher's LSD test should not be a surprise to you:

$$H_0: \mu_i = \mu_j$$

$$H_0: \mu_i \neq \mu_j$$

---

[6] This is pretty good advice in general.

The test statistic might look a little complex, but it really is rather simple in just incorporating the mean square residual from the ANOVA test:

$$t = \frac{\bar{x}_i - \bar{x}_j}{\sqrt{MS_R \left(\frac{1}{n_i} + \frac{1}{n_j} \right)}}$$

It is not too difficult to use this formula to see if there is a significant difference between the Serbia plant and the Montenegro plant at the $\alpha = 0.05$ significance level, as an example. So, looking at the data in Table 14.4, we can see that the mean of population 1 (Serbia) is 16.4 and the mean of population 2 (Montenegro) is 7.8. The MS_R value is 8.9, based on 12 degrees of freedom, which can be found if you use SPSS. As such, and with $n = 5$ for both groups, we can find the test statistic as follows:

$$t = \frac{16.4 - 7.8}{\sqrt{8.9 \left(\frac{1}{5} + \frac{1}{5} \right)}} = 4.56$$

So, taking this value to a t-distribution table shows that for 12 degrees of freedom, $t = 3.055$ for an area of 0.005 in the upper tail. Because our t is greater than this value, we know that the area in the upper tail must be less than 0.005, and because it is a two-tailed test, we double this, to draw the conclusion that our p-value is less than 0.01. Because our p-value is less than 0.05, we can reject the null hypothesis of equal means and conclude that the population mean for the Serbian plant is different from that for the Montenegro plant.

You might find it easier to understand this if instead we were to provide a way to determine how large the difference between sample means has to be in order to reject H_0 for a given situation, which is often done in practice. It is a bit more involved technically (only very slightly), but I think it is easier to understand conceptually. In this case, our test statistic is not t; in fact we rearrange the formula so that we can use the difference between the two means as the test statistic. Check this out:

$$LSD = t_{\frac{a}{2}} \sqrt{MS_R \left(\frac{1}{n_i} + \frac{1}{n_j} \right)}$$

We reject the null hypothesis if:

$$\left| \bar{x}_i - \bar{x}_j \right| > LSD$$

So, for the example we just did, the value for LSD is:

$$LSD = 2.179 \sqrt{8.9 \left(\frac{1}{5} + \frac{1}{5} \right)} = 4.11$$

Again, we can see that the difference between the means of the Serbia and Montenegro plants (8.6) is indeed larger than the LSD value (4.11). We therefore come to the same conclusion. You might also notice that we could use this same LSD value to test the difference between the other pairs of means in the data – because the sample sizes are all the same across the three groups. If the sample sizes were different for each group, you would have to compute the LSD each time. Why not have a go at computing the test for the Serbia and Moldova plants? Then try it for the Moldova and Montenegro plants.

You can also use the LSD value to compute a confidence interval for the difference between two population means:

$$\bar{x}_i - \bar{x}_j \pm LSD$$

This can also provide a reasonably simple hypothesis test, in that if the confidence interval includes zero, you cannot reject the null hypothesis that the two population means are equal.

The Bonferroni Correction

Sounds a bit like a spy thriller, doesn't it? Or one of those hip new bands 'the kids' listen to. Well, sorry to disappoint you, it is not. It is a way of dealing with the problem of experimentwise error that has already been discussed. Remember: if you do multiple *t*-tests to compare groups in any research design with more than two groups, you are going to inflate the overall Type I error rate. The more groups in the design, the greater the problem. The Bonferroni correction was first developed by Carlo Bonferroni, and is nothing more than a simple formula used to adjust the required level of significance for each individual *t*-test, such that the overall Type I error rate (i.e. α) remains at 0.05 (or whatever you would like it to be).

The Bonferroni correction formula is simply α/number of comparisons. In the example above we have three groups, and if we wanted to test all three possible pairwise comparisons (Serbia with Montenegro, Serbia with Moldova, Moldova with Montenegro), we would simply divide our α by 3. Because our significance was 0.05, the formula is simply 0.05/3 = 0.017. So, the level of significance each individual pairwise comparison would have to reach is no longer 0.05, but 0.017. This makes our life slightly more complex, but not much. In fact, you can go back to the Serbia versus Montenegro comparison above and see if it would still remain significant if we applied the Bonferroni correction.

In doing so, you should realize that the *p*-value was shown to be less than 0.01, which means that we still have a significant difference. However, you can realize the trade-off inherent in the Bonferroni correction. Specifically, you lose statistical power. What this means is that for every reduction in Type I error rate, there is a corresponding increase in Type II error (i.e. the error of accepting the null hypothesis when it is not true in the population). By being more conservative, we increase the chance we will miss a 'real' difference. And the more groups you have in your design, the greater this issue becomes. For example, if you had five groups, and therefore 10 possible pairwise corrections, using the Bonferroni correction would result in the level of significance for each pairwise comparison changing to 0.05/10 = 0.005.

Because of this, many researchers try to avoid using the Bonferroni correction in the way shown above, and many other post-hoc comparison methods have been developed. Certainly, the Bonferroni correction when applied to Fisher's LSD is a 'safe' option, but it might be preferable to explore other procedures, such as Tukey's test, or Scheffé's test. In fact, there are many different post-hoc testing procedures available to the informed analyst, and I recommend that if you are using ANOVA frequently – or for mission-critical tasks – go and investigate these and make an informed decision about the Type I/Type II error trade-off inherent in each. In doing so, you can select the right tool for the job.

EXTENDING OUR EXPERIMENTAL DESIGNS

The basic ANOVA design detailed above was applied to a specific experimental design, which, if you recall, I called a completely randomized design.[7] This is the fundamental experimental design. However, there are other experimental designs that can be of major use to you as a business analyst and researcher, of which I will cover two here. Each of these designs requires some modifications to the ANOVA analysis procedure, Before I begin, you might want to refresh your memory of the experimental design terminology, and, if so, I have helpfully provided Back to Basics Box 14.1 for this purpose.

---

[7] Remember that you also applied it to a non-experimental situation too. ANOVA doesn't need experimental data to be used.

back to basics

Box 14.1   Experimental Terminology Recap

Dependent variable: The variable on which you are interested in determining the difference between the groups. Sometimes called the response variable.

Independent variable: A variable you might suspect has an impact on the dependent variable. Sometimes called the factor variable.

Treatments: Different values of the independent variable.

Experimental units: The participants in the experiment.

For example, imagine an experiment where you were interested in whether the amount of exposure to fashion magazines would lead to an increase in the purchase of new shoes. The amount of exposure is the independent variable and the amount of new pairs of shoes purchased is the dependent one. You might have a number of treatment levels for exposure (e.g. high, low and none). A simple completely randomized design would split your experimental units into three groups, each of which received one level of the treatment. You would then measure the dependent variable.

There are many different research questions and designs that can be covered with variants of the basic ANOVA model already shown above. However, there is no way I can cover all of them here; I could write a whole other book on them. That said, this one has taken over five years already, so maybe that is not a good idea.

Anyway, think back to the completely randomized design and in particular the reason for the randomization. Basically, remember that there are two possible sources of variation in our dependent variable. The first is the independent variable – which is the one we are interested in. Yet, there are also many other possible sources of variation, which we often call extraneous factors, or nuisance factors. So, for instance in our sales compensation example, our hypothesis was that the incentive plan (independent variable) caused variation in performance (dependent variable). Yet, we would also expect factors such as intelligence, sales skills, and so forth, to cause variation in performance too. The idea of complete randomization is that these extraneous factors are averaged out across the groups due to the randomization. This is an OK idea, but in reality it should be treated as something of a 'last resort' – to cover those factors that you either do not know about or somehow cannot measure or design into the experiment.

In fact, there are other, more effective ways to take account of extraneous factors, when you have specific expectations about what those factors are going to be. There are two primary methods, which are more or less useful depending on the situation you are dealing with. However, both these methods require some thought before you collect data – in order to make sure you take account of specific variables.

ANCOVA

The simplest method (in my humble opinion) is called ANCOVA – which stands for ANalysis of COVAriance. In this case, we are using an ANOVA, extended to take into account one or more other independent variables. This is a pretty simple extension which I am only going to look at briefly, yet it is very powerful. I also find that it is easier to explain the idea of extraneous variables using ANCOVA, which will prepare you better for the next section – where a few more calculations are involved.

So, consider the sales incentive scheme again from earlier in this chapter. You should remember that the basic situation was that you (the vice president of sales for a large photocopier manufacturer) want to test the most effective incentive plan for your salespeople. There are three possible plans: Plan A where salespeople are paid only on commission; Plan B where there is only a salary paid; and Plan C which is a mix of both. So, incentive plan was our independent variable, and we thought that it would have an effect on performance, our dependent variable. Of course, we would expect some other factors to have some kind of effect too, but we did not really worry about this too much. Our assumption is that the randomization of the study should deal with this issue.

However, what if we really think that the amount of time the salesperson has been in the job of selling photocopiers will have a major influence on their success too? So, those who have been in the job longer will be more likely to be successful in general? In this case, we could actually measure experience, and add it to our model as a covariate, giving us an ANCOVA model rather than a simple ANOVA. In essence, what you do is run a model with the covariate (or covariates) first – equivalent to a regression model – and then enter the independent variable. In this way you are seeing what effect the independent variable has over and above the covariate. We often call this process 'controlling' for the effect of the covariate, or if you want to sound very clever, you could call it 'partialling out' the effect of the covariate.

Basically, the two key reasons to include covariates are (a) to reduce the within-group error variance (i.e. the residual error variance, or SS_R) and (b) to eliminate confounds (i.e. other variables which you know will influence the dependent variable). Both these goals are important, as they lead to a more accurate estimate of the effect of the independent variable.

So, as the VP for sales of the photocopier company, when you get the results of the original incentive study you realize that the research does not take into account the salesperson's experience. You know this is going to be a big influence on performance. Thus, you repeat the study with a new sample and this time include a question asking for each salesperson's total photocopier sales experience in years.

If you remember, our original incentive experiment model looks like this:

$$\text{Sales Performance}_i = \beta_0 + \beta_1 \text{Salary}_i + \beta_2 \text{Mix}_i + \varepsilon_i$$

Adding a covariate will make the model look like this:

$$\text{Sales Performance}_i = \beta_0 + \beta_1 \text{Covariate}_i + \beta_2 \text{Salary}_i + \beta_3 \text{Mix}_i + \varepsilon_i$$

$$\text{Sales Performance}_i = \beta_0 + \beta_1 \text{Experience}_i + \beta_2 \text{Salary}_i + \beta_3 \text{Mix}_i + \varepsilon_i$$

Now, remember that, fundamentally, this is a multiple regression model with dummy variables (Salary and Mix). In fact, adding the covariate should make it even easier to see the connection with multiple regression. You could even run it as a multiple regression in SPSS if you like. As such there is little point in going through the specific working by hand with an example.

However, one thing that might help is if we run it through as an ANCOVA in SPSS to start you off on using computers to analyse this kind of model. To do so, we can use an extension of the sales incentive data set.

Table 14.5 shows the data gathered from an investigation into the sales performance of a team of salespeople. You are interested in determining which method of remuneration results in more sales.

Table 14.5

Incentive	Sales performance	Experience
Commission only	3	5
	1	3
	5	6
	2	4
	2	3
	2	5
	7	11
	2	4
Salaried	7	10
	5	7
	3	6
	5	7
	4	7
	7	11
	6	9
	4	7
Mixed	9	12
	2	3
	6	8
	3	5
	4	7
	4	8
	4	7
	6	5
	4	6
	6	10
	2	3
	8	11
	5	6

The sales performance was scored from 0 to 10 and experience was in years. In order to use SPSS you must first decide how to encode the data. Just to remind you of the different categories (see Chapter 1 for more detail here – this is just a brief recap):

Nominal – Numbers are used only to represent categories (e.g. 1 lecturer, 2 student).

Ordinal – The order in which the data occurred (e.g. first, second, third in a competition) is meaningful, but one cannot draw any conclusions about the differences between the points (e.g. is the difference between first and second the 'same' as that between second and third? What about fourth and fifth?)

Interval – The order is meaningful as above, but now the data is measured on a scale where the differences between points on the scale are now meaningful (e.g. asking people to score their interest on a scale of 0–5, with the difference between 1 and 2 meaning the same as 4 and 5, and so forth).

Ratio – Here, the order and the intervals are meaningful as above, but also the variable you are measuring contains an absolute zero point (i.e. no amount of that variable). For example, age contains a zero point. Here, for example, a person who indicated a 4 on an 'interest' scale would be interpreted to mean that they were twice as interested as someone who indicated a 2.

Importantly, SPSS classifies interval and ratio categories as what are called 'scale' data.

Let's use a step-by-step approach to using SPSS to analyse the data:

Step 1. Decide what we are interested in analysing. In the sales example it is *which remuneration scheme produces the best sales?*

Step 2. Decide how to classify the remuneration schemes. In this case we will use the commission only group as the 'baseline' to compare the other incentive schemes with.

Step 3. Decide how to code the remuneration schemes. The data in this case is nominal so we can assign '1' for commission only, '2' salary and '3' mixed.

Step 4. Decide how to code the remaining data. A scale of 0–10 was used to measure sales performance, and it is feasible to imagine that there is a possible point of 0 performance too, so we will use the 'scale' option in SPSS. The situation is the same for 'experience', which is measured in years.

Step 5. Create the variables in SPSS. Figure 14.3 shows the Variable View window in SPSS.

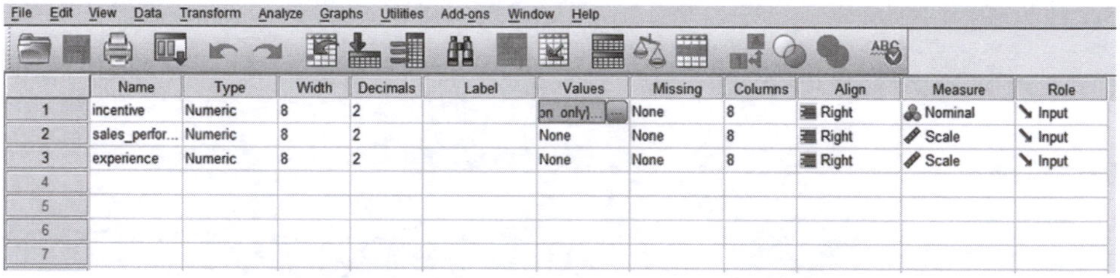

Figure 14.3

Clicking on the 'Values' column for the 'incentive' variable will bring up the dialog box shown in Figure 14.4.

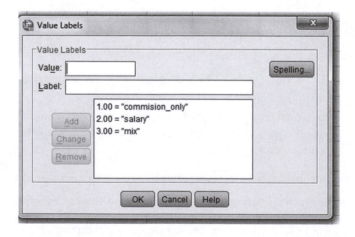

Figure 14.4

This is where we assign the nominal values to the different remuneration schemes.

Step 6. Click on the Data View tab in the bottom left of the SPSS screen and enter your data. Once you have entered it, double check to make sure it has been entered accurately. See Figure 14.5.

	incentive	sales_performance	experience	var
1	1.00	3.00	5.00	
2	1.00	1.00	2.00	
3	1.00	5.00	6.00	
4	1.00	2.00	4.00	
5	1.00	2.00	3.00	
6	1.00	2.00	5.00	
7	1.00	7.00	11.00	
8	1.00	2.00	4.00	
9	2.00	7.00	10.00	
10	2.00	5.00	7.00	
11	2.00	3.00	6.00	
12	2.00	5.00	7.00	

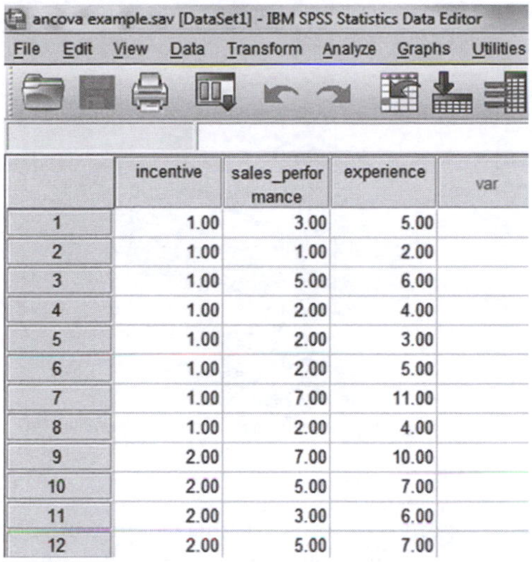

Figure 14.5

Step 7. Analyse the data. Select Analyze → General Linear Model → Univariate as shown in Figure 14.6.

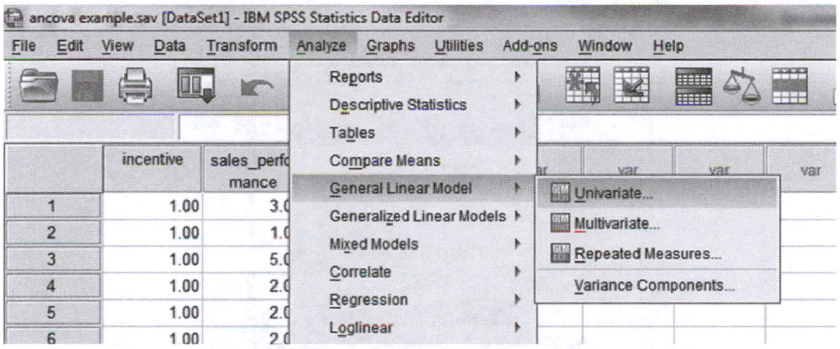

Figure 14.6

You will then see the dialog box shown in Figure 14.7.

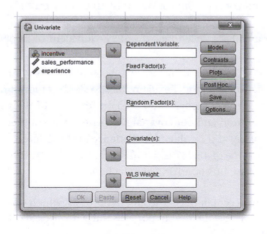

Figure 14.7

Step 8. Drag the variables into the boxes as shown in Figure 14.8. Note that in this example 'experience' is the covariate.

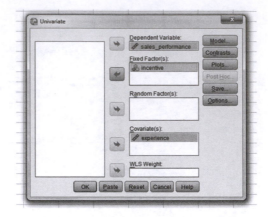

Figure 14.8

Step 9. Decide if you want to do any 'contrasts'. In this case it would be useful to do a contrast that compares the salary and mixed groups with the commission only group. Click on 'Contrasts', 'Simple' and then select the radio button labelled 'First' to select our control group coded as '1', as shown in Figure 14.9.

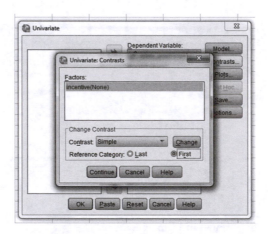

Figure 14.9

Step 10. Interpret the results of the analysis. Figure 14.10 shows you the output from SPSS.

In the source column you will see 'incentive', the SPSS equivalent of SS_M; 'Error' is SS_R and 'Corrected Total' is SS_T.

In this case SS_T has a value of 119.034, which is the total amount of variation in the data. SS_M (value of 1.389) is the amount of variation our model explains and SS_R is the amount of variation due to extraneous factors (17.847). This means our model could account for 1.2% of the variation, extraneous factors accounted for 15% of the variation and our covariate, experience, accounted for most of the 66% variation. This can be seen by looking at the value for experience in the 'Source' column: 78.72 units out of a total of 119.034 units. The F value of 47.247 is significant at the $p < 0.05$ level, which means that there is less than a 5% chance of these results occurring due to chance alone.

Step 11. Decide whether to accept or reject the null hypothesis, which was there is no difference in the means. In this case we can reject the null hypothesis but with the caveat that experience had a large impact on sales performance.

Step 12. Make a recommendation. Over to you...

Between-Subjects Factors

		Value Label	N
incentive	1.00	commision_only	8
	2.00	salary	8
	3.00	mix	13

Tests of Between-Subjects Effects

Dependent Variable: sales_performance

Source	Type III Sum of Squares	df	Mean Square	F	Sig.
Corrected Model	101.187[a]	3	33.729	47.247	.000
Intercept	.191	1	.191	.268	.609
experience	78.720	1	78.720	110.271	.000
incentive	1.389	2	.694	.973	.392
Error	17.847	25	.714		
Total	684.000	29			
Corrected Total	119.034	28			

a. R Squared = .850 (Adjusted R Squared = .832)

Figure 14.10

Before we move on, there is an additional assumption to remember about ANCOVA, over and above the standard assumptions of ANOVA: that is, you must satisfy the assumption of homogeneity of regression slopes across groups. Take a look at Figure 14.11, which shows three different regression slopes for the association between experience (remember, the covariate) and performance, one for each group in the incentive study.

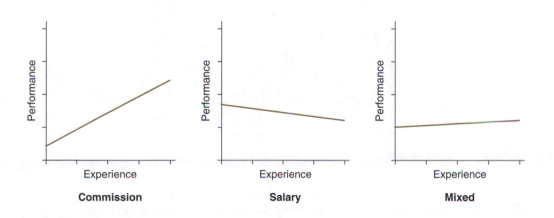

Commission   **Salary**   **Mixed**

Figure 14.11
Example Group
Regression
Slopes

Let me explain why this is an issue. When you run an ANCOVA to analyse data from an experiment, you are basically looking at the relationship between the covariate and the dependent variable for the whole sample, without taking account of the group to which your subjects belong. So, if there is a positive relationship between the covariate (e.g. age) in one group (e.g. the 100% salary incentive group), you assume there is a positive relationship between the covariate and dependent variable in all the other groups. If you cannot make this assumption (i.e. if the regression between the covariate and dependent variable is different across groups), then the regression model is wrong.

While we can view the whole thing using the regression slopes for each group, as shown in Figure 14.11, there is a way of testing this a bit more formally – although it requires an extra step and reanalysis.

What you need to do is run the ANCOVA as a customized model and include the interaction between the covariate and the dependent variable.

In order to do this for our example, you would do the following:

When we were initialling setting up the analysis, the dialog box shown in Figure 14.12 was displayed. If we want to see the interaction between the covariate and the dependent variable, click on the Options button, then select 'Parameter estimates'.

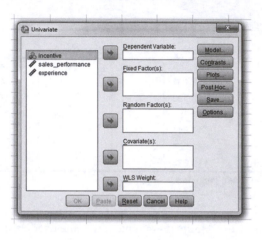

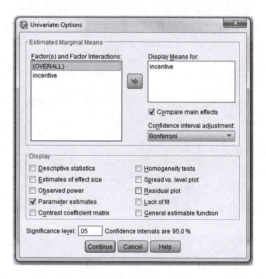

Figure 14.12

Parameter Estimates

Dependent Variable: sales_performance

Parameter	B	Std. Error	t	Sig.	95% Confidence Interval	
					Lower Bound	Upper Bound
Intercept	.054	.513	.106	.916	-1.002	1.111
experience	.685	.065	10.501	.000	.550	.819
[incentive=1.00]	-.477	.401	-1.189	.246	-1.304	.350
[incentive=2.00]	-.406	.385	-1.053	.302	-1.199	.388
[incentive=3.00]	0ᵃ	.	.	.	.	.

Figure 14.13

a. This parameter is set to zero because it is redundant.

With this option selected, Figure 14.13 will be seen in the output. If you look at the 'B' value for experience you will see it is 0.685. This means that for every one-unit increase in experience (in our case one year), you would expect an increase of 68.5% in sales. Be careful with this – it is a generalized result and should not be interpreted literally! In other words, do not use it as a reason to sack someone if their sales performance does not increase by 68.5% for every year they work for you.

RANDOMIZED BLOCK DESIGNS

Another way of taking account of extraneous factors is to use a randomized block design. Here, rather than measuring the extraneous factor and adding it to the model – like we did with ANCOVA above – we design our experiment in such a way as to remove the influence of this extraneous factor. We then slightly modify our calculations and in the end are able to get a more accurate estimate of the true error variance, and as such a better estimate of the effect of our independent variable. The disadvantage of this approach is that it can only be applied to experimental designs, while ANCOVA is able to be used in non-experimental research. Of course, you can actually use both where necessary, including covariates in a randomized block design experiment, but that is a little beyond the scope of this book.

As an example of this design, consider again the sales incentive study. This time, though, imagine that you went beyond thinking that just one single nuisance factor may exist. More specifically, remember that you thought above that the salesperson's experience would have an impact on their performance, so you measured it and included it as a covariate. This is all very well, but there are other ways of taking account of these differences. I am going to extend the sales incentive example here, but you should know that the randomized block design is useful in many other experimental situations, not just those concerning people. Randomized blocks can be considered as a possibility any time there is some nuisance factor that needs to be controlled for. Of course, the decision about 'need' is one for the researcher – in other words, you have to judge how important each nuisance factor is.

In this case, imagine that you think salesperson intelligence might also have some kind of impact on performance, in that more intelligent salespeople will sell more. As such, intelligence will have an effect on their performance, over and above the incentive scheme that is being examined in the experiment. So, salesperson intelligence is a nuisance factor, which differs across salespeople (each salesperson has a different level of intelligence), and this factor will contaminate our MS_E estimate, since it now includes both random error and error due to intelligence.

In order to deal with this, we are going to use essentially each salesperson as their own control, and test each salesperson's performance in response to all three of the different incentive schemes. So, technically, the incentive scheme is the factor of interest (i.e. independent variable) and the salesperson is the blocking factor. It is called a randomized block design because we have to randomize the order in which each incentive scheme (i.e. the treatment) is applied to each salesperson. You cannot use the same order across every salesperson, because, if you do, any differences in performance (the dependent variable) might be due to the order of the application of each scheme. You can use many other factors as blocking factors, though – this is just one example.

So, in order to do this, we take a random sample of $n = 5$ salespeople (this n is chosen purely to allow simple display of the data in this example), who over the next three quarters were given each of the three incentive schemes in turn (remember, the order of administration of the incentive schemes was random, otherwise the order could have an effect on the results). Table 14.6 shows the data for this experiment. Because each salesperson receives each level of the treatment, any variance due to individual difference nuisance factors should be able to be removed. Another way to think about this is that we are administering the same experiment separately to each block (with each salesperson in this case considered as a single block). So, essentially, it does not matter how intelligent the salesperson is. There are other ways of setting up a randomized block design, particularly where you have control of the blocking variable. However, in this case, you cannot really exert any kind of meaningful 'control' over intelligence, so it is best to use this sort of design. In other contexts (e.g. factory production experiments), you would have more control. For example, you could allocate sample elements to different blocks. This kind of thing is called blocking. You could do something *similar* here, by dividing the population of salespeople into groups, based on their intelligence (e.g. high, medium, low), then take a number (say, five) of salespeople from each product line. The block would then be the five salespeople with the same intelligence level. This is a very common design. One thing to remember here is that you still need to assign the salespeople in each block randomly to the different treatments. You can also use what are called incomplete block designs, where not all treatments are applied to each block. However, this sort of design is beyond the scope of this book. You might also think in this particular case that you could measure intelligence and include it as a covariate in an ANCOVA, as done above. You would be right, but what if you could not be confident you were accurately measuring intelligence? The randomized block design does not require you to measure intelligence, because using each salesperson as their own control takes account of individual differences in general. Further, if you were to try to take into account every individual difference factor as a covariate, things would get very unwieldy. Randomized block designs obviate the need for such things.

Table 14.6 Randomized block design data

		100% Commission	100% Salary	Mixed	Block totals	Block means
				Treatments		
	Salesperson 1	121	99	146	366	122
	Salesperson 2	148	87	98	333	111
Blocks	Salesperson 3	228	101	247	576	192
	Salesperson 4	87	89	121	297	99
	Salesperson 5	75	96	63	234	78
Treatment totals		659	472	675	1806	
Treatment means		131.8	94.4	135	361.2	
Grand mean						120.4

ANOVA for Randomized Blocks

The basic idea behind ANOVA for randomized blocks is that you have to partition the total sum of squares SS_T into the sum of squares due to the model SS_M, the sum of squares due to the blocking SS_B and the sum of squares due to residuals SS_R. You should remember most of these terms from our first ANOVA example. What is added here is basically the idea of partitioning out the SS_B from the other sources of error in the model. Formally:

$$SS_T = SS_M + SS_B + SS_R$$

From here, the best way to explain the procedure is actually to do it, and note the key concepts and calculations as we go. So, you will remember that your test statistic for ANOVA is the F statistic, which is the mean square model/mean square error. It therefore stands to reason that we better begin by calculating these values.

Now, for all of the equations for calculating the sums of squares, the following notation will be used:

x_{ij} = value of the data point for treatment j in block i

$\bar{x}_j$ = sample mean for the jth treatment

$\bar{x}_i$ = sample mean for the ith block

$\bar{\bar{x}}$ = grand mean

b = number of blocks

k = number of treatments

To get to the mean squares, we need to calculate SS_M and SS_E. But we also need to calculate SS_T and SS_B. So, let's get on with it! First, SS_T via the following equation:

$$SS_T = \sum_{i=1}^{b} \sum_{j=1}^{k} \left(x_{ij} - \bar{\bar{x}} \right)^2$$

This is a reasonably scary-looking formula, but is actually quite simple. All it says is that you have to take the sum of the squares of each data point minus the grand mean. So, to demonstrate:

$$SS_T = (121 - 120.4)^2 + (99 - 120.4)^2 + (146 - 120.4)^2 + \ldots + (63 - 120.4)^2 = 39527.6$$

Now, because this is a long bit of working, I have not printed all of it – for the other sums of squares I will be able to show the whole thing. Anyway, moving on, we calculate the sum of squares due to the model, SS_M, using the equation:

$$SS_M = b \sum_{j=1}^{k} (\bar{x}_i - \bar{\bar{x}})^2$$

In plain English, all you are doing here is taking the sum of the squares of each treatment mean minus the grand mean, and multiplying by the number of blocks,[8] as follows:

$$SS_M = 5[(131.8 - 120.4)^2 + (94.4 - 120.4)^2 + (135 - 120.4)^2] = 5095.6$$

Beginning to get it? Simple really. Next is the sum of squares due to blocks SS_B, using:

$$SS_B = k \sum_{j=1}^{k} (\bar{x}_i - \bar{\bar{x}})^2$$

You should be able to work out by now that this simply means the sum of the squares of each block mean minus the grand mean, multiplied by the number of treatments:

$$SS_B = 3[(122 - 120.4)^2 + (111 - 120.4)^2 + (192 - 120.4)^2 + (99 - 120.4)^2 + (78 - 120.4)^2] = 22419.6$$

The sum of squares due to error is rather simpler to work out, as:

$$SS_E = SS_T - SS_M - SS_B$$

You can use the earlier results to calculate this:

$$SS_E = 39527.6 - 5095.6 - 22419.6 = 12012.4$$

---

[8] Incidentally, are you beginning to realize why mathematical notation was developed?

Now you have the basic information, you can calculate a simple ANOVA table which includes the mean squares. That said, you will need to know the degrees of freedom for each mean square in order to complete this task. To calculate the mean square due to treatments, MS_M, the degrees of freedom are the number of treatments $k - 1$. For the mean square due to blocks, the degrees of freedom are the number of blocks $b - 1$. For the mean square due to error, the degrees of freedom are $(k - 1)(b - 1)$. For completeness' sake, you should also know that the degrees of freedom for the total variation in the data (e.g. SS_T) are $n - 1$.

So with this in mind, the formulae for the various mean squares of interest are:

$$MS_T = \frac{SS_T}{k - 1}$$

$$MS_B = \frac{SS_B}{b - 1}$$

$$MS_E = \frac{SS_E}{(k - 1)(b - 1)}$$

Now, let's set up that ANOVA table, and then use the information to test the null hypothesis that there is no effect of incentive scheme on sales performance. The ANOVA table is given in Table 14.7.

Table 14.7 ANOVA table for randomized block design

Source of variance	Degrees of freedom	Sum of squares	Mean square	F
Model/treatments	2	5095.6	2547.8	$\dfrac{2547.8}{1501.55}$
Blocks	4	22419.6	5604.9	$= 1.697$
Error	8	12012.4	1501.55	
Total	14	39527.6		

So, in order to conduct the hypothesis test, we need to choose a level of significance, and as usual we will use $\alpha = 0.05$. We know that $F = 1.697$ from Table 14.7, and you should remember that the equation for F is:

$$F = \frac{MS_M}{MS_E}$$

In order to use F we need to know the degrees of freedom. For the numerator, the degrees of freedom are the number of treatments $k - 1 = 3 - 1 = 2$. For the denominator, the degrees of freedom are $(k - 1)(b - 1) = (3 - 1)(5 - 1) = 2 \times 4 = 8$. Our p-value is the area under the F-distribution to the right of $F = 1.697$. So, for an F-distribution with 2 degrees of freedom in the numerator and 8 degrees of freedom in the denominator, $F = 1.697$ lies somewhere below $F_{0.1}$, meaning that our p-value has to be greater than 0.1. This means we are unable to reject the null hypothesis of equal means, and we conclude that our sample does not give us the required evidence to reject H_0.

One final thing to note is that you may be tempted to compute a different F, to try to see the effect of the blocks. For example, you could compute:

$$F = \frac{MS_B}{MS_E}$$

However, it would be a mistake to use this to try to see that 'effect' of the blocks. You did not design this experiment to test the effect of the blocks, you only included the blocking design to remove the variation due to the blocking factor(s). You cannot now go back after the fact and pretend otherwise. One thing you *can* use $F = MS_B/MS_E$ for is to see whether you should continue to use this blocking factor in future experiments. More specifically, if it is significant, you would be justified in concluding that this blocking factor is important in future designs. However, that is all you can conclude, you *cannot* use this to draw a conclusion about a second treatment factor (in this case we said it was 'intelligence'). If you want to draw conclusions about more than one treatment, then a different design needs to be used. Which brings us to…

FACTORIAL EXPERIMENTS: TWO-WAY ANOVA

So, if the blocking design above cannot be used to draw conclusions about a second independent variable, what *do* you do if you want to test more than one treatment factor? In this specific case, what if we looked at those results from the randomized block, and wanted to do another experiment to test whether both incentive scheme and product line had an impact on performance? In this case, where we actually want to draw conclusions about more than one independent variable, we can design a factorial experiment.

Consider this: imagine that the company sells three different photocopier lines. The company suspects that Product A is more attractive to the market than Product B, which in turn is more attractive than Product C. As such, the product line that each salesperson sells will have an effect on their performance, over and above the incentive scheme that is being examined in the experiment. Furthermore, each salesperson specializes in one or another of the product lines. We can design a factorial experiment to test the impact of *both* product line *and* incentive scheme on salesperson performance. Further, we can test the interaction between product line and incentive scheme. That is, does the incentive scheme have more of an effect on performance when the salesperson is selling one or another of the products? For example, if the salesperson sells Product A, is there a larger effect of incentive scheme on performance than when the salesperson sells Product B or C? In fact, factorial designs can be used to include more than two independent variables, using the same basic principles as will be discussed here. However, with three or more independent variables, things can get very unwieldy and hard to explain. So let's focus on two for the present case.

In order to conduct this experiment, we need to sample randomly a number of salespeople from each of the product line specializations. For ease of calculation, let's sample six salespeople from each product line, which would allow us to allocate randomly two salespeople from each specialization to each of the incentive schemes. Remember, random allocation is crucial, and should be used wherever you can in an experimental design.

If you count up the salespeople, this gives a total sample size of 18. Two salespeople from each product line specialization will be allocated to one of the three incentive schemes. So, we have a sample size of two for each treatment, which is also known as having two replications. Of course, you could easily use a larger sample size, and this one is used purely to make the computations I am about to do feasible to show. Anyway, conducting the ANOVA analysis for this design will allow us to gain information on the following effects:

The effect of incentive scheme (factor A) on performance.

The effect of product line (factor B) on performance.

The interaction effect between incentive scheme and product line.

Interaction effects can be hard to explain, but in this example we are referring to whether salespeople specializing in some product lines do better under one incentive scheme, while others do better under a different scheme. If you use an experimental design, you have to use a factorial experiment to study an interaction effect (although you can also study interactions by using modifications of the multiple regression analysis techniques you saw earlier). If we find the interaction effect is significant, it means that the effect of incentive scheme depends on what product line the salesperson specializes in.

ANOVA for Factorial Experiments

Table 14.8 presents the data we collected for this factorial experiment. Remember, there are two sales-people in each cell, hence the multiple data points. The ANOVA analysis is very similar to what you have already done, but just a little more complex, because the formula for partitioning the sums of squares is more complicated:

$$SS_T = SS_A + SS_B + SS_{AB} + SS_E$$

where:

SS_T = the total sum of squares (you remember this – *right?*)

SS_A = the sum of squares due to factor A

SS_B = the sum of squares due to factor B

SS_{AB} = the sum of squares due to the interaction between factor A and factor B

SS_E = the sum of squares due to ... error (just testing)

Table 14.8 Factorial experimental design data

		Factor B: product			Incentive totals	Incentive means
		Product A	Product B	Product C		
	Commission	236	185	150		
Factor A:		198	202	90	1061	176.8333333
incentive	Salary	95	120	75		
		102	135	110	637	106.1666667
	Mixed	170	147	75		
		163	125	97	777	129.5
Product totals		964	914	597		
Product means		160.6666667	152.3333333	99.5		
Grand mean						137.5

Because there are two factors, and one interaction, we actually compute three *F* statistics, and in order to obtain these, we need first to compute a bunch of mean squares to MS_A, MS_B, MS_{AB} and MS_E, which means we also need to compute first the associated sums of squares, as well as SS_T.

Just like before, we are going to go through these formulae together. They look more complex, because there is more to remember. However, ultimately, they are just a small extension of the randomized block equations. Just keep in mind the following notation which will be used:

$\bar{x}_{ijk}$ = value of the data point for the *k*th replicate of treatment *i* of factor A and treatment *j* of factor B

$\bar{x}_i$ = sample mean for all observations in the treatment *i*(factor A)

$\bar{x}_j$ = sample mean for all observations in the treatment *j*(factor B)

$\bar{x}_{ij}$ = sample mean for the observations corresponding to the combination of treatment *i*(factor A)and treatment *j*(factor B)

$\bar{\bar{x}}$ = grand mean

a = number of levels of factor A

b = number of levels of factor B

r = number of replications

n_T = total number of observations in the experiment (equivalent to abr)

Now, some of those descriptions might be unfamiliar, but just follow through the calculations and compare with the numbers in Table 14.8, and it will make sense. Pay particular attention to the mean values in the table. Where things might get a bit hard to understand, I will explain as we go through the calculations.

So, first, let's calculate SS_T; it is the simplest calculation, although it is also the longest, because we have to use every data point. The relevant formula is:

$$SS_T = \sum_{i=1}^{a} \sum_{j=1}^{b} \sum_{k=1}^{r} \left(\bar{x}_{ijk} - \bar{\bar{x}} \right)^2$$

Again, while this looks scary, it basically just means take each data point, subtract the grand mean, square the result and then add them all together, as follows:

$$SS_T = (236 - 137.5)^2 + (198 - 137.5)^2 + (185 - 137.5)^2 + \ldots + (97 - 137.5)^2 = 37732.5$$

Remember, because of the length of this working, it is not possible to show all of it, but you should be able to work it out reasonably easily. So, moving on, SS_A is the sum of squares for factor A – which is the incentive plan. The formula is:

$$SS_A = br \sum_{i=1}^{a} \left(\bar{x}_i - \bar{\bar{x}} \right)^2$$

This is reasonably simple. Remember what b and r represent (look back if you cannot remember). Then it is basically a matter of finding the mean for each level of factor A (incentives), subtracting the grand mean and squaring. But do not forget the multiplications in the formula. See below, and look to pick out the relevant values of Table 14.8 (incentive totals):

$$SS_A = (3)(2)[(176.83 - 137.5)^2 + (106.17 - 137.5)^2 + (129.5 - 137.5)^2] = 15557.33$$

Next, it is time to work out SS_B – the sum of squares for factor B – which is the product type. The formula is:

$$SS_B = ar \sum_{j=1}^{a} \left(\bar{x}_i - \bar{\bar{x}} \right)^2$$

You should be pretty comfortable by now with this. It is essentially the same as the SS_A formula, but instead substituting the means of each level for factor B (product type). Check it out below:

$$SS_B = (3)(2)[(160.67 - 137.5)^2 + (152.33 - 137.5)^2 + (99.5 - 137.5)^2] = 13204.33$$

The next step is to work out SS_{AB}, the sum of squares for the interaction, using the following formula:

$$SS_{AB} = r \sum_{i=1}^{a} \sum_{j=1}^{b} \left(\bar{x}_{ij} - \bar{x}_i - \bar{x}_j - \bar{\bar{x}} \right)^2$$

By now you should be getting good at working these out. What you are doing here is taking the mean for each combination of treatment level, then subtracting both the factor A mean and factor B mean, and adding the grand mean. This might cause you a bit of a hassle, thinking of what the mean for the 'combination' might be. Well, there are nine of these. For example, the mean of the combination of commission and Product A is the mean of the two data points corresponding to that combination. Look at the top left hand corner of the data in Table 14.8 and you will see that the two data points in that combination are

236 and 198. The mean is simply $(236 + 198)/2 = 217$. You should be able to work out the rest for yourself, following along with the working below:

$$SS_{AB} = 2[(217 - 176.83 - 160.67 + 137.5)^2 + (193.5 - 176.83 - 152.33 + 137.5)^2 +$$
$$(120 - 176.83 - 99.5 + 137.5)^2 + \ldots + (92.5 - 129.5 - 99.5 + 137.5)^2 = 4871.167$$

The final step is to calculate SS_E, which you will be relieved to know is a lot simpler than the above calculations:

$$SS_E = SS_T - SS_T - SS_A - SS_B - SS_{AB}$$

I think we are all quite capable of that, don't you? So:

$$SS_E = 37732.5 - 15557.33 - 13204.33 - 4871.167 = 4099.67$$

OK! So, we have the sums of squares. But you will no doubt remember that we are not done yet. We need the mean squares, and then we can calculate the relevant F statistics. Remember, you get a mean square by dividing the relevant sum of squares by its degrees of freedom. For the two-factor experiment, the relevant formulae are:

$$MS_A = \frac{SS_A}{a-1}$$

$$MS_B = \frac{SS_B}{b-1}$$

$$MS_{AB} = \frac{SS_{AB}}{(a-1)(b-)}$$

$$MS_E = \frac{SS_E}{ab(r-)}$$

Furthermore, the degrees of freedom for SS_T are $n_T - 1$.

With these in hand, the relevant F statistics are:

$$\text{Factor A} = \frac{MS_A}{MS_E}$$

$$\text{Factor B} = \frac{MS_B}{MS_E}$$

$$\text{Interaction} = \frac{MS_{AB}}{MS_E}$$

So, with all these in mind, you can create a nice ANOVA table for the results of this two-factor experiment, as can be seen in Table 14.9.

All that is left to do now is test our hypotheses, using the F statistics. Of course, because of the complexity and length of the calculations, you would normally get a computer software package to do the heavy lifting for you, and give you the relevant p-values. But, there is nothing stopping us doing it ourselves. We have the relevant degrees of freedom for each F, and as such we can look up the critical values for $p = 0.05$ in the F-distribution table. If you recall, to work out the critical value you need two different types of degrees of freedom. In this case, the degrees of freedom for the denominator are always those for the error, in this case 9. Then, to establish the critical value for each effect, you simply use the relevant degrees of freedom for the numerator.

Table 14.9 Two-way ANOVA table

Source of variance	Degrees of freedom	Sum of squares	Mean square	F
Factor A	2	15557.33	7778.67	17.08
Factor B	2	13204.33	6602.17	14.49
Interaction	4	4871.47	1217.8	2.67
Error	9	4099.67	455.52	
Total	17	37732.5		

So, in the case of factor A, $F = 17.08$, the degrees of freedom for the numerator are 2, and for the denominator, 9. Looking at the F-distribution for $p = 0.05$, we see that the critical value for the area in the upper tail is 4.26. As such, we can see clearly that the calculated F is greater than the critical value, allowing us to reject the null hypothesis, and suggesting that there is an effect of incentive plan on sales performance. You can draw the same conclusion for factor B, because the degrees of freedom are the same, meaning that the critical value of F for $p = 0.05$ is also 4.26. The calculated F for factor B is 14.49, clearly greater than the critical value. So, we reject the null hypothesis for factor B, and conclude that evidence suggests there is also an effect of product type on sales performance.

When it comes to the interaction, the degrees of freedom of the numerator are 4, with those for the denominator remaining at 9. For $p = 0.05$, the critical value is now 3.63. Since in this case our calculated F is less than the critical value, we have no real evidence to suggest there is an interaction effect.

We can investigate more closely those factors that are found to be significant, to see where the differences lie. For example, it might not be that all three treatment levels are different. Perhaps one is much more different than the others, which drives the overall effect. Looking first at factor A, we can see in Table 14.8 that the sample mean for Commission is 176.8, which is a lot bigger than those for Salary (106.17) and Mixed (129.5). We could do individual post-hoc tests on these differences if we wanted to. Looking at the differences, it does seem likely that there are fairly large differences across them all. The situation is slightly different for factor B, the product type. Look at the mean for Product C, which is 597, whereas the means for Product A (964) and Product B (914) are relatively more similar. It seems likely that the effect here is being driven by Product C, and this may influence the firm to look seriously into whether this product is worthwhile keeping.

Excel and ANOVA

Table 14.10 shows the data collected on the delivery times (in days) from four different suppliers. We will use this data to see which supplier has the greatest variance in delivery times.

Table 14.10

Supplier 1	Supplier 2	Supplier 3	Supplier 4
10	13	16	16
11	10	17	15
15	14	16	20
17	11	20	13
17	15	20	16

We will use what Excel calls 'Anova:single factor', since we are only interested in the variation of the single factor, delivery times. Figure 14.14 shows where to find single-factor ANOVA in the 'Data Analysis' toolbox.

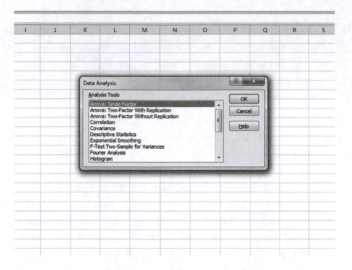

Figure 14.14

You will notice in Figure 14.15 that the data for analysis is located in the cell range A1 to D6, which is entered in the 'Input Range' when you select 'Anova: Single Factor' from the pop-up menu. Do not forget to check the 'Labels in first row' box.

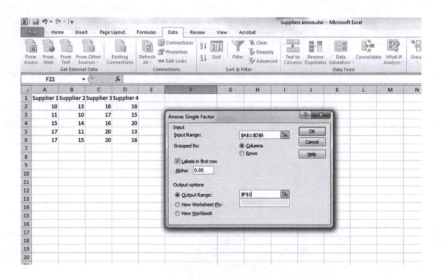

Figure 14.15

Figure 14.16 shows the results from running the analysis. Looking at the summary table, we can see that suppliers 1 and 2 have the least amount of variation in the delivery times. This means that planning for manufacturing can be easier since you know that these two suppliers will probably deliver within approximately four days of the target date.

If we now look at the 'Anova' table we can see that the F value is 3.99 and the p-value 0.03. This tells us that the null hypothesis that there is no difference in the variance in the means can be rejected at the 95% confidence level. We can also see that the F_{crit} value for $\alpha = 0.005$ is 3.24, whereas the F value is 3.99, which again indicates that the null hypothesis should be rejected. Unfortunately, these statistics do not tell us which suppliers are different, only that there is a significant difference between the population means

Anova: Single Factor

SUMMARY				
Groups	Count	Sum	Average	Variance
Supplier 1	5	70	14	11
Supplier 2	5	63	12.6	4.3
Supplier 3	5	89	17.8	4.2
Supplier 4	5	80	16	6.5

ANOVA						
Source of Variation	SS	df	MS	F	P-value	F crit
Between Groups	77.8	3	25.93	3.99	0.03	3.24
Within Groups	104	16	6.5			
Total	181.8	19				

Figure 14.16

for delivery times. Using Excel for two-way ANOVA is very similar, except you have to decide between using 'Anova: Two-Factor Without Replication' and 'Anova: Two-Factor With Replication'. The difference is that with ANOVA with replication you are gathering multiple samples from, say, the same factory (i.e. you are replicating the data – highly recommended).

Using SPSS for ANOVA

You have been asked to rate the performance of five sales offices located in different cities: Bristol, Birmingham, London, Glasgow and Manchester. You have collected five months of data concerning the sales of a particular brand of computer sold at each of the offices, and the data is given in Table 14.11. You have to inform the sales director if all offices are performing at the same level.

Table 14.11

Office	Sales
1	68
1	72
1	75
1	42
1	53
2	72
2	52
2	63
2	55

(Continued)

Table 14.11   (Continued)

Office	Sales
2	48
3	75
3	60
3	82
3	65
3	77
4	48
4	61
4	57
4	64
4	50
5	64
5	65
5	70
5	68
5	53

In order to solve this problem we assume that all offices are performing to the same standard, so therefore our null hypothesis is that there is no differences between them. We will test this at the 0.05 significance level.

Figure 14.17 shows how the data is put into SPSS. In Variable View we enter 'Office' and designate it as nominal data. The sales data will be put under the sales heading with the data classed as scale.

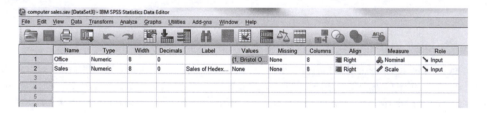

Figure 14.17

Since we have five offices, we allocate each office a number (remember Table 14.11) and provide a descriptive label (Figure 14.18).

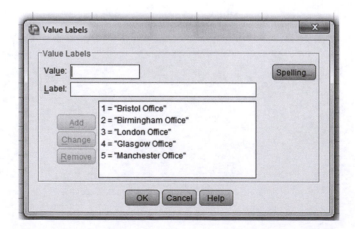

Figure 14.18

Now switch to Data View and enter the data as shown in Figure 14.19.

	Office	Sales	var
1	1	68	
2	1	72	
3	1	75	
4	1	42	
5	1	53	
6	2	72	
7	2	52	
8	2	63	
9	2	55	
10	2	48	
11	3	75	
12	3	60	
13	3	82	
14	3	65	
15	3	77	
16	4	48	
17	4	61	
18	4	57	
19	4	64	
20	4	50	
21	5	64	
22	5	65	
23	5	70	
24	5	68	
25	5	53	
26			

Figure 14.19

Staying in Data View, select <u>Analyze</u> → <u>Compare Means</u> → <u>One-Way Anova</u> (Figure 14.20).

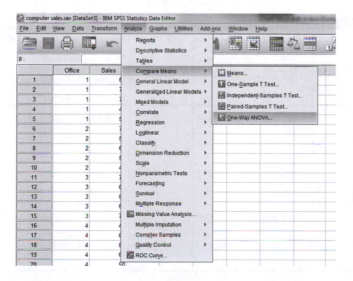

Figure 14.20

In the pop-up box, put Office as the Factor and Sales in the Dependent List box (Figure 14.21).

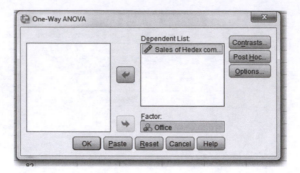

Figure 14.21

Once this is done, go to Options and tick 'Descriptive' and 'Homogeneity of variance test', see Figure 14.22.

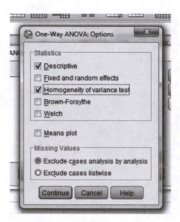

Figure 14.22

Click on Continue then on OK. SPSS will open the Viewer window where the statistics will be displayed. Table 14.12 shows the descriptive statistics so that the mean, etc., can be viewed.

Table 14.12

Descriptives

Sales of Hedex computer system

	N	Mean	Std. Deviation	Std. Error	95% Confidence Interval for Mean		Minimum	Maximum
					Lower Bound	Upper Bound		
Bristol Office	5	62.00	14.018	6.269	44.59	79.41	42	75
Birmingham Office	5	58.00	9.566	4.278	46.12	69.88	48	72
London Office	5	71.80	9.039	4.042	60.58	83.02	60	82
Glasgow Office	5	56.00	6.892	3.082	47.44	64.56	48	64
Manchester Office	5	64.00	6.595	2.950	55.81	72.19	53	70
Total	25	62.36	10.408	2.082	58.06	66.66	42	82

Test of Homogeneity of Variances

Sales of Hedex computer system

Levene Statistic	df1	df2	Sig.
2.130	4	20	.115

ANOVA

Sales of Hedex computer system

	Sum of Squares	df	Mean Square	F	Sig.
Between Groups	756.960	4	189.240	2.054	.125
Within Groups	1842.800	20	92.140		
Total	2599.760	24			

The Levene statistic is not significant and therefore we can be confident that we have homogeneity of variances (one of the assumptions of ANOVA).

The F value for the 'Between Groups' of 2.054 indicates we cannot confidently reject the null hypothesis. The value of the F-ratio, 2.054, at a significance of 0.125 (i.e. greater than 0.05, our stated test value) means that there is a 12.5% chance of this occurring due to other factors. You may decide that this is acceptable, but a more thorough approach would demand you revisit your data and consider other things that could influence your outcomes.

Using Excel for Randomized Block Experiments

To illustrate how to use Excel to perform randomized block design analysis we will use the data shown in Figure 14.23.

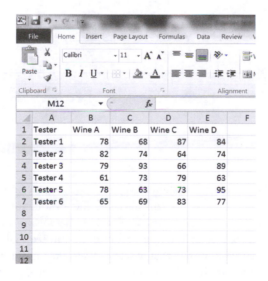

Figure 14.23

We will use this approach since we want to compare the quality of a wine which has been tested by six experts. We need to reduce the variability between the testers so we use the randomized block design, treating each tester as a block. We will use Excel's 'Anova: Two-Factor Without Replication' to analyse the data. Figure 14.24 shows the dialog box which comes up after selecting Data → Anova: Two-Factor Without Replication. A word of warning: Excel will give an error warning if you include labels (a good idea) and do not tick labels in the dialog box.

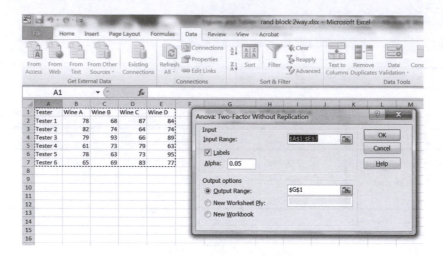

Figure 14.24

Figure 14.24 also shows the data range entered. Once you have completed the dialog box, click on OK and Excel will run the analysis. Figure 14.25 shows the output from Excel. You now need to interpret the results.

SUMMARY	Count	Sum	Average	Variance
Tester 1	4	333	83.25	18.92
Tester 2	4	291	72.75	140.92
Tester 3	4	294	73.50	17.67
Tester 4	4	291	72.75	94.25
Tester 5	4	256	64.00	16.00
Tester 6	4	307	76.75	214.25
Wine A	6	452	75.33	159.87
Wine B	6	474	79.00	120.80
Wine C	6	482	80.33	55.47
Wine D	6	491	81.83	32.57

ANOVA						
Source of Variation	SS	df	MS	F	P-value	F crit
Rows	563.33	5.00	112.67	0.89	0.51	2.90
Columns	942.33	3.00	314.11	2.48	0.10	3.29
Error	1901.67	15.00	126.78			
Total	3407.33	23.00				

Figure 14.25

The first table gives you the summary statistics. Always check this table since it is useful to make sure all your data has been included. The ANOVA table provides the information we need to make our decisions about the analysis. Excel gives us two ways of checking: the *p*-value and the *F* values. Looking at the 'Columns' statistics in the 'Source of Variation' column, we can see that the *F* statistic, 2.48, is less than the critical *F* value of 3.29. This implies that we cannot reject the null hypothesis (i.e. no difference between the mean ratings of the wines). This is confirmed by the *p*-value, which is greater than 0.05, our critical value.

This table also allows us to check to see if there are any significant differences between the testers. Looking at the 'Rows' statistics, we can see that the *F* value is less than the *F* critical value, therefore we cannot reject the null hypothesis. After combining these results we can conclude that the testers are consistent in evaluating the quality of a range of wines.

Using Excel for Factorial Experiments

To demonstrate how to use Excel for factorial experiments, we will analyse data comparing two machines from four different suppliers. We want to know if the quality of the components produced by the machines are comparable. In order to do this we will use Excel's 'Anova: Two-Factor With Replacement'. The data is shown in Figure 14.26.

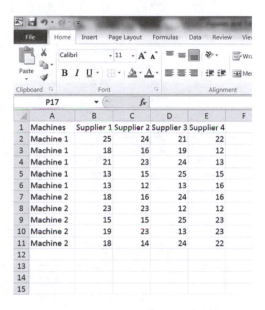

Figure 14.26

This procedure is very similar to the previous one, except this time we must specify how many rows are allocated to each machine; in our case it is five. Figure 14.27 shows the dialog box that needs to be completed in order to run the analysis.

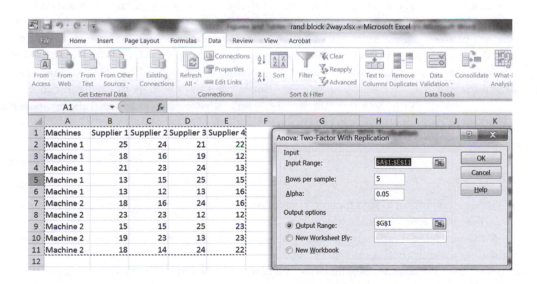

Figure 14.27

Once the analysis has been run, you will see the tables shown in Figure 14.28.

Anova: Two-Factor With Replication					
SUMMARY	Supplier	Supplier	Supplier	Supplier	Total
Machine 1					
Count	5	5	5	5	20
Sum	90	90	102	78	360
Average	18	18	20.4	15.6	18
Variance	27	27.5	22.8	15.3	22.53
Machine 2					
Count	5	5	5	5	20
Sum	93	91	98	96	378
Average	18.6	18.2	19.6	19.2	18.9
Variance	8.3	19.7	42.3	24.7	20.31
Total					
Count	10	10	10	10	
Sum	183	181	200	174	
Average	18.3	18.1	20	17.4	
Variance	15.79	20.99	29.11	21.38	

ANOVA						
Source of Variation	SS	df	MS	F	P-value	F crit
Sample	8.1	1	8.10	0.35	0.56	4.15
Columns	36.5	3	12.17	0.52	0.67	2.90
Interaction	26.9	3	8.97	0.38	0.77	2.90
Within	750.4	32	23.45			
Total	821.9	39				

Figure 14.28

Again, check the summary statistics and make sure everything is OK. We perform the analysis as before, comparing the F values and the p-values. Looking at the 'Interaction' statistics, we can see that the interaction effect between the machines and the suppliers is not significant since the F values are less than the critical value. Once this has been clarified, we can then go on to do our main analysis, comparing the quality of the components. Since the F values of the 'Columns' statistics are much less than the F critical values and the p -values are greater than 0.05, we cannot reject our null hypothesis that the machines produce components to the same standard. In other words, we can be confident that the components being produced by both machines are at the required standard.

Using SPSS

The same procedure is used in SPSS for both randomized block and factorial experiments. This being the case, we will look at doing factorial experiments.

Using SPSS for factorial experiments is reasonably straightforward. It is vital to set up your variables correctly using the rule 'the recorded data of a between-groups variable goes in a single column'. Unlike Excel, where you can create a table which has a more intuitive feel to it, SPSS takes longer to set up. On the plus side, you can perform a much more detailed analysis and specify all sorts of constraints and request different types of information.

We will use the example used with Excel, comparing the output from two machines, and investigate if the components produced are at the required standard. Figure 14.29 shows the data set out in the form required by SPSS. You should notice there are three variables, namely machine, supplier and component, where the first two are nominal and the third scale.

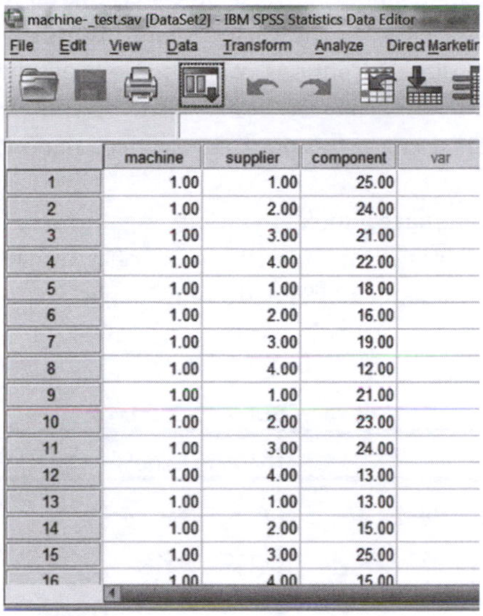

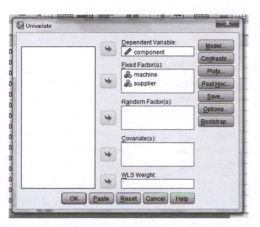

Figure 14.29

To perform the analysis select the Univariate option under General Linear Models found in the Analyze menu (see Figure 14.30).

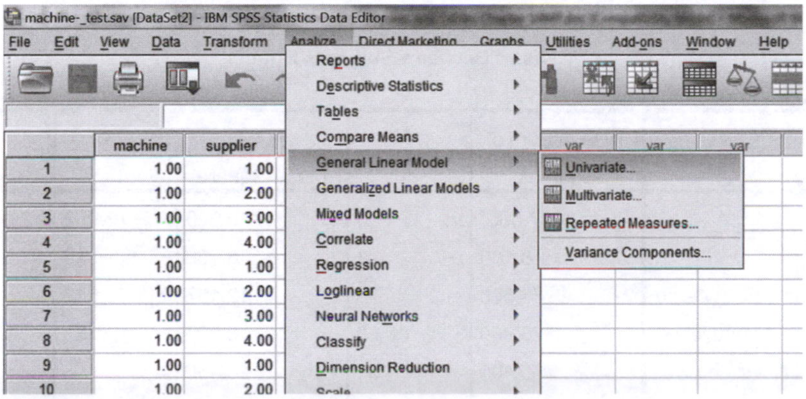

Figure 14.30

Figure 14.31

Figure 14.31 shows the pop-up dialog box where the variables are entered in their appropriate places. As you can see, 'component' is our dependent variable and 'machine' and 'supplier' are the independent variables, or in SPSS speak, the 'Fixed Factors'. Once you have entered your variables in the appropriate places, click on the Model button. By default SPSS does a full factorial analysis, which will suit our requirements. But if you click on the Custom radio button you can select which effects to investigate – have a play and try different options. We will also leave the Sum of Squares option as it is, since this allows both balanced and unbalanced designs. The option we will change is the Intercept as this is not relevant to what we are doing at this point, so uncheck the Include Intercept in Model option. Click on Continue.

Back at the main option screen, have a look at Options. Again there are all sorts of tests you can do, which for now we will leave since we will end up with masses of information which can obscure the main points of the example. Click on OK and let SPSS perform its magic!

Between-Subjects Factors

		Value Label	N
machine	1.00	machine 1	20
	2.00	machine 2	20
supplier	1.00	supplier 1	10
	2.00	supplier 2	10
	3.00	supplier 3	10
	4.00	supplier 4	10

Tests of Between-Subjects Effects

Dependent Variable: component

Source	Type III Sum of Squares	df	Mean Square	F	Sig.
Model	13687.600[a]	8	1710.950	72.962	.000
machine	8.100	1	8.100	.345	.561
supplier	36.500	3	12.167	.519	.672
machine * supplier	26.900	3	8.967	.382	.766
Error	750.400	32	23.450		
Total	14438.000	40			

a. R Squared = .948 (Adjusted R Squared = .935)

Figure 14.32

Figure 14.32 shows the resulting output. As always, check the summary statistics to make sure you have not left anything out and you are analysing what you actually want to analyse. Looking at the 'Test of Between-Subjects Effects' table, we can see the F statistic and its significance. Thankfully the results agree with the Excel output and we can form the same conclusions. One thing I found useful when learning how to use SPSS and Excel to perform data analysis was to compare their respective outputs. Both forms have their strengths and weaknesses. For example, Excel talks about 'sample, columns and interaction' whereas SPSS uses the variable names. Excel gives the critical value for F whereas SPSS gives the significance value.

SUMMARY

Sorry – that was a bit longer than I thought. I mean, 17000 words! But, as I said earlier, ANOVA is probably the other key analysis method you need to get under control. From here on in, you are on your own!!

Just kidding. What I mean is, this marks the end of the chapters where we deal with stuff that *everyone* needs to know. From here on, the last couple of chapters are concerned with the more specialized topics of time series models and quality control. By now, you should be pretty confident with a lot of key basic skills in the quantitative analysis toolkit, and you should also be very proud of yourself! If this is where we part company, then it has been real, it has been fun – in fact, it has been real fun.

For those continuing on, gird your loins. Damn the torpedoes, full speed ahead…

 final checklist

You should have covered and understood the following basic content in this chapter:

☑ Key concepts of experimental design, and with them the reasons behind an ANOVA approach.

☑ How ANOVA can be understood in a regression context.

☑ The calculation of sums of squares, mean squares and associated *F* statistics.

☑ How to test for the significance of the overall effects in ANOVA.

☑ How to use multiple comparison tests to interrogate ANOVA results in more detail.

☑ How to include covariates in an ANCOVA analysis.

☑ How to design a randomized block experiment and use ANOVA to analyse it.

☑ How to design a two-factor factorial experiment and use two-way ANOVA to analyse it.

EXERCISES

1. In the text an example was given on ANCOVA. Rerun the analysis but this time do not use 'experience' as a covariate. The 'Tests of Between-Subjects Effects' table should look like Figure 14.33.

Tests of Between-Subjects Effects

Dependent Variable: sales_performance

Source	Type III Sum of Squares	df	Mean Square	F	Sig.
Corrected Model	22.467[a]	2	11.234	3.025	.066
Intercept	514.650	1	514.650	138.565	.000
incentive	22.467	2	11.234	3.025	.066
Error	96.567	26	3.714		
Total	684.000	29			
Corrected Total	119.034	28			

a. R Squared = .189 (Adjusted R Squared = .126)

Figure 14.33

a. Compare the SS_T, SS_M and SS_R values from the table above with the ones obtained when 'experience' was the covariate. What do these comparisons tell you, particularly the SS_R values?

b. Since the SS_R value indicates that 81.1% of the variation in data is due to extraneous factors, what action would you recommend?

c. Comparing the SS_R value (96.567) with the 'no experience' covariate and the SS_R value with 'experience' as a covariate (17.847), what can you conclude?

d. This time compare the *F* value and its significance. Again, what does this tell you?

2. Table 14.13 shows the yield in kilograms per greenhouse of tomato plants grown in a particular type of soil treated with fertilizers A, B or C.

  a. What form of ANOVA should be used to analyse the variance?
  b. Calculate the mean yields for the different treatments.
  c. Calculate the grand mean for all treatments.
  d. Find the total variation.
  e. Find the variation between treatments.
  f. Find the variation within treatments.

  Perform the calculations by 'hand' and then use Excel and SPSS to compare the results.

Table 14.13

Fert. A	Fert. B	Fert. C
48	47	49
49	49	51
50	48	50
49	48	50

3. Table 14.14 shows the number of defective bolts produced by four different machines on a given day of the week for each of two shifts. Using SPSS perform an analysis of variance to test at the 0.05 significance level whether there is:

  a. a difference in machines
  b. a difference in shifts.
  c. State any conclusions you can draw from the analysis.

Table 14.14

Machine	Shift	Mon	Tue	Wed	Thur	Fri
A	1	6	4	5	5	4
	2	5	7	4	6	8
B	1	10	8	7	7	9
	2	7	9	12	8	8
C	1	7	5	6	5	9
	2	9	7	5	4	6
D	1	8	4	6	5	5
	2	5	7	9	7	10

To run this analysis use the Univariate option in the General Linear Model option of the Analyze menu. Be careful how you assign the independent and dependent variables. You can also run contrasts, post-hoc tests and plot the comparisons, which can be very useful.

To access additional online resources please visit: **https://study.sagepub.com/leepeters**

The Ballad of Eddie the Easily Distracted: Part 15

Certainly, after last week's new experience of actually understanding something a little, and even being able to help Esha a bit, normal service was comprehensively resumed for Eddie this week. Even though he could see that time series models were pretty similar in idea to the regression things he'd worked so hard on earlier in the year, he was struggling a bit to transfer that knowledge over. Even so, he could very easily see how this stuff could be useful in later life – after all, his parents had spent a heck of a long time in the last few years talking about house price movements and economic stuff like interest rates, inflation and so forth. It seemed that all these things were major topics of conversation for 'old people', and they were constantly predicting the future in order to make decisions on what to do. Eddie thought that if they'd had a bit of understanding of forecasting methods like he was learning, maybe they would have made better decisions? In fact, he wondered if the government even had any understanding of these methods, given the stupid decisions they seemed to be making on a daily basis. Eddie stopped dead in his tracks, mildly surprised at the kinds of things he was thinking – 'Wow, I've changed!' he thought.

As he was standing in the middle of the path, lost in thought, he felt a tap on his right shoulder and turned around. No one there. Then he heard a giggle from his left and spun around to see Esha smiling at him. 'What were you so lost in thought about Eddie?' she asked. 'Oh, just thinking about forecasts, would you believe?' he replied. Esha looked surprised: 'Well, I'm just off to study this week's material in the library if you want to come along,' she said. There was a pause. Eddie had been off to town to look at old records. 'Oh, well, OK then. Sounds great!' Eddie thought weirdly; he wasn't even being sarcastic.

Esha's Story: Part 15

Esha was on much more solid ground this week, at least where QUAN101 was concerned. She easily saw the connection between time series models and the regression models she knew so well (and, with Eddie's help, applying them to ANOVA last week had helped even more). Simple: time was considered the independent variable. In fact, there seemed no reason not to include all kinds of other variables in a forecasting model based on regression, and she guessed she'd see that towards the end of the chapter she was reading in the textbook. She was in such a pleasant mood that she was almost skipping off to the library to finish her revision of the topic.

It was at this point that she saw Eddie standing completely still in the middle of the path to the library, staring off into the distance, 'Probably thinking about computers or something,' thought Esha, as she tapped him on the shoulder. She was of course surprised to find that he was in fact thinking of forecasting; he really was a bit of an enigma. Anyway, Esha thought it might be fun to go over the material with him in the library, since he seemed to be on that way anyway ('Wow, he's changed,' she thought). Eddie seemed to pause, and Esha wondered whether he was actually going to see someone else, surprising herself by feeling a bit annoyed at that idea. As they walked off to the library together, both seemingly deep in thought, Esha blurted out without thinking 'Why don't we get a coffee first?', just to fill the silence of course.

TIME SERIES MODELS AND FORECASTING

CONTENTS

 learning objectives

Some of the material gets quite complex here, so try to keep these key learning objectives in mind as you study:

- ☑ Understand the main reason behind forecasting, and what a time series is.
- ☑ Learn what the trend, seasonal, cyclical and irregular components of a time series represent.
- ☑ Learn how smoothing can help to remove irregular components from a stable time series, and the different methods of smoothing: moving averages, weighted moving averages and exponential smoothing.

- ☑ Learn how to use a linear model to model and project a trend in a time series.
- ☑ Learn how to discover and remove seasonal components from a time series.
- ☑ Learn how multiple regression methods can be incorporated into a time series framework to make more accurate forecasts.

We all plan for the future in some way – well, almost all of us. In fact, research has shown that we can predict a lot of future problems for an individual if his or her ability to plan for the future is lower. Certainly, lots of research has shown that organizations that plan for the future are more successful. Good planning enables good management. On an individual basis, many of us plan for the future based on our hunches, or feelings of what 'might' happen. However, it is far from certain that going with our feelings and hunches is the best way to plan for the future in business.

The purpose of this chapter is to introduce various methods of forecasting the future based on quantitative data and analysis. To continue our sales analogy from the last few chapters, imagine you are the sales manager for the photocopier firm we have previously discussed. Your own boss would naturally want you to provide forecasts for the future sales of the various products you were selling. These forecasts would have major impacts on the rest of the business – from recruitment policies to production schedules. So, it should be clear that poor forecasting is a major problem for business. The question is: how do we do 'good' forecasting? After all, if we could predict the future, we probably would not be in the photocopier sales business (or the textbook writing business either, as you will see later in this chapter).

Anyway, if you are the photocopier sales manager, the first thing you are going to need to do is look at the data on your past sales. This is the historical sales data, which makes up a time series. A time series is a set of observations for a single variable measured at points over successive time periods. Using a time series of sales allows you to gain a view of the basic sales level and whether it is increasing or decreasing over time – which is usually called a trend. Looking more closely, you might find that there is some cyclical pattern over a time period, like sales in the first quarter being the peak, and then going down in the second quarter, each year – this is a seasonal pattern. These two characteristics will give you some basic ideas about what to forecast in the future.

Of course, there are plenty of other variables that you might want to use to help you provide a forecast. However, if the only data you use to predict the future value of a variable is the past values of the variable, you are using a time series method. In this case, you are looking for some pattern in the time series and trying to extrapolate that into the future. So, your forecast is based only on past values of the variable. On the other hand, if you assume that the variable you are trying to forecast has some sort of cause–effect relationship with other variables, you could use those other variables in a causal forecasting method. For example, you might think that photocopier sales are in some way influenced by the advertising expenditure of the photocopier firm. You could use historical data on advertising expenditure and sales to develop a regression equation (recall Chapters 10 and 11 where regression models were introduced) showing the relationship between advertising and sales. Using the intended future expenditure for advertising, you could then predict sales. In fact, using regression for forecasting is only a slight extension of the things you have already learnt about regression.

In this chapter, a variety of time series forecasting methods will be introduced and explained. Most of the chapter will focus on these methods, as they require some explanation – although they really are not that complicated. Towards the end of the chapter, though, I will show you how to extend regression modelling into the forecasting domain.

THE COMPONENTS OF A TIME SERIES

A time series is basically the record of some behavioural pattern – be it sales, or whatever. However, it is not quite as simple as that. Usually, we assume that a time series consists of four components:

1. A trend, which is the overall movement in the time series.
2. A cyclical component, which is any recurring pattern above or below the trend that lasts more than one year.
3. A seasonal component, which is any recurring pattern that is less than one year in duration.
4. An irregular component, which is equivalent to a residual factor which catches all the deviations other than the trend, cyclical or seasonal factors.

To begin with, let us clarify that we could create a time series by using measurements every hour, day, week, month, year or whatever – as long as the intervals are regular. Well, actually, you can create and analyse time series where the data is recorded at irregular intervals, but those techniques are more advanced than we can get to here. So, let's stick with regular intervals for this discussion. Now, of course, any time series will usually show random short-term variation, but in general it will also often show a general movement to higher or lower values over a longer period of time. This overall movement is referred to as the trend in the time series, which generally occurs due to the effect of long-run factors like population changes, preference changes and stuff like that.

Take photocopiers, for example. There might very well be major differences each quarter or month over a year in terms of how many photocopiers are sold. However, over a decade or more, you might find some gradual overall trend, as represented in Figure 15.1. This trend seems to be a downward one and is quite well approximated by a straight line. So, it is a linear decreasing trend, over 15 years.

Figure 15.1
Trend for Photocopier Sales Over Time

Of course, there can be many other trend line types. Figure 15.2 shows a couple of non-linear trends, as well as a 'no-trend' situation in panel C. It is important to realize that, without some shift over time, there is no trend, so panel C shows no trend, not a 'flat' trend or anything like that. Of course, do not forget that one type of trend not shown is a linear increasing trend – I figure you can work out what that looks like if you remember that Figure 15.1 is a linear decreasing trend.

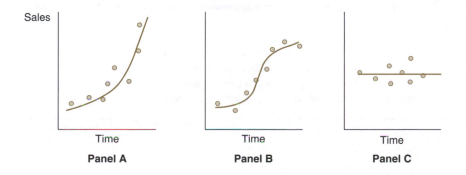

Figure 15.2
Example Non-linear and No Trends

The cyclical component represents a recurring pattern of growth and decline around a basic trend that lasts for more than one year. This is represented in Figure 15.3. You can see the trend is increasing, but there is an obvious cycle above and below this trend over the years. Such cycles are often observed as a result of long-term economic cycles.

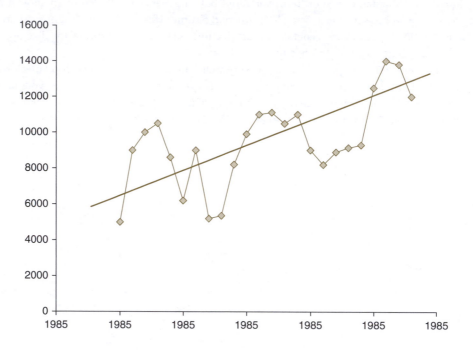

Figure 15.3
Cyclical
Trend

When the cycle occurs over a single-year period, it is known as a seasonal component, rather than a cyclical component. This is observed in many cases – for example, ice cream sales are far higher in summer than winter, and umbrella sales are higher in autumn and spring in most places (apart from the UK where they are high all the time). However, while it is most obvious to talk of seasonal components in terms of one-year cycles, they actually refer to any cycle less than one year in duration. For example, any of you who have to commute to work or school know that traffic has a one-day seasonal component, with peaks (rush hours) in the mornings and afternoons.

Finally, the irregular component can essentially be thought of as a residual, similar to that in a regression model, that catches all the deviation in the time series values other than those captured by trend, cyclical and seasonal components. You might want to think of it as 'error'. It captures short-term, unanticipated, random and non-recurring events that can influence the time series. As such, it is inherently not predictable, and we do not even try to predict its influence on the time series. However, we do try to remove it somehow – usually with the use of what are called 'smoothing' methods. Which we now turn to.

 think it over 15.1

Beware of the black swan! I have only ever seen white swans, so black ones cannot exist. Heed this warning from Nassim Taleb[1] In his book *The Black Swan*, he warns us about ignoring rare and unpredictable events and the extreme impact they can have on our neat, predictable world. Remember that forecasting relies upon the regularity of our data; who knows what the future holds?

---

[1] Nassim Taleb (2008) *The Black Swan: The Impact of the Highly Improbable*. London: Penguin.

SMOOTHING METHODS

Smoothing methods are great – they allow you to go some way at least to removing random fluctuations from the time series. However, they are only really useful when the time series is stable – that is, it does not show any major trend, cyclical or seasonal components. So, it is questionable how useful the basic smoothing methods are for long-term forecasting (although they can be modified). That said, they are quite useful for short-term forecasting tasks.

The Simple Moving Average

The simple moving average method (also known just as the moving average) is reasonably simple and involves using an average of the most recent data points in your time series to make the forecast for the next period. We know, the clue is in the name. By the way, the name is 'moving' average because every time we get a new value in the time series it replaces the oldest value, and a new average is computed. Anyway, the formula is as follows:

$$\text{Simple moving average} = \frac{\sum(\text{most recent } n \text{ data values})}{n}$$

Of course, because the observations used to compute it change, the average changes over time as well. You can see this by using the data in Table 15.1 and the time series in Figure 15.4. This data is 12 months' worth of music downloads from a hypothetical online music store named 'pietunes'.[2]

Table 15.1 Pietunes data

Month	Unique song downloads (000s)
January	95
February	124
March	99
April	110
May	95
June	100
July	115
August	87
September	120
October	100
November	97
December	120

Looking at the time series, it seems like there is some variation present. However, there is no obvious cyclical or seasonal pattern, so our best guess is that the time series is reasonably stable over time. As such, we can use the smoothing methods I am about to cover. I will show how to deal with other situations later on.

---

[2] Needless to say, I didn't have breakfast this morning.

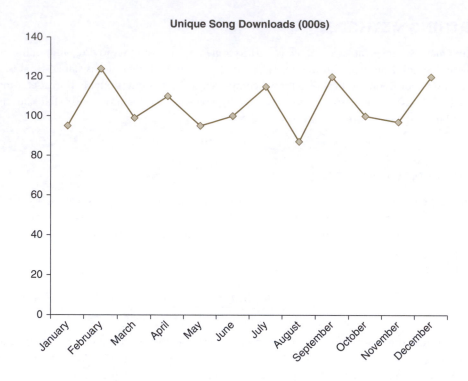

Figure 15.4
Pietunes
Time Series

To use a moving average forecast method, the first decision has to be to select the number of data points to use for the moving average. Here, we will use three points to compute the moving average. It is reasonably typical to use three points, but you can use more – the more points you use, the smoother the moving average that results. So, the first moving average point we can calculate here is for the first three months:

$$\text{Simple moving average (Jan–Mar)} = \frac{95 + 124 + 99}{3} = 106$$

This moving average is used as the forecast for April. It is very important to remember that we are forecasting here. Therefore, it is illogical to use a number to forecast a period that was used to create that forecast – in other words, 106 is not the forecast for March, because March's data point was used to calculate it. Rather, it is the forecast for April. From here, it is pretty easy to calculate the forecasts for the rest of the year.

In fact, this is done for you in Table 15.2, and the resulting forecast is plotted in Figure 15.5. Table 15.2 also contains a number of other interesting values. One is the forecast error. Note that the actual observed value of sales for April is 110, and the forecast value is 106. The forecast error is (rather obviously) the

Table 15.2 Moving average data and calculations

Month	Unique song downloads (000s)	Simple moving average	Forecast error	Squared forecast error	
January	95				
February	124				
March	99				
April	110	106.00	4.00	16.00	
May	95	111.00	−16.00	256.00	
June	100	101.33	−1.33	1.78	

Month	Unique song downloads (000s)	Simple moving average	Forecast error	Squared forecast error	
July	115	101.67	13.33	177.78	
August	87	103.33	−16.33	266.78	
September	120	100.67	19.33	373.78	
October	100	107.33	−7.33	53.78	
November	97	102.33	−5.33	28.44	Mean square forecast error
December	120	105.67	14.33	205.44	
		Totals	4.67	1379.78	*153.31*

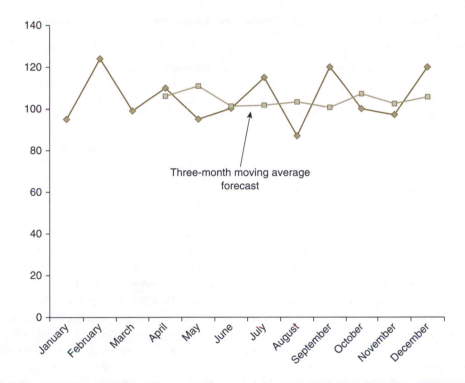

Figure 15.5 Three-Month Moving Average Forecast

difference between the observed value of the data point and the forecast value. Of course, you will also note that the forecast error can be positive or negative, depending on whether the forecast is low or high compared with the actual data point. You can therefore probably guess why we calculate a squared forecast error, but I will keep you in suspense for a little while. Maybe you should have a break now.

The Accuracy of Forecasts

OK, let's talk about accuracy. It seems obvious that the key criterion in selecting which forecasting method to use should be how accurate the results are. Obviously, more accurate is better. You should now realize what we use the squared forecast error values for in Table 15.2. Yes, you can use these to compute a useful measure of the accuracy of your forecast, by taking their average. Using the value for total squared error in Table 15.2, and dividing by the number of periods you forecasted, will give:

Average of the sum of squared errors = 1379.78/9 = 153.31

This value is usually referred to as the mean square error (MSE), as you probably expected. It is a useful way of comparing different forecasting methods on the same time series. For example, in the case of the simple moving average, it may be that different time windows could be more or less accurate – thus, is using two weeks to compute the moving average better than three? What about four? You could use simple trial and error to work this out. Furthermore, there could be *other methods of computing the moving average* that reduce the MSE. Below, I will show you a couple of other methods that have been developed to solve potential problems with the simple moving average, and we will see if they reduce the MSE. However, it is important to realize that using the MSE as a measure of forecast accuracy is making the assumption that the best combination of values to forecast the past will also be best for the future. This is because the MSE can only be computed for errors in prediction of historical data. By definition, you do not yet have the future data to compare the prediction with! And when you do, it is then historical data. Just something to think about…

 think it over 15.2

We may not know the future, but if we view our data critically (take the blinkers off) we can probably identify potential areas that could cause our forecasting to be inaccurate, and develop some contingency plans just in case these events occur. For example, by using historical data I would predict my income is going to increase over the next 10 years. What happens if I am made redundant? My contingency plan is to have enough savings to continue with the lifestyle I aspire to.

The Weighted Moving Average

In the simple moving average, all the data points used to compute the moving average are equally weighted. In other words, they all contribute equally to the resulting average. However, lots of forecasters (often financial analysts) believe that simple moving averages are just too slow to react to changes in trends. One way of solving this problem is to place more importance on more recent data points in a time series when computing the moving average. The typical weighted moving average does just this. Of course, theoretically speaking, you could use a weighted moving average to emphasize any particular data point (e.g. the furthest in the past), but this would be rare, and you would normally have a good reason for doing this. For this reason it would really require you to have an excellent conceptual knowledge of time series analysis and strong feelings about the time series you are analysing. So, to keep things simple, let's stick to the typical case where you wish to put more weight on the more recent data points of a time series when computing a moving average.

So, the first decision you need to make is the same as for the simple moving average – how many data points to use to compute each forecast? Let's keep it simple and stick with three for ease of comparison. Now, let's follow the typical situation and assume that the reason we want to weight the moving average is to emphasize more recent data points. So, we will need to select weights that do this. It is really up to you how to do this, as long as your weighting scheme represents your assumptions. However, one important thing to remember is that the weights *must add up to one* in total. Let me explain through an example recalculation of the April moving average from the simple moving average example. Remember, you used the first three months of the time series to calculate the forecast for April, the fourth month. To compute a weighted moving average, let's make the assumption that the most recent month is most important, the next month back is less important and the furthest month back is least important. It is up to you to create the weights to represent this. I usually use decimal weights rather than fractions. So, check out the example below:

$$\text{Weighted moving average (Jan–Mar)} = (0.2 \times 95) + (0.3 \times 124) + (0.5 \times 99) = 105.7$$

Here, I have given the latest data point a weighting of 0.5, so it contributes most to the final average. The earlier data points get sequentially reducing weights. Note that when you add the weights together, the total is $0.2 + 0.3 + 0.5 = 1$. So we are good. Actually, you might have worked out that, technically speaking, the simple moving average is also weighted – it is just that the weights are equal.[3]

Importantly, note the difference between the simple moving average forecast for April of 106 and the weighted moving average prediction of 105.7. In this case, the weighted moving average is actually a worse forecast for April than the simple one. If you were to recalculate all of the forecasts in Table 15.2 using the weighting scheme above, you would find that the forecasts were less accurate and the MSE was larger (it is in fact 192.6 for the weighted moving average here).

What does this mean? Well, it means that the weighting scheme we used did not represent the variation in the time series. Usually, when a time series is highly variable, using more equal weights results in better predictions. It is only when you strongly believe that more recent observations are better predictors than older ones that you should use a strongly recency-biased weighting scheme like the one I have shown here. Further, it also depends on the length of your time window. Compare the idea of a 3-month window like we are using with, say, a 10-month window. You might be more able to convince yourself that data points 10 months ago were less important than those last month. This will of course vary due to the characteristics of the time series too. So, you can see that there is a lot of thinking that needs to be done when developing weighting schemes for forecasting.[4]

Exponential Smoothing

Exponential smoothing is something I have occasionally been accused of doing over the course of a long evening out on the town. However, such an accusation betrays a total lack of knowledge of forecasting methods, and I usually take that as an invitation to explain what exponential smoothing really is. Often this is not the best conversational tactic. But, regardless, knowledge of exponential smoothing is likely to prove rather valuable in your forecasting career – whether as a forecaster or in interpreting forecasts that you might be shown. This is because exponential smoothing (also known as exponential weighting) is an extremely popular tool in the financial forecasting world. It solves a number of key potential issues with the other moving average techniques above and – eventually – is quite simple in concept and execution. Basically, exponential smoothing uses a weighted average of past data points in the time series, just as the weighted moving average method above does. However, it is a special case, in that you only need to select one weight, the weight for the most recent data point. From there, the other weights are computed automatically and decrease as the data points stretch further into the past.

Therefore, it is clear that exponential smoothing places more emphasis on more recent data points in a time series. Furthermore, as you will see, exponential smoothing uses *all* data points in the time series. Yet, while this may sound like you need a lot of crazy calculations, you will see soon that the whole thing actually reduces down to some reasonably simple calculations. First, let's see the basic exponential smoothing model:

$$F_{t+1} = \alpha Y_t + (1-\alpha)F_t$$

where:

F_{t+1} = forecast of the time series for period $t+1$

Y_t = actual value of the time series in period t

F_t = forecast of the time series for period t

α = smoothing constant ($0 \leq \alpha \geq 1$)

---

[3] You could test this yourself by recalculating the weighted moving average using equal weights, but with a three-period moving average like we are using, it's actually impossible to get perfectly equal weights using decimals. Nevertheless, if you use weights of 0.333333 you'll get virtually indistinguishable results using decimals.

[4] With this in mind, you might want to pay your financial adviser or fund manager a visit and ask how he or she forecasts the market.

What this equation means is that the forecast for any period $t+1$ is a weighted average of the actual value in the previous period t and the forecast for that period t. Also, notice that the weight given to the actual value in period t is α and therefore the weight given to the forecasted value in period t is $1-\alpha$.

Now I can demonstrate that, when using exponential forecasting, the forecast for any period is in fact a weighted average of all previous actual values for that time series. In order to do so simply, I will use a simple time series that contains only three data points: Y_1, Y_2 and Y_3. Let me begin by setting F_1 (the forecast for period 1) equal to the actual value of the time series in period 1 so that $F_1 = Y_1$. As such, the forecast for period 2 can be calculated as:

$$
\begin{aligned}
F_2 &= \alpha Y_1 + (1-\alpha)F_1 \\
&= \alpha Y_1 + (1-\alpha)Y_1 \\
&= Y_1
\end{aligned}
$$

So, the exponential smoothing forecast for period 2 is the actual value of period 1. Now things get interesting, with the forecast for period 3:

$$
\begin{aligned}
F_3 &= \alpha Y_2 + (1-\alpha)F_2 \\
&= \alpha Y_2 + (1-\alpha)Y_1
\end{aligned}
$$

So, the forecast for period 3 depends on the values for periods 1 and 2. Moving to period 4 to cement this, we can substitute the expression for the forecast for period 3 into the forecast for period 4 as follows:

$$
\begin{aligned}
F_4 &= \alpha Y_3 + (1-\alpha)F_3 \\
&= \alpha Y_3 + (1-\alpha)\left[\alpha Y_2 + (1-\alpha)Y_1\right] \\
&= \alpha Y_3 + \alpha(1-\alpha)Y_2 + (1-\alpha)^2 Y_1
\end{aligned}
$$

So, the forecast for period 4 is a weighted average of the first three time series values, and the weights for the Y values sum to one. This does not just work for small time series like this one of three periods. In fact, it can be shown that in a general sense, any exponential smoothing forecast is a weighted average of all previous time series values.

Now, when I first learnt this technique, I began to panic at this point. The enormity of calculating forecasts for large time series seemed to be an impossible challenge. I mean, look above. With three data points, this is manageable, but with time series of any realistic size, it would quickly become a nightmare. However, in reality, you do not have to do it longhand like that. In fact, once you decide on the value for the smoothing constant α you only need two more bits of data. Of course, the smarter ones among you will have worked out already that I was needlessly panicking. Just look at the exponential smoothing equation above. You will see that to forecast the value for any time period $t+1$, all you need to know are the actual and forecast values for the previous period t, which are of course Y_t and F_t. Sweet.

So, with this in mind, check out Table 15.3, which shows the exponentially smoothed forecasts for the pietunes data. Notice that we set the forecast for period 2 equal to the actual value for period 1 to start things off. Doing so shows that the forecast error for period 2 is $124 - 95 = 29$.

Table 15.3 Exponential smoothing forecast

Month	Unique song downloads (000s)	Exponential smoothing forecast	Forecast error	Squared forecast error	Smoothing constant
January	95				0.15
February	124	95	29.00	841.00	
March	99	99.35	−0.35	0.12	
April	110	99.30	10.70	114.54	
May	95	100.90	−5.90	34.84	

Month	Unique song downloads (000s)	Exponential smoothing forecast	Forecast error	Squared forecast error	Smoothing constant
June	100	100.02	−0.02	0.00	
July	115	100.01	14.99	224.56	
August	87	102.26	−15.26	232.95	
September	120	99.97	20.03	401.07	
October	100	102.98	−2.98	8.86	
November	97	102.53	−5.53	30.59	Mean square forecast error
December	120	101.70	18.30	334.85	
		Totals	62.97	2223.39	247.04

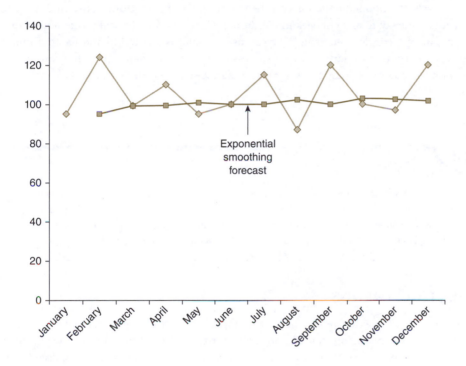

Figure 15.6
Exponential Smoothing Forecast

From there, it is reasonably simple to do the calculation for period 3, once you decide on a smoothing constant, which for now I have chosen to be 0.15:

$$F_3 = 0.15Y_2 + 0.85F_2$$

$$= 0.15 \times 124 + 0.85 \times 95$$

$$= 99.35$$

You can easily generate a forecast for period 4, once you have the actual data for period 3, and so forth. Continuing the calculations will get you the values in Table 15.3, which are then plotted in Figure 15.6. You can see that the exponential smoothing method works well to smooth out the fluctuations in the data. You could also use the data here to get a forecast for the next month – January of the coming year. Simply input the actual and forecast values for December into the formula. That would be a good exercise for you, I think.

Of course, for the February forecast, you would need to wait for the actual January data to come through, and the January results would also let you know how accurate your forecast was.

Speaking of accuracy, let's return to the smoothing constant. You will remember that I used 0.15 above, but any value between 0 and 1 is usable. Of course, some values will result in better forecasts than others, and ideally we would choose the one that minimized the MSE. It is hard to give any exact rules for doing this, but a good rule of thumb is that smaller smoothing constants are better when the time series contains a lot of random variability, whereas larger constants are better if the time series has less random variability. The reasoning behind this is that the larger the smoothing constant, the quicker the forecast adjusts to changes in the time series. If there is a lot of random variability, a large smoothing constant will be over-sensitive and essentially 'chase' what is basically random variation – meaning there is little benefit in using any smoothing method at all. You can see this if you set a smoothing constant of close to 1 (say 0.99) and use the pietunes data. If you do so, you will see that the resulting predicted time series is almost a perfect replication of the unsmoothed time series, but one period behind. What was the point of smoothing it?! On the other hand, forecasts for time series with lower levels of random fluctuations can benefit from larger smoothing constants, as the forecasts will react more quickly to any changes in conditions. That said, it is basically trial and error here, or what we might call 'educated guessing'. We can use the MSE as a criterion and try to minimize it by changing the smoothing constant. But your success in choosing the best smoothing constant will tend to depend on the quality of your 'guesses' about the time series. Or, at least, that is what the financial analysts would like us to think.

 think it over 15.3

We use the word accuracy when we are talking about the results from our prediction calculations, but be careful – it refers to the accuracy of the calculations using a particular method. It does not mean the calculated value will actually occur. It tells us that, providing the historical data we selected is correct and the business environment does not change, our predictions should come true.

PROJECTING TRENDS

The smoothing techniques above are really most applicable to situations where a time series is stable (i.e. one which has only random fluctuations). Of course, nothing is stopping you using them whenever you like, and I have seen plenty of examples of various moving averages being used in situations where there are clear trends and cycles in the data – such as stock market forecasts. The problem is that moving-average-type methods like those above are basically 'mechanical' – just a formula that you plug the historical data into, and out pops a forecast. This idea basically ignores any factors that *cause* changes, and therefore the forecast is usually slow to react to changes in a time series – in other words, such smoothing methods *lag* the trends in a time series, which means that they follow trends rather than predict them. This is a bit of a downer for a forecasting method really. But, on the other hand, smoothing methods are good for their purpose, which is to smooth out random fluctuations.

Much of the rest of this chapter focuses on showing methods of dealing with trends in the data, and I will begin with the most basic method, the use of linear regression trend lines. This technique scores over moving averages when there is a pronounced and consistent long-term trend in the time series, and in particular it does not lag the trend like a moving average does. That said, it is rather simplistic, and it works best as an introduction to more complex methods that are applicable in more realistic situations. Above and Beyond Box 15.1 is a brief digression that explains an extension of this method that is sometimes used by forecasters.

above and beyond

Box 15.1 Linear Regression Indicators

One way to extend the use of linear regression is to compute a new forecast for each data point in a time series, like a moving average. Doing this would essentially amount to plotting the end point of a large series of linear regression lines, one for each consecutive time period. Those end points would be your forecast. You could vary the amount of data you used to compute the linear regression indicator (like varying the time periods used in a moving average). Although you would pay the price of a significant increase in computational complexity and heavy lifting, the forecasts using such a method would be much less lagged than a moving average - they would have a much quicker response to trend changes, in other words. Such a method works best for strong trends and is often used by financial analysts. It is quite a way beyond the scope of this introductory chapter, but, on the other hand, if you think carefully you should be able to work out how to do it yourself. Once you are there, you will probably think of even more interesting ways to forecast. What about combinations of methods? I will touch on this later...

Take a look at Table 15.4, which is an approximate recreation of average UK house prices from 1997 to 2006 (which is the year I bought my first house). The data is not exact, but it is generally representative of the trend and magnitude of house prices in the UK at the time.

Table 15.4 Approximate UK average house price data, 1997–2006

Year	Price (£000s)
1997	55
1998	61
1999	70
2000	75
2001	79
2002	95
2003	110
2004	135
2005	155
2006	160

There is a completely obvious upward trend here, and most analysts would probably agree that a linear trend would be a pretty good representation of the data. Looking at Figure 15.7, you can easily see the trend, and I have also added in a linear trend line. It looks like this trend line provides a pretty good description of the long-term movement in the time series. Of course, this is just a rough guess at the trend line so far, so maybe it is worth thinking about whether it is possible to compute a more accurate trend line. Indeed, we can apply the basic principles of least squares regression, which have been covered

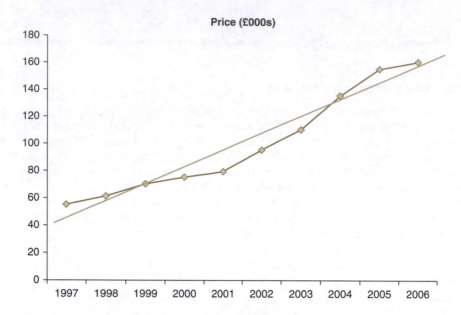

Figure 15.7
Time Series for UK Average House Price 1997-2006

earlier in the book, to time series analysis like this. In essence, what we will do is estimate a relationship between time and house price.

You should recall the basic regression equation from earlier, which describes a linear relationship between an independent variable x and a dependent variable y:

$$\hat{y} = b_o + b_1 x$$

Now, it is helpful to change some of the notation here, because we are dealing with a time series model and therefore the independent variable is time. So, let's change the equation notation to the following:

$$T_t = b_o + b_1 t$$

where:

T_t = trend value of the time series in period t

b_0 = intercept of the trend line

b_1 = slope of the trend line

t = time

Now, do not get confused. Remember, this is the same equation – the notation is just slightly different to remind you that time is involved. So, moving on, we let $t = 1$ for the first data point of the time series, $t = 2$ for the second data point and so on. As such, $t = 1$ is the oldest time point we use. We can use the following equations to compute the estimated regression coefficients:

$$b_1 = \frac{\sum t Y_t - \dfrac{\left(\sum t \sum Y_t\right)}{n}}{\sum t^2 - \dfrac{\left(\sum t\right)^2}{n}}$$

$$b_0 = \bar{Y} - b_1 \bar{t}$$

where:

Y_t = value of the time series for period t

n = number of periods

$\overline{Y}$ = average value of the time series; i.e. $\left(\sum \dfrac{Y_t}{n}\right)$

$\overline{t}$ = average value of t; i.e $\left(\sum \dfrac{t}{n}\right)$

Now, this is looking kind of complicated. However, it makes more sense if you work through it using some data. So, let's go back to the house price data. Table 15.5 shows this data, along with the additional values you need to compute the regression estimates using the formulae above.

Table 15.5 UK house price data regression calculations

t	Y_t	tY_t	t^2
1	55	55	1
2	61	122	4
3	70	210	9
4	75	300	16
5	79	395	25
6	95	570	36
7	110	770	49
8	135	1080	64
9	155	1395	81
10	160	1600	100
Totals	55	995	6497	385
Means	5.5	99.5		

Using the values in Table 15.5, it is a reasonably simple task to compute b_1 and b_0 as below:

$$b_1 = \dfrac{6497 - (55)\left(\dfrac{995}{10}\right)}{385 - \dfrac{(55)^2}{10}} = 12.42$$

$$b_0 = 99.5 - 12.42(5.5) = 31.2$$

So, the equation for the linear trend for UK average house prices, going by the 10-year time series data we have available, is:

$$T_t = 31.2 + 12.42(t)$$

This looks like a pretty solid increasing trend – the sort of thing which, if you observed, you would think seriously about moving heaven and Earth to buy a house, before prices became completely crazy. Right? Basically, the slope of 12.42 indicates that, over 10 years, UK house prices on average experienced growth of about £12420 per year! Assuming this trend is a good indicator of future growth, we could even use it to predict the future, and project later average house prices. All we need to do is substitute the number of the time period into the equation. So, if 2006 is $t = 10$, then substituting $t = 11$ into the equation would allow us to predict for 2007:

$$T_{11} = 31.2 + 12.42(11) = 167.82$$

In fact, this is a reasonable prediction, since going to look at the real data will show an average UK house price for 2007 of around £175000. Wow – success! Thus, we could use this linear regression line to predict even further into the future. What could possibly go wrong?

Well, if you know anything about financial and economic history, you might recall that in 2008 the UK and most of the world experienced a huge financial crash. Indeed, 2007 was the peak of house price inflation in the UK, and by the end of 2008 the housing market (which by then included my house) had lost huge value – the average house price at the start of 2009 was closer to £135000 (2009, coincidentally, is around the time I began writing this book).

So, you can already see one of the disadvantages of the simple linear-regression-based forecasting method here. Without an understanding of the underlying features of the time series (i.e. what is causing it to behave in a certain way) our forecasts run the risk of missing big switches in trends. Simply relying on past data assumes that there will be no change in trend, and therefore you will miss big shifts, like the financial crisis.

There are many extensions to this method. One of these was covered in Above and Beyond Box 15.1. You can probably see how you could use that method to compute rolling forecasts for the next period, one at a time, kind of like a moving average. That might be more accurate than just extrapolating a single trend line. You will also note that the regression method used here models a linear trend (i.e. a straight line). Certainly, there are plenty of techniques available to model non-linear trends, and the regression method can be extended to these too. However, they are well beyond the scope of this introduction, and I will leave such discussion to more advanced specialized texts.

INCORPORATING TREND AND SEASONAL COMPONENTS

Now you know how to forecast a time series with a trend; however, as we saw above, it is dangerous to assume a trend will always continue. In many cases, for example, there are regular cycles, such that a time series will display a regular pattern of increase then decrease. If these cycles are less than one year in duration, we call them a seasonal component, or alternatively refer to the seasonality of a time series.

If you wish to compare different periods of a time series – which is very common in business, economics, finance and similar areas – you need to take account of seasonality. For example, what if I was the CEO of an ice cream company, and I asked my vice president of marketing to comment on how effective our new advertising was? The VP might tell me that ice cream sales are up 10% this month as compared with last month. However, what if the second month was high summer? The comparison would be misleading unless I took the seasonality into account. In other words, the effect of the new advertising would be hidden by the seasonal effect that people eat more ice cream in summer. In fact, once I adjusted for this seasonal effect, I might find that ice cream sales *decreased*!

Removing seasonal components from a time series is known as deseasonalizing the time series, and, once we do this, we can compare periods more usefully, as well as identify trends in the time series. This section presents an approach that is usable when there is both a seasonal and a trend component, as well as when there is just a seasonal component. It is basically a multi-step approach: the first step is new to you and involves deseasonalizing; then, if a trend shows in the deseasonalized time series, you can use the regression methods you already know to estimate it and forecast.

So, let's formalize the situation we are dealing with here. First, let's assume that the time series contains a trend component (T), as well as a seasonal component (S), but let's also assume that it contains a random or irregular component (I). You should already be reasonably familiar with what those components represent in a time series, but, if not, go back and reread the early part of this chapter. Putting these together will give an expression for a multiplicative time series model, as seen below:

$$Y_t = T_t \times S_t \times I_t$$

where:

Y_t = value of time series at time t

T_t = trend component of time series at time t

S_t = seasonal component of time series at time t

I_t = irregular component of time series at time t

It is important to realize that the trend component is expressed in units of whatever is being forecast (i.e. the same units as the time series). This is pretty easy to understand. However, the potential confusion is that the seasonal and irregular components are measured in relative terms – with values above 1 meaning effects above the trend, and values below 1 indicating effects below the trend. This might make more sense once you have worked through an example, and with this in mind take a look at the data in Table 15.6.

Table 15.6 Soup sales quarterly data

Year	Quarter	Sales (litres)
1	1	504
	2	350
	3	198
	4	302
2	1	580
	2	490
	3	225
	4	330
3	1	625
	2	524
	3	301
	4	400
4	1	735
	2	640
	3	440
	4	510

The data in this table is quarterly data for four years of soup sales at the student cafeteria, also plotted in Figure 15.8. Here, there appears to be a clear seasonal component. Assuming that the first quarter begins in January, sales are a lot fewer in the mid-year period. One possible explanation is that, in the northern hemisphere, mid-year is summer, and also when students are on holiday. So, in these summer periods, the cafeteria is likely to have a lot less custom, and also people who do go there might want hot soup a lot less often.

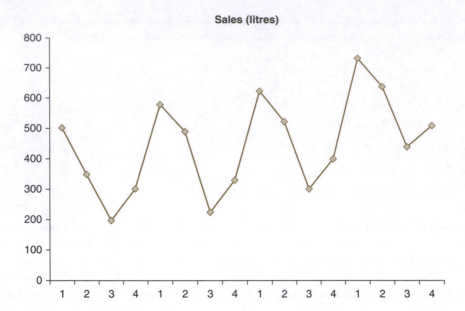

Figure 15.8
Soup Sales
Time Series

What we need to do is somehow separate the trend component from the combined seasonal and irregular components, and we do this by taking moving averages for each year of data. This will be simpler to explain using the data in the example. Basically, we use one year's worth of data for each moving average calculation. Because we have quarterly data, we use four data points for each moving average computation. To compute the first moving average in the example, take the first four quarters of the soup data as follows:

$$\text{First moving average} = \frac{504 + 350 + 198 + 302}{4} = \frac{1354}{4} = 338.5$$

You can see that obviously the calculation gives the average sales per quarter for year 1 of the data. It should be reasonably self-explanatory to compute the second moving average; we drop the value for Q1 of year 1 (504) and add the value for Q1 of the second year (580), as follows:

$$\text{Second moving average} = \frac{350 + 198 + 302 + 580}{4} = \frac{1430}{4} = 357.5$$

From here you should be able to work out that the third moving average is 392.5, the fourth is 399.25 and so on. However, before going further, there is one more thing to think about – caused by the fact that our time series is in quarters.

Consider this, the first moving average is 338.5, which is meant to represent the average quarterly soup sales for the first year. In this sense, 338.5 should represent the 'middle' quarter of the group of quarters used to compute the moving average. *But* where is the 'middle' quarter? In fact, with four quarters there is *no* middle quarter! The value of 338.5 actually corresponds to the last half of Q2 and the first of Q3. The next moving average value (357.5) represents the last half of Q3 and the first half of Q4, and so on.

Is this really a problem, or is it needless nitpicking? Well, the entire point of computing moving averages is to isolate the combined seasonal and irregular components from the trend component. But our moving averages do not directly relate to the original time series quarter periods. To solve this, we need to 'average the averages' – or in other words use the midpoints between each successive pair of moving average values. For example, the first two moving average values are 338.5 and 357.5, with 338.5 corresponding to the first half of Q3 and 357.5 to the last half of Q3. We can use (338.5 + 357.5)/2 = 348 as the moving average value for Q3. This is what we call a centred moving average. Table 15.7 shows all of the moving average calculations explained so far, and you should be able to pick your way through it fairly easily.

Of course, you need only to compute centred moving averages if the number of data points in the moving average calculation is an even number. In this case, there are four quarters. If you used fifths of a year for example instead of quarters, you would not need to compute the centred moving average. But who uses fifths? Anyway, hopefully you get the point.

Table 15.7 Soup sales moving averages

Year	Quarter	Sales (litres)	Yearly moving average	Centred moving average
1	1	504		
	2	350	338.5	
	3	198	357.5	348
	4	302	392.5	375
2	1	580	399.25	395.875
	2	490	406.25	402.75
	3	225	417.5	411.875
	4	330	426	421.75
3	1	625	445	435.5
	2	524	462.5	453.75
	3	301	490	476.25
	4	400	519	504.5
4	1	735	553.75	536.375
	2	640	581.25	567.5
	3	440		
	4	510		

Figure 15.9 shows a plot of the original time series and the centred moving averages. You can see that the centred moving averages smooth out the fluctuations in the time series. In fact, the centred moving averages represent the time series as if there were no seasonal or irregular influences.

At last, we have the ability to identify the seasonal irregular effect in the time series. Doing so is a simple task of dividing each observation by the corresponding centred moving average. For example, Q3 of the first year is the first observation where there is a corresponding centred moving average. The value of the time series in Q3 of year 1 is 198, and the centred moving average is 348. Thus, $198/348 = 0.569$. This is the seasonal irregular value for that point of the time series. Table 15.8 gives all of the seasonal irregular values for the time series. Note that we can only calculate seasonal irregular values for observations where there is a corresponding centred moving average. So, for example, Q1 of year 1 and Q3 of year 4 do not have seasonal irregular values, because we could not calculate centred moving averages for those quarters.

Now, let's go one step further and look at seasonal irregular values for the corresponding quarters from multiple years. Take Q4: the time series gives values of 0.805 for year 1, 0.782 for year 2 and 0.793

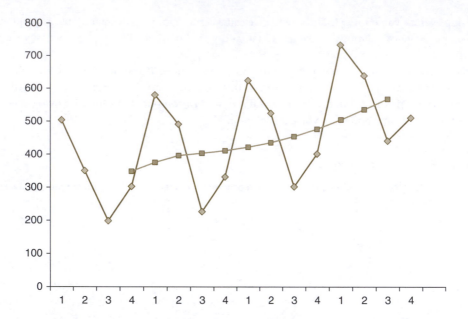

Figure 15.9
Soup Sales
Moving
Average

Table 15.8 Seasonal irregular values

Year	Quarter	Sales (litres)	Centred moving average	Seasonal irregular value
1	1	504		
	2	350		
	3	198	348	0.569
	4	302	375	0.805
2	1	580	395.875	1.465
	2	490	402.75	1.217
	3	225	411.475	0.547
	4	330	421.75	0.782
3	1	625	435.5	1.435
	2	524	453.75	1.155
	3	301	476.25	0.632
	4	400	504.5	0.793
4	1	735	536.375	1.370
	2	640	567.5	1.128
	3	440		
	4	510		

for year 3. It can be seen that because the values are below 1, then in all cases the seasonal irregular component seems to have a below-average influence in the fourth quarter. If we assume that fluctuations across years are mainly due to the irregular component (not the seasonal one) then we can simply average these values to eliminate the irregular component, and be left with an estimate of the seasonal influence for the fourth quarter:

$$\text{Seasonal influence for fourth quarter} = \frac{0.805 + 0.782 + 0.793}{3} = 0.794$$

This value of 0.794 is called the seasonal index for the fourth quarter. Table 15.9 gives seasonal indices for all four quarters calculated in the same basic way. However, there is sometimes a further step that you need to go through, and, coincidentally, we have to in this case, which is a nice piece of design on my part. Basically, the multiplicative model requires that the average seasonal index is 1. Or, in other words, the sum of the four quarterly seasonal indices in Table 15.9 should equal 4. You can see that it does not; in fact it equals 3.97. So, we must adjust this via a simple calculation: we must multiply each seasonal index by the number of seasons divided by the sum of the unadjusted seasonal indices. This is less complicated than it sounds. All the adjusted seasonal indices are given in Table 15.9, but let me give the calculation for Q1. All the figures you need are in Table 15.9, and just remember that the number of quarters is 4:

$$\text{Adjusted seasonal index for quarter } 1 = 1.42 \times \frac{4}{3.97} = 1.44$$

Table 15.9 Seasonal indices and adjusted seasonal indices

Quarter	Seasonal index	Adjusted seasonal index
1	1.42	1.4
2	1.17	1.2
3	0.58	0.6
4	0.79	0.8
Totals	3.97	4

So how do you interpret these values? Well, it is reasonably simple. Q1 seems to be the best for sales, with sales 44% above average quarterly value (adjusted seasonal index of 1.44). The slowest sales quarter is Q3, with sales 41% lower than average quarterly sales. This makes sense for a student cafeteria on a European university campus; most sales come in the winter months (assuming Q1 is in January), and fewer sales come in Q3 when students are mainly on holiday, with sales growing in Q4 as they come back to class and the weather gets colder.

Deseasonalizing the Time Series

The entire point of computing the seasonal indices is to remove the seasonal effect from the time series. Naturally, this is termed deseasonalizing a time series, and you often see deseasonalized time series reported in newspapers and so forth. Or at least you should if they know what they are doing! To explain how to do this, recall first the multiplicative time series model:

$$Y_t = T_t \times S_t \times I_t$$

I hope you can remember what the terms in that model mean. If not, go back to the model earlier in this chapter and recap. OK, moving on, one can simply divide each observation in the time series by the corresponding seasonal index (of course, you have to use the adjusted seasonal index where you have one) to compute the deseasonalized time series. This is done for you in Table 15.10 and graphed in Figure 15.10.

Table 15.10 Deseasonalized time series

Year	Quarter	Sales (litres)	Adjusted seasonal index	Deseasonalized sales
1	1	504	1.44	350.00
	2	350	1.18	296.61
	3	198	0.59	335.59
	4	302	0.80	377.50
2	1	580	1.44	402.78
	2	490	1.18	415.25
	3	225	0.59	381.36
	4	330	0.80	412.50
3	1	625	1.44	434.03
	2	524	1.18	444.07
	3	301	0.59	510.17
	4	400	0.80	500.00
4	1	735	1.44	510.42
	2	640	1.18	542.37
	3	440	0.59	745.76
	4	510	0.80	637.50

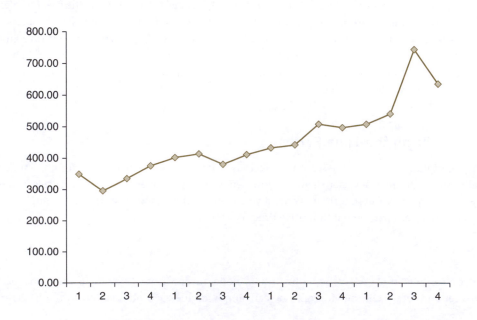

Figure 15.10
Deseasonalized
Time Series

While there remains some random variation in the deseasonalized time series – in particular a bit of a large fluctuation in Q3 of year 4 – there is a pretty clear upward linear trend, don't you think? In order to identify this trend, it is simply a case of using the same procedure that you have already learnt. The hard work was in deseasonalizing it to make this standard procedure usable. So, recall that for a standard linear trend, the estimated sales volume as a function of time will be:

$$T_t = b_0 + b_1 t$$

where:

T_t = trend value of the time series in period t

b_0 = intercept of the trend line

b_1 = slope of the trend line

t = time

You should remember that $t = 1$ is the time of the first data point in the time series, $t = 2$ the second and so forth. In this case, then, $t = 1$ is the first deseasonalized quarterly value and $t = 16$ the final (most recent) value. Table 15.11 shows the deseasonalized values for the time series, and the associated values needed to compute the value of b_1 and b_0 using the formula below:

$$b_1 = \frac{\sum tY_t - \dfrac{\left(\sum t \sum Y_t\right)}{n}}{\sum t^2 - \dfrac{\left(\sum t\right)^2}{n}}$$

$$b_0 = \overline{Y} - b_1 \overline{t}$$

Table 15.11 Working for regression coefficients

t	Y_t (deseasonalized series)	tY_t	t^2
1.00	350.00	350.00	1
2.00	296.61	593.22	4
3.00	335.59	1006.77	9
4.00	377.70	1510.80	16
5.00	402.78	2013.90	25
6.00	415.25	2491.50	36
7.00	381.36	2669.52	49
8.00	412.50	3300.00	64
9.00	434.03	3906.27	81
10.00	444.07	4440.70	100
11.00	510.17	5611.87	121
12.00	500.00	6000.00	144
13.00	510.42	6635.46	169
14.00	542.37	7593.18	196
15.00	745.76	11186.40	225
16.00	637.50	10200.00	256
Totals	136.00	7296.11	69509.59	1496
Means	8.5	456.01	4344.35	93.5

You have used these formulae before, so it should be reasonably straightforward for you now. If not, go back and recap things until you understand what is going on. The key thing to remember is that Y_t refers to the deseasonalized value of the time series at time t, not the actual value. So, using these deseasonalized values, we have the following calculations:

$$\bar{t} = \frac{136}{16} = 8.5$$

$$\bar{Y} = \frac{7296.11}{16} = 456.01$$

$$b_1 = \frac{69509.59 - \dfrac{(136)(7296.11)}{16}}{1496 - \dfrac{(136)^2}{16}} = 22.04$$

$$b_0 = 456.01 - 22.04(8.5) = 268.69$$

And thus:

$$T_t = 268.69 + 22.04t$$

expresses the linear trend component of the time series in question. So, for every time period (i.e. quarter) for the last four years (i.e. 16 quarters), the cafeteria averaged a sales increase of around 22 litres of soup. Making the assumption that this trend (based on past data) is a reasonable indicator for the future, we can use it to forecast the trend in future quarters, simply by substituting in future values for t. So, for example to forecast sales in the next quarter after our data, we substitute in 17 for t as follows:

$$T_{17} = 268.69 + 22.04(17) = 642.69$$

You can probably work out the forecasts for the other quarters in year 5 (i.e. Q18, Q19 and Q20) for yourself. This is pretty cool!

The last thing we need to do (phew!) is to adjust our forecasts by using the seasonal index (remember to use the adjusted seasonal index if you computed one). So, if you have a forecast for Q1 of year 5, you should adjust it using the seasonal index for Q1. I will demonstrate on the forecast computed above, for period 17 – which you should remember is indeed the forecast for year 5, Q1 (period 17 is Q1 of year 5, right?). It is very simple, because you have already done the heavy lifting. The adjusted seasonal index (see Table 15.9) for Q1 is 1.44, so it is simply a case of multiplying your forecast based on trend by the relevant seasonal index. In this case it is:

$$642.69 \times 1.44 = 925.47$$

Again, you should be able to work out the other quarterly forecasts for year 5 by yourself, using the appropriate adjusted seasonal indices from Table 15.9.

Awesome!

Additional Notes on Seasonality

Note that quarterly data has been used throughout the seasonal example above. However, it is perfectly possible to use monthly data and compute monthly forecasts – which is much more useful for some companies. The procedure is just the same, but instead of computing a four-quarter moving average, you create a 12-month moving average. Further, you must compute 12 monthly seasonal indices, not 4 quarterly ones. Simple! Although, admittedly, a bit more work.

Finally, you might have been wondering about the cyclical component of the time series, which has been mentioned earlier. Remember: cyclical components are basically multi-year cycles in the time series – so they are analogous to seasonal components, but over a longer time scale. We can easily extend the model to include a cyclical component:

$$Y_t = T_t \times C_t \times S_t \times I_t$$

However, our problems occur when actually trying to estimate the cyclical component. In principle it should surely be broadly the same as the seasonal component; however, we face a number of practical problems. First, it is rare that we can obtain enough data on the cyclical components, because they are multi-year in nature. Further, cycles often vary in length, which makes things more complicated. As such, if you are interested in learning how to estimate cyclical components, you are best advised to consult a book specifically dedicated to forecasting.

REGRESSION ANALYSIS AND FORECASTING

This book has already covered regression in significant depth (my brain still hurts from writing those chapters), and you might want to refresh your memory by going back to them for a little while. Basically, regression was discussed as a method of predicting the value of one dependent variable from a set of one or more independent variables. While looking at the material in this present chapter, though, some of you might have made a connection between the forecasting techniques covered so far and the regression methods you already learnt. In this section, I will make that connection much clearer.

Think about the time series value that you want to predict as a dependent variable; if you do so, then regression becomes a forecasting tool much more obviously. If you can identify a good set of independent variables, you could develop a regression equation for forecasting future values of a time series. In fact, the fitting of the linear trend line to the UK house price time series in this chapter was a special case of regression. The dependent variable was house price and the single independent variable was time. Above and Beyond Box 15.2 discusses this in a little more depth.

 above and beyond

Box 15.2　What Is Time?[5]

The title to this box is rather philosophical, but what I really mean here is that, in a forecasting context, 'time' is not really considered as being related to the dependent variable. In the house price example, this means that even though the linear trend forecasting example related time as an independent variable to house price as a dependent one, we do not *really* think price is related to time. Rather, we consider time to be a proxy for other variables which actually *are* related to house price (e.g. rising incomes, interest rate decreases), but which are unobservable, or impractical to measure.

We should by now all be in agreement that the real world is a complex place, and we should probably try to represent that complexity as best we can. Usually, it is a reasonably poor representation just to use one independent variable to predict or forecast our dependent variable – even if as shown in Above and Beyond Box 15.2 we might argue that one variable (time) is a proxy for many others. So, we can use multiple regression to add more potential variables of interest to our forecasting model.

[5] Perhaps more importantly, according at least to The KLF, 'What Time Is Love?'

Remember, though, that to estimate a multiple regression model, you need a sample of data points for the dependent variable and all of the independent variables in the model. This makes things a bit complex in a time series situation. Basically, the time series of n periods should provide a sample of n observations of each variable that you want to use in the model. So, for a time series model of k independent variables, we use the following conventions:

Y_t = value of the time series in period t

x_{1t} = value of independent variable 1 in period t

x_{2t} = value of independent variable 2 in period t

x_{kt} = value of independent variable k in period t

Thus, if we need n periods of data for each of the k independent variables, and the time series itself (which is the dependent variable), this data would look something like Table 15.12.

Table 15.12 Example table for regression forecasting data

Period	Time series (Y_t)	x_{1t}	x_{2t}	x_{3t}	.	.	x_{kt}
1	Y_1	X_{11}	X_{21}	X_{31}	.	.	X_{k1}
2	Y_1	X_{12}	X_{22}	X_{32}	.	.	X_{k2}
.	.	.	.	.	.	.	.
.	.	.	.	.	.	.	.
.	.	.	.	.	.	.	.
n	Y_n	X_{1n}	X_{2n}	X_{3n}	.	.	X_{kn}

(header: Value of independent variables)

Of course, there are many different possibilities in terms of choosing independent variables for a regression forecasting model. You already know one of course: you could simply choose time, as was done in the house price forecast. In such a case, you can estimate the trend in the time series by using a linear function of time. So, $x_{1t} = t$ and the estimate regression equation takes the form

$$\hat{y}_t = b_0 - b_1 t$$

Remember that $\hat{y}$ has a hat because it is an estimate of the time series value of Y_t. You should also remember that the b terms represent the estimated regression coefficients. Now, you could actually estimate a more complex model, still only using time, but instead of just one term for time you could actually raise time to various powers. For example, you could make $x_{2t} = t^2$, which would make the model a curvilinear one, rather than a simple linear forecast of the time series. The estimated regression would become:

$$\hat{y}_t = b_0 + b_1 t + b_2 t^2$$

Or, instead, you could use a set of demographic and/or economic factors as independent variables, or virtually any other variable that you might think has an impact on the time series. So, returning to the housing example, you could use the following set of independent variables to forecast house sales:

x_{1t} = price in period t

x_{2t} = number of new houses built in period $t - 1$

x_{3t} = average household income in period t

x_{4t} = average interest rate on mortgages in period t

x_{5t} = population over 18 in period t

In this case, your estimated regression equation would have five independent variables. Of course, whether the model provides a good forecast depends very strongly on whether you have identified a good set of independent variables, and also on whether you can collect high-quality data on these variables. In this sense, you are using what was termed a causal forecasting approach – where you are relating one or more time series (e.g. price, household income, etc., as independent variables) to another (house sales as a dependent variable).

You can also use an autoregressive model. This is simply a fancy name for using previous values of the same time series to predict later values. In other words, assuming the time series values are labelled as Y_1, Y_2, Y_3, ..., Y_n, then with Y_t as the dependent variable you can develop an estimated regression equation relating Y_t to the preceding time series values Y_{t-1}, Y_{t-2}, and so forth:

$$\hat{y}_t = b_0 + b_1 Y_{t-1} + b_2 Y_{t-2}$$

Remember, though, that the above are just examples, not the 'only' things you can do. In fact, you can combine all of these approaches to finding independent variables into one model. Again, though, it is worth consulting a dedicated forecasting textbook if you want to delve more deeply into this stuff.

 above and beyond

Box 15.3 Qualitative Forecasting Approaches

All of the methods looked at in this chapter have been quantitative in nature. This is logical – after all, this is a book about business quantitative analysis! However, forecasting is not always done using quantitative approaches. Sometimes, the historical data we need to do good quantitative forecasts is not available, or even if it is, there may have been major environmental changes or the like, which render historical data less useful for future prediction. In such cases, qualitative forecasts can be used. In fact they are surprisingly common in some situations. Usually qualitative methods rely in one way or another on expert judgements. For example, stock market analysts and investment bankers in a given bank may use expert judgement to predict future movements of the stock market. Indeed, many traders consider their own judgement to be part of their 'competitive advantage' in the marketplace. Of course, quantitative models can also provide inputs into these more qualitative judgements, and forecasts from multiple experts can be combined into one prediction. But the essence of qualitative approaches is that judgement is used, rather than relying on quantitative models.

Qualitative judgements are most useful when there is some clear reason that quantitative forecasts are inappropriate, most often when it is considered that past conditions are unlikely to hold in the future. Of course, such qualitative forecasts depend on the 'quality' of expert judgements, and one should always be cautious in relying on 'experts'. But, equally, one should always be cautious in relying totally on quantitative models too!

USING EXCEL

For the purposes of demonstrating forecasting we will use the latest data from the UK government about people switching their energy suppliers. The data can be found at www.gov.uk/switchingevidence. This data reports the number of households that changed their energy supplier since 2003 and we will use it to see if a trend exists.

The first thing to do is to plot the data to check there is a trend. Figure 15.11 shows the output when the data is plotted by Excel. First thing to observe, there are seasonal patterns within years (the data is divided into quarters) and a trend. One observation you can make is that households changing their energy supplier peaked in 2008. This was the year a major worldwide financial crisis started, so people suddenly became cost-conscious.

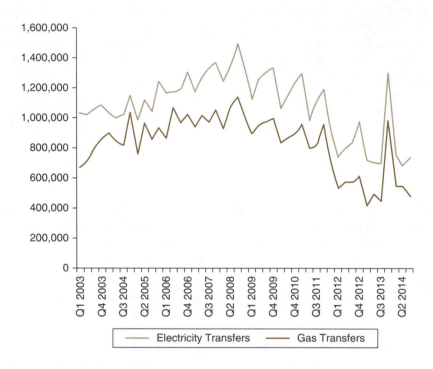

Figure 15.11

Let's start with a three-year moving average analysis. With your data loaded, select Data → Data Analysis and choose Moving Average from the pop-up menu (as shown in Figure 15.12).

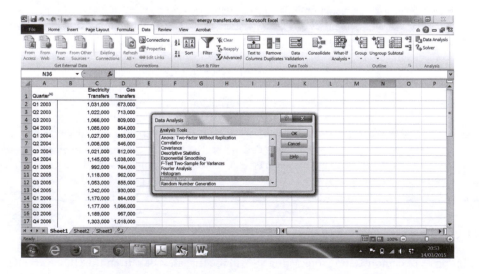

Figure 15.12

Figure 15.13 shows you the selections you can now make. Select your data, your moving average interval (I set mine to 3) and chart output. You can also select to have standard errors reported.

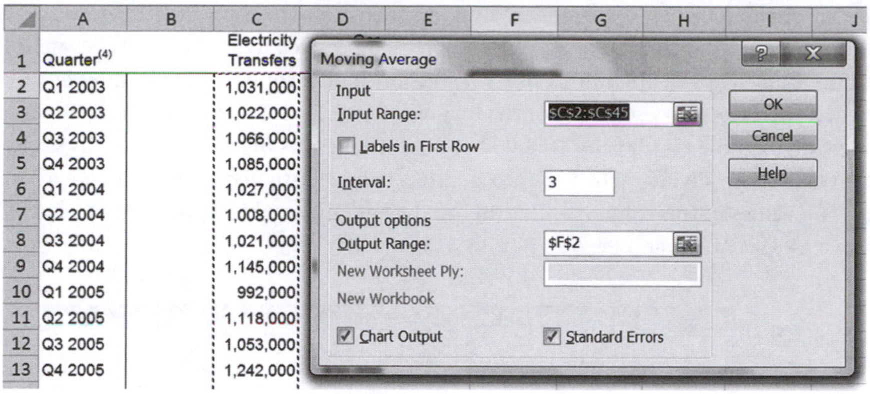

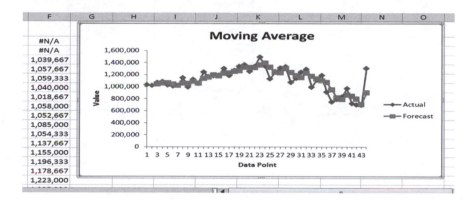

Figure 15.13

The output is shown in Figure 15.14. I would recommend copying and pasting the chart into another sheet so you can enlarge it and get a better idea of the seasonal pattern. Another good idea is to change the labels on the horizontal axis to the actual years.

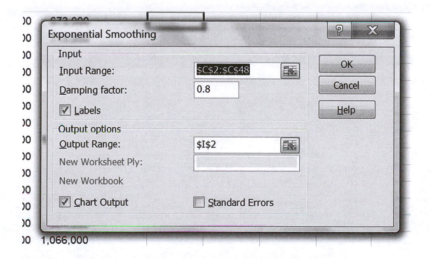

Figure 15.14

We will now use the same data to look at exponential smoothing. As before, select Data Analysis but this time choose Exponential Smoothing. The pop-up dialog box, Figure 15.15, is similar to the moving average one, except you need to enter a damping factor $(1 - \alpha)$. I have chosen 0.8 as an initial guess, but if you want to be more scientific you will need to calculate the MSE value for each smoothing constant α and select the one which has the lowest value for the MSE. As a rule of thumb, if your data contains a lot of variation then a small value for the smoothing constant is preferred.

Figure 15.15

The next technique to look at is regression analysis and forecasting. Using Excel to do this is exactly the same as when we covered regression analysis. If you remember, we attempted to fit a straight line (linear analysis) to our data. We will attempt to use a regression model to forecast the number of households who will switch their electricity supplier for the first quarter of 2014. In order to make the numbers easier to read, I have divided the raw data by 1000000 and put the results in a new column as shown in Figure 15.16. Also, rather than divide each year into quarters, I have assigned a number to each time period (column B). The values in this column will form our dependent variable (if you are not sure why we can do this, have a look at Above and Beyond Box 15.3).

	A	B	C	D
1	Quarter(4)	Period	Electricity Transfers	Electricity Transfers
2	Q1 2003	1	1,031,000	1.031
3	Q2 2003	2	1,022,000	1.022
4	Q3 2003	3	1,066,000	1.066
5	Q4 2003	4	1,085,000	1.085
6	Q1 2004	5	1,027,000	1.027
7	Q2 2004	6	1,008,000	1.008
8	Q3 2004	7	1,021,000	1.021
9	Q4 2004	8	1,145,000	1.145
10	Q1 2005	9	992,000	0.992
11	Q2 2005	10	1,118,000	1.118
12	Q3 2005	11	1,053,000	1.053
13	Q4 2005	12	1,242,000	1.242
14	Q1 2006	13	1,170,000	1.17
15	Q2 2006	14	1,177,000	1.177
16	Q3 2006	15	1,189,000	1.189
17	Q4 2006	16	1,303,000	1.303

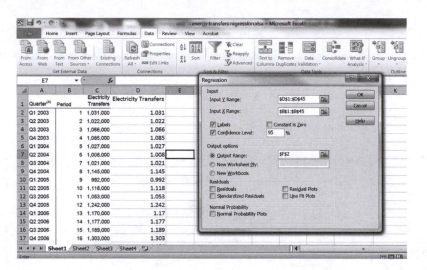

Figure 15.16

Figure 15.17 shows the summary statistics output from Excel. They tell us that our model is not particularly good (R^2 has a value of only 0.076, i.e. our model only accounts for 7.6% impact), the *F* ratio is only 3.48, and so on. But let's use it in an attempt to forecast quarter 1 switches for 2014. According to our model the regression equation is:

$$\hat{y} = 1.21 + 45(-0.005) = 0.985 \times 10^6$$

The actual value was 0.745×10^6, which means our model was out by 240,000 households! We could have saved ourselves a lot of work if we had followed the good advice of always plot your data first since then we would have seen the data behaving as shown in Figure 15.11, not a linear relationship by any stretch of the imagination.

Regression Statistics	
Multiple R	0.276691
R Square	0.076558
Adjusted R Square	0.054571
Standard Error	0.189174
Observations	44

ANOVA

	df	SS	MS	F	Significance F
Regression	1	0.1246104	0.12461	3.482007899	0.069033085
Residual	42	1.50305133	0.035787		
Total	43	1.62766173			

	Coefficients	Standard Error	t Stat	P-value	Lower 95%	Upper 95%	Lower 95.0%	Upper 95.0%
Intercept	1.207521	0.05802454	20.81053	9.61723E-24	1.090422882	1.324619401	1.090423	1.324619
Period	-0.00419	0.00224588	-1.86601	0.069033085	-0.008723203	0.000341526	-0.00872	0.000342

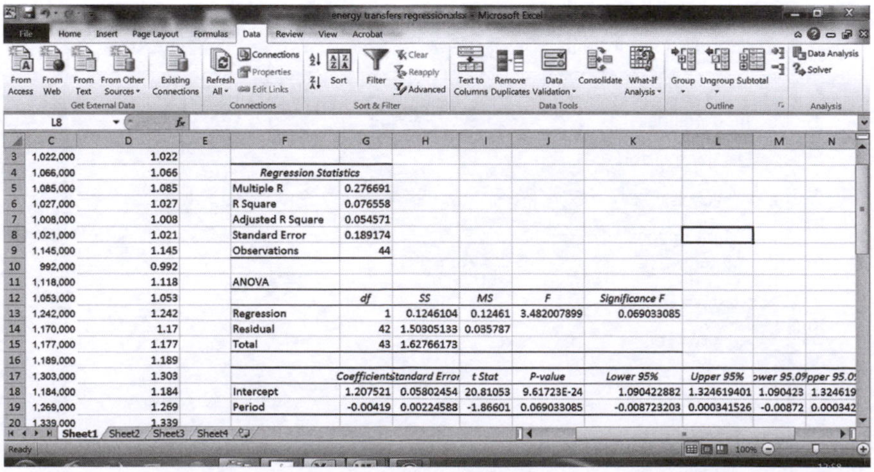

Figure 15.17

One technique we could try is to square the time variable – look at column C in Figure 15.18. We use the same technique as before but this time notice that the single-valued time period and the squared time value are both incorporated into the independent variable range in Excel (see Figure 15.18).

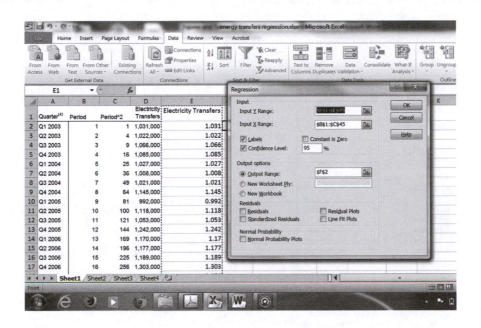

Figure 15.18

Figure 15.19 shows the summary statistics. They report an improvement on the linear model but let's try again to predict quarter 1 switches for 2014:

Using the regression equation $\widehat{y_t} = b_0 + b_1 t + b_1 t^2$

2014 Q1 switches = $0.902 + 0.036(45) - 0.001(45^2) = 0.497$

The difference, this time between actual and projected, is 248,000. This seems to be even worse than the linear model!

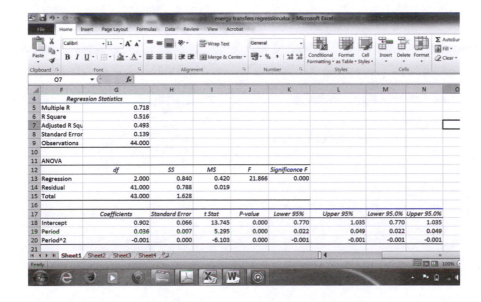

Figure 15.19

Time for a visual check. Figure 15.20 shows the result of right clicking on the data plots and clicking on Add Trendline. For the squared period plot (mathematically known as a quadratic equation), select Polynomial and order 2. It is also worthwhile selecting Display Equation on chart. Figure 15.21 displays the data along with the linear and quadratic trend lines. The quadratic seems to fit the data better, so why when we plug the numbers into the regression equation does it give a worse result than the linear equation?

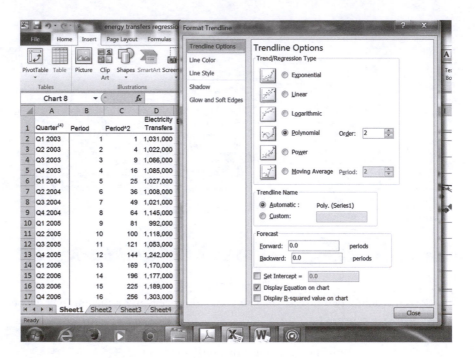

Figure 15.20

Here is another bit of wisdom – if you look again at Figure 15.11, you should see that quarter 4 in 2013 bucked the trend and shot up to 1.302 million transfers and then dropped back to 0.745 million at the start of 2014. Our forecast regression equation is unable to factor in this 'blip' in the data, so always plot your data and look for 'black swans'!

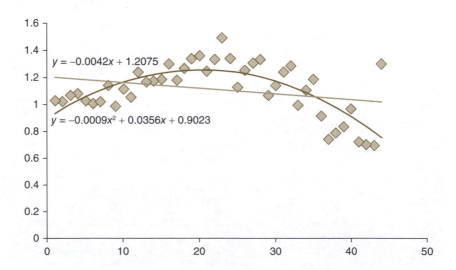

Figure 15.21

This example also illustrates how useful Excel is. You can plot your data and then instruct Excel to add trend lines to give you a visual representation. A particular feature I like is the ability to try different forms of trend lines (linear, polynomial, exponential, etc.) and have the equations displayed. To be honest, I tend to do this before using any fancy calculations, so that I have a good idea of what to expect and any anomalies I need to be aware of.

Seasonality and Trend with Excel

Figure 15.22 shows how we lay out our data in Excel. QTR1, QTR2 and QTR3 are the dummy variables we require to perform the analysis.

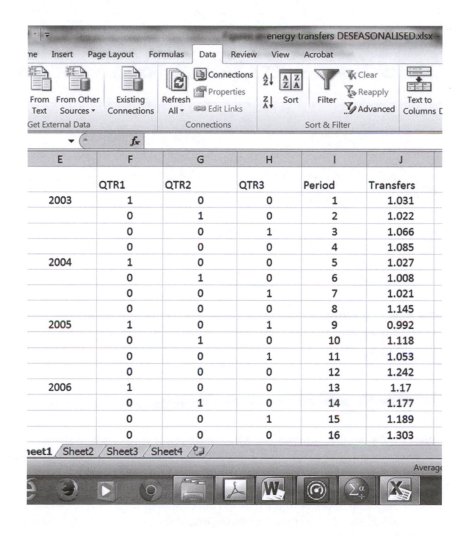

E	F QTR1	G QTR2	H QTR3	I Period	J Transfers
2003	1	0	0	1	1.031
	0	1	0	2	1.022
	0	0	1	3	1.066
	0	0	0	4	1.085
2004	1	0	0	5	1.027
	0	1	0	6	1.008
	0	0	1	7	1.021
	0	0	0	8	1.145
2005	1	0	1	9	0.992
	0	1	0	10	1.118
	0	0	1	11	1.053
	0	0	0	12	1.242
2006	1	0	0	13	1.17
	0	1	0	14	1.177
	0	0	1	15	1.189
	0	0	0	16	1.303

Figure 15.22

Figure 15.23 shows the output. If you look towards the bottom of the figure you will see the coefficients for the dummy variables.

The regression equation would look like:

$$\hat{Y}_{period} = 1.33 - 0.19\,(QTR1) - 0.16\,(QTR2) - 0.09(QTR3) - 0.005(Period)$$

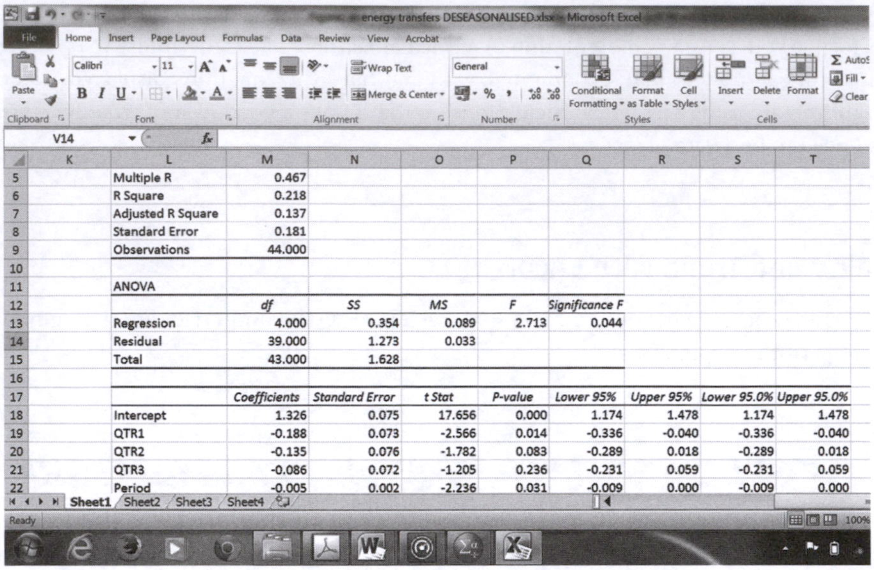

Multiple R	0.467
R Square	0.218
Adjusted R Square	0.137
Standard Error	0.181
Observations	44.000

ANOVA

	df	SS	MS	F	Significance F
Regression	4.000	0.354	0.089	2.713	0.044
Residual	39.000	1.273	0.033		
Total	43.000	1.628			

	Coefficients	Standard Error	t Stat	P-value	Lower 95%	Upper 95%	Lower 95.0%	Upper 95.0%
Intercept	1.326	0.075	17.656	0.000	1.174	1.478	1.174	1.478
QTR1	-0.188	0.073	-2.566	0.014	-0.336	-0.040	-0.336	-0.040
QTR2	-0.135	0.076	-1.782	0.083	-0.289	0.018	-0.289	0.018
QTR3	-0.086	0.072	-1.205	0.236	-0.231	0.059	-0.231	0.059
Period	-0.005	0.002	-2.236	0.031	-0.009	0.000	-0.009	0.000

Figure 15.23

To calculate the projected transfers for 2014 QTR1, the following equation is used (where the subscript $q1$ refers to QTR1):

$$\hat{Y}_{2014q1} = 1.33 - 0.19(1) - 0.16(0) - 0.09(0) - 0.005(45)$$

$$\hat{Y}_{2014q1} = 1.33 - 0.19(1) - 0.005(45) = 0.915$$

According to the forecast for 2014 QTR1, 915,000 households should switch energy suppliers. But as we know, only 745,000 did, a difference of 170,000, which is better than the previous models when seasonality was not taken into account.

SPSS and Forecasting

IBM SPSS Statistics Software (SPSS) makes the whole business of forecasting reasonably straightforward. The procedure we will use is the Time Series Modeler which estimates smoothing, univariate Autoregressive Integrated Moving Average (ARIMA) and multivariate ARIMA (also known as transfer function models). One of the great things about using SPSS is that it incorporates an Expert Modeler procedure. This means we do not have to use trial and improvement to identify an appropriate model; SPSS does the hard work and will select the best-fitting model for our data. We will use the same data that was used with Excel, which can be found in electricity_transfers.sav.

Remembering the golden rule 'eyeball your data', Figure 15.24 shows the plot produced by SPSS.

To get this plot, select Analyze → Forecasting → Sequence Charts as shown in Figure 15.25. As expected it shows a seasonality and a trend.

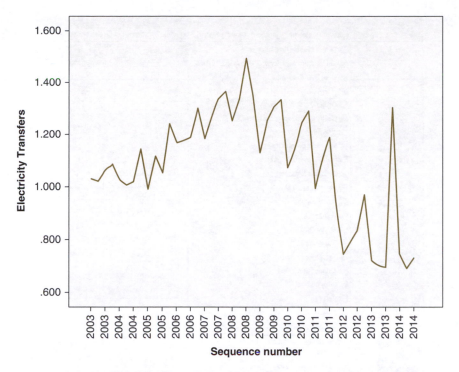

Figure 15.24

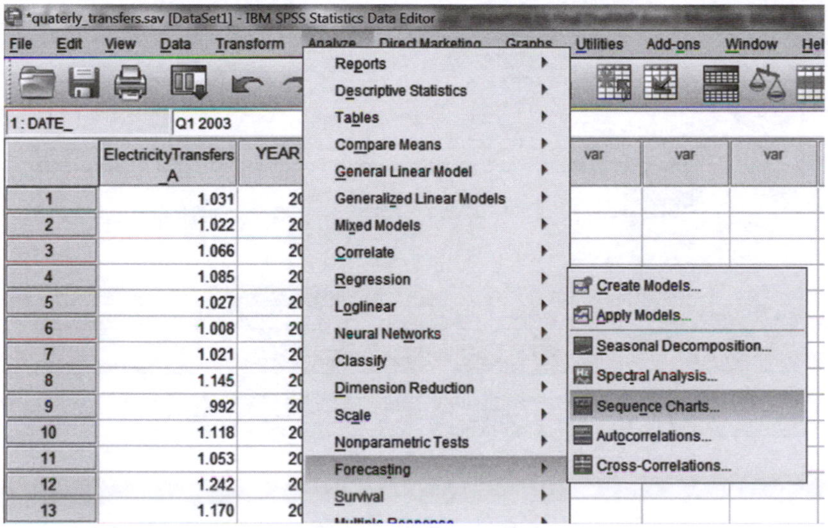

Figure 15.25

Before using the Time Series Modeler, we need to define the structure for our dates. In this instance we will use years and quarters. Figures 15.26–15.28 show the resulting change to the Data View screen.

To analyse this data with the aim of producing a forecast, we need to create a forecasting model. To do this, select <u>Analyze</u> → <u>Forecasting</u> → <u>Create Models</u> (you should be able to see it in Figure 15.25). You will see a pop-up window as shown in Figure 15.29. On the Variables tab, select Electricity Transfers as the dependent variable and transfer it to the Dependent Variables box. In order to perform the analysis a method must be chosen. By default, SPSS selects Expert Modeler which is shown in the Method drop-down box. This is what we will use for now; but as your expertise grows you may wish to choose a particular method in the future which can be found here.

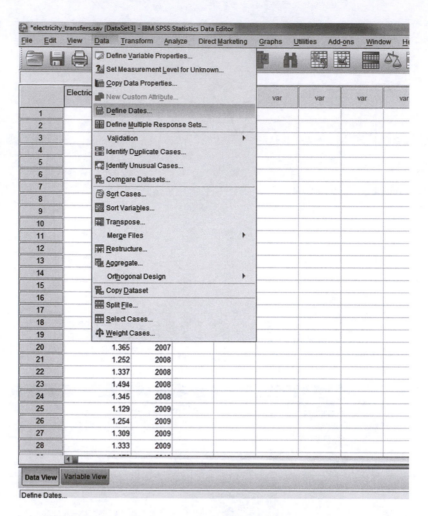

Figure 15.26

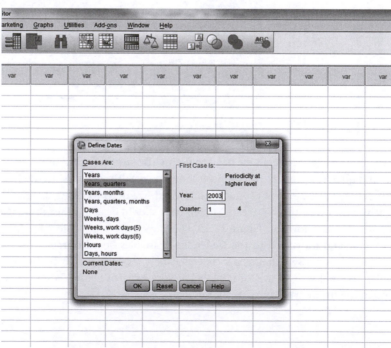

Figure 15.27

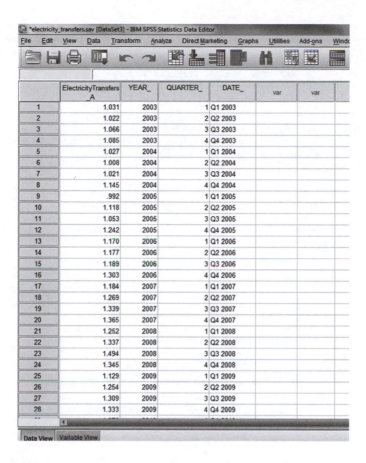

Figure 15.28

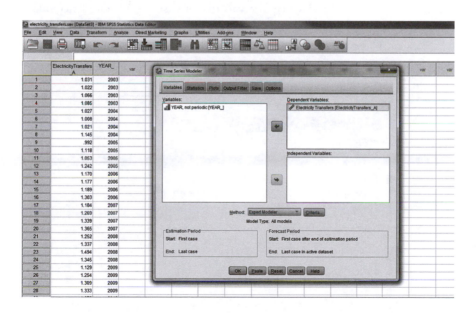

Figure 15.29

The Statistics tab provides options for inclusion in tables displaying the modelling results. Check 'Display fit measures...', which will enable you to specify particular statistics for inclusion in the tables. Figure 15.30 shows the selections which provide information in order to make informed decisions about how good the model is and whether it will be reliable to produce a forecast.

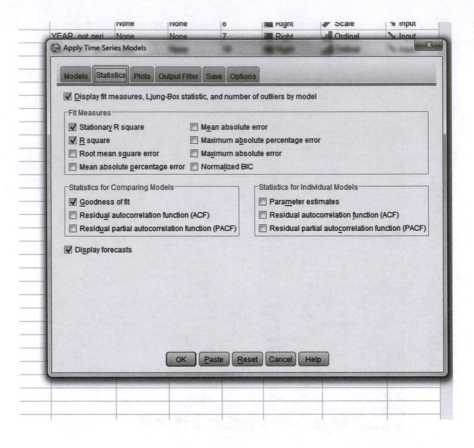

Figure 15.30

The Plots tab provides options for displaying the results. Check the Series box along with 'Observed values', 'Forecasts', 'Fit values', 'Confidence intervals for forecasts' and 'Confidence intervals for fit values'. As shown in Figure 15.31.

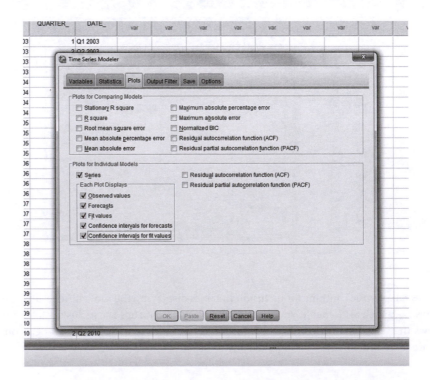

Figure 15.31

The next tab of interest is the Options tab, which is where the forecasting period can be set along with the confidence interval level. In the 'Forecast period' section, you can specify to start the forecast at some point within the actual data. This is useful since you are then able to see how well the model forecasts against known values. To activate this option, check 'First case after end of estimation period through last case in active dataset'. The other available option will produce forecasts beyond the end of the data.

Before the model is run, we need to specify a forecast period. With the data we are using we will specify a year and a month. You can choose any future year and month to see how the model predicts future transfers. I have chosen the year 2020 and the fourth quarter. Figure 15.32 shows the resulting plot.

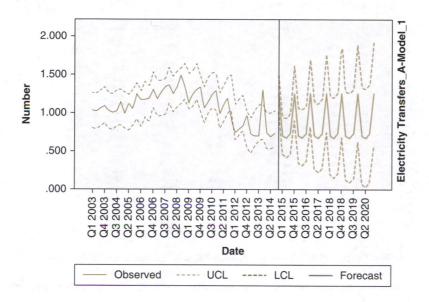

Figure 15.32

Before even looking at the model statistics, a quick look at the plot of the model shows it is not very good. Its forecasting for after 2014 demonstrates a wide variation as can be seen by the plots for the confidence intervals. One thing we could try in an attempt to get a better model is to adjust the data seasonally.

Go back to the Analyze menu and select Seasonal Decomposition. Figure 15.33 shows the pop-up box with the variable we wish to decompose seasonally in the Variables box.

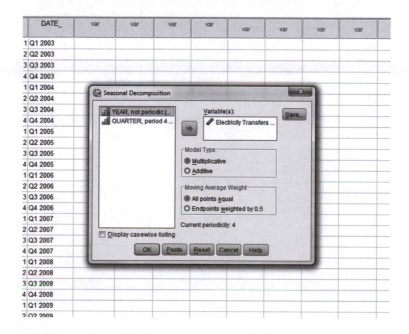

Figure 15.33

Figure 15.34 show the variables that SPSS adds to the original data set. We will be using the seasonally adjusted series (prefix SAS in Data View) since these are the values obtained after removing the seasonal variation in the original series. Figure 15.35 shows the result of running the model again but using the seasonally adjusted data instead of the original data.

	ElectricityTransfers A	YEAR_	QUARTER_	DATE_	ERR#1	SAS#1	SAF#1	STC#1	var	var
1	1.031	2003	1	Q1 2003	1.04198	1.12684	.91495	1.08144		
2	1.022	2003	2	Q2 2003	.97683	1.04675	.97636	1.07157		
3	1.066	2003	3	Q3 2003	.98982	1.04113	1.02389	1.05184		
4	1.085	2003	4	Q4 2003	.95692	1.00018	1.08481	1.04521		
5	1.027	2004	1	Q1 2004	1.06666	1.12246	.91495	1.05232		
6	1.008	2004	2	Q2 2004	.98930	1.03241	.97636	1.04358		
7	1.021	2004	3	Q3 2004	.95740	.99718	1.02389	1.04156		
8	1.145	2004	4	Q4 2004	.99923	1.05549	1.08481	1.05630		
9	.992	2005	1	Q1 2005	1.00811	1.08421	.91495	1.07549		
10	1.118	2005	2	Q2 2005	1.04510	1.14507	.97636	1.09566		
11	1.053	2005	3	Q3 2005	.92299	1.02844	1.02389	1.11425		
12	1.242	2005	4	Q4 2005	.99081	1.14490	1.08481	1.15552		
13	1.170	2006	1	Q1 2006	1.07290	1.27876	.91495	1.19186		
14	1.177	2006	2	Q2 2006	1.00064	1.20550	.97636	1.20473		
15	1.189	2006	3	Q3 2006	.96150	1.16126	1.02389	1.20776		
16	1.303	2006	4	Q4 2006	.98103	1.20113	1.08481	1.22436		
17	1.184	2007	1	Q1 2007	1.02586	1.29406	.91495	1.26144		
18	1.269	2007	2	Q2 2007	1.01170	1.29973	.97636	1.28470		
19	1.339	2007	3	Q3 2007	1.00582	1.30776	1.02389	1.30020		
20	1.365	2007	4	Q4 2007	.96001	1.25829	1.08481	1.31070		
21	1.252	2008	1	Q1 2008	1.01550	1.36838	.91495	1.34749		
22	1.337	2008	2	Q2 2008	1.00514	1.36938	.97636	1.36237		
23	1.494	2008	3	Q3 2008	1.07658	1.45915	1.02389	1.35536		
24	1.345	2008	4	Q4 2008	.94891	1.23985	1.08481	1.30661		
25	1.129	2009	1	Q1 2009	.96672	1.23395	.91495	1.27643		
26	1.254	2009	2	Q2 2009	1.01875	1.28437	.97636	1.26073		
27	1.309	2009	3	Q3 2009	1.02120	1.27846	1.02389	1.25192		
28	1.333	2009	4	Q4 2009	1.00149	1.22879	1.08481	1.22696		

Figure 15.34

As you can see from the plot, there is little improvement. If you look at the plot you will see that the problem is being caused by the 'spike' at the end of 2013. One solution may be to try using the data just prior to this 'spike' and see if that produces a better model.

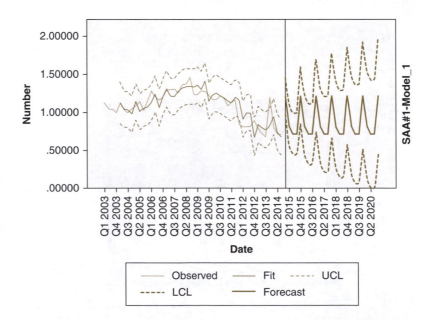

Figure 15.35

Finally SPSS produces the usual model statistics tables for you to interpret (see Figure 15.36) which, if you just used them to make a judgement, would probably say it is a good model since $R^2 = 0.707$. So the final moral for this chapter is: if possible plot your data so you can see what is going on.

Model Statistics

Model	Number of Predictors	Model Fit statistics		Ljung-Box Q(18)			Number of Outliers
		Stationary R-squared	R-squared	Statistics	DF	Sig.	
Electricity Transfers-Model_1	0	.280	.707	10.684	16	.829	0

Figure 15.36

SUMMARY

Well, I have to say that writing this chapter was pretty interesting for me! Forecasting has always been something I have shied away from in the past, and time series models have been a mystery to me for many years. In light of this chapter, though, it can be seen that they are reasonably simple extensions of the regression approach. In fact, an understanding of forecasting methods will prove to be highly useful in general life, with so much of today's world dependent on economic variables, and forecasting playing such a key role in our current affairs.

From here, we are so close to finishing our journey through quantitative analytics for business that I bet you can almost taste it! I certainly can. It is a nice flavour. In the next chapter – *the final one* – many mysteries will be revealed. But, mainly, we will focus on using quantitative analysis to perform quality control tasks, a key task for the modern business analyst.

 final checklist

You should have covered and understood the following basic content in this chapter:

- ☑ The main reason behind forecasting, and what a time series is.
- ☑ What the trend, seasonal, cyclical and irregular components of a time series represent.
- ☑ How smoothing can help to remove irregular components from a stable time series, and the different methods of smoothing: moving averages, weighted moving averages and exponential smoothing.

- ☑ How to use a linear model to model and project a trend in a time series.
- ☑ How to discover and remove seasonal components from a time series.
- ☑ How multiple regression methods can be incorporated into a time series framework to make more accurate forecasts.

EXERCISES

1. Table 15.13 shows the data on transformers used within the electricity supply industry. The total number of losses column records the number of transformers that became unusable due to failure. The cost column reports the cost in dollars to the industry.

   a. Could a moving average technique be used to predict failures for subsequent years? Explain your answer, giving reasons why the technique is suitable or unsuitable for this type of analysis.
   b. How could you validate your answer to part (a)?

Table 15.13

Year	Total no. of losses	Cost
1997	19	15742834
1998	25	35121
1999	15	397389
2000	20	93323695
2001	15	13890684
Total	94	123389723

    c. Select and use a suitable number of data points to predict the number of failures the industry could expect in 2002.

    d. Based on your answer to part (c), what advice would you give to the power industry?

2. Table 15.14 shows the life expectancy at birth for someone who lives in Glasgow, Scotland.

Table 15.14

Year	Life expectancy (years)
2000–2	68.9
2001–3	69.1
2002–4	69.3
2003–5	69.9
2004–6	70.4
2005–7	70.7
2006–8	70.7
2007–9	71.2
2008–10	71.8
2009–11	72.2
2010–12	72.6

    a. Plot the data and comment on the trend in life expectancy.

    b. Using a suitable moving average method, predict the life expectancy for someone born in the period 2011–13.

    c. Comment on the reliability of your forecast in terms of economic prosperity, advances in medicine, improvements in lifestyle and possible future events.

    d. What type of organization(s) would use and perhaps benefit from this data?

3. Table 15.15 represents the attendance at my mathematics lectures from 2006 to 2014.

Table 15.15

Year	Attendance
2006	142
2007	163
2008	157
2009	149

Year	Attendance
2010	138
2011	141
2012	140
2013	132
2014	147

a. Calculate the three-year moving averages.
b. Using a smoothing constant of 0.3, exponentially smooth the series.
c. Repeat part (b), with a smoothing constant of 0.1.
d. Compare and interpret the results from parts (b) and (c).

4. The data in Table 15.16 shows the yearly salaries of a Band 6 nurse working for the National Health Service in the UK over a five-year period.

Table 15.16

Year	Salary
2009	25783
2010	27072
2011	27613
2012	27613
2013	27613

a. Using a linear regression forecasting technique, project what a Band 6 nurse could expect to earn in five years' time.
b. Comparing your result with the data in the table, is the projected salary realistic?
c. Explain why your projected salary may not actually occur.
d. Give an explanation why the nurse's salary did not increase in value between 2011 and 2013.

5. Cornwall is a county in the south west of the UK. It is largely dependent upon tourism as the main wealth generator. You have been asked by the Cornwall Tourist Board to project the income from tourism for next year. In order to provide a realistic projection, you will need to answer the following questions:

a. What are the factors that you would take into account?
b. What assumptions would you make?
c. List some of the factors that could adversely affect your projection.

6. National statistics used by such organizations as the UK government in monitoring and formulating policy are provided by the Office for National Statistics. If you follow the link http://www.ons.gov.uk/ons/datasets-and-tables/index.html it will take you to data sets the ONS produces. Go to the 'Regional Labour Market: headline indicators for the West Midlands'; you will see in the top right of the data set the words 'seasonally adjusted'.

a. Why does this data need to be seasonally adjusted?
b. Suggest a method for performing the seasonal adjustment calculation.
c. Use Excel to perform the calculations and compare the results with the ones you compute by hand.
d. Use SPSS to perform your calculations and compare the ones computed by hand, the ones Excel produces and the ones SPSS gives.

To access additional online resources please visit: **https://study.sagepub.com/leepeters**

The Ballad of Eddie the Easily Distracted: Part 16

Eddie was in many ways relieved to reach the end of QUAN101, and correspondingly the end of the textbook. He thought also that the person who'd written the cursed thing was also pretty pleased to finish it (and he was in fact right about that). But, on the other hand, he couldn't help but admit that he was almost beginning to enjoy the subject. After his strange epiphany last week about forecasting being useful, he was beginning to see the use in all kinds of the tools he was being taught. For example, even if he never went into quality management, the ideas of quality control made quite a lot of sense to him.

In particular, he'd seen quite a lot of Esha in the last couple of weeks. They'd got on quite nicely when they went for coffee last week, and as such had seen each other a few more times. 'Of course,' Eddie thought, 'it's always connected to work somehow, but it doesn't always feel that way.' Anyway, to stop himself dwelling on that, he started to apply some of the process control concepts he was reading about. He thought about 'rating' how positive his interactions were with Esha each time he saw her, and plotting them on a chart. If he could somehow work out what the expectations of these interactions were, he could work out whether things were getting kind of weird or not – he chuckled at the term used in the textbook, 'out of statistical control'. He was beginning to wonder whether that was in fact a rather appropriate term for how he felt about things right now.

Esha's Story: Part 16

Esha was looking forward to the end of term, and also to her exams. She always kind of liked a good exam, with all of the focus and challenge that it entailed. She was also looking forward to going home to see her parents and old school friends and sharing stories of all the weird and wonderful things that had happened this year. Just a few more weeks of concentration and studying and she could relax for the summer. 'Maybe,' she thought, 'this might even be the last time I can take such a long break!' She had a feeling her life would get busier and busier as she moved forwards and so was determined to earn a good break this time around.

That said, she couldn't help feeling a strange sort of pang when she thought about Eddie. He was such an odd boy, she thought, but she couldn't help smiling when she thought of all the silly things he did and said. She'd definitely miss him when she went home for the summer. Immediately as the thought popped into her head, though, she pushed it away. The last thing she needed was to be going all weird over some silly boy – especially because she could never seem to tell what he was going to do next. It was a bit like the acceptance sampling she was learning about in the QUAN101 class this week. If she took a sample of their different meetings, she could set up some expectations of how many weird 'Eddie-isms' (as she had taken to calling them) were acceptable before she decided Eddie was just *too* odd. It was kind of a cool idea, but when she started working out what would correspond to Type I and Type II errors in this situation, she got a bit confused about exactly what she was deciding about. 'Well I suppose the best thing to do is keep reading about it, but on the other hand I wonder whether Eddie's studies are going OK. Maybe I should check…' Esha thought, picking up her mobile phone.

16

USING STATISTICS FOR QUALITY CONTROL

CONTENTS

 learning objectives

This is the final chapter, but do not let your concentration slip! Make sure you focus on achieving the following learning objectives:

☑ Understand how we can use statistics to give us evidence about whether or not a manufacturing (or other) process is in or out of control (and by extension that even really abstract statistical and quantitative concepts do have a practical use!).

☑ Learn how to create a control chart, by computing the LCL and UCL, in situations where the population mean and standard deviation are known, as well as when they are unknown.

☑ Learn how to create the different $\bar{x}$, R, p and np control charts.

☑ Learn how acceptance sampling works, and the definitions of producer and consumer risk.

☑ Learn how the binomial distribution can be used along with an acceptance sampling program to compute the likelihood of accepting a lot of raw material with a given number of defective items, and how to create an operating characteristic curve from this information.

☑ Learn how to use this knowledge to choose the most useful acceptance sampling plan, which balances out consumer and producer risk at levels appropriate to the specific situation.

So, here we are at the final chapter of the book. And, let me tell you, if you are feeling some relief at that, then please be assured that this is absolutely nothing compared with the relief I am feeling. I am also very proud of you all for getting this far, and I hope that each and every one of you has grown in confidence. But mutual (I assume) admiration aside, this chapter is an interesting one in many ways. Here, we move completely from 'basic' techniques to applications of the tools you learned earlier. While the previous chapter started that process – building on regression to show how we could predict trends in data (e.g. financial results) – here we build on probability theory and other techniques to develop methods of determining whether or not some process is achieving a set quality standard. This sort of thing is directly applicable to many different business processes and situations, and as such this is one of the more immediately practical parts of the book.

In fact, quality control is an area where you could say that statistical methods are really the only way of working out with any confidence whether or not standards of quality are being met, and this makes them essential to modern business practice. Of course, we must think about what 'quality' is in this context, for these methods to make sense. When we talk in this chapter about 'quality' we are referring to some 'characteristic' that a given product or service must have. In other words, the quality control process is one of determining whether the product or service meets the required standards. To do so, one could of course inspect every single product/service that is made or performed. However, this seems rather unfeasible for mass-production situations, or in anything other than very specific service contexts. So, usually, quality control comes down to performing a series of measures and tests on a sample of products/services to ensure that quality standards are being met. But, of course, you will already have worked out that, if you take a sample of the whole population, you are dealing with probability in terms of the chances of the results from the sample also applying to the population. In fact, if you remember, I have given quality control examples in earlier chapters, such as the Milan shoe factory (Chapter 6, hypergeometric probability). There are others too; see if you can find them (remember motorcycle helmets?).

In any case, the present chapter will explain in some detail two critical methods of quality control that use statistics. The first is called statistical process control and is essentially the creation and use of control charts to keep an eye on production processes. The basic goal of statistical process control is to make decisions on whether the process should be continued or modified to achieve a predefined quality standard (e.g. error rate, tolerance, etc.) The second method is called acceptance sampling, and it is basically a method of making decisions about whether or not to accept a batch of items based on the quality of a sample.

STATISTICAL PROCESS CONTROL

Before we start, let me set the scene for you. In this section, I am talking about quality control as it would apply to a typical production process. That is, a process where some product is manufactured continuously. In such a case, how do we determine that the production process is achieving the required standard? In almost all cases, this is done by taking a sample of the output of the process and inspecting it. Based on the results of that inspection, a decision will be made either to continue the process as it is, or to make some change to it to increase quality. No matter how advanced or well run a production process is, there will always be situations which may lead to errors and thus failing quality standards. For example, tools wear out over time, poor-quality materials from a supplier can be a problem, and operators (who are, after all, only human) can make mistakes. Statistical process control is a way of monitoring quality so that poor quality can be caught early and remedied.

There are two possible causes of quality variations in a production process, in a general sense at least. First, assignable causes are those things that are under the control of the manufacturer in some way. For example, tools wearing out, human error, bad materials and so forth. These causes are controllable, and therefore the process can be adjusted to correct for them. However, if the quality variations are down to common causes, this is out of the control of the manufacturer. Common causes are analogous to random errors in the process; they are basically random fluctuations in material quality, conditions and so forth. They are not controllable, and therefore the process cannot be corrected for them. The key task of statistical process control is to judge the likelihood that the observed variations in quality are due to assignable causes (in which case we adjust the process) or common causes (in which case we do not). Some of you will start to make the connection here to the other material in this book, particularly about hypothesis testing.

think it over 16.1

Some big companies rely upon smaller companies that manufacture components for them (this is known as the supply chain). Many large companies put the supply chain process out to tender (i.e. smaller companies 'bid' for the work). Whose problem is it if one of the supply chain manufacturers consistently supplies components that are outside of the required tolerances, and what do you do to rectify the problem? The company in question is a preferred supplier.

When we detect assignable causes, we judge that the process is out of control and take action to bring it back to the level of quality defined as acceptable. However, if the variation in quality is solely due to common causes, we conclude the process is in control (or *in statistical control*) and take no action. If this is confusing, consider this: we have to assume there will be *some* variation in any process, and our task is basically to work out how likely that variation is to be random (in which case we do not worry about it), or caused by some controllable problem (in which case we do something). So, it is clear that the basic principles of statistical process control should be essentially the same as those for hypothesis testing that were covered earlier. If you consider the null hypothesis H_0 to be that the process is in statistical control, and H_1 to be that it is out of control, things may become clearer. Take a look at Table 16.1, which collects this together with the concepts of Type I and Type II errors to help you make the connection.

Table 16.1 Statistical process control and error

Decision	State of process	
	H_0 = true **Process in statistical control**	H_0 = false **Process out of control**
Continue process	Correct decision	Type II error (allow out-of-control process to continue)
Change process	Type I error (adjust in-control process)	Correct decision

Control Charts

The fundamental tool in statistical process control is the control chart. A control chart provides a visualization that the decision maker can use to decide whether variation in a process's output is down to common causes or assignable causes – in other words, whether it is in or out of control. There are multiple different types of control charts, which are classified by the data they present. Different types of control charts contain different measurements on the vertical axis and time on the horizontal. As such, they all share basic similarities, and there is no need to go into equal depth with all types.

Beginning with the most basic control chart, the $\bar{x}$ chart is appropriate to use if the quality outcome of a given process can be measured as some kind of quantitative variable, such as length, height, temperature, weight, or the like. As such, it is pretty easy to see that any decision on whether a process is in or out of control will be naturally based on the mean value for the relevant quality measure that is found in a sample of the production process. Figure 16.1 shows a basic $\bar{x}$ chart. The vertical axis would represent the scale for the variable of interest, and the centre line would represent the mean of that process when the process is in control. Every time one takes a sample from the production process, one computes a sample mean $\bar{x}$ and then plots that on the control chart. The two lines labelled UCL (Upper Control Limit) and LCL (Lower Control Limit) are used to determine whether the process is in or out of control. These lines are drawn at points on the vertical axis so that when the process is truly in control, the value of the sample mean $\bar{x}$ has a high probability of being between the two lines. Conversely, values of $\bar{x}$ falling outside the lines provide statistical evidence that the process is out of control. Obviously, you might be thinking, the trick is in getting the position of those lines at the right place.

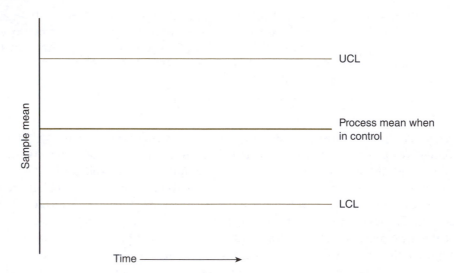

Figure 16.1
Basic Control Chart

As time moves on, you add more and more data points to the chart, moving from left to right over time of course. When you plot a point on the chart, you test a null hypothesis that the process is in control. If you do not quite understand how, then the next section will explain it much more clearly. But before we move on, you should be aware that the $\bar{x}$ chart is by no means the only control chart possible. In fact, you can create control charts for the number of defective items in a sample (*np* chart), the proportion of defects in a sample (*p* chart), or the range of measurements in a sample (*R* chart). The basic structure of the charts is the same as in Figure 16.1, but the difference is that the vertical axis measures something different. For example, the *np* chart would have a vertical axis that measured the number of defective items in the sample. All of these charts will be shown in the following sections – but they are really just variations on a theme, and simply use different skills you have already acquired from earlier sections in the book.

Creating an $\bar{x}$ Chart Where the Process Mean and Standard Deviation Are Known

Just like any other mean hypothesis test, the simplest example to start with is when we know the population mean and standard deviation. Of course, in this situation, we refer to the population as the process, but the basic ideas are the same as you already know. So, let's consider this task in light of a typical example. Imagine a company that makes BBQ Sauce – BBQCo. I like BBQ sauce, and when I buy a 250 ml bottle of it, I expect to get 250 ml. So, BBQCo, like almost any other similar firm, operates an automated production line that fills the bottles. The company knows that when its process is in control, the mean filling of each bottle would be $\mu = 255$ ml, with a standard deviation $\sigma = 2$. As usual in such a situation, the company also assumes that the filling volume of each bottle is normally distributed, as shown in Figure 16.2.

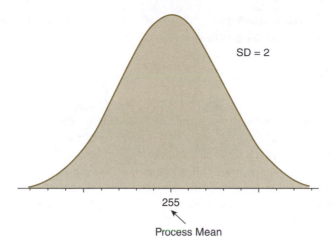

SD = 2

255
Process Mean

Figure 16.2
Distribution
of Bottle
Filling

We can use the sampling distribution of $\bar{x}$ (which you should remember from earlier chapters in this book) to calculate the variation that could be expected in the $\bar{x}$ values for a process which is in control. That said, it is probably a while since you have come across this concept, so maybe a recap of key issues is important. First, remember that the expected value of the sample mean $\bar{x}$ is equal to μ. So, for any sample of size n, the equation for the standard error of the mean – which is another name for the standard deviation of $\bar{x}$ – is:

$$\sigma_{\bar{x}} = \frac{\sigma}{\sqrt{n}}$$

Furthermore, because we are assuming that the filling volumes of the process are normally distributed, the sampling distribution of $\bar{x}$ is also normally distributed, whatever the sample size. As such, we know that the sampling distribution of $\bar{x}$ is a normal distribution, with a mean of μ and a standard deviation of $\sigma_{\bar{x}}$ as shown in Figure 16.3.

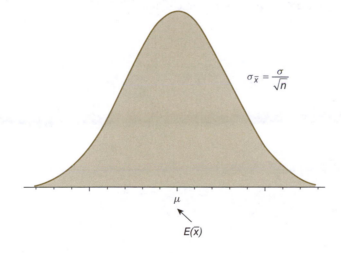

$$\sigma_{\bar{x}} = \frac{\sigma}{\sqrt{n}}$$

μ

$E(\bar{x})$

Figure 16.3
Normal
Distribution
(Again...)

So, as you might expect, we use the sampling distribution of $\bar{x}$ to calculate what values of $\bar{x}$ are expected if the process is in control. While we can use virtually any decision rule to do this (just as we can use any statistical significance level in a hypothesis test), common practice in quality control is to consider that any value of $\bar{x}$ which is within three standard deviations above or below the mean value is reasonable for an in-control process. If you remember, around 99.7% of the area of a standard normal distribution is between ±3 standard deviations of the mean. So, the decision rule in this case is that if $\bar{x}$ is within the interval $\mu - 3\sigma_{\bar{x}}$ to $\mu + 3\sigma_{\bar{x}}$, then we assume the process is in control. You can then easily convert this into the language of the control chart using the following:

$$UCL = \mu + 3\sigma_{\bar{x}}$$

$$LCL = \mu - 3\sigma_{\bar{x}}$$

So, with this in mind, we can work through the BBQCo example in more depth. Assuming that the process distribution is as shown in Figure 16.2, and the sampling distribution of $\bar{x}$ is as shown in Figure 16.3, what would typically happen is some kind of quality control inspector would draw regular samples (let's say one per hour) and take the mean filling volume as a way of determining whether the process is in control or not. In this case, let's say the inspector takes nine bottles of BBQ sauce for each sample. Before deciding whether or not the process is in or out of control, the inspector would need to compute the UCL and LCL as follows:

$$UCL = \mu + 3\sigma_{\bar{x}}$$
$$= 255 + 3\left(\frac{2}{\sqrt{9}}\right)$$
$$= 255 + 3(0.67)$$
$$= 255 + 2.01$$
$$= 257.01$$

$$LCL = \mu - 3\sigma_{\bar{x}}$$
$$= 255 - 3\left(\frac{2}{\sqrt{9}}\right)$$
$$= 255 - 3(0.67)$$
$$= 255 - 2.01$$
$$= 252.99$$

Figure 16.4 shows the control chart with the results of a 12-hour period of samples. As you can see, for period 12, the sample mean is below the LCL, indicating a process that is out of control. What is needed now is corrective action to get the process back in control.

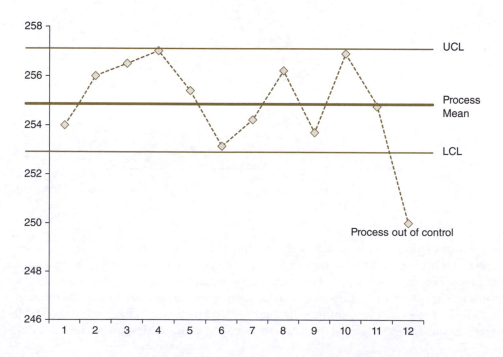

Figure 16.4
BBQCo
Sauce
Control
Chart

Creating an $\bar{x}$ Chart Where the Process Mean and Standard Deviation Are Not Known

Of course, in most situations, you do not know the true mean of the process, or the true standard deviation. Rather, you need to compute an estimate of these values by using samples of the process when it is in control. The obvious potential problem here is how to decide whether the process is in control without the control chart, but without the process mean and standard deviation you cannot compute the control chart. So, in some ways, it is a bit like a chicken and egg problem.

More common therefore is to use the range of a sample rather than the standard deviation to examine the variation in a process. This has the further advantage of being pretty easy to compute, and provides a good estimate of the standard deviation, with the addition of one or two bits of information, as I will show you.

So, let's move to another example. Imagine that I run an e-commerce website for fashion clothing. Once a regular customer (i.e. one who has pre-registered his or her main details) selects one or more items, and moves to the checkout area of the site, I have a process which should result in the customer's completing the transaction within 100 seconds. If the average time for transaction completion is greater or less than this, I consider the process out of control and look to see if there are technical problems with the site, and remedy them if necessary.

So, let's imagine that I use the tools from the e-commerce site to take random samples of the transaction time for 10 customers every hour, for 10 hours. Table 16.2 gives the summary data from these 10 samples – specifically the mean transaction time for each sample and the range of the data in each sample. Remember, the range is simply the difference between the longest and shortest transaction times in each sample.

Table 16.2 E-commerce site transaction time data

Sample number	Sample range	Sample mean
1	9.4	99.5
2	11.2	102.6
3	14.1	98.1
4	9.9	101.4
5	10.5	99.8
6	9.6	98.4
7	13.2	103.2
8	17.8	102.2
9	12.9	97.6
10	13.8	98.4
Overall mean		**100.12**
Average range	**12.24**	

We can use this data to give us some important information. First, we estimate the process mean by calculating the overall sample mean – or, in other words, the 'mean of the means' – using the following formula (which is kind of obvious once you think about it):

$$\bar{\bar{x}} = \frac{\bar{x}_1 + \bar{x}_2 + \dots + \bar{x}_k}{k}$$

where:

$\bar{x}_j$ = mean of the jth sample $j = 1, 2, \dots, k$

k = number of samples

You can see from Table 16.2 that the overall sample mean is 100.12. This will be used as the centre line of the control chart. The next step is to work out how to calculate UCL and LCL. For this we can use the average range across the samples. It again is reasonably self-explanatory to compute this as:

$$\overline{R} = \frac{R_1 + R_2 + \ldots + R_k}{k}$$

where:

R_j = range of the jth sample j=1,2,...,k

k = number of samples

Again, you can see from Table 16.2 that the average range in this case is 12.24

So, recall from earlier in this chapter that any sample mean that was within ±3 standard deviations of the process mean was considered in control, and we used that knowledge to compute the UCL and LCL. But in this case we do not have a process mean or standard deviation, so we must use estimates. This complicates matters somewhat, and requires us to use what some might term a bit of 'statistical magic'. But it is not really like that at all. Basically, it can be shown[1] that the average range of a set of samples from a population is related to the population standard deviation by a constant called d_2 that depends on the sample size. What you really need to know is that this constant is helpfully tabulated for you, for each sample size, in Table 16.3, along with some other ones that will be used for the rest of the examples in this section. So, first things first, the process standard deviation can be estimated by the formula:

$$\hat{\sigma} = \frac{\overline{R}}{d_2}$$

Now, this is already super-helpful. But cleverer minds than mine went further, and realized that they could help out by doing a bit more arithmetic for us. So they created another constant, which again depends on the sample size, A_2. This constant is calculated as:

$$A_2 = \frac{3}{d_2 \sqrt{n}}$$

It is also tabulated in Table 16.3. Some of the more advanced among you will probably be able to work out how that saves you a lot of computation, and why it is kind of obvious. However, it is not necessary to worry about that particularly at this point. What will be useful to you is that, taken together, we now have estimates of the process mean and the process standard deviation, which can be used to create the UCL and LCL on our control chart.

Just to recap, the process mean is estimated by the overall sample mean $\overline{\overline{x}}$, and an estimator $\hat{\sigma}$ for the process standard deviation is computed by the formula given above. We can use these with the equations you have already seen in earlier sections to compute the UCL and LCL, by substituting in the new estimates where the old process values would be. If you are very keen on this, then it would be a good exercise for you.

However, the result of all of this could be considerably simplified by using the A_2 constant above, which eventually reduces to the following:

$$UCL = \overline{\overline{x}} + A_2 \overline{R}$$
$$LCL = \overline{\overline{x}} - A_2 \overline{R}$$

The only thing you need to know now is the sample size to use when reading the constants off the table. In this case, we had a sample size of 10 for our control samples. This computes to d_2 = 3.087 and A_2 = 0.308.

---

[1] Although the proof is well outside the scope of this book.

Table 16.3 Quality control constants table

Subgroup size	A_2	d_2	D_3	D_4
2	1.88	1.128	-	3.268
3	1.023	1.693	-	2.574
4	0.729	2.059	-	2.282
5	0.577	2.326	-	2.114
6	0.483	2.534	-	2.004
7	0.419	2.704	0.076	1.924
8	0.373	2.847	0.136	1.864
9	0.337	2.97	0.184	1.816
10	0.308	3.078	0.223	1.777
11	0.285	3.173	0.256	1.744
12	0.266	3.258	0.283	1.717
13	0.249	3.336	0.307	1.693
14	0.235	3.407	0.328	1.672
15	0.223	3.472	0.347	1.653
16	0.212	3.532	0.363	1.637
17	0.203	3.588	0.378	1.622
18	0.194	3.64	0.391	1.608
19	0.187	3.689	0.403	1.597
20	0.18	3.735	0.415	1.585
21	0.173	3.778	0.425	1.575
22	0.167	3.819	0.434	1.566
23	0.162	3.858	0.443	1.557
24	0.157	3.895	0.451	1.548
25	0.153	3.931	0.459	1.541

From here, it is child's play to compute the UCL and LCL:

$$A_2\overline{R} = 0.308 \times 12.24$$
$$= 3.77$$
$$\text{UCL} = \overline{\overline{x}} + A_2\overline{R}$$
$$= 100.12 + 3.77$$
$$= 103.89$$
$$\text{LCL} = \overline{\overline{x}} - A_2\overline{R}$$
$$= 100.12 - 3.77$$
$$= 96.35$$

You can see the control chart in Figure 16.5. From the chart, it is clear that the process looks to be in control across the 10 samples. Nice work.

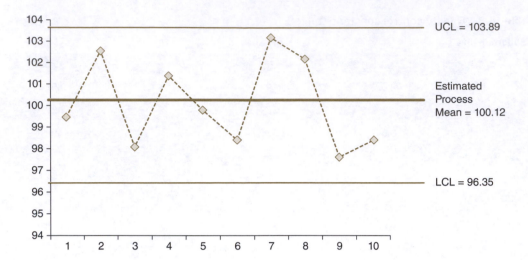

Figure 16.5
E-commerce
Control
Chart

Creating an R Chart

Rather than looking at deviations from some mean value, it is actually very common to look at the variability of a given process. In other words, using the e-commerce example from just above, can we control the variability of the transaction time? In many cases, that is actually more important. We can use the R chart to do so. In order to create an R chart, you need to think about the range of a sample as a random variable in its own right, with its own mean and standard deviation. In this sense then, the average range $\bar{R}$ functions as the mean of the range variable. But, how do we estimate the standard deviation of $\bar{R}$? Well, this is where Table 16.3 comes in again. While the proof cannot be shown here, it is the case that we can estimate the standard deviation of the range with the following formula:

$$\hat{\sigma}_R = \frac{d_3}{d_2}\bar{R}$$

As you might have worked out from Table 16.3, the values of the constants d_3 and d_2 are dependent on the sample size. You might also wonder where d_3 is. Well, do not worry, you will find out soon that, because of some clever stuff, we do not really need those values by themselves in this situation, so d_3 is not in the table. Anyway, let's move on. We already know that the process is considered in control if the sample value is within ±3 standard deviations of the mean. So with this knowledge we can compute the UCL and LCL for the R chart as:

$$UCL = \bar{R} + 3\hat{\sigma}_R = \bar{R}\left(1 + 3\frac{d_3}{d_2}\right)$$

$$LCL = \bar{R} - 3\hat{\sigma}_R = \bar{R}\left(1 - 3\frac{d_3}{d_2}\right)$$

Now, we could save ourselves some trouble if we did some of these calculations in advance – which is exactly what has been done in Table 16.3. So, let:

$$D_4 = 1 + 3\frac{d_3}{d_2}$$

$$D_3 = 1 - 3\frac{d_3}{d_2}$$

That would let us write the UCL and LCL as:

$$UCL = \bar{R}D_4$$
$$LCL = \bar{R}D_3$$

So, of course, D_3 and D_4 are given in Table 16.3, which shows why we do not really need values for d_3 itself in this case. Moving back to the e-commerce example, we can see that with $n = 10$, $D_3 = 0.223$ and $D_4 = 1.77$. Given that $\bar{R} = 12.24$, it is really easy to compute the control limits for the R chart:

$$\text{UCL} = 12.24 \times 1.77$$
$$= 21.66$$
$$\text{LCL} = 12.24 \times 0.223$$
$$= 2.73$$

Figure 16.6 shows the control chart. You can see that the process seems to be in control at this point.

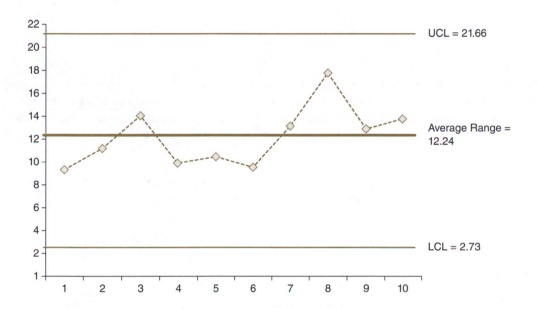

Figure 16.6
E-Commerce Site R Chart

Creating a p or an np Chart

In other quality control cases, what we are more interested in is the proportion of defective or non-defective items in a sample. This is actually a pretty common situation. Imagine a production line that makes T-shirts. No matter how good the line, there will always be some defects. The company should decide whether it should check every item (time consuming and expensive) or instead operate a quality control system where it only checks a sample of items. If the latter, the company will define a percentage of defects, below which it considers the line is working in control, and above which is cause for concern (i.e. out of control). So, imagine in this situation that the company considers a defect rate of 2% to be acceptable, which works out to a proportion of 0.02.

What we need here is to work out the sampling distribution of p, and of course you should remember this was given much earlier in the book. Now, we can apply it to a really useful situation. The first thing to remember is that π represents the expected value (i.e. the mean) of p, the proportion of defective items when the process is in control. So, the first task is to compute the standard error of the proportion using the following formula:

$$\sigma_p = \sqrt{\frac{\pi(1 - \pi)}{n}}$$

think it over 16.2

Does the formula above remind you of a particular distribution? The particular distribution had only two outcomes - similar to process control.

One thing you do need to take into account, however, is that (as was discussed in earlier chapters) the sampling distribution of p can only be assumed to approximate a normal distribution if the sample size is large. Again, though, we raise the question as to 'what is large?' Well in the case of p, we need our sample n to fulfil the following two conditions:[2]

$$n\pi \geq 5$$

$$n(1 - \pi) \geq 5$$

So, one can summarize the above by suggesting that – if the sample size is large enough – the sampling distribution of p is approximated by a normal distribution with a mean of π and a standard deviation of σ_p.

From here, it is yet again simple to work out the UCL and LCL, because the formula remains the same:

$$\text{UCL} = \pi + 3\sigma_p$$
$$\text{LCL} = \pi - 3\sigma_p$$

So, returning to the T-shirt example, say we take a sample of 250 shirts from the line; $n = 250$ and $\pi = 0.02$. We can compute the standard error as:

$$\sigma_p = \sqrt{\frac{0.02(1-0.02)}{250}} = \sqrt{\frac{0.0196}{250}} = \sqrt{0.000078} = 0.00885$$

Inserting that into the equations for the control limits, we get:

$$\text{UCL} = \pi + 3\sigma_p$$
$$= 0.02 + 3(0.00885)$$
$$= 0.047$$

$$\text{LCL} = \pi - 3\sigma_p$$
$$= 0.02 - 3(0.00885)$$
$$= -0.00655$$

You will note that the LCL is a negative number. In this case, because it is illogical to have a proportion lower than zero, we consider the LCL to be equal to zero. With these values, it would be simple to set up a control chart and plot samples of T-shirts on it for quality control.

However, if the proportion of defective items for an in-control process is not known, you can still use the method above – albeit with a higher risk. Basically, you can estimate the proportion by using sample data. What you need to do is take multiple samples of size n from the process when it is in control, and then determine the proportion of defective items in each sample. If you sum all the sample data, and treat it as one large sample, you can then compute the proportion of defective items in the entire data

[2] Remember, these are just rules of thumb, and other sources can sometimes give alternatives (e.g. I've read sources which suggest 10 should be the cut-off value, not 5). Basically, the principle revolves around the idea that p is not too close to 0 or 1, and the closer it gets, the larger the sample has to be to make up for it. In this sense, p is really the limiting factor, rather than the sample size n.

set, and take this as an estimate of π. This estimate can then be used to estimate the standard error of the proportion and, from there, the LCL and UCL. Of course, as I have already mentioned regarding other control charts, the problem is how to know if the process is in control when you take the sample, since you often determine whether or not it is in control using the control chart! This makes the process a little risky, but sometimes it is the best we can do.

So, if we can compute a p chart for the proportion of defects, it stands to reason that we could do the same for the number of defects in a sample. Indeed, this is called an np chart. Here, the principles are pretty much the same as for the p chart: n is the sample size, and π represents the probability of observing a defective item when the process is in control. Of course, this value is identical to the proportion of defective items in a given sample when you think about it. When the sample is large enough (and the rules of thumb are the same as for the p chart), the distribution of the number of defective items in a sample of size n can be considered to approximate a normal distribution with a mean of $n\pi$ and a standard deviation of:

$$\sqrt{n\pi\,(1-n)}$$

As such, for the T-shirt example above, where $n = 250$ and $\pi = 0.02$, the number of defective T-shirts in a sample of 250 is approximated by a normal distribution with a mean of $n\pi = 250(0.02) = 5$ and a standard deviation of:

$$\sqrt{250 \times 0.02 \times 0.98} = 4.9$$

Again (just to cement this in your head), the control limits for the np chart are three standard deviations above and below the expected number of defects when the process is in control. The general formulae for them are:

$$\text{UCL} = n\pi + 3\sqrt{n\pi(1-\pi)}$$
$$\text{LCL} = n\pi - 3\sqrt{n\pi(1-\pi)}$$

For the T-shirt example with $n = 250$, and $\pi = 0.02$, UCL = 5 + 3(4.9) = 19.7 and LCL = 5 − 3(4.9) = −9.7. Again, because the LCL is negative, we set it to zero in the control chart (you cannot have less than zero defects!). So, if the number of defective T-shirts in the sample is greater than 19, you would consider the process out of control.

Most of you are probably thinking 'What's the point of the np chart, when it gives exactly the same conclusion as the p chart?' Indeed, you would be right – the conclusions from both charts are always the same. However, sometimes, a quality control engineer might consider that the users of the control chart might find it easier to interpret an np chart than a p chart. A good analyst always considers how the analysis will be used, just as much as how 'technically perfect' it is.

One other thing to remember about the np chart is that you must always take a sample of the same size. That is, if you draw up the control chart using a sample size n of 250, then all other samples you take to plot on the chart must also be 250. This makes total sense, because if you had a sample of 2500, then even if it was in control, the expected value of the number of defects would be 50. Think about that!

above and beyond

Box 16.1   Interpreting Control Charts

It is likely that you already understand pretty clearly that data points outside the control limits (i.e. UCL and LCL) are statistical evidence that a process is out of control, and therefore that some corrective action should be taken. However, there are other - more subtle - ways of using control charts, which revolve around interpreting trends and patterns in the data over time. For example, there may be an

(Continued)

(Continued)

observable trend over time for the data points to tend towards one of the limits, but none may yet be observed outside the limits. In such cases, this could be a warning that some aspect of the process is 'drifting' towards being out of control. This can happen because machinery may wear out, or the environment (e.g. temperature, etc.) may change. There may also be a problem building with operator fatigue, or laxity. Or, if the pattern of data points is such that almost all the points are on one side of the mean, some shift may have occurred in the process, which might indicate a potential problem. Maybe the materials have changed? Or maybe some specific issue in the machinery is at the root of this? As such, it is not only their ability to provide statistical evidence that makes control charts useful.

ACCEPTANCE SAMPLING

Acceptance sampling is a way of deciding whether or not to accept a lot of some raw material or other sort of input into a production process. Just to clarify, a 'lot' is defined here as some group of items (the number of items in the lot is not really important). As such, while control charts deal with the end result of a production process, acceptance sampling deals with the inputs into that process. This is a common situation in most manufacturing operations. Say I run a company that makes high-end leather jackets. Of course, it is highly unlikely that I breed my own cows and run a leather tanning operation myself. Most likely, I buy in my leather from a specialist leather producer. In all such operations, it is highly important to make sure the quality of my raw materials is up to scratch. I can use acceptance sampling methods to decide whether to accept or reject a batch of raw materials, on the basis of some specified quality criterion. It is a pretty simple process for anyone who – like yourself – is trained in fundamental statistics to devise a statistical procedure for this purpose, and it basically revolves around the following set of steps:

1. You receive a lot of raw materials.
2. You draw a sample of the material for inspection.
3. You inspect the sample for quality.
4. You compare the results of your inspection with a pre-specified quality criterion.
5. If quality is satisfactory, you accept the lot, and then send it to production (or whatever end-user is relevant).
6. If quality is unsatisfactory, you reject the lot, and decide on a course of action (possibly involving angry phone calls to your supplier).

You will probably already see where the statistical techniques you have learned throughout this book will help in making the accept/reject decision. Indeed, it all revolves around the hypothesis testing method that has formed the basis of so much of the material. In this case, the null and alternative hypotheses are:

H_0: the lot is good quality

H_1: the lot is poor quality

Of course, as you probably are already thinking, the hypothesis testing procedure also has the potential for error, which was previously described as Type I and Type II errors. In this case, a Type I error would be rejecting a lot that is good quality, and Type II error would be accepting a lot that is of poor quality. Table 16.4 shows the four potential outcomes of this procedure: two correct and the two potential errors. In this context, a Type I error is considered to be a risk to the supplier of the lot (i.e. that a good-quality lot will be rejected) and is thus called the producer's risk. Conversely, a Type II error is considered a risk for the user of the lot (i.e. that a poor-quality lot will be accepted and used in production) and is therefore known as the consumer's risk. Of course, the values of producer and consumer risk are linked (as one increases, the other decreases), and are analogous to our statistical significance decisions that have been discussed in earlier chapters. As such, they can be controlled by whoever designs the acceptance sampling procedure.

Table 16.4 Outcomes of acceptance sampling

	Quality of the lot	
Decision	H_o = **true** **Lot is of good quality**	H_o = **false** **Lot is of poor quality**
Accept lot	Correct decision	Type II error (accept poor-quality lot)
Reject lot	Type I error (reject good-quality lot)	Correct decision

Acceptance Sampling in Practice

Let's imagine StyleCo, a company that manufactures high-quality suits, which are then sold under various high-end prestige brand names. StyleCo of course does not manufacture all the parts which go to make up its suits, and in particular it sources its fabric from a number of suppliers, each of whom of course claims their fabric to be of superior quality. If StyleCo uses poor-quality fabric (say, with blemishes or holes), the ensuing suits will be poor and will be returned by the brand-name fashion houses (who of course will have their own acceptance sampling procedures).

The fabric comes in long rolls (called 'bolts'). StyleCo needs to test whether the fabric it gets is high enough quality, but testing is time consuming and thus expensive, because the bolts are long, and the testing process is detailed. As such, StyleCo simply cannot justify testing every bolt it receives, and instead needs to use an acceptance sampling plan to monitor quality. What this entails is selecting a sample of size n bolts from each lot, and testing that sample for defects. The head of quality control also needs to decide how many defects is 'too many', and this is termed the acceptance criterion – that is, the maximum number of defects that can be found in the sample and still indicate an acceptable lot. Of course, this number depends on a number of factors, including how important the particular component/material is for ultimate production, and also issues such as safety of the end product. Because StyleCo's key selling point is the quality of its suits, the company decides that the acceptance criterion $c = 0$. It also decides to take a sample of $n = 10$ bolts of fabric.

The actual process of acceptance sampling is pretty simple – the quality control inspector takes a random sample of 10 bolts of fabric from each shipment and inspects for defects. If zero defects are found, the lot is accepted; if more than zero defects are found, the lot is rejected.

If that is all there is to it, you might wonder why a statistical textbook is needed to explain it. Indeed. However, the real meat of acceptance sampling is not in the actual implementation of the plan. Rather, it is in the evaluation of the acceptable risk of errors that are possible. In other words, it is a case of balancing the producer risk (Type I error) against the consumer risk (Type II error) so that both are considered acceptable. This is done by implementing a kind of 'scenario' analysis (very similar in concept to the power analysis you did in prior chapters). In other words, one assumes that a lot has some known proportion of defective items, and then computes the probability of accepting that lot if one were using the given acceptance sampling plan. If you vary the known proportion of defective items, you can examine the effect of the sampling plan on both types of risks, and thus choose the best one for your purposes.

 think it over 16.3

Some of you might be thinking 'Producer risk is not my problem if the company is in my supply chain.' Consider the scenario where one of your suppliers does not always supply you with good-quality items (i.e. within acceptable limits). But on the other hand, you can rely upon this supplier to deliver on time and, occasionally, if you need extra items at short notice, it is willing to employ its staff on overtime to help you out. As the production manager, how would you deal with this situation?

Applying this to the StyleCo example, assume that the company has just received a big shipment of fabric bolts, and that in fact 5% of the bolts contain some defect. The question becomes: for a lot with 5% defects, what is the probability of accepting the lot using a given acceptance sampling plan – for example, the $n = 10$, $c = 0$ plan explained above? First, recall that each bolt of fabric can be either defective or non-defective, so we have a dichotomous situation. Secondly, remember that the sample size is large. Because of these two key features, the number of defective items in the sample has (or can be approximated by) a binomial distribution, which allows us to use the binomial probability function as follows:

$$p(x) = \frac{n!}{x!(n-x)!}\pi^x(1-\pi)^{(n-x)}$$

where

n = sample size

π = the proportion of defective items in the lot

x = the number of defective items in the sample

$p(x)$ = the probability of x defective items in the sample

It is reasonably simple to apply this to the StyleCo example, where $n = 10$ and $\pi = 0.05$ (i.e. the lot actually contains 5% defective bolts as above). We calculate the probability of observing zero defective bolts of fabric in the sample as follows:

$$p(0) = \frac{10!}{0!(10-0)!}(0.05)^0(1-0.05)^{(10-0)}$$
$$= \frac{10!}{0!(10-0)!}(0.05)^0(0.95)^{(10)}$$
$$= (0.95)^{10}$$
$$= 0.599$$

OK, there were a few tricks used there to simplify what is a reasonably tedious calculation. If you are really confused, check out Back to Basics Box 16.1 – which is the first time it has appeared for a while! I think it might be handy for some readers who are still baffled by what happens sometimes in calculations.

 back to basics

Box 16.1   Clever Tricks...

In order to save yourself some annoyingly pointless calculations, you can employ a few tricks for this formula, which might help out. First, you need to know that $0! = 1$. That solves a few problems. Then, when you work out the first bit of the equation, which is $10!/0!(10 - 0)!$, you will realize it actually simplifies to $10!/1 \times (10)!$. I have added that multiplication symbol just to make things totally clear, but you probably did not need me to. Anyway, in doing so, just to take you another step, you will see immediately that this actually simplifies to $10!/10!$. Or in other words, 1. Which means that the first part of the equation in this case (but not always) simplifies to 1. The next trick to remember is that anything to the power of 0 also equals 1. Which means that the next bit of this equation $(0.05)^0$ also simplifies to 1. Which leads us to something like $1 \times 1 \times (0.95)^{10}$. Which of course is the same as $(0.95)^{10}$, which, as you can calculate in milliseconds with a calculator, is 0.599.

Of course, if your sampling plan had different values than the one I created, you would not necessarily be able to do this, but even so, I think it is nice to see how you can use some clever knowledge of maths to save yourself some work.

So, you can see that with the sampling plan of $n = 10$ and $c = 0$, we have a 0.599 probability of accepting a lot with 5% defective bolts of fabric. In turn, this gives us a $1 - 0.599 = 0.401$ probability of rejecting the lot.

Now, without my clever tricks detailed in Back to Basics Box 16.1, this is a seriously involving piece of calculation. One way to do it is to use an Excel spreadsheet. But (trust me on this) setting up the calculation is also pretty tedious and offers many opportunities to make silly errors which will throw your results out. So, what is usually done is to consult tables of binomial probabilities. If you go to one of these very helpful tables, you can immediately see that our calculated answer for the probability of accepting a lot with 5% defective items is correct. You can also see that the corresponding probability of accepting a lot with 10% defective items is 0.349 when using the sample acceptance sampling plan of $n = 10$ and $c = 0$. While you are there, you can also see the corresponding probabilities of accepting lots with 1% defective items, 2%, 3% and so forth. These probabilities are summarized in Table 16.5. This is kind of cool, but what is even cooler is that you can plot these, as is done in Figure 16.7. This type of plot is called an operating characteristic curve, or OC curve, for the $n = 10$, $c = 0$ acceptance sampling plan.

Table 16.5 Acceptance probabilities for StyleCo for different per cent defective bolts and a sampling plan of $n = 10$ and $c = 0$

Per cent defective in lot	Probability of accepting lot
1	0.904
2	0.817
3	0.737
4	0.665
5	0.599
10	0.349
15	0.197
20	0.107
25	0.056

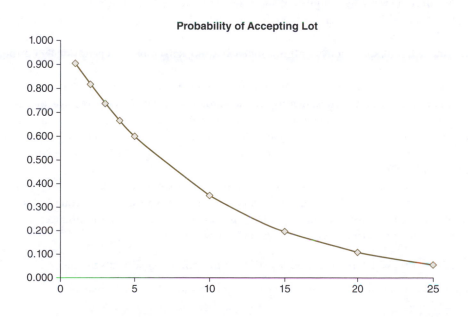

Figure 16.7 Operating Characteristic Curve for StyleCo with a Sampling Plan of $n = 10$ and $c = 0$

Of course, who is to say that our $n = 10$, $c = 0$ plan is the best? We could consider other ones, with different sample sizes and/or different acceptance criteria. First, imagine increasing c from 0 to 1, but keeping $n = 10$. For a lot with 5% defective items, the probability of accepting the lot with this new sampling plan is 0.914. It is easy to see that this is much, much larger. In fact, we could calculate OC curves for various sampling plans in this way, and Figure 16.8 does exactly this. I am not totally sure if it is the coolest figure in the book, but it certainly comes close.

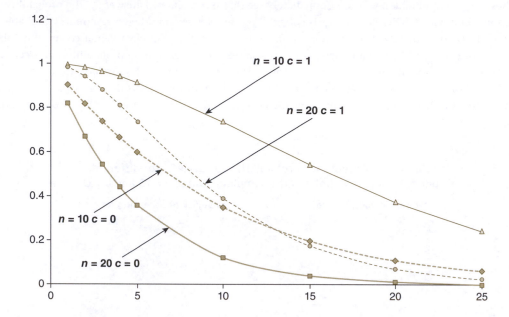

Figure 16.8
OC Curves for Different Sampling Plans

Choosing Which Acceptance Plan to Use

Looking at Figure 16.8, you can see a few obvious things. First, the $n = 20$, $c = 0$ planning always gives the lowest probabilities of accepting the lot. Of course, it also then gives the highest probabilities of rejecting the lot. Conversely, the $n = 10$, $c = 1$ plan gives the opposite: the highest probabilities of accepting the lot, and the lowest of rejecting. The question is: how do you choose which plan is best? Well, it is kind of subjective in some ways. But, ultimately, someone has to decide what levels of producer risk and consumer risk they are willing to tolerate. In other words, what levels of Type I (rejecting a good-quality lot/producer risk) and Type II (accepting a poor-quality lot/consumer risk) are you willing to tolerate? This is a balancing act, and, quite honestly, it is a somewhat subjective one. It depends really on the factors that are inherent to the business itself. For example, how critical is the particular item to the production process, or to product safety? In the case of StyleCo, high-quality fabric is absolutely crucial, so the company would probably prioritize consumer risk and look to minimize it. This would have knock-on effects for the suppliers, who would be tolerating more producer risk. In turn, this might have an impact on the contracts that were made between StyleCo and the suppliers. For a less crucial component, a manufacturer may be wishing to tolerate more consumer risk, perhaps in return for more favourable terms from suppliers when drawing up contracts.

Anyway, it is impossible for a textbook to tell you how to decide what levels of risk to tolerate in your business. But what it can do is show you how to choose a good sampling plan, once you have chosen those levels. To do so, we need first to define two values: p_0 will be used to control for producer risk; and p_1 to control for consumer risk. From here, we invoke some new notation:

α = producer risk, which is the probability of rejecting a lot with p_0 defective items.

β = consumer risk, which is the probability of accepting a lot with p_1 defective items.

So, let's go back to StyleCo. Imagine that the managers decide that $p_0 = 0.02$ and $p_1 = 0.2$. We can use the OC curve in Figure 16.9 to demonstrate the basic principles. Using $p_0 = 0.02$ gives a producer risk of around $1 - 0.81 = 0.19$, while $p_1 = 0.2$ gives a consumer risk of approximately 0.11. So, if the manager is willing to tolerate a 0.19 probability of rejecting a lot with 2% defective bolts of fabric (producer risk), and at the same time a 0.11 probability of accepting a lot with 20% defective bolts (consumer risk), then the $n = 10$, $c = 0$ plan is fine.

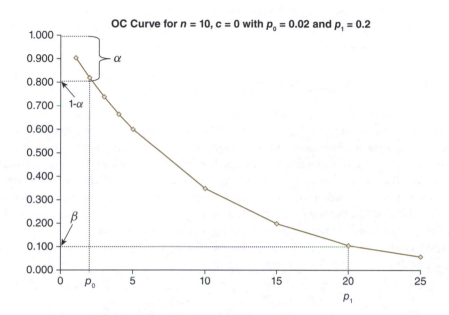

Figure 16.9

But what if StyleCo wants to reduce consumer risk? In this case, I think it might be that the company would be more likely to try to trade off more producer risk for a lower consumer risk. So, imagine it is only willing to tolerate a 0.015 probability of accepting a lot with 20% defective bolts (consumer risk), but is willing to tolerate a 0.35 probability of rejecting a lot with 2% defective bolts (producer risk). All of a sudden, the $n = 10$, $c = 0$ plan has a lower than required producer risk, but an unacceptable consumer risk. In other words, the consumer risk of 0.19 is way too high for our managers at StyleCo, and we need a new plan. In fact, if you look at Figure 16.8, you can see that the $n = 20$, $c = 0$ plan seems to do a decent job of this. In fact, this little exercise also shows how changing the number of items we sample from the lot can have a major effect on the probabilities of accepting/rejecting a lot. Of course, you should expect this, with your statistical knowledge. Remember: sample size is a crucial consideration in hypothesis testing.

Final Notes on Acceptance Sampling and Quality Control

It is important to realize that an introductory textbook such as this can never provide exhaustive information on specific issues like quality control. In fact, there are entire qualifications you can obtain on statistical quality control and such topics. It is clear that, in most cases, multiple different sampling plans need to be explored to determine which gives the best balance of consumer and producer risk. It would probably seem that creating such things would be rather laborious. However, statistical quality control is an industry in itself, of course, and there are many sources to consult for tables of various sampling plans. More advanced texts on statistical quality control will address far more issues than this chapter can ever hope to. For example, in real life you would definitely consider the cost of sampling when you are deciding the best plan. Further, you can also design multi-stage acceptance sampling plans, where you take sequential samples and make decisions on whether to proceed in a step-by-step process. If you need information on these issues, it is best to consult dedicated quality control textbooks. Enjoy that for your summer reading.

think it over 16.4

Does ethics have a role in the cut-throat world of business? Imagine you are the production manager for a company which manufactures safety-critical medical products such as replacement heart valves. Your ideal supplier who meets your acceptable consumer risk requirements is too expensive and would reduce your profit margin. Do you use products from a different supplier which are cheaper, but not of the same high quality, so you can maintain your profit margin (i.e. increase your consumer risk requirement)?

SPSS AND STATISTICAL PROCESS CONTROL

IBM SPSS Statistics Software (SPSS) is capable of producing control charts of various sorts. First of all we will look at variable charts since they are intended to be used in analysing the state of a process where parameters such as diameter, flow rates and temperature are measured. We will then look at how we can track attributes such as defects using *p* and *np* charts. The data to be used can be found in fasteners.spv.

First, when we wish to track variables in set time periods, we use the X-bar chart with either an R chart if we are interested in the spread of the sample range, or an S chart if the sample standard deviation is of interest. The individual and moving range chart is used if one sample is taken per time period. This chart measures the spread in terms of the range of two or more consecutive samples.

All of SPSS's control charts can be found under the Quality Control item in the Analyze pull-down menu (Figure 16.10).

Figure 16.10

Figure 16.11a shows the control chart options once Control Charts has been selected from the Analyze pull-down menu. Select 'X-bar, R, s' (the default option) from the available options and click on Define.

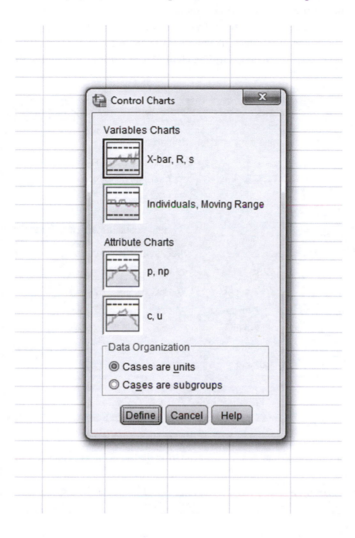

Figure 16.11a

Figure 16.11b

The X-bar, R, s: Cases Are Units dialog box (Figure 16.11b) allows you to select the parameters you wish to analyse. Put 'Diameter' in the Process Measurement box and 'Time' in the Subgroups Defined by box. Click on Statistics. Enter 50.5 in the upper specification limit box, 50.4 in the lower specification box and 50.45 in the target box. In the Process Capability Indices group, select CP, CpU, CpL, K, CpM and Z-out. In the Process Performance Indices group, select PP, PpU, PpL, PpM and Z-out. Above this group, select 'Actual % outside specification limits'. Click on Continue. Figure 16.12 shows the menu with these boxes ticked.

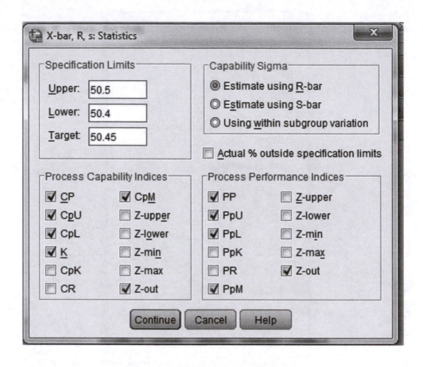

Figure 16.12

Click on Control Rules in the X-Bar, R, s: Cases Are Units dialog box. In this box, check 'Select all control rules' (Figure 16.13).

Click on Continue, then on OK in the Control Rules in the X-Bar, R, s: Cases Are Units dialog box.

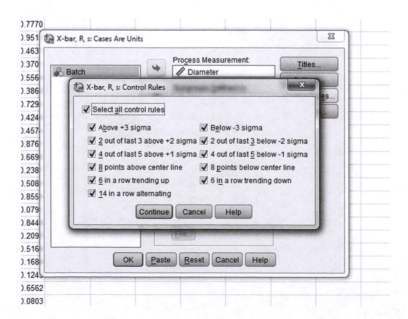

Figure 16.13

The chart shown in Figure 16.14 is the output from the analysis. The 'Range' chart shows that the majority of sample ranges are within the control limits; only point 8 violates the rules. SPSS calculates the control limits so that the expected amount of variation in the sample ranges due to common causes of variation are present. You have probably worked out that the solid line is the average and the dashed lines represent the upper and lower control limits (UCL and LCL respectively). SPSS highlights in red any points that cause a rule violation.

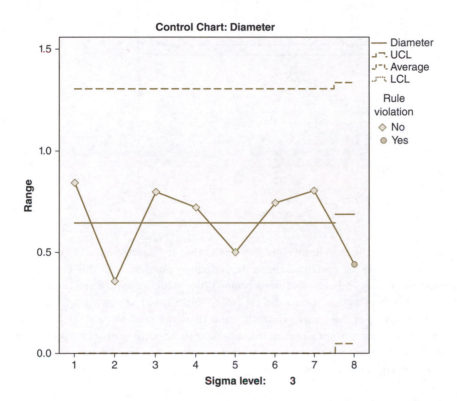

Figure 16.14

Once the R chart has been examined and it seems the process is not out of control, we will examine the X to look at the sample means and see if the variation is within the control limits calculated from the amount of variation expected due to common causes. Figure 16.15 shows the control chart. You can see the upper specification (U Spec) was set at 50.5, the Average (sample means) is 50.472984 and the lower specification (L Spec) is set to 50.4. None of the points violate any of the control rules but you can see that points 1, 3, 5, 7 and 8 are outside the specification limits. Perhaps the point of most concern is point 5, which is way below the lower specification limit but is still within the lower control limit. If the original data is consulted, it can be seen that this point occurs during time period 5. In fact, during this time period there are several points which are low and therefore further investigation is needed. If time period 5 is the fifth hour of the working day, it could be around lunch time and the production staff may be a bit sluggish after lunch! Other factors may be the cause, so do not be too quick to jump to conclusions.

Rather than just rely upon the visual representation of the data, the process statistics shown in Figure 16.16 should be consulted. Looking at the capability indices, CP is the measure (the ratio) of the difference between the specification limits to the observed process variation. Ideally CP should be equal to or greater than one to indicate a process is capable; a low value of 0.065 is of real concern! CpL and CpU give an indication of whether the process variability is symmetric about the mean. If the process variability is symmetric, the values of CpL and CpU will be close to CP. The values given in Figure 16.16 again tell us we have a problem. The K value indicates whether the process mean is a good

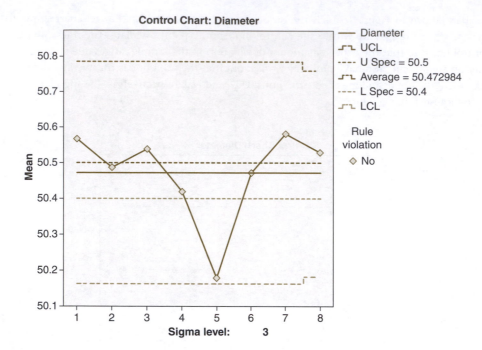

Figure 16.15

approximate of the specification limits. Ideally a small value of K along with a large value of CP would indicate the process is within specification. Again, we have a problem with the data we are analysing. CpM measures the process capability to stay on target (the value set earlier, see Figure 16.12). Finally, the performance indices are similar to the capability indices, but are based on the overall process variability rather than just the sample variability and therefore tend to be more conservative. If the performance indices are much smaller than the capability indices, there may be a problem due to non-random variation in the process. There is not a huge difference in our indicators, so it is unlikely there are non-random events affecting the process.

Process Statistics

Capability Indices	CP[a]	.065
	CpL[a]	.095
	CpU[a]	.035
	K	.460
	CpM[a,b]	.065
	Est. % Outside SL[a]	84.6%
Performance Indices	PP	.060
	PpL	.087
	PpU	.032

The normal distribution is assumed. LSL = 50.4 and USL = 50.5.

a. The estimated capability sigma is based on the mean of the sample group ranges.

b. The target value is 50.45.

Figure 16.16

In summary, the statistics indicate there is a problem with the process and thus indicate further investigation is required.

The *p* Chart – Monitoring Defective Items

The *p* chart can be used to identify the number of defective or non-conforming units in the production process. Load the file defects.sav which is the data obtained from a shoe manufacturer's quality control inspector.

As before we will use Control Charts found under Quality Control in the Analyze menu. This time select 'p, np' charts and check 'Cases Are Subgroups' in the Data Organization group. Once you have clicked on Define, you can then enter the analysis parameters, as shown in Figure 16.17.

Click on Control Rules and check 'Select all control rules'. Click on Continue and on OK.

Figure 16.18 shows the chart produced by SPSS.

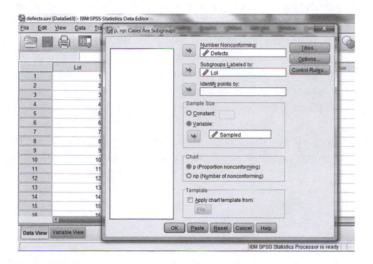

Figure 16.17

Looking at Figure 16.18, we can see that all points are within the control limits. The upper control limit is shown as variable since the sample sizes varied by the collection period. The lower limit is not visible since it is flush with the horizontal axis. The control limits represent the amount of variation in the defects when

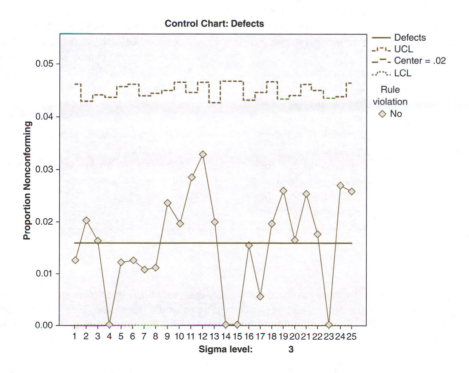

Figure 16.18

only common causes of variation are taken into account. Each point on the chart represents the sample ratio of defects to the total number inspected within each subgroup which we defined to be the 'lot'.

In summary, the control chart indicates that the manufacturing process is producing shoes within acceptable limits (SPSS uses a sigma level of 3) and there do not appear to be any obvious patterns which could indicate a problem. Also, SPSS does not report any rule violations.

SUMMARY

This chapter was written with two things in mind. First, it stands on its own as a useful introduction to what is a super-important topic in the real business world – where statistical analysis plays a vital role every day in ensuring the things we buy and rely on are up to standard. However, in a broader sense it shows how the fundamental concepts that have been treated in this book – such as hypothesis testing and probability – are more than just abstract concepts. They are things that you might have to use every day later in your life. Without these fundamental ideas, we would be relying on assumptions and judgement to make decisions. However, with the tools of statistics and quantitative analysis in our armoury, we are able to improve our decisions, rely less on 'gut feel', and in the end be better businesspeople.

Do not let anyone ever tell you that maths, statistics and models are no use to ordinary people. Even the most abstract things such as knowing that $0! = 1$ can end up being incredibly useful in your later life.

Promise.

Oh, and well done.

 final checklist

You should have covered and understood the following basic content in this chapter:

- ☑ In a general sense, how we can use statistics to give us evidence about whether or not a manufacturing (or other) process is in or out of control.
- ☑ How to create a control chart, by computing the LCL and UCL, in situations where the population mean and standard deviation are known, as well as when they are unknown.
- ☑ How to create the different $\bar{x}$, R, p and np control charts.
- ☑ How acceptance sampling works, and the definitions of producer and consumer risk.
- ☑ How the binomial distribution can be used along with an acceptance sampling program to compute the likelihood of accepting a lot of raw material with a given number of defective items, and how to create an operating characteristic curve from this information.
- ☑ How to use this knowledge to choose the most useful acceptance sampling plan, which balances out consumer and producer risk at levels appropriate to the specific situation.
- ☑ That even the most seemingly abstract mathematical knowledge has a practical use somewhere.

EXERCISES

1. You are the quality control manager in charge of a facility that manufactures silicon wafers for the semiconductor industry. Part of the process involves using acid baths where the temperature must be maintained between 18 and 22 degrees centigrade. The ideal temperature is 20 degrees centigrade. The file temp.sav contains the data collected over three shifts at different times. There are five acid baths which you are

responsible for. If the temperature rises above 23 degrees centigrade, the acid will vaporize and become a serious health risk, and if it drops below 17 degrees centigrade, it is ineffective.

a. Using SPSS select a suitable chart to monitor the process.
b. Interpret the information.
c. Decide if the process is operating within safe limits.
d. State any conclusions or recommendations.

2. You have landed your dream job: quality control director for a company that makes teddy bears. There are five production facilities scattered across the globe. In order to maintain standards each factory is expected to sample 20 production runs (lots) and take a sample of 20 teddies. The factories then send their data to you for analysis. The data can be found in teddy.sav.

a. Using a suitable chart, monitor the defects from each factory.
b. Analyse and identify any potential problems.
c. State any conclusions or recommendations.

 To access additional online resources please visit: **https://study.sagepub.com/leepeters**

APPENDIX

A.1 Standard Normal (z) Table

Entries in the table give the area under the curve between the mean and z standard deviations above the mean. For example, for $z = 1.28$ the area under the curve between the mean and $z = 0.3997$

z	0.00	0.01	0.02	0.03	0.04	0.05	0.06	0.07	0.08	0.09
0.0	0.0000	0.0040	0.0080	0.0120	0.0160	0.0199	0.0239	0.0279	0.0319	0.0359
0.1	0.0398	0.0438	0.0478	0.0517	0.0557	0.0596	0.0636	0.0675	0.0714	0.0753
0.2	0.0793	0.0832	0.0871	0.0910	0.0948	0.0987	0.1026	0.1064	0.1103	0.1141
0.3	0.1179	0.1217	0.1255	0.1293	0.1331	0.1368	0.1406	0.1443	0.1480	0.1517
0.4	0.1554	0.1591	0.1628	0.1664	0.1700	0.1736	0.1772	0.1808	0.1844	0.1879
0.5	0.1915	0.1950	0.1985	0.2019	0.2054	0.2088	0.2123	0.2157	0.2190	0.2224
0.6	0.2257	0.2291	0.2324	0.2357	0.2389	0.2422	0.2454	0.2486	0.2517	0.2549
0.7	0.2580	0.2611	0.2642	0.2673	0.2704	0.2734	0.2764	0.2794	0.2823	0.2852
0.8	0.2881	0.2910	0.2939	0.2967	0.2995	0.3023	0.3051	0.3078	0.3106	0.3133
0.9	0.3159	0.3186	0.3212	0.3238	0.3264	0.3289	0.3315	0.3340	0.3365	0.3389
1.0	0.3413	0.3438	0.3461	0.3485	0.3508	0.3531	0.3554	0.3577	0.3599	0.3621
1.1	0.3643	0.3665	0.3686	0.3708	0.3729	0.3749	0.3770	0.3790	0.3810	0.3830
1.2	0.3849	0.3869	0.3888	0.3907	0.3925	0.3944	0.3962	0.3980	0.3997	0.4015

z	0.00	0.01	0.02	0.03	0.04	0.05	0.06	0.07	0.08	0.09
1.3	0.4032	0.4049	0.4066	0.4082	0.4099	0.4115	0.4131	0.4147	0.4162	0.4177
1.4	0.4192	0.4207	0.4222	0.4236	0.4251	0.4265	0.4279	0.4292	0.4306	0.4319
1.5	0.4332	0.4345	0.4357	0.4370	0.4382	0.4394	0.4406	0.4418	0.4429	0.4441
1.6	0.4452	0.4463	0.4474	0.4484	0.4495	0.4505	0.4515	0.4525	0.4535	0.4545
1.7	0.4554	0.4564	0.4573	0.4582	0.4591	0.4599	0.4608	0.4616	0.4625	0.4633
1.8	0.4641	0.4649	0.4656	0.4664	0.4671	0.4678	0.4686	0.4693	0.4699	0.4706
1.9	0.4713	0.4719	0.4726	0.4732	0.4738	0.4744	0.4750	0.4756	0.4761	0.4767
2.0	0.4772	0.4778	0.4783	0.4788	0.4793	0.4798	0.4803	0.4808	0.4812	0.4817
2.1	0.4821	0.4826	0.4830	0.4834	0.4838	0.4842	0.4846	0.4850	0.4854	0.4857
2.2	0.4861	0.4864	0.4868	0.4871	0.4875	0.4878	0.4881	0.4884	0.4887	0.4890
2.3	0.4893	0.4896	0.4898	0.4901	0.4904	0.4906	0.4909	0.4911	0.4913	0.4916
2.4	0.4918	0.4920	0.4922	0.4925	0.4927	0.4929	0.4931	0.4932	0.4934	0.4936
2.5	0.4938	0.4940	0.4941	0.4943	0.4945	0.4946	0.4948	0.4949	0.4951	0.4952
2.6	0.4953	0.4955	0.4956	0.4957	0.4959	0.4960	0.4961	0.4962	0.4963	0.4964
2.7	0.4965	0.4966	0.4967	0.4968	0.4969	0.4970	0.4971	0.4972	0.4973	0.4974
2.8	0.4974	0.4975	0.4976	0.4977	0.4977	0.4978	0.4979	0.4979	0.4980	0.4981
2.9	0.4981	0.4982	0.4982	0.4983	0.4984	0.4984	0.4985	0.4985	0.4986	0.4986
3.0	0.4987	0.4987	0.4987	0.4988	0.4988	0.4989	0.4989	0.4989	0.4990	0.4990

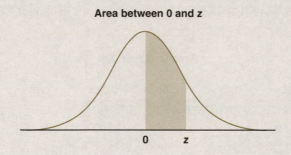

Area between 0 and z

A.2 Student's *t* Table

Entries in the table give *t* values for an area or probability in the upper tail of the *t* distribution. For example, with 8 degrees of freedom and a 0.05 area in the upper tail, $t_{0.05} = 1.86$ (rounded to 2 decimal places)

Area in Upper Tail

df	0.40	0.25	0.10	0.05	0.025	0.01	0.005	0.0005
1	0.324920	1.000000	3.077684	6.313752	12.70620	31.82052	63.65674	636.6192
2	0.288675	0.816497	1.885618	2.919986	4.30265	6.96456	9.92484	31.5991
3	0.276671	0.764892	1.637744	2.353363	3.18245	4.54070	5.84091	12.9240
4	0.270722	0.740697	1.533206	2.131847	2.77645	3.74695	4.60409	8.6103
5	0.267181	0.726687	1.475884	2.015048	2.57058	3.36493	4.03214	6.8688
6	0.264835	0.717558	1.439756	1.943180	2.44691	3.14267	3.70743	5.9588
7	0.263167	0.711142	1.414924	1.894579	2.36462	2.99795	3.49948	5.4079
8	0.261921	0.706387	1.396815	1.859548	2.30600	2.89646	3.35539	5.0413
9	0.260955	0.702722	1.383029	1.833113	2.26216	2.82144	3.24984	4.7809
10	0.260185	0.699812	1.372184	1.812461	2.22814	2.76377	3.16927	4.5869
11	0.259556	0.697445	1.363430	1.795885	2.20099	2.71808	3.10581	4.4370
12	0.259033	0.695483	1.356217	1.782288	2.17881	2.68100	3.05454	4.3178
13	0.258591	0.693829	1.350171	1.770933	2.16037	2.65031	3.01228	4.2208
14	0.258213	0.692417	1.345030	1.761310	2.14479	2.62449	2.97684	4.1405
15	0.257885	0.691197	1.340606	1.753050	2.13145	2.60248	2.94671	4.0728

df	0.40	0.25	0.10	0.05	0.025	0.01	0.005	0.0005
16	0.257599	0.690132	1.336757	1.745884	2.11991	2.58349	2.92078	4.0150
17	0.257347	0.689195	1.333379	1.739607	2.10982	2.56693	2.89823	3.9651
18	0.257123	0.688364	1.330391	1.734064	2.10092	2.55238	2.87844	3.9216
19	0.256923	0.687621	1.327728	1.729133	2.09302	2.53948	2.86093	3.8834
20	0.256743	0.686954	1.325341	1.724718	2.08596	2.52798	2.84534	3.8495
21	0.256580	0.686352	1.323188	1.720743	2.07961	2.51765	2.83136	3.8193
22	0.256432	0.685805	1.321237	1.717144	2.07387	2.50832	2.81876	3.7921
23	0.256297	0.685306	1.319460	1.713872	2.06866	2.49987	2.80734	3.7676
24	0.256173	0.684850	1.317836	1.710882	2.06390	2.49216	2.79694	3.7454
25	0.256060	0.684430	1.316345	1.708141	2.05954	2.48511	2.78744	3.7251
26	0.255955	0.684043	1.314972	1.705618	2.05553	2.47863	2.77871	3.7066
27	0.255858	0.683685	1.313703	1.703288	2.05183	2.47266	2.77068	3.6896
28	0.255768	0.683353	1.312527	1.701131	2.04841	2.46714	2.76326	3.6739
29	0.255684	0.683044	1.311434	1.699127	2.04523	2.46202	2.75639	3.6594
30	0.255605	0.682756	1.310415	1.697261	2.04227	2.45726	2.75000	3.6460
inf	0.253347	0.674490	1.281552	1.644854	1.95996	2.32635	2.57583	3.2905

t table with right tail probabilities

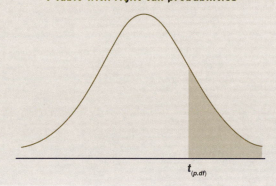

$t_{(p,df)}$

A.3 Chi-Square Table

Entries in the table give χ^2_α values, where α is the area in the upper tail of the chi-squared distribution. For example, with 7 degrees of freedom and 0.05 area in the upper tail, $\chi^2_{.05} = 14.07$ (rounded to 2 decimal places).

Area in Upper Tail

df	.995	.990	.975	.950	.900	.750	.500	.250	.100	.050	.025	.010	.005
1	0.00004	0.00016	0.00098	0.00393	0.01579	0.10153	0.45494	1.32330	2.70554	3.84146	5.02389	6.63490	7.87944
2	0.01003	0.02010	0.05064	0.10259	0.21072	0.57536	1.38629	2.77259	4.60517	5.99146	7.37776	9.21034	10.59663
3	0.07172	0.11483	0.21580	0.35185	0.58437	1.21253	2.36597	4.10834	6.25139	7.81473	9.34840	11.34487	12.83816
4	0.20699	0.29711	0.48442	0.71072	1.06362	1.92256	3.35669	5.38527	7.77944	9.48773	11.14329	13.27670	14.86026
5	0.41174	0.55430	0.83121	1.14548	1.61031	2.67460	4.35146	6.62568	9.23636	11.07050	12.83250	15.08627	16.74960
6	0.67573	0.87209	1.23734	1.63538	2.20413	3.45460	5.34812	7.84080	10.64464	12.59159	14.44938	16.81189	18.54758
7	0.98926	1.23904	1.68987	2.16735	2.83311	4.25485	6.34581	9.03715	12.01704	14.06714	16.01276	18.47531	20.27774
8	1.34441	1.64650	2.17973	2.73264	3.48954	5.07064	7.34412	10.21885	13.36157	15.50731	17.53455	20.09024	21.95495
9	1.73493	2.08790	2.70039	3.32511	4.16816	5.89883	8.34283	11.38875	14.68366	16.91898	19.02277	21.66599	23.58935
10	2.15586	2.55821	3.24697	3.94030	4.86518	6.73720	9.34182	12.54886	15.98718	18.30704	20.48318	23.20925	25.18818
11	2.60322	3.05348	3.81575	4.57481	5.57778	7.58414	10.34100	13.70069	17.27501	19.67514	21.92005	24.72497	26.75685
12	3.07382	3.57057	4.40379	5.22603	6.30380	8.43842	11.34032	14.84540	18.54935	21.02607	23.33666	26.21697	28.29952
13	3.56503	4.10692	5.00875	5.89186	7.04150	9.29907	12.33976	15.98391	19.81193	22.36203	24.73560	27.68825	29.81947
14	4.07467	4.66043	5.62873	6.57063	7.78953	10.16531	13.33927	17.11693	21.06414	23.68479	26.11895	29.14124	31.31935
15	4.60092	5.22935	6.26214	7.26094	8.54676	11.03654	14.33886	18.24509	22.30713	24.99579	27.48839	30.57791	32.80132
16	5.14221	5.81221	6.90766	7.96165	9.31224	11.91222	15.33850	19.36886	23.54183	26.29623	28.84535	31.99993	34.26719
17	5.69722	6.40776	7.56419	8.67176	10.08519	12.79193	16.33818	20.48868	24.76904	27.58711	30.19101	33.40866	35.71847
18	6.26480	7.01491	8.23075	9.39046	10.86494	13.67529	17.33790	21.60489	25.98942	28.86930	31.52638	34.80531	37.15645

(Continued)

(Continued)

df	.995	.990	.975	.950	.900	.750	.500	.250	.100	.050	.025	.010	.005
19	6.84397	7.63273	8.90652	10.11701	11.65091	14.56200	18.33765	22.71781	27.20357	30.14353	32.85233	36.19087	38.58226
20	7.43384	8.26040	9.59078	10.85081	12.44261	15.45177	19.33743	23.82769	28.41198	31.41043	34.16961	37.56623	39.99685
21	8.03365	8.89720	10.28290	11.59131	13.23960	16.34438	20.33723	24.93478	29.61509	32.67057	35.47888	38.93217	41.40106
22	8.64272	9.54249	10.98232	12.33801	14.04149	17.23962	21.33704	26.03927	30.81328	33.92444	36.78071	40.28936	42.79565
23	9.26042	10.19572	11.68855	13.09051	14.84796	18.13730	22.33688	27.14134	32.00690	35.17246	38.07563	41.63840	44.18128
24	9.88623	10.85636	12.40115	13.84843	15.65868	19.03725	23.33673	28.24115	33.19624	36.41503	39.36408	42.97982	45.55851
25	10.51965	11.52398	13.11972	14.61141	16.47341	19.93934	24.33659	29.33885	34.38159	37.65248	40.64647	44.31410	46.92789
26	11.16024	12.19815	13.84390	15.37916	17.29188	20.84343	25.33646	30.43457	35.56317	38.88514	41.92317	45.64168	48.28988
27	11.80759	12.87850	14.57338	16.15140	18.11390	21.74940	26.33634	31.52841	36.74122	40.11327	43.19451	46.96294	49.64492
28	12.46134	13.56471	15.30786	16.92788	18.93924	22.65716	27.33623	32.62049	37.91592	41.33714	44.46079	48.27824	50.99338
29	13.12115	14.25645	16.04707	17.70837	19.76774	23.56659	28.33613	33.71091	39.08747	42.55697	45.72229	49.58788	52.33562
30	13.78672	14.95346	16.79077	18.49266	20.59923	24.47761	29.33603	34.79974	40.25602	43.77297	46.97924	50.89218	53.67196

Right tail areas for the chi-square distribution

X^2

A.4 *F* Distribution Tables

There are four tables here, one for each of the major alpha (α) values (0.1, 0.05, 0.025 and 0.01), where α is the area in the upper tail of the chi-square distribution. So, for example, with 5 denominator degrees of freedom (on the vertical), and 6 numerator degrees of freedom (on the horizontal), and an 0.5 area in the upper tail, you would go to the *F* table for $\alpha = 0.05$, and look up the value, which would be $F_{.05} = 4.95$

F Table for Alpha=0.1

Numerator Degrees of Freedom

Denominator Degrees of Freedom	1	2	3	4	5	6	7	8	9	10	12	15	20	24	30	40	60	120	INF
1	39.86346	49.50000	53.59324	55.83296	57.24008	58.20442	58.90595	59.43898	59.85759	60.19498	60.70521	61.22034	61.74029	62.00205	62.26497	62.52905	62.79428	63.06064	63.32812
2	8.52632	9.00000	9.16179	9.24342	9.29263	9.32553	9.34908	9.36677	9.38054	9.39157	9.40813	9.42471	9.44131	9.44962	9.45793	9.46624	9.47456	9.48289	9.49122
3	5.53832	5.46238	5.39077	5.34264	5.30916	5.28473	5.26619	5.25167	5.24000	5.23041	5.21562	5.20031	5.18448	5.17636	5.16811	5.15972	5.15119	5.14251	5.13370
4	4.54477	4.32456	4.19086	4.10725	4.05058	4.00975	3.97897	3.95494	3.93567	3.91988	3.89553	3.87036	3.84434	3.83099	3.81742	3.80361	3.78957	3.77527	3.76073
5	4.06042	3.77972	3.61948	3.52020	3.45298	3.40451	3.36790	3.33928	3.31628	3.29740	3.26824	3.23801	3.20665	3.19052	3.17408	3.15732	3.14023	3.12279	3.10500
6	3.77595	3.46330	3.28876	3.18076	3.10751	3.05455	3.01446	2.98304	2.95774	2.93693	2.90472	2.87122	2.83634	2.81834	2.79996	2.78117	2.76195	2.74229	2.72216
7	3.58943	3.25744	3.07407	2.96053	2.88334	2.82739	2.78493	2.75158	2.72468	2.70251	2.66811	2.63223	2.59473	2.57533	2.55546	2.53510	2.51422	2.49279	2.47079
8	3.45792	3.11312	2.92380	2.80643	2.72645	2.66833	2.62413	2.58935	2.56124	2.53804	2.50196	2.46422	2.42464	2.40410	2.38302	2.36136	2.33910	2.31618	2.29257
9	3.36030	3.00645	2.81286	2.69268	2.61061	2.55086	2.50531	2.46941	2.44034	2.41632	2.37888	2.33962	2.29832	2.27683	2.25472	2.23196	2.20849	2.18427	2.15923
10	3.28502	2.92447	2.72767	2.60534	2.52164	2.46058	2.41397	2.37715	2.34731	2.32260	2.28405	2.24351	2.20074	2.17843	2.15543	2.13169	2.10716	2.08176	2.05542
11	3.22520	2.85951	2.66023	2.53619	2.45118	2.38907	2.34157	2.30400	2.27350	2.24823	2.20873	2.16709	2.12305	2.10001	2.07621	2.05161	2.02612	1.99965	1.97211
12	3.17655	2.80680	2.60552	2.48010	2.39402	2.33102	2.28278	2.24457	2.21352	2.18776	2.14744	2.10485	2.05968	2.03599	2.01149	1.98610	1.95973	1.93228	1.90361
13	3.13621	2.76317	2.56027	2.43371	2.34672	2.28298	2.23410	2.19535	2.16382	2.13763	2.09659	2.05316	2.00698	1.98272	1.95757	1.93147	1.90429	1.87591	1.84620
14	3.10221	2.72647	2.52222	2.39469	2.30694	2.24256	2.19313	2.15390	2.12195	2.09540	2.05371	2.00953	1.96245	1.93766	1.91193	1.88516	1.85723	1.82800	1.79728
15	3.07319	2.69517	2.48979	2.36143	2.27302	2.20808	2.15818	2.11853	2.08621	2.05932	2.01707	1.97222	1.92431	1.89904	1.87277	1.84539	1.81676	1.78672	1.75505
16	3.04811	2.66817	2.46181	2.33274	2.24376	2.17833	2.12800	2.08798	2.05533	2.02815	1.98539	1.93992	1.89127	1.86556	1.83879	1.81084	1.78156	1.75075	1.71817
17	3.02623	2.64464	2.43743	2.30775	2.21825	2.15239	2.10169	2.06134	2.02839	2.00094	1.95772	1.91169	1.86236	1.83624	1.80901	1.78053	1.75063	1.71909	1.68564
18	3.00698	2.62395	2.41601	2.28577	2.19583	2.12958	2.07854	2.03789	2.00467	1.97698	1.93334	1.88681	1.83685	1.81035	1.78269	1.75371	1.72322	1.69099	1.65671
19	2.98990	2.60561	2.39702	2.26630	2.17596	2.10936	2.05802	2.01710	1.98364	1.95573	1.91170	1.86471	1.81416	1.78731	1.75924	1.72979	1.69876	1.66587	1.63077
20	2.97465	2.58925	2.38009	2.24893	2.15823	2.09132	2.03970	1.99853	1.96485	1.93674	1.89236	1.84494	1.79384	1.76667	1.73822	1.70833	1.67678	1.64326	1.60738

Denominator Degrees of Freedom	1	2	3	4	5	6	7	8	9	10	12	15	20	24	30	40	60	120	INF
21	2.96096	2.57457	2.36489	2.23334	2.14231	2.07512	2.02325	1.98186	1.94797	1.91967	1.87497	1.82715	1.77555	1.74807	1.71927	1.68896	1.65691	1.62278	1.58615
22	2.94858	2.56131	2.35117	2.21927	2.12794	2.06050	2.00840	1.96680	1.93273	1.90425	1.85925	1.81106	1.75899	1.73122	1.70208	1.67138	1.63885	1.60415	1.56678
23	2.93736	2.54929	2.33873	2.20651	2.11491	2.04723	1.99492	1.95312	1.91888	1.89025	1.84497	1.79643	1.74392	1.71588	1.68643	1.65535	1.62237	1.58711	1.54903
24	2.92712	2.53833	2.32739	2.19488	2.10303	2.03513	1.98263	1.94066	1.90625	1.87748	1.83194	1.78308	1.73015	1.70185	1.67210	1.64067	1.60726	1.57146	1.53270
25	2.91774	2.52831	2.31702	2.18424	2.09216	2.02406	1.97138	1.92925	1.89469	1.86578	1.82000	1.77083	1.71752	1.68898	1.65895	1.62718	1.59335	1.55703	1.51760
26	2.90913	2.51910	2.30749	2.17447	2.08218	2.01389	1.96104	1.91876	1.88407	1.85503	1.80902	1.75957	1.70589	1.67712	1.64682	1.61472	1.58050	1.54368	1.50360
27	2.90119	2.51061	2.29871	2.16546	2.07298	2.00452	1.95151	1.90909	1.87427	1.84511	1.79889	1.74917	1.69514	1.66616	1.63560	1.60320	1.56859	1.53129	1.49057
28	2.89385	2.50276	2.29060	2.15714	2.06447	1.99585	1.94270	1.90014	1.86520	1.83593	1.78951	1.73954	1.68519	1.65600	1.62519	1.59250	1.55753	1.51976	1.47841
29	2.88703	2.49548	2.28307	2.14941	2.05658	1.98781	1.93452	1.89184	1.85679	1.82741	1.78081	1.73060	1.67593	1.64655	1.61551	1.58253	1.54721	1.50899	1.46704
30	2.88069	2.48872	2.27607	2.14223	2.04925	1.98033	1.92692	1.88412	1.84896	1.81949	1.77270	1.72227	1.6673	1.63774	1.60648	1.57323	1.53757	1.49891	1.45636
40	2.83535	2.44037	2.22609	2.09095	1.99682	1.92688	1.87252	1.82886	1.79290	1.76269	1.71456	1.66241	1.60515	1.57411	1.54108	1.50562	1.46716	1.42476	1.37691
60	2.79107	2.39325	2.17741	2.04099	1.94571	1.87472	1.81939	1.77483	1.73802	1.70701	1.65743	1.60337	1.54349	1.51072	1.47554	1.43734	1.39520	1.34757	1.29146
120	2.74781	2.34734	2.12999	1.99230	1.89587	1.82381	1.76748	1.72196	1.68425	1.65238	1.60120	1.54500	1.48207	1.44723	1.40938	1.36760	1.32034	1.26457	1.19256
inf	2.70554	2.30259	2.08380	1.94486	1.84727	1.77411	1.71672	1.67020	1.63152	1.59872	1.54578	1.48714	1.42060	1.38318	1.34187	1.29513	1.23995	1.16860	1.00000

F Table for Alpha=0.05

Numerator Degrees of Freedom

Denominator Degrees of Freedom	1	2	3	4	5	6	7	8	9	10	12	15	20	24	30	40	60	120	INF
1	161.4476	199.5000	215.7073	224.5832	230.1619	233.9860	236.7684	238.8827	240.5433	241.8817	243.9060	245.9499	248.0131	249.0518	250.0951	251.1432	252.1957	253.2529	254.3144
2	18.5128	19.0000	19.1643	19.2468	19.2964	19.3295	19.3532	19.3710	19.3848	19.3959	19.4125	19.4291	19.4458	19.4541	19.4624	19.4707	19.4791	19.4874	19.4957
3	10.1280	9.5521	9.2766	9.1172	9.0135	8.9406	8.8867	8.8452	8.8123	8.7855	8.7446	8.7029	8.6602	8.6385	8.6166	8.5944	8.5720	8.5494	8.5264
4	7.7086	6.9443	6.5914	6.3882	6.2561	6.1631	6.0942	6.0410	5.9988	5.9644	5.9117	5.8578	5.8025	5.7744	5.7459	5.7170	5.6877	5.6581	5.6281
5	6.6079	5.7861	5.4095	5.1922	5.0503	4.9503	4.8759	4.8183	4.7725	4.7351	4.6777	4.6188	4.5581	4.5272	4.4957	4.4638	4.4314	4.3985	4.3650
6	5.9874	5.1433	4.7571	4.5337	4.3874	4.2839	4.2067	4.1468	4.0990	4.0600	3.9999	3.9381	3.8742	3.8415	3.8082	3.7743	3.7398	3.7047	3.6689
7	5.5914	4.7374	4.3468	4.1203	3.9715	3.8660	3.7870	3.7257	3.6767	3.6365	3.5747	3.5107	3.4445	3.4105	3.3758	3.3404	3.3043	3.2674	3.2298
8	5.3177	4.4590	4.0662	3.8379	3.6875	3.5806	3.5005	3.4381	3.3881	3.3472	3.2839	3.2184	3.1503	3.1152	3.0794	3.0428	3.0053	2.9669	2.9276
9	5.1174	4.2565	3.8625	3.6331	3.4817	3.3738	3.2927	3.2296	3.1789	3.1373	3.0729	3.0061	2.9365	2.9005	2.8637	2.8259	2.7872	2.7475	2.7067
10	4.9646	4.1028	3.7083	3.4780	3.3258	3.2172	3.1355	3.0717	3.0204	2.9782	2.9130	2.8450	2.7740	2.7372	2.6996	2.6609	2.6211	2.5801	2.5379
11	4.8443	3.9823	3.5874	3.3567	3.2039	3.0946	3.0123	2.9480	2.8962	2.8536	2.7876	2.7186	2.6464	2.6090	2.5705	2.5309	2.4901	2.4480	2.4045
12	4.7472	3.8853	3.4903	3.2592	3.1059	2.9961	2.9134	2.8486	2.7964	2.7534	2.6866	2.6169	2.5436	2.5055	2.4663	2.4259	2.3842	2.3410	2.2962
13	4.6672	3.8056	3.4105	3.1791	3.0254	2.9153	2.8321	2.7669	2.7144	2.6710	2.6037	2.5331	2.4589	2.4202	2.3803	2.3392	2.2966	2.2524	2.2064
14	4.6001	3.7389	3.3439	3.1122	2.9582	2.8477	2.7642	2.6987	2.6458	2.6022	2.5342	2.4630	2.3879	2.3487	2.3082	2.2664	2.2229	2.1778	2.1307
15	4.5431	3.6823	3.2874	3.0556	2.9013	2.7905	2.7066	2.6408	2.5876	2.5437	2.4753	2.4034	2.3275	2.2878	2.2468	2.2043	2.1601	2.1141	2.0658
16	4.4940	3.6337	3.2389	3.0069	2.8524	2.7413	2.6572	2.5911	2.5377	2.4935	2.4247	2.3522	2.2756	2.2354	2.1938	2.1507	2.1058	2.0589	2.0096
17	4.4513	3.5915	3.1968	2.9647	2.8100	2.6987	2.6143	2.5480	2.4943	2.4499	2.3807	2.3077	2.2304	2.1898	2.1477	2.1040	2.0584	2.0107	1.9604
18	4.4139	3.5546	3.1599	2.9277	2.7729	2.6613	2.5767	2.5102	2.4563	2.4117	2.3421	2.2686	2.1906	2.1497	2.1071	2.0629	2.0166	1.9681	1.9168
19	4.3807	3.5219	3.1274	2.8951	2.7401	2.6283	2.5435	2.4768	2.4227	2.3779	2.3080	2.2341	2.1555	2.1141	2.0712	2.0264	1.9795	1.9302	1.8780
20	4.3512	3.4928	3.0984	2.8661	2.7109	2.5990	2.5140	2.4471	2.3928	2.3479	2.2776	2.2033	2.1242	2.0825	2.0391	1.9938	1.9464	1.8963	1.8432

Denominator Degrees of Freedom	1	2	3	4	5	6	7	8	9	10	12	15	20	24	30	40	60	120	INF
21	4.3248	3.4668	3.0725	2.8401	2.6848	2.5727	2.4876	2.4205	2.3660	2.3210	2.2504	2.1757	2.0960	2.0540	2.0102	1.9645	1.9165	1.8657	1.8117
22	4.3009	3.4434	3.0491	2.8167	2.6613	2.5491	2.4638	2.3965	2.3419	2.2967	2.2258	2.1508	2.0707	2.0283	1.9842	1.9380	1.8894	1.8380	1.7831
23	4.2793	3.4221	3.0280	2.7955	2.6400	2.5277	2.4422	2.3748	2.3201	2.2747	2.2036	2.1282	2.0476	2.0050	1.9605	1.9139	1.8648	1.8128	1.7570
24	4.2597	3.4028	3.0088	2.7763	2.6207	2.5082	2.4226	2.3551	2.3002	2.2547	2.1834	2.1077	2.0267	1.9838	1.9390	1.8920	1.8424	1.7896	1.7330
25	4.2417	3.3852	2.9912	2.7587	2.6030	2.4904	2.4047	2.3371	2.2821	2.2365	2.1649	2.0889	2.0075	1.9643	1.9192	1.8718	1.8217	1.7684	1.7110
26	4.2252	3.3690	2.9752	2.7426	2.5868	2.4741	2.3883	2.3205	2.2655	2.2197	2.1479	2.0716	1.9898	1.9464	1.9010	1.8533	1.8027	1.7488	1.6906
27	4.2100	3.3541	2.9604	2.7278	2.5719	2.4591	2.3732	2.3053	2.2501	2.2043	2.1323	2.0558	1.9736	1.9299	1.8842	1.8361	1.7851	1.7306	1.6717
28	4.1960	3.3404	2.9467	2.7141	2.5581	2.4453	2.3593	2.2913	2.2360	2.1900	2.1179	2.0411	1.9586	1.9147	1.8687	1.8203	1.7689	1.7138	1.6541
29	4.1830	3.3277	2.9340	2.7014	2.5454	2.4324	2.3463	2.2783	2.2229	2.1768	2.1045	2.0275	1.9446	1.9005	1.8543	1.8055	1.7537	1.6981	1.6376
30	4.1709	3.3158	2.9223	2.6896	2.5336	2.4205	2.3343	2.2662	2.2107	2.1646	2.0921	2.0148	1.9317	1.8874	1.8409	1.7918	1.7396	1.6835	1.6223
40	4.0847	3.2317	2.8387	2.6060	2.4495	2.3359	2.2490	2.1802	2.1240	2.0772	2.0035	1.9245	1.8389	1.7929	1.7444	1.6928	1.6373	1.5766	1.5089
60	4.0012	3.1504	2.7581	2.5252	2.3683	2.2541	2.1665	2.0970	2.0401	1.9926	1.9174	1.8364	1.7480	1.7001	1.6491	1.5943	1.5343	1.4673	1.3893
120	3.9201	3.0718	2.6802	2.4472	2.2899	2.1750	2.0868	2.0164	1.9588	1.9105	1.8337	1.7505	1.6587	1.6084	1.5543	1.4952	1.4290	1.3519	1.2539
inf	3.8415	2.9957	2.6049	2.3719	2.2141	2.0986	2.0096	1.9384	1.8799	1.8307	1.7522	1.6664	1.5705	1.5173	1.4591	1.3940	1.3180	1.2214	1.0000

F Table for Alpha=0.025

Numerator Degrees of Freedom

Denominator Degrees of Freedom	1	2	3	4	5	6	7	8	9	10	12	15	20	24	30	40	60	120	INF
1	647.7890	799.5000	864.1630	899.5833	921.8479	937.1111	948.2169	956.6562	963.2846	968.6274	976.7079	984.8668	993.1028	997.2492	1001.414	1005.598	1009.800	1014.020	1018.258
2	38.5063	39.0000	39.1655	39.2484	39.2982	39.3315	39.3552	39.3730	39.3869	39.3980	39.4146	39.4313	39.4479	39.4562	39.465	39.473	39.481	39.490	39.498
3	17.4434	16.0441	15.4392	15.1010	14.8848	14.7347	14.6244	14.5399	14.4731	14.4189	14.3366	14.2527	14.1674	14.1241	14.081	14.037	13.992	13.947	13.902
4	12.2179	10.6491	9.9792	9.6045	9.3645	9.1973	9.0741	8.9796	8.9047	8.8439	8.7512	8.6565	8.5599	8.5109	8.461	8.411	8.360	8.309	8.257
5	10.0070	8.4336	7.7636	7.3879	7.1464	6.9777	6.8531	6.7572	6.6811	6.6192	6.5245	6.4277	6.3286	6.2780	6.227	6.175	6.123	6.069	6.015
6	8.8131	7.2599	6.5988	6.2272	5.9876	5.8198	5.6955	5.5996	5.5234	5.4613	5.3662	5.2687	5.1684	5.1172	5.065	5.012	4.959	4.904	4.849
7	8.0727	6.5415	5.8898	5.5226	5.2852	5.1186	4.9949	4.8993	4.8232	4.7611	4.6658	4.5678	4.4667	4.4150	4.362	4.309	4.254	4.199	4.142
8	7.5709	6.0595	5.4160	5.0526	4.8173	4.6517	4.5286	4.4333	4.3572	4.2951	4.1997	4.1012	3.9995	3.9472	3.894	3.840	3.784	3.728	3.670
9	7.2093	5.7147	5.0781	4.7181	4.4844	4.3197	4.1970	4.1020	4.0260	3.9639	3.8682	3.7694	3.6669	3.6142	3.560	3.505	3.449	3.392	3.333
10	6.9367	5.4564	4.8256	4.4683	4.2361	4.0721	3.9498	3.8549	3.7790	3.7168	3.6209	3.5217	3.4185	3.3654	3.311	3.255	3.198	3.140	3.080
11	6.7241	5.2559	4.6300	4.2751	4.0440	3.8807	3.7586	3.6638	3.5879	3.5257	3.4296	3.3299	3.2261	3.1725	3.118	3.061	3.004	2.944	2.883
12	6.5538	5.0959	4.4742	4.1212	3.8911	3.7283	3.6065	3.5118	3.4358	3.3736	3.2773	3.1772	3.0728	3.0187	2.963	2.906	2.848	2.787	2.725
13	6.4143	4.9653	4.3472	3.9959	3.7667	3.6043	3.4827	3.3880	3.3120	3.2497	3.1532	3.0527	2.9477	2.8932	2.837	2.780	2.720	2.659	2.595
14	6.2979	4.8567	4.2417	3.8919	3.6634	3.5014	3.3799	3.2853	3.2093	3.1469	3.0502	2.9493	2.8437	2.7888	2.732	2.674	2.614	2.552	2.487
15	6.1995	4.7650	4.1528	3.8043	3.5764	3.4147	3.2934	3.1987	3.1227	3.0602	2.9633	2.8621	2.7559	2.7006	2.644	2.585	2.524	2.461	2.395
16	6.1151	4.6867	4.0768	3.7294	3.5021	3.3406	3.2194	3.1248	3.0488	2.9862	2.8890	2.7875	2.6808	2.6252	2.568	2.509	2.447	2.383	2.316
17	6.0420	4.6189	4.0112	3.6648	3.4379	3.2767	3.1556	3.0610	2.9849	2.9222	2.8249	2.7230	2.6158	2.5598	2.502	2.442	2.380	2.315	2.247
18	5.9781	4.5597	3.9539	3.6083	3.3820	3.2209	3.0999	3.0053	2.9291	2.8664	2.7689	2.6667	2.5590	2.5027	2.445	2.384	2.321	2.256	2.187
19	5.9216	4.5075	3.9034	3.5587	3.3327	3.1718	3.0509	2.9563	2.8801	2.8172	2.7196	2.6171	2.5089	2.4523	2.394	2.333	2.270	2.203	2.133
20	5.8715	4.4613	3.8587	3.5147	3.2891	3.1283	3.0074	2.9128	2.8365	2.7737	2.6758	2.5731	2.4645	2.4076	2.349	2.287	2.223	2.156	2.085

Denominator Degrees of Freedom	1	2	3	4	5	6	7	8	9	10	12	15	20	24	30	40	60	120	INF
21	5.8266	4.4199	3.8188	3.4754	3.2501	3.0895	2.9686	2.8740	2.7977	2.7348	2.6368	2.5338	2.4247	2.3675	2.308	2.246	2.182	2.114	2.042
22	5.7863	4.3828	3.7829	3.4401	3.2151	3.0546	2.9338	2.8392	2.7628	2.6998	2.6017	2.4984	2.3890	2.3315	2.272	2.210	2.145	2.076	2.003
23	5.7498	4.3492	3.7505	3.4083	3.1835	3.0232	2.9023	2.8077	2.7313	2.6682	2.5699	2.4665	2.3567	2.2989	2.239	2.176	2.111	2.041	1.968
24	5.7166	4.3187	3.7211	3.3794	3.1548	2.9946	2.8738	2.7791	2.7027	2.6396	2.5411	2.4374	2.3273	2.2693	2.209	2.146	2.080	2.010	1.935
25	5.6864	4.2909	3.6943	3.3530	3.1287	2.9685	2.8478	2.7531	2.6766	2.6135	2.5149	2.4110	2.3005	2.2422	2.182	2.118	2.052	1.981	1.906
26	5.6586	4.2655	3.6697	3.3289	3.1048	2.9447	2.8240	2.7293	2.6528	2.5896	2.4908	2.3867	2.2759	2.2174	2.157	2.093	2.026	1.954	1.878
27	5.6331	4.2421	3.6472	3.3067	3.0828	2.9228	2.8021	2.7074	2.6309	2.5676	2.4688	2.3644	2.2533	2.1946	2.133	2.069	2.002	1.930	1.853
28	5.6096	4.2205	3.6264	3.2863	3.0626	2.9027	2.7820	2.6872	2.6106	2.5473	2.4484	2.3438	2.2324	2.1735	2.112	2.048	1.980	1.907	1.829
29	5.5878	4.2006	3.6072	3.2674	3.0438	2.8840	2.7633	2.6686	2.5919	2.5286	2.4295	2.3248	2.2131	2.1540	2.092	2.028	1.959	1.886	1.807
30	5.5675	4.1821	3.5894	3.2499	3.0265	2.8667	2.7460	2.6513	2.5746	2.5112	2.4120	2.3072	2.1952	2.1359	2.074	2.009	1.940	1.866	1.787
40	5.4239	4.0510	3.4633	3.1261	2.9037	2.7444	2.6238	2.5289	2.4519	2.3882	2.2882	2.1819	2.0677	2.0069	1.943	1.875	1.803	1.724	1.637
60	5.2856	3.9253	3.3425	3.0077	2.7863	2.6274	2.5068	2.4117	2.3344	2.2702	2.1692	2.0613	1.9445	1.8817	1.815	1.744	1.667	1.581	1.482
120	5.1523	3.8046	3.2269	2.8943	2.6740	2.5154	2.3948	2.2994	2.2217	2.1570	2.0548	1.9450	1.8249	1.7597	1.690	1.614	1.530	1.433	1.310
inf	5.0239	3.6889	3.1161	2.7858	2.5665	2.4082	2.2875	2.1918	2.1136	2.0483	1.9447	1.8326	1.7085	1.6402	1.566	1.484	1.388	1.268	1.000

F Table for Alpha=0.01

Numerator Degrees of Freedom

Denominator Degrees of Freedom	1	2	3	4	5	6	7	8	9	10	12	15	20	24	30	40	60	120	INF
1	4052.181	4999.500	5403.352	5624.583	5763.650	5858.986	5928.356	5981.070	6022.473	6055.847	6106.321	6157.285	6208.730	6234.631	6260.649	6286.782	6313.030	6339.391	6365.864
2	98.503	99.000	99.166	99.249	99.299	99.333	99.356	99.374	99.388	99.399	99.416	99.433	99.449	99.458	99.466	99.474	99.482	99.491	99.499
3	34.116	30.817	29.457	28.710	28.237	27.911	27.672	27.489	27.345	27.229	27.052	26.872	26.690	26.598	26.505	26.411	26.316	26.221	26.125
4	21.198	18.000	16.694	15.977	15.522	15.207	14.976	14.799	14.659	14.546	14.374	14.198	14.020	13.929	13.838	13.745	13.652	13.558	13.463
5	16.258	13.274	12.060	11.392	10.967	10.672	10.456	10.289	10.158	10.051	9.888	9.722	9.553	9.466	9.379	9.291	9.202	9.112	9.020
6	13.745	10.925	9.780	9.148	8.746	8.466	8.260	8.102	7.976	7.874	7.718	7.559	7.396	7.313	7.229	7.143	7.057	6.969	6.880
7	12.246	9.547	8.451	7.847	7.460	7.191	6.993	6.840	6.719	6.620	6.469	6.314	6.155	6.074	5.992	5.908	5.824	5.737	5.650
8	11.259	8.649	7.591	7.006	6.632	6.371	6.178	6.029	5.911	5.814	5.667	5.515	5.359	5.279	5.198	5.116	5.032	4.946	4.859
9	10.561	8.022	6.992	6.422	6.057	5.802	5.613	5.467	5.351	5.257	5.111	4.962	4.808	4.729	4.649	4.567	4.483	4.398	4.311
10	10.044	7.559	6.552	5.994	5.636	5.386	5.200	5.057	4.942	4.849	4.706	4.558	4.405	4.327	4.247	4.165	4.082	3.996	3.909
11	9.646	7.206	6.217	5.668	5.316	5.069	4.886	4.744	4.632	4.539	4.397	4.251	4.099	4.021	3.941	3.860	3.776	3.690	3.602
12	9.330	6.927	5.953	5.412	5.064	4.821	4.640	4.499	4.388	4.296	4.155	4.010	3.858	3.780	3.701	3.619	3.535	3.449	3.361
13	9.074	6.701	5.739	5.205	4.862	4.620	4.441	4.302	4.191	4.100	3.960	3.815	3.665	3.587	3.507	3.425	3.341	3.255	3.165
14	8.862	6.515	5.564	5.035	4.695	4.456	4.278	4.140	4.030	3.939	3.800	3.656	3.505	3.427	3.348	3.266	3.181	3.094	3.004
15	8.683	6.359	5.417	4.893	4.556	4.318	4.142	4.004	3.895	3.805	3.666	3.522	3.372	3.294	3.214	3.132	3.047	2.959	2.868
16	8.531	6.226	5.292	4.773	4.437	4.202	4.026	3.890	3.780	3.691	3.553	3.409	3.259	3.181	3.101	3.018	2.933	2.845	2.753
17	8.400	6.112	5.185	4.669	4.336	4.102	3.927	3.791	3.682	3.593	3.455	3.312	3.162	3.084	3.003	2.920	2.835	2.746	2.653
18	8.285	6.013	5.092	4.579	4.248	4.015	3.841	3.705	3.597	3.508	3.371	3.227	3.077	2.999	2.919	2.835	2.749	2.660	2.566
19	8.185	5.926	5.010	4.500	4.171	3.939	3.765	3.631	3.523	3.434	3.297	3.153	3.003	2.925	2.844	2.761	2.674	2.584	2.489
20	8.096	5.849	4.938	4.431	4.103	3.871	3.699	3.564	3.457	3.368	3.231	3.088	2.938	2.859	2.778	2.695	2.608	2.517	2.421

Denominator Degrees of Freedom	1	2	3	4	5	6	7	8	9	10	12	15	20	24	30	40	60	120	INF
21	8.017	5.780	4.874	4.369	4.042	3.812	3.640	3.506	3.398	3.310	3.173	3.030	2.880	2.801	2.720	2.636	2.548	2.457	2.360
22	7.945	5.719	4.817	4.313	3.988	3.758	3.587	3.453	3.346	3.258	3.121	2.978	2.827	2.749	2.667	2.583	2.495	2.403	2.305
23	7.881	5.664	4.765	4.264	3.939	3.710	3.539	3.406	3.299	3.211	3.074	2.931	2.781	2.702	2.620	2.535	2.447	2.354	2.256
24	7.823	5.614	4.718	4.218	3.895	3.667	3.496	3.363	3.256	3.168	3.032	2.889	2.738	2.659	2.577	2.492	2.403	2.310	2.211
25	7.770	5.568	4.675	4.177	3.855	3.627	3.457	3.324	3.217	3.129	2.993	2.850	2.699	2.620	2.538	2.453	2.364	2.270	2.169
26	7.721	5.526	4.637	4.140	3.818	3.591	3.421	3.288	3.182	3.094	2.958	2.815	2.664	2.585	2.503	2.417	2.327	2.233	2.131
27	7.677	5.488	4.601	4.106	3.785	3.558	3.388	3.256	3.149	3.062	2.926	2.783	2.632	2.552	2.470	2.384	2.294	2.198	2.097
28	7.636	5.453	4.568	4.074	3.754	3.528	3.358	3.226	3.120	3.032	2.896	2.753	2.602	2.522	2.440	2.354	2.263	2.167	2.064
29	7.598	5.420	4.538	4.045	3.725	3.499	3.330	3.198	3.092	3.005	2.868	2.726	2.574	2.495	2.412	2.325	2.234	2.138	2.034
30	7.562	5.390	4.510	4.018	3.699	3.473	3.304	3.173	3.067	2.979	2.843	2.700	2.549	2.459	2.386	2.299	2.208	2.111	2.006
40	7.314	5.179	4.313	3.828	3.514	3.291	3.124	2.993	2.888	2.801	2.665	2.522	2.369	2.288	2.203	2.114	2.019	1.917	1.805
60	7.077	4.977	4.126	3.649	3.339	3.119	2.953	2.823	2.718	2.632	2.496	2.352	2.198	2.115	2.028	1.936	1.836	1.726	1.601
120	6.851	4.787	3.949	3.480	3.174	2.956	2.792	2.663	2.559	2.472	2.336	2.192	2.035	1.950	1.860	1.763	1.656	1.533	1.381
inf	6.635	4.605	3.782	3.319	3.017	2.802	2.639	2.511	2.407	2.321	2.185	2.039	1.878	1.791	1.696	1.592	1.473	1.325	1.000

A.5 Binomial Probabilities

Entries in the table give the probability of k successes of n trials of a binomial experiment where p is the probability of success for one trial. For example, with 8 trials and $p = 0.05$, probability of 3 successes is 0.0054. Note, the blank cells are probabilities of less than 0.0000 and are thus not printed for the sake of clarity in the table.

Entry is $P(X = k) = \binom{n}{k} p^k (1 - p)^{n-k}$

n	k	.01	.02	.03	.04	.05	.06	.07	.08	.09
2	0	.9801	.9604	.9409	.9216	.9025	.8836	.8649	.8464	.8281
	1	.0198	.0392	.0582	.0768	.0950	.1128	.1302	.1472	.1638
	2	.0001	.0004	.0009	.0016	.0025	.0036	.0049	.0064	.0081
3	0	.9703	.9412	.9127	.8847	.8574	.8306	.8044	.7787	.7536
	1	.0294	.0576	.0847	.1106	.1354	.1590	.1816	.2031	.2236
	2	.0003	.0012	.0026	.0046	.0071	.0102	.0137	.0177	.0221
	3				.0001	.0001	.0002	.0003	.0005	.0007
4	0	.9606	.9224	.8853	.8493	.8145	.7807	.7481	.7164	.6857
	1	.0388	.0753	.1095	.1416	.1715	.1993	.2252	.2492	.2713
	2	.0006	.0023	.0051	.0088	.0135	.0191	.0254	.0325	.0402
	3			.0001	.0002	.0005	.0008	.0013	.0019	.0027
	4									.0001

n	k	.01	.02	.03	.04	.05	.06	.07	.08	.09
5	0	.9510	.9039	.8587	.8154	.7738	.7339	.6957	.6591	.6240
	1	.0480	.0922	.1328	.1699	.2036	.2342	.2618	.2866	.3086
	2	.0010	.0038	.0082	.0142	.0214	.0299	.0394	.0498	.0610
	3		.0001	.0003	.0006	.0011	.0019	.0030	.0043	.0060
	4						.0001	.0001	.0002	.0003
	5									
6	0	.9415	.8858	.8330	.7828	.7351	.6899	.6470	.6064	.5679
	1	.0571	.1085	.1546	.1957	.2321	.2642	.2922	.3164	.3370
	2	.0014	.0055	.0120	.0204	.0305	.0422	.0550	.0688	.0833
	3		.0002	.0005	.0011	.0021	.0036	.0055	.0080	.0110
	4					.0001	.0002	.0003	.0005	.0008
	5									
	6									
7	0	.9321	.8681	.8080	.7514	.6983	.6485	.6017	.5578	.5168
	1	.0659	.1240	.1749	.2192	.2573	.2897	.3170	.3396	.3578
	2	.0020	.0076	.0162	.0274	.0406	.0555	.0716	.0886	.1061
	3		.0003	.0008	.0019	.0036	.0059	.0090	.0128	.0175
	4				.0001	.0002	.0004	.0007	.0011	.0017
	5								.0001	.0001
	6									
	7									
8	0	.9227	.8508	.7837	.7214	.6634	.6096	.5596	.5132	.4703
	1	.0746	.1389	.1939	.2405	.2793	.3113	.3370	.3570	.3721
	2	.0026	.0099	.0210	.0351	.0515	.0695	.0888	.1087	.1288
	3	.0001	.0004	.0013	.0029	.0054	.0089	.0134	.0189	.0255
	4			.0001	.0002	.0004	.0007	.0013	.0021	.0031
	5							.0001	.0001	.0002
	6									
	7									
	8									

n	k	.10	.15	.20	.25	.30	.35	.40	.45	.50
2	0	.8100	.7225	.6400	.5625	.4900	.4225	.3600	.3025	.2500
	1	.1800	.2550	.3200	.3750	.4200	.4550	.4800	.4950	.5000
	2	.0100	.0225	.0400	.0625	.0900	.1225	.1600	.2025	.2500

(Continued)

(Continued)

n	k	.10	.15	.20	.25	.30	.35	.40	.45	.50
3	0	.7290	.6141	.5120	.4219	.3430	.2746	.2160	.1664	.1250
	1	.2430	.3251	.3840	.4219	.4410	.4436	.4320	.4084	.3750
	2	.0270	.0574	.0960	.1406	.1890	.2389	.2880	.3341	.3750
	3	.0010	.0034	.0080	.0156	.0270	.0429	.0640	.0911	.1250
4	0	.6561	.5220	.4096	.3164	.2401	.1785	.1296	.0915	.0625
	1	.2916	.3685	.4096	.4219	.4116	.3845	.3456	.2995	.2500
	2	.0486	.0975	.1536	.2109	.2646	.3105	.3456	.3675	.3750
	3	.0036	.0115	.0256	.0469	.0756	.1115	.1536	.2005	.2500
	4	.0001	.0005	.0016	.0039	.0081	.0150	.0256	.0410	.0625
5	0	.5905	.4437	.3277	.2373	.1681	.1160	.0778	.0503	.0313
	1	.3280	.3915	.4096	.3955	.3602	.3124	.2592	.2059	.1563
	2	.0729	.1382	.2048	.2637	.3087	.3364	.3456	.3369	.3125
	3	.0081	.0244	.0512	.0879	.1323	.1811	.2304	.2757	.3125
	4	.0004	.0022	.0064	.0146	.0284	.0488	.0768	.1128	.1562
	5		.0001	.0003	.0010	.0024	.0053	.0102	.0185	.0312
6	0	.5314	.3771	.2621	.1780	.1176	.0754	.0467	.0277	.0156
	1	.3543	.3993	.3932	.3560	.3025	.2437	.1866	.1359	.0938
	2	.0984	.1762	.2458	.2966	.3241	.3280	.3110	.2780	.2344
	3	.0146	.0415	.0819	.1318	.1852	.2355	.2765	.3032	.3125
	4	.0012	.0055	.0154	.0330	.0595	.0951	.1382	.1861	.2344
	5	.0001	.0004	.0015	.0044	.0102	.0205	.0369	.0609	.0937
	6			.0001	.0002	.0007	.0018	.0041	.0083	.0156
7	0	.4783	.3206	.2097	.1335	.0824	.0490	.0280	.0152	.0078
	1	.3720	.3960	.3670	.3115	.2471	.1848	.1306	.0872	.0547
	2	.1240	.2097	.2753	.3115	.3177	.2985	.2613	.2140	.1641
	3	.0230	.0617	.1147	.1730	.2269	.2679	.2903	.2918	.2734
	4	.0026	.0109	.0287	.0577	.0972	.1442	.1935	.2388	.2734
	5	.0002	.0012	.0043	.0115	.0250	.0466	.0774	.1172	.1641
	6		.0001	.0004	.0013	.0036	.0084	.0172	.0320	.0547
	7				.0001	.0002	.0006	.0016	.0037	.0078
8	0	.4305	.2725	.1678	.1001	.0576	.0319	.0168	.0084	.0039
	1	.3826	.3847	.3355	.2670	.1977	.1373	.0896	.0548	.0313
	2	.1488	.2376	.2936	.3115	.2965	.2587	.2090	.1569	.1094
	3	.0331	.0839	.1468	.2076	.2541	.2786	.2787	.2568	.2188

n	k	p								
		.10	.15	.20	.25	.30	.35	.40	.45	.50
	4	.0046	.0185	.0459	.0865	.1361	.1875	.2322	.2627	.2734
	5	.0004	.0026	.0092	.0231	.0467	.0808	.1239	.1719	.2188
	6		.0002	.0011	.0038	.0100	.0217	.0413	.0703	.1094
	7			.0001	.0004	.0012	.0033	.0079	.0164	.0312
	8					.0001	.0002	.0007	.0017	.0039

n	k	p								
		.01	.02	.03	.04	.05	.06	.07	.08	.09
9	0	.9135	.8337	.7602	.6925	.6302	.5730	.5204	.4722	.4279
	1	.0830	.1531	.2116	.2597	.2985	.3292	.3525	.3695	.3809
	2	.0034	.0125	.0262	.0433	.0629	.0840	.1061	.1285	.1507
	3	.0001	.0006	.0019	.0042	.0077	.0125	.0186	.0261	.0348
	4			.0001	.0003	.0006	.0012	.0021	.0034	.0052
	5						.0001	.0002	.0003	.0005
	6									
	7									
	8									
	9									
10	0	.9044	.8171	.7374	.6648	.5987	.5386	.4840	.4344	.3894
	1	.0914	.1667	.2281	.2770	.3151	.3438	.3643	.3777	.3851
	2	.0042	.0153	.0317	.0519	.0746	.0988	.1234	.1478	.1714
	3	.0001	.0008	.0026	.0058	.0105	.0168	.0248	.0343	.0452
	4			.0001	.0004	.0010	.0019	.0033	.0052	.0078
	5					.0001	.0001	.0003	.0005	.0009
	6									.0001
	7									
	8									
	9									
	10									
12	0	.8864	.7847	.6938	.6127	.5404	.4759	.4186	.3677	.3225
	1	.1074	.1922	.2575	.3064	.3413	.3645	.3781	.3837	.3827
	2	.0060	.0216	.0438	.0702	.0988	.1280	.1565	.1835	.2082
	3	.0002	.0015	.0045	.0098	.0173	.0272	.0393	.0532	.0686
	4		.0001	.0003	.0009	.0021	.0039	.0067	.0104	.0153
	5				.0001	.0002	.0004	.0008	.0014	.0024
	6							.0001	.0001	.0003
	7									

(Continued)

(Continued)

n	k	.01	.02	.03	.04	.05	.06	.07	.08	.09
	8									
	9									
	10									
	11									
	12									
15	0	.8601	.7386	.6333	.5421	.4633	.3953	.3367	.2863	.2430
	1	.1303	.2261	.2938	.3388	.3658	.3785	.3801	.3734	.3605
	2	.0092	.0323	.0636	.0988	.1348	.1691	.2003	.2273	.2496
	3	.0004	.0029	.0085	.0178	.0307	.0468	.0653	.0857	.1070
	4		.0002	.0008	.0022	.0049	.0090	.0148	.0223	.0317
	5			.0001	.0002	.0006	.0013	.0024	.0043	.0069
	6						.0001	.0003	.0006	.0011
	7								.0001	.0001
	8									
	9									
	10									
	11									
	12									
	13									
	14									
	15									

n	k	.10	.15	.20	.25	.30	.35	.40	.45	.50
9	0	.3874	.2316	.1342	.0751	.0404	.0207	.0101	.0046	.0020
	1	.3874	.3679	.3020	.2253	.1556	.1004	.0605	.0339	.0176
	2	.1722	.2597	.3020	.3003	.2668	.2162	.1612	.1110	.0703
	3	.0446	.1069	.1762	.2336	.2668	.2716	.2508	.2119	.1641
	4	.0074	.0283	.0661	.1168	.1715	.2194	.2508	.2600	.2461
	5	.0008	.0050	.0165	.0389	.0735	.1181	.1672	.2128	.2461
	6	.0001	.0006	.0028	.0087	.0210	.0424	.0743	.1160	.1641
	7			.0003	.0012	.0039	.0098	.0212	.0407	.0703
	8				.0001	.0004	.0013	.0035	.0083	.0176
	9						.0001	.0003	.0008	.0020
10	0	.3487	.1969	.1074	.0563	.0282	.0135	.0060	.0025	.0010
	1	.3874	.3474	.2684	.1877	.1211	.0725	.0403	.0207	.0098
	2	.1937	.2759	.3020	.2816	.2335	.1757	.1209	.0763	.0439

					p					
n	k	.10	.15	.20	.25	.30	.35	.40	.45	.50
	3	.0574	.1298	.2013	.2503	.2668	.2522	.2150	.1665	.1172
	4	.0112	.0401	.0881	.1460	.2001	.2377	.2508	.2384	.2051
	5	.0015	.0085	.0264	.0584	.1029	.1536	.2007	.2340	.2461
	6	.0001	.0012	.0055	.0162	.0368	.0689	.1115	.1596	.2051
	7		.0001	.0008	.0031	.0090	.0212	.0425	.0746	.1172
	8			.0001	.0004	.0014	.0043	.0106	.0229	.0439
	9					.0001	.0005	.0016	.0042	.0098
	10							.0001	.0003	.0010
12	0	.2824	.1422	.0687	.0317	.0138	.0057	.0022	.0008	.0002
	1	.3766	.3012	.2062	.1267	.0712	.0368	.0174	.0075	.0029
	2	.2301	.2924	.2835	.2323	.1678	.1088	.0639	.0339	.0161
	3	.0852	.1720	.2362	.2581	.2397	.1954	.1419	.0923	.0537
	4	.0213	.0683	.1329	.1936	.2311	.2367	.2128	.1700	.1208
	5	.0038	.0193	.0532	.1032	.1585	.2039	.2270	.2225	.1934
	6	.0005	.0040	.0155	.0401	.0792	.1281	.1766	.2124	.2256
	7		.0006	.0033	.0115	.0291	.0591	.1009	.1489	.1934
	8		.0001	.0005	.0024	.0078	.0199	.0420	.0762	.1208
	9			.0001	.0004	.0015	.0048	.0125	.0277	.0537
	10					.0002	.0008	.0025	.0068	.0161
	11						.0001	.0003	.0010	.0029
	12								.0001	.0002
15	0	.2059	.0874	.0352	.0134	.0047	.0016	.0005	.0001	.0000
	1	.3432	.2312	.1319	.0668	.0305	.0126	.0047	.0016	.0005
	2	.2669	.2856	.2309	.1559	.0916	.0476	.0219	.0090	.0032
	3	.1285	.2184	.2501	.2252	.1700	.1110	.0634	.0318	.0139
	4	.0428	.1156	.1876	.2252	.2186	.1792	.1268	.0780	.0417
	5	.0105	.0449	.1032	.1651	.2061	.2123	.1859	.1404	.0916
	6	.0019	.0132	.0430	.0917	.1472	.1906	.2066	.1914	.1527
	7	.0003	.0030	.0138	.0393	.0811	.1319	.1771	.2013	.1964
	8		.0005	.0035	.0131	.0348	.0710	.1181	.1647	.1964
	9		.0001	.0007	.0034	.0116	.0298	.0612	.1048	.1527
	10			.0001	.0007	.0030	.0096	.0245	.0515	.0916
	11				.0001	.0006	.0024	.0074	.0191	.0417
	12					.0001	.0004	.0016	.0052	.0139
	13						.0001	.0003	.0010	.0032
	14								.0001	.0005
	15									

(Continued)

(Continued)

n	k	.01	.02	.03	.04	.05	.06	.07	.08	.09
20	0	.8179	.6676	.5438	.4420	.3585	.2901	.2342	.1887	.1516
	1	.1652	.2725	.3364	.3683	.3774	.3703	.3526	.3282	.3000
	2	.0159	.0528	.0988	.1458	.1887	.2246	.2521	.2711	.2818
	3	.0010	.0065	.0183	.0364	.0596	.0860	.1139	.1414	.1672
	4		.0006	.0024	.0065	.0133	.0233	.0364	.0523	.0703
	5			.0002	.0009	.0022	.0048	.0088	.0145	.0222
	6				.0001	.0003	.0008	.0017	.0032	.0055
	7						.0001	.0002	.0005	.0011
	8								.0001	.0002
	9									
	10									
	11									
	12									
	13									
	14									
	15									
	16									
	17									
	18									
	19									
	20									

n	k	.10	.15	.20	.25	.30	.35	.40	.45	.50
20	0	.1216	.0388	.0115	.0032	.0008	.0002	.0000	.0000	.0000
	1	.2702	.1368	.0576	.0211	.0068	.0020	.0005	.0001	.0000
	2	.2852	.2293	.1369	.0669	.0278	.0100	.0031	.0008	.0002
	3	.1901	.2428	.2054	.1339	.0716	.0323	.0123	.0040	.0011
	4	.0898	.1821	.2182	.1897	.1304	.0738	.0350	.0139	.0046
	5	.0319	.1028	.1746	.2023	.1789	.1272	.0746	.0365	.0148
	6	.0089	.0454	.1091	.1686	.1916	.1712	.1244	.0746	.0370
	7	.0020	.0160	.0545	.1124	.1643	.1844	.1659	.1221	.0739
	8	.0004	.0046	.0222	.0609	.1144	.1614	.1797	.1623	.1201
	9	.0001	.0011	.0074	.0271	.0654	.1158	.1597	.1771	.1602
	10		.0002	.0020	.0099	.0308	.0686	.1171	.1593	.1762
	11			.0005	.0030	.0120	.0336	.0710	.1185	.1602
	12			.0001	.0008	.0039	.0136	.0355	.0727	.1201
	13				.0002	.0010	.0045	.0146	.0366	.0739
	14					.0002	.0012	.0049	.0150	.0370
	15						.0003	.0013	.0049	.0148
	16							.0003	.0013	.0046
	17								.0002	.0011
	18									.0002
	19									
	20									

A.6 Poisson Probabilities

Entries in the table give the probability of x occurrences for a Poisson process with the mean of λ. For example, when $\lambda = 1.5$, the probability of 2 occurrences is 0.251

For a given value of λ, entry indicates the probability of a specified value of x.

λ

x	0.1	0.2	0.3	0.4	0.5	0.6	0.7	0.8	0.9	1.0
0	0.9048	0.8187	0.7408	0.6703	0.6065	0.5488	0.4966	0.4493	0.4066	0.3679
1	0.0905	0.1637	0.2222	0.2681	0.3033	0.3293	0.3476	0.3595	0.3659	0.3679
2	0.0045	0.0164	0.0333	0.0536	0.0758	0.0988	0.1217	0.1438	0.1647	0.1839
3	0.0002	0.0011	0.0033	0.0072	0.0126	0.0198	0.0284	0.0383	0.0494	0.0613
4	0.0000	0.0001	0.0003	0.0007	0.0016	0.0030	0.0050	0.0077	0.0111	0.0153
5	0.0000	0.0000	0.0000	0.0001	0.0002	0.0004	0.0007	0.0012	0.0020	0.0031
6	0.0000	0.0000	0.0000	0.0000	0.0000	0.0000	0.0001	0.0002	0.0003	0.0005
7	0.0000	0.0000	0.0000	0.0000	0.0000	0.0000	0.0000	0.0000	0.0000	0.0001

λ

x	1.1	1.2	1.3	1.4	1.5	1.6	1.7	1.8	1.9	2.0
0	0.3329	0.3012	0.2725	0.2466	0.2231	0.2019	0.1827	0.1653	0.1496	0.1353
1	0.3662	0.3614	0.3543	0.3452	0.3347	0.3230	0.3106	0.2975	0.2842	0.2707
2	0.2014	0.2169	0.2303	0.2417	0.2510	0.2584	0.2640	0.2678	0.2700	0.2707
3	0.0738	0.0867	0.0998	0.1128	0.1255	0.1378	0.1496	0.1607	0.1710	0.1804
4	0.0203	0.0260	0.0324	0.0395	0.0471	0.0551	0.0636	0.0723	0.0812	0.0902

(Continued)

(Continued)

λ

x	1.1	1.2	1.3	1.4	1.5	1.6	1.7	1.8	1.9	2.0
5	0.0045	0.0062	0.0084	0.0111	0.0141	0.0176	0.0216	0.0260	0.0309	0.0361
6	0.0008	0.0012	0.0018	0.0026	0.0035	0.0047	0.0061	0.0078	0.0098	0.0120
7	0.0001	0.0002	0.0003	0.0005	0.0008	0.0011	0.0015	0.0020	0.0027	0.0034
8	0.0000	0.0000	0.0001	0.0001	0.0001	0.0002	0.0003	0.0005	0.0006	0.0009
9	0.0000	0.0000	0.0000	0.0000	0.0000	0.0000	0.0001	0.0001	0.0001	0.0002

λ

x	2.1	2.2	2.3	2.4	2.5	2.6	2.7	2.8	2.9	3.0
0	0.1225	0.1108	0.1003	0.0907	0.0821	0.0743	0.0672	0.0608	0.0550	0.0498
1	0.2572	0.2438	0.2306	0.2177	0.2052	0.1931	0.1815	0.1703	0.1596	0.1494
2	0.2700	0.2681	0.2652	0.2613	0.2565	0.2510	0.2450	0.2384	0.2314	0.2240
3	0.1890	0.1966	0.2033	0.2090	0.2138	0.2176	0.2205	0.2225	0.2237	0.2240
4	0.0992	0.1082	0.1169	0.1254	0.1336	0.1414	0.1488	0.1557	0.1622	0.1680
5	0.0417	0.0476	0.0538	0.0602	0.0668	0.0735	0.0804	0.0872	0.0940	0.1008
6	0.0146	0.0174	0.0206	0.0241	0.0278	0.0319	0.0362	0.0407	0.0455	0.0504
7	0.0044	0.0055	0.0068	0.0083	0.0099	0.0118	0.0139	0.0163	0.0188	0.0216
8	0.0011	0.0015	0.0019	0.0025	0.0031	0.0038	0.0047	0.0057	0.0068	0.0081
9	0.0003	0.0004	0.0005	0.0007	0.0009	0.0011	0.0014	0.0018	0.0022	0.0027
10	0.0001	0.0001	0.0001	0.0002	0.0002	0.0003	0.0004	0.0005	0.0006	0.0008
11	0.0000	0.0000	0.0000	0.0000	0.0000	0.0001	0.0001	0.0001	0.0002	0.0002
12	0.0000	0.0000	0.0000	0.0000	0.0000	0.0000	0.0000	0.0000	0.0000	0.0001

λ

x	3.1	3.2	3.3	3.4	3.5	3.6	3.7	3.8	3.9	4.0
0	0.0450	0.0408	0.0369	0.0334	0.0302	0.0273	0.0247	0.0224	0.0202	0.0183
1	0.1397	0.1340	0.1217	0.1135	0.1057	0.0984	0.0915	0.0850	0.0789	0.0733
2	0.2165	0.2087	0.2008	0.1929	0.1850	0.1771	0.1692	0.1615	0.1539	0.1465
3	0.2237	0.2226	0.2209	0.2186	0.2158	0.2125	0.2087	0.2046	0.2001	0.1954
4	0.1734	0.1781	0.1823	0.1858	0.1888	0.1912	0.1931	0.1944	0.1951	0.1954
5	0.1075	0.1140	0.1203	0.1264	0.1322	0.1377	0.1429	0.1477	0.1522	0.1563
6	0.0555	0.0608	0.0662	0.0716	0.0771	0.0826	0.0881	0.0936	0.0989	0.1042
7	0.0246	0.0278	0.0312	0.0348	0.0385	0.0425	0.0466	0.0508	0.0551	0.0595
8	0.0095	0.0111	0.0129	0.0148	0.0169	0.0191	0.0215	0.0241	0.0269	0.0298
9	0.0033	0.0040	0.0047	0.0056	0.0066	0.0076	0.0089	0.0102	0.0116	0.0132
10	0.0010	0.0013	0.0016	0.0019	0.0023	0.0028	0.0033	0.0039	0.0045	0.0053
11	0.0003	0.0004	0.0005	0.0006	0.0007	0.0009	0.0011	0.0013	0.0016	0.0019
12	0.0001	0.0001	0.0001	0.0002	0.0002	0.0003	0.0003	0.0004	0.0005	0.0006
13	0.0000	0.0000	0.0000	0.0000	0.0001	0.0001	0.0001	0.0001	0.0002	0.0002
14	0.0000	0.0000	0.0000	0.0000	0.0000	0.0000	0.0000	0.0000	0.0000	0.0001

λ

x	4.1	4.2	4.3	4.4	4.5	4.6	4.7	4.8	4.9	5.0
0	0.0166	0.0150	0.0136	0.0123	0.0111	0.0101	0.0091	0.0082	0.0074	0.0067
0	0.0679	0.0630	0.0583	0.0540	0.0500	0.0462	0.0427	0.0395	0.0365	0.0337
1	0.1393	0.1323	0.1254	0.1188	0.1125	0.1063	0.1005	0.0948	0.0894	0.0842
2	0.1904	0.1852	0.1798	0.1743	0.1687	0.1631	0.1574	0.1517	0.1460	0.1404
3	0.1951	0.1944	0.1933	0.1917	0.1898	0.1875	0.1849	0.1820	0.1789	0.1755
4	0.1600	0.1633	0.1662	0.1687	0.1708	0.1725	0.1738	0.1747	0.1753	0.1755
5	0.1093	0.1143	0.1191	0.1237	0.1281	0.1323	0.1362	0.1398	0.1432	0.1462
6	0.0640	0.0686	0.0732	0.0778	0.0824	0.0869	0.0914	0.0959	0.1002	0.1044
7	0.0328	0.0360	0.0393	0.0428	0.0463	0.0500	0.0537	0.0575	0.0614	0.0653
8	0.0150	0.0168	0.0188	0.0209	0.0232	0.0255	0.0280	0.0307	0.0334	0.0363
9	0.0061	0.0071	0.0081	0.0092	0.0104	0.0118	0.0132	0.0147	0.0164	0.0181
11	0.0023	0.0027	0.0032	0.0037	0.0043	0.0049	0.0056	0.0064	0.0073	0.0082
12	0.0008	0.0009	0.0011	0.0014	0.0016	0.0019	0.0022	0.0026	0.0030	0.0034
13	0.0002	0.0003	0.0004	0.0005	0.0006	0.0007	0.0008	0.0009	0.0011	0.0013
14	0.0001	0.0001	0.0001	0.0001	0.0002	0.0002	0.0003	0.0003	0.0004	0.0005
15	0.0000	0.0000	0.0000	0.0000	0.0001	0.0001	0.0001	0.0001	0.0001	0.0002

λ

x	5.1	5.2	5.3	5.4	5.5	5.6	5.7	5.8	5.9	6.0
0	0.0061	0.0055	0.0050	0.0045	0.0041	0.0037	0.0033	0.0030	0.0027	0.0025
1	0.0311	0.0287	0.0265	0.0244	0.0225	0.0207	0.0191	0.0176	0.0162	0.0149
2	0.0793	0.0746	0.0701	0.0659	0.0618	0.0580	0.0544	0.0509	0.0477	0.0446
3	0.1348	0.1293	0.1239	0.1185	0.1133	0.1082	0.1033	0.0985	0.0938	0.0892
4	0.1719	0.1681	0.1641	0.1600	0.1558	0.1515	0.1472	0.1428	0.1383	0.1339
5	0.1753	0.1748	0.1740	0.1728	0.1714	0.1697	0.1678	0.1656	0.1632	0.1606
6	0.1490	0.1515	0.1537	0.1555	0.1571	0.1584	0.1594	0.1601	0.1605	0.1606
7	0.1086	0.1125	0.1163	0.1200	0.1234	0.1267	0.1298	0.1326	0.1353	0.1377
8	0.0692	0.0731	0.0771	0.0810	0.0849	0.0887	0.0925	0.0962	0.0998	0.1033
9	0.0392	0.0423	0.0454	0.0486	0.0519	0.0552	0.0586	0.0620	0.0654	0.0688
10	0.0200	0.0220	0.0241	0.0262	0.0285	0.0309	0.0334	0.0359	0.0386	0.0413
11	0.0093	0.0104	0.0116	0.0129	0.0143	0.0157	0.0173	0.0190	0.0207	0.0225
12	0.0039	0.0045	0.0051	0.0058	0.0065	0.0073	0.0082	0.0092	0.0102	0.0113
13	0.0015	0.0018	0.0021	0.0024	0.0028	0.0032	0.0036	0.0041	0.0046	0.0052
14	0.0006	0.0007	0.0008	0.0009	0.0011	0.0013	0.0015	0.0017	0.0019	0.0022
15	0.0002	0.0002	0.0003	0.0003	0.0004	0.0005	0.0006	0.0007	0.0008	0.0009
16	0.0001	0.0001	0.0001	0.0001	0.0001	0.0002	0.0002	0.0002	0.0003	0.0003
17	0.0000	0.0000	0.0000	0.0000	0.0000	0.0000	0.0001	0.0001	0.0001	0.0001

(Continued)

(Continued)

λ

x	6.1	6.2	6.3	6.4	6.5	6.6	6.7	6.8	6.9	7.0
0	0.0022	0.0020	0.0018	0.0017	0.0015	0.0014	0.0012	0.0011	0.0010	0.0009
1	0.0137	0.0126	0.0116	0.0106	0.0098	0.0090	0.0082	0.0076	0.0070	0.0064
2	0.0417	0.0390	0.0364	0.0340	0.0318	0.0296	0.0276	0.0258	0.0240	0.0223
3	0.0848	0.0806	0.0765	0.0726	0.0688	0.0652	0.0617	0.0584	0.0552	0.0521
4	0.1294	0.1249	0.1205	0.1162	0.1118	0.1076	0.1034	0.0992	0.0952	0.0912
5	0.1579	0.1549	0.1519	0.1487	0.1454	0.1420	0.1385	0.1349	0.1314	0.1277
6	0.1605	0.1601	0.1595	0.1586	0.1575	0.1562	0.1546	0.1529	0.1511	0.1490
7	0.1399	0.1418	0.1435	0.1450	0.1462	0.1472	0.1480	0.1486	0.1489	0.1490
8	0.1066	0.1099	0.1130	0.1160	0.1188	0.1215	0.1240	0.1263	0.1284	0.1304
9	0.0723	0.0757	0.0791	0.0825	0.0858	0.0891	0.0923	0.0954	0.0985	0.1014
10	0.0441	0.0469	0.0498	0.0528	0.0558	0.0588	0.0618	0.0649	0.0679	0.0710
11	0.0245	0.0265	0.0285	0.0307	0.0330	0.0353	0.0377	0.0401	0.0426	0.0452
12	0.0124	0.0137	0.0150	0.0164	0.0179	0.0194	0.0210	0.0277	0.0245	0.0264
13	0.0058	0.0065	0.0073	0.0081	0.0089	0.0098	0.0108	0.0119	0.0130	0.0142
14	0.0025	0.0029	0.0033	0.0037	0.0041	0.0046	0.0052	0.0058	0.0064	0.0071

λ

x	7.1	7.2	7.3	7.4	7.5	7.6	7.7	7.8	7.9	8.0
0	0.0008	0.0007	0.0007	0.0006	0.0006	0.0005	0.0005	0.0004	0.0004	0.0003
1	0.0059	0.0054	0.0049	0.0045	0.0041	0.0038	0.0035	0.0032	0.0029	0.0027
2	0.0208	0.0194	0.0180	0.0167	0.0156	0.0145	0.0134	0.0125	0.0116	0.0107
3	0.0492	0.0464	0.0438	0.0413	0.0389	0.0366	0.0345	0.0324	0.0305	0.0286
4	0.0874	0.0836	0.0799	0.0764	0.0729	0.0696	0.0663	0.0632	0.0602	0.0573
5	0.1241	0.1204	0.1167	0.1130	0.1094	0.1057	0.1021	0.0986	0.0951	0.0916
6	0.1468	0.1445	0.1420	0.1394	0.1367	0.1339	0.1311	0.1282	0.1252	0.1221
7	0.1489	0.1486	0.1481	0.1474	0.1465	0.1454	0.1442	0.1428	0.1413	0.1396
8	0.1321	0.1337	0.1351	0.1363	0.1373	0.1382	0.1388	0.1392	0.1395	0.1396
9	0.1042	0.1070	0.1096	0.1121	0.1144	0.1167	0.1187	0.1207	0.1224	0.1241
10	0.0740	0.0770	0.0800	0.0829	0.0858	0.0887	0.0914	0.0941	0.0967	0.0993
11	0.0478	0.0504	0.0531	0.0558	0.0585	0.0613	0.0640	0.0667	0.0695	0.0722
12	0.0283	0.0303	0.0323	0.0344	0.0366	0.0388	0.0411	0.0434	0.0457	0.0481
13	0.0154	0.0168	0.0181	0.0196	0.0211	0.0227	0.0243	0.0260	0.0278	0.0296
14	0.0078	0.0086	0.0095	0.0104	0.0113	0.0123	0.0134	0.0145	0.0157	0.0169
15	0.0037	0.0041	0.0046	0.0051	0.0057	0.0062	0.0069	0.0075	0.0083	0.0090
16	0.0016	0.0019	0.0021	0.0024	0.0026	0.0030	0.0033	0.0037	0.0041	0.0045
17	0.0007	0.0008	0.0009	0.0010	0.0012	0.0013	0.0015	0.0017	0.0019	0.0021
18	0.0003	0.0003	0.0004	0.0004	0.0005	0.0006	0.0006	0.0007	0.0008	0.0009
19	0.0001	0.0001	0.0001	0.0002	0.0002	0.0002	0.0003	0.0003	0.0003	0.0004
20	0.0000	0.0000	0.0001	0.0001	0.0001	0.0001	0.0001	0.0001	0.0001	0.0002
21	0.0000	0.0000	0.0000	0.0000	0.0000	0.0000	0.0000	0.0000	0.0001	0.0001

λ

x	8.1	8.2	8.3	8.4	8.5	8.6	8.7	8.8	8.9	9.0
0	0.0003	0.0003	0.0002	0.0002	0.0002	0.0002	0.0002	0.0002	0.0001	0.0001
1	0.0025	0.0023	0.0021	0.0019	0.0017	0.0016	0.0014	0.0013	0.0012	0.0011
2	0.0100	0.0092	0.0086	0.0079	0.0074	0.0068	0.0063	0.0058	0.0054	0.0050
3	0.0269	0.0252	0.0237	0.0222	0.0208	0.0195	0.0183	0.0171	0.0160	0.0150
4	0.0544	0.0517	0.0491	0.0466	0.0443	0.0420	0.0398	0.0377	0.0357	0.0337
5	0.0882	0.0849	0.0816	0.0784	0.0752	0.0722	0.0692	0.0663	0.0635	0.0607
6	0.1191	0.1160	0.1128	0.1097	0.1066	0.1034	0.1003	0.0972	0.0941	0.0911
7	0.1378	0.1358	0.1338	0.1317	0.1294	0.1271	0.1247	0.1222	0.1197	0.1171
8	0.1395	0.1392	0.1388	0.1382	0.1375	0.1366	0.1356	0.1344	0.1332	0.1318
9	0.1256	0.1269	0.1280	0.1290	0.1299	0.1306	0.1311	0.1315	0.1317	0.1318
10	0.1017	0.1040	0.1063	0.1084	0.1104	0.1123	0.1140	0.1157	0.1172	0.1186
11	0.0749	0.0776	0.0802	0.0828	0.0853	0.0878	0.0902	0.0925	0.0948	0.0970
12	0.0505	0.0530	0.0555	0.0579	0.0604	0.0629	0.0654	0.0679	0.0703	0.0728
13	0.0315	0.0334	0.0354	0.0374	0.0395	0.0416	0.0438	0.0459	0.0481	0.0504
14	0.0182	0.0196	0.0210	0.0225	0.0240	0.0256	0.0272	0.0289	0.0306	0.0324
15	0.0098	0.0107	0.0116	0.0126	0.0136	0.0147	0.0158	0.0169	0.0182	0.0194
16	0.0050	0.0055	0.0060	0.0066	0.0072	0.0079	0.0086	0.0093	0.0101	0.0109
17	0.0024	0.0026	0.0029	0.0033	0.0036	0.0040	0.0044	0.0048	0.0053	0.0058
18	0.0011	0.0012	0.0014	0.0015	0.0017	0.0019	0.0021	0.0024	0.0026	0.0029
19	0.0005	0.0005	0.0006	0.0007	0.0008	0.0009	0.0010	0.0011	0.0012	0.0014
20	0.0002	0.0002	0.0002	0.0003	0.0003	0.0004	0.0004	0.0005	0.0005	0.0006
21	0.0001	0.0001	0.0001	0.0001	0.0001	0.0002	0.0002	0.0002	0.0002	0.0003
22	0.0000	0.0000	0.0000	0.0000	0.0001	0.0001	0.0001	0.0001	0.0001	0.0001

λ

x	9.1	9.2	9.3	9.4	9.5	9.6	9.7	9.8	9.9	10
0	0.0001	0.0001	0.0001	0.0001	0.0001	0.0001	0.0001	0.0001	0.0001	0.0000
1	0.0010	0.0009	0.0009	0.0008	0.0007	0.0007	0.0006	0.0005	0.0005	0.0005
2	0.0046	0.0043	0.0040	0.0037	0.0034	0.0031	0.0029	0.0027	0.0025	0.0023
3	0.0140	0.0131	0.0123	0.0115	0.0107	0.0100	0.0093	0.0087	0.0081	0.0076
4	0.0319	0.0302	0.0285	0.0269	0.0254	0.0240	0.0226	0.0213	0.0201	0.0189
5	0.0581	0.0555	0.0530	0.0506	0.0483	0.0460	0.0439	0.0418	0.0398	0.0378
6	0.0881	0.0851	0.0822	0.0793	0.0764	0.0736	0.0709	0.0682	0.0656	0.0631
7	0.1145	0.1118	0.1091	0.1064	0.1037	0.1010	0.0982	0.0955	0.0928	0.0901
8	0.1302	0.1286	0.1269	0.1251	0.1232	0.1212	0.1191	0.1170	0.1148	0.1126
9	0.1317	0.1315	0.1311	0.1306	0.1300	0.1293	0.1284	0.1274	0.1263	0.1251
10	0.1198	0.1210	0.1219	0.1228	0.1235	0.1241	0.1245	0.1249	0.1250	0.1251
11	0.0991	0.1012	0.1031	0.1049	0.1067	0.1083	0.1098	0.1112	0.1125	0.1137
12	0.0752	0.0776	0.0799	0.0822	0.0844	0.0866	0.0888	0.0908	0.0928	0.0948
13	0.0526	0.0549	0.0572	0.0594	0.0617	0.0640	0.0662	0.0685	0.0707	0.0729

(Continued)

(Continued)

λ

x	9.1	9.2	9.3	9.4	9.5	9.6	9.7	9.8	9.9	10
14	0.0342	0.0361	0.0380	0.0399	0.0419	0.0439	0.0459	0.0479	0.0500	0.0521
15	0.0208	0.0221	0.0235	0.0250	0.0265	0.0281	0.0297	0.0313	0.0330	0.0347
16	0.0118	0.0127	0.0137	0.0147	0.0157	0.0168	0.0180	0.0192	0.0204	0.0217
17	0.0063	0.0069	0.0075	0.0081	0.0088	0.0095	0.0103	0.0111	0.0119	0.0128
18	0.0032	0.0035	0.0039	0.0042	0.0046	0.0051	0.0055	0.0060	0.0065	0.0071
19	0.0015	0.0017	0.0019	0.0021	0.0023	0.0026	0.0028	0.0031	0.0034	0.0037
20	0.0007	0.0008	0.0009	0.0010	0.0011	0.0012	0.0014	0.0015	0.0017	0.0019
21	0.0003	0.0003	0.0004	0.0004	0.0005	0.0006	0.0006	0.0007	0.0008	0.0009
22	0.0001	0.0001	0.0002	0.0002	0.0002	0.0002	0.0003	0.0003	0.0004	0.0004
23	0.0000	0.0001	0.0001	0.0001	0.0001	0.0001	0.0001	0.0001	0.0002	0.0002
24	0.0000	0.0000	0.0000	0.0000	0.0000	0.0000	0.0000	0.0001	0.0001	0.0001

x	λ = 20	x	λ = 20	x	λ = 20	x	λ = 20
0	0.0000	10	0.0058	20	0.0888	30	0.0083
1	0.0000	11	0.0106	21	0.0846	31	0.0054
2	0.0000	12	0.0176	22	0.0769	32	0.0034
3	0.0000	13	0.0271	23	0.0669	33	0.0020
4	0.0000	14	0.0387	24	0.0557	34	0.0012
5	0.0001	15	0.0516	25	0.0446	35	0.0007
6	0.0002	16	0.0646	26	0.0343	36	0.0004
7	0.0005	17	0.0760	27	0.0254	37	0.0002
8	0.0013	18	0.0844	28	0.0181	38	0.0001
9	0.0029	19	0.0888	29	0.0125	39	0.0001

A.7 Critical Values for the Durbin–Watson Test of Autocorrelation

Entries in the table give the critical values for a one-tailed Durbin–Watson test for autocorrelation. For a two-tailed test, simply double the level of significance.

Durbin-Watson statistic: Significance points of d_L and d_u at 5% level of significance

k' = number of explanatory variables excluding the constant term

obs	$k'=1$		$k'=2$		$k'=3$		$k'=4$		$k'=5$	
N	d_L	d_u	d_L	d_u	d_L	d_u	d_L	d_u	d_L	d_u
6	0.610	1.400	-	-	-	-	-	-	-	-
7	0.700	1.356	0.467	1.896	-	-	-	-	-	-
8	0.763	1.332	0.559	1.777	0.368	2.287	-	-	-	-
9	0.724	1.320	0.629	1.699	0.455	2.128	0.296	2.588	-	-
10	0.879	1.320	0.697	1.641	0.525	2.016	0.376	1.414	0.243	2.822
11	0.927	1.324	0.658	1.604	0.595	1.928	0.444	2.283	0.316	2.645
12	0.971	1.331	0.812	1.579	0.658	1.864	0.512	2.177	0.379	2.506
13	1.010	1.340	0.861	1.562	0.715	1.816	0.574	1.094	0.445	2.390
14	1.045	1.350	0.905	1.551	0.767	1.779	0.632	2.030	0.505	2.296
15	1.077	1.361	0.946	1.543	0.814	1.750	0.685	1.977	0.562	2.220
16	1.106	1.371	0.982	1.539	0.857	1.728	0.734	1.935	0.615	2.157
17	1.133	1.381	1.015	1.536	0.897	1.710	0.779	1.900	0.664	2.104
18	1.158	1.391	1.046	1.535	0.933	1.696	0.820	1.872	0.710	2.060

(Continued)

(Continued)

obs N	k'=1 d_L	d_u	k'=2 d_L	d_u	k'=3 d_L	d_u	k'=4 d_L	d_u	k'=5 d_L	d_u
19	1.180	1.401	1.074	1.536	0.967	1.685	0.859	1.848	0.752	2.023
20	1.201	1.411	1.100	1.537	0.998	1.676	0.894	1.828	0.792	1.991
21	1.221	1.420	1.125	1.538	1.026	1.669	0.927	1.812	0.829	1.964
22	1.239	1.429	1.147	1.541	1.053	1.664	0.958	1.797	0.863	1.940
23	1.257	1.437	1.168	1.543	1.078	1.660	0.986	1.785	0.895	1.920
24	1.273	1.446	1.188	1.546	1.101	1.656	1.013	1.775	0.925	1.902
25	1.288	1.454	1.206	1.550	1.123	1.654	1.038	1.767	0.953	1.886
26	1.302	1.461	1.224	1.553	1.143	1.652	1.062	1.759	0.979	1.873
27	1.316	1.469	1.240	1.556	1.162	1.651	1.084	1.753	1.004	1.861
28	1.328	1.476	1.255	1.560	1.181	1.650	1.104	1.747	1.028	1.850
29	1.341	1.483	1.270	1.563	1.198	1.650	1.124	1.743	1.050	1.841
30	1.352	1.489	1.284	1.567	1.214	1.650	1.143	1.739	1.071	1.833
31	1.363	1.496	1.297	1.570	1.229	1.650	1.160	1.735	1.090	1.825
32	1.373	1.502	1.309	1.574	1.244	1.650	1.177	1.732	1.109	1.819
33	1.383	1.508	1.321	1.577	1.258	1.651	1.193	1.730	1.127	1.813
34	1.993	1.514	1.333	1.580	1.271	1.652	1.208	1.728	1.144	1.808
35	1.402	1.519	1.343	1.584	1.283	1.653	1.222	1.726	1.160	1.803
36	1.411	1.525	1.354	1.587	1.295	1.654	1.236	1.724	1.175	1.799
37	1.419	1.530	1.364	1.590	1.307	1.655	1.249	1.723	1.190	1.795
38	1.427	1.535	1.373	1.594	1.318	1.656	1.261	1.722	1.204	1.792
39	1.435	1.540	1.382	1.597	1.328	1.658	1.273	1.722	1.218	1.789
40	1.442	1.544	1.391	1.600	1.338	1.659	1.285	1.721	1.230	1.786
45	1.475	1.566	1.430	1.615	1.383	1.666	1.336	1.720	1.287	1.776
50	1.503	1.585	1.462	1.628	1.421	1.674	1.378	1.721	1.335	1.771
55	1.528	1.601	1.490	1.641	1.452	1.681	1.414	1.724	1.374	1.768
60	1.549	1.616	1.514	1.652	1.480	1.689	1.444	1.727	1.408	1.767
65	1.567	1.629	1.536	1.662	1.503	1.696	1.471	1.731	1.438	1.767
70	1.583	1.641	1.554	1.672	1.525	1.703	1.494	1.735	1.464	1.768
75	1.598	1.652	1.571	1.680	1.543	1.709	1.515	1.739	1.487	1.770
80	1.611	1.662	1.586	1.688	1.560	1.715	1.534	1.743	1.507	1.772
85	1.624	1.671	1.600	1.696	1.575	1.721	1.550	1.747	1.525	1.774
90	1.635	1.679	1.612	1.703	1.589	1.726	1.566	1.751	1.542	1.776
95	1.645	1.687	1.623	1.709	1.602	1.732	1.579	1.755	1.557	1.778
100	1.654	1.694	1.634	1.715	1.613	1.736	1.592	1.758	1.571	1.780
150	1.720	1.746	1.706	1.760	1.693	1.774	1.679	1.788	1.665	1.802
200	1.758	1.778	1.748	1.789	1.738	1.799	1.728	1.810	1.718	1.820

FURTHER READING

Essentials of Contemporary Business Statistics, 5th Edition, by Thomas A. Williams, Dennis J. Sweeney and David R. Anderson, 2012, South-Western Cengage Learning.

Understanding Statistics, by Graham Upton and Ian Cook, 1996, Oxford University Press.

Basic Business Statistics: Concepts and Applications, 12th Edition, by Mark L. Berenson, David M. Levine and Timothy C. Krehbiel, 2012, Pearson Education.

Probability and Statistics, 2nd Edition, Schaum's Outlines, by Murray R. Spiegel, John J. Schiller and R. Alu Srinivasan, 2011, McGraw-Hill.

IBM SPSS Categories 22 available at ftp://public.dhe.ibm.com/software/analytics/spss/documentation/statistics/22.0/en/client/Manuals/IBM_SPSS_Categories.pdf

IBM SPSS Forecasting 22 available at ftp://public.dhe.ibm.com/software/analytics/spss/documentation/statistics/22.0/en/client/Manuals/IBM_SPSS_Forecasting.pdf

Foundations of Behavioral Research, 4th Edition, by Fred N. Kerlinger and Howard Lee, 1999, Wadsworth.

Experimental and Quasi-Experimental Designs for Generalized Causal Inference, 2nd Edition, by William R. Shadish, Thomas D. Cook and Donald T. Campbell, 2001, Houghton Mifflin.

Internet, Phone, Mail and Mixed-Mode Surveys: The Tailored Design Method, 4th Edition, by Don A. Dillman, Jolene D. Smyth and Leah Melani Christian, 2014, Wiley.

Taking the Fear out of Data Analysis, 2nd Edition, by Adamantios Diamantopoulos and Bodo Schlegelmilch, 1997, Cengage Learning.

Statistical Models: Theory and Practice, 2nd Edition, by David A. Freedman, 2009, Cambridge University Press.

Statistics, 4th Edition, by David A Freedman, Robert Pisani and Roger Purves, 2007, Cambridge University Press.

Discovering Statistics Using IBM SPSS Statistics, 4th Edition, by Andy Field, 2013, Sage.

Applied Multiple Regression/Correlation Analysis for the Behavioral Sciences, 3rd Edition, by Jacob Cohen, Patricia Cohen, Stephen G. West and Leona S. Aiken, 2002, Routledge.

A Student's Guide to Analysis of Variance, by Maxwell J. Roberts and Riccardo Russo, 1999, Routledge.

Principles of Forecasting, by J. Scott Armstrong, 2001, Springer.

Principles of Business Forecasting, by Keith Ord and Robert Fildes, 2012, Cengage Learning.

Introduction to Statistical Quality Control, 7th Edition, by Douglas C. Montgomery, 2012, Wiley.

Doing Business Research, by Nick Lee with Ian Lings, 2008, Sage.

INDEX